Constitutional Change: Amendment Politics and Supreme Court Litigation Since 1900

Constitutional Change: Amendment Politics and Supreme Court Litigation Since 1900

Clement E. Vose

A Twentieth Century Fund Study

Lexington Books
D.C. Heath and Company
Lexington, Massachusetts
Toronto   London

Published simultaneously in Canada.

Printed in the United States of America.

International Standard Book Number: 0-669-83519-6.

Library of Congress Catalog Card Number: 72-1965.

For John and Celia

The Supreme Court must continue to decide only those cases which present questions whose resolution will have immediate importance far beyond the particular facts and parties involved.

Chief Justice Fred M. Vinson, 1949

We have no constituency. We serve no majority. We serve no minority. We serve only the public interest as we see it, guided only by the Constitution and our own consciences.

Chief Justice Earl Warren, 1969

Contents

List of Figures   ix

List of Tables   xi

Foreword by M.J. Rossant   xiii

Preface   xv

Introduction: Approaches to Constitutional Change   xxiii

Part One	Issues and Episodes	1
	Limiting the Population and the Suffrage	3
Chapter 1	The Eugenics Movement	5
Chapter 2	The Grandfather Clause	21
Chapter 3	Woman Suffrage	47
	Provincial Issues vs. Cosmopolitanism	67
Chapter 4	Prohibition	69
Chapter 5	Lawyers for Repeal	101
Chapter 6	The Catholic School Issue	139
	The Movement to Protect Workers	161
Chapter 7	The Brandeis Brief	163
Chapter 8	Early Minimum Wage Movement	179
Chapter 9	The Minimum Wage Overruling	197
	Judicial Conservatism Overcome	241
Chapter 10	The Amendment Stalement	243

Chapter 11   Social Policies As Jurisdictional Issues   257
Chapter 12   The White Primary Overruling   287

Part Two   **Findings and Recommendations**   327

Chapter 13   Litigation in the Web of Social Movements   329
Chapter 14   Amendment as Legislative Politics   341
Chapter 15   Recommendations   361

                Bibliography   373

                Notes   393

                Index   437

List of Figures

2-1   Percentage of Blacks in Total Maryland Population: 1910   27

2-2   Percentage of Blacks in Total Oklahoma Population: 1910   36

3-1   Woman Suffrage in 1919   54

4-1   Wet and Dry Record of States in 1916   73

4-2   Wet and Dry Record of States in 1919   74

12-1   Percentage of Blacks in Total Texas Population: 1910   292

13-1   Genealogy of Conservative Organizations   333

List of Tables

4-1	Anti-Saloon League Briefs in Supreme Court Cases	95
7-1	Justices' Alignment on Maximum Hour Laws	174
8-1	Justices' Alignment on Minimum Wage Laws	195
12-1	White and Black Population in Ten Southern States	304
12-2	Justices' Alignment on Holding Primary Elections	323

Foreword

The study undertaken by Clement Vose for The Twentieth Century Fund deals with the most enduring framework of modern democracy. In sponsoring this study the Trustees of the Fund, impressed with the durability and flexibility of the Constitution, felt that an examination of its adaptability would be both timely and useful in an era when the nation's institutional structure has come under increasing criticism and pressure for change.

Although the specific cases chosen for research by Mr. Vose have now become part of constitutional history, the study speaks to current concerns because it deals with the forces and pressure groups that generate and resist change. Mr. Vose has uncovered enormous amounts of fresh material in his research, material that provides insight on the wide variety of personalities and groups that have engaged in constitutional battle. Today new groups are taking up new causes, but the process of constitutional change in the United States still follows many of the same routes and encounters many of the same obstacles described in this study.

Perhaps the key finding in the study, one that is suggested implicitly rather than explicitly over and over again, is that the Constitution is a remarkably tough document that has nevertheless been responsive to economic, social and political developments. The case studies demonstrate that it also is a human document, both in terms of its influence on the lives and well-being of all citizens and in terms of the actions and reactions of those who have been most intimately involved in seeking to effect its modification or reinterpretation. The study shows that efforts to bring about change inevitably are preceded by individual concerns and accompanied by healthy conflict between opposing interests.

Constitutional change, moreover, is not left simply to lawyers and jurists. Many different individuals and interest groups have played prominent roles in the continuous debate that has maintained the vitality of the Constitution. It can be questioned whether every amendment has been constructive or progressive. But there can be no question that the changes wrought have reflected and responded to the will of the public. Since the public sometimes undergoes a thorough shift of mind and heart, it is hardly surprising that the Constitution, in specific issues like prohibition and its subsequent repeal, has experienced reversal as well.

Mr. Vose is a constitutionalist, but his research has led him to suggest some reforms in procedure governing future constitutional change. Whatever the response to them, I believe that his study of constitutional change makes a contribution to all who are interested and especially to those who are involved in constructive criticism of this nation's moral and intellectual arrangement for responsible government.

The fund is grateful to Mr. Vose for his dedicated labor in shedding so much light on so complicated and complex an area. I hope that every reader will benefit from his study.

M.J. Rossant
Director, The Twentieth
Century Fund

February 1972

Preface

These studies of court cases and constitutional amendments are part of the work I began some twenty years ago, work that has so far been published in articles and in a book titled *Caucasians Only: The Supreme Court, the NAACP and the Restrictive Covenant Cases.*[1] The numerous in-depth reports of the politics of litigation prepared by others during this period are listed in the bibliography of the present work. The methodology used in such studies relies heavily on the existence of interlocking manuscript collections, office files, official records and interviews. This may restrict the subjects and definitely limits the episodes that can be examined because the needed materials may not be known, were not preserved, or are not available for study. Locating and handling the archival sources pertinent to unraveling social and political aspects of litigation are among the most intriguing challenges of modern scholarship.

The studies of the politics of constitutional amendments in this book are based on many previously untapped sources. The papers of the Massachusetts Anti-Suffrage Association in the Massachusetts Historical Society revealed the serious and durable opposition to the Nineteenth Amendment. The papers of Alexander Lincoln in the Schlesinger Library at Radcliffe College show how an organization named the Sentinels of America opposed the prohibition, woman suffrage and child labor amendments. Surprisingly, one letter in those papers led me to Harrison Tweed in New York who found old files of the Voluntary Committee of Lawyers, Inc. covering in rich detail the steps taken by a group of attorneys to ratify the Twenty-first Amendment repealing national prohibition. These papers have since found their way into the Collection on Legal Change at Wesleyan University. Not all the amendments of this century are examined in this book, but I believe new light is shed on those that are. Moreover, the prohibition, repeal, and woman suffrage amendments represent fundamental constitutional change that expressed shifting social attitudes. All eleven amendments adopted and many others advocated since 1900 are discussed.

Relative to amendments, Supreme Court decisions are so numerous that only a sample can be treated by the methodology of exhaustive background history. The choice of subjects came about in several different ways. I discovered that the organizations engaged in amendment controversies also went to court, so attention is given here to the litigation conducted by the Anti-Saloon League of America, the Sentinels of America, the Maryland League for State Defense and others. The National Consumers' League papers were available in the Library of Congress and the league's role in general in wage and hour cases well known. Once into the history of a particular string of cases, participation of other organizations becomes known; in this instance the opposition of business organizations was difficult to document while that of the National Woman's Party, owing to papers at the Schlesinger Library, was easy. NAACP litigation is legendary and the chapters on the court battles over the ballot for blacks relate one facet. I had already written of NAACP strategy on housing and, with the papers in the Library of Congress having a twenty-five year limit on access, was unable to study the major education cases or others of the 1950s and 1960s. These constraints account, in part, for studies of the grandfather clause and the white primary in this book. There is surely no more certain way of demonstrating that an organization participates in litigation than to choose for study those known to do so.

Several cases were selected for inquiry precisely because they did *not* exhibit the stigmata of group conflict. *Buck v. Bell*[2] was surely connected to the eugenics movement and possibly to organizations within that movement, but how? *Pierce v. Society of the Sisters*[3] pitted Protestants against Catholics but there was no inkling that Scottish Rites Masons and the Knights of Columbus were engaged. The official documentation in litigation ordinarily conceals facts of sponsorship and support beyond naming the parties and their counsel. More could be learned of the *Pierce* case because papers of the Oregon Attorney General and of the Archdiocese of New York could be examined. The *Social Security Cases*[4] could likewise be seen in a new light because information from back files of lawyers in Boston and Birmingham were obtained.

Few topics, cases, organizations and lawyers are included in this book compared to the many I considered and approached. Some acknowledgment of the courtesies extended in this exploration must be made. The legal programs generated out of the labor movement and the New Deal proved too vast to pursue, as stimulating interviews with Thomas Harris and Philip Levy and the array of papers in many repositories came to indicate. This sense of helplessness was reinforced by the kindnesses of Walter Gordon Merrit in describing the origins and history of the American Anti-Boycott Association and of Lambert Miller in discussing the more recent concerns of the National Association of Manufacturers. Efforts to give close study to the American Liberty League was stymied by the dearth of available papers. A somewhat different block appeared upon reviewing the papers of the National Child Labor Committee in the Library of Congress, when it was discovered that there was voluminous material on congressional enactment of the Fair Labor Standards Act of 1938 but almost nothing on subsequent litigation. The story of that organization and the early child labor cases has already been thoroughly described in published books.

The history of the American Civil Liberties Union begged for attention and, while interviews with Melvin Wulf and Osmond K. Fraenkel started me down that path, the sheer bulk of ACLU papers at Princeton University dampened any realistic prospect of preparing one. In the same way the movement for birth control legislation held great attraction, but study of the papers of Margaret Sanger and associations connected to her work at Smith College and the Library of Congress showed this would be a major study in itself. This was a source of disappointment because of the sparkling interviews I had with Morris L. Ernst, Harriet Pilpel and others.

The complex of Jewish legal action organizations could not be included here, and yet I remain indebted to Joseph Robison and Leo Pfeffer of the American Jewish Congress, Samuel Rabinove and Harry J. Alderman of the American Jewish Committee, and Sol Rabkin of the Anti-Defamation League of B'nai B'rith for opening their libraries and their minds to me.

I also pursued to a point several other possibilities. The subject of immigration was viewed through the papers of the Immigration Restriction League in the Houghton Library at Harvard University and in the activities of the American Immigration and Citizenship Conference in New York. In the end the subject seemed too remote from constitutional change as displayed in other episodes in this book. A dramatic instance of litigation in the field of naturalization was the denial of citizenship in the 1920s to Rosika Schwimmer, the pacifist who would not swear to bear arms for the United States, but her voluminous papers in the New York Public Library remain closed.

Listing these options tells something of the macroscopic world of constitutional law and history. Every case in the *United States Reports* surely has not merely a human story behind it but is often fraught with antagonistic social movements, the interplay of shifting interest groups, and the conflicts over strategy and tactics within organizations and law offices engaged in litigation. All cases cannot be treated as equals but there remain countless litigations that merit examination in detail.

Comprehensive constitutional history is being renewed with the most significant events in this century treated in no less than three different multivolume studies recently published or scheduled for publication during the next year. *Court and Constitution in the Twentieth Century* in two volumes by William F. Swindler is a richly documented history covering the years from 1889 to 1968.[5] The New American Nation Series under the general editorship of Henry Steele Commager and Richard B. Morris, planned to include five volumes on constitutional history, already boasts of two, *The Development of the American Constitution, 1877-1917* by Loren Beth (1971) and *The Constitution in Crisis Times, 1918-1969* by Paul L. Murphy (1972).[6] Each of these books is interpretative, and broad gauged and also contains accomplished bibliographical essays. A still more ambitious scholarly monument is *The Oliver Wendell Holmes Devise History of the Supreme Court of the United States* in twelve large volumes prepared by nine authors under the general editorship of Paul A. Freund.[7] Early volumes show that this is a work based essentially on primary manuscript sources and court records. The volumes on this century soon to appear are *National Expansion and Economic Growth, 1888-1910* by Philip C. Neal and Owen M. Fiss; *The Judiciary and Responsible Government, 1910-1921* and *1921-1930*, two volumes by Alexander M. Bickel; and *Depression, New Deal, and the Court in Crisis, 1930-1941* by Paul A. Freund.

I have not attempted the kind of coverage expected in standard constitutional histories. For one thing the episodes treated are highly selective. For another, little use is made of secondary sources, even the many notable judicial biographies available. This means that interplay among the justices is minimized and events surrounding the preparation of litigation given maximum attention. The emphasis on group participation is further highlighted by the special bibliography at the end of this book.

I cannot hope to acknowledge, let alone repay, the debts I feel to the numerous people who have made this book possible, but I will strive to name many of them.

The libraries I have used substantially in Connecticut are the Wesleyan University Library, the Connecticut State Library and the Yale University Libraries. The Library of Congress, especially the Manuscript Division, has been used heavily. In Maryland the Baltimore Sunpapers Library and the Enoch Pratt Free Library were used. In Boston my chief work was at the Massachusetts Historical Society and in Cambridge the Schlesinger Library at Radcliffe College. A visit to the Michigan Historical Collections in Ann Arbor was especially productive. Numerous trips to New York City led to reliance on the Library of the Association of the Bar of the City of New York; the Department of Special Collections, Columbia University Libraries; the New York Historical Society; and the New York Public Library, particularly the Manuscript Division. The Corrigan Memorial Library, St. Joseph's Seminary, Yonkers, New York contains the Archives of the Archdiocese of New York. Study in the Southern Historical Collection, Manuscripts Department in the University of North Carolina Library in Chapel Hill was also profitable.

Invaluable aid was obtained by correspondence with other libraries, chief among them being the Frances E. Willard Memorial Library for Alcohol Research, National Woman's Christian Temperance Union in Evanston, Illinois; the Margaret I. King Library, University of Kentucky, Lexington, and the Louisville Free Public Library; the Public Library of Cincinnati and Hamilton Counties, the American Jewish Archives in Cincinnati and the Columbus Public Library in Ohio; the Oklahoma Historical Society in Oklahoma City; the Oregon State Archives, Oregon State Library in Salem; and the American Philosophical Society Library in Philadelphia.

Scattered through the notes and the list of manuscript sources in the bibliography are many, many implied acknowledgments. Even there one may find oversights and further will be risked here by naming many individuals who provided aid to me. Several persons mentioned in these pages granted interviews, correspondence and also provided papers for my use. On eugenics in chapter 1, J. Easley Edmunds, Jr. and Dr. Benedict Nagler of Lynchburg, Virginia; Mrs. William R. Smith of Sweet Briar, Virginia; Frances Hassencahl of Euclid, Ohio provided indispensable information. On the grandfather clause in chapter 2, information about the situation in Oklahoma was obtained from libraries listed elsewhere in these acknowledgments, but visits to Baltimore to see William L. Marbury, Jr. put all of Maryland's politics from the Civil War onward in a new light. His patience and interest in reading this chapter is also appreciated. That subject and others, including woman suffrage discussed in chapter 3, were enlarged by conversations in Baltimore with Thomas F. Cadwalader, a lawyer who had actively opposed adoption of the Nineteenth Amendment.

Understanding the movement for prohibition, discussed in chapter 4, was enhanced by examining papers of the Anti-Saloon League of America held by the successor organization now named the American Council on Alcohol Problems in Washington, D.C. The papers are now in the Michigan Historical Collections. Clayton M. Wallace in Washington was helpful in this respect. A conversation with Robert C. Dalton and D. Vincent Hurley of the United States Brewers Association, Inc. in New York and a long interview with Bernard Hershkopf, who had been in the brief in the *National Prohibition Cases of 1920*,[8] were of special value. Chapter 5 on repeal rests heavily on the papers of Joseph H. Choate, Jr., whose use was made possible by Dickerman Hollister and Joseph H. Choate, III. These papers and those of Harrison Tweed concern the activities of the little-known Voluntary Committee of Lawyers, Inc., active in the years 1927-33. Tweed himself helped open these papers, made his office available for my use, introduced me to another surviving member of the committee, George Roberts, and read and criticized drafts of this chapter. Later, David Kyvig read and commented on this chapter and provided me a copy of his doctoral dissertation on the Association Against the Prohibition Amendment. Facts about the Oregon Catholic school case in chapter 6 depended on letters from John C. Veatch, a Portland lawyer who was counsel in the companion case concerning the Hill Military Academy. Griffith R. Dye, Jr. of Cincinnati gave me a copy of his study of Louis Marshall. For chapters 7, 8, and 9 on wage and hour issues and the National Consumers' League, I had occasional conversations and correspondence over a long period with Mary W. Dewson, Elinore M. Herrick, Elizabeth Brandeis, Emily Sims Marconnier, Elizabeth Magee and Vera Mitchell. Many of the women associated with this movement early in the century are accorded masterful short biographies in *Notable American Women*, published in 1971. I am indebted to the general editor of *NAW*, Edward T. James, and to individual authors who permitted me to read drafts of their sketches prior to publication.[9]

The director and staff of the Schlesinger Library at Radcliffe College exemplified the marvelous aid that manuscript librarians can accord a stranger. Chapter 10, on the conservative efforts to amend the Constitution during the 1920s to prevent progressive enactments, grew out of examination of papers brought to my attention in the Schlesinger Library. James Kelleher recalled the activities of Alexander Lincoln from his vantage point in the State House in Boston.

The test cases against the Social Security Act of 1935, described in chapter 11, brought by Boston and Birmingham law firms for their business clients, are seen here through the files of the lawyers. The files of Nutter, McClennen & Fish in Boston were opened to me by George P. Davis. Mr. Davis, a member of the firm since 1918 and the plaintiff in the landmark case of *Helvering v. Davis* (1937), has also been a generous host, correspondent and conversationalist. The closely related case of *Steward Machine Company v. Davis* (1937) concerned a different Davis but was a similar challenge to the Social Security Act. The test case was conducted by William Logan Martin. I am indebted to S. Eason Balch, the senior partner in the firm of Martin, Balch, Bingham, Hawthorne and Williams, for correspondence and information about Judge Martin and the litigation.

The history of litigation over the Texas white primary from 1921 to 1944, set forth in chapter 12, rests substantially on two sets of papers in the Library of Congress. There are the voluminous papers of the National Association for the Advancement of Colored People and the separate papers of Arthur B. Spingarn, the New York lawyer who for many years was president of the NAACP.

Wesleyan University provided me with the physical setting and sabbaticals that have enabled me to study the subject of constitutional change over some years. A leave from all my university duties in 1969-70 enabled me to accept full-time support for this study from the Board of Trustees of the Twentieth Century Fund. This gave me a research budget appropriate to the endeavor as well as the support and interest of the fund's staff. Those who gave me particular aid include M.J. Rossant, the director, John E. Booth, associate director, Gordon Weil and Richard Rust. Nancy MacKenzie copyedited the manuscript with skilled care. My budget enabled me to employ for short periods two research assistants, Albert D. Cover and Brian Sullivan. Continuous assistance in numerous tasks at every phase of the study has been given by my secretary, Mrs. Mildred Carter.

I am also grateful for the comments and criticisms of several persons. They are Leon D. Epstein, David Fellman, Fred I. Greenstein, Russell D. Murphy, Hubert J. O'Gorman, James L. Payne and Roger Spegele who read all or parts of the manuscript. I have elsewhere mentioned the value for me of readings of certain chapters by David Kyvig, William L. Marbury, Jr., George Roberts and Harrison Tweed. At the fund all or parts of the manuscript were read by Nancy MacKenzie, Charles Pepper, M.J. Rossant, Richard Rust, Pearl Schwarz and Gordon L. Weil. Finally there were readers whose names remain unknown to me who prepared reports for publishers considering the manuscript. These were exceptionally well done and, with all the other comments, have saved me some errors.

This occasion affords an opportunity to salute the staff of the Wesleyan University Library beginning with Wyman W. Parker and Michael Durkan, the librarian and assistant librarian. Perhaps twenty members of the staff aided me in some way, but I wish to single out the circulation and reference librarians who worked in my behalf on what must have seemed to them a daily and regular basis. These include Grace Bacon, Harold L. Geisse, Jr., Joan Jurale, Gertrude M. McKenna, Brian D. Rogers, Edmund A. Rubacha and Kathleen Witten.

My wife, Doris Foran Vose, has responded enthusiastically to the intellectual stimulation I felt at many points in this study. She and our children, John and Celia, evidently enjoyed, vicariously or as companions, the traveling engendered by the project. They have also found my bizarre work habits occasions for creativity. They will now have an opportunity to examine the results.

Introduction: Approaches to Constitutional Change

Scope

The many changes in constitutional law since 1900 have affected the economic, political, social and legal status of everyone in this country. These changes have been accompanied by an enlargement of national power as against the states and an expanding role of the federal courts in supervising and, often, initiating public policy.

This study will give particular attention to two forms of American constitutional change. One is the process of national constitutional amendments, those advocated and proposed as well as those adopted. The other—the most distinctive and dramatic technique of constitutional change in this century—is the process by which the United States Supreme Court has overruled the Court's previous decisions.

Changes in the fundamental law occur in other ways but these are touched upon only incidentally. It is an open secret that Congress and the president, collectively and independently, make basic policy. This has been particularly true in war-making. But domestic crises also have spawned statutes or executive orders which are fundamental in character and have been accepted as legitimate without being tested in the courts. If the United States had no written Constitution, the government, the governed and students of constitutional development would be less oriented to litigation. We would probably pay more attention to the social and political ingredients in every manifestation of constitutional change.

The objective of this study is to show how these ingredients have contributed to a number of notable changes wrought by Supreme Court decisions and by constitutional amendments. This is a multiple enterprise. The research approach may seem somewhat idiosyncratic and a mutant of archival history of the sort that political scientists and legal scholars rarely engage in, with a political analysis that does not emerge in most historical narratives. A long time span—this entire century so far—is reviewed. To avoid a multivolume work, some parts are examined minutely and others in less detail. Essentially the book assumes that the Constitution we had in 1900 has changed in many ways and engages in a series of test borings to discover how change takes place.

The organized formal and group life of litigation outside of the Court is of special interest. This is one of the most important and least appreciated aspects of American political development. It is still poorly understood today, but it is best studied by old-fashioned techniques: archival immersion, interviews with surviving participants and narrative connections. This study isolates some events and specializes in certain aspects of them, revealing many historical events that have never before been reported. Given the nature of constitutional litigation and of the amendment process, the broad time period offers a number of advantages.

The full scope of constitutional change is so enormous that many other case studies might have been substituted for those presented here. The rise of the labor movement with the constitutional rights given to workers to organize and bargain collectively could have been examined; instead, a detailed history of the movement for protective wage and hour legislation is offered. The constitutional struggle for ending birth-control legislation could have been substituted for the story of eugenical sterilization. The political, social and legal differences among Protestants, Catholics and Jews in the United States may be illustrated in numerous ways. The choice here was the 1925 Oregon compulsory school law.

Race relations law also has many facets but, not wishing to repeat the ground covered in an earlier book on northern housing discrimination, the focus here is on southern discrimination against ballots for blacks. After inquiring into voting according to race, it was inviting to look at voting according to sex. The Fifteenth Amendment of 1870 has always required strong enforcement; otherwise discrimination against blacks was easily accomplished. But while opposition to voting by women was strong and strident, the Nineteenth Amendment of 1920 was as close to being automatically carried out as a change in the Constitution can be.

The matter of law enforcement in the United States is classically told by the story of national prohibition of alcoholic beverages and its repeal, in which the Twenty-first Amendment negated the Eighteenth. Neither an amendment nor a statute, nor the Prohibition Bureau could bring drinking practices into accord with the Constitution. Luckily, by finding untapped legal files, the story of repeal from a new perspective is told here for the first time. The point is that these episodes almost all draw on unused or little-used sources. But one could certainly write about constitutional change by relying on different sources and different topics.

The Constitution has yielded to changing social attitudes about race, religion and women's rights; about the place of workers and trade unions; about alcohol and sex. The chief objective in this book is to show those interested in law the advantages of studying these social changes rather than merely reading judicial decisions, constitutional amendments and other official documents.

It is equally important to notice the changes in governmental institutions over several decades. Supreme Court majorities have differed in outlook markedly during this century. To generalize, the Court was dominated by activist-conservatives until 1937. That is, the majority believed it a proper judicial function to invalidate legislation found unconstitutional. The measure of constitutionality often coincided with the social, economic and political outlook of those justices. In that era, Oliver Wendell Holmes, Jr., Louis D. Brandeis, Harlan F. Stone and Benjamin Cardozo often dissented, for they believed that the Court should abide by legislative decisions unless clearly mistaken. These justices saw the entire work of the Court in these terms. Brandeis in particular championed progressive legislation as the means to constitutional change and deplored judicial intrusion.

Since 1937 the Supreme Court was dominated, sometimes fully, by justices who were activist-liberals. This trend reached its apogee in the Warren Court from 1953 to 1969. Many of those who had criticized the conservative use of judicial power found that it was not the activist philosophy they objected to but the ends it had worked toward in the hands of conservatives. In contrast, critics of the Warren Court favored a much more restrained or more conservative approach. In 1971, the appointees of President Richard Nixon appear to be moving the Supreme Court backward to more restraint or more conservatism—or both.

In the American federal system the institutions are continually changing because of population movements and attitudinal differences in constituencies. Changes take place in state governments as well as in Congress, in the federal courts and throughout the federal executive. They are fundamental to constitutional law and a generous sampling of them will be found in this book.

The most obvious feature of constitutional change in this century has been the change in institutional clienteles. Before 1900 and up to 1937 judicial review was championed by businessmen and their conservative lawyers. It was opposed by Progressive reformers, the settlement-house movement and lawyers "for the people." As a last resort, the progressives advocated the income tax amendment (adopted in 1913), popular election of senators and the woman suffrage amendment. They also supported the prohibition amendment, but were frustrated in the 1920s in seeking curbs on the Supreme Court and in ratification of the child labor amendment.

All this changed when liberals captured the presidency and Congress and then persuaded the Supreme Court that national power to regulate the economy was provided in the Constitution. Between 1937 and 1944 the Supreme Court lost its business champions and gained the confidence of civil rights and civil liberties advocates. Not always fully, to be sure. But as the Court moved actively to extend constitutional protections to minorities, it not only gained a new set of defenders but also gained critics. Soon "Impeach Earl Warren" was heard and previous defenders of judicial power questioned its use while critics discovered that true democracy required that judges with life tenure make some of its fundamental rules.

This switch in roles over several decades, then, explains the emphasis in this study on the politics of constitutional amendments. It is a subject illumined by history. Proponents of amendments to the United States Constitution commonly assert this form of change to be majoritarian and democratic as against the judicial usurpers. This was true in the Abolitionist revulsion to *Dred Scott* when the Thirteenth, Fourteenth and Fifteenth Amendments were urged and adopted. It was true of the progressives who worked for the income tax, child labor and other amendments. It is true in recent and current urgings to overturn

Supreme Court rulings on other issues. Few scholarly studies of amendment politics are adequate because this legislative process is considered outside the province of students of litigation and largely ignored (perhaps because of its federal character) by students of Congress or state legislatures. And students of the judiciary have usually slighted the amendment process because the topic is more legislative. This neglect of amendments reflects poorly on how we have conceived of the scope of the American political system. The present study represents an attempt to repair this gap.

Constitutional change in our time has been accomplished by a web of events the most dramatic of which have been Supreme Court *overrulings*. I do not mean reversals of lower court decisions but the overturning of precedent. Yet, although the Supreme Court of the United States has overruled its own earlier determinations of law in more than a hundred cases, we continue to have a precedent-oriented legal system. But overrulings are significant and deserve study because they amount to invalidations and reversals in forms of judicial values.

Among the overrulings to be given close scrutiny will be those on state minimum wage laws for women in 1937 and primary elections that included white voters only in 1944. These are samples that suggest patterns in other overrulings such as cases on school segregation in 1954, legislative reapportionment in the 1960s, and changes in the position of taxpayers to challenge public policy in federal court in the 1970s. Other cases than overrulings will, of course, be studied. The public has pretty well comprehended such common judicial behavior as dissenting opinions and disagreements on the bench, but the pathology of overrulings and their values have not been similarly absorbed.

Scholars are turning close attention to what happens when the words of law change. It is not just the president, as Harry Truman once remarked, who gives orders and finds that nothing happens, but Congress and the Supreme Court as well. What is the "impact" of Supreme Court decisions? What is the nature and level of "compliance"? The breadth of this study enables us to consider in detail the most famous failure of compliance in the century—the breakdown of the national prohibition of alcoholic beverages between 1919 and 1933. This affords a yardstick against which readers may measure the success in enforcing the decisions of the Warren Court on segregation, apportionment, defendants' rights and the prohibition of school prayers.

Thus, constitutional change will be seen throughout this book both in terms of what the Constitution and the amendments mean and what authoritative institutional bodies *say* they mean, and in terms of the impact of new amendments and Supreme Court overrulings and other decisions on society.

Explanatory Variables

In seeking to give historical breadth to this political science study of constitutional change and to give case-study depth to history, a number of particular

inquiries are made over and over again. A series of explanatory variables—
"hypotheses" is too scientifically ambitious—will be drawn upon. Alone, each
offers little novelty. But each has its own intellectual history and deserves
attention at the outset. How is each variable presently regarded and what are its
benefits and drawbacks as applied to the development of constitutional change?
Several different themes of explanation will be applied in the body of the study
itself. It will become obvious that in trying to comprehend factors accounting
for constitutional change, this book relies on shifting explanatory combinations.

Casebooks are inherently inadequate for illustrating the nature of constitutional change. Ordinarily their purpose is limited to the exposition of currently
accepted rules; supplements and new editions ensure that students are alerted to
the latest authoritative rulings of the Supreme Court. But if one facet of coping
with change is learning the current rules, surely another is ascertaining those
factors which accounted for the Court's departure from the old rules. The study
of what the Constitution means today should be the beginning rather than the
end of formal courses in the subject. Interpretations of constitutional change not
only have serviceability for practicing lawyers but also hold a significant
educational value for all citizens in achieving a broader understanding of the
Supreme Court. One wonders if the rigid snapshot of constitutional law
encapsulated in the casebook of 1910, 1930, 1950 or 1970 does not, in some
small degree, account for the cries of outrage heard from prominent lawyers,
judges, professors and laymen over Supreme Court overrulings.

A central task in preparing case histories or studies in the nature of
constitutional change is to strike a balance among the various factors that shape
the end result. What are the contributions of social environment, of technical
developments, of chance and of personality? The sheer complexity of the
subject perhaps accounts for the existence of many narrow and often contradictory interpretations of the Court. Students of any complex subject tend to
specialize, which results in overemphasis of one conditioning factor where many
may be present.

Another source of contradiction comes from oversimplifying, often through
honest interpretation in an attempt to aid understanding. And then there are the
disgruntled of each generation who sum up their view of the Supreme Court in a
quip such as "What's the Constitution among friends?" The quips, the conclusions of specialists and the broad interpretations have been repeated uncritically
when the insights which many of them display deserve to be accommodated as
only *part* of the knowledge of the subject. The detailed topical history affords
an approach to this end. Through the study of cases and amendments, we may
discover what truth lies in the various views of Supreme Court behavior, first in
specific instances and then in more generalized ways.

The many detailed studies of constitutional change published during the last
decade show hardly a trace of theory. They are a welcome departure from the
recitation of doctrinal development found in survey histories of constitutional

development. Indeed, they are precisely the kinds of books that will contribute to superior histories of legal change. Yet these case studies (for which, see the Bibliography) gallop forward with detail that give broad stretches of attention to the litigants and none to the lawyers, stress the justices but neglect public opinion, comment on social movements but ignore the particular organizations financing a key case. Authors of these studies often seem unaware that they are making important interpretive choices and there is rarely a discussion of the possible explanations available nor of the sources or data needed to support one or another of them.

Besides adding new detailed studies to the literature of constitutional change this book asserts the importance of introducing explanatory variables as a guide to understanding this gnarled subject. It will also discuss several instances of constitutional change in this century by searching for and examining several variables and settling for somewhat different explanations as each situation dictates. The judges, who seem at times to be the ultimate factor in decision-making independence, will be looked upon as just one factor. Another will be the lawyers conducting the litigation. A third will consider the parties to the cases and, most particularly, their connections with voluntary associations. At times this relationship will be reversed when organizations supporting test cases clearly use the parties as pawns in constitutional litigation.

In addition to keeping these somewhat elusive elements in mind, each of the studies in this book is an expression of some facet of a social movement. While a social movement can hardly be treated as a concrete entity, examples will be connected, where possible, to an intellectual elite on the one hand and to mass public opinion on the other.

These explanatory variables will be discussed individually and then brought together in each of the episodes of constitutional change treated in this book.

Judges

Working habits of a number of judges harmonize with an assumption in this book that the Supreme Court approaches many cases in terms of broad intellectual and social considerations. When Felix Frankfurter came to the Court in 1938, for example, he brought with him a background of academic discipline. Soon he was preparing historical studies of subjects being debated in public, in the law reviews, in lower courts. Anticipating constitutional questions about constitutional constraints on search and seizure, for example, he and his law clerks examined the English background and wrote an essay on their findings and filed it for eventual use.

Frankfurter's files were replete with polished studies of this sort which could be used in a case for decision. This was true even though Frankfurter insisted on a traditional view that narrowly construed the business of the Court and limited social issues within the confines of particular cases and controversies before it. But since many cases take four years to reach the Court, it needs little prescience to know that certain pathbreaking, controversial statutes or administrative orders will be tested, especially when the officers of legal defense funds announce their planned test cases in the newspapers.

Like most men appointed to the Court, Hugo Black had reached fifty upon his appointment in 1937. As a United States senator from Alabama he had acquired a national outlook in dealing with national problems and he had a thoughtful, philosophical mien. But he was not a scholar, as Holmes, Brandeis and Cardozo were. Upon coming to the Court and wishing to make up for any inadequacy he might have felt, Black began to read purposefully and sought further stimulation by inviting authors to his chambers and to his home. When Alexander Meiklejohn, the great philosopher of free speech, died in 1965 and was being eulogized at the annual meeting of the American Association of University Professors, Mr. Justice Black joined the tribute to Meiklejohn, whom he called this "great man and his works."

Dr. Meiklejohn [cherished] . . . the great ideals of liberty that I find in the First Amendment. . . . While he and I did not see eye to eye as to the exact scope of the absolute terms used in that amendment, we did fully agree that a country dedicated to freedom as ours is must leave political thoughts, expressions, and discussions open to the people if it hopes to maintain that freedom. Dr. Meikle- john and I joined in another belief—and I cannot say much more in my three minutes. Neither he nor I opposed full freedom to fully discuss both sides of any public question, no matter how unpopular one side may be. We agreed that where a belief can be argued against, there likewise must be freedom to argue for it.

I am here today to express my appreciation, my admiration, and indeed my affection for a man who fought so valiantly—so gently in language but so firmly in conviction—for his belief that if this country is to remain free, the minds, the tongues, and the pens of people must not be shackled.[1]

These are only samples of ways justices of the Supreme Court are issue- oriented and think thematically about constitutional matters. Certainly the cases become a focus and they then become problem-solvers in a somewhat different way from professional men in other fields. Moreover, there are nine justices and their relationships may be significant. These are not always as edifying as the intellectual styles of Frankfurter and Black suggest.

The outcries over the behavior of justices, headlined not long ago by the Senate battles over Abe Fortas, Clement Haynsworth, G. Harrold Carswell and William Rehnquist have again proved that men appointed to the bench are as human as men elected to six-year terms as legislators. An unhappy by-product has been the further withdrawal of judicial papers, making it more difficult to document the immediate and recent past in interpersonal Supreme Court relations than for the period before, say, 1937. Following Mr. Justice Black's death in 1971 it was learned that he had destroyed most of his judicial papers because he objected to the writings of scholars about the inner conflicts of the justices.

But no study of the Court can ignore its members and, while this one does not dwell on the personal and philosophical attributes of the justices, it does note the changing attitudes of men in service and their responses to a particular problem over time. It is safe to assume—and indeed to think otherwise would be unrealistic—that federal judges in the 1970s are reading federal commission reports on urban violence and campus disruptions, academic studies on I.Q. tests, the debate over Jensenism, biographies of Margaret Sanger, the experience of New York State with its new abortion law and the latest *Harvard Law Review* article on capital punishment. Issues relating to these matters are already before the Court or soon will be and judges do not wait for a mechanical signal on the docket to look for their gavels.[2] Thus an effort is made to gear judicial behavior to social movements, intellectual developments, the work of voluntary associations engaged in litigation, the skill of lawyers practicing before the Court and, to a limited extent, the interaction among the justices. Of course, the membership of the Court makes a difference although the method of this book intentionally minimizes the importance of individual justices on the seamless Supreme Court, where the fascinations of overlapping service are endless.

The backgrounds of Supreme Court justices are often isolated as the determinants of a decision. When a majority of the Court ruled a state minimum wage law invalid, Mr. Justice Stone found it "difficult to imagine any grounds, other than our own personal economic predilections," for the decision.[3] Some scholars, like Fred Rodell, have seen a direct inescapable line between personal, social, and economic background and constitutional decisions.[4] Yet John Schmidhauser states that "investigation of the relative influence of social background factors upon judicial interpretation has scarcely progressed beyond the speculative stage."[5] His conclusion to a preliminary study was that the influence of background factors has been only to set "implicit limits on the scope of theoretical decision-making possibilities."[6]

Judicial biography cannot end with social background as the major determinant of policy preferences, for men take on new commitments as judges. It may be, as Pritchett and others have claimed, that judicial attitudes toward values can be plotted to show a conservative-liberal split on the Supreme Court.[7] Others have departed altogether from analyzing judicial behavior and conceived of decision-making as a game or in terms of a mathematical model.[8] A danger in these approaches, as with the emphasis on social factors, arises when the quality of judicial open-mindedness is underplayed.[9] The extent to which judges can effectively antisepticize personal views or passions in given cases will be difficult to pinpoint, but it is a factor that cannot be excluded from analysis.

The crowning complexity in the judicial process of the Supreme Court—the interaction among the justices—is surely the most difficult to grasp. Popular writing about the Court has often given great play to the personal animosities which arise between justices.[10] An account by Westin, based on his extensive study of the life of the first John Marshall Harlan, shows that these rivalries may bear on such seeming trivialities as the framing of a headnote in the Court reports.[11] It is not clear how actual decisions may be colored by this factor. Indeed, the intra-Court picture made available in Alexander Bickel's study of Brandeis emphasizes reason and statesmanship in the internal deliberations of the justices.[12] The requirements of secrecy, the length of time which passes between decision and disclosure, indeed, the inconclusive nature of the debate over full disclosure—all contrive to make accurate contemporary analysis of the factor of interaction difficult.[13]

Lawyers

Lawyers—as advocates, writers and professors—convey both their own ideas and those of others into the forums where judicial policy is set. A single statement about the connections between bench and bar in constitutional litigation is impossible to make because lawyers vary enormously in their values, imaginativeness, intelligence, audacity and style. There are lawyers who are intellectuals as well as specialists, who have a view of social change that permits them to serve clients successfully through decades of uncertainty. Such a man was Walter Gordon Merritt, who fought trade unions and the boycott in the Danbury Hatters case, beginning in 1902, and who became an apologist for thirty years for the policies embodied in the National Labor Relations Act, until his death in 1968. Merritt prepared some twenty cases in the Supreme Court for employer organizations.

Similarly, lawyers like Thurgood Marshall, Constance Motley, Robert L. Carter and Jack Greenberg adjusted to the changing wishes and possibilities of the civil rights organizations they served between the 1930s and the 1970s. These included the National Association for the Advancement of Colored People, the NAACP Legal Defense Fund and the Conference of Black Lawyers. The adroit lawyer senses what ideas must be placed in the minds of the justices and they have the skills to utilize books, law reviews, newspapers, reports of study commissions and other broad instruments of communication as well as to prepare effective legal papers.

It has ever been so. It will be a theme in this book to see the different ways in which the work of lawyers contributes to constitutional change. Judge Simeon Baldwin once said that the development of law "is primarily the work of the lawyer. It is the adoption by the judge of what is proposed at the bar."[14] Applying this theory, Twiss showed how, in the years between 1880 and 1935, lawyers like John A. Campbell, Joseph H. Choate and William D. Guthrie linked the currents of economic laissez faire to protective rules of constitutional law.[15]

Although the advocates of the last century who placed new concepts before the judges sometimes originated them, often they drew their ideas from legal textbooks. The influence of Thomas M. Cooley, Christopher G. Tiedeman and John F. Dillon, the most prolific law writers of the day, has been traced in an important study which broadens the work of Twiss; its thesis is that these authorities, "not less than the judges and the lawyers, were responsible for the popularization within their profession of constitutional principles which encompassed the laissez-faire policies demanded by industrialists."[16]

Lawyers need not play all-powerful roles in constitutional change to make major contributions. In 1970, Abe Fortas spoke a basic truth about this, with some hyperbole, in observing:

To a considerable extent, the vast social decisions of the past decade may be traced to litigation lawyers who had the ingenuity and the skill to shape the issues and to carry them through the maze of the courts, sensitively and astutely. In substantial measure, it was the Warren Court that opened the new frontier of life in this nation; but the decisions handed down by the Warren Court would never have existed except that lawyers shaped the issues and brought the cases to it. It was lawyers who pointed the way and who made possible the advances toward the goal of comprehensive dignity which our Constitution embodies. It was lawyers, engaged in the great and ever-new practice of law. It was they who saw the conflicts in justiciable terms; who framed the issues, marshalled the facts and the concepts of the law; and who shaped and guided the cases to the point of decisions.[17]

Fortas's words have an authentic ring and testify to the significance of the lawyer who funnels societal conflict to the courts for adjudication.

Intellectuals

Officially, the grist of the Supreme Court mill—in the form of records, petitions, briefs and oral arguments—is the work of lawyers who are members of the Court's own bar. These lawyers and the justices have sometimes made creative and significant intellectual contributions. Yet, they inhabit and partake of a larger intellectual climate, which affects them in wondrous ways. Many lay writers, philosophers, scientists, historians and social scientists have helped to shape American constitutional development, often without intention. The growing practice of thorough citation of the sources of decision in Court opinions scarcely matches the ultimate influences at work.

The jurisprudential school of legal realism often carped at the "inarticulate major premise" found lurking in conservative opinions from the late nineteenth century into the 1930s. The most celebrated complaint is in the dissent of

Mr. Justice Holmes in the *Lochner* case. The Court struck down a state statute limiting the working time of bakers to ten hours, calling this an undue, unconstitutional interference with the freedom of contract. Holmes said this was "decided upon an economic theory which a large part of the country does not entertain," and declared, "The Fourteenth Amendment does not enact Mr. Herbert Spencer's *Social Statics*."[18] The briefs did not mention, nor did the opinion of the Court cite the English social philosopher's book. Yet Spencer's theories surely registered in this outcome and in many others during that era, for his vision matched the conception of the constitutional order entertained by a prominent sector of the bench and bar in the United States at the turn of the century. This summary by Professor Joad spells out what Spencer had in mind in 1850:

Social Statics is a description of society as Spencer conceives that it ought to be, the ideal condition of political organization being envisaged as one of static repose. . . . Spencer's description of the function of the state is little more than a list of the functions it should renounce. There must be no regulation of industry, which should be left to the free play of individual activities, since Spencer's ideal man is also an economic man. There must be no established, or state, church, no organized colonization, no poor relief, no social legislation, nothing in short in the way of collective organization to interfere with the law of natural selection.[19]

Many more technical notions also come to be judicial formulations with hardly a word about their origin. An amusing instance came to light recently through publication of correspondence between the economist Richard T. Ely and Mr. Justice Holmes. In 1900 Ely defined "monopoly" to embody exclusiveness or unity, the suppression of competition in order to pursue unified tactics to control prices. As a professor with psychic and financial rewards in mind, Ely was upset to find his phrasing in a Supreme Court opinion without benefit of attribution. He complained to Holmes:

I see that the U.S. Supreme Court has adopted absolutely and almost word for word my definition of monopoly—that is, if the opinion of Mr. Justice McKenna in *National Cotton Oil Co. v. Texas* 197 U.S. 129 may be taken as the doctrine of the Court. The justice uses the quotation marks, saying, "to quote another," etc. but does not mention my *Monopolies and Trusts*. . . . It took me years to work out this definition. . . . I know that in opinions private authors (except of law books) are seldom mentioned but is that quite fair? . . . the recognition of my work would have been very welcome.[20]

Recently the courts have not only been guided by the scholarly work of nonlawyers but have also more readily acknowledged such guidance. The literature on this subject includes Corwin's astuteness in apprehending the Court's venture as a national school board, Shapiro's survey of several roles (including the Court as expert in labor relations, tax and antitrust policy and as political scientist and economist), and Miller's critique of the justices' capabilities as historians.[21]

In studying the Supreme Court it must be appreciated that law is a scholarly pursuit, that judicial opinions are intellectual statements and that all manner of ideas are bootlegged into the thinking of the justices.

Groups and Movements

A theory that judicial decisions are primarily responses to the machinations of specific pressure groups must also be taken into account. In 1908, Arthur Bentley wrote that there were "luminous instances of the same group pressures which operate through executives and legislatures, operating also through supreme courts and bringing about changes . . . which must be interpreted directly in terms of pressures of group interests."[22] Yet in discussing an example, Bentley explained he did not mean "that the justices consciously forced the law to fit the case, nor that they showed any traces whatever of demagogism or of subserviency to popular clamor."[23] And, in answer to David Truman's description of the judicial process in terms of access by pressure groups, Walter Berns said that such groups "must come armed with sound arguments, addressed to reason. The proposition that the judicial process can be understood in terms of the pressure exerted by groups cannot be maintained—unless that pressure takes the form of constitutional arguments. And this kind of pressure may be exerted by an insignificant author of a law review article."[24]

Although it is apparent that important constitutional questions are pursued to the Supreme Court by organized groups, it does not follow that this necessarily accounts for a particular decision. For one thing, important organizations often support opposing positions. For another, the effectiveness of interest groups in American government generally has been widely questioned. One essay on the state of the art, calling the counts in the indictment against pluralist theory "numerous," asserts that the main criticism of the pluralist or interest group emphasis in political science is its "conservative bias on the one hand and irrelevance on the other."[25]

Until the 1950s the assertions by Arthur Bentley and David Truman that interest groups did engage in litigation had so little empirical support that a master of political science like V.O. Key omitted the topic entirely from his leading text, *Politics, Parties and Pressure Groups*.[26] Early studies took the form of minute examination of the history of particular litigations where organizations—identifiable by letterhead and usually by incorporation—seemed to link broad interests in society to individual parties of interest in Supreme Court cases.[27]

Organizations support legal action most frequently because individuals lack the necessary time, money and skill. Even with no delays, a case takes an average of four years to pass through two lower courts to the Supreme Court. A series of cases on related questions affecting the permanent interest of a group may extend over two decades or more. The constant attention that litigation demands, especially when new arguments are being advanced, makes the employment of regular counsel—supplemented by a legal staff of some size and by volunteer lawyers—both economical and practical. Parties also pay court costs and meet the expense of printing the record and briefs. So organizations are usually better able than individuals to provide the continuity demanded in litigation. Some individuals do maintain responsibility for their own cases even at the Supreme Court level, but this is increasingly difficult under modern conditions.

The form of group participation in court cases is set by such factors as the type of proceeding, standing of the parties, legal or constitutional issues in dispute, the characteristics of the organization and its interest in the outcome. Perhaps the most direct and open participation has been by organizations which have been obliged to protect their rights and privileges. Robert Horn has shown that a modern constitutional law of association has developed out of Supreme Court cases concerning churches, trade unions, political parties and other organizations.[28] The cases have sometimes placed organizations as parties, but more often the organization supports a member or an officer in litigation. Perhaps one example will suffice.

The constitutional concept of religious freedom has been broadened in recent years by the Supreme Court decisions in cases involving members of the sect known as Jehovah's Witnesses. Most of the cases began when a Jehovah's Witness violated a local ordinance or state statute. From 1938 to 1958, when their litigation work largely ceased, the Witnesses, incorporated as the Watch Tower Bible and Trace Society and represented by their counsel, Hayden Cooper Covington, won forty-four of fifty-five cases in the United States Supreme Court. As a result Jehovah's Witnesses came to enjoy

the rights to solicit from house to house, to preach in the streets without a license, to canvass apartment buildings regardless of the tenants' or owners' wishes, to be recognized as ministers of an accredited religion and thus be exempt from the draft, to decline to serve on juries, and to refuse to salute or pledge allegiance to the flag.[29]

While the studies of interest group activity in court cases were well documented and made only the modest claim that it was one factor, albeit a neglected factor in the total judicial process, they were mostly ignored by lawyers, law professors, journalists and laymen, but were found attractive and valid by many social scientists. Most of the published commentary has been uncritical—with two exceptions. Danelski says "description of a broad universe of legal phenomena" has been the main contribution of the "group-process approach." "The future importance of one approach," he concludes, "turns on whether it is able to offer sophisticated explanation based on verifiable theory, and not merely careful description of legal-governmental processes."[30] The chief critic of these studies has been Nathan Hakman, who has complained that "a view of Supreme Court litigation as 'a form of political action' or 'pressure group activity' has become deeply embedded in scholarly folklore."[31]

Lest constitutional case histories be drawn too narrowly, it is proper to agree with Mr. Justice Jackson's view that "the ultimate function of the Supreme Court is nothing less than the arbitration between fundamental and ever-present rival forces or trends in our organized society."[32] He believed that in this way "the technical tactics of constitutional lawsuits . . . [may be seen as] part of a greater strategy of statecraft in our system."[33] And Mr. Justice Frankfurter, prior to his appointment to the Court, noted:

From Marshall's day to this the pages of the Supreme Court Reports present a cinematograph of the movements of our society, revealing, under our "peculiar jurisprudence," the clash of forces in terms of ordinary lawsuits resolved by the judicial process. Already the substance of Supreme Court decisions begins to bear the aspects of these times. Subtly the impregnating intellectual climate of an era also affects the Court. This is so by the very nature of our Constitution, by virtue of the vague concepts that have to be applied and the "moods" that have to be conveyed—a very different thing, be it noted, from the shallow implications of Mr. Dooley's "th' supreme coort follows th' iliction returns."[34]

Heberle uses the term *social movement* to denote "a wide variety of collective attempts to bring about a change in certain social institutions or to create an entirely new order," with Gusfield agreeing but supplying the phrasing "socially shared demands for change in some aspect of the social order."[35] These writers make numerous further refinements. With a commitment to understanding constitutional change over considerable stretches of time it becomes necessary to move away from arbitrary limits.

Thus, in studying the Supreme Court we move away from the single term or even era—such as the Roosevelt or Warren Courts—to a longer institutional span. We move away, also, from the single case or group of cases to the development of a topic over a generation or more. This study will take account of particular cases, particular justices and particular outcomes just as it will be concerned with individual intellectuals and lawyers, and with small organizations. But over time it is possible to see a larger pattern; the notion of the social movement appears to be a useful one in putting together interests and tendencies which may exhibit unawareness, incohesiveness, rivalry and an incapacity to work single-mindedly in the same direction. We recognize in American life over the last century powerful movements by workers, women, blacks and others in their own behalf and a proliferation of altruistic social movements for defendants' rights, child laborers and the insane. This is the purpose behind exploring the utility of the term social movements in comprehending constitutional change.

Perhaps the term social movement gives scarce comfort to social scientists still experiencing difficulty with "interest group." David Truman in 1951 used *interest group* to refer to "any group that, on the basis of one or more shared attitudes, makes certain claims upon other groups in the society for the establishment, maintenance, or enhancement of forms of behavior that are implied by the shared attitudes."[36] Shared attitudes are not enough; the group must also emerge with a common response "observable as demands or claims upon other groups in society."[37] Studies of the judiciary employing the term have tended to reduce it to interests organized as voluntary associations. In the current study the tendency is to treat voluntary associations singly and, when a cluster or series, to treat them as a social movement.

Part One:
Issues and Episodes

**Limiting the Population
and the Suffrage**

1 The Eugenics Movement

In 1927 the sexual sterilization of a feeble-minded woman under a Virginia statute was upheld as constitutionally valid by the United States Supreme Court.[1] The woman's due process and equal protection claims shrank before the superior public, societal interest promoted by sterilization. Mr. Justice Holmes spoke dramatically for an eight-to-one majority. As a wounded hero of the Civil War, Holmes had always celebrated the manly sacrifices of battle and acquiesced in *Buck v. Bell* in those terms, saying, "We have seen more than once that the public welfare may call upon the best citizens for their lives."[2] From this, Holmes thought "those who already sap the strength of the state" could be called upon for the lesser sacrifice of sexual sterilization.

The master of judicial restraint did more than defer to the Virginia legislature, which had enacted the sterilization statute in 1924,[3] and the State courts. He enthusiastically endorsed the compulsory operation of salpingectomy upon Carrie Buck as she herself, her illegitimate daughter and her mother were all inmates in the State Colony for Epileptics and Feeble Minded. "It is better for all the world," said Holmes, "if instead of waiting to execute degenerate offspring for crime, or to let them starve for their imbecility, society can prevent those who are manifestly unfit from continuing their kind."[4] That he saw so few, and such dark, alternatives must be one reason he endorsed sterilization. The prevention of smallpox was cited as parallel, always the key public health precedent—established by a seven-to-two margin when Holmes first went to the Court.[5] And so Holmes concluded with a ringing battle cry that won easy, right-thinking converts to the eugenics movement. "The principle that sustains compulsory vaccination is broad enough to cover cutting the Fallopian tubes. Three generations of imbeciles are enough." To which, for the sake of everlasting academic hilarity, Professor Thomas Reed Powell added, "Mr. Justice Butler dissenting."

Buck v. Bell is a landmark case that endorsed and legitimized the eugenics movement in the United States. Although compulsory procreative sterilization got an important boost, there was insufficient scientific and public support after 1930 to sustain the eugenics movement. The statutes in most states gradually fell into disuse.

Compulsory sterilization has practically ceased in the United States, as the life of the movement for it has died out. *Buck v. Bell* remains, as they say, "good law"; it has not been overruled, the Court having had no occasion to do so. There remain eugenic sterilization laws in twenty-six states, their provisions seldom carried out.

The history of compulsory sterilization in Germany during the years offers an ironic contrast to the American situation. The racial views of the Nazis were expressed in eugenic legislation that prevailed from 1933 to 1945. Compulsory as well as punitive sterilizations carried out in Nazi Germany were condemned in the Nuremburg War Crime Trials and the laws were abolished by the Allies in 1946. They have not been reenacted.[6]

We shall consider in some detail the history of *Buck v. Bell* and the 1924 Virginia "Act to provide for the sexual sterilization of inmates of State institutions in certain cases." This requires attention to the subject of eugenics, defined recently as "an applied science that seeks to maintain or to improve the genetic potentialities of the human species."[7] Donald Pickens wrote in 1968:

The Great Depression of 1929 and the rise of genetics marked the decline of eugenics as an organized movement and as a creed among intellectuals and social leaders. Environmentalism, based on a fuller understanding of culture and individual development, contributed to the demise of Galtonian eugenics. Fascists with their programs of racial purity completed the process of disenchantment for Americans with racial reforms.[8]

It was not quite this neat. Compulsory sterilization has continued in some states to this day and eugenics has found new applications in concern with mutations from radiation, for example. Yet there has been wide acceptance of the warning made to the Supreme Court in 1927 by the lawyer I.P. Whitehead in his brief for Carrie Buck. He called the Virginia statute a eugenics law, not a public health law, and labeled the eugenics advocates Plantonic guardians who wished to "establish in the state the science of medicine and a corresponding system of judicature."[9] In concluding his argument, Whitehead prophesied doom:

A reign of doctors will be inaugurated and in the name of science new classes will be added, even races may be brought within the scope of such a regulation and the worst forms of tyranny practiced. In the place of the constitutional government of the fathers we will have set up Plato's Republic.

To which it can only be added that Mr. Justice Holmes (and Willis Van Devanter, James McReynolds, Louis D. Brandeis, Chief Justice William Howard Taft, George Sutherland, Edward Sanford and Harlan F. Stone) disagreed.

The founder and patron saint of eugenics was the remarkably versatile and brilliant English scientist Sir Francis Galton, who introduced the term in 1883. Galton established separate reputations as an explorer, in geography and in the development and application of statistical methods to the weather. He was a cousin of Charles Darwin and, after 1859, Galton gradually transformed himself into an anthropologist and eugenist.[10] His main objective became the improvement of the race of man. Researches in heredity and statistics were essential to carry the work forward. In *Hereditary Genius* (1869) Galton saw a mix of early environment and opportunity combining with natural ability. He was exceptional in opposing the theory of the inheritance of acquired characteristics. Hence he advocated the search for methods to improve inherited characteristics, both physical and mental. For this quest, Galton coined the term "eugenics" in his book *Inquiries Into Human Facility* in 1883. He devoted many papers and public lectures to the subject and won an important following among psychologists and biologists in England, the United States and elsewhere.

In the United States, there were many expressions of interest in the study and application of eugenics. Alexander Graham Bell had a pioneer interest in eugenics. The careless and sensational tradition in the study of heredity can be dated from 1875 by the study of the Juke family by Richard Louis Dugdale, in a report of the Prison Association of New York, published under the title of *The Jukes, A Study in Crime, Pauperism, Disease and Heredity* (1875). Of 709 persons of "Juke" blood, Dugdale found persistence of crime, venereal disease and illegitimacy, which had cost New York State more than a million dollars. This conclusion persuaded Dugdale and much of the public that inheritance was more important than environment in determining character. Arthur H. Estabrook brought the Dugdale study up to date in 1915 and argued for sterilization as proper treatment for criminals instead of prison.

The major advocates in American eugenics were Charles Benedict Davenport, David Starr Jordan, Edward M. East, and Henry H. Laughlin, of whom Pickens wrote:

The common denominator among these men's theories was the supreme importance of heredity in man and his civilization: that the unfit must be eliminated or at least limited in number and the fit encouraged to increase their numbers, an objective achieved through a scientific knowledge and social application of heredity.[11]

This leadership cast the American eugenics movement with racist ideas, favorable to immigration restriction. It combined original scientific research with strong emphasis on organization and the application of eugenics to public policy.

Davenport, a biology professor at the University of Chicago at the turn of the century, persuaded the trustees of a newly created philanthropic foundation, Carnegie Institution of Washington, to establish in 1904 a Station for Experimental Evolution at Cold Spring Harbor, on the north shore of Long Island, New York. To Davenport, the study of biology and the institutions he directed supported his own social views that there were superior races in mankind, that racial hybrids were inferior, that miscegenation should not be permitted, that geography also played a part and that immigration to the United States should be restricted. Davenport distrusted cities and he saw "germ plasm" as the key to eugenic control. Germ plasm was the hereditary material, as contrasted to the hereditary body cells, passed from generation to generation. If the laws of eugenics could become laws adopted by governments then society could ensure victory for the biologically superior.

The Eugenics Record Office as a Pressure Group

In 1910 Mrs. Mary Williamson (Averell) Harriman funded the Eugenics Record Office at Cold Spring Harbor. This adjoined the facilities of the Carnegie Institution already directed by Davenport and was endorsed by the American Genetics Association. With a maintenance fund from Mrs. Harriman, scientists at Cold Spring Harbor now increased research on human inheritance, collected and indexed data and issued reports. The first Eugenics Record Office Bulletin in 1911 was entitled *Heredity of Feeblemindedness*, by Henry H. Goddard. Dr. Davenport, the director of the Record Office, and the staff conducted extensive investigations among prison inmates and the feeble-minded under state care to learn the effect of marriage among defective persons upon future generations.

Mrs. Harriman was well pleased and on January 1, 1918, transferred the office buildings and land to the Carnegie Institution of Washington and provided an endowment of $300,000 toward its maintenance. Her ultimate interest in eugenics was not research for its own sake but a basis for an action program. The benign picture of the thoughtful, generous philanthropist painted by her biographers[1 2] is offset by Mrs. Harriman's passion for the swift and sure correction of human deficiencies by means of applied eugenics. This confidence was expressed by her at a public meeting in 1915 when she declared, "What is the matter with the American people? Fifteen million must be sterilized!"[1 3]

The Eugenics Record Office, from 1910 to 1940, was the functional equivalent of an interest group. In particular, Harry Laughlin and his closest associate at the office, Arthur Estabrook, spread the eugenics creed by publications, correspondence, travel for consultations and lectures, and by conducting training institutes for field workers in eugenics. They developed legislative proposals which culminated in a "Model Eugenical Sterilization Law." When test cases developed they were commonly in correspondence with state officials and the lawyer for the state with advice on how to select a patient for a test case, how to gather the appropriate evidence and how far to go with an appeal.

They acquired considerable expertise in litigation and in the tactics of the adoption and application of eugenics policy from experience in many states. Their advocacy of eugenics policies in the states was as persistent and broad-scaled for the Eugenics Record Office as it would have been if that office had a more telling label, such as the "Society for the Promotion of Eugenical Sterilization through Legislation, Enforcement and Legal Defense."

The political side of the activities fostered by the Eugenics Record Office is shown by many publications and by the work of Harry H. Laughlin. In 1914, he sought to advance this program in a Record Office bulletin entitled "The Legal,

Legislative and Administrative Aspects of Sterilization." Fact finding had a central function for eugenists, for sterilization could follow only when there was convincing evidence that a human flaw was obvious and that it was, in fact, hereditary. Davenport and Laughlin consequently worked up a how-to-do-it kit combining the tasks of genealogy with those of biology and published this in 1915 as another bulletin of the Record Office.[14] These bulletins had a wide audience and, through staff travel and the organization of training institutes, the basic message of eugenics action was put across.

The late nineteenth century witnessed a sharp rise in immigration and an even sharper increase in public correctional institutions and private charities. Men and women concerned with these forms of social service were alarmed over these developments and were susceptible to panaceas offered to arrest and solve them. The new science of eugenics gave a certain comfort to many second, third and older generation Americans by indicating that their stock was genetically superior to the newer immigrants and that the inmates of mental hospitals were poor, helpless victims of hereditary infirmities. This belief enabled them to salve their consciences and adopt a positive program of immigration restriction on the one hand and eugenical sterilization on the other. Both programs were thought sensible and pragmatic public policy and not at all the narrow, self-serving program it appears to observers from another time or place.

Illustrative of the scientific conservation, genealogical and race-inspired mix of the eugenics movement were the papers delivered to the Second International Congress of Eugenics, held at the American Museum of Natural History in New York, September 22-28, 1921. There were many scientific papers of interest only to biologists, botanists and statisticians, but the meeting had a marked political side. In the address of welcome, Henry Fairfield Osborn, calling himself a paleontologist and geologist, forcefully urged a restrictive national immigration policy, saying, "We are engaged in a serious struggle to maintain our historic republican institutions through barring the entrance of those who are unfit to share the duties and responsibilities of our well-founded government."[15]

He also expressed fear that "the purest New England stock is not holding its own. The next stage is the no-child marriage and the extinction of the stock which laid the foundations of the republican institutions of this country."[16] This was all spelled out in one of the papers entitled "The Mayflower Pilgrims."[17] In it Sarah Louise Kimball of the California Genealogical Society showed to her satisfaction that a number of presidents and other men of prominence and achievement could trace their family line back to Plymouth Rock. Another indicator of the social objectives of the congress is seen in the service of Madison Grant as its treasurer and Laughlin as secretary of publications.

State Sterilization Legislation

Sterilization operations had begun in state mental hospitals late in the nineteenth century and a snarl of legislative, administrative and judicial policy and practice grew up in conjunction with other aspects of the eugenics movement. Thus there were some three decades of state governmental activity in eugenics prior to the Supreme Court case of *Buck v. Bell*. A thumbnail history of the early Indiana experience will display how the vagaries of chance and legal ambiguity affected eugenic practice.[18] In phase one, from 1899 to 1907, vasectomy operations on convicts at the state reformatory at Jeffersonville were regularly practiced. These sterilizations were performed by a physician, Dr. H.C. Sharp, "Under the general laws governing surgical practice in the state." No other information about the legal basis of his actions is available but it is authoritatively stated that "his motives were purely eugenical."[19]

In phase two this practice was given a firmer legal foundation with the enactment in 1907 of a specific statute empowering a committee of experts to act with the regular institutional physician and board of managers of all institutions to authorize sterilization. It applied to "confirmed criminals, idiots, rapists and imbeciles." This Indiana law permitted these agents to proceed when they judged an inmate to be unimprovable and unfit for procreation and ordained simply that the surgical operation shall be "the safest and most effective." During the next phase beginning in 1909 this law was effectively nullified and operations ceased because of the opposition of the new governor of Indiana. He was Thomas R. Marshall, governor from 1909 to 1913, vice president of the United States from 1913 to 1921 and famous for having once said, "What this country needs is a good five cent cigar."

Phase four came with an administration that favored enforcement of the 1907 statute but first prudently sponsored a court case to settle legal uncertainties. This came immediately after World War I and an ample account of the circumstances of the litigation is available from a field report from Arthur Estabrook in Indiana to Cold Spring Harbor. He explained that Governor James P. Goodrich asked the institutions to comply with the vasectomy law and the reformatory at Jeffersonville proceeded to appoint a Sterilization Board. But, according to Estabrook,

... institutional officials, especially the physicians involved, were more or less fearful because of the seeming unconstitutionality of the act, and so were rather afraid to go ahead merely on the governor's wish, so he took some money from his contingent fund, secured a very good lawyer from Jeffersonville as counsel for plaintiff, instructing the lawyer to test the constitutionality of the act on every possible ground of there being any errors in the same. The lawyer selected was Wilmer T. Fox, a high type man of good intellectual and social traits.

Warren Wallace Smith, the subject in this case, was selected as the plaintiff in the case, because he had been convicted of incest and sent to the reformatory, coming under the classification of rapist in the act.

It was explained to Smith that he was chosen for the case, that the act of sterilization was not going to be carried out, that this was to be a test case and he agreed to the proposition. ... In view of the fact that this test case is a friendly case, and there was to be no argument about the facts, I feel you will not need any particular data concerning Smith's career in the reformatory. However, Smith is probably a high-grade imbecile, coming from a more or less degenerate family in Wayne County, was sent to the reformatory . . . for incest on his half-sister . . . February 13, 1919, for two to twenty-one years.[20]

Yet Laughlin correctly anticipated the flaws in this test case in Indiana. It was evident from Estabrook's reports that Wilmer T. Fox would discharge his duties as appointed counsel for Smith in a thoroughly competent manner. Among the objections Fox urged was "that the medical profession is not yet agreed on diagnoses in the mental field and also they did not agree on the effects of sterilization, and . . . the judiciary must protect the people until such an agreement takes place." Fox said that he and other constitutional lawyers in Indiana were concerned that the statute "creates increased punishment with no court action," thereby combining the legal profession's hostility to the development of administrative law with a sound enough sense of innate procedural fairness. Another flaw lay in the choice of Warren Smith to bring the injunction to test the validity of the act because there was insufficient hereditary information about him. The objections of Fox were sustained and in December 1919 a state trial judge granted a permanent injunction against the chief physician and board of the reformatory at Jeffersonville on the ground that the Indiana sterilization act of 1907 was unconstitutional "because it denies to the persons subject to it the right to free administration of justice in open court."[21] This judgement was affirmed in 1921 by the Indiana Supreme Court.[22]

The Indiana experience between 1899 and 1921 was unique, but not untypical of the complex conflict engendered in other states by the issue of eugenical sterilization which aroused strenuous opposition in one branch of state government or another. Typically early bills provided for sterilization of inmates of various correctional institutions and were directed either at convicted criminals or persons with mental illness. They gave large discretion to directors or to committees of physicians employed by the state and often omitted any formal review otherwise.

Whether legislation had a primitive, therapeutic or hereditary motive and whatever its substance and procedure, objections stopped it at some level in many states. In addition to Pennsylvania in 1905 there were gubernatorial vetoes there again in 1921, in Oregon in 1909, Vermont and Nebraska in 1913, and Idaho in 1919. Occasionally state attorneys general were asked to rule these laws invalid but declined to do so in California in 1910 and Connecticut in 1912. Test cases were pressed in eight states. The Washington Supreme Court held the act in that state constitutional in 1912, but the courts in seven states invalidated sterilization statutes.[23]

The eugenists at Cold Spring Harbor followed the legal panorama with close interest and, with the care that specialized advocates often lavish on a subject, developed more thorough approaches to overcome obstacles. In 1922 Laughlin came forward with a full-scale bible for the legal program of the eugenics movement—*Eugenical Sterilization in the United States*. In its preface he says:

This volume is intended primarily for practical use. It is designed to be of particular service to four classes of persons: First, to law-makers who have to decide upon matters of policy to be worked out in legislation regulating eugenical sterilization; second to judges of the courts, upon whom, in most states having sterilization statutes, devolves the duty of deciding upon the constitutionality of new statutes, and of determining cacogenic individuals and of ordering their sexual sterilization; third, to administrative officers who represent the state in locating, and in eugenically analyzing persons alleged to be cacogenic, and who are responsible for carrying out the orders of the courts; and fourth, to individual citizens who, in the exercise of their civic rights and duties, desire to take the initiative in reporting for official determination and action, specific cases of obvious family degeneracy.[24]

Laughlin's hoped-for audience included lay vigilantes who could discharge their own "civic rights" by reporting "obvious family degeneracy." The chief audience remained legislators, judges and administrators.

Laughlin's book contains texts of all the state laws on the books by 1922, statistical summaries of enforcement and a detailed review of litigation growing out of the several statutes in Washington, New Jersey, Iowa, Michigan, New York, Nevada, Indiana and Oregon. Several bills passed by legislatures had been vetoed by the governor and seven state sterilization statutes had been invalidated by courts because of procedural inadequacies. But in 1922 Laughlin declared that the experimental period for legislation was over and "it is now possible to enact a just and eugenically effective statute on this subject."[25]

He then set forth the full text for a "Eugenical Sterilization Law," which would be "AN ACT to prevent the procreation of persons socially inadequate from defective inheritance, by authorizing and providing for the eugenical sterilization of certain potential parents carrying degenerate hereditary qualities." The law would establish an Office of State Eugenicist to protect society from defectives. The law provided for a most elaborate and careful administrative procedure full of provisions for notice and hearing and for judicial review but, as Walter Berns observed in a critique published many years later,[26] there was an assumption about who the law covered and what the effect of the law would be that should scorch the thinnest sensibilities about the meaning of substantive due process.

The definitions show how incredibly careless and abusive this model was. The law would apply to individuals in these groups of persons: "A socially inadequate person is one who by his or her own effort . . . fails chronically in comparison with normal persons, to maintain himself or herself as a useful member of the organized life of the state." This would not embrace the old, the young and the infirm if the "ineffectiveness is adequately taken care of by the particular family in which it occurs." "The socially inadequate classes" was defined more sweepingly to include the feeble-minded, insane, criminalistic "including the delinquent and wayward," epileptic, inebriate "including drug habituates," diseased "including the tuberculous, the syphilitic, the leprous," blind, deaf, deformed and dependent "including orphans, ne'er-do-wells, the homeless, tramps and paupers." The law would also apply against a category of persons called "a potential parent of socially inadequate offspring," at least one-fourth of whose possible offspring would, on the average, "according to the demonstrated laws of heredity, most probably function as socially inadequate persons." Such a parent would be given the legal label of "cacogenic person" and under all the procedural safeguards could be subjected, against an individual's will, to eugenical sterilization.

In 1936, Laughlin received an honorary degree in medicine from the University of Heidelberg, presented through the German Consul General in New York. Dr. H. Borchers made the presentation to Laughlin on December 8. The degree is in German and English and reads in part:

We honor him [Laughlin] as the pioneer of successful pioneer[s] of practical Eugenics and the farseeing representative of racial policy in America.
Drawn up and announced at Heidelberg on June 30, 1936.

Laughlin's letter of acceptance was sent to Heidelberg on August 11, 1936, and in it he said he was "greatly honored to accept this degree from the University of Heidelberg, which stands for the highest ideals of scholarship and research achieved by those racial stocks which have contributed so much to the foundation blood of the American people." He ended his letter by saying:

I consider the conferring of this high degree upon me not only as a personal honor, but also as evidence of a common understanding of German and American scientists of the nature of eugenics as research in and the practical application of those fundamental biological and social principles which determine the racial endowments and the racial health—physical, mental, and spiritual—of future generations.[27]

Buck v. Bell as a "Friendly Suit"

The letter of the Virginia law was followed by the superintendent of the State Colony for Epileptics and Feeble-Minded (in Colony, Virginia, near Lynchburg) as proceedings against Carrie Buck unfolded. He petitioned a three-member special board to order her sterilization on the grounds that she was a "moral delinquent—had just given birth to a mentally defective child before admissions" and had "a mental age of 9 years and feeble-minded of the moron class." (Record, p. 9.) Born July 2, 1906, in Charlottesville, Carrie Buck was committed to the State Colony before her eighteenth birthday. Her mother, Emma Buck, was already a legally committed inmate; her father, Frank Buck, was dead.

The Circuit Court of Amherst County in July 1924 appointed Robert G. Shelton to act as guardian of Carrie Buck "to defend her rights and interests" in the proceedings. Those proceedings before the board were held in September with Colonel Aubrey E. Strode as attorney for the superintendent (A.S. Priddy, later succeeded in office by John Hendren Bell) and I.P. Whitehead, attorney for R.G. Shelton, guardian and friend of Carrie Buck. Cross-examination at the hearing stressed the safety of the operation, the possible rehabilitation of the victim and alternative care. Without the operation it seemed likely "that both for her protection and the protection of society she must be kept in custody and confinement until her child-bearing age is past." (Record, p. 27.) With sterilization, on the other hand, Carrie Buck "could leave the Colony and enjoy the liberty and blessings of outdoor life, become self-supporting, and thereby relieve the Commonwealth of Virginia of the burden of the support of her under custodial care." (Record, p. 9.) Her talents were evidently meager although she could, at least, "help out around the house."

Asked at the hearing if she had a comment on having the operation performed on her, Carrie Buck answered, "No, sir, I have not, it is up to my people." (Record, p. 27.) On September 30, 1924, the board ordered the superintendent to have a competent physician perform, "after not less than 30 days from the date of this order, the operation of salpingectomy upon the said Carrie Buck." (Record, p. 28.)

The sterilization ordered by the board was carried to the Circuit Court of Amherst County, where the eugenic argument was amplified. The record was dramatically filled by observations of Harry Laughlin in answer to questions agreed to by opposing counsel, propounded in behalf of the superintendent. Laughlin's deposition was taken before a notary public at his office at Cold Spring Harbor.

Laughlin's deposition in *Buck v. Bell* for the trial court brought a nationally prominent eugenist directly into this key case. A movement may account for a statute but then its fulfillment and application depend upon government officials possessing great discretion and overwhelming duties. Advocates of a statute commonly follow up their legislative work by urging administrators to put a favorable policy into action. In a court test of administrative and legislative authority, advocates in a movement reappear again, often with the latest and most polished arguments. Laughlin had by 1924 become a well of knowledge on political and legal tactics as the Eugenics Record Office went well beyond research in advocating public policy.

The deposition was one means of placing the professional eugenic viewpoint before the courts. Several points were made. Laughlin made a long-distance analysis of the hereditary nature of Carrie Buck's family, relying on a Red Cross nurse in Charlottesville to "try to work out their line." (Record, p. 33.) On sketchy facts the nurse said of the family: "These people belong to the shiftless, ignorant, and worthless class of anti-social whites of the South." (Record, p. 33.) Laughlin concluded that Carrie Buck's feeble-minded character stemmed from heredity, not environment, for she had been in a foster home after the age of four, had an opportunity for schooling but yet "was sexually very immoral, and finally bore an illegitimate child." (Record, p. 34.) Upon this basis Laughlin believed she fell within the scope of the Virginia statute as she was "a potential parent of socially inadequate or defective offspring." (Record, p. 35.)

Eugenic findings were entered in the record of *Buck v. Bell* through Laughlin's deposition for the Amherst County court. As this was a test case, Laughlin was asked to "outline the results of scientific investigations tending to show that feeble-mindedness is likely to be transmitted to offspring from a feeble-minded parent." (Record, p. 30.) Laughlin submitted a number of his own publications and those of the Eugenics Records Office and spoke to the record of the "many hundreds of manuscript pedigrees of families with feeble-minded members." From his studies he concluded that "both feeble-mindedness and other intelligence levels are, in most cases, accounted for by hereditary qualities." (Record, p. 35.) He cited a number of studies by eugenists about the English experience under the Mental Deficiency Act in force in Britain since 1914.

The message was that, despite some objections, sterilization was appropriate in many cases. It worked and was salutary for both individual and society and, if anything, more action was called for. The methods of eugenics could serve the government in the administration of sterilization statutes. Laughlin favored the English proposal by Dr. Gibbons that "in case of a feeble-minded man or woman, or those having such a family history of insanity as would render in the highest degree probable mentally defective children, one or both could be sterilized before granting the certificate." (Record, p. 37, quoting R.A. Gibbons, "Sterilization of Mental Defectives," in the *British Medical Journal*, August 11, 1923, pp. 226-28.)

Laughlin's concluding words included these: "Modern eugenical sterilization is a force for the mitigation of race degeneracy which, if properly used, is safe and effective." (Record, p. 40.) And, finally, "I believe that the Virginia statute is, in the main, one of the best laws thus far enacted in that it has avoided the principal eugenical and legal defects of previous statutes, and has incorporated into it the most effective eugenical features and the soundest legal principles of previous laws." (Record, p. 41.) The trial court upheld the board, the Virginia Supreme Court and the United States Supreme Court affirmed.

On Octber 19, 1927, Carrie Buck was sterilized, later left the institution, and married and settled down. According to the records, her illegitimate daughter, who lived with a Mrs. Dobbs in Charlottesville, Virginia (and died at age nine of measles), was reported to have been "very bright." The hospital records contained no definite evidence that the child was "feeble-minded."[28]

Buck v. Bell exemplifies judicial restraint at work as Justice Holmes's opinion of the Court first expressed the famous skepticism that led him so regularly to defer to the legislature: "In view of the general declarations of the legislature and the specific findings of the [Virginia] court obviously we cannot say as matter of law that the grounds do not exist, and if they exist they justify the result." But he goes much further than a presumption of validity and seems, quite certainly, to have endorsed the concept of eugenical sterilization as wise public policy.

If all sides in a case announced to the Supreme Court that they had a mutual, unopposed interest in resolving the legal issues raised, the matter would be dropped promptly. Pritchett put the principle that the Supreme Court does not decide such cases this way:

From the principle that a lawsuit must pit against each other parties with adverse legal interests grows the practice in the federal courts of refusing to accept so-called "friendly suits." Obviously, if the interests of the opposing parties are actually not adverse, then motivation for bringing out all the relevant facts will be lacking, and the trial court will have no assurance that justice is being done. Particularly is this important when the constitutionality of a federal statute is being attacked, because both parties might actually be antagonistic to the statute.[29]

Although Pritchett notes exceptions in stockholder cases, and although all authorities recognize some slippage in the application of this doctrine, there has been almost no appreciation, or at least declaration, that numerous Supreme Court cases are conceived and carried forward by lawyers posing as opponents while, in fact, allied in conducting a friendly suit. They dare not announce this out of fear of jeopardizing the chance of having the issue adjudicated. They may even do a lawyerlike job of "bringing out all the relevant facts" for, after all, intelligence and acumen will do this job far better than being adversaries.

It is a fiction that the Supreme Court does not accept "friendly suits," for the Court does so—unknowingly for the most part. The Court makes no independent investigation of the origins of its cases. The "friendly suit" is not the only vehicle that obliterates the search for the truth and for the wise formulation of public policy by the courts. Thurman Arnold showed long ago that the celebrated adversary process, which he called "trial by combat,"[30] also shielded the truth and was a costly and inefficient means of policy-making, as well. Probably every procedure has weaknesses and strengths. Here, in the constitutional testing of mandatory eugenical sterilization, is a chance to see how a "friendly suit"— not previously so identified—served the Supreme Court and the public.[31]

Buck v. Bell may confidently be denominated a "friendly suit" for its complete absence of a devoted and informed critic of eugenical sterilization for insane persons. This was true in the sense that one social movement was at work on both sides of litigation. It was also true in its specifics as counsel were not simply social friends, which is quite beside the point, but associates in improving and reforming the mental hospitals of Virginia.

Although Thurman Arnold and others have correctly diagnosed weaknesses in the adversary method, the "friendly suit" dressed up as an encounter between opposing interests is equally inadequate, if for quite different reasons. In *Buck v.*

Bell, the expertise in the record was one-sided as Laughlin's deposition was not subjected to critical examination. Carrie Buck's lawyer had neither the resources nor the desire to search for experts who might contradict Laughlin. Mr. Justice Butler no doubt opposed the Virginia statute, not on procedural grounds but for moral reasons rooted in his Catholicism.[32] If counsel had offered the Catholic viewpoint and other criticisms of sterilization in his brief, some justices might have had second thoughts and Butler might have had at hand in usable form materials for a spoken instead of a silent dissent.

Yet, we are all time-bound, and with the eugenics movement at its height in 1927 the Court was its prisoner. Otherwise the justices might have put off the issue; they might not have accepted for review any case at that time. Or they might, as they so commonly had done in the past, and have continued to do, have accumulated cases—stacked them up—so the issue of eugenical sterilization could be reviewed in the context of several statutes, in several states, with the resultant multiplication of counsel and of interest. The decision in *Buck v. Bell* publicized the subject. It is obviously desirable for a subject to be advertised *in advance* of a constitutional decision so that the public, the interested parties, the media and scholars may examine and debate the issues.

From Compulsory to Voluntary Sterilization

The assumptions of Galtonian eugenics—that there are good genes and bad, that these are identifiable and that government should sterilize carriers of bad genes—were fiercely and effectively criticized both before and after Mr. Justice Holmes delivered the opinion in *Buck v. Bell*. Governors Pennypacker and Marshall, many legislators, some lawyers and popular writers, Catholic theologians, and leading biologists belatedly attacked the racial improvement ambitions of eugenics and questioned the scientific claims of the movement.

As early as 1911, Charles A. Boston, a noted New York City lawyer, spoke out against compulsory sterilization at the New York Academy of Medicine.[33] Perhaps G.K. Chesterton foresaw the dangers of eugenical sterilization best of all when he published a book in 1927 entitled *Eugenics and Other Evils*. He correctly anticipated how eugenical sterilization could readily become a keystone to a regime like Nazi Germany under Hitler when he called the eugenics movement part of a "modern craze for scientific officialism and strict social organization."[34] Looking back it is this view, by an English essayist, that is more in tune with the spirit of American constitutional law in 1970 than the endorsement of Mr. Justice Holmes in the same year of 1927.

In his 1930 encyclical on *Christian Marriage in Our Day*, Pope Pius XI labeled eugenic sterilization a crime, insisting that as "public magistrates have no direct power over the bodies of their subjects ... they can never directly harm, or tamper with the integrity of the body, either for the reasons of eugenics or for any other reason."[35]

Pius XI's criticisms were both moral and scientific, in keeping with the claim of the church that its "condemnation of contraceptive sterilization has been consistent and current with medical practice."[36] Soon after the surgical technique of salpingectomy became a reality and eugenists urged its use, the Holy Office, in 1895, "declared that no active or passive procedure that was undertaken with the express purpose of sterilizing a woman was permitted."[37] From then on, "the theologians of the church recognized it as an immoral invasion of human integrity."[38]

Leading scientists within the framework of the eugenics movement now ridiculed and rejected "the slow and tedious methods of selective breeding" and insisted that social change was "a matter of social factors, not racial."[39] The *coup de grâce* was administered in 1932 by Herbert J. Muller, later a Nobel laureate, when he addressed the Third International Eugenics Congress. He admitted that eugenics could still apply to imbecility but that, otherwise, Galtonian eugenics merely projected class bias and could not be a respectable scientific enterprise.[40]

The generally complex problem of defining and studying legal compliance with statutory and judicial commands is reflected specifically in recent history of sterilization of humans in the United States. Punitive sterilization was declared unconstitutional by the Supreme Court in the case of *Skinner v. Oklahoma* in 1942.[41] But in holding that mentally healthy prisoners could not be sterilized, the Court did not reconsider the *Buck v. Bell* rule that the feebleminded could be. And yet the rule has eroded. What does this mean? For one thing, by 1970 compulsory sterilization under twenty-eight state statutes was "statistically insignificant" with only 488 cases reported in 1963, the last year for which reports are available.[42] Voluntarism has asserted itself. Instead of the feeble-minded being sterilized, people with the highest intelligence are today being sterilized. Ardent biologists voluntarily bind themselves to have no more than two children and then proselytize the world to join them.[43]

In 1969, the Board of Directors of the Association for Voluntary Sterilization, Inc., resolved that "to prevent increasing overpopulation, American parents in general, irrespective of race, economic status, educational background, or age range, should adopt as a social and family ideal the principle of the two-child family."[44] While operations upon state hospital inmates mandated by statute have virtually vanished, "over two million Americans have chosen voluntary contraceptive sterilization."[45] Some 100,000 persons in the United States annually choose voluntary sterilization.

This is a profound change in temper from the eugenic evangelism of the 1920s to sterilize the "unfit" to the effort in the 1960s and 1970s to persuade the fit to submit voluntarily. This transformation requires legal change, too, as many states once restricted voluntary sterilization. This was an anomaly compared to the eugenics laws, but is accountable to the earlier nineteenth-century disdain for birth control legislation.[46]

Practical developments rarely coincide neatly with legislative and judicial declarations. Neither *Buck v. Bell* nor the twenty-eight state eugenic statutes on the books in 1970 require sexual sterilization; but they authorize operations under certain conditions. In practice the number of surgical sterilization operations upon imbeciles (persons who in today's gentler parlance might be spoken of as merely retarded) in state institutions is close to zero. The authorizing legislation will likely be repealed or revised in many states but it is not at all certain that the Supreme Court of the United States will get an opportunity for overruling *Buck v. Bell*.

The Supreme Court barely missed an opportunity to review its 1927 ruling in *Buck v. Bell* when it noted probable jurisdiction on February 4, 1969, of an appeal in the case of *Cavitt v. Nebraska*.[47] The chief question presented was whether a Nebraska statute under which sterilization may be made a condition for release of a mental defective was unconstitutional. The case began when the patient, Gloria Cavitt "indicated that she did not desire to have the operation."[48] The Board of Examiners of the Mentally Deficient in Nebraska ordered the operation over objections of Gloria Cavitt's appointed guardian, Vincent L. Dowding, then a practicing attorney in Beatrice, Nebraska. He appealed the case to the district court of Gage County and won but the state gained reversal in the Nebraska Supreme Court. In the meanwhile, the Nebraska legislature repealed the sterilization law, adding an amendment "to provide that no sterilization could be done even though a pending Court order indicated otherwise. This amendment was specifically added to take care of the Cavitt case." The repealer went into effect in December 1969. Gloria Cavitt was accordingly released from the Beatrice State Home without sterilization and the case was entirely mooted. The Supreme Court then simply dismissed the appeal without further proceedings.[49]

The appeal to the Supreme Court in *Cavitt v. Nebraska*[50] had all the earmarks of an argument whose time had come. Three modern constitutional claims were stressed. One questioned whether due process was met where "Gloria Cavitt was ordered sterilized without any statutory requirement that there be a finding that her mental deficiency be inherited by her offspring." Another raised the equal protection issue, noting that the Nebraska law applied "only to inmates of the Beatrice State Home and not to the general public or the other state institutions where mentally deficient patients are committed and housed and where poverty or wealth is a factor in the decision of the Board of Examiners of Mentally Deficient on whether or not to order sterilization." The statement also questioned whether the Nebraska law was "repugnant to the Eighth Amendment of the United States Constitution where no statutory limitations are placed on the type of sterilization operation that may be used and where hysterectomy operations have been performed under the statutes."

This recent experience suggests uncertainty about the Supreme Court's opportunity to review its dictum that "three generations of imbeciles are enough." Clearly, three generations are not enough to make predictions. More-over, one writer states that 89 percent of mentally deficient persons are born to normal parents.[51] How well we know that there are retarded children in the families of royalty, the famous and other worthies. The fact is that the justices have probably changed their minds and, anyhow, they are not the same justices who sat on *Buck v. Bell*. But the important fact is that since 1927 the position of most biologists, physicians, modern-day advocates of population control have concluded that compulsory sterilization is immoral, inhumane and unscientific. They do not all agree about voluntary sterilization, but that is the path of the future. This change has not yet been reflected fully in formal constitutional law but the shift is nonetheless real.

2

The Grandfather Clause

Chance does, indeed, have much to do with the origination of cases decided in the Supreme Court of the United States. In 1915 the grandfather clause cases came from Oklahoma and Maryland.[1] Lineal descendants of persons qualified to vote before the Fifteenth Amendment's adoption in 1870 were excused from literacy tests. But Oklahoma, in 1910, was the last of seven states to include the grandfather clause in its constitution. (The clause forbade a person to vote who was not himself eligible or a descendant of someone who was eligible to vote on January 1, 1869.) South Carolina in 1895, Louisiana in 1898, North Carolina in 1900, Alabama in 1901, Virginia in 1902 and Georgia in 1908 had already done so.[2] And the Maryland legislature in 1908 had applied a grandfather clause to voter registration in only one city, Annapolis. It is customary for the Supreme Court, in reviewing claims of constitutional transgression, to sample rather than to survey, as a legislative investigating committee might do. Two sides resourcefully devoted to a cause are said to be essential to spawning test cases for Supreme Court review. This necessary condition definitely prevailed in Maryland and Oklahoma, where it apparently did not in states farther south. It was not, then, altogether fortuitous that the grandfather clause cases originated in these two border states.

This is another exploration in strategies of constitutional change. As such, the uniquenesses in the controversy as well as aspects common to other litigations will be searched out. Any voting case exhibits the irony of minority adjudication of majoritarian practices. The fundamental issue is over the definition of the constituency, that is, the qualification for participation in the polity. In 1910 in the United States, it is well to recall, universal manhood suffrage was less than a hundred years old. In England, Macaulay had ridiculed that notion in the 1830s. Women had not yet won national suffrage either in England or in the United States. The secret Australian ballot was still a novelty. The Fifteenth Amendment to the United States Constitution, providing that no person shall be denied the right to vote "on account of race, color, or previous condition of servitude," was forty years old. This is simply to argue that definitions of the electorate were not completely settled; there were arguments about qualifications unique to that time. If disagreement over fundamentals is the essence of constitutional debate—as it is—then the condition prevailed in good measure in the states of Maryland and Oklahoma in the era of the grandfather clause cases.

Opposing arrays of the population over a public issue is a common prior condition for a constitutional "test case" in the Supreme Court. In this instance, in Oklahoma some 100,000 votes opposed adopting the grandfather clause in a 250,000 vote referendum. In Maryland, proposals to disfranchise Negroes were debated for a decade or more before the most limited kind of measure was enacted by the legislature. Nor is a test case ordinarily simply manufactured in the sense of being contrived, arranged and invented out of whole cloth. The demands of the judicial process will, of course, be served, but this is different. Factions in a political dispute will find lawyers (or is it the other way around?) when, having lost in other arenas, they are prepared to do battle in the courts. More often than not in American constitutional practice particular organizations sponsor the ensuing litigation. If they are lucky enough to have their values and interests shared by the executive branch of government it may be possible to have their cause represented by the state. The organizations vary with the issue. Real estate boards and neighborhood associations will appear in housing cases, granges and commodity groups in farm cases, churches in religious freedom cases. Political parties are the pertinent organizations in disputes over the size and definition of the electorate.

The grandfather clause cases from Oklahoma and Maryland afford instances of political party functioning as an interest group by sponsoring constitutional litigation.[3] This fact requires recasting old conceptions. In turning to the courts, as Socialists and Republicans did to retain blacks within their constituencies, political parties wanted to protect themselves. Democrats sought to exclude blacks from the electorate by means of legislation, but they had no hesitation in defending that legislation in the courts. The commitment to litigation was made by state central committees in Oklahoma and at least some of the lawyers engaged in the cases were authorized to do so by the party organization. In all cases, the lawyers for the parties were prominent members of competing political parties.

To triumph in elections political parties sometimes go to court. Indeed, going to court is ordinarily only an incidental event in the life of any voluntary organization. A notation that organizations support a test case does not mean they monopolize. One expects to see expressions of interest which are at once both narrower and broader than an organizational concern suggests. What I have in mind are the striking individuals with larger-than-life theories. To them, a test case offers an opportunity, and a dramatic one, to espouse their political theory and hopefully contribute to fashioning a usable building block for the constitutional order they seek.

We shall see that to advocates in Maryland like William L. Marbury and in Oklahoma like Robert Lee Williams the grandfather clause was simply one expedient to achieve white supremacy in the social, political and legal orders. Marbury had a passionate desire, shared with fellow Baltimore barristers, to see the Fourteenth and Fifteenth Amendments set aside. Thus he grasped the chance afforded by the test case over the grandfather clause to bring the Supreme Court around to his persuasion. It happens to be characteristic of many Supreme Court cases that a different utopia is presented by the other contenders. That opposite view was offered in these cases by Moorfield Storey, who filed the very first Supreme Court brief ventured by the National Association for the Advancement of Colored People. To him, this test case could be a step up the long road to an equalitarian and fair society as well as one where a racial test for voting would be anathema.

Race is the central ingredient in these test cases, and it is central because the ultimate issue was the place of blacks in the American constitutional order. The lower court judges and the Supreme Court justices who sat on these cases knew they were doing that, even as they practiced the arcane and the practical skills of their craft. But because law develops from a welter of societal conflict, over centuries, its accomplished practitioners are saturated with its values. These are different from their predilections about race, class, church and party. This is why it is relevant to look closely at the legal features of these test cases. The larger struggle is naturally reflected in some aspects of the judicial process at the same time many requirements of constitutional litigation are fulfilled quite apart from the subject matter in dispute.

Disfranchisement in Maryland

Economically, socially and politically Maryland—and especially Baltimore—after the Civil War were microcosms of national tensions between northern and southern values. The ambivalence was generations old. All the conflicting feelings had been acerbated during the war and, of course, time had only rechanneled and not fundamentally altered these sentiments. At the end of the Civil War Baltimore bankers and merchants decided their "primary job was to help the South get back on its feet in a business way."[4] Hamilton Owens, the great editor of the *Baltimore Sun*, in his economic history of Baltimore wrote of this era in this way:

It was the men of the quality of Johns Hopkins and Enoch Pratt who determined the course that Baltimore was to follow after the war. The wisdom of the course they suggested was so apparent that it became almost a religion with Baltimoreans to regard themselves as the appointed guardians of Southern economic welfare.[5]

In race relations the dominant, though not the unanimous view of Maryland politicians was quintessentially southern in two senses that are germane here. One was its overwhelming opposition to the entrance of blacks into the political life of the state. In 1869 Senator William Pinkney Whyte voted against proposing the Fifteenth Amendment to the Constitution to the states. The notable lawyer and diplomat Reverdy Johnson was perhaps the most esteemed Maryland public man in the mid-nineteenth century, with an honorable southern record. From

1817 onward he practiced law in Baltimore. Representing the defense in the *Dred Scott Case,*[6] Reverdy Johnson was perhaps the major influence in the Supreme Court's ruling that Congress had no power to prohibit slavery in the territories. Looking upon secession as treason, he stood with the Union at the outset of the Civil War, but opposed Lincoln's reelection in 1864 because he regarded the Emancipation Proclamation as unwise. As United States senator from Maryland he was first on one side, then on the other with behavior common to border-state politicians with the result that he won the epithet "trimmer" from his opponents. The sentiments of Whyte and Reverdy Johnson were widely shared in Maryland for decades after the Civil War and just about universally believed in by men in the Democratic party of the state.

But like the more recent Democratic parties of the South so brilliantly analyzed by V.O. Key, Jr., Maryland Democrats from Reconstruction to World War I had their own brand of factionalism. The dominant power after 1867 was Arthur Pue Gorman, who combined economic influence, as president of the Chesapeake & Ohio Canal Company, with political power, as a United States senator from Maryland. Gorman's ally in Baltimore was I. Freeman Rasin, and together they fashioned a political machine in state and city that was a prototype of the age. The redoubtable newspaperman Frank R. Kent associated the sudden advent of black voting with "vote-buying and election bribery in Maryland." He said:

In 1871 the start of this sort of corruption [buying the vote] began, and the Democrats were responsible for it, they being the ones who first found it profitable to pay the negroes to stay away from the polls. The practice grew greatly from that date, and no campaign that followed has been free from it. From buying the negroes the next step was buying the white men, and it did not take many years of this sort of thing before the politics of Maryland became thoroughly steeped in corruption.[7]

The Gorman machine was repeatedly challenged by a Democratic reform faction which sometimes won independents and Republicans to its side. The reform element in the Democratic party of Maryland worked for nonpartisan and independent judges in a critical 1882 contest and won. They sought the Australian ballot, favored civil service reform and opposed political corruption. One of the intellectual leaders among the reformers was Colonel Charles Marshall, a lawyer in Baltimore with a large practice after the Civil War. Around 1880 his nephew William L. Marbury entered the office to read law and begin practice in an association that continued to Marshall's death. Both took to the stump in the so-called new judges fight in 1882 when their allies included the *Baltimore Sun*, which "daily thundered against the iniquities of the bosses and the necessity of defeating them at the polls."[8]

Many a bruising battle occurred between the Gorman and the reform factions in Baltimore and Maryland politics and, by all accounts, elections were danger-

ous affairs. Poll watchers were ordinarily armed and Marbury, an increasingly successful and prominent lawyer in Baltimore, always wore a pistol when he went to vote in nineteenth-century elections. There were real battles; men risked their lives on election days.

While the reform Democrats sought fair primaries, the secret ballot and an end to buying votes, they joined their opponents in the Gorman-Rasin machine in deploring black suffrage and worked to accomplish black disfranchisement in a "lawful manner." A wider southern influence registered in each disfranchisement effort and each also occasioned factional and interparty collisions typical of Maryland politics. First came an "understanding clause" in the form of a state constitutional amendment prepared by John P. Poe and offered to the voters in 1905. This had been taken with a modification from the Mississippi constitution of 1890 and required voters to read and understand any section of the constitution. This was opposed by the reform Democrats and by Republicans also, but for markedly different reasons.

The Poe amendment had been prepared at the request of Senator Gorman to disfranchise the black but was opposed by reformers because they feared it to be unconstitutional and believed it would bring back the era of fraudulent elections. Although Marbury favored legislation in Maryland "as will bring the suffrage of the Negroes within the narrowest limits permitted by the Constitution," he opposed the Poe amendment. It would not accomplish its stated purpose—the elimination of the black vote. If it did do this there would be a terrible side effect, namely the serious endangering of the right of suffrage by the white people of the state. Finally, the discretion placed in the hands of registrars would give new opportunities to the Gorman political faction to control elections.

The Poe amendment also encountered stiff opposition from Republicans in Maryland, led by Charles J. Bonaparte, who expressed an unusual cosmopolitanism at war with some, though not all, of the typical southern enthusiasms of Baltimore Democrats. His grandfather was Napoleon Bonaparte's brother Jerome, King of Westphalia, who married Elizabeth Patterson of Baltimore; his parents were Jerome Bonaparte and Susan May Williams, a New Englander. Charles J. Bonaparte was educated at a French school near Baltimore, graduated from Harvard College in 1872 and from Harvard Law School in 1874. Independently wealthy, he also had a successful law practice and as a mugwump in politics was a prominent figure in countless good causes of the day; a "patrician reformer" as one biographer called him.[9]

As attorney general of the United States from 1905 to 1909, Bonaparte conducted fifty-six cases for the government in the Supreme Court, personally arguing forty-nine. Of the total, thirty-nine were decided in favor of the government position and seventeen against.[10] Bonaparte is today best remembered as originator of the idea of a "special detective force" in the Department of Justice which eventually led to the establishment of the Federal Bureau of Investigation.[11] In March 1909 he returned to law practice in Baltimore.

Bonaparte and other Republicans in Maryland opposed the Poe amendment in 1905 and, in combination with Marbury and the reform Democrats, persuaded the electorate to defeat it in the November 1905 referendum. The effort to disfranchise blacks in Maryland then took its second incarnation in a state constitutional amendment proposed by the legislature to a referendum of the people in 1908. Called the Straus amendment after the attorney general of Maryland, Isaac L. Straus, the Maryland grandfather clause amendment was drafted by a large group of lawyers, including William Marbury. They were intimates of Governor Austin Crothers, who made the clause part of his political platform. On this issue the two parties met head-on, for the Republican party nationally was then championing its services to blacks since the time of Lincoln, boasting of the number of Afro-Americans appointed to office in the Roosevelt administration in contrast to the ante-bellum attitudes of Democrats.[12] From his station in Washington, Attorney General Bonaparte railed against the measure as immoral, unfair and undemocratic and unrepublican.

As with the understanding clause of the Poe amendment in 1905, so too did the grandfather clause of the Straus amendment go down to defeat at the polls in 1909. Frank Kent reported that in the campaign "the two figures most prominently to the front on the Democratic side were Governor Crothers and William L. Marbury, who stumped the state, spoke together in many meetings and everywhere did their utmost for the ticket and the suffrage amendment. This time the *Baltimore Sun* supported the disfranchising amendment. Kent himself evidently favored the grandfather clause from the tone of his report of its defeat at the polls:

Its defeat was a bitter blow to the men who believed the best interest of the state demanded the elimination of the illiterate and venal negro vote. Its defeat convinced them that the last hope of carrying through such an amendment in Maryland had been lost.[13]

Although the voters of Maryland rejected the addition of a grandfather clause to the state constitution the legislature had already quietly, through ordinary local legislation, applied one to the city of Annapolis, in Anne Arundel County.

The racial demography of Maryland in 1910 suggests why the legislature adopted a grandfather clause for one locality when unable to do so statewide.[14] Several counties in northwestern Maryland contained virtually no blacks, although there were more than 25 percent in twelve out of the twenty-three counties (see figure 2-1). The total population of Maryland was 1,062,639, of which 232,250 were blacks. Thus the division in the 1910 census was 82 percent white and 18 percent black. Turning to Annapolis, the census of 1910 reported a total population of 8,601. As women were not eligible to vote, the census counted 2,688 males of voting age in the city of Annapolis, of whom 863 were blacks.

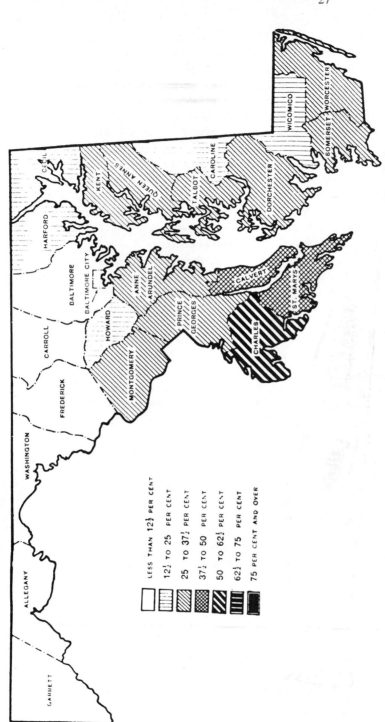

Figure 2-1. Percentage of Blacks in Total Maryland Population: 1910. Source: United States Bureau of the Census, Census of Population, 13th Decennial Census, 1910.

In any event, a grandfather clause was provided for in Maryland legislation signed by Governor Crothers on April 8, 1908, entitled, "An Act to fix the qualification of voters at municipal elections in the City of Annapolis and to provide for the registration of said voters."[15] It provided that only "lawful male descendants of any person who prior to January 1, 1868" had been entitled to vote in Maryland or another state would qualify. This referred back to a time when Maryland's constitution limited voting to white persons.

Local legislation like this did not require ratification as had changes in the state constitution. Marbury had been placed in a position of considerable influence by the election of Governor Crothers in 1907 and this was one of the results, although his efforts to win legislation to disfranchise blacks throughout Maryland had failed. Marbury now stood ready to see the Annapolis grandfather clause enforced and defended in the courts, together with Isaac Straus, who was also the first Jewish lawyer elected to state office.

It is important to recall that during the same time Marbury was active in attempting to disfranchise the black, he was promoting progressive legislation. He persuaded the governor to promise enactment of a direct primary law, a workmen's compensation law, and a law for the regulation of public utilities. Marbury also urged amendments to strengthen the existing laws regulating the hours of work and prohibiting child labor and, after the election of Governor Crothers, he actually drafted these measures which the legislature adopted. During all this period, Marbury also actively promoted further civil service reform.[16]

Three black citizens, each with a personal history suited to test the grandfather clause, sought to register in Annapolis in June 1909. The form of papers filed was identical but each man made a somewhat different claim and so three separate cases originated in the events of that month. Each case was carried to the Supreme Court, though grouped for argument and decision under the first, initiated on behalf of John B. Anderson. He was the eldest of the three, born in 1835, and would have been eligible to vote at any election in Anne Arundel County before the Civil War but for the word "white" in the constitution of Maryland then in force. Anderson served in both the Army and Navy during the war, had sustained injuries and drew a pension. Beginning in 1868, Anderson voted at municipal elections and for thirty-eight years he had also voted for the members of the General Assembly of Maryland.[17]

On June 7, 1909, Anderson filed a two-page letter with the Registrar of Voters, beginning, "Gentlemen: I apply for and demand registration as a legal voter of the City of Annapolis qualified to vote at the municipal elections held therein." After setting forth his qualifications, and asserting the unconstitutionality of the grandfather clause, he concluded, "I respectfully warn you that to refuse me registration as herein requested will deprive me of a right and privilege secured to me by the Constitution and Laws of the United States, and will render you, or such of you as shall join in such refusal, liable to me in a proper

proceeding for redress."[18] One officer, Clarence M. Jones, voted to register Anderson, but two, Charles E. Myers and Claude Kalmey, were opposed.

William H. Howard was born in Annapolis in 1874 and "his grandfather, like himself, was of the negro race, and was nearly of the same very dark complexion." His grandfather also would have been able to vote prior to 1868 except for the word "white" in the Maryland constitution. Howard was a lawyer, a member of the bar of the state of Maryland. He registered to vote at the age of twenty-one and had voted regularly in elections in Annapolis since 1895. When Howard appeared before the registrars on June 14, 1909, Mr. Myers used the words, "Here's another one of them." Otherwise the officials were silent in voting two to one to refuse registration.

The applicant in the third case, Robert Brown, had been born a slave in 1848, and so his father was not qualified to vote until after 1868. The record indicates that Brown could not write. He also presented himself to the officers in Annapolis and was denied registration by a two to one vote.

These cases were joined for trial in the Circuit Court of the United States for the state of Maryland with the plaintiffs bringing a civil suit for damages under the provisions of one of the surviving sections of the act of Congress of April 20, 1871, as follows:

Every person who under color of any statute, ordinance, regulation, custom or usage of any state or territory, subjects or causes to be subjected any citizen of the United States, or other person within the immunities secured by the Constitution and laws, shall be liable to the party injured in an action at law, suit in equity, or other proper proceeding for redress.[19]

That the challenge of the Maryland grandfather clause for Annapolis was a planned test case, and not merely a casual encounter that developed unexpectedly into a constitutional showdown, is shown by the record. The transcript plainly shows that the black voters, Anderson, Howard and Brown, took all the correct steps under the tutelage of their lawyers to establish grounds for a successful challenge.

They, their fathers or grandfathers would have been qualified prior to January 1, 1868, but for the word "white" in the Maryland constitutional provisions then in force. But this word, they argued, "was subsequently in legal effect expunged by the adoption of the Fifteenth Amendment." The denial of these applications deprived the three blacks of the right to vote in an election in the city of Annapolis on July 12, 1909. Their lawyers promptly took their cases into the United States District Court in Baltimore in an ingenious and forceful attack on the Maryland grandfather clause and on the ruling of the election officials. They sought damages from the two judges of elections.

Charles J. Bonaparte and other counsel had settled upon this strategy to document the officials' refusal to register the black voters, thereby establishing grounds for damages.[20] The declaration prepared by Bonaparte and other counsel could hardly have been more pointed. The plaintiff Anderson said "that he then and there and always was, and is now of the negro race and black color, and by reason of his said race and color and for no other reason whatsoever," he was prior to January 1, 1868, excluded from the election franchise in Maryland and at Annapolis.[21] This was an action at law based ultimately, of course, on the contention and for the purpose of having the grandfather clause invalidated as contrary to the Fifteenth Amendment. That they turned to the concept of libel is remarkable in light of observations made in recent years on the infrequent reliance of blacks on this claim. In his provocative lectures on *The Negro and the First Amendment*, Harry Kalven has asserted that blacks apparently had such low esteem that no injury to reputation was conceivable.[22] But in *Anderson v. Myers* the concept of defamation was developed by Bonaparte in this way:

And the plaintiff has been thereby deprived of the right to vote at an election held at the said City of Annapolis (July 12, 1909) and of the right to vote at all future elections in the said City and is subject to an unjust stigma and aspersion of his character and status as a citizen, and his feelings have been greatly wounded and he is subjected to humiliation and obloquy and brought into public scandal, infamy and [distress], and the plaintiff claims five thousand dollars damages.[23]

The Republican State Central Committee of Maryland sponsored these cases against the Annapolis grandfather clause, cases that were six years in court, from 1909 to 1915. When Bonaparte dropped out in 1913 he repeated that the case was "generally regarded, and I think rightly, as under the control of the Republican State Central Committee."[24]

Anderson's declaration was filed in the Circuit Court of the United States for the District of Baltimore on July 30, 1909. A demurrer in response, for Myers and Kalmey, was filed December 9 by lawyers for the defendant officials, William L. Marbury, Ridgely P. Melvin and Isaac L. Straus. The case was heard by Judge Thomas J. Morris, who had been appointed in 1879 by President Hayes. Judge Morris announced his decision in the *Anderson*, *Howard* and *Brown* actions against Myers and Kalmey on October 28, 1910 in a single, comprehensive opinion.[25] This he did on the basis of pleadings to settle the questions of law at issue between the parties.

He held that the Maryland grandfather clause for Annapolis municipal elections was unconstitutional, as violating the Fifteenth Amendment. As the officials enforced an invalid law and deprived them from voting solely because of their race the plaintiffs were entitled to recover damages against the defendants under the Act of Congress of April 20, 1871. Perhaps the most interesting feature of the opinion of Judge Morris was his holding that the Fifteenth Amendment is not limited to congressional elections but applies to the right to vote at state or municipal elections as well. Thus the demurrers of Marbury,

Melvin and Straus were overruled. There were then stipulations by the parties waiving a jury trial and Judge Morris, in February 1911, rendered a verdict against the defendants and entered a judgment of damages of $250 in favor of each of the plaintiffs.

The grandfather clause and William L. Marbury lost. But Marbury was committed to carrying the issue to the Supreme Court of the United States. In the meanwhile, the national mood was changing and Marbury thought, on the whole, in his favor. He was an enthusiastic Wilson man and the National Democratic Convention of 1912 was held in Baltimore. A number of delegates stayed with the Marburys during the convention and Wilson's nomination and subsequent election were considered by them a triumph for southern values. After Wilson's inauguration in March 1913 the executive branch segregated its black employees and registered a preference for white superiority in a number of ways. But, of course, the grandfather clause issue would be considered by the Supreme Court, a part of the government that is presumed to be aloof from immediate shifts in an administration.

Disfranchisement in Oklahoma

Oklahoma is one of the handful of twentieth-century American states; its founding fathers lived in our own time. A special census of population in 1907, taken by the Bureau of the Census to apportion United States representatives from the new state, found that less than 30 percent were native-born Oklahomans. Many of the outlanders prominent in the transformation of Oklahoma from territorial status to statehood were from the South and among these was Robert Lee Williams, born in Alabama.[26] Williams worked his way through Southern University, later named Birmingham-Southern, won admission to the bar in 1891 and an M.A. degree in 1892. He began law practice in Troy, Alabama and moved in 1896 to Indian Territory in the Oklahoma region. Democratic politics became a passion with him and within that interest he was a committed southern Democrat, opposed to Republicans and to blacks, and devoted to bringing Oklahoma into the Union as a white man's state. This was a cause he shared with many others, but his outstanding political and legal skill enabled Williams to attain great public success.

It is the continuity of association with black disfranchisement in Oklahoma which brings Robert Lee Williams center stage in this account. Other men were more important at some points. But unusual turns of fate brought Williams into the grandfather clause and other registration disputes on black suffrage at crucial points. This was because of the string of public offices he occupied and because he believed it was unwise, immoral and unfortunate for anyone except white men to vote. This feeling was bolstered by the fact that most blacks were Republican! Williams first appeared in the long controversy over black access to the polls in Oklahoma in 1910 when the state supreme court reviewed the adoption of the grandfather clause amendment to the constitution.

The grandfather clause added to the Oklahoma constitution in 1910 was embedded in this amendment:

No person shall be registered as an elector of this State or be allowed to vote in any election herein, unless he be able to read and write any section of the constitution of the State of Oklahoma; *but no person who was, on January 1, 1866, or at any time prior thereto, entitled to vote under any form of government, or who at that time resided in some foreign nation, and no lineal descendant of such person, shall be denied the right to register and vote because of his inability to so read and write sections of such constitution.* (Italics supplied.)

To a skeptical Oklahoma journalist, writing a breezy state history, the grandfather clause meant "the ignorant white man, native or immigrant, should have the right to vote; the Negro must qualify by written test in the hands of precinct election officials, many little better versed than he."[27] The leading mover was Fred P. Branson of Muskogee, chairman of the Democratic State Central Committee and also the Oklahoma election board. Initiative petitions, circulated by the Democratic State Committee, gained 43,140 signatures filed with the secretary of state in June 1910. The proposed grandfather clause, said Branson, "is copied from the constitution in the state of North Carolina, which provision was adopted in 1900, and after litigation in the courts, the validity of the same was upheld by the highest tribunal of the nation."

The grandfather clause probably could not have been included in the Oklahoma constitution of 1906 because that document had to be approved by a Republican president and a Congress still solicitous of black voters. Precedent shows that at this stage in the process of gaining statehood, Congress and the administration reigned. Thus, in 1866, provision in the constitution of the new state of Colorado limiting the franchise to white males was vehemently protested by Senator George F. Edmunds of Vermont and was withdrawn.[28]

In Oklahoma, the Department of Justice under Charles J. Bonaparte was engaged in reviewing the phrasing of the enabling act and clearly would have opposed black disfranchisement under a grandfather clause.[29] Once Congress accepts a new constitution and votes admission, a state can change provisions by amendment without further congressional supervision. Oklahoma in 1910 exemplified this practice when, through its initiative and referendum, voters authorized removal of the state capital from the small community of Guthrie to Oklahoma City. The special election was held on June 11, 1910. The population of Guthrie was static, staying under 12,000, while Oklahoma City doubled between the 1907 special census and 1910, from 32,452 to 64,205. Guthrie's claim conclusively failed in the landmark case, *Coyle v. Smith*, where removal to Oklahoma City, allowed by the Oklahoma Supreme Court, and Judge Williams, was affirmed by the Supreme Court of the United States with the opinion of Mr.

Justice Lurton.[30] The basic rule in *Coyle v. Smith* the power to locate a state's seat of government and to control many other conditions relating wholly to internal matters, is beyond the control of Congress. This insistence of "equal footing" with other states won so early in its history, expressed a genuine southern feeling about Oklahoma's place in the Union. It was a spirit that the grandfather clause episode also expressed.

Opponents of the grandfather clause attacked the adoption procedure as well as its substance. There was little chance of success as statehood had been sought to end the inferiority of territorial status as well as to enter the Union on equal terms. At the convention elected to draft a state constitution, delegate W.A. Ledbetter opposed a resolution supporting the United States Constitution as the highest and paramount law. He won. The founding fathers of Oklahoma were pronounced states rights men seasoned by the Progressive spirit then abroad in the land.

The Oklahoma constitution of 1907 provided for primary elections and direct election of a dozen state officials. The initiative and referendum, patterned after the 1902 Oregon law, were included. "The initiative is a device," according to a standard definition, "by which any person or group of persons may draft a proposed ordinance, law or constitutional amendment and by securing in its behalf a designated number of signatures may require that such proposal be submitted to the voters for their acceptance or rejection."[31] In Oklahoma, signatures of 5 percent of the qualified voters were enough to require a vote. Secretary of State Smith found the grandfather clause petitions sufficient and placed the question on the ballot in the statewide primary election scheduled for August 2, 1910. The grandfather clause was adopted by a close vote, 130,000 to 100,000.

Controversy and litigation swirled around numerous aspects of the grandfather clause but the climactic preliminary test—before the ultimate denial of the vote to blacks in an election—came in October 1910 over the lawfulness of its adoption. This was the case of *Atwater v. Hassett* in the Oklahoma Supreme Court.[32]

The Republican party in Oklahoma bent every effort to fight the grandfather clause during the summer of 1910. This was the most urgent business at the Republican state convention in July. There was incessant activity with a strong campaign to defeat the grandfather clause in the referendum, followed by charges of election irregularities.

Blacks in Oklahoma resisted the grandfather clause on a broad front, too. But they were bound to work with the Republicans, as they said, "to free ourselves from this damnable yoke of oppression placed upon us by the Haskell Democrats of this state." Several black organizations, such as the Constitutional League, the Protective League and the Fourth and Fifth Congressional League joined in this effort.

There was dissension in black ranks over allying with the Republicans and at a meeting in October in Chickasha the leadership deserted to the Socialist party.[33] A new organization was formed called the Association of Amalgamated Negro Organizations. Resolutions favored woman suffrage, and opposed the poll tax and grandfather clause. The meeting also memorialized Congress to reduce Oklahoma representation in the House "in proportion to the number of black citizens disfranchised by the grandfather amendment to the constitution." President of the new association was J.A. Johnson and the secretary was C.A. Buchanan of Guthrie, editor of the *Safeguard*, a weekly black newspaper. Republican votes were said to have put over the grandfather clause and the assembly was told, "The negroes should keep their hands on their pocketbooks and let Jim Harris [chairman of the Republican State Committee] make his own fight for the grandfather clause." In blaming Republicans for conditions in Oklahoma resolutions of the meeting declared that the Socialist party "was the only party that has truly befriended the negro." Accordingly, "the entire socialist platform was adopted and negroes were urged to support the socialist ticket."

In the meanwhile, in litigation, black organizations, Republicans and Socialists were pushing in the same direction against Democrats in and out of office. Out of perhaps ten cases that were started, only *Atwater v. Hassett* reached the Oklahoma Supreme Court for decision. The action was begun by a black who was represented by Wiley Jones, attorney for the Association of Amalgamated Negro Organizations. The attorneys for the state were leading Democrats W.A. Ledbetter and Charles B. Stuart. An *amicus curiae* brief was filed for the Republicans by John Burford. The claims were that the referendum should be disallowed because it was held on the day of a primary rather than the general election. The more important second claim was that the grandfather clause violated the Fourteenth and Fifteenth Amendments as well as the enabling act of Oklahoma.

The Oklahoma Supreme Court, on October 26, 1910, two weeks prior to the general election, ruled that the grandfather clause was valid. Justice Robert Lee Williams wrote the opinion for a unanimous court. He relied on Supreme Court decisions of the previous two decades which had upheld state disfranchisement of blacks when the relevant legislation was not explicit in doing so. His favorite example was *Williams v. Mississippi*.[34] He insisted that the grandfather clause had to be read as simple genealogical good sense for it would exclude many aliens but include descendants of free blacks from northern states. This disingenuous interpretation completely ignored the electoral history of the grandfather clause in Oklahoma and in other states, prominently displayed in the press of the day, that the grandfather clause was intended to disfranchise blacks. Justice Williams's sense of its purpose was developed into a sound, appropriate and constitutional classification. He called this "a classification based on reason."[35] Justice Williams then showed that there was a biblical basis for his thought which he apparently equated with reason, saying that under the grandfather clause "any person who was entitled to vote under a form of government on or prior to said date is still presumed to be qualified to exercise such right, and the presumption follows as to his offspring—that is, that the virtues and intelligence of the ancestor will be imputed to his descendants, just as the inequity of the fathers may be visited upon the children unto the third and fourth generation."[36] Justice Williams insisted, "This does not apply to any one race, but to every race that falls within this qualification." *Atwater v. Hassett* was not appealed. The election would proceed with the grandfather clause exclusion considered valid by all Oklahoma officials.

Several characteristics of the Oklahoma population as depicted by the Census Bureau in 1910 are informative.[37] The total of 1,657,155 is broken down in a number of ways. Two-thirds of the population was born outside the state with the percentage of Oklahoma-born blacks somewhat higher than for whites. The total population was 87.2 percent white, 8.3 percent black, and 4.5 percent Indian. Illiteracy figures were compiled for persons over ten years of age and showed rates to be 17.7 percent among blacks, 9.8 percent among foreign-born whites and 3.3 percent among native whites. Geographical distribution, according to the census, showed that "in 62 of the 76 counties blacks constitute less than 12.5 percent of the population, in 8 counties from 12.5 to 25 percent, and in 6 the proportion exceeds one-fourth." Kingfisher County, where the *Guinn* case originated, was 1 of the 8 counties in the next to largest proportion of blacks. There were 2,392 in a county population of 18,825 (see figure 2-2). Detailed percentages are not given for Union Township; its total population in 1910 was a mere 736.

Republicans particularly continued to champion black voters in protesting steps toward adoption of the grandfather clause amendment to the Oklahoma constitution. The national Republican platform of 1908 had specifically spoken up for the black vote, in these words:

We demand equal justice for all men, without regard to race or color; we declare once more, and without reservation, for the enforcement in letter and spirit of the Thirteenth, Fourteenth and Fifteenth Amendments to the Constitution, which were designed for the protection and advancement of the Negro, and we condemn all devices that have for their real aim his disfranchisement for reasons of color alone as unfair, un-American and repugnant to the supreme law of the land.[38]

The Association of Amalgamated Negro Organizations was apparently right to trust Socialists in Oklahoma to lead opposition to the grandfather clause, although black equality was not a particular concern of the national Socialist movement during this era. This may have been true at the national level, and in many states but it definitely does not hold for Oklahoma, where the executive committee of the Socialist party vehemently protested the grandfather clause. But the most persistent and effective tactician in the Socialists' campaign against the grandfather clause was Patrick S. Nagle of Kingfisher. He questioned the

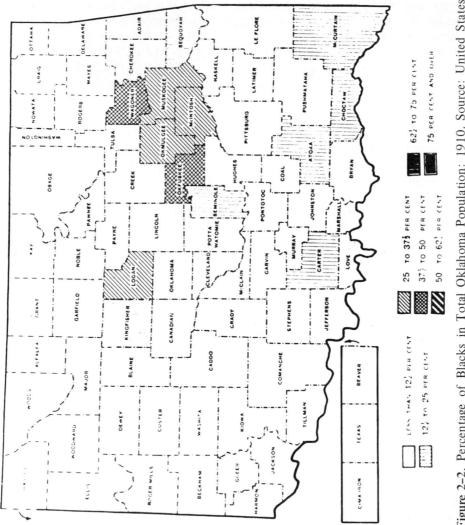

Figure 2-2. Percentage of Blacks in Total Oklahoma Population: 1910. Source: United States Bureau of the Census, Census of Population, 13th Decennial Census, 1910.

validity of the initiative in June 1910, the referendum in August and the first election under the clause in November. There was a great flurry of litigation but it was Nagle's work which contributed most to beginning the test case which eventually resolved the question in the United States Supreme Court.

Nagle's advice to black voters was an excited mixture of aggressiveness, hostility, fear and devotion. They should go to the polls unarmed to avoid provoking Democrats who would cause a disturbance and call it a race war. They should demand the right to vote. If refused "go to the nearest Justice of the Peace and swear out a warrant for the Democratic Election Board, or such members as refuse to allow you to vote." Nagle explained that every refusal of the board to allow a Negro to vote was a separate offense and, accordingly, "let every negro who is so refused swear out a warrant and keep arresting them as fast as they give bail." If armed resistance was encountered, then blacks would be justified in replying with force.

His ardent Socialist views are summed up in his instructions telling what "the black section of the working class must do to be saved." These are his words:

And now in conclusion I wish to say to the negro that what is written here is said in the name of those who are directing the great movement of the working class throughout the world. We do not stand for you because you have any God given rights, or because you are "guaranteed" anything under any constitution of any "Enabling Act" or because it is "Eternally right," or because of the "Golden Rule" or the "Sermon on the Mount." We stand for you because you belong to the working class. Here we take our stand and from this rock we shall never be shaken.[39]

Negro voters in Union Township, Kingfisher County, were denied ballots by election officers Frank Guinn and J.J. Beal. Complaints were made in the manner recommended and United States Attorney John Embry took charge of the case. The defendants were indicted and arraigned. They were very well defended by lawyers for the Democratic State Committee who were aided by funds collected by supporters of the grandfather clause. "As a private citizen Bob Williams sought to help Guinn and Beal fight the case and raised funds to help defray court expenses."[40] He was at the time chief justice of the state supreme court. Guinn and Beal pleaded not guilty and were tried, in September 1911, before a jury which found a verdict against them. They were convicted and sentenced to serve one year in the penitentiary at Leavenworth, Kansas, and each to pay a fine of one hundred dollars.[41]

Supreme Court Decision, 1915

Advocates of the grandfather clause as a legal means of black disfranchisement took the initiative in carrying the *Guinn* case from Oklahoma and the *Myers* case from Maryland to the United States Supreme Court. As losers in federal trial courts in 1911 they had almost a legally binding right of review. This was invoked in the Oklahoma case by seeking certification of the case to the Supreme Court by the Circuit Court of Appeals in St. Louis. That court, by the approval of three judges on December 16, 1912,[42] sought instructions of the Supreme Court upon the question of whether the grandfather clause was void insofar as black citizens of the United States, otherwise qualified to vote, were debarred from voting in congressional elections. Such a certificate from an intermediate appellate court was binding. The Supreme Court of the United States was bound by that act to review the *Guinn* case on the merits. The clerk placed *Guinn v. United States* on the Supreme Court docket in the October term, 1912 as No. 923. The case would be reviewed, but not soon.

Myers v. Anderson and the two companion cases from Maryland had reached the Supreme Court a year earlier when, on May 17, 1911, Judge Morris in Baltimore had issued an order allowing a writ of error.[43] This case had been docketed in the October term, 1911, and continued in the October term, 1912, as No. 365. As attorneys for the defendant election registers, William L. Marbury and his staff had listed eighteen assignments of error to supplement the petition for a writ of error. Nearly all of these referred back to their demurrer to the declaration of the plaintiff. The contentions were well developed early in the litigation. The briefs in the Supreme Court would be built on premises and claims made earlier.

These were years when the Court was considerably behind in its business. The *Guinn* and *Myers* cases stood still during the October 1912 term and were redocketed and, finally, set down for oral argument in the October 1913 term. In fact, *Guinn and Beal v. United States* was argued in the chamber of the Supreme Court in the basement of the Senate on October 17, 1913, with *Myers v. Anderson* following the next month, on November 11.

The membership of the Supreme Court had been recently reconstituted by the unusual string of vacancies filled by President William Howard Taft during his last two years or so in the White House. He had the uncommon opportunity in a single administration to make five nominations, including one for the chief justiceship, which he solved by elevating Mr. Justice Edward D. White of Louisiana. Three justices who continued were Joseph McKenna, Oliver Wendell Holmes, Jr., and William R. Day. In 1910 President Taft nominated Governor Charles Evans Hughes of New York, a progressive Republican, and a former judicial colleague in Cincinnati, Horace Lurton of Tennessee. In 1911 he named Willis Van Devanter and Joseph R. Lamar and, in 1912, Taft's fifth appointment was Mahlon Pitney. As Supreme Courts go, this was a relatively new and untried group which took the two cases on the grandfather clause under advisement in the autumn of 1913.

Briefs for Reversal

The arguments supporting the validity of the grandfather clause were rooted in ante-bellum constitutional theory. This, after all, was inherent in the purpose and its symbolic name, and the arguers in the Supreme Court personally believed in the constitutional world of their fathers. Thus they argued that the Fourteenth Amendment had nothing to do with voting, the Fifteenth Amendment concerned only racial distinctions on the face of a statute, and that, after all, perhaps those amendments were unconstitutional anyhow. There were attacks, too, on the validity and applicability of the surviving sections of the Enforcement Acts used in these cases. The theme was presented variously in four briefs, three in the *Guinn* case and one in the *Myers* case.

William L. Marbury, with Ridgley P. Melvin, Annapolis city attorney, and William L. Rawls, prepared a brief for the plaintiffs in error in the Annapolis cases of 122 pages.[44] Its attack on the validity of the Fifteenth Amendment is its most striking feature. Marbury's theory of the Fifteenth Amendment drew heavily from an article in the *Harvard Law Review* in 1910 by his Baltimore friend, Arthur W. Machen.[45] His emphasis was upon the limit in Article Five, the amending clause, against any amendment which would deprive a state of its "equal representation in the Senate" without its consent. Maryland had not voted ratification of the Fifteenth Amendment and was thereby exempted from its strictures against disfranchisement. Marbury's point was that "the right to determine for itself who shall constitute its electorate, is one of the functions essential to the *existence* of a state."[46] Marbury's brief built its theory of the Fifteenth Amendment upon strict legal definition of a "state" drawn from precedents in the Southern tradition like *Texas v. White*, where the Supreme Court in 1869 ruled, in effect, that the Civil War had not occurred as the Constitution did not permit succession.[47] This was combined with a social definition of the word "electorate" in accord with theories that political community depended on racial homogeneity. There were no explicit references to particular racial theorists but the brief expounded Marbury's own philosophy at considerable length.

Assuming that the Fifteenth Amendment, construed to be applicable to State elections, is "an amendment" within the meaning of that term as employed in Article V. of the Constitution, it falls within the express prohibition therein contained against any amendment which would deprive a State of its equal suffrage in the Senate, without its consent.

For it is submitted that any amendment which would have the effect under any possible circumstances of converting one of the States of the Union into an Asiatic State or an African State by compelling the white people to permit Asiatics or Negroes to vote upon the same terms as themselves, would be in substance and effect depriving the original State—the State which assented to and was contemplated and meant by the Constitution—of all representation in the Senate.

For, as we have already seen, "a State in the ordinary sense of the Constitution is a political community of free citizens occupying territory of defined boundaries and organized under a government sanctioned and limited by a written Constitution, and *established by the consent of the governed*." Texas vs. White, 16 Wall. It is *such* States that constitute the United States. . . .

It is, therefore, respectfully submitted that to construe the words "right of citizens of the United States to vote" in the Fifteenth Amendment to include the right of citizens of a *State* to vote at State or municipal elections, would give it a construction which would render it absolutely unconstitutional and void.[48]

Other contentions in Marbury's brief pale alongside his sweeping, grand theory of the inapplicability of the Fifteenth Amendment to protect black suffrage in Maryland. The brief did contain a detailed defense of the grandfather clause as a nonracial measure which would deny the vote to some whites and permit it to some blacks, as there was only a date and not a color bar. Marbury also reviewed the post-Civil War civil rights laws, stressing those that were repealed or invalidated as showing the limits of the Fourteenth and Fifteenth Amendments.

There were two main briefs supporting Guinn and Beal's enforcement of the Oklahoma grandfather clause against blacks who requested ballots in the 1910 election. One was submitted by five Democratic lawyers from Oklahoma, C.B. Stuart, A.C. Cruce, W.A. Ledbetter, Norman Haskall and C.G. Hornor. Their seventy-four-page brief was submitted in April, 1913.[49] But in the fall another brief was submitted and the oral argument was made by Joseph Weldon Bailey, who had recently resigned as United States senator from Texas.[50] A stormy figure, Bailey was a congressman from 1890 to 1900 and a senator from 1901 to 1913. As House minority leader of the Democrats, he urged war against Spain in 1898. Although he championed the income tax amendment, Bailey opposed such Progressive measures as the initiative, referendum and recall and, later, battled both prohibition and woman suffrage. His biographer states that "in 1909, President Taft offered Bailey a place on the Supreme Court bench, which he declined."[51] He had attacked President Theodore Roosevelt for inviting Booker T. Washington to dinner at the White House. After resigning his Senate seat, Bailey took up a full-time law practice in Washington.

These briefs duplicated Marbury's in spirit although their views on the Fifteenth Amendment were not the same. They argued only that the grandfather clause was valid because the Fourteenth and Fifteenth Amendments simply did not extend far enough to touch it. The suffrage was said to be a state matter and for this contention the writings of Wilson, Willoughby and Jameson were invoked. Regulation of the suffrage was part of the reserved powers of states and the grandfather clause was not discriminatory on its face.

An *amicus curiae* brief by J.H. Adriaans of Washington, D.C. in the *Guinn* case attacked both the Fourteenth and Fifteenth Amendments in an exhaustive, polemical brief which made the Marbury argument seem tame by comparison.

Citing 359 cases where these amendments had been construed by the Court, Adriaans declared: "The objective of the present brief is to challenge directly the validity of the [Fourteenth] Amendment; to deny that it was ever legally adopted; to deny that it is part of the Constitution."[52] Because the subject was "large, comprehensive, and intricate, Adriaans then divided it into sixteen branches. He then reviewed in detail the proposal and ratification of the amendment, noting every conceivable procedural question mark. The Fifteenth Amendment was examined in a similar manner. Toward the end of the argument Adriaans exhibits perhaps the most virulent racist feelings ever expressed in a legal brief. "The time is ripe," he said, "to settle the status of the Negro race."[53] In a vulgar, racist tirade he pictured coexistence as impossible, urging that, "in sheer self-defense, the white race owes to itself the duty of making a stand for its life."[54]

Adriaans condemned the Fourteenth and Fifteenth Amendments as unconstitutional on grounds of flawed procedure in their adoption, a basically different objection from Marbury and Machen's theory that the Fifteenth Amendment was objectionable for substantive reasons. Adriaans' was an argument that was heard for decades after the Civil War. He argued that ratification of the Fourteenth Amendment by southern states was under duress and that after 1868 most rescinded their actions.

Brief for Affirmance

The brief for affirmance of Judge Morris's invalidation of the Annapolis grandfather clause was filed by Edgar H. Gans, Morris A. Soper and Daniel R. Randall.[55] The brief repeated the constitutional arguments made below and now relied on the opinion of Judge Morris for further support.

The first of three briefs for affirmance in the *Guinn* case was presented for the United States government by Solicitor General John W. Davis.[56] He had been in President Wilson's administration just six months when the case was argued so his position simply followed upon the record and conviction won in the trial court by an earlier Republican United States attorney in Oklahoma.

An *amicus curiae* brief was filed by two prominent Oklahoma Republicans, one of whom, John Embry, had been the prosecutor of Guinn and Beal earlier. He was joined by the lawyer for the Oklahoma Republican State Committee, John H. Burford.[57] These two briefs followed the same themes, that the Court must look behind the purpose of a statute to see its intent and effect. Their scrutiny showed that the grandfather clause affected blacks, not whites.

The NAACP

The National Association for the Advancement of Colored People, then only four years old, entered the *Guinn* case with an *amicus curiae* brief which marked its first appearance before the Supreme Court of the United States.[58] Moorfield Storey, the Boston attorney who was president of the NAACP, prepared the brief and filed it. Although this was the first of the NAACP cases, it was not at all a novelty because the association's legal program was really a continuation of efforts by three other organizations which had tried to use litigation to protect the rights of blacks. An elaboration on the early NAACP recourse to legal redress will place the *Guinn* brief in perspective.

In its membership, purpose and approaches the early National Association for the Advancement of Colored People, after its formation in 1909, took up where three older organizations left off. The militant Niagara Movement lasted only five years. Rudwick says that "after the NAACP was formed, Du Bois asked all of the Niagara alumni to support it."[59] Bishop Alexander Walters, as the last president of the National Afro-American Council, was among the six blacks who signed the call for the NAACP. A third organization with some experience in litigation, the Constitutional League of the United States, did not dissolve immediately but actually sought to merge with the NAACP. John E. Milholland, the sometimes scheming president of the league, signed the NAACP call in 1909, but after much bickering the association declined to merge with the league. Yet the historian of the NAACP found that "the first case of real significance undertaken by the association was the peonage case of Pink Franklin" which it took over from the failing hands of the Constitutional League.[60]

The Franklin case displayed so many complexities in the American legal system that, at its conclusion in the fall of 1910, the executive committee of the NAACP was easily persuaded to establish a legal redress department as soon as possible. Pink Franklin was an illiterate farmhand who was arrested in South Carolina for leaving his employer after receiving advances on his wages, a violation of a state law. An altercation over serving a warrant for his arrest developed and Franklin, in self-defense, shot and killed an officer. He was indicted, tried, judged guilty of murder and sentenced to be executed. But after hectic efforts of the NAACP, Governor Martin F. Ansel of South Carolina commuted the sentence to life imprisonment. Several years later, in 1919, Franklin was paroled.

During these first years the NAACP dealt for the first time with problems that would come up again and again through its history. So-called anti-intermarriage, or miscegenation laws were resisted in a number of states. Housing segregation ordinances were contested in Louisville and Baltimore, first in the city council, then in the courts. There were criminal law cases. Early in the period, Gilchrist Stewart, a black lawyer with the Constitution League, worked effectively with Charles H. Studin, law partner of Spingarn, in public accommodation cases in New York City.

Simultaneous with the grandfather clause cases in the Supreme Court, the NAACP began its persistent opposition to residential segregation in American cities. The Baltimore City racial zoning ordinance, passed May 15, 1911, was one of the first to fall in a case conducted by the association. In the case of *State v.*

Gurry, the Maryland Supreme Court invalidated the ordinance on the ground that its applicability to property owned prior to its passage took away vested rights. However, that court found no objection under the Fourteenth Amendment, saying the ordinance was "for the preservation of peace, prevention of conflict and ill-feeling, between white and colored persons in Baltimore City, and for promoting the general welfare of the city."[61] The Baltimore Branch of the NAACP sponsored the case and it was argued by a black lawyer, W. Ashbie Hawkins of Baltimore, with A. Ames Brooks of the NAACP Legal Redress and Legislative Committee in New York. In this case the defense of the ordinance by the Baltimore City Solicitor S.S. Field was aided by Edgar Allan Poe, Maryland's attorney general, and by William L. Marbury.[62]

Minutes of meetings of the NAACP Board of Directors in this period show that Hawkins had notified New York about the Annapolis grandfather clause case. Nothing more is known nor is it clear why Storey filed in the Oklahoma case only. Charles J. Bonaparte had been praised by Storey for his work in defeating the Straus amendment in 1909.[63] It may have been that the NAACP aided the Annapolis case directly. Bonaparte, at least, suggested that "the scanty resources of the nominal plaintiffs" might be supplemented by "the National society of which Mr. Oswald Villard is President" and which recently had met in Baltimore.[64] Charles F. Kellogg has credited Storey with persuading John W. Davis to carry the Oklahoma case to the Supreme Court.[65] Storey was no doubt in correspondence but, of course, the advocates of the grandfather clause appealed these cases and the Justice Department was already deeply involved. There has also been a tendency to speak as though the *Guinn* case was an NAACP victory; this is hardly fair to the lawyers who had worked for years on these cases prior to the NAACP entry as an *amicus*.

Moorfield Storey's brief for the NAACP aimed its barbs at the travesty of admitting Oklahoma into the Union under an enabling act which forbade racial distinction and then permitted virtual repeal of the provision by means of the grandfather clause amendment.

The enabling act is . . . significant as showing that Oklahoma obtained admission to the Union only with the most definite understanding that the rights of her citizens were to be in no way dependent on considerations of race or color. Indeed, the prohibition of distinctions on account of race or color indicates a desire on the part of Congress to prevent such distinctions as to all civil and political rights whatever—even as to those, if any there be, not already protected by the Constitution.

If the amendment now in question can stand, it means that a state received into the Union on these stringent terms may, immediately after her admission, make sport of her solemn obligations and by a transparent subterfuge set at naught the Constitution of the United States itself. The real question for decision is whether the court is to be "deceived by the mere phraseology" into permitting such a flagrant breach of the fundamental law. To this question, it is submitted, there can be only one answer.[66]

The Supreme Court Decisions

The political alignment within the Supreme Court explains the long delay encountered in deciding the fate of the grandfather clause. It concerned the presence on the Court of Justice Horace H. Lurton, a Tennessee veteran of the Confederate Army, who was easily won to William L. Marbury's view that the Fifteenth Amendment to the federal Constitution had been invalidly adopted and that it was not binding on the state of Maryland. Marbury learned that "this so shocked his colleagues that they held up the decision until Justice Lurton retired."[67] After a severe illness he retired in 1914 and died soon afterward. Appointed in Lurton's place was James Clark McReynolds, attorney general in the first Wilson administration, also from Tennessee. Mr. Justice McReynolds took no part in the consideration and decision of these cases so that the Court's decisions were unanimous. The opinions by Mr. Chief Justice White were announced on June 21, 1915.

The Court came down hard for affirmance in both the Oklahoma and Maryland cases. The grandfather clause in each state was held void because it violated the Fifteenth Amendment. The Chief Justice agreed that the Fifteenth Amendment did not confer suffrage on anyone but it did prohibit the states from depriving any person of the right of suffrage on account of race, color or previous condition of servitude. There was also no question but that the Fifteenth Amendment's provisions applied to state and municipal as well as to federal elections. In both cases the grandfather clause provisions were ruled to be so inextricably bound to other election regulations in the same laws that the whole was invalidated. Thus in two separate decisions the grandfather clauses were erased from the books in Oklahoma and Maryland.

Compliance

The reactions to the invalidation of the grandfather clause varied in Maryland and Oklahoma. Voting by blacks was already practiced in Maryland generally and the loss of the Annapolis registration law made it impossible for William L. Marbury and like-minded men to push further on this front. In Oklahoma, the widespread support of disfranchisement among white Democrats encouraged other methods of election control.

The editor of the *Daily Oklahoman* looked upon the invalidation of the grandfather clause as a tactical defeat only. He led the search for a new method of black disfranchisement in which "no stickler for constitutional rights could find a technical flaw."[68] Unquestionably, the decision was final; therefore Oklahoma must act. The newspaper advocated an "understanding clause" as the most workable method of excluding blacks from voting. Its aim was to maintain white supremacy in Oklahoma:

. . . The white people of Oklahoma, who are responsible for this common-wealth's status in the galaxy of states feel that they alone should continue to direct its affairs; that they alone are competent to direct such affairs. . . . The state has done prodigiously well under the exclusive rule of the white man. Would you care to live within its borders if its destinies were entrusted exclusively to the black man? It might be worth mentioning, *en passant*, that in some counties the latter holds the balance of power.

If, under the Oklahoma laws, the precinct inspectors should be given the right, exercisable at their discretion, to examine a would-be voter as to his educational qualifications, it would insure the casting of a high-grade vote throughout the state. These inspectors might, for instance, cause the applicant at the booth to read a section of the constitution, and, as a still further precaution, question him as to his understanding of its provisions and meaning. This would have the effect of throwing out about all of the undesirable vote.[69]

Advocacy of an understanding clause was only one of several possible courses of action suggested by Oklahoma Democrats "to prevent illegal and illiterate voting in this state." E.J. Giddings, attorney for the Democratic State Central Committee, picked on the federal conspiracy statute as a target. Giddings argued that when the Enforcement Acts were repealed in 1894 Congress would probably have eliminated the conspiracy law if it had been thought applicable to elections. The remedy, therefore, according to Giddings, was repeal. "Repeal the conspiracy statute," he said, "and then there will be no federal statute giving federal courts jurisdiction to punish state election officials."[70]

Giddings combined his racial bias with a fundamental ingredient of Progressivism in attacking the Supreme Court for invalidating the Oklahoma grandfather clause. This was judicial review, judges holding a law adopted by a state's majority invalid. As a remedy, he urged "an amendment to the federal constitution, prohibiting the courts of the country declaring unconstitutional laws passed by the people."

On an immediate, practical matter, Giddings said that Oklahoma Democrats should appeal to the president to pardon the convicted election officials.

Giddings's view of the grandfather clause was unique in one respect—immigration control. He felt that blacks would not move into a state which denied them the franchise. And so, like the *Daily Oklahoman* editor, Giddings recommended an understanding clause as the most effective substitute for the grandfather clause restriction. This is the pungent language Giddings used to express the thought: "The people demand, and they are going to have, a law in this state to prevent a horde of Negro immigrants. They do not want them, and their wishes shall be respected, notwithstanding the Republican notion that the more Negroes there are in Oklahoma the more Republican votes there are in consequence."[71] This account, and other newspaper articles, made it seem certain there would be action in Oklahoma. Governor Williams announced he would have no plans for an immediate legislative session but he was trusted to come up with something. As a former state supreme court justice upholding the validity of the grandfather clause he "will know better what to do than a layman."[72]

However well understood the function of a case like *Guinn v. United States* is to the constitutional order, there is natural interest in the fate of election officers under sentence of a year and a day in the United States penitentiary at Leavenworth, Kansas. What, then, became of Frank Guinn and J.J. Beal? After the Supreme Court decision the Circuit Court of Appeals in St. Louis, on October 8, 1915, affirmed the judgment of the District Court. Time was then allowed for a pardon effort set in motion by the Oklahoma delegation in Congress. Under Article Two of the Constitution the president "shall have power to grant reprieves and pardons for offenses against the United States."[73] This is a very broad, discretionary power, fully within the prerogative of the president and sought annually by hundreds of persons convicted of federal offenses. The heavy administrative responsibilities had long since been handled by the pardon attorney in the Department of Justice with actions of the president ordinarily taken upon the recommendation of the attorney general. This was so in the case of Guinn and Beal as the attorney general called them "uneducated men—farmers—" who followed the instructions of the governor of Oklahoma in enforcing the grandfather clause in 1910. There was "no doubt that colored men were illegally deprived by them of the right to vote." But a pardon was recommended because these "men were honestly and fairly attempting to perform their duties as election officers under a law of their State which they believed to be constitutional and valid."[74] Without further comment, on January 17, 1916, President Wilson ordered pardons granted. The men were taken to Oklahoma City and introduced to the legislature, which gave them an ovation.[75]

The Oklahoma legislature enacted a new registration scheme signed into law by Governor Williams on February 26, 1916. Those who had voted in the 1914 general elections remained registered. Those who had not—among them blacks excluded from voting then by the grandfather clause—had to apply for registration during a restricted period, April 30 to May 11, 1916, with an extension of six weeks for absentees. This arrangement survived for twenty years before it came under attack in a litigation decided by the Supreme Court in *Lane v. Wilson* in 1939.[76]

Women Suffrage

A concise history of constitutionally assured woman suffrage shows that Congress, on June 4, 1919, proposed "The right of citizens of the United States to vote shall not be denied or abridged by the United States or by any state on account of sex." Ratification was completed on August 18, 1920, when the thirty-sixth state (Tennessee) approved the proposed amendment. On August 26, 1920, the Secretary of State Bainbridge Colby certified that this proposal had become the Nineteenth Amendment to the United States Constitution.

Opponents of woman suffrage are now thought to have been knaves and fools[1] and the achievement of woman suffrage regarded as inevitable. The history of the achievement of woman suffrage is a many-told tale and will merely be sketched here as background for several aspects of constitutional change.

There was actually a rather respectable opposition to woman suffrage by prominent scholars and intellectuals. There were organizations of men and of politically active women, too, working to stop the movement for woman suffrage. They helped to keep Congress from voting to propose an amendment from 1869, when it was first introduced, to 1919. Even then they persuaded seven legislatures to reject ratification. Following this, the opponents of woman suffrage went to the Supreme Court, arguing that the Nineteenth Amendment was invalid and that the justices could so hold, just as they could invalidate a statute. They failed again and this lost a feature of a constitutional world they treasured. While swift compliance followed their defeat, neither their fears nor the suffragettes' hopes were altogether realized by feminine voting behavior.

National woman suffrage transformed both sides in ways that impinged on other major controversies of American constitutional politics. The suffragettes split into several factions. Nearly all became Democrats or Republicans, but the activists continued an additional interest in one or more women's organizations. Led by Carrie Chapman Catt, the National League of Woman Voters organized in February 1920 as the moderate successor organization to the National American Woman Suffrage Association. The league was satisfied with assurance of the right to vote and dutifully set about enunciating thoughtful choices on public issues. More militant suffragettes were already pushing forward to advanced positions and in 1923 began to lobby for an additional constitutional amendment declaring: "Equality of rights under the law shall not be denied or abridged by the United States or any state on account of sex." This was one of the feminist goals of Alice Paul and the National Woman's party after 1917. The National Woman's party worked fruitlessly for decades for its equal rights

47

amendment and scorned ameliorative, incremental measures such as protective labor legislation for women.

Opponents to woman suffrage feared that Socialists like Florence Kelley, pacifists like Jane Addams and Jeannette Rankin, and social workers like Julia Lathrop and Grace Abbott would lead naïve women voters to bring in a political revolution. Many such organizations with roots in the nineteenth century were concerned over *how* women would vote if they could.

One organization, the National Association Opposed to Woman Suffrage, led by Mrs. Arthur Dodge, voiced its opposition in a newspaper called *The Woman Patriot* and its sadness over ratification of the Nineteenth Amendment. It continued publication into the 1930s and fought against the Sheppard-Towner Maternity Act, the child labor amendment, and other "evils" of socialism, pacifism and feminism. These were women, it should be remembered, who had been politically active for more than a generation in a desperate effort to stop the advance of woman suffrage.

The social and political attitudes stirred by the contest over woman suffrage, then, had antecedents and left in its wake significant patterns of behavior. The achievement of woman suffrage by amendment requires that attention be given to the nature of the amending process in this instance. Also, there were a group of lawyers so certain of the wrongness and unconstitutionality of the Nineteenth Amendment that they were willing to break lances in the Supreme Court on this issue. Even without the amendment and the litigation, the achievement of sexual emancipation symbolized—however imperfectly—by woman suffrage is a major constitutional event in any society.

Antisuffrage Activity

In the 1870s women of education and means in Boston and Cambridge organized to oppose extension of the suffrage by the state legislature. They succeeded in countering the movement for woman suffrage over half a century, reporting that "from 1882 onwards a remonstrance followed every petition" from the suffragettes.[2] "Their first achievement was inducing Mr. Francis Parkman to write an article published in the *North American Review*, the basis of many later papers."[3] Parkman, the most accomplished and honored historian of his day, a graduate of the Harvard Law School, laid out a set of conservative objections to woman suffrage that would have won the admiration of Edmund Burke. Parkman's article dwelled on sexual differences that equipped men and women for separate spheres of activity. He deduced that in the politics of the United States voting by women would spread "principles of pure humanitarianism" in ways beneficial to the political spoils system, harmful to the cities and favorable to the interests of the Catholic Church. To Parkman, as to nearly everyone who advocated or opposed woman suffrage, speculation on its impact was the important thing, as these passages show:

The evils of universal female, as of universal male suffrage, would be greatest in dense industrial populations. In the country, they would be less felt, and least of all in the rough and simple life of the thinly-settled borders, or the far West. Like other political evils, they would reach their climax in great cities. The government of these is difficult enough already. To make it impossible would be madness. . . .

Those who wish the Roman Catholic Church to subvert our school system, control legislation, and become a mighty political force, can not do better than labor day and night for female suffrage. This, it is true, is opposed to every principle and tradition of that great Church, which, nevertheless, would reap from it immense benefits. The priests have little influence over a considerable part of their male flock; but their power is great over the women, who would repair to the polls at the word of command with edifying docility and zeal.[4]

As the early feminists were abolitionists as well, so did the remonstrants against woman suffrage in Massachusetts grow out of narrow traditions. These remonstrants resented the moral posture of William Lloyd Garrison, a leading abolitionist who took up the cause of women's rights.

To Mr. Garrison especially, the appearance of a handful of women as remonstrants was the signal for a torrent of abuse. The Abolitionists were the idealists, all other persons were blinded by passion and prejudice, and their descendants could never be trusted.[5]

During the nineteenth century in Massachusetts the women remonstrants were represented by men. John Lowell, a learned United States judge in Massachusetts, spoke at legislative hearings on their behalf. So did Louis D. Brandeis, who appeared before a committee of the Massachusetts legislature on January 28, 1884, and argued against woman suffrage. Francis Parkman followed him the next day. The following year, on March 10, at a hearing in the Green Room of the State House in Boston, Brandeis opened for the remonstrants. An editor of the Brandeis letters says that to Brandeis the vote "was not a right, but a privilege that imposed certain duties peculiar to the male sex." Brandeis's opposition "seemed to revolve around a typical nineteenth-century view of the 'proper' roles of men and women."[6] As time went on, and especially after 1892 when the remonstrants began a more elaborate and formal organization, able spokesmen were employed to speak at what they called "the Annual Woman Suffrage Hearing." Charles R. Saunders, a graduate of the Harvard Law School in 1887 and later a member of the legislature, served the organized women remonstrants as counsel. Another figure of eminence in Boston on this side was Frank Foxcroft, a journalist for the *Youth's Companion* and Boston newspapers, who worked anonymously as editor of the *Remonstrance*, an antisuffrage publication.[7]

Woman suffrage edged slowly forward during the last part of the century. Several western states adopted it across the board and in the East ground was given in local elections or on special subjects. School suffrage for women had been adopted by the legislature in Massachusetts in 1879 and extensions were pressed regularly thereafter. The informal committees of antisuffragists were alarmed in 1894 when a bill conferring suffrage upon women in municipal elections passed the House and came within seven votes of enactment by the Senate. The following year the Massachusetts legislature submitted the question of municipal suffrage to a state-wide referendum that included all persons qualified to vote for school committees. Even with women voting, a majority of 133,447 voted "No" to the question "Is it expedient that municipal suffrage be granted to the women of Massachusetts?" The antisuffrage forces continued to prevail in the state but in the 1890s their organizations took on a more organized style and regularity. The ironic truth was that their efforts to stop women as a political force were attracting these more conservative ladies to the political life they claimed to deplore.

The women antisuffragists appear to have been continuously organized from the 1870s on. What began as the "Massachusetts Remonstrants Against the Extension of Suffrage to Women," became, in 1916, the "Woman's Anti-Suffrage Association of Massachusetts." By 1918, the antisuffragists had formed an alliance with the Public Interests League and had convinced themselves that woman suffrage and feminism were the moral equivalent of socialism and pacifism. During the last several years prior to adoption of the Nineteenth Amendment in 1920 the Massachusetts Anti-Suffrage Association was served by Mrs. Harriet Frothingham as recording secretary. She would later, in the 1920s, lend her name to the annals of Supreme Court litigation in the famous taxpayer case of *Frothingham v. Mellon*.

In New York, perhaps the most persistent opponent of woman suffrage was Everett Pepperell Wheeler, who chaired the Man Suffrage Association Opposed to Political Suffrage for Women beginning in 1912. Like many of his counterparts in this campaign, Wheeler had a background of nineteenth-century liberalism but in fighting woman suffrage toward the end of his life he opposed a host of other "evils." In 1917 he helped organize the American Constitutional League, whose purpose was "to uphold and defend the American Constitution against all foreign and domestic enemies." With this organization, Wheeler continued the fight against the Nineteenth Amendment after 1920 by challenging its validity in the United States Supreme Court.

Wheeler was "closely associated with many of the great movements for social and political reform in New York City" from the time of the Civil War onward.[8] Descended from a colonial family, he graduated from the College of the City of New York in 1856 and then from the Harvard Law School. He was one of the founders of the Bar Association of the City of New York and was active in the American Bar Association for decades.

He was in the generation of liberalism expounded by Samuel J. Tilden and Grover Cleveland, and as he lived on into the twentieth century he found fault with most of the Progressive innovations. He opposed state wage and hour laws and child labor legislation. He urged forceful measures against crime and unmercifully criticized a Sing Sing prison warden who had questioned the efficacy and morality of capital punishment. Wheeler was especially outraged at Progressive proposals for the recall of judges, calling Theodore Roosevelt "no true American" for backing the idea.[9] This was the context of changing institutional structures and practices which helps to explain how Wheeler came to oppose woman suffrage with such tenacity.

His tirades against the suffragists were bluntly answered on one occasion when Mrs. Carrie Chapman Catt demanded that he withdraw a leaflet distributed by the Man Suffrage Association.[10] The leaflet said that the "accepted leaders" of the suffragists were "opposed to the doctrine that the family is the unit of society and the state." To which Mrs. Catt wrote, "The inference from that statement, when taken in conjunction with the context of the rest of the leaflet, is that I hold immoral views and am an enemy to home and family. I am not. The association's statement in regard to me is false." Calling the leaflet "libelous" and "cunningly designed to mislead" she demanded its withdrawal and gained it.

The small organizations Wheeler led against woman suffrage had offices in the same building, had a carry-over membership, overlapping leadership and the same objectives. The Man Suffrage Association apparently continued on until 1919 when it gave way to other antisuffrage organizations. Wheeler and his associations worked through the American Constitutional League in sponsoring the case of *Fairchild v. Colby* to challenge the validity of the Nineteenth Amendment in the Supreme Court.

In 1919 in Maryland long-time resistance to women suffrage blossomed into an organization known as the Maryland League for State Defense.[11] This was to be a "strong organization of influential men to protest against the ratification of the woman suffrage amendment. Thirty-five prominent men were announced as members of the board of managers of the league, including William L. Marbury. The first aim of the Maryland League for State Defense was not merely to persuade the legislature to vote against ratification but to positively reject the proposed amendment. Following is part of the league's initial statement prepared by William L. Marbury:

To the People of Maryland:
  The Congress of the United States recently adopted a resolution to submit to the several States for ratification or rejection a proposed amendment to the Constitution of the United States whereby, if the said amendment should be ratified, woman suffrage will be forced upon every State of the American Union, whether such States wish it or not.
  Its [the Maryland League for State Defense] object is to oppose by all lawful means the ratification by the General Assembly of Maryland of the pending Woman Suffrage Amendment, thereby to preserve for the people of Maryland the right which they have possessed since colonial days to determine for them-

selves who shall be entitled to vote at their own elections and thus preserve the essential feature of the sacred right of local government.

As it turned out, the league was successful in its first endeavor—the Maryland General Assembly voted to reject the woman suffrage amendment on February 24, 1920. Soon afterward, leaders of the league turned to the courts to stop certification of ratification as illegal.

The activities of the antisuffragists in Massachusetts, New York and Maryland, the writings and activities of Henry St. George Tucker of Virginia, Everett P. Wheeler and William Marbury were being duplicated in many parts of the country, especially over ratification politics. In 1911 various state groups against woman suffrage had organized.[12] *The Woman Patriot*—mentioned earlier—was "Dedicated to the Defense of Womanhood, Motherhood, the Family and the State AGAINST Suffragism, Feminism and Socialism." The president of the association was Mrs. James W. Wadsworth, Jr., whose husband was a senator from New York. Many other officers and board members were wives of prominent men.

The writing in *The Woman Patriot* was pathologically xenophobic, hysterically despairing at every setback and rhapsodic over every achievement.

The National Association Opposed to Woman Suffrage and its various affiliates and allies across the country put on a terrific campaign to stop ratification. They adroitly employed two special tactics—referendum elections and litigation—in states where they were unable to defeat legislative ratification. There was no want of intelligence or of persistence in the antisuffrage campaign, and the association kept close tabs on the amendment situation during the period after June 4, 1919, when the amendment was officially proposed to the states.

One of the pleasures for minorities in the American political world is counting the small number of votes needed to *stop* adoption of a policy. Under the Constitution a two-thirds vote in the Senate to confirm a treaty or prevent closure of debate means one-third plus one to stop it. To prevent the overriding of a presidential veto only one-third plus one in either house is required. To ratify an amendment to the Constitution, three-fourths of the states must approve. To prevent ratification, one-fourth plus one must refuse approval. Thus do factions use fractions to their advantage. There being then forty-eight states in the Union, thirty-six were required for ratification while thirteen were required for rejection. By October 1919 the antisuffrage faction reviewing the amendment situation reported sixteen ratifications and three rejections (Alabama, Georgia and Virginia), with a referendum call suspending ratification in the state of Ohio. "It will be seen that the suffragists need twenty more ratifications," chortled *The Woman Patriot*, "while the anti-ratificationists need only *nine* states in addition to Alabama, Georgia, Virginia and Ohio to get the amendment *rejected!*"[13] Listing the dates in 1920 that legislatures were to meet, it concluded that of nine convening in regular session "*seven* are counted upon as likely to *reject*!" Everything looked rosy then. In fact, things turned out gloom-ily as only four other states rejected (South Carolina, Maryland, Mississippi and Louisiana) for a total of seven with thirty-eight voting ratification. Three did not act at all.

It must be remembered that the Nineteenth Amendment did not change the situation of nonvoting to voting overnight. Women were already voting in many states and the amendment merely increased this more rapidly and, of course, universally (see figure 3-1).

Nineteenth Amendment Court Cases

The readiness of an interest group to use procedures created by its ideological opponents is demonstrated by the reliance of antisuffragists on popular refer-enda to halt ratification of the Anthony amendment in many states. The initia-tive and the referendum, after all, had been often adopted to perfect the consti-tutional world of Progressives. The extension of this twin reform was one of the keystones of the National Popular Government League, of Theodore Roosevelt and of Robert M. LaFollette and his followers. It is not untypical for factions which lose in one forum to chastise that forum as "undemocratic," "unrepre-sentative," and under the control of a small, self-interested elite. It may very well be true.

In any event, the antisuffragists battling state legislative ratification in 1919 and 1920 were in the same spot that Progressives had been in many times before when adverse measures were adopted and the language and action of the referendum were pressed into service. Most state constitutions had built in the referendum for the ratification of amendments proposed by legislatures, an understandable two-step method to distinguish an amendment from ordinary state statutes.

The antisuffragists, seeing legislative ratification of the Anthony amendment gaining, claimed that federal amendments should be submitted to state referen-dum elections as well. This would be more *democratic* and, besides, the United States Constitution does not confer legislative power on state legislatures alone but to the whole electorate. This was the gist of the antisuffragist argument. "It is a striking fact," they said, "that we find the advocates of the woman suffrage movement *always aligned* against any referenda to the voters. It is so much easier to control a terrorized card-indexed politician than it is to *convince* the people." They went on: "The test of democracy is our trust in the people. By this test the suffragists are aligned solidly with autocracy and with the Federal 'centralization of power' which always breeds autocracy."[14] Antisuffragists campaigned for referenda in Maine, Massachusetts, Oklahoma, New Mexico and Ohio. There were referendum clauses in twenty-two state constitutions.

Voters in Ohio at the general election in November 1918 extended the refer-

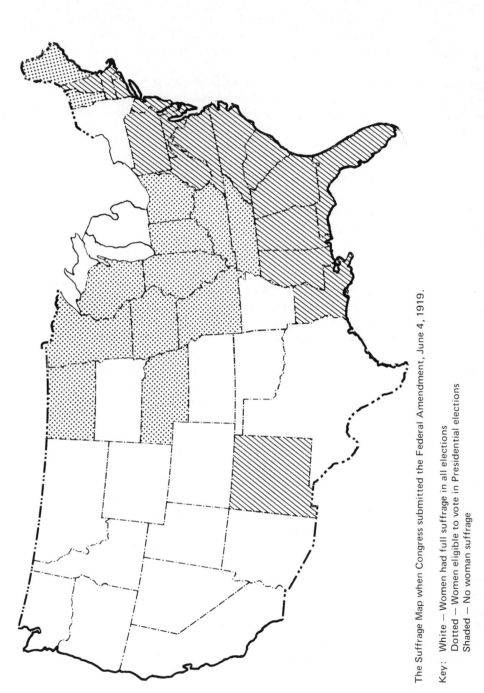

The Suffrage Map when Congress submitted the Federal Amendment, June 4, 1919.

Key: White — Women had full suffrage in all elections
      Dotted — Women eligible to vote in Presidential elections
      Shaded — No woman suffrage

Figure 3-1. Woman Suffrage in 1919. Source: Elizabeth Cady Stanton, Ida Husted Harper and others, editors, *The History of Woman Suffrage*, 6 vols., National Woman Suffrage Association, Vol. 6, 1900–1920 (1922), p. 627.

endum to the ratification by the state legislature of proposed amendments to the federal Constitution. The Ohio provision read: "The people also reserve to themselves the legislative power of the referendum on the action of the general assembly ratifying any proposed amendment to the Constitution of the United States." In Ohio, the prohibition amendment intended to establish national prohibition was approved by the legislature on January 7, 1919, and this action was counted officially among the thirty-six states required for ratification as stated in the proclamation of the Eighteenth Amendment on January 27, 1919.

Wets called "foul" and insisted the state constitutional requirement be followed, urging the secretary of state of Ohio to submit the question of ratification to referendum. Dry forces went to court to stop what they said was a needless expense and a procedure violating Article Five of the United States Constitution. The suit by the drys was begun in a state court in Columbus by George S. Hawke, a citizen who was also a taxpayer and a voter, to enjoin Secretary of State Harvey C. Smith, "from spending the public money in preparing and printing forms of ballot for submission of a referendum."[15] Hawke and the drys lost, as a demurrer to his petition was sustained. The planned referendum, jeopardizing the already certified Eighteenth Amendment, was approved successively by three Ohio courts, including the state supreme court. Wets were aroused and active in opposing Hawke's suit while drys were jubilant over the prospect of a referendum held valid by the Ohio courts. Wets now carried Hawke's case to the United States Supreme Court, where the Ohio referendum requirement was pressed as a violation of Article Five of the federal Constitution, an issue argued and decided in Washington in the spring of 1920.[16]

Meanwhile in Columbus, an essentially identical train of events had occurred with the federal woman suffrage amendment, ratification by the Ohio legislature falling on June 16, 1919. The antisuffragists then petitioned Ohio's secretary of state to suspend ratification until a referendum could be held in 1920. To enjoin Secretary Smith from printing ballots and proceeding to conduct a referendum, Hawke again initiated legal action. True to form, the court of common pleas, the court of appeals and then the Ohio Supreme Court decreed that the referendum be held.[17] Now a plaintiff in the suffrage cause, Hawke then sought and obtained review by writ of error in the Supreme Court of the United States.[18]

The two cases by George S. Hawke, the dry suffragist, raised precisely the same constitutional question: whether the Ohio requirement that legislative ratification of a federal amendment be referred to the voters is consistent with Article Five of the federal Constitution. The Supreme Court ruled unanimously, with Mr. Justice Day delivering the opinion of the Court, that the Ohio referendum requirement was constitutionally invalid. He stated his reasons fully in the case on prohibition,[19] and rested the women suffrage case on that precedent. Both were decided on June 1, 1920.

Mr. Justice Day's opinion in the *Hawke* cases is an important interpretation of the words of Article Five of the Constitution, which provides:

The Congress, whenever two-thirds of both houses shall deem it necessary, shall propose amendments to this Constitution, or, on the application of the legislatures of two-thirds of the several states, shall call a convention for proposing amendments, which, in either case, shall be valid to all intents and purposes, as part of this Constitution, when ratified by the legislatures of three-fourths of the several states, or by conventions in three-fourths thereof, as the one or the other mode of ratification may be proposed by the Congress; provided, that no amendment which may be made prior to the year one thousand eight hundred and eight shall in any manner affect the first and fourth clauses in the ninth section of the first article; and that no state, without its consent, shall be deprived of its equal suffrage in the Senate.[20]

Day said that the people had established the Constitution and there provided for future amendment through their representatives in Congress. When Congress made a choice between the two methods of ratification and designated state legislatures it was within its powers. The Ohio constitution in 1918 had spread legislative authority in that state to embrace a popular referendum and applied it to federal amendments in these words: "The people also reserve to themselves the legislative power of the referendum on the action of the general assembly ratifying any proposed amendment to the Constitution of the United States."

This meant that the Supreme Court had only one question to determine: What is meant by legislatures? Day was concerned with the original understanding rather than with what a majority of the voters of Ohio felt should be meant in 1918, thus his phrasing of the issue was: "What did the framers of the Constitution mean in requiring ratification by 'legislatures'?" From analysis of the text of the Constitution, Day found the term had certain meaning. "A legislature was then the representative body which made the laws of the people. The term is often used in the Constitution with this evident meaning." Consequently, the Court ruled the Ohio referendum requirement invalid as a violation of Article Five of the United States Constitution.

Hawke v. Smith, cases number one and two, display the common alliance of drys and suffragists, on the one hand, against wets and antisuffragists, on the other. Nor was this merely a coincidence in strategic and tactical needs, for there is plenty of evidence of affiliation of these two groups. Not that they were totally congruent, but the Populists and Progressives of the first part of the twentieth century tended to appeal to a rural and religious puritanism that set them against the cities and the saloon. Their faith in direct democracy led them to champion woman suffrage. At least this seems to explain the fact that in both *Hawke* cases, the same plaintiff and the same lawyers worked to protect both the Eighteenth and the Nineteenth Amendments against a referendum vote sought by wets and antisuffragists. They were not slavishly devoted to the referendum; not when this method of checking a legislature was being used against themselves. The chief lawyer was J. Frank Hanly, a former governor of Indiana, with Hawke himself, Arthur Hellen, Charles B. Smith, James Bingham and Remster Bingham.

The Anti-Saloon League of America also filed a brief covering both cases and consequently opposed a potentially dangerous referendum that might upset the chances for woman suffrage as well as the already signed, sealed and delivered prohibition amendment. Wayne B. Wheeler of the national office and James A. White of Ohio prepared the *amici curiae* brief for the Anti-Saloon League. The National Woman's party did not reciprocate and the lawyers who filed their *amici curiae* brief in the *Hawke* case against a referendum on the woman suffrage amendment probably were not themselves drys. Moreover, the National Woman's party was so insistently single-minded in its quest for women's rights that log-rolling, or concern over a side issue would have been out of character.

Attorney General John G. Price of Ohio had little choice but to defend the legality and the appropriateness of the referendum on ratification voted into the state constitution in 1918. It appears that he sought out or at least accepted other talents to help to ensure that a referendum would be held. He placed the defense of the state's new practice in the hands of Lawrence Maxwell of Cincinnati, a former solicitor general of the United States, and was aided on the brief by Judson Harmon and B.W. Gearheart. This group of lawyers then, in effect, represented "the people of the State of Ohio," Secretary of State Smith and the wets in *Hawke v. Smith, No. 1* and the antisuffragists in *Hawke v. Smith No. 2*.

George Hawke had hoped to win support and funds from the National American Woman Suffrage Association, but Mrs. Catt declined to take over the cases and would not contribute to the costs after the victory. Hawke himself contributed money and rather desperately sought some reimbursement from the suffragists.[22] Earlier Mrs. Catt had said that fighting the referendum elections around the country would cost a million dollars and Hawke was bitter that his victory was credited to the suffragists when they contributed nothing to gain it, telling Mrs. Catt:

The world takes it for granted that you and your Association instigated and backed the referendum litigation with all your resources, both intellectual and financial. It has already given you credit for this great legal move which checkmated all the opposing forces and won what was without question the paramount contest of the century. One instance of this is seen in the enclosed marked article by Ida Husted Harper in the Indianapolis News of June 5th, 1920, "Court's Decision Gives Suffragists Much Joy." She says that the Hawke case was "backed by the National Suffrage Association." But this impression that you are entitled to the credit for this legal triumph will grow stronger with time and will eventually become universal.[23]

Even after losing the *Hawke v. Smith* referendum case on June 1, 1920, and seeing woman suffrage proclaimed as the Nineteenth Amendment to the United States Constitution, the National Association Opposed to Woman Suffrage held to its esteem for the Supreme Court of the United States and looked forward to the Court showing itself "outside of politics" by siding with the antisuffragists in the new round of litigation against the Nineteenth Amendment then being brought by William L. Marbury's Maryland League for State Defense and Everett P. Wheeler's American Constitutional League.[24]

Months before the woman suffrage amendment achieved ratification, the opponents began thinking about a constitutional challenge in the courts. The first person to put forward the idea was J.A. Adriaans, the Washington, D.C. lawyer who had earlier been absorbed in exposing the evils of black suffrage and the unconstitutionality of the Fifteenth Amendment. In 1908 he wrote a pamphlet contending that blacks lacked sufficient native intelligence to vote. His view of women was equally contemptuous. Adriaans believed that court cases should be started before the thirty-sixth state ratified the woman suffrage amendment, and he outlined his ideas in conversation with J.S. Eichelberger, field secretary of the American Constitutional League in Washington. Eichelberger naïvely believed Adriaans was a master of constitutional politics and promptly sped the ideas for litigation on to Mary Kilbreth, then president of the National Association Opposed to Women Suffrage:

Mr. Adriaans suggests that [eleven named organizations] present a petition to the Supreme Court of the United States "praying leave to file an original bill of injunction against the Secretary of State and the Attorney General to enjoin the former from proclaiming and the latter from enforcing the proposed amendment to the Constitution known as the 19th, or Susan B. Anthony amendment prior to the holding of referendums thereon in certain States, and pending the legal decision of the validity of alleged ratification in certain other States, in order to prevent the Secretary of State from proclaiming an amendment which may be illegal or premature." [Uncertainty] may imperil the validity of the 1920 elections.[25]

Eichelberger added that he was sending this suggestion on at the same time to Marbury, Judge Leser, Wheeler and others. This started a flurry of telegrams, telephone calls and letters.

Marbury took exception to the type of action Adriaans and Eichelberger suggested, saying that if an original proceeding was to be taken, "it ought to be taken by a state."[26] This was so, he explained, because of the problem of "standing" to bring an original action in the Supreme Court. Suits by organizations had no hope of consideration but they might help by urging a state to bring action in its own name. He suggested trying the attorney general of Maryland with whom he had contact and with whom Marbury could probably work. Eichelberger was impressed with Marbury's letter and conceded that Adriaans had his limitations as a counselor on Supreme Court practice. He learned from the clerk of the Supreme Court that what had to be done to bring a suit in the name of a sovereign state was for the state attorney general simply to act by virtue of his inherent power. Eichelberger consulted Wayne Wheeler and other lawyers in Washington and was fully persuaded that Adriaans was wrong and Marbury right in dictating how to proceed.

Actually, with the 1919 October term of the Supreme Court ending in early June 1920 it was nearly impossible to organize a passable case quickly. Also, the lawyers were busy men with private practices and public careers in motion. Harry Tucker begged off from participating in a case against the amendment because he was preoccupied in a campaign for governor of Virginia. Not that he had lost his dislike of the amendment, as he told Everett Wheeler. "The acid test of a republican form of government," he wrote, "is that the state should have the right to determine who should be its officers and who should be its voters. If either one is denied, the republican form of government is also denied."[27] And so the cases took a little longer than had been hoped.

Several million women voted in the national elections in the fall of 1920 in which Republican Warren G. Harding and Calvin Coolidge were elected president and vice president. The only woman to be elected to Congress was the ultraconservative Mrs. Alice M. Robertson of Oklahoma.

The erstwhile opponents of woman suffrage might have let well enough alone, but they proceeded to test the Nineteenth Amendment in court, eventually getting a written ruling by the Supreme Court on March 10, 1922.[28] This litigation ended all thought of reversing woman suffrage and ensured national compliance. We shall briefly review the arguments in these two cases and the Court's ruling.

As it happened, the constitutional challenge of the Nineteenth Amendment followed neither the approach first suggested by Adriaans nor Marbury's more careful counterproposal. There were two cases, both begun in trial courts and carried by appeal to the Supreme Court of the United States and both brought in the name of an individual, rather than an organization. But antisuffrage sponsorship was perfectly plain. The plaintiff in the first case was Charles S. Fairchild, but the official record of the case, true to the form of constitutional litigation, did not hint that he was president of the American Constitutional League. On July 7, 1920, a suit was filed for Fairchild in the federal trial court in the District of Columbia against the secretary of state (then Bainbridge Colby; soon to be Charles Evans Hughes) from proclaiming the woman suffrage amendment and against the attorney general (then A. Mitchell Palmer; soon to be Harry Daugherty) from enforcing it.

The court took only a week to rule against Fairchild and that decree was affirmed by the Court of Appeals of the District of Columbia. Thus the Nineteenth Amendment was proclaimed and women voted long before this case reached the United States Supreme Court. When it did, in the 1921-22 term, the lawyers for Fairchild were listed in this order: William L. Marbury, Thomas F. Cadwalader, Everett P. Wheeler and Waldo G. Morse. Wheeler also filed a separate brief. The case was argued in the Supreme Court in Washington on January 23, 1922.[29]

The Maryland League for State Defense, under Marbury's direction, took a different course, starting on October 12, 1920, in Baltimore when women were registering as qualified to vote under the terms of the Nineteenth Amendment. At the board of registry of the seventh precinct of the eleventh ward, Oscar Leser led members of the League for State Defense in challenging the registration of two women. Marbury then filed a bill asking the court of common pleas to strike from the registration books the names of the two women, whose right to vote was questioned.[30] The women were Cecilia S. Waters and Mary D. Randolph, the first identified as white, the second as "colored." The women were, in fact, registered, and they voted in the presidential election of 1920. The complainants were aggrieved at this action and sought to have the names removed "because the persons registered are disqualified under the Constitution and laws of the State of Maryland and of the United States of America to vote at any election hereinafter to be held."

The bill of complaint was brought by members of the league as citizens, voters and taxpayers. It insisted that the "so-called Nineteenth Amendment," so-called being colloquial for alleged, was not a part of the Constitution. There were really two basic reasons why this was so, according to Marbury's complaint. For one, suffrage within a state was "wholly outside of the scope and purpose" of the amending power and woman suffrage certainly could not be foisted upon the state of Maryland, whose legislature had rejected and refused to ratify the federal amendment. For another, procedural quirks in the legislative ratification in the states of West Virginia, Missouri and Tennessee made actions there illegal and could not be counted among the thirty-six states necessary to ratify a proper amendment.

The trial of these issues in the case of *Leser v. Garnett* was conducted before Judge Heuisler in the court of common pleas in Baltimore for four days in December 1920. An account of the trial stresses the group affiliation of lawyers on both sides.[31] The case was opened by Marbury for the Maryland League for State Defense and he was joined by Cadwalader, and by State Senator George Arnold Frick, chairman of the Judiciary Committee of the Maryland Senate, also a member of the league. Frick, a leading Democratic lawyer, was active in championing states rights and had traveled to various states in 1919 and 1920 to oppose ratification of woman suffrage.[32] These three were joined at the counsel table by Everett P. Wheeler, executive chairman of the American Constitutional League.

It is difficult today to appreciate the self-confidence these opponents of women suffrage felt as they argued that week before a devoted following. Because the trial judge was amiable, and wished everyone a Merry Christmas as he took the case under advisement, the antisuffragists were sure they would win. They did not. Their petition to strike the names of the two women from the registry of voters was dismissed. The next year this was affirmed by the court of appeals of the state of Maryland.[33] In the October term 1921-1922, the Supreme Court reviewed both the *Fairchild* case from the District of Columbia and the *Leser* case from Maryland. Briefs were filed, oral argument was held consecutively in January 1922 and rulings were made in both cases on February 27, 1922.

The elaborate arguments William Marbury had made in the *Myers* case that the Fifteenth Amendment was unconstitutional were now dusted off and repeated with regard to the Nineteenth Amendment. Remember that Marbury was a highly respected lawyer in Baltimore, that the arguments he made against the power of the federal government to regulate the suffrage in a state had been accepted by a majority of legislators in Maryland and several other states. Many lawyers in the country who did not care at all for the southern view of the Fifteenth Amendment had been aroused by the success of the Anti-Saloon League in winning the prohibition amendment. Marbury also received encouragement from still another group of people who were aroused by the threat of a child labor amendment. His views were well formulated and widely known for they essentially were those put forward by Arthur Machen, by Tucker and in law review articles of his own.[34] These were not obscure pieces published in fifth-rate publications but were issued from the law schools at Harvard, Yale and Virginia. Marbury and his associates must have felt all the more encouraged when, at the oral argument in Washington, the Solicitor General James M. Beck saluted the patriotism of the American Constitutional League in its work.[35] Yet Everett P. Wheeler was ailing and could not attend. His companion in arms, Waldo G. Morse, spoke briefly but both arguments were carried by Marbury and his devoted assistant Cadwalader.

Time has stood still in Thomas F. Cadwalader's view of the good, the true and the beautiful in social as well as constitutional matters. A visitor to his Baltimore office in the 1960s in Baltimore's old Fidelity Building entered a nineteenth-century world. On sooty walls were portraits of Robert E. Lee, Grover Cleveland, Andrew Jackson, John C. Calhoun and Grandfather Cadwalader. Moving toward the end of his ninth decade, Cadwalader talked of more lost causes, of the possible segregationist Maryland Petition Committee gaining a referendum on Maryland's open occupancy statute. He ranked his friend, George Washington Williams, a Baltimore contemporary and insatiable racist, as impractical. In 1966 Williams brought action in the United States District Court for Maryland to require President Lyndon Johnson to declare the Fourteenth Amendment improperly ratified and, hence, invalid. Although calling this action a futile gesture, Cadwalader, in his own name and with his own funds, prepared an *amicus curiae* brief endorsing the ultimate correctness of this view of the amendment.

On a roll call of constitutional issues, Cadwalader was vehement in condemning the prohibition amendment and the Volstead Act, the woman suffrage amendment and the Sheppard-Towner Maternity Act, the child labor amendment and the New Deal. In 1948 he filed a brief *amicus curiae* for Baltimore neighborhood improvement associations in the *Racial Restriction Covenant Cases*. Having inherited family property and being chiefly concerned in estate work in recent decades, he had ample time for causes, wrote innumerable letters to the editors of the Baltimore newspapers and contributed to perhaps twenty conservative organizations.

Forty-five years after, Cadwalader vividly remembered the decisions of the Supreme Court handed down on February 27, 1922. The Court ruled unanimously against *Fairchild* and *Leser*, against their sponsors and their lawyers Marbury, Wheeler and Morse, and their junior associate at the bar, Cadwalader. The opinion of the Court in each case was by Mr. Justice Brandeis.[36] Here was a nice piece of irony in itself for, as we have seen, Brandeis, nearly forty years earlier, had represented the antisuffragist position in Massachusetts. Exactly when he changed his mind is uncertain, but it came some time after his marriage to Alice Goldmark, who was active in the drive for woman suffrage. By 1911 he publicly advocated the extension of suffrage and in 1915 was working for it. A close student of his life has said this of Brandeis: "As he became increasingly familiar with women in public life, notably his sister-in-law, Josephine Goldmark, he evidently changed his mind about their intellectual ability and their role in a modern society."[37]

Cadwalader had no complaint about Brandeis's beliefs but complained that the reasoning followed in disposing of the cases on the precedent of *Myers v. Anderson* was what hurt. Brandeis said that since the Court had ruled the Fifteenth Amendment valid and since the Nineteenth Amendment was similarly styled then it was also valid. To which Cadwalader lamented, "We never admitted the premise. I don't accept the theory that the Fifteenth Amendment is a valid part of the Constitution."[38]

The two woman suffrage cases were disposed of differently by the Supreme Court. Mr. Justice Brandeis found that Fairchild's alleged interest did not afford a proper basis for a decision on the merits. "It is frankly a proceeding to have the Nineteenth Amendment declared void," wrote Brandeis. He continued,

In form it is a bill in equity; but it is not a case within the meaning of section 2 of Article Three of the Constitution which confers judicial power on the Federal courts, for no claim of plaintiff is "brought before the courts for determination by such regular proceedings as are established by law or custom for the protection or enforcement of rights, or the prevention, redress, or punishment of wrongs."[39]

Brandeis then disposed of the matter by stressing that citizens, taxpayers and voters had no right as such to bring cases to the Supreme Court. These were his words:

Plaintiff has only the right, possessed by every citizen, to require that the government be administered according to law, and that the public moneys be not wasted. Obviously this general right does not entitle a private citizen to institute in the Federal courts a suit to secure by indirection a determination whether a statute, if passed, or a constitutional Amendment about to be adopted, will be valid.[40]

Leser v. Garnett passed this procedural hurdle as the Court accepted the case on certiorari while rejecting it on a writ of error; this was done because the laws of Maryland authorize such a suit by a qualified voter against the board of registry. Brandeis then dealt with the merits, first in the way that stung Cadwalader. That the Fifteenth Amendment is valid, said Brandeis, "although rejected by six states, including Maryland, has been recognized and acted on for half a century." The Nineteenth Amendment "is in character and phraseology precisely similar" to the Fifteenth and the idea that the latter is invalid "cannot be entertained." Brandeis also turned down the second contention which was that some of the ratifying states violated their own procedural rules in acting on the Nineteenth Amendment. This really was the point raised by *Hawke v. Smith* and this was one authority invoked against the contention. Finally, Brandeis for the Court ruled that "As the legislatures of Tennessee and West Virginia had power to adopt the resolutions of ratification, official notice to the Secretary [of State], duly authenticated, that they had done so, was conclusive upon him, and being certified to by his proclamation, is conclusive upon the courts."[41]

Conclusion

Just as the feminist movement was a by-product of industrialization, urbanization and mass education, so woman suffrage as a political goal and then as a practice has been an expression of feminism. It is remarkable that such a powerful movement had so few direct and obvious expressions in American constitutional controversy. In its broadest sense, of course, the transformation in the place of women in society from, say, the Seneca Falls Convention for Women's Rights in 1848 to the situation of today has been profound. But like the development of competitive political parties the place of women in the American polity has occurred very largely without benefit of constitutional rhetoric—whether in the original document and its amendments, in federal statutes or in court decisions.[42] Speaking strictly of woman suffrage, however, there appears to be a series of object lessons in constitutional change which provide a counterpoint to other examples of the phenomena. These are points to reflect upon:

  1. Feminists interested in political rights, from the 1860s onward, used the gamut of tactics—petitions, demonstrations, polemics, propaganda, and litigation and legislation.

  2. Advocates of woman suffrage in the 1850s and 1860s were allied with abolitionists and freedmen and, together, sought a federal constitutional amendment barring discrimination in voting "on account of race, color and previous condition of servitude" (the Frederick Douglass amendment) or "on account of

sex" (later called the Susan B. Anthony amendment). The alliance with blacks collapsed when the Douglass amendment was adopted as the Fifteenth Amendment of the United States Constitution in 1870 and the Anthony provision against discrimination on account of sex failed in Congress.

3. Following this, woman suffrage advocates broke into two major—and many minor—camps to pursue different paths to their goal. Susan B. Anthony and Elizabeth Cady Stanton stressed an amendment of the Constitution after first trying litigation to win political rights for women under the Fourteenth Amendment. Stressing this national path, Stanton and Anthony named their organization the National Woman Suffrage Association. At the same time Lucy Stone focused on the states and sought action there through the American Woman Suffrage Association. Year by year, decade by decade territories and states were added to the woman suffrage ranks either by amending their own constitutions or adopting statutes.

4. The tactic of incrementalism worked. By 1919, when Congress voted to propose the Anthony amendment, seventeen states had full woman suffrage, and fourteen other states permitted woman suffrage in presidential elections. This left seventeen states and some of these permitted women to vote in school or other municipal elections. While there was fierce resistance in Massachusetts among this last group and there was strong opposition even where women could already vote, the most persistent and settled opposition was in the southern states. Thus at some point the recalcitrant states which would not vote woman suffrage themselves, could have it imposed on them by three-fourths of the other states through a constitutional amendment. At that point the Anthony amendment was championed by both those in the Anthony school of thought and the Lucy Stone school.

5. If the woman suffrage amendment is seen as a necessary tactic to force woman suffrage upon the few states whose legislatures would not themselves permit women to vote, then the shape of the opposition will quickly be appreciated. For one thing, as states in the southern tradition were seriously opposed it is clear they had two things on their minds. One was the fear that this would bring black women to the polls. The other one was the related and deeply ingrained view of states rights, that so sensitive and fundamental a matter as suffrage was intended to be, should be and must be left to the states. Persons who were anxious over the new immigration were also concerned about granting suffrage to women. At least this, rather than race, seems to account for resistance to woman suffrage in Pennsylvania, New Jersey, New York and in New England. In Maryland and in some other states these two considerations combined and leading opponents to the Fifteenth Amendment and to black voting there were also against woman suffrage.

6. When opponents to woman suffrage organized, they also used a wide variety of tactics. It will be of particular interest here that while Susan B. Anthony and other suffragists were unsuccessful in the 1869-72 period with litiga-

tion so were the antisuffragists unavailing when they carried three cases to the United States Supreme Court between 1920 and 1922. Each side accepted the results of the judicial decisions against themselves and turned to other tactics or to other topics.

7. What about compliance? Prior to the Supreme Court decision in *Minor v. Happersett* in 1873, there was some voting by women counted. That decision closed this possibility and so, it must be noted, was complied with by registrars everywhere. The various state constitutions and statutes were complied with. So was the Nineteenth Amendment upon its ratification in 1920. This does not mean that all women voted but that no woman was denied the vote "on account of sex." This contrasts sharply with the absence of compliance and the resistance to the Fifteenth Amendment. Clearly there are factors about compliance not to be found in the words of the Constitution. The Nineteenth Amendment was an instant success in 1920; one student of the subject thinks it would not have succeeded in 1870 for she has written:

Like earlier efforts to make provisions for woman suffrage part of the Fourteenth and Fifteenth amendments, the Anthony and Minor cases demonstrated that the time was not ripe for woman suffrage. To try to bring it about by judicial fiat was a long step ahead of social realities; to win it through act of Congress was politically an impossibility.[43]

Compliance with the Fifteenth Amendment was starkly different as citizens, both men and women, were denied the vote "on account of race and color" for decades after ratification in 1870. Whatever else it tells us, it is obvious that no legal decree wins compliance simply because of its form, and a policy placed in the United States Constitution does not necessarily carry more weight than the same order adopted as a statute, issued as a presidential executive order or issued as a ruling by the Supreme Court. The variables at work here will be dealt with further in this book.

8. Upon the achievement of universal woman suffrage in the United States under the Nineteenth Amendment large numbers of women previously absorbed as suffragists or antisuffragists had time on their hands. There is often a void in great achievements even when, perhaps more often when, there is a sense of genuine and sincere gratification. Women feel depression after childbirth; men after retirement from a successful career. Large numbers of people were not profoundly affected by the ratification of the Nineteenth Amendment but to those in, around and against the movement it was a time of radical readjustment. The experiences shared in the conflicts over suffrage were rapidly displaced by new public issues as we shall later observe. There were at least five major lines of action followed by men and women deeply involved in the suffrage campaign.

One was the middle course led by Carrie Chapman Catt, who transformed the National American Woman Suffrage Association into the National League of Women Voters. This organization was devoted to the education of women on public issues and saw nonpartisanship as a necessary condition for their work. The League of Women Voters encouraged members to join and work in a political party of their choice, but league officers could not run for or hold party office. Another course was taken by the women in the Congressional Union, who formed the National Woman's Party and still others in the Lucy Stone League. These militantly feminist organizations have not survived as important groups but have been replaced by other activist groups, such as women's liberation. A third group of women in politics stressed regular party organization and have been Republicans and Democrats in ways that have not made sex a particularly important or central issue. This was true of Frances Perkins, Eleanor Roosevelt, Clare Boothe Luce, Margaret Chase Smith, Edith Green and Shirley Chisholm, among many others. A fourth group has been active in pressure group politics and is differentiated by the particular group. These are women who were suffragists or in the suffragist tradition. These are women not primarily associated with either the League of Women Voters or with a militant feminist organization, nor with a political party, although they may be members. They may even be readily identifiable as Democrats or Republicans, but Florence Kelley was foremost as the leader of the National Consumers' League, Jane Addams of the settlement-house movement, Coretta King with her husband in the Southern Christian Leadership Conference, Constance Baker Motley with the NAACP Legal Defense Fund, and Jeannette Rankin, Rosika Schwimmer and Joan Baez with the peace movement.

Finally, the women who opposed woman suffrage and their political descendants are people on the right who feared the vote because they saw it as an entering wedge for socialism, pacifism and bolshevism.

Provincial Issues vs. Cosmopolitanism

4 **Prohibition**

In 1920 Bernard Hershkopf was counsel for the United States Brewers' Association. Together with Robert Crain, William D. Guthrie and Elihu Root he sought to persuade the Supreme Court that the Eighteenth Amendment had been improperly adopted, that it invaded personal liberty, was an illegal invasion of states rights, was inapplicable to states that had not ratified it and that the Court had the authority to, and should hold, the amendment unconstitutional.[1] The Court was unanimous in declining to interfere, and national prohibition was the law of the land for nearly fourteen years, from January 29, 1920, to December 5, 1933. In recalling those days recently, Hershkopf said, "Prohibition is deader than a doornail," and asked why anyone should be interested in it today.[2] Is there a reasonable answer? I believe there are several answers.

For one, prohibition ranks as one of the broadest and deepest social and morally motivated movements in American history, similar in some ways to the antislavery movement, to the civil rights movement and to the peace movement of the 1960s. It was a crusader's movement, appealing to the traditions of puritanism and Protestantism which have had a part in generating most of the major social movements in the United States. As a significant social movement, the goal of prohibition was looked upon by advocates as a panacea, as a means of cleansing the unwashed, whose inferior habits and values were ruining American civilization. Their attack was broad-scaled. While the most obvious evils of alcoholism, of the saloon, of poverty were stressed, the movement for prohibition also condemned the greedy brewers and hotels, the trade unionists employed in the brewing industry and one and all who declined to endorse their bout with king alcohol with the fervor of evangelical Protestantism.

This was a movement generating legal change, moreover, which nearly succeeded in drying out the Constitution. Led by lawyers in the Anti-Saloon League, the prohibition movement sought to make "the manufacture, sale, or transportation of intoxicating liquors" within and into the United States unconstitutional. That this policy became part of the Constitution could have been only a rhetorical achievement, but it was far more than that. Dry forces also worked for total compliance and their activity, though besmirched by ultimate failure, affords one of the enduring lessons on the difficulties of durable constitutional change in the American system.

The problems of compliance with the Eighteenth Amendment, with the enforcement laws of Congress, with federal administrative orders and with the many comparable laws, rules and orders in the states are worthy of exploration by persons interested today in the difficulties of law enforcement.

The politics of the amending process is also remarkably illuminated by examining the adoption of twin amendments: the Eighteenth Amendment ushering in prohibition and the Twenty-first repealing it. The juxtaposition of interests where drys and wets switched sides in favoring and opposing an amendment shows how ephemeral may be a group's attachment to a procedure—like constitutional amendments *per se*, for example. There have been few amendments to the United States Constitution ratified (twenty-six over 200 years) but there is a constant chatter about amendments, their merit, efficacy and possibility. The prohibition and repeal episodes offer a special dimension to the study of constitutional change in the twentieth century.

Finally, proof of the importance and breadth of the prohibition movement is registered by the remarkable number of side effects it produced in American constitutional law. The courts were flooded with thousands of cases arising out of enforcement, and the Supreme Court was obliged to deal for the first time with some enduring issues which, by themselves, had no necessary connection with prohibition but concerned fundamental constitutional problems. Thus the first great search and seizure case of *Olmstead v. United States*[3] concerned wire tapping to obtain information about suspected bootlegging. *Tumey v. Ohio*[4] dealt with self-enrichment for a local judge whose remuneration depended on convictions; this case arose over a prohibition violation. There were many others, as will be seen, which were unimagined by those who supported the temperance movement at the beginning. Social movements simply have a way of producing an almost endless procession of ancillary legal and political problems. This is perhaps a fair measure of the power and significance of such movements.

Nor are there recent political science or constitutional law studies of prohibition and repeal, and there are, in fact, few scholarly studies at all of these matters. As we shall see, it appears to be a fact that there is now no study whatever of repeal based upon the newly available manuscript sources on this subject for the 1920s and early 1930s. The opportunity to prepare the first account of these events, with all its pitfalls, has obvious attractions.

Taking these points together, with an understanding that prohibition is "deader than a doornail" we shall see a movement that took several generations to come to fruition and yet failed. We shall also see a movement that insisted on utilizing government to make people toe the line. That such a powerful movement failed in this ambition must surely afford some lessons to any group that might wish to get people to behave in certain ways. Prohibition raises few if any passions today and so we can look back at the record, with a contemporary glance, to be sure, and search objectively for any lessons of constitutional change it may offer.

Drying Out the Constitution

The Founding Fathers did not, according to the records of the Philadelphia Convention of 1787, consider forbidding the manufacture, transportation, sale or consumption of intoxicating liquors. They had neither the urge of self-denial nor a sense that the government of a nation should enact sumptuary legislation. The temperance movement which spread across the land in the nineteenth century only gradually steered its way toward the goal of incorporating its passion in the Constitution. This may safely be called a grass-root movement. Moral suasion sometimes accompanied by local license laws came first. Organizations with more aggressive techniques, like the Sons of Temperance, developed in several states. A dynamic leader, Neal Dow in the state of Maine, drafted the first state-wide prohibition measure which kept Maine officially dry from 1851 to 1933. Dow served for a decade as mayor of Portland, gave rousing lectures throughout the country and in Scotland and England as well, and in 1872 was the presidential nominee of the Prohibition party. Yet, in some twenty presidential elections the Prohibition candidate not once polled more than 2.2 percent of the total vote cast. It is a maxim of political science that parties cannot survive without winning elections. And in presidential politics even the 13.5 percent won by George Wallace in 1968 did not give him the balance of power he sought. As a single issue, zealous prohibitionists learned that they should form organizations that, among other things, endorsed candidates but did not run them. Yet, very early in the temperance movement some advocated sweeping, legalized prohibition. This is seen in a resolution of the National Prohibition convention in Chicago, in September 1869:

That the traffic in intoxicating beverages is a dishonor to Christian civilization, inimical to the best interests of society, a political wrong of unequal enormity, subversive of the ordinary objects of government, not capable of being regulated or restrained by any system of license whatever, but imperatively demanding for its suppression effective legal prohibition by both state and national legislation.[5]

The Woman's Christian Temperance Union was a more powerful force against liquor than the Prohibition party, but its ambitious alliances with other reform groups and parties often made it unworkable. Frances E. Willard, born in upstate New York, educated in Wisconsin and Illinois, became national president of the new WCTU in 1874. A Puritan interested in science, she became an ardent Methodist at this time. In those days of temperance crusades, "bands of women appeared everywhere—on the streets and in the saloons—singing and praying against the sin of the liquor traffic. Frances Willard joined one of these bands in Pittsburgh and delivered her first prayer in public kneeling on the sawdust floor of a Market Street saloon."[6] The WCTU became a major national organization, an adjunct of feminism which supported numerous reform programs and sought to forge an alliance in the 1890s with the Populist party. The WCTU is one of the oldest continuously organized groups in the country but it never placed heavy emphasis on governmental action, though its members surely approved of prohibition. One of today's leaders has recently said: "The primary program of the Woman's Christian Temperance Union has been on education and the protection of the home."[7] It appears that the WCTU never participated in litigation, and so, despite its membership, finances and prominence, seems to have stressed direct rather than governmental action.[8]

Temperance became an increasingly popular cause toward the end of the nineteenth century and new local and state restrictions on liquor abounded. Several western state constitutions, including that of Kansas in 1880, were amended to prohibit the importation and sale of intoxicating liquor within their borders. Interestingly, in Kansas this led to one of the most famous episodes of dry hostility to drinking when Carry Nation, a woman associated with the WCTU, began her celebrated agitation to rid the state of drinking. "So far as she had a definite theory of action, it was that since the saloon was illegal in Kansas, it was permissible for any citizen to force his way in and destroy not only liquor but furniture and fixtures. Saloon property, she avowed, 'has no rights that anybody is bound to respect.' "[9] Fame and support followed in her wake as Carry Nation used her hatchet in what she envisaged as a divine crusade to wreck saloons, furniture and liquor stocks valued in the thousands. She was arrested about thirty times in as many states for disturbing the peace. Carry Nation "visited several American universities, including Harvard and Yale, which she denounced as 'hellholes'; the students greeted her with wild burlesque."[10] In this account of constitutional change, the story of Carry Nation stands out in several ways. She represented the American vigilante tradition. She expressed the moralistic righteousness that her vision of the truth stood at a higher level than ordinary mortals, especially those in government. In these beliefs especially she left a heritage to fellow prohibitionists who criticized her methods but imitated them all the same, even if in muted ways.

Sentiment across the country was affected by the crusading activity of the Prohibition party and the WCTU. Native Yankees and their kin in the West were ready for this agitation. The temperance cause struck a deep chord in the American consciousness as it linked up with the puritanical virtues of hard work and progress, which appeared to be threatened by urbanization and immigration. It is difficult to appreciate today that organizations like the Grand Army of the Republic, embracing the veterans of the Civil War, and the counterpart Confederate Veterans, were essentially dry organizations but they were. The time was ripe for a highly organized political movement to bring the country to the dry decades of the early twentieth century. That organization—the Anti-Saloon League of America—was not alone in working toward national prohibition but it was at the forefront.

Before turning to the league itself and its success in making the Eighteenth Amendment part of the Constitution at the end of World War I, it is well to note that most of the states were already dry prior to nationally ordained prohibition. By 1916 some twenty-three states had prohibited intoxicating beverages within their borders (see figure 4-1). But by the time the Eighteenth Amendment came under consideration, thirty-three states had included essentially the same provision in their own constitutions (see figure 4-2). Thus the Eighteenth Amendment

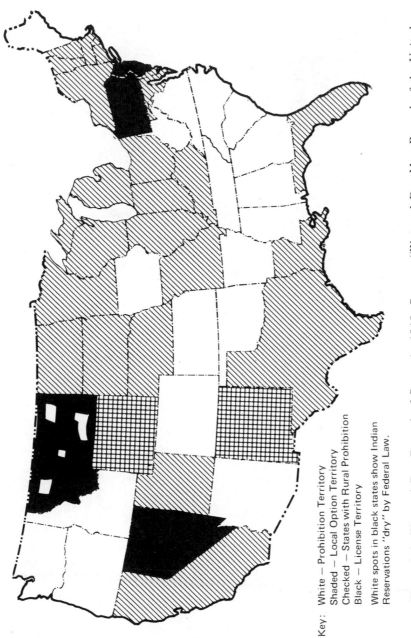

Key: White — Prohibition Territory
Shaded — Local Option Territory
Checked — States with Rural Prohibition
Black — License Territory

White spots in black states show Indian
Reservations "dry" by Federal Law.

Figure 4-1. Wet and Dry Map Record of the United States in 1919. Source: "Wet and Dry Map Record of the United States," The American Issue Publishing Company, Westerville, Ohio, n.d.

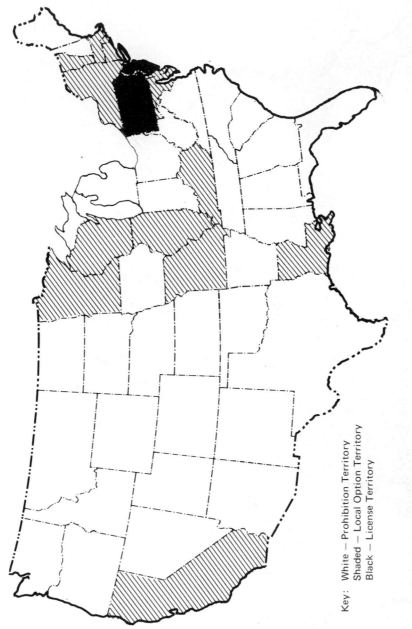

Key: White — Prohibition Territory
Shaded — Local Option Territory
Black — License Territory

Figure 4–2. Wet and Dry Record of States in 1919. Source: *Wet and Dry Map Record of the United States,* The American Issue Publishing Company, Westerville, Ohio, n.d.

made sure that the holdouts would be forcibly made prohibition states. In the end, only the state of Rhode Island failed to ratify the Eighteenth Amendment and this failure, as we shall see, became one of the several slender reeds for contending in the Supreme Court that the Eighteenth Amendment was subject to judicial review and was invalid, a proposition the justices did not accept. With the adoption of the Eighteenth Amendment in 1919, to become effective in January 1920, and of the implementing Volstead or National Prohibition Act, a social movement of several decades reached its apogee.

After it was over, the prohibition era was called "the great experiment" but its sponsors had intended and expected it to be a permanent constitutional change. As a major change that faded and was reversed by the Twenty-first Amendment in 1933, national constitutional prohibition raises several intriguing issues. What was the social character of the movements contesting this issue? What role did voluntary organizations play in bringing about national prohibition? Why was it possible to achieve this through national legislation and through the constitutional amendment procedure? The federal courts cooperated with the prohibition policies expressed by the federal statutes and the Eighteenth Amendment in a period where they interfered with other social policies. What litigation arose out of the temperance movement? Did temperance lawyers participate in court cases and what was the judicial record on the subject? Why was compliance with national prohibition a serious difficulty even though the policy was written into the Constitution, supported by federal statutes, enforced by the executive branch with heavy appropriations from Congress and supported by the courts? These are questions this chapter will seek to answer. The further matter of how repeal came about, through the adoption of the Twenty-first Amendment, will be examined in Chapter 5.

Wayne Wheeler: Prohibition Lawyer

Wayne Bidwell Wheeler was an Anti-Saloon man from his college days at Oberlin College until his death in 1927, and he became a lawyer expressly to serve the interests of his chosen organization. His college essays and orations frequently lambasted the evils of alcohol, and the Oberlin professors who founded the Anti-Saloon League of Ohio urged Wheeler on. A Baptist, he attended the first public union service of the Ohio League in Oberlin on June 4, 1893, heard the Reverend Howard Hyde Russell, organizer of the league speak, and signed a pledge card agreeing to pay twenty-five cents a month support. Wheeler believed at the outset that this association offered a better means than a political party, including the Prohibition party, of gaining temperance reform.

Recalling the first meeting of the Ohio Anti-Saloon League, Wheeler said:

The simplicity and practical nature of the new organization captured me. It offered a chance for united effort to people who agreed on prohibition but disagreed on nearly everything else. It went direct to the people of the churches—the genuine altruists and idealists of the nation. It ignored all sectarian, political, racial, sectional and other subdivisions.[11]

As a volunteer before graduation in 1894 and as a paid field secretary afterward, Wheeler's first tasks were to speak in the churches and to get out the dry vote in elections to the Ohio legislature. He chose to study law to serve the temperance cause. He seems to have sensed the void and to have plunged purposely ahead. His publicity secretary has woven the texture of those law school days:

The Anti-Saloon League had no lawyer. Wheeler saw the opportunity for a lawyer who was a League man. Soon after his entrance into the organization, he began the study of law with a Cleveland attorney. For a year he studied law on trains, in hotel rooms, or wherever he happened to be. He was giving full-time service to the League, as superintendent of the Cleveland district, besides speaking two or three times on Sunday in the churches. At the end of this year's study, he entered the Western Reserve University at Cleveland, from which he graduated in 1898 with the degree of LL.B. During the whole period of his law course, he continued on the staff of the League, speaking on Sunday and doing such other work during the week as Rev. Purley A. Baker (later state and national superintendent), then superintendent of the Cleveland district, assigned to him.[12]

Wheeler was shrewd, persistent and farseeing. A practical sense led him to seek punishment at the polls for wets and neutrals and to gain administrative posts in government for drys. As a kind of one-man legal center, Wheeler was a law writer (in publications like *The Law of Ohio Relating to Intoxicating Liquors* in 1900 and *Federal and State Laws Relating to Intoxicating Liquors* in 1916), and a polemicist (as in his *How to Enforce National Prohibition* in 1927) as well as a man capable of drafting legislation and defending it in litigation.[13] He drafted legislation at all levels and developed persuasive arguments for legislative friends to use in debate. Wheeler learned the legislative process thoroughly— at every level from common council to Congress. He had an important hand in preparing the Webb-Kenyon Act of 1913 and the Volstead Act of 1919 as well as in the strategic considerations of obtaining the Eighteenth Amendment to the Constitution. Wheeler also learned the importance of appropriations for and administration of dry laws and regularly guided the officials concerned. He became a past master at litigation. In Ohio between 1900 and 1915 he is said to have worked in 2,000 local cases to enforce dry laws. From 1915 to 1927 he was the chief counsel for the temperance, meaning the enforcement side, in cases in the Supreme Court of the United States.

Starting in the 1840s advocates of prohibition worked through every governmental nook and cranny to rid the country of alcohol. The movement's banner of success was variously marked "local option," "state-wide prohibition," the "bone-dry law" or "national prohibition." Prohibitionists were moralistic in theory, often pragmatic in practice, and Wayne Wheeler combined the two. Not until 1913 did nation-wide prohibition become the professed, announced goal of the Anti-Saloon League of America. In a sense this sweeping objective was an aberration in a movement previously marked by an incremental, grass-roots, do-what-can-be-done outlook.

The temperance crusade success collided with the hard reality of a federal legal system in a national economy. The checkerboard of prohibition laws could not circumvent national transportation, which made all areas of the country potential markets for alcohol. Local and state enforcement in the dry jurisdictions simply could not stop the liquor traffic, and the drys sought national governmental assistance. They first advocated nation-wide prohibition by constitutional amendment in 1856 when, according to Cherrington's chronology, "The Sons of Temperance inaugurates the movement for National Constitutional Prohibition. (The amendment is adopted sixty-three years later.)"[14] Yet there was no substantial movement for a constitutional amendment until 1913 when the Anti-Saloon League of America endorsed this path. By then the advocates of temperance had had vast experience with Congress and the courts in backing up state prohibition laws.

When the temperance movement won state prohibition laws and then national legislation supporting those laws, the wets went to court. Lawyers for breweries, distilleries and their various trade associations and allies asserted that states had gone beyond the limits of their police powers and that Congress had unconstitutionally yielded its powers to regulate commerce among the states.

Joseph Hodge Choate told the Supreme Court in 1888 that the Kansas prohibition law inflicted an overwhelming economic loss on the brewer he represented, a loss that deprived him of liberty and property without due process of law. His plea was unavailing. In an age when regulatory legislation was often invalidated as an infringement of property rights, the Supreme Court looked at prohibition as a necessary and valid community protection. Thus the police power of the state was chosen as the higher value because, as the opinion of the Court held, "all property in this country is held under the implied obligation that the owner's use of it shall not be injurious to the community."[15] Although temperance advocates often complained about ineffective enforcement and the permissiveness of trial court judges toward prohibition laws, they were generally well pleased with the Supreme Court's constitutional rulings on the subject.

When the Supreme Court failed to stretch the commerce clause enough to suit prohibitionists, Congress was persuaded to do so. This resulted in major innovative national legislation twice, in the Wilson Act of 1890 and in the Webb-Kenyon Act of 1913. The Wilson Act was aimed at reinforcing state prohibition laws which had sought to regulate interstate shipments of liquor in its original kegs. This would overcome the Supreme Court's 1888 ruling that an Iowa statute requiring an interstate railroad to obtain a license from the auditor of the destination county before bringing liquor into the state violated the commerce clause.[16]

The Court followed this in 1890 with the invalidation of enforcement of the Iowa prohibition law against an interstate shipment of liquor in the "original packages," a form of transit held sacred since Chief Justice Marshall's *Brown v. Maryland* decision in 1827.[17] This precipitated the Wilson Act, a key congressional victory for the drys.

The federal Wilson Act of 1890 supported enforcement of prohibition in the dry states by subjecting all intoxicating liquors transported there "for use, consumption, sale or storage therein" to state laws "enacted in the exercise of its police powers." The statute provided specifically that these liquors "shall not be exempt therefrom by reason of being introduced therein in original packages or otherwise."[18]

A case testing the Wilson Act began the day after enactment when one Rahrer in Kansas sold a certain keg and bottle shipped to him by a Missouri distiller. Rahrer was arrested for violating the Kansas prohibition law, now supported by the Wilson Act. Rahrer sought and won a writ of habeas corpus in a federal court and the respondent sheriff appealed to the Supreme Court. The wets' argument was that Congress had given away or delegated its own power under the commerce clause to the state, a view rejected by the Court. In an opinion by Chief Justice Melville W. Fuller, the Court upheld the congressional conclusion "that the common interests did not require entire freedom in the traffic in ardent spirits."[19]

The victory for the drys in Congress, in the Wilson Act, and in the Supreme Court in the Rahrer case, moved the temperance movement further along to national prohibition. They were searching for *complete* prohibition. Every legislative election, the composition of all the courts whether filled through appointment or election, and increasingly the designation of administrative officials came to concern the leaders of the Woman's Christian Temperance Union, the Anti-Saloon League and countless local organizations at work for temperance across the country. At the constitutional level the next large quest was stronger national legislation to clamp down on out-of-state intrusions on the increasing number of states with prohibition laws.

The national ascendancy of the temperance movement is exhibited in several ways in the Webb-Kenyon Act of 1913, adopted by a lame-duck Congress over the veto of the lame-duck President William Howard Taft. A firmer legal basis was needed to stop the burgeoning express companies from transporting liquor from wet states to individual customers in dry states. This was not a resale commercial transaction, but concerned state laws prohibiting a common carrier from transporting intoxicating liquors into a state "even when intended for personal use." A dry coordinating committee worked in Washington for years to devise a legislative formula satisfactory to at least a majority and, if possible, to two-thirds of each house. Beginning in earnest in 1911 this was, if one may use the phrase, a valuable dry run for temperance forces. Soon after the Webb-Kenyon victory they launched the great drive for total national prohibition by constitutional amendment. The Webb-Kenyon experience included electioneering, drafting, conferring and compromising, lobbying, coping with opposition from President Taft, Attorney General Wickersham and leading senators like George Sutherland of Utah and Elihu Root of New York. After enactment of the Webb-Kenyon Act the temperance movement organized a major court test, successfully managed by Wayne Wheeler. All this took place between 1911 and 1915. The Eighteenth Amendment followed swiftly upon these developments and in a similar pattern with the focus on the elections of 1916, the two-thirds vote for proposal in Congress in 1917, ratification by the states in 1918 and 1919, followed by enforcement legislation and court tests in the 1920s.

The constitutional testing of the Webb-Kenyon Act was initiated in West Virginia and pursued to the Supreme Court by Anti-Saloon League leaders. A new state-wide prohibition law went into effect in West Virginia on July 1, 1914, and a report by the League's state superintendent boasted of the organization's vigilante role in law enforcement.[20] He explained that the liquor interests had deluged the state with mail-order advertisements and were ready to challenge the new law and the Webb-Kenyon Act with it.

The West Virginia tax commissioner, a lawyer named Fred O. Blue, served also as the new commissioner of prohibition. Working closely with officials of the West Virginia League, Blue sought an injunction in the federal district court to restrain the express companies from bringing liquor into West Virginia to fill mail orders. Blue was joined by Wheeler in arguing this case before the Circuit Court of Appeals in Richmond, which made a decision favorable to them on January 13, 1915. Wheeler also joined Blue in the Supreme Court of the United States in arguing the James Clark Distilling Company cases. They rehearsed their oral arguments ahead of time by playing the devil's advocate in turn to cover every imaginable argument concerning the validity of the Webb-Kenyon Act. The cases were first argued in Washington on May 10 and 11, 1915, but in the following October term the Court ordered rebriefing and reargument, which did not take place until November 8 and 9, 1916. This appears to have been a consequence of the Hughes resignation and the drawn-out contest over the Brandeis appointment each of which had a strongly disruptive effect. After reargument, the Court's decision came swiftly enough, being announced on January 8, 1917.

It is rather remarkable to consider that the argument for the validity of the Webb-Kenyon Act, a United States statute, depended solely on the argument in the Supreme Court by the general counsel of a voluntary association and a state official. Wayne Wheeler said over and over again that John W. Davis, solicitor general of the United States, should have joined in the defense of the act before the Supreme Court.

A further effort by wets to weaken the Webb-Kenyon Act led to another Supreme Court case victory for the drys in which Wheeler participated. This took the form of a challenge to the validity of enactment by arguing that the two-thirds vote overriding President Taft's veto did not accord with the constitutional requirement. It is evidence of the significance of the temperance movement that cases on all manner of subjects were churned up in its wake and illustrates once more how questions of procedure ordinarily arise out of heated substantive controversy. The case was *Missouri Pacific Railway Company v. Kansas*[21] with the railroad placing its appeal of a conviction under the Webb-Kenyon Act on a contention that the veto clause of the Constitution had been violated. That clause[22] provides that for a bill disapproved by the president to become law it shall be repassed by two-thirds of the Senate and House of Representatives. Counsel for the railroad insisted this meant two-thirds of the total membership of each house, but the argument of Kansas and of Wheeler in a separate brief prevailed. The Court ruled unanimously that the two-thirds vote of each house required to pass a bill over a veto means two-thirds of a quorum.

The scope of Wheeler's work during his first year with the Anti-Saloon League in Washington was set forth in his own summary:

The Webb-Kenyon Interstate Liquor Shipment case argued and won in the Supreme Court.

Brief prepared on State and Federal Laws covering over twenty-five cases in State and Federal Courts.

Aided by personal counsel, visitation, and by sending briefs and drafts of laws to most of the states that have enacted state prohibition this year.

Have filed briefs and given information to Post Office Department, Justice Department, and some other Departments in the preparation of opinions, liquor bulletins and other documents which affect the liquor traffic. I have also prepared a large number of memorandum briefs for Congressmen in connection with the fight for advanced prohibition legislation in the courts.

Aided New Hampshire in its legislative fight for State Prohibition, and in the special Congressional fight which followed.

A large part of the time of the attorney for the National League has been given to legislative work at Washington, and in the special field work in securing the votes of the doubtful Congressmen. In pursuing this work, I have visited over twenty states; have spoken nearly every Sunday, and in several campaigns, raising funds for the State and National League and helping in state-wide election fights; have raised over $40,000 in cash and subscriptions for State and National work at these meetings.

Have prepared copy for the second edition of the compilation of the liquor laws, State and Federal.

Have been in touch with the law enforcement officials and League attorneys in nearly all the states, giving counsel and working out the law enforcement program.[23]

These were the activities that led Muskingum College and Oberlin College to honor Wayne Bidwell Wheeler with the degree of Doctor of Laws.

The Anti-Saloon League of America

In its heyday of success in the first quarter of the twentieth century, the Anti-Saloon League of America had all the assets a voluntary association bent on political action could ask for.[24] The idea of the league had been put into action in Ohio and in the District of Columbia in 1893 at a time when hundreds of temperance societies were at work. The formula of focusing on the saloon through nonpartisan political action had a narrow attraction around which numerous other organizations and thousands of individuals could rally. At the instigation of the Reverend Alpha J. Kynett and the Reverend Luther B. Wilson of the Methodist Episcopal Church and a Roman Catholic leader, John Ireland, first archbishop of St. Paul, Minnesota, and long an advocate of total abstinence, the Anti-Saloon League of the District of Columbia issued a call for a national convention in 1895. Some 161 delegates from forty-seven organizations responded and met at the Calvary Baptist Church in Washington, D.C. on December 17, 1895. There the American Anti-Saloon League, later renamed the Anti-Saloon League of America, came into existence.

The first national superintendent—today's coinage would be executive director—was the Reverend Howard H. Russell, whose organizing skills had been demonstrated in the Ohio Anti-Saloon League, the premier state league. From Columbus he moved to open state leagues across the country on the Ohio model. His approach was to bypass the existing temperance organizations and use cooperating churches, particularly the Methodist, Baptist, Presbyterian and Congregational, as a base to develop a truly national league. These churches had a ready-made army of temperance believers that enabled the hierarchical approach to work. Timberlake has described this astonishingly simple, thorough formula as follows:

Russell applied himself at once to the task of organizing additional state leagues. To facilitate the work, he drew up model constitutions to guide the various subdivisions within each state. The basic unit was to be the church antisaloon league. . . . The next larger unit was to be the local antisaloon league, which would embrace all local organizations interested in temperance. . . . Next up the ladder was to be the county antisaloon league which would comprise the heads of all local antisaloon leagues in the county.

To cap the structure in each state was to be a state antisaloon league, which would consist of a superintendent and his assistants, and a board of trustees who would represent the various organizations affiliated with the state league. The boards of trustees were to control and govern the state leagues. Although they were ultimately to become elective, the boards of trustees were initially appointed from above in order to prevent them from being captured and destroyed by unfriendly partisans. The state superintendents were to oversee the work in each state. Upon them devolved the burden of building up their respective organizations and supervising all league activities, one of the most important of which was to lobby at the state legislature.[25]

This formula was not an instant success as there were many financial and personnel problems early in the years. Yet during his tenure from 1895 to 1903, Russell saw the establishment of the Anti-Saloon League in forty states with a total of 300 full-time, paid workers.

Under the leadership of the Reverend Purley A. Baker from 1903 to 1913, the Anti-Saloon League of America took hold as a significant national organization. Its internal government and financial base was perfected. Its first legislative goals were achieved. There was an annual conference of state superintendents and other officials from 1898 onward to teach and to learn the most effective tactics, to train and indoctrinate workers in the principles and methods of the league. Through the years almost all paid workers had attended these sessions, and by 1913 some thirty-four state superintendents had emerged from an Ohio Anti-Saloon apprenticeship. This network of friends and associates gave the league a true federal structure yet centralized in a way that made the organization "capable of moving quickly and with one mind to achieve its aims."[26]

The Anti-Saloon League could not have survived without a grass roots that supported it with two essential ingredients, dollars and ballots. The key fund-raising technique was an individual pledge on subscription cards often distributed in churches on the occasion of an "Anti-Saloon Field Day." On a field day a league agent entered the pulpit as a guest of the local minister, gave the latest Anti-Saloon word, solicited funds and urged the congregation to vote for league-endorsed candidates. True, John D. Rockefeller and John D. Rockefeller, Jr., staunch Baptists, were heavy contributors, and other rich men gave, too, but most funds came from small gifts. By 1910 the total annual income of the state leagues was a million dollars and ten years later achieved an annual high of $2.5 million. This permitted a growth of paid staff to 1,500 in 1915 and more in the drive for national prohibition.

For its three departments of work, which were agitation, legislation and law enforcement, the Anti-Saloon League established its own publishing house in 1909 at Westerville, Ohio, close to Columbus. This was an ideal location for swift national distribution of the thirty-one different state editions of *The American Issue* with a monthly circulation of 500,000 copies, put out by the American Issue Publishing Company, Inc., directed by Ernest H. Cherrington. The Westerville plant grew with the circulation of *The American Issue*, reaching 16 million in 1919. Yearbooks, pamphlets, briefs, new journals and even encyclopedias on temperance came forth from the plant. The American Issue Publishing Company not only spread antisaloon propaganda far and wide but made money for the league at the same time.

Apportionment and the Eighteenth Amendment

The power of the temperance idea in American life, loud and clear as it was, could not have achieved national constitutional prohibition without the presence of temperance organizations. Millions of new immigrants from Europe during this period came from societies where drinking was condoned. Few were Protestants in the American evangelical mold; most were Catholics and many were Jews. Thus there were marked social differences between the native Baptists and Methodists of small-town U.S.A. and the aliens and new citizens who possessed an unimpressive illiteracy or a threatening cosmopolitanism. The immigrant could hardly win and was condemned for clannishness and other un-American ways. Gusfield has brilliantly illustrated the whole issue of temperance in American life over several generations as a symbolic crusade.[27]

Explanations of prohibition have overlooked the contribution which apportionment of Congress during the 1890-1930 period may have made in transforming admittedly strong sentiment into constitutional law. The goal of the two-thirds vote was achieved repeatedly by the temperance movement, in overriding the Taft veto of the Webb-Kenyon Act in 1913, in proposing the prohibition amendment to the states in 1917, and in overriding the Wilson veto of the Volstead Act in 1919. The proposition that Congress had a peculiar apportionment in these years and that this worked to make the two-thirds vote possible needs fuller study than can be given here. Yet it is possible from the most elementary facts about the apportionment of both House and Senate to see its probable impact on the outcome of these votes. The facts also bear on the ratification of the Eighteenth Amendment where three-fourths of the state legislatures were needed. The development of statehood itself is, therefore, a good place to begin this speculation.

The last of territories within the continent to become states were coincidentally strongly marked by temperance sentiment. The final ten, which became states between 1889 and 1912, raised the number to forty-eight and achieved the total needed to block ratification of the proposed constitutional amendment from nine to thirteen. These ten were Washington, Montana, North Dakota and South Dakota in 1889; Idaho and Wyoming in 1890; Utah in 1896; Oklahoma in 1907; and Arizona and New Mexico in 1912. In fact, the seven states admitted before the final ten turned out in the crucial votes on prohibition between 1890 and 1930 to be overwhelmingly dry. It will be recalled that these states were Minnesota in 1858, Oregon in 1859, Kansas in 1861, West Virginia in 1863, Nevada in 1864, Nebraska in 1867, and Colorado in 1876. None of the controversies occurring at each point of entrance revolved around temperance; it simply was a coincidence that temperance sentiment emerged as predominate in these states. If the areas from which these states were formed had remained territories or been cut into fewer states, national constitutional prohibition would have been far more difficult to achieve.

To the idea of temperance, its social status basis and the admittedly resourceful voluntary associations must be added some of the facts of American political geography of the 1911-31 era when national prohibition was achieved. The admission of Oklahoma to statehood in November 1907, New Mexico in January 1912 and Arizona in February 1912 had the effect of adding six dry United

States senators who held almost consistently on every key vote during the next twenty years. Indeed, all of the states entering the Union after the Civil War naturally were western, sparsely settled, religiously Protestant and politically Progressive. This combination coincided with a temperance attitude whipped up first toward state-wide and then nation-wide prohibition. The overriding of the Taft veto by two-thirds of the Senate and the fact that by 1919 thirty-three of the forty-eight states had significant dry legislation on their books illustrates the well-rooted constituency of the temperance movement.

The history of apportionment in the House of Representatives in this era is a further classic amplification of a political expression. The apportionment was controlled by the rural interests speaking for temperance—as a simple summary of key figures shows. For one thing, the apportionment following the 1910 census was the last in which the total membership of the House was increased. It rose 10 percent, from 391 in 1900 to 435 in 1910, and this meant that the slow-growing Bible-belt areas kept congressmen as not a single state lost representation in that decade. Oklahoma jumped from an initial five in 1907 to eight after the 1910 apportionment while the urban states of Illinois, Massachusetts, New Jersey and Texas added just two each. California added just three, Pennsylvania four and New York six. All in all the apportionment of 1910 aided the rural interests in the House, and this situation was destined to prevail for the next twenty years for in 1920 no agreement on apportionment could be reached.

This was the only occasion in the history of the country that Congress did not comply with the Constitution's positive mandate to reapportion representatives among the states "within every subsequent term of ten years" of the initial enumeration of 1790.[28] Thus the tilt of the 1910 apportionment became ever more pronounced in favor of the Bible-belt, temperance-minded, Progressive, rural, small states and against the agnostic and Catholic, sophisticated and cosmopolitan—though often politically conservative—states with growing city populations. The Anti-Saloon League recognized the great advantage in having constitutional representative system in its favor and toward the end of the 1920s its leaders sought desperately to move further against the alien spirit it feared would put an end to national prohibition. It is easy now to see that the Johnson Anti-Immigration Act of 1924 was, in a sense, a by-product of the temperance movement for it would have reduced immigration from the countries of southern and eastern Europe which did not disdain wine and liquor. The act would continue to admit substantial numbers from the British Isles and a goodly number from northern continental Europe.

This mood might have been advanced further if the views of Bishop James J. Cannon of the Anti-Saloon League had carried. He became a staunch advocate of a constitutional amendment introduced in 1927 by Representative Gale H. Stalker of Elmira, New York. The Stalker amendment would have cut representation from areas with immigrant populations, thereby maintaining the disproportionate native influence. Virginius Dabney has summarized the appeal of the idea which Cannon declared to be "the most important legislative proposition before the country."

One of Bishop Cannon's objectives in 1929 and for several years thereafter was to secure the adoption of a constitutional amendment excluding aliens from the population count on which congressional apportionment is based. The bishop had obtained endorsement for this "Stop Alien Representation" amendment from the Virginia anti-Smith Democratic convention of 1929. On this subject he wrote: "I hold the position that the great mass of aliens who are in this country without any naturalization and who are herded very largely in urban centers are a great menace to our national life. I am in sympathy with the law to prevent these unnaturalized aliens from having a quasi-representation in the halls of Congress.[29]

The amendment was approved by the House Judiciary Committee but is now almost lost to memory.

The Personal Liberty Leagues

Ordinarily prohibition laws did not affect "personal use" of alcoholic beverages, a fact stemming from the power of the idea of individual liberty felt by drys as well as wets. That this omission arose from legal and constitutional considerations is simply to acknowledge the feedback from the political ideal of personal liberty. This was a sufficiently broad slogan to be a rallying point for people and sections with sharply different political traditions. The theme is, of course, far older than the nation itself.

"Personal liberty laws" had been the answer given by several northern state legislatures to federal enforcement of the Fugitive Slave Laws of 1793 and 1850.[30] These laws, forbidding the use of state law-enforcement assistance in returning fugitive slaves were enacted in Vermont in 1842, Massachusetts in 1843, Connecticut in 1844, New Hampshire in 1846, Pennsylvania in 1847, and Rhode Island in 1848. After the federal act of 1850 broadened the Fugitive Slave Act of 1793, the states escalated their defiance and, in effect, nullified the national policy. More northern states acted to thwart federal policy. Public buildings could not be used to hold fugitives, no state official could help, and citizens cooperating in catching or holding fugitives were treated as kidnappers and faced severe penalties. During the 1850s the personal liberty laws were strengthened and new laws passed in Michigan, Maine, Wisconsin, Ohio, New York, New Jersey and Illinois. Thus the term personal liberty came from a tradition of defying abusive laws, and doubtless some of the men of the anti-slavery crusade were still around half a century later to condemn prohibition laws as wrong.

Southern states gained a similar view of states rights from jousting with the Abolitionists, fighting the national government in the Civil War and being subjected to the Force Acts during Reconstruction. The liquor interests opposing prohibition struck this chord in the South over and over and often enough gave aid and comfort to the many personal liberty leagues which sprang up across the country to combat the temperance movement. Just as the words "temperance" and "antisaloon" turned out to be code words for "prohibition" in the lexicon of the wets, so were "local self-government" and "personal liberty" euphemisms for drink.

The etymology of these terms is scarcely as interesting as their adoption by a succession of organizations opposed to progressive reforms from the New Freedom to the New Deal. Thus when Henry St. George Tucker spoke for local self-government in his Storrs Lectures at Yale in 1916, he was opposing the woman suffrage amendment. There is evidence, too, that the organizers of personal liberty leagues opposing prohibition were the direct antecedents of the men in 1934 who formed the American Liberty League to combat Franklin D. Roosevelt and the New Deal. An amusing indication of this is contained in records of the Maryland Division of the Association Against the Prohibition Amendment.[31]

Three documents show how Baltimore opponents to prohibition in 1917 plagiarized a Boston workers' appeal to vote "no license" in a 1916 Massachusetts referendum. The first sheet lists the officers of the Trades Union Liberty League of Massachusetts, grouped around a line illustration of the Statue of Liberty. The officers appear to be sons of Ireland to a man: Casey, Cody, Gerraughty, Hines, Kelliher, Nash, Thornton, Ward and Young, representing the Bartenders', Bottlers' and Drivers', Brewery Workers, Coopers', Engineers' and Firemen's local unions in Boston and Lawrence. Two slogans appear at the top of the page: "Home Rule for Our Cities and Towns," and "Liberty and Union Now and Forever."

The next letterhead is of the Personal Liberty League of Maryland with the identical line cut of the Statue of Liberty with a letter in 1917 seeking a legislative candidate's position on prohibition. The plot is the same but with a different cast of characters evidenced by chief officers C.L. Schanberger, M.K. Schellenberger and J.A. Banz. The executive board included a Curry, Cronin and Sullivan but the Irish were outnumbered by German names. There is no clear evidence, but the leaders of the Personal Liberty League of Maryland appear to have included brewery managers and owners, perhaps some allied consumers and, considering the printer's bug on the letterhead, trade unionists as well. By 1920 most of these were members of the Maryland Division of the Association Against the Prohibition Amendment with an even broader citizenship, and the Personal Liberty League of Maryland appears to have discontinued.

The third item links the Baltimore organization to the first one in Boston. It is a printed election appeal from Boston, dated July 15, 1916, from the Trades

Union Liberty League of Massachusetts marked up and adapted to serve as an appeal from the Personal Liberty League of Maryland. There is nothing shocking about it and nothing really to give it ranking in the history of plagiarism and imitation. Yet it shows something about the art of borrowing among political organizations as "Trades Union" is crossed out for "Personal," "Massachusetts" in favor of "Maryland," "No License in your city or town" for "Prohibition in Baltimore and Baltimore County," and so on through the document.

The nature of these liberty leagues, so far as we can discern, shows that wet sentiment was organized and active even before the leagues were outflanked by national constitutional prohibition. The organization in 1919 of the Association Against the Prohibition Amendment makes it clear that the campaign for repeal was under way even before ratification of the Eighteenth Amendment. The Irish in Boston and the Germans in Baltimore provided a solid and growing electoral base of wet sentiment, too, one with an unlikely Catholic and Lutheran alliance to challenge the evangelical moralism of the Anti-Saloon League. Within a decade of national prohibition the power of this urban vote was strongly evident.

Litigation by Wets, 1917-20

The unavailing efforts of wets to stop ratification of the Eighteenth Amendment either through legislative or judicial action did not deter them from litigation after the advent of national constitutional prohibition. Two significant major efforts reached the Supreme Court of the United States, one in 1920, the other in 1931, but they were similar in arguing that judicial review of a constitutional amendment was within the power of the Court. The liquor industry itself, led by the United States Brewers' Association and a number of corporations engaged in the trade, together with some independent-minded wets, mounted a formidable series of cases in 1920. They were answered by the United States government, which was then obliged to defend the law of the land, specifically the Eighteenth Amendment and the Volstead Act, numerous attorneys general of the states, and the Anti-Saloon League. Altogether the litigation, gathered together by the reporter of the Supreme Court under the rubric of the *National Prohibition Cases*, brought a clash of interest groups in litigation which exemplifies American constitutional combat in the courts. In commenting on the lawyers participating in these cases, Swisher agreed with Corwin that not for sixty years had "a more notable array of counsel stood up before the Court, while the *amici curiae* filing briefs in the cases comprised half the state attorneys general of the Union."[32]

The United States Brewers' Association, organized in 1862, had a formidable organization which included about 95 percent of the brewers of the country. The traditions, the leaders and the style of the brewing industry in the United

States were so ethnically German that the ups and downs of American nativism affected many things about the trade. Strong anti-German sentiment was evidenced in the Know-Nothing period of the 1850s, during the Franco-Prussian War and, of course, in World War I. The Brewers' Association used German as their official language during its first decade and went bilingual as a concession to the Boston delegation only in 1872.

In a sense a law—the Revenue Act of 1862—brought the brewers together on more than a local or regional basis for the first time. The leaders of the movement had already engaged an attorney in New York, John J. Freedman, to "give an opinion on the spirit and letter of the law" taxing beer.[33] The organization at first was small, informal and semi-official without a name or title. At first called the Lager-beer Brewers' Association, it was soon also spoken of as the National Brewers' Association or Brewers' Congress. Incorporated in New York on May 12, 1875 as The United States Brewers' Association, it was only then that its objectives were officially spelled out in a constitution, some of which follow:

The . . . Association is established to secure cooperation among the Brewers of the United States in furthering and protecting the interests, general welfare and prosperity of the brewing trade. More especially to guard their interests, as affected by federal and state legislation; to protect themselves, . . . against an oppressive arbitrary or unjust administration of the Internal Revenue Laws relating to the manufacture and sale of malt-liquors; to refute and repel the unjust aspersions and ill-advised action of the so-called temperance party against the manufacture and use of fermented malt-liquors, and to vindicate the truth, based upon the experience of all civilized nations, that by the popular use of fermented beverages the cause of rational temperance is most surely advanced and best sustained.[34]

Already, by 1875, the Brewers' Association was becoming preoccupied with the "unjust aspersions and ill-advised action of the so-called temperance party." By World War I, the Brewers had a larger, more prosperous, better organized association, but one that was on the defensive on many fronts. In 1913, there were nine committees: Finance, Federal Relations, Advisory, Vigilance, Labor, Publication, Membership, Crop Improvement, and Transportation and Rates.[35] But the topics of discussion and concern in those years were the Webb-Kenyon bill, the prohibition movement, saloon reform, prospective legislation, judicial decisions; with polemics against the eugenists' claim that children of drinking parents were inferior, on the abuse of alcohol, on woman suffrage and Catholics and prohibition. In a word, the United States Brewers' Association was smack in the middle of every social, political and economic controversy touched off by the temperance movement and the advancing momentum toward prohibition.

Factional interests and changes in technical procedures and business methods within the liquor industry must be touched upon briefly to account for the success of the temperance movement by 1920.[36] For one thing, competition between beer and hard liquor for the drinking man's dollar was fierce. By 1870 the brewers were trying to assuage and to ally with the drys by portraying beer as a beverage of moderation, calling whisky the source of alcoholism. Some prohibitionists accepted this while others claimed the former led to the latter.

Unionization of the brewing industry illustrates how everything seemed to be turned to the advantage of dry propaganda. Here was an industry growing in concentration and bigness employing many highly skilled persons. By 1900 there were many craft unions organized, in part along industrial lines. Coopers, maltsters, teamsters, firemen, engineers, glassblowers and, servicing the industry, teamsters, bartenders and waitresses, all of whom had organizations. All of the growing pains known to unionization—strikes, picketing, lockouts, scab labor, jurisdictional fights and the like—were present. Yet the Anti-Saloon League pictured unionization as a benign brewers' program to get out the wet vote. During Senate hearings in 1918 the United States Brewers' Association was accused of deciding in concert "for political reasons that in order to secure or endeavor to secure the help and cooperation of organized labor in political contests it was expedient to unionize the industry."[37]

Another sin by the brewers was their ethnicity and religion. Many of the owners were Bavarian Catholics and, as mentioned, the German language predominated for years. Even the first closed-shop agreement on the West Coast (drawn up in Portland, Oregon, in 1891) was written in both German and English.[38] The workers were also German or, equally unappetizing to the Baptists and Methodist drys, Irish Catholics. Nativist suspicion of these two groups turned into overt hostility at many junctures from the 1840s onward and, as temperance feelings grew among Anglo-Scotch Protestants, the German and Irish Catholics were scorned for their associations with the drinking business, too. Freemasonry can be identified on the dry side during the nineteenth century, as in 1867 the Grand Lodge of Good Templars of Pennsylvania declared they would not vote in elections "for men who countenance the liquor traffic, or degrade their official position by the use of intoxicating liquors."[39] The 1916 Easter uprising in Ireland and the 1917-18 American war against Germany further sobered American opinion of Irish and German brewers in the United States.

This résumé of the predicament of the liquor industry on the eve of national prohibition can be concluded with some weaknesses on the economic side. The industry had been substantially nationalized and concentrated in a few great dynasties by the turn of the century. This was in common with development in other fields which brought with it such corrective efforts as the Sherman Anti-Trust Act of 1890 and the muckraking of the "beer barons." By 1900 the beer field was dominated by national companies, notably Schlitz, Pabst, Anheuser-Busch and Liebmann. Concentration had grown among the manufacturers of hard liquor as well, with brands like Old Crow and Old Grand-Dad while companies like Park and Tilford, and Fleischmann became prominent nationally.

Taxation of beer and ardent spirits became a two-edged sword in the struggle over prohibition. The Revenue Act of 1862 had brought in tremendous funds from the industry to pay for the Civil War, and the brewers, in particular, boasted of the taxes they paid. In time the drys turned this point around by insisting that the financial contribution the brewers made to the government was immoral, gave the brewers political power and was, in effect, a sales tax robbing the poor, which wreaked more costly social havoc than any profit the government could gain from taxation. A prohibitionist put it this way: "The American citizen sanctions and sustains the public drink trade, not that it is good, but because he thinks it pays him well."[40]

Finally, there was a fatal economic tie between brewers and the corner saloon, upon which Frances Willard, Carry Nation, Wayne Wheeler, Bishop Cannon and their followers concentrated their fire. The brewers owned and franchised saloons in the same way that oil companies later established filling stations and national chains in quick food service developed. In other words, the breweries competed for favorable corner locations and set up a townsman in business with the requirement that he sell only company brands. In a small area one might find a Ruppert saloon, a Schlitz saloon and one run by a whisky company or a local brewery. The large national breweries owned chains of hotels, too, as they still do in Britain and Germany. But supervision was inadequate and the competition so severe that there were beer wars just as, all too rarely, in recent times an automobile driver is blessed to find a gasoline war raging among service stations.

By 1912 the United States Brewers' Association was giving serious attention at its national meetings to the saloon problem, but it could not gain the initiative against the attacks of the Anti-Saloon League of America. In a propaganda war, the brewers could not "muster the same backing of mass appeal, of religious fanaticism, of moral indignation" as the Anti-Saloon League.[41] Rectitude they had in abundance, but they could not contrive to convey their own values to a neutral—let alone to a dry—public. They did not have the political base or the style to follow the exhortation of Boston's mayor, John F. (Honey-Fitz) Fitzgerald, who welcomed the 1912 Brewers' convention by saying they should "take care that the law-makers of state and nation are correctly informed as to your business, . . . to [show] that the business is properly conducted."[42]

The movement toward national prohibition under the Constitution advanced swiftly during the World War I era. In December 1913, 4,000 men and women of the Anti-Saloon League climaxed their annual convention in Washington with a march to the Capitol carrying a resolution for the submission of a prohibition amendment. The Webb-Kenyon Act was in force but efforts to broaden national statutory support for state prohibition continued at the same time the prohibition amendment was pushed. In December 1914 the House vote for the measure was 197 for and 190 against, a majority, but short of the required two-thirds vote. The Anti-Saloon League concentrated on the election of 1914 and then the election of 1916 to vote in a dry Congress. Meanwhile, the number of states with prohibition laws was increasing. In the 1916 national elections, a predominately dry Congress was elected and was seated, under the lame-duck system then in effect, in December 1917. "Many hours before the country knew whether Hughes or Wilson had triumphed," said Wayne Wheeler, "the dry workers throughout the nation were celebrating our victory. We knew that the prohibition amendment would be submitted to the states by the Congress just elected."[43]

America's entry into World War I on April 6, 1917, intensified the cry for prohibition. A food-control bill urged early in the war by President Wilson was promptly shaped into a wartime prohibition statute to reduce the food materials allowed for the manufacture of alcoholic beverages. A series of measures was enacted by Congress, each delegating considerable discretionary powers to the president and executive departments and agencies for enforcement. The drys thus successfully wrapped the flag around prohibition. Wartime prohibition measures were nearly as severe and complete in limiting brewing and distilling as the Eighteenth Amendment and the Volstead Act were intended to be. And sure enough, in December 1917 the national prohibition amendment was officially proposed by Congress and state ratification was under way and completed by January 1919, well before wartime prohibition was scheduled to end.

The sweeping political victory of the drys during and immediately after World War I was attacked, perhaps unrealistically, in a series of lawsuits mounted by the distillers and brewers. Owing to the length of a typical appellate litigation these cases did not reach the Supreme Court until nation-wide prohibition was a political fact, an event hardly lost on the justices. A series of key cases resulting in the formal, constitutional legitimization of national prohibition was settled in the Supreme Court in the 1919-20 term. The first three cases dealt with wartime prohibition while a group of seven test cases, decided June 1, 1920, validated the Eighteenth Amendment and the Volstead Act passed under its powers. The alignment of counsel for the wets and drys in these cases is of interest.

Having dealt directly against prohibition in Congress and the courts for a full decade before the Volstead Act, Robert Crain was in touch with the ablest lawyers in the country sharing the views of his chief client, the United States Brewers' Association. Crain was obviously in touch with developments on the litigation front although he appeared in few cases as counsel. There was a tradition in the association, one emulated by numerous other national organizations, that litigation might as well start naturally at the local level, that using attorneys conversant with local conditions—including the inclinations of judges and juries in their regions—and with support from local clients was the best way to start test cases. Thus, in the major test of wartime prohibition one case began in Kentucky, the other in New York; and though both tests were lost in the Supreme Court, there was some hope kindled that the justices would not always uphold prohibition as valid under the Constitution.[44] Counsel for the brewers included two men of vast experience at the Supreme Court bar, Levy Mayer of Chicago and William Marshall Bullitt of Louisville in the Kentucky case, with Walter C. Noyes the prime lawyer in the New York case supported by Levi Cook and George R. Beneman as *amici curiae.* The United States was represented by Solicitor General Alex C. King and Assistant Attorney General William L. Frierson in each case, supported in the first by an *amici* brief filed on behalf of the Anti-Saloon League of America by Wayne B. Wheeler and R.C. Minton. The results were most unsatisfactory to the wets and cheering to the drys as Mr. Justice Brandeis for a unanimous Court upheld the statute as a valid exercise of congressional power.

Victory in the Standard Brewery case,[45] in which the Court held against Treasury Department and Internal Revenue Service constructions of the wartime prohibition statute, was the sole achievement for the brewers' lawyers before America went bone-dry. Administrative rulings that taxed all beer containing ½ of 1 percent of alcohol were held beyond the intent of Congress. The Baltimore lawyers William L. Marbury and William Rawls conducted one of these cases and they brought the other case to William D. Guthrie in New York. Marbury and Guthrie were then at the peak of their careers at the bar and knew each other.

Guthrie won lasting fame in 1895 when, in association with Joseph H. Choate, he helped persuade the Supreme Court that Congress lacked constitutional power to tax incomes. Guthrie was then a member of the famous Cravath firm but early in the twentieth century formed his own firm in New York—Guthrie, Bangs, and Van Swerington. Hard-driving and correct, Guthrie was a man who seemed to a colleague untouched by human warmth and love, but his reputation as the "compleat reactionary," urged by Twiss, is unjust.[46] For instance, he argued and won the *Silverthorne* case, holding against an unreasonable search and seizure, a keystone of the modern law of privacy. Guthrie also successfully defended the principle of rent-control laws immediately after World War I even though this was the kind of victory that drove away wealthy business clients. We shall see later in these pages that Guthrie was also prominent as counsel to the archbishop of New York in helping to win what must be regarded as a liberal victory in the *Pierce* case for the right of parochial and private schools to exist. These activities show Guthrie to have been complex; they do not contradict the fact that generally speaking his clients were rich and his interests were markedly conservative.

Bernard Hershkopf, fresh from Columbia Law School upon joining the Guthrie firm in 1909, recently recalled that with their reputation and the victory in the *Standard Brewery* case they were "called to the attention of the Brewers, whose president was a man named Feigenspan." Christian Feigenspan, who owned a brewery in Newark and later controlled breweries in Albany and New Haven was the kind of man Hershkopf calls "a dead game sport—if you licked him, he got up and said, 'When do we fight again?' "[47]

Coordinating the litigation against the Eighteenth Amendment was Robert

Crain, general counsel of the United States Brewers' Association. The national prohibition cases gave Feigenspan and Crain plenty to fight for and they turned again to the ablest lawyers they could find. There is no reason to doubt that they were not pleased with Guthrie but, while the sequence is unclear, they also tried and failed to enlist William L. Marbury and Charles Evans Hughes as part of their team. Both men declined but Hughes turned up on the other side, presenting a dry *amici curiae* brief for half of the attorneys general of the states. The Guthrie firm took charge, with Hershkopf doing much of the research and brief-writing and feeding ammunition to allied lawyers in the various cases. Crain was listed on the briefs with Guthrie and Hershkopf and, again, former Senator Elihu Root joined in making an argument before the Supreme Court along with Guthrie.

The seven prohibition cases of 1920, like the five school segregation cases of the 1950s, represented the complex nature of the American system of government, its jurisprudence and the character of the enterprise under attack. In terms of Supreme Court practice, two were original cases brought on behalf of the states of Rhode Island and New Jersey while the other five were appellate cases drawn in federal district courts to enjoin United States district attorneys or collectors of Internal Revenue from enforcing the Volstead Act. These five cases came from states where the industry was particularly important to the local economy: Kentucky, Missouri and Wisconsin in the West; Massachusetts and New Jersey in the East. The distillers' chief case, prepared by Mayer and Bullitt, was *Kentucky Distilleries & Warehouse Company v. Gregory.* The United States Brewers' Association employed Guthrie, Hershkopf, Root and Crain to prepare its main case, *Christian Feigenspan, Inc. v. Bodine.* The Brewers were also behind the original case for Rhode Island where they aided the attorney general of the state, Herbert A. Rice, and also filed a brief *amici curiae.* Altogether the names of fifty-four lawyers appeared on one or more of the briefs submitted to the United States Supreme Court in the seven cases. Other notables on the wet side included Alexander Lincoln, then an assistant attorney general of Massachusetts and later active in major constitutional matters for the far right organization called the Sentinels of the Republic. Another was Congressman Patrick Henry Kelley, who submitted the case of *Dempsey v. Boynton* alone. A Michigan member of the House of Representatives from 1913 to 1923, Kelley, in arguing before the Court while a sitting member of Congress, was following a relatively common practice. Yet, his position of attacking the constitutionality both of an amendment and a duly-enacted federal statute in the Supreme Court raises disturbing questions about congressmen who continue the professional practice of law, receive fees for work outside of clear congressional functions and who carry their losing battles against legislation outside the halls of Congress to the third branch of government. This is a subject we will have occasion to canvass more fully toward the end of this book.

Defense of the Eighteenth Amendment fell to the executive branch of the federal government, ironically the only branch omitted from participation in the adoption of constitutional amendments. For a group of such momentous cases the attorney general himself often appears in court but even though the original cases named him as a party, A. Mitchell Palmer was personally a wet, was preoccupied with matters of internal security and, in the spring of 1920, was actively seeking the Democratic nomination for president. The government's defense, in all seven cases, were presented by Alex C. King, solicitor general of the United States, with William L. Frierson, assistant attorney general. They were aided informally in many ways by Wayne Wheeler. The Anti-Saloon League also filed *amici curiae* briefs in four of the seven cases. These cases, with citations, are listed in table 4-1 and detail all of the briefs filed on behalf of the Anti-Saloon League of America in Supreme Court cases.

In Hershkopf's recollections, Feigenspan was the key man in promoting the attack on the amendment and the Volstead Act. In his words, "Feigenspan was it. He had the guts that would sustain that kind of a hopeless case. And it was hopeless, and they knew it was, and I told them so, and Guthrie said he feared so! Nevertheless, you had to make the fight." Hershkopf had many meetings with the leading brewers, especially Liebmann and Feigenspan and he admired each of them. "Feigenspan was a trump," he recalled, the kind of a client one gets once in a lifetime. "Leibmann had much more brains than Feigenspan: Leibmann was a thinking dog, Feigenspan was a fighting dog."

The argument that Guthrie and Hershkopf stressed was that the federal government did not have the kind of national police power in any form that would sustain sumptuary legislation of the scope contemplated by the Eighteenth Amendment and enacted in the Volstead Act. A summary of all the arguments made against the amendment, the act and their application would fill pages.

The Supreme Court, on June 1, 1920, unanimously upheld the validity of the prohibition amendment and the National Prohibition or Volstead Act. There were a medley of separate concurring opinions by Chief Justice White and by McReynolds, Clarke and McKenna, but there was majority support for a set of eleven points set forth by Mr. Justice Van Devanter. His conclusions were simply that the amendment had been validly adopted, that the subject was within the purview of the amending power and that the Volstead Act was an appropriate piece of legislation under this new constitutional provision. Henceforth there was to be much litigation over the enforcement of prohibition but only modest and eccentric cases over the constitutionality of the Eighteenth Amendment and the Volstead Act and other congressional legislation under the amendment. Thus, in 1921 there was a further amendment case along the lines of *Hawke v. Smith*,[48] questioning the validity of ratification, specifically the provision that the states must act within seven years of proposal by Congress. Ten years later, a group of New York lawyers went to elaborate lengths to again adumbrate the substantive claims made in the *National Prohibition Cases* that the Eighteenth Amendment was beyond the legitimate powers of government, especially considering the attitudes of the framers of the Constitution.[49]

Table 4-1
Anti-Saloon League of America Briefs in Supreme Court Cases

The Anti-Saloon League of America, organized in 1893, with branches developed in every state went to court often as an ally of local and state government and the United States government. Wayne Bidwell Wheeler, 1869-1927, was the most notable lawyer of the Anti-Saloon League, serving as general counsel, 1915-1927, after two decades of leadership in the Ohio League. "In Ohio he appeared as attorney in the courts in the successful prosecution of more than 2000 cases of prohibition violations." James A. White, 1872-1949, was one of many dry lawyers whose activities were confined to the local and state level. A leader of the Ohio Anti-Saloon League, White said he "prosecuted about 250 saloon cases yearly for 10 years up to 1919," but he was active later, too. Upon adoption of the Eighteenth Amendment, Wheeler and his associate and successor, Edward B. Dunford, 1890-1966, regularly prodded, advised and aided the United States government in its defense of the amendment and enforcement of national prohibition. Other Anti-Saloon League lawyers on briefs were ordinarily associated with a case from the time of its initiation at the trial level.

This is an original listing of Anti-Saloon League cases drawn from reports of the Legal Department of the league and checking the *United States Reports*. Litigation by the League was barely noticed in Peter Odegard's *Pressure Politics*, published in 1927.

Webb-Kenyon Act Cases

(1) *Clark Distilling Co. v. Western Maryland Railway Co. and State of West Virginia. Clark Distilling Co. v. American Express Co. and State of West Virginia*. 242 U.S. 311 (1917). The Court upheld the Webb-Kenyon Act (1913) allowing states to forbid shipment into the state of intoxicating liquors, despite the interstate nature of the commerce. "Mr. Wayne B. Wheeler argued the cause and filed a brief for the state of West Virginia." "Mr. Fred O. Blue also argued the cause and filed a brief for the state of West Virginia." Wheeler argued for the right to exclude liquor from commerce as a deleterious product and against the right of the individual to use it given its harmful nature. The Attorney Generals of the following states filed a brief as *amici curiae*; Alabama, Arizona, Georgia, Idaho, Iowa, Kansas, Mississippi, North Carolina, North Dakota, Oklahoma, Oregon, South Carolina, Tennessee, Virginia, Washington. *The dry position won*.

(2) *Missouri Pacific Railway Co. v. Kansas*, 248 U.S. 276 (1919). The Webb-Kenyon Act of 1913 had been adopted when Congress overrode a veto by President Taft. Wet interests in the Missouri Pacific Railway case claimed the statute was improperly enacted, saying the veto clause intended that two-thirds of the *total* membership of each House must vote to override. The Court ruled the Constitution meant two-thirds of the number present and voting within a *quorum*. James P. Coleman and S.M. Brewster, Attorney General of Kansas, submitted the main brief for the State. "Mr. Wayne B. Wheeler also submitted the cause." *The dry position won*.

State Police Power

(3) *Crane v. Campbell*, 245 U.S. 304 (1917). The Court upheld an Idaho prohibition statute making the mere possession of whiskey for personal use a criminal offense. This was held to be within the police power of the state, not abridging personal liberties protected by the Fourteenth Amendment. Mr. T.A. Waters, Attorney General of Idaho, argued the cause and filed a brief for Campbell, a sheriff, who was defendant in error. "Mr. Wayne B. Wheeler also filed a brief for defendant in error." *The dry position won*.

Table 4-1 (cont.)

War-time Prohibition Act Cases

(4) *Hamilton vs. Kentucky Distilleries & Warehouse Co.*, 251 U.S. 146 (1919). The Court upheld the War-time Prohibition Act of Nov. 21, 1918 as a constitutional exercise of the war power on the theory that even though the armistice had come the power of Congress to judge emergency needs continued. The Department of Justice represented Hamilton, a collector of Internal Revenue in Western Kentucky. "Messrs. Wayne B. Wheeler and R.C. Minton filed a brief as amici curiae." *The dry position won.*

(5) *United States v. Standard Brewery, Inc.*, 251 U.S. 264 (1920). A case construing the War-time Prohibition. *Held*, administrative rulings by Treasury and Internal Revenue that beer containing 1/2 of 1 percent of alcohol is taxable and intoxicating went beyond the statute as enacted by Congress. In this and a related case, the brewers were represented by William L. Marbury, Elihu Root and William D. Guthrie. Assistant Attorney General William L. Frierson and Solicitor General Alex C. King acted for the United States. Their position was supported by the Anti-Saloon League. "Messrs. Wayne B. Wheeler and Andrew Wilson filed a brief as amici curiae." *The dry position lost.*

Cases on the Constitutionality of the Eighteenth Amendment

(6) *Hawke v. Smith*, no. 1, 253 U.S. 221. Decided June 1, 1920. The Court ruled that a State (Ohio) could not submit a proposed constitutional amendment to a statewide referendum; only the state legislatures could decide the issue of ratification. Mr. Frank J. Hanly with whom Mr. George S. Hawke, Mr. Arthur Hellen, Mr. Charles B. Smith, Mr. James Bingham and Mr. Remster A. Bingham were on the brief for plaintiff in error. "Mr. Wayne B. Wheeler and Mr. James A. White, by leave of the court, filed a brief as amici curiae." *The dry position won.*

(7) *Hawke v. Smith*, no. 2, 253 U.S. 232. Decided June 1, 1920. The Court ruled identically with the first Hawke case. This case concerned the Nineteenth Amendment (Woman Suffrage) rather than the Eighteenth. Most of the lawyers were in both cases. "Messrs. Wayne B. Wheeler and James A. White also filed a brief as amici curiae." Ohio's ratification of the Woman Suffrage Amendment was sustained and, consequently, *the dry position won.*

(8) The United States Brewers Association and the distillers initiated numerous challenges of the validity of the Eighteenth Amendment. Seven of these cases were joined together for argument in March 1920 and decided together on June 1, 1920. The Court concluded, in an announcement by Mr. Justice Van Devanter, that the Eighteenth Amendment and the Volstead Act of October 28, 1919 were valid exercises of national power by Congress. The first listed case was *Rhode Island v. Palmer* but the Official Reporter grouped all seven together in the *United States Reports* under the title "National Prohibition Cases," 253 U.S. 350 (1920). The Justice Department spoke for the amendment and the Volstead Act in all seven cases. *Amici curiae* briefs for this position were filed in two cases for twenty-three states by their attorneys general and Charles Evans Hughes. The Anti-Saloon League filed *amici* briefs in four of the cases. In *Dempsey v. Boynton*, 253 U.S. 350 (1920), "Messrs. Wayne B. Wheeler, George S. Hobart, G. Rowland Monroe, R.C. Minton, and James A. White filed a brief as amici curiae." *The dry position won.*

(9) In *Kentucky Distilleries & Warehouse Co. v. Gregory*, 253 U.S. 350 (1920), Messrs. Wheeler, Hobart, Monroe, Minton and White also filed a brief as *amici curiae*. As above, *the dry position won.*

(10) In *Christian Feigenspan, Inc. v. Bodine*, 253 U.S. 350 (1920), Messrs. Wheeler, Hobart, Monroe, White, B.L. Hicks, E.L. McIntyre, and Walter H. Bender filed a brief as *amici curiae*. As above, *the dry position won.*

Table 4-1 (cont.)

(11) In *Sawyer v. Manitowoc Products Co.*, 253 U.S. 350 (1920), for the Anti-Saloon League of America, Messrs. Wheeler, Hobart, White, Hicks, McIntyre and Bender filed a brief as amici curiae. As above, the *dry position won.*

Cases Under National Prohibition

(12) *United States v. Yuginovitch*, 256 U.S. 350 (1921). The Court upheld a lower court (and the defendant) ruling that certain liquor revenue laws were repealed by the Eighteenth Amendment and thus the U.S. could not indict on their basis. Wayne B. Wheeler filed as *amicus curiae*, supporting the United States position. He argued that these statutes could coexist with the Eighteenth Amendment and that legislation could not be repealed by implication. *The dry position lost.*

(13) *Corneli v. Moore*, 257 U.S. 491 (1922). Decided Jan. 30, 1922, with three related cases. The Court ruled (in favor of the U.S. position) that liquor legally purchased and stored in government warehouses prior to the Volstead Act could not be removed for use as alcoholic beverage. Wayne B. Wheeler filed a brief as *amici curiae*, supporting the U.S. position. He argued that courts had and should realize that the objective was to prohibit the drinking of alcohol. *The dry position won.*

(14) *Cunard Steamship Co. v. Mellon*, 262 U.S. 100 (1923). Decided with eleven related cases, April 30, 1923. In one of these cases *United American Lines, Inc. v. Stuart* "Messrs. Andrew Wilson and Wayne B. Wheeler filed a brief as *amici curiae.*" The Court ruled that intoxicating liquors may be served on ships on the high seas, but not in territorial waters. The Anti-Saloon League brief argued that the Eighteenth Amendment was to be liberally construed. Only when exemptions are mentioned specifically should they be assumed. *With respect to territorial waters the dry position won; on the high seas the dry position lost.*

(15) *Brambini v. United States*, 267 U.S. 584 (1925). *Per curiam* decision dismissing appeal for conviction of violating prohibition in California. Case below, 192 Cal. 19, 218 Pac, 569. "Messrs. U.S. Webb, Edward B. Dunford, Arthur W. Hill and Wayne Wheeler for defendants in error." *The dry position won.*

(16) *Lambert v. Yellowley*, 272 U.S. 581 (1926). Decided Nov. 29, 1926. The Court upheld Congress' power under the Eighteenth Amendment to limit the amount of liquor prescribed by a doctor for "medicinal purposes." "Messrs. Wayne B. Wheeler and Edward B. Dunford filed a brief as amici curiae." Wheeler argued that Congress as well as the states possessed police powers in this area. He stated that the need to regulate consumption of alcohol as a beverage required regulation as a non-beverage, and that if the power to prohibit exists, then the power to regulate also exists. *The dry position won.*

(17) *Tumey v. Ohio*, 273 U.S. 510 (1927). Decided March 7, 1927. The Court ruled that the States could not allow municipalities to set up special courts to try prohibition violations in such a way as to deny defendants due process (by allowing mayors or town officials who would gain monetarily from convictions to serve as judges). "Messrs. Wayne B. Wheeler and Edward B. Dunford argued the cause and with Messrs. D.W. Murphy and Charles M. Earhart filed a brief for defendants in error. Messrs. Wayne B. Wheeler, Edward B. Dunford, D.W. Murphy, Charles M. Earhart and the Attorney General of Ohio filed an additional brief for the defendant in error." Wheeler argued that a mayor should not be disqualified as a judge, and that the courts cannot declare a policy different than that of the legislatures. *The dry position lost.*

Counsel for state organizations in the Anti-Saloon League of America began cases in 1933 questioning ratification of the Twenty-first Amendment. None of these cases reached the United States Supreme Court.

The *Sprague* case at the end of the decade created something of a sensation as the federal district judge in New Jersey, William Clark, agreed with the claims of the wets and on December 16, 1930, actually held the Eighteenth Amendment *invalid.*[50]

This was because ratification had been by state legislatures rather than by constitutional conventions. Judge Clark's twenty-page opinion was not highly regarded at the time, even by lawyers for the wets in the case,[51] but it was symptomatic of at least two things of significance for constitutional change. One was the fact that the case for Sprague was prepared by prominent conservatives, Julius Henry Cohen and Selden Bacon, and drew four *amici* briefs from colleagues like Jeremiah M. Evarts of Windsor, Vermont, a leading Republican, Henry W. Jessup, Austen G. Fox (who had led the fight in 1916 against the confirmation of Louis D. Brandeis to be associate justice of the Court), Eliot Tuckerman and William H. Crichton-Clarke. There was a huge wing of the American bar that not only detested prohibition but also regarded the Eighteenth Amendment as unconstitutional straight through the entire period of the great experiment.

Another symptom was the emphasis placed by Judge Clark on ratification by convention. Conservatives were then frustrated by the rural state legislatures so maladroitly (literally) apportioned and districted, and he was expressing a view that came to be a part of the argument for repeal. It was strategic and tactical to insist that repeal be done through ratification by state convention, as we shall see, but the intellectual and ideological groundwork had to be laid, too. The opinion of Judge Clark did just that. In reversing Judge Clark, Mr. Justice Roberts, in an opinion for a unanimous Supreme Court, reiterated what was said in the *National Prohibition Cases*, that the "Amendment by lawful proposal and ratification has become part of the Constitution." It is said that Professor Edward S. Corwin of Princeton University had coached Clark and that Roberts knew of this when he wrote snidely that the district court had erred "not as a result of analysis of Article 5 and Amendment 10, but by resorting to 'political science,' the 'political thought' of the times, and a 'scientific approach to the problem of government." Neither the opinion of Judge Clark nor the reversing opinion of Mr. Justice Roberts are otherwise notable.

This failure to resist prohibition through litigation showed an appropriate judicial restraint in coping with the temperance movement, a powerful movement to be sure but not one without limits. The question of its staying power would be settled in the political arena as most lawyers of the day well knew. Bernard Hershkopf was one lawyer who so believed at the time the *National Prohibition Cases* were argued in Washington in March 1920. The lawyers, wet and dry, all had lunch together in the Senate restaurant while they were waiting for their cases. Wayne B. Wheeler and other Anti-Saloon League lawyers as well as Root, Guthrie, Crain and, perhaps, Christian Feigenspan were there on an occasion when Hershkopf made his prediction. "In fact I told Wheeler and some others—and the brewers—that that would be the first amendment to be repealed; and it was." They asked him why, and Hershkopf said, "We adopted this out of altruism: those who drink and can restrain themselves would like to help those who can't. But that will wash off very quickly. Nothing dies so fast as self-imposed virtue. And as this is an incursion on a man's personal liberty—you don't understand the American people if you think they're going to let it be."[52]

Lawyers for Repeal

The adoption of national prohibition of alcoholic beverages as national policy in 1919 has been fully documented and explained; repeal of that policy in 1933 has not. This chapter is an effort to explain how public sentiment for repeal was expanded and harnessed to win the Twenty-first Amendment to the Constitution.[1] Who were the movers, what were the conditions and how were the tactics developed for repeal of national prohibition?

Scholars have identified the sponsors of prohibition as provincial socially, Protestant in religion and Progressive in politics. Peter Odegard in *Pressure Politics* described the Anti-Saloon League as one of the most powerful of these sponsors. The league, as an organization of Protestant churches was most responsible for the adoption of the Eighteenth Amendment. James Timberlake has identified the leading drys as Progressives who also believed other social welfare reform could be achieved by national legislation.[2] Finally, the sociologist Joseph Gusfield saw the politics of temperance as a clash of life styles.[3] According to Gusfield, the policy of national prohibition was the assertion by country people of their style and their values as central national values. Prohibition expressed their quest for political and social dominance.

Odegard's book has long held an honored place in American social science but it was published five years before repeal and had no sequel even though the adoption of the Twenty-first Amendment repealing prohibition clearly equals that of the adoption of the Eighteenth. Yet, Gusfield asserts that "the repeal of the Eighteenth Amendment has never been subject to a scholarly analysis."[4]

The specific tactics employed in the proposal and ratification of the Twenty-first Amendment should be of special interest, for there have been few amendments and fewer political studies. If an advocacy organization like the Anti-Saloon League was essential to prohibition, an opponent organization would have seemed necessary for repeal. And if the views of Odegard and Gusfield are correct, the persons working for repeal would be cosmopolitan, urban and urbane. But no sure conclusions can be drawn about the politics of repeal and the attributes of wets without a detailed, step-by-step narrative of the adoption of the Twenty-first Amendment.

A number of conditions seem to explain the absence of studies of repeal. The adoption of the Twenty-first Amendment in 1933 was vastly overshadowed by economic depression and the advent of the New Deal under President Franklin D. Roosevelt, and most scholars interested in the period of the 1930s were attracted to more stirring topics than repeal. It also offered no particular connection with other events and other problems and did not appear to raise compelling questions for scholarly inquiry. Or perhaps adoption of the Twenty-first Amendment raised too many questions in diverse fields. A kind of jurisdictional problem is raised by a topic like repeal for political science, as it has been organized as a discipline. It is difficult to achieve a comprehensive view of an event when only one aspect interests students of constitutional law, political parties, interest groups, public opinion, legislation and federalism. Exploiting an issue like repeal may be a virtue of approaching politics by looking for constitutional change. Finally, the availability of information about the proposal and ratification of the Twenty-first Amendment has been slender. Official records existed but they were far from enough. Unless the movers, their organization and their tactics could be identified and studied closely none of the questions about repeal could be adequately answered. But vital records have recently become available; the inquiry can proceed.

The Organized Bar on Record

Lawyers played resourceful and creative roles in 1933 in the adoption of the Twenty-first Amendment to the United States Constitution. Their participation began some five years earlier when some convivial New York attorneys resolved to work for restoration of national sanity, which they saw threatened by prohibition. Almost as a joke, one of these men recounted, a dozen or so New York City friends set out in 1927 to persuade the organized bar to formally condemn the Eighteenth Amendment. They incorporated as the Voluntary Committee of Lawyers and moved step by step with the times to win repeal.

The Voluntary Lawyers tapped bar association opinion through referenda, by dramatizing favorable highlights of the Wickersham Report. (The Wickersham Commission was appointed by President Herbert Hoover to investigate the methods of enforcement of the Eighteenth Amendment.) They also petitioned and visited "party leaders" in 1932 to attack prohibition in Democratic and Republican platforms, and by initiating model state laws for ratifying conventions and pressing them on confused but receptive governors and legislatures. The committee did not have prescience. Yet, in a time of bleakness, nurtured with hope and hard work, the VCL was to effect legal change when conditions were ripe. This chapter discusses the sequence of events in which the VCL acted to move toward adoption of the Twenty-first Amendment; after its success the committee promptly disbanded.

In 1968, forty years after the Voluntary Committee of Lawyers was formed, two survivors of the board of managers discussed the spirit of their group. George Roberts recalled that the founders all had convivial drinking in common. They were embarrassed to see the bar associations shrink from taking a public stance against national prohibition. Earlier, the founders had opposed the

Eighteenth Amendment during its adoption between 1918 and 1920. But the atmosphere of the 1920s was so intimidating, Roberts explained, that he lacked nerve at first to discuss prohibition in his own Baptist church in Brooklyn.

These records and recollections, along with the public history of the prohibition era, afford a detailed reconstruction of the role played by lawyers behind the Twenty-first Amendment. Lawyers are indispensable to constitutional litigation, but their part in the adoption of amendments has been less appreciated. After considering the process of amendment, attention will be directed to a series of questions about the Volunteer Committee of Lawyers, the social character of its membership, its organization, effective leaders, financial resources, and the related political proclivities of its members.

The VCL did not begin as a formal organization. Financial records show May 5, 1928, as the first pay day for Mrs. Helena P. Rhudy, who was to serve as executive director of the Voluntary Committee of Lawyers.[5] So there was a fair amount of activity prior to filing in December 1928 for a certificate of incorporation under the Membership Corporations Law of the state of New York. The nine directors of the new corporation, called managers, were Joseph H. Choate, Jr., Henry W. DeForest, George W. Martin, Arthur H. Masten, Samuel H. Ordway, Kenneth M. Spence, Harrison Tweed, George Westervelt and Clifton P. Williamson. These men were typically graduates of Ivy League colleges (chiefly the Harvard Law School), they were cosmopolitan and then stood—or would soon stand—among the leaders of the New York bar. On January 22, 1929, their organization became officially recognized under New York law as the Voluntary Committee of Lawyers, Incorporated, with its stated purpose being "to preserve the spirit of the Constitution of the United States. Its immediate purpose is to bring about the repeal of the so-called Volstead Act and the Eighteenth Amendment."[6]

The managers were clear about the corporation's objective but did not, in 1929, propose to work directly for a repeal amendment. Rather, the committee set as its first task the persuasion of other lawyers throughout the country to join in advocating repeal. It sought to persuade them by stressing their professional importance and public influence. The bar was qualified to judge; it was under a traditional and imperative duty to speak. The charter of the Voluntary Committee of Lawyers, Inc., gave this responsibility as its only specific plan of action:

In furtherance of its purposes, the corporation will . . . encourage the adoption of resolutions by Associations of members of the Bar throughout the country holding that the Eighteenth Amendment and the Volstead Act violate the basic principles of our law and government and encroach upon the powers properly reserved to the States and the people; that the attempt to enforce them has been productive of such evils and abuses as are necessarily incident to a violation of those principles, including disrespect for law, obstruction of the due administration of justice, corruption of public officials, abuse of legal process, resort by the

Government to improper and illegal acts in the procurement of evidence, and infringement of such constitutional guaranties as immunity from double jeopardy and illegal search and seizure.[7]

The original prospectus of the Voluntary Committee acknowledged the unusual character of the work at hand.[8] "We do not render professional services or give legal advice to those accused of violating the law." Under the circumstances created by the adoption of national prohibition by the Eighteenth Amendment, these lawyers were to work outside the familiar terrain of constitutional litigation in the courts and ordinary lawmaking in Congress. "The enactment of a federal statute which lacks support by the public conscience is a serious matter, but the adoption of a constitutional amendment which lacks such support is fraught with even more serious consequences." And, the prospectus noted, "a statute may be repealed by a majority, but a constitutional amendment can be repealed only with the concurrence of three-fourths of the states." It added that its aims were "purely educational" and disavowed any intention "to take part in political activities or political controversies."

While eschewing politics, the committee shrewdly worked from strength as they sought protest declarations against prohibition first from the sure-bets. Resolutions were quickly adopted by the Law Association of Philadelphia, the Association of the Bar of the City of New York, and the Bar Association of Boston. The committee's literature emphasized that all endorsements of repeal expressed "the most representative opinion of the Bar." Of course, the organized bar in the United States has never enlisted as members all of the lawyers in active practice. By beginning with the most cosmopolitan cities the committee was working with a select group whose economic position and social outlook harmonized with the quest for repeal. That there was dissent at all seems remarkable today and yet the resolutions in these cities carried by just three to one.

The committee invited memberships from all parts of the country, by circulating an appeal to the 20,000 members of the American Bar Association. Soon hundreds of lawyers sent in letters and, often, small contributions to join the list. Mrs. Rhudy traveled through the South and Southwest and then into western Pennsylvania and upstate New York to find key supporters. The campaign for support was vigorously pressed. In 1929 and 1930 the bar associations in the cities of San Francisco, St. Louis, Detroit and Washington, D.C., and of the states of New Jersey, and Virginia went on record for repeal.[9]

Opponents claimed that the bar was an inappropriate forum for debating prohibition and voting on the merits of repeal. In seeking an endorsement from the largest prize of all, the American Bar Association, the Voluntary Committee moved deliberately. At the October 1929 ABA meeting in Memphis the committee was officially represented by several members of the board of managers and by Mrs. Rhudy. At "a very informal sort of headquarters" the committee worked "to lay a foundation for formal action at the meeting in Chicago in October, 1930."[10]

There appear to have been fringe benefits to the Voluntary Committee campaign for bar association pledges for repeal. There was a narrow, business attraction noticed by the cold eye of a social scientist forty years later when reading an observation like this, from Philadelphia: "Younger members of the Bar are glad to take on this work for the sake of the contacts it gives them."[11] There were the larger social contacts maintained by the board of managers even after resolutions were won.

Constitutional amendment procedures prescribed in Article Five, as written in 1787, are exclusively federal, as Congress proposes and 75 percent of the states must ratify. Constitutional change by amendment must be organized in the states as well as in Washington. The development of an extensive membership list, totalling 3,626 on October 27, 1932, and some experience in the practicalities of winning votes for repeal, gave a valuable country-wide footing to the VCL program. Still, it made sense for ultimate purposes that 80 percent of the membership eventually was outside New York.

In New York City the leaders were continuously busy building enthusiasm and understanding. There were frequent luncheon meetings featuring talks by the foremost advocates of repeal. On February 15, 1930, for instance, Austen G. Fox presided over a luncheon attended by 400 lawyers and physicians at the Plaza Hotel. The headquarters at 25 Cedar Street was maintained throughout the existence of the committee. An impressive series of reports and statements criticizing prohibition flowed from this office. The main thrust in its first few years was to develop a feeling among lawyers that imposing prohibition by constitutional amendment was terribly, viciously wrong. By pressing this view and by organizing lawyers who felt it most deeply, the committee was laying a superb basis for the day of ratification which, until 1932, was hardly mentioned since they would not have believed the time was right.

The Wickersham Commission Report

Criticism of the national prohibition on drinking had been made by lawyers well before adoption of the Eighteenth Amendment,[12] but it was after 1928 that the critics gained a broader audience and a growing respectability. The Voluntary Committee of Lawyers contributed to turning around national presumptions about prohibition. The occasion for this change was the appointment by President Hoover in 1929 and the report in 1931 of the National Commission on Law Observance and Enforcement, known popularly as the Wickersham Commission.

At his inaugural on March 4, 1929 President Hoover promised "to appoint a national commission for a searching investigation of the whole structure of our Federal system of jurisprudence, to include the method of enforcement of the Eighteenth Amendment and the causes of abuse under it."[13] Hoover asserted the right of citizens who did not like a law "openly to work for its repeal" but he supported prohibition and intended his new commission to work within its framework. "Its purpose," he declared, "will be to make such recommendations for reorganization of the administration of federal laws and court procedure as may be found desirable."

President Hoover's appointment of George W. Wickersham as chairman of the commission seemed almost foreordained. A generous-minded conservative and leader of the New York bar, and attorney general under President Taft, he was endorsed by drys as well as wets and neutrals. Spontaneous advice came to Hoover from all sides and the press reported his consultations with Chief Justice Taft, Justice Stone, Charles Evans Hughes (later to be named Chief Justice by Hoover), Attorney General Mitchell, and Senator Borah. Wickersham was well known to Hoover. George Roberts of the Voluntary Committee of Lawyers has recalled that he and Secretary of State Henry L. Stimson urged Wickersham's appointment on the president during a White House visit in the spring of 1929.

The ten other Wickersham Commission members were former Secretary of War Newton D. Baker of Cleveland, a prominent Democrat; federal judges William S. Kenyon, Paul J. McCormick and William I. Grubb, former Chief Justice Kenneth Mackintosh of the Supreme Court of Washington, Dean Roscoe Pound of Harvard Law School, President Ada L. Comstock of Radcliffe College, Henry W. Anderson of Virginia, Monte M. Lemann of New Orleans, and Frank J. Loesch of Chicago.[14]

Hoover's conception of a broad study beyond problems associated with prohibition was reinforced by the academic community and social-action organizations which persuaded the commission to study a wide range of criminal law problems.[15] The commission staff in Washington, whose secretary was Max Lowenthal, prepared studies on prosecutions, the deportation laws, the federal courts, penal institutions, probation and parole. The report on criminal statistics led directly to establishment of the *Uniform Crime Reports* of the Federal Bureau of Investigation. Some of the fourteen reports of the Wickersham Commission were monographs prepared by noted experts like Miriam Van Waters on the child offender, Edith Abbott on crime and the foreign born, David H. Monroe and Earle W. Garrett on the police, Zechariah Chafee, Jr., and Walter H. Pollak on lawlessness and law enforcement. Each report was published and publicized individually—there was even scandal in the suppression by the commission of the Tom Mooney case,[16] a *cause célèbre* of the era—but little was done by Congress on their account. Overshadowing all was the only pamphlet-size publication, the second of fourteen reports of the Commission, entitled *Report on the Enforcement of the Prohibition Laws of the United States.*[17] The report was made public on January 20, 1931.

Full of facts though it was, the report ended in a welter of confusion through the separate concluding statements of each of the eleven commissioners. Of the eleven, only Monte M. Lemann did not sign the report's conclusions, the first of which read: "The Commission is opposed to repeal of the Eighteenth Amendment."[18] This view was underlined by President Hoover in submitting the report to Congress as he wrote: "The Commission, by a large majority, does not favor the repeal of the Eighteenth Amendment as a method of cure for the inherent abuses of the liquor traffic."[19] He added: "I am in accord with this view." The report might have complicated unduly the campaign for repeal had not the VCL board of managers published a persuasive interpretation of its meaning, arguing that it "merits the thorough examination which seems to have been denied it by the President, the public, and a portion of the press; and that when so examined, it will be found to constitute the strongest argument that has yet been made for the repeal of the Eighteenth Amendment."[20]

The board of managers addressed their statement to the members of the Voluntary Committee of Lawyers, urging them still "to advocate, and to work for, immediate unqualified repeal."[21] The board believed "a most effective means to that end is the dissemination among the public of a knowledge of the findings of fact of the Wickersham Commission." This view was also adopted by other wet organizations, particularly the Association Against the Prohibition Amendment (AAPA), which later distributed a similar gloss on the *Report on the Prohibition Laws*.[22]

This skillfully argued VCL critique, made up almost wholly of quotations, drew first from the Wickersham Commission facts on prohibition and then exploited the confusion inherent in the eleven statements of the commissioners. It will suffice here to show just what the board of managers concluded from these two aspects of the report. With impressive documentation, they stated:

These findings of fact, concurred in by all the members of the Commission, fully support the conclusions of the Board of Managers of the Voluntary Committee of Lawyers (1) that the Eighteenth Amendment being a police regulation, has no proper place in the Constitution of the United States; (2) that it is unenforceable because it has not the support of law-abiding citizens; (3) that it does not tend to bring about temperance; (4) that it tends to increase crime and corruption; and (5) that it impairs the due administration of justice and causes disrespect for law.[23]

Although ten of the eleven commissioners did support the conclusion that the Eighteenth Amendment should not be repealed, there was wide disagreement over what should be done to carry out dry national policy.

The 1932 Party Platforms

Committed wets organized numerous special-interest committees to widen support for repeal. In addition to the AAPA tapping businessmen since 1920, and the VCL working with the bar since 1928, there were committees of physicians and trade unionists. The American Hotel Association was organized with several committees and the Women's Organization for National Prohibition Reform included a Woman's Hotel Committee. The wets most politically active in working for repeal appear often to have had positive party allegiances. It is really not clear how they divided because, among the leaders of the wets, were a remarkable number of Republicans and Democrats. Indeed, there were special committees for repeal in each of the two great national political parties. The AAPA and VCL worked hand in hand with these committees and with these politicians in seeking national party endorsements of repeal in the 1932 platforms.

The Republican Citizens' Committee Against National Prohibition in February 1932 included on its organization committee these four familiar VCL names, in a list of thirty-one: in New York, Joseph H. Choate, Jr.; in Delaware, Lammot du Pont; in Michigan, Henry B. Joy, president of the Packard Motor Car Company; and in Pennsylvania, Raymond Pitcairn, then temporary chairman of the committee. Pitcairn, a journalist who later attacked the New Deal regularly in his nationally syndicated column, was especially active in trying to convert Republicans to make theirs the party of repeal. His correspondence with Choate reveals him as a showman, ready to get President Hoover's attention with a joke when nothing else seemed to work effectively.

Republican wets during the 1920s were disheartened that Presidents Harding, Coolidge and Hoover each strongly supported prohibition and thereby identified their party as dry. This taxed their party loyalty just as the effort to convert the leadership and rank-and-file Republicans to repeal taxed their ingenuity. One incident in 1932 helps fill in the portrait of cosmopolitan repealers by showing how lively and addicted to fun they were. It was a stunt, a hoax, the brainchild of Pitcairn, who devised a bogus newspaper to shake up the Republican party. Here is part of a contemporary report of the hoax:

A newspaper was published in Utopia yesterday.

Its editors blandly disregarded the cramping limitations of fact and built their paper around an eight-column headline on the first page, which startled the country with the announcement, "Hoover Demands Prohibition Repeal."

Below it is a long story of a hypothetical message to Congress which President Hoover might make. It is told as if he really had on a mythical "February 30" asked Congress to set about abolishing national prohibition.

The rest of the page is devoted to accounts of the nation's reactions to this message, headed by such titles as "Nation's Leaders Hail Hoover Move as Turning Point," "Democrats Fume as Nation Lauds Hoover Message," "Stocks Soar High as Optimism Runs Riot on Exchange," "National Jubilee Planned at Philadelphia," and "Bishop Declares Rule by Churches to be Un-American."

The "Herald-Times" was distributed free on the streets of Philadelphia, New York, Washington, Baltimore, Chicago, St. Louis, Cincinnati, New Orleans, San Francisco and other cities yesterday.

At the very top of the first page of the Herald-Times is the announcement, "All Imaginary—More's the Pity," and a notice that "statements contained herein are imaginary and not to be attributed to their pretended authors."

But a lot of people—especially drys—missed that. A glance at the first page of the paper threw them into consternation. The [Philadelphia] *Record* received a score of calls from persons who took the Herald-Times seriously and wanted confirmation on the glad tidings or the fearful news, according to their sentiments on the prohibition question.[24]

Pitcairn wrote Choate and other Republicans on his committee that "the reception accorded our Herald of Good Times has exceeded our fondest hopes."[25]

On May 31, 1932 the Voluntary Committee of Lawyers sent a resolution, signed by fifty-three leaders of the bar, to President Hoover, an incumbent certain of renomination.[26] A number of Democrats who were possible nominees for president received the same resolution. They were Franklin D. Roosevelt, governor of New York; Albert C. Ritchie, governor of Maryland; John N. Garner, speaker of the House and a Representative from Texas; Alfred E. Smith, Democratic nominee in 1928; John W. Davis, Democratic nominee in 1924; and Newton D. Baker. There is a contrast here not only in numbers but in the fact that Hoover had opposed repeal in his 1928 campaign and had not really changed, while the several Democrats included some famous wets, particularly Ritchie and Smith, and Roosevelt's public position was close to theirs. The resolution was issued to the press and efforts were made to place it in the hands of convention delegates of both parties.

The resolution argued that the parties and candidates must not be equivocal on repeal. All were urged to stand against prohibition, which was as a tyrannical intrusion on the life of citizens. It went on to declare that party allegiance was nothing compared to the crisis all Americans faced. "The question whether the Republican or the Democratic party shall run the government," it declared, "is subordinate to the question whether our traditional form of government is to continue at all." It was this stance, apparently, which permitted these wets, lawyers all, to claim to speak as professionals. As they put it: "This resolution expresses the views of lawyers as lawyers, irrespective of personal party allegiance."

The VCL position was presented to the resolutions committee of the Republic National Convention by Ralph M. Shaw of Chicago. He was joined by Joseph H. Choate, Jr., and by W.W. Montgomery, Jr., of Philadelphia. The Republican plank did not endorse repeal outright but it did favor submission of an amendment to the states and it came down hard on convention rather than legislative ratification: "Such an amendment should be promptly submitted to the states by Congress, to be acted upon by state conventions called for that sole purpose . . . and adequately safeguarded so as to be truly representative."[27] This phrase was an achievement for the committee. President Hoover campaigned on this platform. But in favoring the regulation of liquor by the states Hoover was so cautious that he was clearly "drier" than the Democratic platform and the Democratic candidate Roosevelt.

The Democratic platform called for immediate and unqualified repeal, which pleased the Voluntary Committee as it "exactly embodied the views of our members."[28] The committee added: "We do not believe we are presumptuous in asserting that the inclusion of the phrase that the vote on a repeal amendment be 'truly representative' was due at least in part to the efforts of our representatives." The repeal plank of the Democratic party platform of 1932 read as follows: "We advocate the repeal of the Eighteenth Amendment. To effect such repeal we demand that Congress immediately propose a constitutional amendment to truly representative conventions in the states called to act solely on that subject."[29]

The wet mandate of the 73rd Congress was not destined to be expressed immediately by them. In any event, the president had no formal, official or essential part in the constitutional amendment process. The 73rd Congress was not scheduled to meet for thirteen months, and could not be called into special session until the 72nd Congress passed out of existence on March 3, 1933. In fact it was the lame-duck 72nd Congress that voted by the necessary two-thirds in each house to submit a repeal amendment to the states, an indication that the force of the November 1932 mandate was so powerful that it affected a Congress standing by the wayside.

Thus did the last lame-duck Congress respond positively to public opinion! The 72nd Congress had been elected in November 1930; its first session ran from December 7, 1931 to July 16, 1932. During that session on March 2, 1932, Congress voted to submit the lame-duck amendment to the states. It would end the terms of the president and vice president at noon on the twentieth day of January every fourth year; it would make Congress assemble at least once in each year on January 3rd, unless otherwise provided by law. The proposed amendment was ratified so rapidly by the necessary thirty-six legislatures that it was proclaimed as part of the Constitution on February 6, 1933.[30] The ratification of the Twentieth Amendment on that date ensured that the 72nd Congress which had earlier proposed it would, itself, be the last (and of course the 72nd) lame-duck Congress. Two weeks later, on February 20, this same 72nd Congress officially proposed the repeal amendment to the states.

Congress Submits Repeal

A familiar statement to students of politics is that "proposal is a neutral act allowing the states to decide." Its intent is to persuade those opposed and those on the fence to cast votes to accomplish the initial, formal, though indispensable phase of a larger procedure for action. It is an argument that certainly wins votes. This stance, in a legislative body like Congress, for a member who is neutral personally or is buffeted by constituents of conflicting persuasions, gets him off the hook. The amendment procedure under the United States Constitution is similar to many other governmental decision-making procedures not only in possessing two key steps but also in the wide appreciation of their different political attributes. Perhaps the chief comparisons will cast some light.

Debate over whether clearance at a preliminary stage of decision-making is neutral or discretionary and, therefore, political boils up from time to time in many contexts. In the United States House of Representatives the rules committee clears legislation for floor action. In the Supreme Court of the United States the justices annually select 150 cases from 3,000 for full review on the merits. The certiorari, and other mechanisms by which selection operates have drawn a huge critical literature revealing that while some justices are less overtly policy-minded than others, this stage of selection is absolutely crucial because without it the Court cannot consider effective action on an issue.

With respect to amendments to the United States Constitution, step one (the proposal by Congress) is inevitably different from step two (ratification by the states). When further distinctions are made, the differences are magnified. Politics is never static for the fundamental reason that time and circumstance change daily for a growing population. In our minds dates like 1914, 1919 and 1933 evoke remarkably different images of life in the United States. If so, Congress reflected these images in one way; the state legislatures in another. The prohibition amendment was proposed to the legislatures in 1918; the repeal amendment to state conventions in 1933. And so both time and the institution relied upon were different. In 1919, moral values and patriotism combined with skilled and vigorous organizational efforts to win a national concensus for prohibition. In 1933, urban centers that were subject to depression, gang wars and widespread flouting of the law combined with equally skilled organizations to vote in repeal.

Speaking for the Association Against the Prohibition Amendment, its president, Henry H. Curran argued in January 1932 that there existed "a strong, widespread sentiment and demand from the people" for repeal. He gave several indications: (1) The six states petitioning Congress for repeal, including New York and Illinois, held 23.4 percent of the country's population and paid 55.5 percent of the federal income tax payments for 1930; (2) Nine states with even more impressive totals of population and tax payments refused to either ratify the Eighteenth Amendment or to adopt enforcement laws or else rescinded those laws afterward; (3) In recent elections, wet candidates like Dwight Morrow in New Jersey and Senator Bulkley in Ohio had won over drys and prohibitionists; (4) The American Bar Association called for repeal by a vote of 13,779 to 6,340, and the American Legion asked for submission by 1,008 to 394; (5) "We know, for instance, that the Literary Digest's poll in 1922 showed 20.6 percent for repeal, but that poll in 1930 showed 40.4 percent for repeal, 29.1 percent for modification, and only 30.5 percent for enforcement." (6) The coming national party convention platform votes were anticipated by this example of changing sentiment: "We know that, although not a single state platform contained a repeal plank in 1928, there was a call for repeal in twenty-one different state platforms in 1930." (7) And, finally, there was the Wickersham report on prohibition, which "contains overwhelming evidence that conditions exist which have created a public demand for prompt relief."

These arguments were made to congressmen well over a year prior to their action in submitting the question of repeal to the states for action in state conventions. The final votes came on February 16 and 20, 1933, but the softening-up process for congressmen of uncertain and uneasy persuasions on this subject had been going on for years.

The champion of the conservative wets was James Montgomery Beck, in 1932 a Republican congressman from Philadelphia at the end of a career in which he had served as solicitor general of the United States and ambassador to Great Britain.[31] William D. Guthrie in New York, Ralph Shaw in Chicago, Alexander Lincoln in Boston and Thomas Cadwalader in Baltimore may also be called conservative wets. In a poll in the winter of 1932-33, a sampling of the VCL registered over 50 percent support for this viewpoint.

By contrast with the states-oriented conservative wets was a group whose most articulate spokesmen were A. Mitchell Palmer and Joseph H. Choate, Jr. They were pragmatists in the sense that they conducted the campaign for repeal as a single issue without worrying unduly over implications for other issues, past or prospective. They were virtuosos in politics and, although pragmatists, they could move with ease on the level of constitutional abstraction: "I entirely agree with you that he [Beck] begs the whole question by assuming beforehand the false premise that the Constitution is a compact between the states."[32] As lawyers, they were skilled at wielding precedents: "He [Beck] seems to utterly ignore the long line of cases which have settled beyond doubt that it is a compact made by and for the people in their sovereign capacity."[33] They were confident, highly intelligent men ready to learn from the learned as their correspondence with Professor Edward S. Corwin of Princeton suggests. Corwin told them that he thought "Congress has full discretion" in the matter of calling or not calling state conventions.[34] Corwin urged that if Congress was to stipulate details on state conventions that it enact a statute so providing separate from the resolution submitting an amendment to such conventions. Above all, Palmer, Choate and other pragmatist wets worked tirelessly to establish ratification procedures which would, in the end, repeal prohibition. In planning for this goal they were not sentimental conservatives but prudent, practical men.

During December 1932 Palmer and Choate exchanged letters nearly every day and each was in correspondence with hundreds of other lawyers throughout the country. Of these, Palmer told Choate, "none has been so helpful as yours."[35] Their aim was to draft a measure for congressional action which would bring about convention machinery to capture and legitimize wet sentiment in the country. They so feared the legislatures as warped institutions under dry control that they gambled to offend by thinking up the strictest possible sanctions to ensure creation of "representative" and wet conventions. They knew they could not be too strict, and they worked to moderate their own hard line, in order to develop a plan that stood a chance to succeed. Palmer finally put together a bill for congressional consideration in response to which Choate wrote: "On first reading your draft struck me as too radical to have any chance of acceptance. Study of it has changed this view, and I rather think it represents the best, if not the only, practical scheme."[36] Gradually the Palmer plan emerged under which Congress, to the fullest extent thought acceptable, would prescribe and control the ratification process.

A pragmatist wet like A. Mitchell Palmer saw the conventions only one way—as nondeliberative, rubber stamps. Under his bill, wets would ensure, through a congressional requirement, that state conventions would be organized efficiently to vote repeal, and repeal alone. "It seems to me that the principle we must work on," Palmer wrote in December 1932, "is that we should have what amounts to a popular referendum in the states going through the forms of constitutional requirement. Thus, we would elect the delegates to the convention in such a manner that the people would know when the votes were counted, how many states would ratify and the conventions would simply register the will of the people."[37] In spelling out how this would work, Palmer returned again and again to the analogy of the electoral college, which he knew thoroughly from his years in Congress, from his finessing role behind Wilson in 1912 and his own quest for the Democratic presidential nomination in 1920. As an old pro, Palmer's phrasing of the analogy is of interest. He called his plan "in strict accord" with electing a president:

The framers of the Constitution contemplated that the electoral college should be a deliberative Convention but the drift of public sentiment in America away from a representative democracy has by long continued usage, changed the system entirely. And today we have a popular referendum in the election of the President and Vice-President but adhering to the constitutional form.[38]

And so ratification conventions would be mere form, referendums in fact. Palmer did not regard a legally binding pledge necessary:

No matter how these delegates are elected, there would be no method of compelling them to carry out the will of the people as expressed at the election. Neither is there any such method with regard to presidential electors, but God help the electoral college in any state which should repudiate the vote of the general election.

The concept of the conventions as nondeliberative bodies was understood. Members of the Voluntary Committee of Lawyers and the members of the executive committee knew why. Henry Alan Johnston concurred in Palmer's view in reaction to reading an early draft of his plan. He congratulated Palmer for having

hit upon a scheme which with very slight amendments, if any, should be acceptable to the people of the several states, without arousing the antagonisms of those who still belong to the "Old School."

The point might be raised that conventions, thus formed, will not be, in reality, deliberative bodies; but from a practical standpoint they will be more truly representative of the will of the people of the several states, than if they were deliberative; and I can see no more force in that objection than if they were made against the electoral college.[39]

Choate thought deliberative conventions were "probably contemplated" by the framers of the Constitution, adding

but the situation does not demand deliberative bodies since the conventions have no power except that of giving a yes or no answer to the question whether the repealing amendment should be ratified. Moreover, the Supreme Court would hardly upset ratification because the practical rather than the theoretical requirements of the situation had been met. Your type of convention would certainly do the job for which conventions were wanted—the ascertainment of the will of the people in the several states.[40]

A much-argued problem among the pragmatist wets was the extent to which Congress would actually control the elections for delegates to the state ratifying conventions. Palmer started out at the extreme position of total control. Choate, Johnston and others complained that this would frighten away congressional support, especially from southerners. Palmer relented but only after the issue had been thoroughly aired, in the press as well as in committee correspondence.

Choate's idea, broached in identical letters to John W. Davis and James M. Beck at the end of November 1932, was to have Congress set the date but to allow the states to conduct elections of convention delegates. As protection against truancy by any state, Choate provided automatically for a congressionally called election. Congress would pay for these conventions as an added lure.[41] It was just at this point that Palmer's views appeared in published form for wide distribution. Choate asked Palmer for a dozen copies for the Voluntary Committee of Lawyers, saying he had read the brief "with interest and admiration."[42] But he made no bones over being troubled by Palmer's view that Congress should govern every aspect of ratifying conventions in the states:

I do not believe we can swing the opinion of the bar to general acceptance of your view to do any good. If we cannot, the repealing amendment will probably be submitted for ratification by conventions to be called and regulated by the legislatures. In that event, every word of your argument will be used by the drys afterward in an attempt to show that the ratification was unconstitutional in that the state legislatures had no power in the premises.[43]

Choate sent Palmer his November 30 letter to Beck to suggest a way out of the dilemma.

The members of the executive committee of the VCL all believed Palmer's plan went too far. Johnston thought the plan was wrong legally and wrong politically and, furthermore, felt that public sentiment was so against prohibition that nothing too clever was needed. He wrote: "It is my personal belief that if you could check up on thirty-six or more legislatures who will probably ratify straight repeal, we will get the job done much quicker through that process than through conventions."[44] Johnston worried that Palmer's brief "would probably do a great deal of harm to the cause of repeal."[45] And after all executive committee members had read the Palmer brief and conferred, Choate again advocated his compromise, that "would leave every state which wished to do so, free to constitute its own convention."[46]

Choate's argument, supported by the executive committee, won over both Shouse, president of the AAPA, and A. Mitchell Palmer.

By Christmas 1932 there was a stalemate between the schools of thought represented by Beck, who wanted to leave all details to the state legislatures and Palmer, who insisted Congress must set the conditions of convention ratification. The Beck and Palmer views, printed in separate pamphlets, were distributed widely. At this point Choate and the executive committee ordered a hundred copies of both men's statements to send to a part of the membership of the Voluntary Committee "to get a cross section of the opinion of the bar on the subject which the committee could afterward publish."[47] This was done and there the matter rested as 1933 dawned.

Existing records and memories do not permit pinpointing the date when wets in the states resolved to take initiative in planning ahead for conventions to ratify a repeal amendment should one be submitted by Congress. Two Baltimore lawyers, Arthur Machen and William Marbury, who were prominent members of the committee and who had long before urged convention ratification of all federal amendments, appear to have been first in formulating such a plan on the ground that convention ratification of an amendment had a superior legitimacy to legislative ratification. Early in 1933 their bill was ready for introduction in the general assembly of Maryland providing an election law under the subtitle "Conventions to Pass on Proposed Amendments to the Constitution of the United States." Johnston told Palmer that "the provisions of this bill are similar in many respects to the bill which you have drafted for congressional action on the same subject."[48] Machen had elaborated his views in a *Harvard Law Review* article in 1910; Marbury followed the same theme in the same journal in 1918. Together they had questioned the lawfulness of the Fifteenth Amendment against racial exclusion and opposed the prohibition, woman suffrage and child-labor amendments. They lived, thought, spoke and acted on their principles of lessening federal authority; they did so daily, regularly, without letup, without a possibility of reconsideration, through their long careers as lawyers in Baltimore. Machen and Marbury had been thinking about the subject of state ratification conventions for so long that it seems entirely likely that the Maryland convention bill, drafted by Machen, was the first in this newest chapter in the struggle for repeal.

The 1932 platform formula for "representative conventions" with the happy November mandate convinced repealers that the popular vote was there to be harnessed if at-large elections were arranged. Machen drafted one of the early bills for Maryland and sent it to Choate at the request of Jouett Shouse. "[T]he only thing in which I am interested," Machen wrote, "is the underlying idea of making the members of the convention the same sort of figureheads that presidential electors have become, and of submitting the question of repeal or continuance of the Eighteenth Amendment to a statewide popular vote."[49] Yet Machen's bill followed Maryland's "firm tradition" that constitutional conventions contain members from each county of the state. Choate said "it would be unsatisfactory for the first act to be passed, which would be certain to be widely copied, to call for election by districts." Of course he realized "in safely Wet states a convention elected by districts would be much easier to get and would be perfectly safe."[50] Machen was able to set Choate at ease as he explained his plan more completely. The delegates, it seemed, would be residents of the different counties but this provision, according to Machen, would be deprived "of all efficacy by binding the delegates to vote in accordance with the result of the statewide referendum . . ."[51]

Reflecting on Machen's proposed convention bill for Maryland, Johnston saw a need for an enabling clause in any congressional submission resolution. "It has occurred to me," he wrote Palmer, "that if several other states should enact similar legislation to that which is proposed by Mr. Machen and Mr. Marbury for the state of Maryland, it would be advisable to have incorporated in any proposed congressional bill a provision which would permit those states which have appropriate legislation to follow the provisions of their own code."[52]

In the end, that is in mid-February 1933, Congress voted by the necessary two-thirds of each house to submit a repeal amendment to the states. The numerous provisions for controlling the establishment of ratifying conventions in the states were not acceptable to enough members of Congress to be included. The proposed amendment had the overriding virtue of simplicity; the corollary of simplicity was virtually limitless discretion to the states. The text of the amendment, as proposed February 20, 1933, and as ratified December 5, 1933, as the Twenty-first Amendment to the Constitution of the United States stated:

Section 1. The eighteenth article of amendment to the Constitution of the United States is hereby repealed.

Section 2. The transportation or importation into any State, Territory or possession of the United States for delivery or use therein of intoxicating liquors, in violation of the laws thereof, is hereby prohibited.

Section 3. This article shall be inoperative unless it shall have been ratified as an amendment to the Constitution by conventions in the several States, as provided in the Constitution, within seven years from the date of the submission hereof to the States by the Congress.[53]

By this time the Voluntary Committee of Lawyers, having anticipated the vacuum, were well prepared to guide the states in forming ratifying conventions.

The Model Ratifying Convention

The standstill of the Voluntary Committee over the Beck and Palmer formulas and the uncertainty of congressional action continued through January 1933. Then from Michigan and Wisconsin came suggestions that the committee formulate a model law to take advantage of the state legislation timetable. Most legislatures were in session but the time for filing new bills and the period afterward for available action was limited. The correspondents suggested that where legislatures were in session steps be taken to enact a general law providing for ratifying conventions ready to be organized if Congress proposed a special amendment.

The first of these cogent suggestions was volunteered to the committee by Albert K. Stebbins of Milwaukee. In Wisconsin, he pointed out, there were no statutory provisions of any kind relative to a state-ratifying convention. He assumed, correctly, that this was true in practically all of the states. He suggested a law with a mandatory convention call, election and meeting at specified times after submission of a constitutional amendment. "With such legislation upon the books," wrote Stebbins, "it would be impossible to delay action in the event that any amendment is submitted to the state for ratification" by convention.[54] But thirty-six states would need to ratify and there should be uniformity. Stebbins was sanguine if united action were begun: "I think I could secure such legislation in Wisconsin without very much difficulty, but it would be of slight value to do so in this state unless similar action was taken in other states."

This galvanized the executive committee. They agreed with Stebbins's "admirable" suggestion and promised to urge into action VCL members whose state legislatures were in session. In communicating with Stebbins for the committee, Choate warned against district elections along the lines of the typical legislature. "This will be perfectly safe in a state certain to be wet, but would be exceedingly dangerous in some of the states which still have dry legislatures." Choate suggested therefore that the bill "adopt the analogy of the presidential electors and provide for the election of delegates at large in the same manner as the electors from the state are chosen." As this procedure "adopts a normal state method" it should "not excite much opposition."[55]

The executive committee promptly followed up, "suggesting by telegram to one of its members in each state of which the legislature is now in session (except Wisconsin, New Jersey and Maryland where the job is already being done) that an attempt be made to procure legislation of the kind in question."[56] Stebbins had got them moving again.

What civics books do not tell about private initiative in anticipation of legislative action is nicely told by the Voluntary Committee of Lawyers in early 1933. The telegram of January 30 deserves enshrinement:

Executive Committee of Voluntary Committee of Lawyers believes that repealing amendment should require ratification by conventions stop This will involve delay of years unless legislatures now sitting act promptly stop Each can and should now provide by statute how convention for its state should be constituted, and that it be called and function when Congress proposes an amendment requiring such ratification stop Won't you initiate such enactment in your state stop Letter follows.[57]

Letters the same day spelled out the reasoning behind this request. Again, it took the opportunity to point out, "We think that in order to insure a real expression of public opinion the conventions wherever possible should be elected not by districts but at large."[58]

At this time the committee, working on entirely new ground, was really desperately uncertain about each new move. But Choate in particular kept in motion even while despairing of his effectiveness. The day he telegraphed VCL members in the states for legislative action he also wrote Palmer: "Mr. Shouse has asked me to have our Committee try to draft a model bill. I doubt if we can do this in time to be of any use, but I am going to have a crack at it. I shall welcome any suggestions."[59] Choate telephoned Professor Noel T. Dowling of the Department of Legislative Research in Columbia University for help and, in a day's time, obtained a draft of a bill.[60] As always, Choate's first concern was to develop a model bill calling for election-at-large.[61] He then rushed the draft to a handful of lawyers who had experience with election law seeking reactions before perfecting and printing the model law. Choate wrote: "This paper, though carefully drawn in consultation with Professor Dowling, is still strictly a first draft and will not be sent out by the Voluntary Committee unless it has been approved by several experts in election law, after which, of course, it may present an entirely different appearance."[62] The election experts called upon were John Godfrey Saxe, John T. Dooling, Robert C. Cumming and Abraham S. Gilbert, all lawyers in New York City. They were asked to join together as soon as possible in a conference on the subject and Choate concluded, "It is necessary that whatever is done in this matter be done with the utmost possible speed so I should be greatly obliged if you will telephone me on receipt of this whether you can take it up."[63]

By the end of the first week in February there were many cross requests and exchanges of the bills proposed already in New Jersey, Maryland and Wisconsin. Variants of these were prepared hastily in other states, Wyoming, for example,[64] or the time for filing new bills passed for want of a draft, as in Oregon.[65] The regrets from Oregon sum up the frustration the VCL agent felt with "only one more day left after I received your telegram, in which bills could be introduced."

He added: "If Congress follows what I gather is the opinion of a large number of lawyers and passes the buck to the states, it might be that Oregon will have to suffer a two-years' delay which may be imputable to me, and which I should very keenly regret; but, as indicated, there was nothing which I could do under the circumstances."[66] Within this same week agents in twenty-two states acknowledged the VCL telegram of January 30.

Not all legislatures were rushed. In Florida the regular session would convene in April, so there was plenty of time for careful drafting. The Voluntary Committee representative in Florida wrote that he had copied some of the provisions of the New Jersey and Maryland bills and adopted ideas about the others. He then redrafted his own bill for Florida and sent it to New York for criticism.[67] Uniformity both in the substance of policy and in the procedure of its agencies has been largely missing in the American state government. The Voluntary Committee of Lawyers knew this all too well and for this reason had its own representatives, men who knew the law and the ropes, in each state. After receiving the first news shock of what could or could not be done in the various states, Choate was able to field the local problems quite smoothly.

During this hectic time, the undocumentable word was out that the 72nd Congress, the last of the lame ducks, was going to propose repeal before it went out of business at midnight, March 3, 1933. The proposal for convention ratification in fact cleared the United States Senate on February 16. Its vote heightened urgency for preparatory action in the states all the more. The joint resolution proposing the repeal amendment passed the U.S. House of Representatives on February 20. In that month of February the files of the Voluntary Committee of Lawyers in New York bulged with letters from Jouett Shouse. Shouse, a Kentucky native, former Kansas congressman, and chairman of the Democratic National Committee, 1929-32, between Raskob and Farley, actively opposed national prohibition from the beginning. The AAPA had been formed in 1919. With repeal in sight Shouse was at the height of his powers and was pushing hard. After all these dry years with convention ratification an essential plank in the repeal platform, the actual drafting of a model state law still had to be accomplished the last minute. But the excitement in the states was having an influence on congressmen. Without a letup Shouse pressed Choate for his draft:

I am wondering whether you do not have in such shape as you can give it out a copy of the bill that you and your associates have prepared. As pointed out a few days ago, the time for the introduction of new acts is about to expire or indeed has already expired in a number of legislatures now in session.

Therefore, it would seem highly desirable to get to our friends at the earliest moment possible some form of bill even though it needs to be corrected later on. I am eager to see a copy of the legislation that you propose. Won't you let me have it as soon as you can?[68]

On February 11, just a day after the prodding letter from Shouse came in, Choate finished the model—but with one important change and scattered lesser ones.[69] The big change was in agreeing with critics of election-at-large by preparing an alternative bill combining this plan with election by districts.

The climactic point came on February 24 for Choate and the executive committee of the Voluntary Committee of Lawyers, Inc. In Washington, "the enrolled joint resolution was delivered on February 20, 1933, to the Secretary of State Henry L. Stimson, who on the next day sent certified copies of it to the respective governors of the forty-eight states."[70] The file copy of the letter sent by Choate on the heels of the resolution on February 24 is addressed to each governor. The letter described the draft bill, the alternate draft bill and the memorandum. The letter is of some interest as it displays a stodgy, stilted, formal, respectable front which stresses "careful study," and "all possible expert advice." There is also emphasis on conventions which are "simple," "inexpensive," and "truly representative," but the objective was clear:

The Voluntary Committee of Lawyers (a national organization of lawyers opposed to Prohibition, having some 4,000 members distributed throughout every part of the country) has for months been conducting a careful study of the difficulties attending the ratification of amendments to the Federal Constitution by Conventions. Having reached the conclusion that while Congress has power to constitute such conventions, it could and presumably would, adopt and throw its authority behind Conventions constituted by the State Legislatures, the Committee concluded that each State could and should provide for such Conventions beforehand, so as to be ready, if and when Congress should submit the expected Repeal Amendment, and so that by getting the authority of both Congress and the States behind each Convention, all questions of constitutionality might be eliminated. To aid such Legislatures as might take this view, the Committee prepared . . . a Draft Bill intended to create, in the simplest and least expensive manner, a "truly representative" Convention, to pass upon any Amendment which the Congress might hereafter propose. It also prepared an Alternative Draft Bill for use in States to which the preferred measure might prove unacceptable, and a Memorandum explaining both. These were presented by members of the Committee to members of most of the Legislatures now in session, and bills based on them have been introduced in many States. For your information, we enclose three sets of these papers, which we believe should be of service in considering whatever measure may be pending in your State.

We call your attention particularly to the method of nomination suggested in the Draft Bill, which is the result of exhaustive consideration, and which we believe to be the only method yet suggested which does away with the risk that a division of votes among an unnecessary number of candidates may bring about a minority victory, and at the same time enables the people, without expense, to choose their own official ticket for each side of the controversy.[71]

Within a week of the repeal's proposal the governors had these attractive, clearly printed prescriptions for action. Representatives of the VCL visited many governors to follow through on the model bill. In Ohio, Governor White "seemed receptive, and said it was the first presentation of the fundamental reasons why the delegates should be selected at large. He seemed favorably impressed, and said he would consider it with an 'open mind.' "[72]

Coping with Dry Litigation

A distinct shift in strategy between wet and dry forces took place in 1933. The proposal of a repeal amendment to the states for action by conventions put the drys on the defensive and they responded in many states with a series of actions intended to delay and defeat ratification. From the adoption of the Eighteenth Amendment until then, the wets had been obliged to litigate; now it was the drys' turn to go to court.[73] When they could not stop the inexorable movement toward repeal in a legislature or governor's office, they turned to litigation. No great cases resulted and none ever reached the United States Supreme Court. But wets were threatened by many suits in the states and their alertness contributed to stopping them. Most actions concerned some alleged flaw in the procedures of state election laws and in the special ratifying conventions being called into being. All were, in essence, open and shut cases of drys versus wets.

Advice and activity in litigation concerning ratification of the repeal amendment became an unexpected major function for Choate and the Voluntary Committee of Lawyers beginning in March 1933. Choate was in correspondence with associates of the VCL, the AAPA and other lawyers working for repeal on the subject of litigation in Maine, New York, Alabama, Pennsylvania, Ohio, Missouri and Vermont. Lawyers in Florida and Maryland approached him about initiating test cases on behalf of the repeal forces. Choate's involvement varied with the state and the situation but in all instances he seems to have offered something important in the way of guidance and in some his role was crucial. State lawyers, facing an immediate, local problem tended to exaggerate difficulty; Choate saw the national situation and calmed his allies in the field.

Choate's confidence in winning repeal saw him counseling other lawyers against bringing test cases to clear in advance the validity of its processes. A Jacksonville lawyer urged in late 1932 that upon submission of a repeal amendment and adoption of one state convention law a taxpayer's suit be brought to settle all the constitutional issues.[74] Choate thought ill of the idea. He saw no purpose in inviting endless delay, saying, "The machinery of ratification will be started as soon as your proposed test case could be begun and I rather think that in the ensuing race, ratification would win. It looks to me," he continued, "as though we shall have to rely on the overwhelming probability that if ratification is secured the Supreme Court will bow to the expressed will of the people just as it did in upholding the original amendment."[75]

In April, Edgar Allen Poe, a descendent of the poet and a leading Baltimore lawyer devoted to repeal, told Shouse and Choate that there should be a taxpayer's suit "to determine whether or not Mitchell Palmer's theory of calling conventions is correct."[76] He wanted the question "determined immediately while Congress is in session so that should the Supreme Court support Mr. Palmer's view, the necessary legislation could be put through immediately." Shouse was clear that the AAPA "will be governed by Mr. Choate's advice in the matter."[77] Choate again saw no merit in going to court when the repeal movement was doing so well elsewhere. "It may be that in taking this position," he wrote, "we are gambling with the whole enterprise and refusing to take the safe course. On the whole, however, I cannot help being more afraid of the possibilities of the proposed suit than of letting matters take their course."[78] Poe had written in great detail exactly how and why he believed a suit could and should be brought; Choate very promptly gave him an answer in kind. While he graciously called Poe's plan ingenious and attractive he was certain that the "balance of risk is against it."[79] Choate feared that confusion and delay would result if the drys were given any straw to grasp when repeal was moving so quickly through the ratification stage in many states. This snuffed out all possibility that wets would seek court tests of their own favored procedures for repeal.

One suit by the drys which went but a short distance was begun in the Court of Common Pleas of Dauphin County, Pennsylvania.[80] The case was never heard even in this trial court, but surviving in the Choate Papers is an *amicus curiae* brief of thirty-one pages submitted by William Sheafe Chase.[81] It is a curious, idiosyncratic document bitterly assailing the wet steamroller strategy in the adoption of repeal. Chase represented several dry organizations, including the International Reform Federation, the National WCTU, the National Temperance Society, the National Civic League, the National United Committee for Law Enforcement. The brief aimed at persuading the Supreme Court of the United States "to pronounce the so-called state ratifying convention in Pennsylvania to be null and void—because it is neither representative nor deliberative, but merely a referendum."[82] Otherwise a new method of amendment would be legalized.

The Chase brief *amicus curiae* in the Pennsylvania case bluntly attacked the Voluntary Committee of Lawyers and, in so doing, pointed up and acknowledged their influence and achievement. The brief was dated October 23, 1933, when repeal was all but assured, so that it could be comprehensive in commenting on the committee. Relying on an article of Noel Dowling,[83] Chase stated that the convention law under attack did not originate in Pennsylvania. Indeed, except for Maine, thirty-nine state convention laws adopted in 1933 were essentially alike. He wrote that "the similarity of the 39 laws gives the appearance of being drawn by one brain, working for an employer who is wet and anxious to give every advantage to the liquor traffic."[84] He called this "a striking illustration of how the legislative development of the law may be advanced by private organizations." The brief then moved to a direct assessment of the VCL:

Shortly after Congress proposed the Amendment, draft bills to provide for conventions were submitted for legislative consideration by the Voluntary Committee of Lawyers, chiefly through the efforts of Joseph H. Choate, Jr. These bills had an immediate and substantial effect upon a large part of the legislation which followed.[85]

There was no incisiveness, no hard logic in this *amicus curiae* brief for the dry forces in Pennsylvania, for it simply presented a rather artless, muckraking attack on the activities of wets in working to adopt the repeal amendment. Everything was wrong. The nomination of delegates in most states was by petitions, officials or special committees, rather than by direct primary laws; the election of delegates on an at-large basis, then totaling twenty-two states, wrongly gave the urban vote a superior opportunity over the rural; pledging of delegates in advance combined with wet-dry slates on all ballots but Maine's was wrong. It must be remarked that the political analysis and summary of this brief *amicus curiae* by William Sheafe Chase has a certain persuasiveness but as a basis for legal action, particularly as set forth here, the argument is confused and ineffective. It is a dry tract of the times, and nothing more.

With proposal of a repeal amendment facing them in the states, the dry forces lacked nearly all traces of the morale, purpose and organization that had motivated them in the adoption of prohibition fifteen years before. There seemed to be no national coordination against ratification of repeal, only a series of hit-or-miss efforts by local drys. Even this feeble effort might have worked since rejection or inaction in thirteen states would prevent ratification of the repeal amendment. In fact, ten states did hold to the dry line as South Carolina elected a dry convention, North Carolina voted not to hold a convention and the legislatures of the eight states of Georgia, Kansas, Louisiana, Mississippi, Nebraska, Oklahoma, North Dakota and South Dakota did not take effective action. Montana would not hold its election and convention until mid-1934. This meant that only two other states needed to be kept in the dry column to stop ratification. Of course, the situation in 1933 was so fluid that a calculation like this could not then be made; we can see the lineup only at the end and appreciate the closeness of the result. But both sides were certainly making calculations daily about each other's chances. And if only two states were needed to foreclose early ratification, drys mounted strong court tests in Maine, Alabama, Missouri and Ohio. Choate was in close touch with the members of the Voluntary Committee of Lawyers in these states who were close to the cases.

In Maine, the premier law firm of the state, Verrill, Hale, Booth and Ives, kept Choate informed about its difficulties. In March 1933 Robinson Verrill wrote about his problems: "As Chairman of the Maine Division of the Association Against the Prohibition Amendment, I have been assisting my partner Robert Hale in the adaptation of the form of bill prepared by the Voluntary Committee of Lawyers, Inc. for presentation to the Maine legislature."[88] The VCL or, in Maine, the Weeks bill was introduced and referred to committee in competition with the Murchie bill, designed by drys. Wishing "to forestall an unsatisfactory compromise bill," Verrill asked for alternative suggestions and guidance from Choate for whom he outlined the precise obstacles faced in the Maine legislature. In the key passage he noted:

Several arguments have been advanced against the Weeks Bill, particularly that it is wet and that it is Democratic. Those arguments may be disregarded as there are obvious answers. The principal objections to the bill have been raised by the Republicans who are in the majority in the legislature and who were elected to the legislature on a dry state platform. Their arguments are, first, that conventions are by nature and in law deliberative bodies. Second, that election of pledged delegates destroys the deliberative function, hence resulting in an unconstitutional action, and third, that representation must be based upon districts. The latter is, of course, political and is based upon the theory that the country districts and small towns have supported a dry Republican party in Maine for many years.[87]

Verrill sought answers to the criticisms being advanced against the VCL bill: Must the convention be deliberative? Can delegates be pledged? What about election at-large?

Choate answered Verrill's questions about Maine the same day he received them. In a long detailed letter,[88] he distinguished between conventions whose purpose is to draft a constitution and must be deliberative and those currently assembling to ratify or not to ratify a single proposition for which a yes or no answer could be the only response. Choate also repeated his standard argument for election at-large and nomination slates with generous remarks about Verrill's work and the desirability of compromising if necessary to accomplish ratification in Maine. Choate included up-to-date developments in other states and a reasoned and full argument for the position of the Voluntary Committee of Lawyers. Verrill was most appreciative, and replied, "I feel sure that if the people of the state are given a reasonable opportunity, they will vote to repeal the Eighteenth Amendment."[89] Verrill's associate, Hale, was also optimistic, feeling they might win an even better bill than the VCL model:

. . . We are standing out for an election of delegates at large. I enclose copy of the bill as introduced by Senator Weeks prepared by my associates and myself in this office. The likelihood now appears to be that the legislature will pass a bill for a convention of five delegates chosen at large, nominations on the ratification and anti-ratification tickets to be made by the Governor, President of the Senate, Speaker of the House and Chief Justice. This would suit me better than my own bill. The simpler we can make the convention the better.[90]

Choate was "a little afraid of the plan for a convention of a few delegates only, elected on nominations by the governor."[91] He advised that the convention should be legally capable of deliberating without being rigged. While he certainly believed legislation should be designed to result in ratification, Choate was too wise a lawyer to think formulation of state convention laws could be oversimple and machinelike.

In just two weeks' time Hale's optimism was shattered by the success of dry forces in obtaining a favorable "advisory opinion" from the Supreme Judicial Court of Maine and in moving their own convention bill through the legislature. Maine has long been one of only a half-dozen states permitting, indeed requiring, the highest state court to file opinions on hypothetical questions, without the adversary process at work, when submitted by the governor or the legislature.[92] Hale condemned the bill reported out by committee and expressed his remorse.

If you examine the bill carefully I think you will agree with me that it is one of the very worst bills that has been passed in any state. The reason is this. The principal opponent of our bill in the legislature had the happy thought of invoking the provisions of our state constitution to ask the Justices of the Supreme Judicial Court several questions. . . . [In substance] the opinion is to the effect that the choice of a convention consisting entirely of delegates at large is unconstitutional under the Federal Constitution and that the classification of delegates is not warranted. The opinion also insists upon a deliberative convention so-called. I am surprised at the opinion which seems to me a somewhat extraordinary document. . . .

I can make no more humiliating confession but the fact that we have been completely out-maneuvered by the Christian Civic League which, however, would not have prevailed against us but for the assistance which it received from our Supreme Judicial Court.[93]

When the dry convention bill, providing for the election of delegates to an eighty-member convention, became law, Hale repeated his hurt and his fear to Choate. "I am sorry but I don't think that we can do anything except try to get a decent body of men elected to the convention. Whether the convention votes for ratification or against it, its vote will be without significance or value so far as public opinion goes."[94]

The depression Robert Hale of Maine felt was understandable but inappropriate. Earlier he was overconfident about the legislature's likely action; now he was overly pessimistic over the coming election and convention. Later, as a Republican congressman from Maine's First District, he was rather constantly off-balance in his views about the New Deal, even commiting his discouraged thoughts to print in a national magazine.[95] As it happened in Maine, Democratic Governor Louis J. Brann made a much more sanguine, and correct, assessment of the chance for ratification of repeal. The Committee on Prohibition of the American Hotel Association in New York, responding to a talk with Choate, telephoned Arthur L. Race of the Copley Plaza in Boston about the Maine situation and, in turn, Race "asked some of his friends to get busy."[96] At the same time he wrote Governor Brann, who provided a calm estimate of prospects in Maine:

I have your letter in regard to the Constitutional Convention, and I do not believe there will be any difficulty in getting a very clear decision on the Eighteenth Amendment under the proposed plan. The Court ruled that we could not classify on the ballot the different candidates as either for or against, but I thoroughly believe that no man or woman will be permitted to place on the ballot, or at least receive a considerable number of votes unless they declare their position either one way or the other on this question.

I think the plan is all right, and while I would have liked to have a smaller convention, it perhaps is the best we can do under the circumstances; in any event Maine has a convention, and also has passed the Beer Bill. In all, quite a little hurdle for the Old State of Maine.[97]

Eighty wet delegates were elected on September 11 and the convention unanimously voted ratification on December 6, the day after ratification of the Twenty-first Amendment had been officially certified in Washington.

Wets failed in their litigation during the 1920s to stop or dent the prohibition amendment and Volstead Act. The Supreme Court upheld the procedures followed in adopting that amendment. Now that the tide had turned, the drys were, if anything, even less successful in attacking the procedures for convention ratification of the repeal amendment. Their strong, ingenious bid in Maine, the oldest prohibition state of all, ended in ineffective failure. And what had been true in the cases started by drys in New York, Pennsylvania and Maine was also the result in Alabama, Ohio and Missouri.

Avoiding Extraneous Issues

A group of 4,000 lawyers opposing prohibition certainly had no other policy position in common. One dissent from a solicitation sums up the discordance. A simple pledge card turned up at the VCL office one day with this handwritten sentence: "On account of your contention that Congress can override the ultimate sovereignty of the several states I must decline to support your organization. Thos. F. Cadwalader."[98] He was harking back to the Beck-Palmer dispute now mooted by formal proposal of the repeal amendment. Choate asked him to reconsider with this appeal to practicality: "Knowing that the bar is hopelessly divided between those who think that Congress can constitute the ratifying conventions and those who think that only the states can do so, the Executive Committee has been trying to make the question unimportant by getting the authority of *both* Congress and the state behind each convention."[99] This reply convinced Cadwalader the VCL would do anything "to secure repeal one way or another" and "would gladly see conventions called under an Act of Congress if that would conduce to a quicker result."[100] Their real reason, he told Choate, "is because you think Congress is more likely to provide for delegates at large in the several states, which will thus give to the large urban vote in the northern states complete control of their conventions." Cadwalader's point was rooted in his antediluvian empathy with the powder train of troubles befalling the states "in the sixties." His fears were that a congressional provision for elections to state ratifying conventions might be an entering wedge later permitting the federal government to conduct and police them. Choate tried again to explain, then let the matter rest.[101]

As 1933 wore on the repeal effort was ever more auspicious while the New Deal looked ominous to some lawyers in the Voluntary Committee. John S. Wise, Jr. then urged VCL to send to its members copies of a James M. Beck speech "on the destructive effect of the recovery legislation on the Constitution."[102] It would cost little because Beck would help and the views of lawyers would be requested. Wise believed the replies would "furnish valuable material for the defense of the Constitution and might enable the Committee to render important service in the future."[103] Choate submitted the suggestion by letter to the executive committee and with his own and six other negatives he put an end to the project so far as the VCL was concerned.[104] The reasons harmonized: "I feel also that until the Eighteenth Amendment is out of the Constitution the Voluntary Committee should not extend its efforts in other directions."[105] The Beck speech was called "political and to some extent partisan and rather extreme in many of its statements and its metaphors."[106] The men were sympathetic to Beck but thought the New Deal not too outlandish in such a desperate time. "I do not want to rock the boat when some honest people in Washington are doing their very best to work out a plan which will meet the needs of the situation. The situation is so very extraordinary that our liberties may have to be suspended for a time."[107] There was a consistent feeling that the VCL should stick to its task but always with a sense of willingness to consider other objectives later on.

Straight through the Depression and the first New Deal year of 1933, the Voluntary Committee of Lawyers hewed to its purpose of accomplishing repeal of the Eighteenth Amendment. Against strong political distraction offering fresh excitement, the organization, commanded by the executive committee of the board of managers, took a consistent line. To some members, the Roosevelt administration was an inviting target, and individuals took an occasional shot at it. But as an organization, there was strict, exclusive attention to the repeal of the prohibition amendment.

Choate's Triumph in Repeal

Because the record from which this account of the repeal of the Eighteenth Amendment has been drawn is the file kept by Joseph H. Choate, Jr., there is no question but that his role has been overdrawn. It can hardly be otherwise. But it was not Choate's wish or ambition that his part be celebrated; there are numerous indications of self-effacement. The fact is that Choate's colleagues in the Voluntary Committee of Lawyers and in the larger repeal movement all credited Choate, in 1933 and since, with the glory. The leading news magazine of the day, the *Literary Digest*, gave Choate the chief credit in the lawyers' campaign.[108] This role was again stressed upon Choate's death, at ninety-one, on January 19, 1968.[109] His character and career cast light on the repeal campaign.

Through family, school and profession, Joseph H. Choate, Jr., was a part of a world of trained talent, cosmopolitanism, wealth, experience and political understanding. He was past forty in 1917 when his famous father died. By then he was firmly established as a senior partner in the Wall Street firm of Choate, Byrd, Leon and Garretson, a trustee of the Mutual Life Insurance Company, and the Bank of New York. The elder Choate had won high fame in 1895 by persuading the Supreme Court to hold a federal income tax law unconstitutional.[110] His associate counsel was William D. Guthrie, with whom he opposed New York State ratification of the income tax, or Sixteenth Amendment in 1910.[111] Choate Senior had represented liquor interests in the leading 1888 case of *Mugler v. Kansas.*[112]

In 1899 during his service as ambassador to England, his son interrupted his studies at the Harvard Law School to serve for a time as third secretary of the embassy. A quiet, faded drawing of the two Choates was still on the office wall upon the death of the son in the winter of 1968. By the turn of the century Joseph H. Choate, Sr. was acknowledged to be the leader of the New York bar. His reputation for conservatism was confirmed when the National Consumers' League failed to win his help in defending the Oregon ten-hour law. From Choate, Mrs. Florence Kelley turned to Louis D. Brandeis of Boston,[113] who then helped the league create the first sociological brief named after him.

Joseph H. Choate, Jr. enlarged upon his associations and the family prestige through work for the American chemical industry. During World War I, he conducted the chemical section of the Alien Property Custodians Bureau concerned especially with German patents and German control of chemical factories located in the United States. Head of the Bureau was A. Mitchell Palmer, who had represented Pennsylvania in Congress from 1909 to 1915 and, as a staunch Democrat, had supported Wilson for the nomination in 1912. As Alien Property Custodian, Palmer set out to reduce the domination of Germany over the American chemical and dyestuff industry. In a 1919 report to Congress, Palmer explained that this objective was facilitated by the organization of a new corporation known as the Chemical Foundation, Inc. with the stockholders drawn from the important American chemical manufacturers. Joseph H. Choate, Jr. was named general counsel of this company. Its specific purpose, according to the charter of the Chemical Foundation, was to acquire by purchase German patents and to hold them as trustee for American industry, "for the Americanization of such institutions as may be affected thereby, for the exclusion or elimination of alien interests hostile or detrimental to the said industries and for the advancement of chemical and allied science and industry in the United States."[114] This was a turbulent subject politically and complex legally, and it occupied Choate at least until 1926 when, in the Supreme Court case of *United States v. Chemical Foundation, Inc.*, he finally defeated the attack of "vicious and unscrupulous violence, by every corrupt and pro-German influence, backed by the Department of Justice under the egregious Dougherty."[115] In the 1926 case fellow counsel included John W. Davis and Moorfield Storey.

There is a certain parallel in Choate's service as counsel to the Chemical Foundation, Inc., which was formed to free the American companies from German control, and his devotion to the Voluntary Committee of Lawyers, Inc., formed to free the liquor industry and the consumer from the dry embrace of national prohibition. His work as a dollar-a-year man in the chemical side of the Alien Property Custodian's Bureau of Investigation in 1917 and 1918 preceded affiliation in the private arena; his later service in Washington, as chairman of the Federal Alcohol Administration in 1933-35, followed his efforts for repeal.[116] A man who is counsel to one industry moves rather easily into working for another nearby. Joseph H. Choate, Jr., in his fifties during the life of the Voluntary Lawyers, was a well-known name to those in the overlapping American worlds of business, finance, law and politics. He surely found it easy and natural to work with other leaders of the New York bar, with Pierre S. du Pont, Chairman of the executive committee of the Association Against the Prohibition Amendment, with Congressman James M. Beck of Philadelphia, with Jouett Shouse, John W. Davis and A. Mitchell Palmer.

As repeal looked more and more like a sure thing, Choate and the Voluntary Committee of Lawyers reaped considerable praise.[117] It began as early as April when Irenee du Pont wrote: "At the Executive Committee meeting of the Association Against the Prohibition Amendment there were some very nice things said about you. I think that as one of the members I know you well enough to write you to say that I think you have done a 'hell of a good job' for the repeal of the Eighteenth Amendment."[118] A few days later, Pierre S. du Pont thanked Choate, "for your courage and your generous giving of time." Du Pont believed lawyers were indispensable to the repeal movement, saying: "So much of what is now before us is of legal nature that those of us not trained in law are not very helpful. I take this opportunity to extend my congratulations and thanks for what you have accomplished."[119]

Election of convention delegates in four states on September 7, 1933, sealed repeal. Kentucky would become the thirty-third state when its convention met on November 27 and then the states of Ohio, Pennsylvania and Utah, all meeting on December 5, would achieve thirty-six ratifications and repeal. The executive committee planned its final report for the activities of the Voluntary Committee of Lawyers, Inc., for publication on November 8. This was the time of triumph and Choate was showered with congratulatory messages. Jouett Shouse tele-graphed Choate:

In the hour of repeal victory I want to attest to the invaluable work done by you particularly in connection with legislative matters necessary to the conventions in the states as well as to all legal questions involved in a very difficult situation stop I have said to our executive committee that I feel the cause owes you a great debt and I shall take occasion publicly a little later to voice that feeling and the appreciation of all of us who with you have been working for repeal.[120]

Among many other congratulations to Choate, two offer something special in felicity and emphasis. A New Bedford lawyer wrote simply: "This is to let you know that, as is presumably the case with many thousands of other persons, I think that you and the committee of the Voluntary Committee of Lawyers have done a wonderful piece of work in bringing about repeal."[121] The last letter said: "Your work in connection with the repeal has been pure patriotism."[122]

The Voluntary Committee of Lawyers

This rare organization, which was dissolved upon accomplishing its single purpose of ridding the Constitution of national prohibition, may now be examined closely. Its records and the Choate correspondents have provided a description of the steps taken in winning repeal. Here attention is directed to the internal organization of the committee and then to three aspects of the VCL leadership to ascertain the social background, financial support, and wider political outlook of its members. The results are relevant to the concluding section, where explanation of the success of repeal in 1933 is considered.

The executive committee of the board of managers was critical to VCL success as its members shared a social and political goal and the professional skills to gain it. Possible deviance was overcome by their uniting in style and agreement about their single purpose. Each was sufficiently affluent to work or contribute money at junctures of need. An "angel" contributed office space and a simple but efficient office force kept up to date, planning ahead and publicizing accomplishments. After an awkward beginning, the treasurer's work was taken over by Harrison Tweed who, on the day of ratification, closed the books by contributing a final $6.16 from his own pocket. Joseph H. Choate, Jr. was indispensable. Though untitled, he took the boldest initiative and applied impressive balance and perspective in counseling other lawyers in almost every state upon the most suitable strategy and tactics. Self-effacing though competent and confident, Choate turned to the executive committee on any issue needing clarification. He held the committee in esteem as a resource while the committee was thoroughly satisfied with him.

Like all organizations coping with the American federal system of government, the VCL had its own central-local relations to keep intact. Several factors worked in its favor. Lawyers disliking prohibition knew that both central leadership and decentralized action were required to achieve repeal. New York was the common center of command in such campaigns, and repeal lawyers in the various states were delighted to work with and acknowledge the superior skill of Choate. The executive committee's prominence, dignity and low-keyed approach also earned cooperation in the states.

The neutral quality of its title, Voluntary Committee of Lawyers, helped attract lawyers adverse to party work or to an avowed pressure group like the Association Against the Prohibition Amendment. Its role as a single-issue organization—not for a catch-all of causes—also made the VCL appealing to many lawyers. Its exclusiveness helped, too, for while some of its ardent lawyer members joined or worked in one or more of the other wet organizations, the committee's restriction on membership only to lawyers enhanced its prestige and effectiveness.

It took less than ten months in 1933 from the official steps of congressional proposal to state ratification, due in large part to the rising tide of criticism that had begun some ten years earlier and the work of the Voluntary Committee of Lawyers over the preceding five years. The VCL patience in building its own experience, expertness and reputation is impressive. The programs chosen to put it on the map and to prepare informally for the occasion of formal amendment action were the lawyers' functional equivalent of advertising. As early as 1927 the committee formulated its plan of winning bar association support for repeal. It was resourceful in "interpreting" the Wickersham Commission report to the press and public. It was adroitly nonpartisan in urging Republicans and Democrats in 1932 to give platform endorsement to repeal. All of these well-planned and executed activities contributed to the formal action in 1933. Merely counting the days it took for the official steps to take effect without attention to what made the official steps possible is chronology without history and procedure without politics. Both are false to understanding the ingredients of constitutional change, as the VCL's experience demonstrates.

What did the lawyers' campaign for repeal cost and how was it paid for? Financial records of the Voluntary Committee of Lawyers, kept by the treasurer Harrison Tweed, provide precise answers. Expenditures were nearly $6,000 in 1928; about $12,000 a year in both 1929 and 1930; about $16,000 in 1931; some $12,000 in 1932 and about $9,000 in 1933. Total income and expenditures amounted to $67,000. The main commitment for funds was for the maintenance of an office and its personnel: salaries (for the secretary Mrs. Francis Smith Clarke, and the executive director Mrs. Helena P. Rhudy) claimed 65 percent; printing expenses 25 percent; rent 5 percent; postage 5 percent. Some years there were travel expenses for Mrs. Rhudy. The decision to identify the organization, to incorporate it, to have an office and maintain continuity through regular reports and publications meant a basic budget was necessary, but the work of the lawyers themselves was entirely voluntary. If an estimate were made of the value of the services of lawyers like Choate and other members of the executive committee of the board of managers the VCL's budget would be very high.

Leaders not only gave their time to the purpose of the organization; they also made the heaviest direct financial contributions. Twenty-five percent of the total funds were contributed by a dozen members of the executive committee; nine of them donated more than $1,000 over the five-year period and of these, only three reached $2,000. The largest amount given by anyone was $2,300. The money was received in relatively small amounts during the life of the organization. Altogether more than 500 lawyers contributed; some 125 gave amounts of $100 or more.

The committee counted on contributions of $100 or more to support its work. The Great Depression reinforced this approach as broad appeals for funds were both costly and seemed less fruitful. Mrs. Rhudy in April 1931 summed up plans: "Last year we found that as a result of economic conditions general letters of appeal were scarcely justified. Therefore, this year, it was decided if possible to have the committee budget underwritten by those in a position to contribute $100 or more."[123] The allocation was for seven lawyers to contribute $500 of which only two more were needed; fourteen lawyers to give $250 of which eight were needed; and other contributions of $100 each of which twenty had been received. The next year, in July, when Choate sent a check for $500 he told Tweed this would be his "last large contribution."[124] Everything about the financial record shows the Voluntary Committee of Lawyers to have been entirely voluntary and it was, in this respect, as in others what Tweed has recently called it—"A lawyers enterprise."

Biographical information about the leaders of the VCL enables us to judge the social characteristics of the lawyers who worked for repeal.[125] It negates the conclusions of Timberlake and Gusfield about the social status and political preferences of the advocates of prohibition.[126] Detailed information on fifteen members of the board of managers affords a basis for some generalization.

Of the fifteen, all but one was born in New York City—one was born in Albany, New York. Dates of birth ranged from 1891, making the youngest forty-two in the year of repeal, to 1855, for two who were seventy-eight years of age in 1933. The median age was fifty-six. Twelve of the group had been undergraduates of Ivy League colleges, including four from Harvard and three from Yale, the exceptions having graduated from Williams, Washington University and the University of Kansas. The law school pattern was similar, with all but two receiving the LL.B. from prestigious places. Williamson from the New York Law School and Wood from Kansas were the exceptions. Otherwise the law schools represented were Virginia and Pennsylvania once, Columbia four, and Harvard six. In New York practice, all fifteen were members of the Association of the Bar of the City of New York and appear to have been members of established firms. Club memberships, location of homes, religious affiliations where indicated, contribute to an impression of high status in New York.

These were men devoted to expressing what their associate in the Bar Association of the City of New York, Elihu Root, had called "the public profession of the law." All were trustees of one or more charitable organizations. Ordway was for many years chairman of the executive committee of the Civil Service Reform Association. Tweed was a leading figure in the Legal Aid Society of New York. These were the kinds of nonpartisan interests through which these lawyers expressed their generous instincts of uplift and improvement. Subsequent to the work of the Voluntary Committee of Lawyers, there were other outlets suitable to the times. In the 1940s this was sometimes civil liberties; in later years civil rights.

The Voluntary Committee of Lawyers, Inc. sought repeal of national prohibition, and it was achieved. It was an elite group led by some of New York City's top lawyers and with associates in virtually every state in the country. Its opposition to prohibition arose in large part from personal traits of urban background, Ivy League education, professional and social status. These characteristics contrasted sharply with the advocates of prohibition who tended toward provincial, small city and rural backgrounds. The VCL did not seek to reach the masses; they worked through lawyers who, in turn, used experience and know-how to gain ratification of the Twenty-first Amendment in a sufficient number of states. Expenses were borne by the lawyers themselves with several hundred contributing. There is no evidence that liquor interests supported the VCL in any way although it is quite plausible that some of the lawyers enjoyed or would later obtain clients in the industry. The facts as they stand appear to support a social interpretation of the VCL more than an economic interpretation. The committee formed upon an impulse to overcome a constitutional amendment which offended the members' sense of a sane society. Their view of the legal order grew as much from this sense as from professional training or outlook. Their political world, in the age of Hoover, was one of *laissez faire* and of state responsibility, which national prohibition, enforced from Washington, violated. All in all, the Voluntary Committee of Lawyers, Inc., contributed enormously to the campaign to repeal the Eighteenth Amendment.

An Assessment of Repeal

A key parliamentary tactic in the movement to repeal the prohibition amendment was "convention ratification." This tactic was not chosen by a cabal but rather was a form of constitutional change which at once satisfied several needs. One was to question and expose the method of legislative ratification as undemocratic and illegitimate. During the first third of the century, Progressives had repeatedly condemned state legislatures as unrepresentative and irresponsible; against this estimate, their ratification of the Eighteenth Amendment could be pictured as somehow improper. The legislatures were depicted as dominated by narrow, rural types grafting their prejudices against the city on the hallowed Constitution. Another need was to make a positive argument that state convention ratification was superior because there could be a special election on a single subject to produce delegates and then there could be miniature Philadelphias around the country deliberating on constitutional change; this attractive image concealed an essential political need for advocates of repeal. In practice the purpose of the repealers was to organize the state-ratifying conventions to give their cause the best possible political expression, de-emphasizing or even eliminating the revered concept of deliberation in favor of delegate elections on an at-large basis, between competing slates pledged for or against repeal. Pledged as they were the delegates were thereby stripped of discretion in the same manner as presidential electors had come to be by more than a century of political practice.

The attack on state legislatures had been launched by Populists and Progressives who had for years urged the popular election of United States senators as an alternative to legislative selection. This reform, which became law by the adoption of the Seventeenth Amendment to the Constitution in 1913, was only one of many efforts during the Progressive era to remedy what were considered undemocratic aspects of the legislatures. Ironically, the alleged organizational and procedural deficiencies of state legislatures came next to be criticized by conservatives. The criticism arose over the substantive programs of Progressives who turned to reform by means of constitutional amendments when ordinary acts of Congress, such as child labor, were invalidated by the Supreme Court. Conservatives like Joseph Choate, Sr. and William D. Guthrie objected to the income tax amendment, which became the Sixteenth Amendment in 1913. Elihu Root, as United States senator from New York, opposed adoption of the Seventeenth Amendment, ratified in 1913, to do with the election of senators.

Conservative opposition, including Senator James Wadsworth, Everett P. Wheeler of New York, William Marbury of Baltimore and Representative Henry St. George Tucker of Virginia believed Congress and the state legislatures were exceeding their authority in bringing national woman suffrage into the Constitution through the Nineteenth Amendment. These men, and many others, also were convinced that prohibition of alcoholic beverages was an inappropriate subject matter for the Constitution. Most objected to the child labor amendment proposed to the legislatures by Congress in 1924. Southern politicians and friends of the South, chiefly Democrats, also continued during all these years to question the legitimacy of the Thirteenth, Fourteenth and Fifteenth Amendments, adopted at the conclusion of the Civil War. Each of these different issues had contributed to an intellectual posture regarding constitutional amendments sponsored by the forces of reform. Objecting to the substance of these amendments, critics also found fault with the procedures which made their adoption possible.

Thus convention ratification became a shibboleth for conservative critics of Progressive amendments and a formula for action in repealing the prohibition amendment in particular. It was not an idea spawned by a particular person or organization; rather convention ratification was a watchword for a broad and divisive movement. Certainly convention ratification of the Twenty-first Amendment was not invented in Congress, in 1933, as a means of speeding ratification. Rather the convention method of ratification represented a long-term reaction, an ideological stand against legislative ratification and a practical political method for actually achieving repeal.

We have seen that the VCL, with Choate in the lead, stayed with the issue through 1933 until ratification was assured. Numerous members of the committee were elected to the various state-ratifying conventions. Thus, these lawyers not only worked to frame convention rules in the state legislatures and through the state governors but also were concerned with possible upsetting litigation, the elections of delegates and to the organization and action of the conventions. Part of their strength lay in the fact that the VCL was a one-issue organization both in theory and practice.

Other organizations contributed to the repeal of the Eighteenth Amendment by their efforts in Congress and in stimulating public feeling against national prohibition. Captain William H. Stayton and Jouett Shouse persuaded the lame-duck Congress in February 1933 to submit repeal to the states. Their Association Against the Prohibition Amendment, like the VCL, had representatives in every state. Its pamphlets and news releases produced an enormous amount of favorable cartoons, columns, news stories and editorials in newspapers and magazines through the 1920s. Mrs. Charles H. Sabin's Woman's Organization for National Prohibition Reform, as well as other organizations, also played important propaganda roles.

The American public did not adopt the Twenty-first Amendment because it was manipulated by organizations; there were many reasons—economic, social, political—for the change. Every man had his own experience with prohibition and a preponderant number came to believe it did not work. There was widespread flouting of the law; there were large untaxed profits made by the bootleggers; there were gang wars and police corruption. Even nondrinkers came to see the brewing and distilling industry as an economic asset. Purchases of grain, corn and other commodities would benefit farmers. The industry would give employment to many workers plying all sorts of trades—glass-blowers, teamsters, bartenders. Most important, products of the industry could be taxed by state government as well as by the United States government. During the boom years of the 1920s this was not a telling argument but it rapidly became significant after the 1929 crash. This is not the place to review the economic aspects of the campaign for repeal but it is perfectly obvious that economic conclusions as well as social ones contributed importantly to a public favorable to repeal.

There was not only a glacial movement from dry to wet opinion in the United States during these years but there was also a change in the constituency of the nation. The population was growing rapidly and its composition was shifting. In 1920 the total population was 105,710,046; in 1930 the census was 122,775,046. Immigration was not as high as it had been in previous decades but it was still an important factor, even after 1924 when the national origins quota was adopted by Congress; between 1921 and 1930 4,107,209 immigrants entered the United States compared to 5,735,811 between 1911 and 1920. At the same time and partly because of immigration, the country's population shifted away from rural predominance. The proportion of American population designated rural by the census of 1910 was 54.3 percent; in 1920 it was 48.8 percent and in 1930 it fell to 43.8 percent. Immigrants as well as other urban residents favored or at least accepted drinking. In the long run national prohibition seemed bound to lose. Other social indicators such as travel abroad, more farm and small-town children going away to college and the noisy entrance of veterans into public life through the aegis of the American Legion fed skepticism of prohibition.

The American electorate changed even more drastically than the overall population during the 1920s as immigrants and their children from both the period before and after 1910 became citizens and began registering and voting in huge numbers. According to V.O. Key, the presidential election of 1928 was critical in registering a basic realignment in the electorate. He showed that Alfred E. Smith, the Democratic candidate, made gains over previous Democrats in all the New England states. Key wrote: "When one probes below the surface of the gross election figures it becomes apparent that a sharp and durable realignment also occurred within the electorate, a fact reflective of the activation by the Democratic candidate of low-income, Catholic, urban voters of recent immigrant stock."[127] Hoover's showing in the South and his election tended to conceal the realignment Key spotted. But the durability of this shift was evident in the 1930 congressional elections and in the 1932 election of Roosevelt.

There were other political signals in addition to the strong urban vote of Democrats that told of rising wet sentiment in the United States during the 1920s. The polls of the *Literary Digest*, whose accuracy is of course questionable, reflected a desire for repeal. There were also state-wide referenda on the issue of liquor control when the voters of Massachusetts, New York, Wisconsin and some others decided against continuing state-enforced prohibition. If the opportunity to vote for delegates to ratifying conventions had come before 1933 there would, in all likelihood have been a wet vote in most if not all states. The delay in voting until after the 1932 elections meant that the electorate would be very different indeed from that before 1920. The actual vote in 1933 showed this to be true as wet majorities were easily amassed in thirty-seven states.

In sum, the repeal of prohibition was accomplished by a strong combination of leadership and followership, by elite organizations with special skills and an electorate with ballots. Prohibition had been supported by a native and nativist population with its roots in a progressivism hostile to cosmopolitan, urban values. By means of an alliance between the urbane, highly educated, high status old family members of the Voluntary Committee of Lawyers and other organizations, especially the AAPA, and the new immigrants and newer arrivals in the cities who were often Catholic, Jewish, poor and bilingual, national prohibition was brought to an end.

The Catholic School Issue

If the Hill Military Academy, numerous schools conducted by the Society of the Sisters and other privately run institutions were to continue in business in Oregon after September 1926, the State Compulsory Education Act had to be erased before that date. Having lost at the polls in 1922, lawyers for these institutions felt they had to go to court to stress the inherent rights of parents to choose their children's schools and the constitutional right of private schools to exist. They petitioned the federal district court for an injunction restraining Governor Walter M. Pierce and other state officials from attempting to enforce the act. A preliminary injunction was issued on March 31, 1924, but Governor Pierce and his associates appealed the cases to the United States Supreme Court, where they were argued the following March and decided June 1, 1925.[1] The decrees of the United States District Court for Oregon were affirmed unanimously. The decision was the lead story and lead editorial in the *New York Times* which declared:

Yesterday's decision by the Supreme Court holding invalid the Oregon school law is none the less welcome for being expected. The statute set aside was born of prejudice. It would have required parents in Oregon to take all their children between the ages of 8 and 16 out of private or parochial schools and send them to the public schools of the state. The measure professed to be one of equality, but it was plainly directed most intolerantly at a single class. It was one of the most hateful by-products of the Ku Klux Klan movement, which now happily seems to be dying out. The Supreme Court does not deny the right of the state to pass compulsory education laws, but it holds that the guarantees of religious freedom and individual liberty are violated when the attempt is made to say exactly how and where children shall be educated. . . .[2]

The editorial correctly identified the act as expressing Ku Klux Klan venom toward the Roman Catholic Church. It was apt to say further that, in a larger sense, the Oregon law had a kinship with the Tennessee Anti-Evolution School Law which William Jennings Bryan, the Nebraska Populist, was then defending. There was an intolerance circulating in the land which managed to translate itself into statutory law in a few states. It was an inchoate movement, from the grass roots, similar in spirit to Prohibition but poorly organized and less successful. The fundamentalist, nativist mind conjured up a specter of an alien threat which it identified—in ways that seem grossly inconsistent and contradictory—in Tennessee as the teachings of Charles Darwin, in Nebraska as the German language, in Oregon as the Catholic Church, and, generally, as the doctrines of Marx and Lenin. The schools were seen as a pivotal arena whose power to affect the future was greatly exaggerated.[3] Recent research findings by historians of church-state relations and of American educational history provide ample documentation of the view that the Oregon act of 1922 was inspired by the Ku Klux Klan, with Freemasonry and with patriotic organizations such as the Sons of the American Revolution.[4] From the papers of Patrick Joseph Cardinal Hayes, it will also be possible in this chapter to demonstrate something of the complexity of Catholic response and the remarkable range of support the church received from organizations not always its most dependable allies.

In commenting on the decision of the Supreme Court in the *Pierce* cases in June 1925, the *New York Times* editorial made two further observations which call for comment in turning to the opinion of the Court itself. The *Times* noted that "it is an enactment by a state which the Supreme Court has decided to be repugnant to the Constitution" and hoped there would be no "outcry against confiding such tyrannical powers to judges." These were days, after all, when the Court had been holding social legislation of both the federal and state governments invalid over and over again. The Progressive outrage over the power of the Court boiled for a generation or more.

What was especially interesting here, however, was the *Times* view that this was a law passed by the "rednecks," and that despite majority support in the state of Oregon, the Court was right to use its wisdom and its power to invalidate that law. And while it was Mr. Justice Oliver Wendell Holmes who perceived that "general propositions do not decide concrete cases," the *Times* leaned on just such an utterance, and one by Holmes, to justify the Court's action. Holmes had once said that the power of judicial review over Congress was not essential but "that he did not see how our government could survive if the Supreme Court were deprived of the power to void acts of state legislatures." The *Times* agreed with the nine justices that the need for a "federal tribunal to maintain the rights of the citizen when they are invaded by local legislation has never been more evident than in the case of this Oregon School law." Upon reading this in Cambridge, Felix Frankfurter promptly wrote a letter to the *Times* calling the Oregon school law a "bad" law and elucidating the "general proposition," saying

Perhaps some of your readers will be interested to see the exact words of Mr. Justice Holmes, inasmuch as the observation had a much more specific and restricted direction than is conveyed by your paraphrase. What is said will be found in his *Collected Legal Papers*, pages 295-6:

"I do not think the United States would come to an end if we lost our power to declare an act of Congress void. I do think the Union would be imperiled if we could not make that declaration as to the laws of the several states. For one in my place sees how often a local policy prevails with those not trained to national views, and how often action is taken that embodies what the commerce clause was meant to end."[5]

As a political issue and as a large issue of constitutional policy, *Pierce v. the Society of the Sisters* concerned questions of the right of churches and their communicants to conduct their education outside governmentally run schools. Transformed into legal issues in the early 1920s, the case turned on questions framed in the rhetoric and reflecting the state of the art of constitutional adjudication of that day. The broader issues of religious freedom recognized by the *New York Times* of 1925 and, indeed, of nearly everyone interested in this litigation at the time and since, was not, in fact, touched or alluded to in the opinion for the Supreme Court by Mr. Justice McReynolds. Instead, he dealt with this as he dealt with most cases where a popular branch of government wished to regulate a railroad, an electric utility or a machine tool plant. The language of his opinion for the unanimous Court was strictly about property rights and, at that, about property rights of corporations.

McReynolds observed with evident satisfaction that the appellees in the cases, the Society of the Sisters and the Hill Military Academy, were corporations. Under interpretations of "persons" in the due process clause of the Fourteenth Amendment corporations' business and property interests can properly claim protection. This was enough to justify equitable relief to prevent the impending injury the Compulsory Education Act would inflict. "The suits were not premature" because the law was not to be effective until September 1, 1926. "The injury to appellees was present and very real," McReynolds declared; "not a mere possibility in the remote future." He concluded, "If no relief had been possible prior to the effective date of the act, the injury would have become irreparable."[6]

McReynolds' opinion in *Pierce* also held that the Oregon act "unreasonably interferes with the liberty of parents and guardians to direct the upbringing and education of children under their control."[7] Like the decisions on child labor legislation in that era, the idea of parental guidance and control over the child as against the demands of the state was powerfully felt by most Supreme Court justices in the 1920s. As familiar social and constitutional doctrine, McReynolds' was succinct, stating his view of the matter in three sentences:

Rights guaranteed by the Constitution may not be abridged by legislation which has no reasonable relation to some purpose within the competency of the state. The fundamental theory of liberty upon which all governments in this Union repose excludes any general power of the state to standardize its children by forcing them to accept instruction from public school teachers only. The child is not the mere creature of the state; those who nurture him and direct his destiny have the right, coupled with the high duty, to recognize and prepare him for additional obligations.[8]

Freemasonry and the Klan

As an initiative measure, the Compulsory Education Act was adopted in a popular election campaign and not negotiated through the Oregon state legislature. The initiative was a procedural alternative to the regular legislative process and its Progressive boosters hailed this method of legislation as a popular, more democratic form. Reflecting on this claim, it is misleading to see democracy as a practice which is a matter of "some, more, most." Better to appreciate that any procedure carries consequences, many unforeseen, and that it may blow up in the faces of its instigators. Provision for direct initiation of legislation clearly means that at a given moment in time a concerted campaign can take advantage of momentary feelings to adopt new laws later regarded as imprudent even by their original endorsers.

In an American legislative body ideas are converted into bills, hearings and research follow, complaints and criticisms register which redrafting may take into account. Details differ radically and the legislative process hardly deserves blind adulation. But placed back to back to legislation by initiative, the regular methods of lawmaking by organized legislatures, the initiative has gross inadequacies. Nor is there executive guidance or the threat of a veto at play in the initiative method. These weaknesses are quite evident in the adoption of the Oregon Compulsory Education Act of 1922.

Legislative majorities in both houses could not have been mustered for a bill outlawing private and parochial schools in Oregon. Certainly Governor Ben Olcott would have vetoed in any event and overriding that was out of the question. In June 1922 opponents of private education set the initiative procedure in motion by filing necessary papers and the text of a statute with the secretary of state in order to have it voted upon in the November election. "Be it enacted by the people of the state of Oregon," the proposal began.[9] In form, this was a bill for the amendment of a single section (section 5259) of the Oregon school law on the books. It applied to children between the ages of eight and sixteen years, making it a misdemeanor for any parent or guardian not to send children in their charge to a public school. There were exceptions for (a) physically disabled children, (b) children who had completed the eighth grade, (c) children who lived long distances from public schools, and (d) individual children in extraordinary circumstances who might be tutored or given private instruction. The penalties for noncompliance were harsh. Each day's avoidance would be a misdemeanor subject to a fine of not less than $5 nor more than $100 with imprisonment between two and thirty days in the discretion of the court. The act would be in force and take effect after the first day of September 1926.

As the authors of the Oregon initiative procedure believed in the rationality and perfectibility of man, they provided for an official pamphlet setting forth pros and cons of each question to be distributed by mail "to every voter in the state" fifty-five days prior to an election.[10] Under the law the secretary of state was obliged to include any arguments filed by any "person, committee or organization" for or against an initiative measure. The pamphlet distributed by Secretary Sam A. Kozer in August 1922 read, officially, as "A measure to amend section 5259, Oregon Laws, relating to compulsory education, to be submitted to the legal electors of the State of Oregon for their approval or rejection at the regular general election to be held November 7, 1922."[11]

The affirmative argument for the Compulsory Education Act was made in the official pamphlet by eleven men who sponsored the measure and who appeared to speak for Masonic lodges in Oregon. At least in this public document they declared that

The inspiration for this act is the following resolution:

Resolved, That we recognize and proclaim our belief in the free and compulsory education of the children of our nation in public primary schools supported by public taxation, upon which all children shall attend and be instructed in the English language only without regard to race or creed as the only sure foundation for the perpetuation and preservation of our free institutions, guaranteed by the Constitution of the United States, and we pledge the efforts of the membership of the order to promote by all lawful means the organization, extension and development to the highest degree of such schools, and to oppose the efforts of any and all who seek to limit, curtail, hinder or destroy the public school system of our land.

The above resolution was adopted by the Supreme Council, A.&S. Rite, for the Southern Jurisdiction of the United States, May 1920.

Grand Lodge of Oregon, A.F.&A.M., June 1920.

Imperial Council, A.A.O. Nobles Mystic Shrine, June 1920.[12]

The emphasis was on "assimilation and education of our foreign-born citizens" and how the public school could do the job if social integration were first required. "Mix the children of the foreign born with the native born, and the rich with the poor. Mix those with prejudices in the public school melting pot for a few years while their minds are plastic, and finally bring out the finished product—a true American."[13] This was the essence of the argument advanced for voting the proposal into law.

This was one of the rare occasions in twentieth-century political history when Freemasonry had come into public view as an open opponent of Catholicism. *The New Age*, a monthly publication of the Supreme Council of the 33rd Degree, Ancient and Accepted Scottish Rite, issued since 1904, often opposed Catholic candidates for public office and, especially in the first third of the twentieth century, opposed parochial school education and immigration from Catholic countries. The Southern Jurisdiction of the Scottish Rite enrolls 32nd degree Masons in thirty-three Southern and Western states, Oregon included.

Enmity between Catholicism and Freemasonry, muted almost to the point of ecumenism in recent years, is more than two centuries old—practically as old as the Masonic movement itself. Roman Catholics are forbidden to seek membership in any Masonic group by a series of papal documents condemning Freemasonry as a rival religion.[14] This is so because Freemasonry "includes temples and altars, prayers, a moral code, worship, vestments, feast days, the promise of reward or punishment in the afterlife, a hierarchy, and initiation and burial rites."[15] As Masons are mostly Protestants their social and political activities have been of most concern to Catholics. There is nothing monolithic about the organization as there were major, minor, auxiliary and quasi-Masonic organizations in the United States with over four million members in 1970. That Freemasonry is not united is shown by the opposition to outlawing parochial schools registered in Oregon by a number of leading Masons in the state.[16]

These Masons believed that some Ku Klux Klan members had infiltrated their organization although it may very well have been a different phenomenon—men already in Masonic lodges becoming Klansmen. It is really impossible to say what the relationship might have been between members of a secret society such as the Masons and men in a clandestine, or more secret group, which the Klan was.

In the *Official Pamphlet* on the Compulsory Education Bill against the endorsement inspired by the Scottish Rite Masons were seven different negative arguments. One was submitted by the Catholic Civil Rights Association and signed by leading Catholic lawyers. They insisted that private schools had high standards, that their curriculum was supervised by the state, that private institutions have been the "salvation of our democracy" by keeping the public schools "from becoming autocratic and arbitrary." They appealed strongly to the anxieties of Oregon voters when they declared that the measure "will create a tremendous burden of taxation." With only eight persons to the square mile, Oregon needed new settlers to bring development and prosperity but, they declared, "Immigration is not attracted by freak legislation, and many at whom measures of this kind are aimed will prefer to live in other states where a more liberal spirit prevails."[17]

Among much Catholic activity the organizing work and speeches of Father Edwin V. O'Hara, archdiocesan superintendent of education in Oregon, were most notable. O'Hara had chaired the state minimum wage board, had worked energetically and effectively for protective labor laws in Oregon, and had acquired a national reputation as a liberal priest. The charming and courageous O'Hara was legendary as a speaker—he had once accepted a challenge to public debate by an atheist street speaker haranguing a crowd in Portland. He kept in touch with Roger Baldwin of the American Civil Liberties Union in New York and with Father John J. Ryan of Catholic University in Washington about the impending Oregon school law. Highly esteemed as he was by the Catholic hierarchy, O'Hara organized the Catholic Truth Society of Oregon as a militant group of priests set up to persuade Protestants that the church had only benign ends in conducting parochial schools.

His biographer asserts that O'Hara was the "obvious champion of the Catholic cause" and that he "enlisted influential people from among his non-Catholic friends to join in committees which he supplied with ammunition for a propaganda campaign to bring the facts to light." It is said, too, that he worked closely with John P. Kavanaugh, a leading Catholic lawyer, and others both in the election campaign against the initiative measure and later in managing the litigation.[18]

The arguments opposing the school law published in the *Official Pamphlet* mailed to all voters were repetitious, with claims of state confiscation of property, of the danger of state control of the child and of religious intolerance. Negative statements were filed by the Evangelical Lutheran Synod, by Episcopalians, by four private nonsectarian schools, including the Hill Military Academy, by the Seventh Day Adventists of Oregon, by a group of twenty-five Oregon ministers who were members of the Presbyterian Church and by an unaffiliated or at least unidentified group of citizens. With these statements, together with a noisy campaign over the referendum question in which the incumbent Governor Ben Olcott openly opposed and his challenger Walter Pierce quietly supported the school law, the Oregon electorate had a surfeit of information about the proposal. Proponents have an advantage in such a campaign for their initiative meant that they had opportunity for advance planning. The habitual voter participates in referendum elections and zealous supporters of a measure do also, but in a general election with a long ballot there are always many who skip voting on referenda.

Accounts of the adoption of the Oregon Compulsory Education Act on November 7, 1922, conventionally stress the part of the Ku Klux Klan in the campaign. It is to be expected that Klan members exaggerated their significance and it is also likely that opponents did the same. Though it is certain the Klan organization was organized in Oregon and participated, it is more notable that the Masonic lodges openly supported the measure and that some of the most prominent figures in Oregon public life, Walter M. Pierce and Wallace McCamant among them, were on the side of this law.

The Ku Klux Klan was vehemently anti-Catholic and its intention to put parochial schools out of business was fanatic enough to abolish all private schools with them. The approval of the measure which became law in November 1922 showed, indeed, that old-time American nativism, or one hundred percent Americanism could be registered at the polls. No doubt a radical faction of Protestants, most of whom were Masons and some of whom were Klansmen, led the crusade, but they were followed by thousands who were less committed though brought to a fair pitch of frenzy in 1922. The law was approved by approximately 53 percent of those voting.[19] Considering that the population of Oregon in the religious census of 1916 registered only 8 percent Catholic, a huge number of Protestants voted against the Compulsory School Law in 1922. Also, there were no doubt degrees of anti-Catholicism, many far short of the virulence of the Ku Klux Klan.

The law, the Ku Klux Klan and Pierce were opposed by the incumbent Republican, Ben Olcott. Then just over sixty, Pierce's view of the public school as appropriate for the education of *all* children can be comprehended against his background. Although he won a law degree from Northwestern in 1896, Pierce had Populist views befitting his years as a farmer and as a teacher and school superintendent. He also practiced law in small-town Oregon for a decade and speculated successfully in land. As a state senator, as governor from 1923 to 1927 and then, from 1933 to 1943, a United States congressman, Walter Pierce enjoyed a long public career in which to establish positions on issues. Called "a lifelong prohibitionist" who waged his first public campaign against liquor in the 1880s, Pierce also advocated federal and state income taxes, the popular election of United States senators, the public ownership of utilities, and the initiative and referendum. For ten years in Congress Pierce said he "was a New Dealer, and proud of it."[20]

Pierce was a Mason and an Odd Fellow as well as a member of the Grange and the Farmers' Union. When Margaret Sanger and Harrison Tweed sought a congressman in the 1930s to file bills to alter the Comstock limitations on the dissemination of birth-control information, Pierce was their man.[21] At any rate, this web of interests and beliefs make a plausible outline of some of the sources explaining how Walter Pierce's opposition to private and parochial schools might have been sustained.

McCamant came to Oregon in 1890 from Lancaster, Pennsylvania, where he had studied law for two years following graduation at the head of his class from Lafayette College. For two years, 1917-19, a member of the Oregon Supreme Court, McCamant opposed many Progressive reforms and was an outspoken critic of the idea of the recall of judges urged by Theodore Roosevelt and Hiram Johnson. It was entirely in keeping with his regular Republicanism that he should make the speech in 1920 nominating Calvin Coolidge for vice president. Their philosophies coincided as, for example, "McCamant was active in efforts to reform the teaching of American history so as to eliminate radicalism and disrespect for American institutions."[22] A Presbyterian, a 33rd degree Mason, McCamant was a self-styled genealogist, historian and patriot who served nearly two decades as president of the Oregon Society of the Sons of the American Revolution and then, in 1921-22, was president general of the national society of the Sons of the American Revolution.

These associations are in keeping with McCamant's argument for the Oregon Compulsory Education Law which, he insisted, would reduce class hatred. "I don't know any better way to fortify the next generation against that insidious poison," McCamant declared, "than to require that the poor and the rich, the people of all classes and distinction, and of all different religious beliefs, shall meet in the common schools, which are the great American melting pot, there to become . . . the typical American of the future."[23] McCamant urged adoption of the law and then defended its constitutionality in the United States District Court in Oregon.

The Catholic Legal Defense

The litigation against the Oregon Compulsory Education Act of 1922 was inspired by Catholic insistence on parochial schooling, sponsored by an intelligent and sensitive hierarchy, financed by a combination of lay and clerical organizations and conducted by outstanding Catholic lawyers with well-earned national reputations. This combination won to its side a remarkable array of public editorial support and briefs *amici curiae* in the *Pierce* cases themselves. This was no sudden affair. Each ingredient to the alliance had a long past.

The genuine opposition to the Oregon law by many non-Catholics is attested in litigation by the Hill Military Academy. This private school in Portland depended primarily upon students from the Northwest whose homes were considerable distances from any schools. They were therefore sent to the academy, which was a boarding school. The school's attorney in 1922 was John C. Veatch, a graduate of the University of Oregon in Eugene, who served as an instructor at the Hill Military Academy while he studied law at the university branch in Portland.

When the Oregon statute was passed prohibiting private schools, John Veatch "made a strenuous effort through the Catholic organizations in Portland to get them to start suit to determine the validity of that statute. . . . [He] could get no action from the Catholic institutions but the Hill Military Academy could not delay because the very existence of that statute prevented the academy from making contracts with instructors and contracts with parents for the education of sons in the succeeding year. So [he] filed suit on behalf of the academy and that compelled the Catholic institutions to come into the case."[24]

Considering the evidence of Catholic planning for a test case within two months following adoption of the Oregon law on November 7, 1922, the church obviously would have taken spontaneous action. The Hill Military initiative broadened the issue, however, and its authentic self-interest in opposing the constitutionality of the school law proves that its pursuit of litigation was independently inspired.

The Knights of Columbus, a fraternal benefit society of Catholic men, swung into action swiftly. The supreme board of directors acted at its regular quarterly meeting. The board heard from three Oregon Catholic leaders, Archbishop Alexander Christie of Oregon City, his principal legal adviser John P. Kavanaugh, and Brother P.J. Hanley, state deputy of the Knights of Columbus.[25] They requested "the Knights of Columbus to finance the suit to test the constitutionality of the Oregon School Law."[26] A committee of the board was appointed to consider the situation in detail and report at the same Chicago meeting its recommendations for action, which it did. The committee chairman was Luke E. Hart, then supreme advocate of the Knights of Columbus, a lawyer and later, in the 1950s, the prime mover to persuade Congress to insert the words "under God" in the Pledge of Allegiance. Hart's committee reported back on the same day, recommending that if Archbishop Christie

should make a formal request upon the Supreme Board of Directors, the Supreme Knight should say . . . that the Knights of Columbus would undertake the financing and backing of litigation involved in testing the constitutionality of the Compulsory Education Bill; that we will now advance ten thousand dollars for the purpose of financing this litigation; . . . that we feel that this is a big issue confronting the Catholic people of the country and that the Knights of Columbus as a Catholic organization ought to meet the request of the Bishop; that if we are going into this we ought to be allowed to take the whole responsibility; that we are willing to do it whether the question arises in Oregon or in any other State.[27]

The assertion that the Knights helped with the Hill Military Academy case is only one of the puzzling aspects about the financial side of the legal action against the Oregon school law. Another is the disbursement of funds. Available records and recollections simply do not indicate the extent to which there were fees for legal services paid to the lawyers for the Catholic interests. The substantial briefs and the traveling from Oregon to Washington would have been costly. But there were also other contributions in addition to those made by the national office and the subordinate councils of the Knights of Columbus. These were moneys made available through the hierarchy.

Support for legal action by the hierarchy was expressed chiefly by the National Catholic Welfare Conference, formed in 1919 as an "agency of the Archbishops and Bishops of the United States to organize, unify and coordinate Catholic activities for the general welfare of the Church."[28] The American Bishops' Committee also met in Chicago in January 1923 and it was reported immediately afterward that "the outstanding result of the gathering was the unanimous decision to get behind a test of the Oregon school law in both state and federal Courts with all of the moral, spiritual and financial aid necessary, and to use every legitimate means to secure the law's repeal."[29] While the Knights of Columbus were promptly forthcoming with money for Archbishop Christie, the organized hierarchy was tardy yet not at all niggardly. More than a year after the Supreme Court decision in *Pierce v. Society of the Sisters*, the chairman of the Bishops' Committee was still trying to make good his promise to contribute $10,000 and sought a contribution from Cardinal Hayes of New York.[30] Hayes promptly sent a check for $500 but exclaimed that he was "at a loss to know just what quota of the total amount I should assume."[31]

The available information suggests contributions to fight the Oregon school law amounted to well over $20,000. It is definite that the Knights of Columbus contributed $10,000, and the hierarchy, whether formally through the Bishops' Committee or through its arm, the National Catholic Welfare Conference, also contributed $10,000. It would be interesting to learn whether the Catholic lawyers in Oregon or William D. Guthrie, the nationally prominent Catholic lawyer who took charge of the case in the Supreme Court, received fees. This is not unique to this litigation. The costs of Supreme Court litigation remain a difficult and intriguing subject of investigation.

Meanwhile, quite apart from financial support, the lawyers for Archbishop Christie had chosen to bring action in the United States District Court of Oregon on behalf of the Society of the Sisters of the Holy Names of Mary and Jesus. This religious order, one of hundreds in the United States and Canada with parochial schools in a few places, had been founded in Canada in 1843, in the United States in 1859.[32] The society was the oldest and largest religious community of women in the archdiocese of Portland in Oregon, although in 1923 conducting fewer than ten high schools and grammar schools in the state. The bill of complaint for the plaintiff Society was filed on December 22, 1923, by Bowerman & Kavanaugh, Malarkey, Seabrook & Dibble, Emmons & Lusk, and Frank J. Lonergan, all of Portland.

The Catholic complaint was based entirely on the corporate status of the society, its license from the state to conduct schools, the value of the schooling provided to the children enrolled and to the public well-being, and the economic loss the society would suffer if put out of business by state law. Except for clearly stating that the society was a Catholic order and that its schools were parochial, the complaint said nothing of the First Amendment to the United States Constitution. The emphasis was on the deprivation of property without due process of law that the Oregon provision would bring about. Point five in the complaint did speak of religion and conscience, though not in terms of the free exercise clause or the separation clause of the First Amendment, alleging that the "pretended law" to go into effect in 1926

attempts to control the free exercise and enjoyment of religious opinions and to interfere with the rights of conscience in violation of Section 3 of Article I of the Constitution of the State of Oregon, and of that Clause of Section 1 of Article XIV of the Amendments to the Constitution of the United States, which provides that no state shall deprive any person of liberty without due process of law.[33]

The Catholic lawyers felt they had no speedy or adequate remedy at law (that is, they did not wish damages although their losses would be substantial) and consequently asked that the governor and attorney general and other state officials be enjoined and restrained from enforcing the "pretended law" after September 1, 1926.

The Hill Military Academy, as we have seen, was represented by John C. Veatch, who made much the same complaint in the three-judge District Court. The academy had grown out of an Episcopal school established in 1852 but reorganized in 1901 by Joseph A. Hill, an 1878 graduate of Yale.[34] Although having an Episcopal history, the Hill Military Academy called itself "undenominational" in the 1920s. It then had an enrollment of about 120 boarding and fifty day students—boys aged six to eighteen—with a faculty of twenty. It counted about 3,000 alumni and, according to later accounts, sent out a national appeal to them and others for funds to fight the Oregon school law of 1922.[35] Veatch has said that he "handled the academy's case entirely alone and did not conduct the litigation in the name of the law firm with which I was connected. The principal reason for this was due to a lot of local controversy in which I didn't want the other members of the law firm to be involved."[36] He and Dan Malarkey argued the case before the district court.

Opposing counsel to the society and to the academy, for Governor Pierce and Attorney General Van Winkle were Van Winkle himself, Stanley Myers, the state district attorney and the private firm of McCamant & Thompson of Portland. The case was heard by William B. Gilbert, circuit judge, and Charles E. Wolverton and Robert S. Bean, district judges, and on March 31, 1924, they unanimously held in an opinion by Wolverton that in adopting the Oregon Compulsory Education Act the state "exceeded the limitations of its power" and, in denying the right of parochial and private schools to operate, and of the right of parents and guardians to send their children and wards to such schools as they may desire, contravened the due process clause of the Fourteenth Amendment.[37] The court issued preliminary injunctions restraining the defendant Oregon state officials from threatening or attempting to enforce the act.

The state officials determined that they should appeal this decision to the Supreme Court of the United States. As a state law had been invalidated under an interpretation of the United States Constitution, there was no question the case would be heard. And as 1924 was again an election year, these officials had almost no other course considering that the law had been adopted by a popular majority. Applications for writs of error were prepared and filed during the spring of 1924, but the Supreme Court did not reach the case until the following year.

The Masonic Lawyers for Pierce

The day following the district court's invalidation of the Oregon school law, Wallace McCamant advised one of the attorneys for the state that "we have a period of three months within which to take an appeal to the Federal Supreme Court."[38] Stating that the question of an appeal "is primarily for your office to determine," McCamant made his own judgment evident by placing the decision on this ground: "I suppose it is a duty owing to the Oregon electorate to carry a matter so important as this through to the court of last resort." He also indicated what the Masons would wish, saying: "I will be unable to advise you without some little delay as to what will be the attitude of the Scottish Rite bodies at whose instance I have appeared in the litigation. My impression is that they will want the case carried up."[39] McCamant was soon assured that Attorney General Van Winkle believed the case should be appealed to the Supreme Court and that the other state officials hoped McCamant's clients would arrange to have him continue his connection with the case.[40]

It is fascinating to see how the work—the financing, the credit and publicity— is handled when a state attorney general cooperates closely with an interest group in conducting litigation. Van Winkle had options he did not take, chiefly dropping the whole matter and not carrying an appeal. But like so many public officials before and since he welcomed every assistance he could get from outsiders. He and McCamant conducted a straightforward correspondence in bringing the appeal along, but there were tacit understandings reflecting their awareness that a fully aired public relationship could be damaging. McCamant was delighted that the attorney general would appeal, adding: "We are corresponding with our people on this subject and will be able to give you an answer shortly as to the further pleasure of the Masonic bodies which I have more particularly represented. . . . I think the expense of preparing and printing the record on appeal should be borne by the state [but] it is probable that the Scottish Rite bodies will take care of the expense of printing the brief."[41] Later, to make sure that Oregon would, indeed, finance at least half of the appeal, McCamant sought and obtained assurances from Governor Pierce and Secretary of State Sam A. Koser that the state would take care of it.[42]

McCamant, meanwhile, was doing most of the work but was not sure whether his clients would care for the credit or notoriety of carrying the case to the Supreme Court. "In accordance with our understanding," he told Van Winkle, "I have prepared the papers which I understand to be necessary to perfect our appeal" in the Society of the Sisters and Hill Military Academy cases.[43] Originals and copies were sent along to Van Winkle. "If you find these papers in due form," McCamant wrote, "will you kindly sign all of them except the citation? Will you also have Governor Pierce join with you in signing the bond on appeal and will you make arrangements to have the bond signed by some surety."[44] Although McCamant persistently labored on the appeal, he did not appear as a matter of record and that being so he told Van Winkle he thought "you would better cover the original papers with your own official covers and return to me."[45] Early in planning the appeal, McCamant explained his clients' ambiguity on this in these words:

The Supreme Council of the Scottish Rite, which is my client in this matter, is still deeply interested in the litigation and will undoubtedly put forth some effort in the Supreme Court. It is not yet certain that they will desire their counsel to be listed as solicitor of record for the defendants, and for this reason I am keeping my name off the papers. You will be advised at a later date of the conclusions of the Supreme Council on the above matter, and I hope that there may be the same spirit of cooperation in the Supreme Court which obtained in the lower court.[46]

With the two cases on the Supreme Court docket in the 1924-25 term, another lawyer representing the Masons entered the picture, George Earle Chamberlain, then practicing law in Washington, D.C., had had an illustrious Oregon political career. Though born in Mississippi and educated at Washington and Lee University, he had settled in Oregon at the age of twenty-two in 1876. He soon entered public life as a Democrat, served in the legislature, was attorney general from 1891 for four years, governor of Oregon from 1903 to 1909 and United States senator from 1909 to 1921. As chairman of the Senate Military

Committee during World War I, Chamberlain became the "father of the selective draft law."[47]

Isaac H. Van Winkle, a Willamette University law graduate in 1901, practiced in an age when public officials commonly accepted voluntary assistance from private interests. Perhaps that age has not passed and may never pass. Working for the state was not a full-time position, at all; Van Winkle also served on the faculty of the College of Law at Willamette from 1905 to 1927, the last twelve years as dean. In *Who's Who in America*, he listed himself as Republican, Methodist, Woodman, Artisan, Kiwanian. Welcoming Chamberlain as an associate "in this important and somewhat loaded litigation" he made clear that his "only anxiety" in conducting the Oregon school cases "is not to appear to shirk my official duty in any respect on account of the issues involved." To ensure this he suggested that they split the cases so that Chamberlain would handle the governor's case and Van Winkle the case for himself as attorney general.

This is precisely how the division of counsel was made. Both the Hill and Society cases were aimed at the same top officials in the state, Governor Pierce, Attorney General Van Winkle, the District attorney for Multnomah County Myers and others. A brief in both cases was filed by George E. Chamberlain, his Washington law partner, Peter Q. Nyce, and Albert H. Putney. As their brief was very substantially the work of Wallace McCamant, who continued to send copy, make suggestions and generally work over their shoulders, it is evidently fair to view both briefs as not merely in harmony with the views of the Scottish Rite Masons but the work of their lawyers, as well.[48]

The brief filed for Governor Pierce by Chamberlain, Putney and Nyce insisted that the school legislation was a state matter untouchable by federal power. If the compulsory school laws of other states were valid so was Oregon's, for it was a plain and valid exercise of the police power. This was a wise exercise of the police power, a fine expression of the people's wisdom because only "a compulsory system of public school education will encourage the patriotism of its citizens, and train its younger citizens to become more willing and more efficient defenders of the United States in times of public danger."

The brief prepared by McCamant and filed officially by Willis S. Moore and Isaac H. Van Winkle for appellant Van Winkle stressed similar themes and also insisted that neither due process nor religious liberty, nor the obligation of contracts was unconstitutionally disturbed by the compulsory school law. The provisions of a corporation charter as well as contracts made by a corporation are subject to modification and annulment under the police power, the brief said. Since the state may compel attendance at some school it follows, they argued, that the legislature may choose the means of achieving this policy.

A late petition to file an *amicus* brief came to the Court from attorneys for the Public School Defense League of Detroit, Michigan. This was an organization seeking in Michigan a state constitutional amendment similar to the Oregon school law. The Court ordinarily insists that all briefs be filed before oral argument, and as this brief was received much later the petition to file was rejected by Chief Justice William Howard Taft.[49] This was a technical ruling as the printed petition and motion for leave to file was accepted by the clerk of the Supreme Court and is to be found in bound copies of the records and briefs in the *Pierce* cases. The argument in the document filed by the Public School Defense League was openly anti-Catholic. Having examined the teachings of the Roman Catholic Church, the brief asserted that the Roman Catholic Church taught, among other things

That the Pope has the right to annul any law;
    That education outside of the Catholic church is a "damnable heresy";
    That the state has no right to educate;
    That any attempt on the part of the state to educate is usurping the power of the church;
    That our public system of education is vicious and that the church should do everything in its power against the public schools;
    That our public system of education is vicious and should not be permitted to exist;
    That any Catholic parent who sends his children to the public school may be excluded from the sacraments.[50]

The league argued that holding the Oregon law invalid would have an adverse impact in other states, saying:

In Michigan and Detroit local conditions are such that a decision in this case might be especially unfortunate for them because of the large and somewhat aggressive foreign population. In Michigan alone 153,000 children are taken from the public schools and turned over to be educated by private institutions.[51]

These words, the briefs for Oregon prepared by lawyers for the Masons, and the related documents reviewing electoral arguments for voting in the school law placed a full record of Ku Klux Klan, Freemasonry and Protestant nativist contentions before the Supreme Court. Artless they were, but they were truly sociological briefs even if of the plain, provincial variety. Would these assertions about and fears of the Roman Catholic Church move the Supreme Court of 1925?

In arguing that the school law does not deprive any person of liberty without due process of law, Chamberlain's brief for Governor Pierce distinguished precedents invalidating legislation. The Arizona antialien labor law was properly voided because an alien's own liberty to contract was directly affected.[52] The Nebraska law forbidding the teaching in any modern language, other than English, in any school "merely decided that the parents had some rights of control over the education of their children."[53] Decisions upholding state regulatory legislation harmonized with the Oregon school law, according to

Chamberlain. State compulsory vaccination against smallpox upheld in 1905, a favorite precedent for health, education and welfare advocates, was stressed.[54]

That precedents, and the phrasing of judicial opinions from bygone days can mesmerize lawyers is shown by Chamberlain's emphasis on the well-known 1837 *Miln* case.[55] Mr. Justice Philip P. Barbour, in his most notable opinion, there justified an 1824 New York State act "concerning passengers in vessels arriving in the port of New York." Ship masters were required to report details about arriving passengers and cargo to the mayor of the city. In dissent, Mr. Justice Joseph Story believed the statute contravened an exclusive power of Congress to regulate commerce. But the eight members of the Court thought otherwise and in his 1925 brief for Pierce, ex-Senator Chamberlain found Justice Barbour's words justification for the Oregon school law, writing:

In the case of *Mayor, etc. of New York v. Miln* (11 Peters 102, 97 L. Ed. 648), the Supreme Court of the United States said:

"We think it as competent and as necessary for a State to provide precautionary measures against the moral pestilence of paupers, vagabonds, and possibly convicts, as it is to guard against the physical pestilence which may arise from unsound and infectious articles imported, or from a ship, the crew of which may be laboring under an infectious disease."

The discretionary powers of a state are broad enough to permit it to decide that compulsory attendance at public schools is a proper "precautionary measure against the moral pestilence of paupers, vagabonds, and possibly convicts."

The voters of Oregon who adopted the new school law for their state had the right to base their action on the belief that the fact that the great increase in juvenile crime in the United States followed so closely after the great increase in the number of children in the United States who were not attending public schools, was more than a coincidence.

... In the case of *Mayor, etc. of New York v. Miln* (supra), the Supreme Court was considering the evil effects upon a State of the immigration of ignorant foreigners, unacquainted with and lacking in sympathy with, American institutions and ideals. In this connection, it should be remembered that the vast majority of children not now attending the public schools of Oregon who will be compelled to do so by the new statute, are either themselves immigrants or the children of immigrants.[56]

Representing Masonic bodies, lawyer Chamberlain also looked ahead and imagined how a right to conduct private schools could enable subversives to utilize the principle for malign ends. It was essential to consider the kinds of private schools which may be established in the future. Chamberlain was clearly speculating but, considering the views of his clients, the slur on Catholic schools was surely intended. This is what he said:

At present the vast majority of the private schools in the country are conducted by members of some particular religious belief. They may be followed, however, by those organized and controlled by believers in certain economic doctrines entirely destructive of the fundamentals of our government.

If the Oregon school law is held to be unconstitutional it is not only a possibility but almost a certainty that within a few years the great centers of population in our country will be dotted with elementary schools which instead of being red on the outside will be red on the inside.

Can it be contended that there is no way in which a state can prevent the entire education of a considerable portion of its future citizens being controlled and conducted by bolshevists, syndicalists and communists?[57]

William D. Guthrie As Counsel to Cardinal Hayes

As chief counsel for Catholic interests in the *Pierce* case, William D. Guthrie brought to the case a vast experience as a lawyer and a churchman. Thirty years earlier, in 1894, he had argued the *Income Tax Cases* in league with Joseph Hodge Choate, and was credited with persuading the Supreme Court to rule that Congress lacked authority to tax incomes. In that connection, Guthrie had worked avidly to prevent ratification of the Sixteenth Amendment. His talents as a writer, speaker and advocate in defense of corporate and other propertied interests led Twiss to make Guthrie a major villain in the movement in which economic conservatism was accepted as gospel under the Constitution.[58] Guthrie had a worldly background of a boyhood in France and frequent later travels to England, France and Italy. He had an excellent command of French and a sense and knowledge of historical change matched by few lawyers of his generation. He was admitted to the bar at age twenty-one in 1880.

Guthrie argued numerous cases in the Supreme Court of the United States, had lucrative corporate accounts and won enough estate cases to make him a wealthy man. As a scholar he delivered the Storrs Lectures at Yale Law School in 1908 and was Ruggles Professor of Constitutional Law at Columbia from 1913 to 1922. Guthrie was a man of ardent convictions on constitutional issues which rose directly from a philosophy of man and the state. If he opposed the income tax by legislation then he would also oppose its imposition by constitutional amendment. So, too, did he oppose the Eighteenth Amendment, for he believed prohibition was beyond the powers of government to ordain as it intruded on personal habits and individual preferences of behavior. He had the same objection to the child labor amendment which, he felt, would disturb parental authority.

These views were in harmony with the social views of the leading American Cardinals O'Connell of Boston and Hayes of New York. As a devout and deeply concerned Catholic, Guthrie was the single most prominent figure in the litigation attacking the constitutionality of the Oregon school law of 1922.

The early part of the case was conducted in Oregon, but on appeal to the Supreme Court it became too important for the American hierarchy to leave to local counsel. Accordingly, arrangements were made through Cardinal Hayes of the New York archdiocese to have Guthrie enter the litigation.

As in so many pivotal Supreme Court cases, this was not a neutral technician at work but a lawyer who by native inclination and by long experience could speak effectively and with confidence for the interests he represented. Thus his philosophy of the relationship between church and state, of the nature of religious freedom, of the values of parochial religious training and of the rights of property under the Fourteenth Amendment were as one in the mind of William D. Guthrie. It can truly be said that in representing the church in the *Pierce* case, Guthrie did so with mind, heart and soul.[59]

Guthrie believed the Catholic parochial schools not only had a constitutional right to function but, far beyond that defensive claim, should be reimbursed for the savings they brought to local governments.[60] He did not urge a mechanical formula for he did not wish to supplant or harm the public schools. In fact, his ideas about government payments to parochial schools were trial balloons for he thought that talk was needed, that the subject should be opened up to discussion.

He was obsessed by the claim that at that time "the immediate saving to the City of New York alone from the parochial schools was fully $7,500,000 per annum, and that not one penny of this saving was being contributed by the City or State to the cost of educating and training these Catholic children."[61]

During a time when Catholics were under attack from many Protestants, Guthrie's sword was inappropriate for many in the church who believed in stressing the shield. Guthrie complained there was "altogether too much temporizing and compromising for fear of stirring up religious prejudice."[62] He was prepared for temporary setbacks because he was convinced of long-run success. In 1920, Guthrie was still militantly urging this position.

Guthrie's public pronouncements were of particular concern to Hayes. As chancellor of the archdiocese after 1903 and auxiliary bishop to John Cardinal Farley beginning in 1914, Hayes was a key man in educational politics in New York State even before he was created a cardinal in 1924. In the New York State Constitutional Convention of 1915 he was in regular touch with Guthrie, and with Catholics who were members of key committees there. Hayes was exceedingly pleased with Guthrie's performance, and he told him so directly, to Guthrie's great satisfaction.[63] Hayes sincerely respected Guthrie's abilities and influence which was all the more reason why the lawyer could not be permitted publicly to advocate government aid to parochial schools. Now, in 1920, the secretary to Archbishop Hayes asked the leader of the Catholic Educational Association to convey this to Guthrie:

... I write to advise you that his Grace, the Most Reverend Archbishop, would like you to write very frankly to Mr. Guthrie and tell him that it has been consistently maintained by the hierarchy that it would be inopportune to bring up the question of partial support for our parochial schools from public funds. As we all know, there is a division of opinion among the hierarchy on the subject, and it has been quite generally agreed that such an agitation at this time would be highly inopportune.

It is also suggested by his Grace that you intimate to Mr. Guthrie the advisability and propriety of calling to see Archbishop Hayes at his earliest convenience and before determining upon the scope of his paper for the conference. I trust that this letter is quite clear.[64]

The archbishop of New York was the prime leader of American Catholics by this time. While the church in America never enjoyed a perfectly ordered, unanimous facade, the numbers and wealth, traditions and talent of the New York archdiocese placed it in the forefront. It was Hayes's decision in the 1920s to battle against Progressive programs of maternity aid, child labor regulation and federal aid to education. This appealed to conservative Protestants and to many Catholics who shared Hayes's fear that government programs designed to protect mothers, children and benefit the public schools would bring an unwanted secularism that would impair traditional religious and family relationships.

Protestant and Jewish Briefs

The arguments made by Lutherans, Episcopalians and Seventh Day Adventists in the 1922 campaign in Oregon were elaborated and turned toward constitutional points in briefs *amici curiae* for these groups in the Supreme Court. John Veatch again represented the Hill Military Academy so that there was marked participation by Protestants in the litigation. This was not merely the inclination of church leaders but also expressed the strategy that William D. Guthrie and Louis Marshall, a lawyer leading the American Jewish Committee, agreed was wise. Each was familiar with nativist Protestants who, by hating Jews and Catholics, called themselves one hundred percent Americans, but Ku Klux Klan members could better be described as two hundred percent Americans for they hated the whole human race![65] One observer has spoken of the geographical ubiquity of the KKK.

The new Klan was anti-Negro in the South, anti-Japanese in California, anti-Mexican in the Southwest, anti-Catholic in the Midwest, even anti-French-Canadian in New England, and anti-Semitic where Jews had not "assimilated."[66]

The Klan had to be fought, but how to fight it was what worried Louis Marshall. This question of strategy comes up often in American political life for those who wish to halt the appeal of a radical or reactionary person, organization or movement. One approach is to enter the field of political combat head-on in a duel, another to ignore the opponent. In this instance it was Marshall's view that an indirect fight should be made—but in the name of, and by, Protestants rather than by Jews, Negroes and Catholics, who were chief targets of the Ku Klux Klan. He thought the best way to fight was through the Protestant churches because the Klan masqueraded as a Protestant organization. This was quite an elaborate view of tactics for he believed it was up to

the American people to repudiate the tenets of Klanism; Marshall felt that they must find the Klan an insult to their intelligence, and regard its iniquitous doctrines with contempt and impatience. As President of the American Jewish Committee, he was adamant in seeking to prevent a controversy between the Klan and the Jews. He argued that the B'nai B'rith, as a Jewish secret society, should not attempt to combat the Klan; it was the very secrecy of the Klan which was deplored and feared, and it had to be fought in the open. The Klan, he noted, had attacked the Knights of Columbus for being a secret organization. He also cautioned strongly against Catholics and Negroes taking public action against the work of the Klan, because by such opposition, Catholics, Negroes and Jews could be accepting a challenge which he looked upon as beneath the dignity of all three groups. Fearing reprisals and recriminations that Catholics and Jews were attacking Protestantism, he declined to offer any financial assistance to anti-Klan candidates in the South.[67]

Catholic leaders believed the Klan should not be met with a frontal attack and that, if ignored, it would go away. This was not the universal approach toward the Klan though it was shared by Guthrie and Marshall. Another preeminent member of the New York bar, John W. Davis, felt obliged to speak out against the Klan during his campaign in 1924 as the Democratic candidate for president.[68] Here was a Protestant speaking, just the man in Marshall's view to condemn the intolerance and prejudice of the Klan. Marshall was deeply disappointed when conservatives, especially a fellow Republican like Calvin Coolidge, did not come out against the Klan in the mid-1920s while the Progressives, led by Robert M. LaFollette, did so.

Yet in this major litigation of *Pierce v. Society of the Sisters*, with Masons and the Klan having promoted the school law and with Masons making the major defense effort in the courts, Marshall believed Jews should join in the alliance to have the law invalidated. His friend Guthrie appealed to Marshall for help and their briefs were complementary.[69]

What resulted was a rather spectacular set of briefs on behalf of the constitutionality of private and parochial schools, insisting that the American system of education did and should include options for students, parents, teachers, administrators and benefactors. Truly, on this side of the question against the validity of the Oregon law which gave the state a monopoly in education, there was an array of interests and arguments which make the proceeding seem more like a major legislative hearing than a litigation between two parties. Both sides were in earnest and the law, if untouched by legislative repeal or judicial review, would put private and parochial schools out of business in Oregon.

There were main briefs for the parties, one by William D. Guthrie and another by the Oregon Catholics led by John Kavanaugh on behalf of the Society of the Sisters. John Veatch prepared a brief for the Hill Military Academy and, with Guthrie and Kavanaugh, appeared in oral argument before the Court in its Old Senate Chamber on March 16 and 17, 1925. Separate *amici curiae* briefs were also filed for the American Jewish Committee, the Lutherans, Episcopalians and Seventh Day Adventists. These churches ran some parochial schools but they were widely scattered and, in fact, there were no Jewish schools in Oregon.

As a matter of national public policy these lawyers argued the value of alternatives, of pluralism in education. Variety in schooling was touted as superior and, of course, as the American way. The Oregon law was spoken of repeatedly as giving the state a "monopoly" over education, a monopoly which would end competition and lower standards. "If the children of the country are to be educated upon a dead level of uniformity and by a single method," said Marshall's brief for the American Jewish Committee, "then eventually our nation would consist of mechanical robots and standardized Babbitts."

The constitutional claims made in these several briefs were also repetitious, developing along the same lines used in and accepted by the federal district court. This was a ground-breaking case. The Court had little experience with claims made on behalf of religious liberty nor had they much with litigation concerning education. This was true for the lawyers and they consequently sang the familiar strains of the taking away of property without due process of law. Thus the battle was at two levels, one over social policy and the other over the application of constitutional phrases then in vogue which could most readily be called up as a basis for making the invalidation of the Oregon school law stand.

Pluralism in American Education

That the Supreme Court should go against Governor Pierce, the Oregon electorate and the Masonic sponsors of the appeal and go against them unanimously nine to zero seems something of a marvel. In simple institutional terms there were a number of things the decision accorded with, however. The Court was accustomed to holding state legislation invalid on grounds of due process violations. The fact that the legislation was adopted as an initiative measure in Oregon would not have been held against it but neither was this any consideration in the minds of those justices for upholding the measure. A three-judge federal district court had already enjoined enforcement of the law and so the nine members of the Supreme Court were affirming the court below. Nor was this legislation sweeping the country. Efforts to enact similar laws had been attempted in a few states but the Klan movement, the strength of the Masons and of Fundamentalist Protestants were, in general, only strong enough to cause turmoil and consternation. Moreover, the arguments of Chamberlain, of McCamant for Van Winkle, tended toward an excessiveness that was far to the right of members of the Court, who were themselves staunch conservatives.

It is interesting that Mr. Justice James Clark McReynolds prepared and delivered the opinion of the Supreme Court in *Pierce v. Society of the Sisters* as he was, perhaps, its most provincial member in terms of the geography of the mind. A Protestant from Tennessee, he was not a man of cosmopolitan breadth like Holmes, Brandeis or Sutherland or Chief Justice Taft. That there was an occasion for such an opinion is also a curiosity, for the kind of pluralism in education which has for decades characterized the United States did not originate or flow from this decision. Rather it can be said only that the *Pierce* case afforded an occasion for the Court to speak and, in a sense, to give some ordered legitimacy to the kind of dual system at the elementary and secondary levels of education enjoyed in the country.

In affirming the lower court's ruling against the constitutionality of a state compulsory education statute which seeks to outlaw private and parochial school education the Supreme Court was riding with the status quo. Enforcing the ruling was simple. In Oregon, the schools conducted by the Society of the Sisters and other Catholic and church-affiliated schools as well as the Hill Military Academy and other nonsectarian schools continued to operate without question. In other states, similar legislation had this further strike against it and no similar legislation has been enacted. Clearly, the Court was not asking for the establishment of more private schools; it was simply saying that their creation could not be stopped by a state.

This was the first of the landmark constitutional cases on the relationship of government to religious education. We shall have occasion, later, to reflect on the fact that five decades after the Oregon episode was won by cosmopolitan forces seeking diversity in education, there arose a strong movement by racial separatists to champion private schools and, if necessary, to dismantle the public school in the process. The opposing religious forces in the *Pierce* case in Oregon in the early 1920s make a poignant contrast to the contest over the schools today on the issue of racial integration.

The Movement to Protect Workers

7 The Brandeis Brief

For the first third of the twentieth century, until the transitional period 1937-41, the legal position of trade unions and the constitutionality of numerous forms of protective labor legislation were debated steadily in the press and universities, in party meetings and public forums, in state legislatures and Congress and, of course, in the courts. The police power of the states—that is, the inherent power of government to attend to the health, welfare and morals of its citizens—was generally sufficient for courts to justify the prohibition of alcoholic beverages, to ban birth-control clinics, limit prostitution and censor obscene books and magazines, proscribe racial integration both in public places and in marriage. We have seen that the Supreme Court of the United States also approved a state eugenical sterilization law.

There is no single "police power" clause for the federal government in the American Constitution, but the Court has found adequate authority elsewhere for national regulation of practices offensive to members of Congress. Again, this was approved by the Court when Congress acted on sex and morals. Then the judiciary relied on the commerce, postal and tax clauses. The power of Congress "to regulate Commerce with foreign nations, and among the several states, and with the Indian tribes," gradually became the most used basis for assertion of a federal police power. For instance, the federal Lottery Act of 1895, penalizing the interstate carriage of lottery tickets, was sustained as constitutional by the Supreme Court in 1903.[1] In its ambition to protect morals, Congress frequently used its prohibitory powers to support the states. The Webb-Kenyon Act of 1913, as we have seen, helped dry states to enforce prohibition. The Mann "White Slave Traffic" Act of 1910, upheld in the *Hoke* case and broadened in *Caminetti*, demonstrates that both Congress and the Court saw the national police power as virtually limitless when the regulated practices were sufficiently scorned.[2]

The Populists of the 1890s and the Progressives in the twentieth century brought into public life a "new morality," not readily accommodated under the police power. The new morality saw capitalist and industrialist, rather than gambler, pimp and bootlegger, as sinning against society. Factory conditions were deplorable, city slums loathsome, housing horrendous, the legal rights of children, women and all workers in dangerous industries virtually nonexistent. A social movement emerged in the 1890s to study these conditions and act against them. The movement was led by no one person but was, rather, an amalgamation of brilliant critics like Lincoln Steffens and Upton Sinclair; dedicated young

163

women like Florence Kelley and Jane Addams; able lawyers like Clarence Darrow and Louis D. Brandeis; and politicians like Robert LaFollette and Hiram Johnson—all innovators creating new social institutions, novel legislation, sophisticated sanctions and inducements and changing conceptions of constitutional law.

For a generation or more they worked toward governmental protections for employees' safety on the job, humane hours, a living wage, compensation for injuries, unemployment insurance and retirement security. They focused on particular deprivations at certain points, on the untrained immigrant, child labor, migrant labor or night work for women. An untoward event such as the Pullman Strike of 1895 elevated Governor John Peter Altgeld of Illinois and Eugene V. Debs in the radical imagination. The Triangle Laundry Fire in New York in 1911 evoked public feeling for conditions in the needle trades and their championship by the International Ladies Garment Workers' Union—the ILGWU. The Danbury Hatters Case, won for the employers by the American Anti-Boycott Association in litigation that dragged on for fifteen years after 1902, aroused enormous public sympathy for the workers because of the treble damages awarded by the court.

Through the half century from 1890 to 1940 the Populists, Progressives and Liberals were insurgents on the make, gradually persuading the majority of the rightfulness of government intervention to protect both unions and unorganized workers. They argued that the police power afforded correct constitutional grounds to support these assertions of governmental power. Lawyers for business interests who had often convinced judges of the primacy of constitutional limitations during the first three-and-a-half decades of the twentieth century found their arguments unavailing from 1937 on. These interests, which had hallowed the judicial process and the power of the courts and had questioned the amendment process, now shifted their faith in institutions and their governmental philosophy to fit new conditions.

The social workers, economists, politicians and lawyers who believed in protective labor legislation and in trade unionism thought out and learned the strategy and tactics of American constitutional change as they went along. They did not always foresee the particular obstacles to be encountered in their quest for reform. They were interested in improving the lot of ordinary men, women and children and, while they were ready to fight for their altruistic beliefs, they did not appreciate in advance that sweeping constitutional changes would be required. In fact, they became engaged in constitutional warfare at just about every conceivable level: winning federal and state legislation, working for amendments to the Constitution, criticizing the judicial function as practiced by conservative activists, attacking the right-wing bar and its associations, being concerned with judicial appointments and—in that connection—fighting off the conservative attack on President Wilson's nomination of Louis D. Brandeis in 1916 and joining the successful assault on President Hoover's nomination of John J. Parker to the Supreme Court in 1930.

A degree of specialization and coincident interlocking cooperation marked individual careers and organizations moving toward these goals. The settlement houses in Boston, New York, Rochester, Cleveland, Chicago and elsewhere were educational and research centers generating and encouraging reform. Small networks clustered around particular issues: the National Consumers' League concentrated on state wage and hour legislation; the National Child Labor Conference worked for national legislation and then a child labor amendment; the American Association for Labor Legislation was more of an academic clearinghouse especially concerned with the plight of organized labor.

Rivalry arose over the scarce resources of votes and money, over priorities, over strategy and tactics, and came when strong personalities like Florence Kelley and Felix Frankfurter clashed. In what seemed to opponents to be a monolithic force, there were also fundamental differences in the labor reform movement. There were deep ideological differences between Socialists and Communists on the one hand, and between them and traditional go-slow incrementalists on the other. Women divided after 1920 between the militant National Woman's Party working for an equal rights amendment and those who favored statutory protection for women and, indeed, all workers. Some like Jeanette Rankin and Rosika Schwimmer concerned themselves chiefly with pacifism and political rights.

Perhaps the most divisive conflict among champions of working people affecting the struggle for legislation and for the constitutional acceptance of that legislation was between trade union leaders and leaders of voluntary associations such as the NAACP and National Consumers' League. Here a man like Samuel Gompers saw a clear self-interest for his American Federation of Labor in organizing a trade, limiting entrance into it and bargaining hard with an employer for the best possible conditions of work. He distrusted government intrusion. Gompers consequently shared neither the goals nor the techniques of social reform organizations seeking to improve the lot of the unorganized who could not or would not help themselves.

Opposition to legislation and workers' rights was similarly specialized, overlapping and beset with disagreement. Industries differed from each other and there was economic competition within a field. Business leaders scaled from intransigence to those who welcomed unionization and protective legislation. As in earlier parts of the book we will follow especially the prominent lawyers who represented conservative interests.

The time span of the book affords opportunities to note two major transitions for members of the bar. The first concerns lawyers who led the fight against the Eighteenth Amendment, who witnessed the 1932 election, then repeal and, finally, the unveiling and progress of the New Deal. This will take the form of a discussion of the famous National Lawyers' Committee of the American Liberty League, composed of some sixty attorneys who insisted, in pamphlets and radio talks and eventually at the bar of the Supreme Court, on the unconstitutionality of a dozen or more New Deal statutes.

Another question concerns the adjustment of both friend and foe to a realignment (perhaps this would today be called restructuring) of national institutions as the presidency and Supreme Court were liberalized and the Congress and the constitutional amendment process became tilted in a more conservative direction. This is a subject that will be opened up in this part of the book but elaborated upon in the succeeding part.

We will look at promise and reality; at rhetoric and compliance. Again the treatment is topical and selective. It will be seen that even in identical topics the precise path from emergence as a public issue to constitutional accommodation can be radically different. These contrasts in shading explain why we will now consider, from the turn of the century to about 1940, the topics of maximum hours, minimum wages, collective bargaining, social security and child labor. The ordering follows the calendar of the ruling of constitutionality, not of the origin or recognition of the problem.

National Consumers' League Lawyers

Beginning in 1899 the National Consumers' League aided in the successful struggle to enact, enforce and defend protective labor legislation. The publication in the 1930s of magazines to inform shoppers of the best buy, and the "new consumerism" of the 1970s has eclipsed the NCL's idealistic purpose in organizing "to have consumers use their buying power, their economic and political power, to compel the payment of decent wages."[3] Consumer action as a method of reform developed during the 1890s when many men and, especially, educated women became conscience-stricken over the miserable working conditions created by industrialism.[4] Correction came only after the public was aroused, and this came only after facts and figures about conditions were provided. The leaders were individuals who did not experience in their own daily lives the factory working conditions they sought to change. Rather they were shocked by the very helplessness of the men, women and children whom they acted to protect.

In the first years of the twentieth century, activity in consumer organizations had great prestige among socially prominent women across the country. Directors or officers of state leagues included the names of Choate, Morgan and Vanderbilt in New York; Gardiner, Lawrence, Peabody, Phillips and Shaw in Massachusetts; Fels in Pennsylvania; Garfield, Hanna and Mather in Ohio; Kent, McCormick and Root in Illinois; and Sensenbrenner in Wisconsin. Not only did the society leaders in the league contribute most of the money, but they also participated actively in the work of the league. This was true of Eleanor Roosevelt and Frances Perkins, both of whom devoted much time to the organization during its early years.

As a true federation of organizations in the North and West, state consumer leagues often enjoyed the endorsement, wealth and leadership of the outstanding civic leaders of the day. After service as attorney general, Charles J. Bonaparte served as president of the Consumers' League of Maryland and won the praise of James Cardinal Gibbons for its goals. In Massachusetts, Edward A. Filene backed the league for proving that "the consumer can exert a decisive influence over business, if he will take the trouble." Filene is best known for his department store, its famous "automatic bargain basement," his association with Lincoln Steffens in the "Boston 1915" movement and his establishment and endowment of the Twentieth Century Fund to perpetuate research into social and economic change. This was the type of man drawn into NCL activity.[5]

The life of Florence Kelley is almost a biography of the National Consumers' League since she served as its general secretary from its origin in 1899 until her death in 1931. Her qualifications for the position were ideal. Daughter of William D. Kelley, a Pennsylvania congressman known as "Pig Iron" because of his protectionist views, she early gained a firm grasp of public affairs and politics. One of the first women to graduate from Cornell University, Florence Kelley also earned a law degree from Northwestern. After college she studied for three years in Zurich. Here she became interested in socialism and translated into English Friedrich Engels's *The Condition of the Working Class in England*. Her personal acquaintance with Engels and her assertion that she was a Socialist made Florence Kelley in her lifetime and beyond a target of obloquy by pious critics of the programs she endorsed.[6]

Back in the United States with two children after an unsuccessful marriage in Europe, she resumed her maiden name but with a "Mrs." in front of it. Soon Florence Kelley was a resident of Hull House, an intimate friend of Jane Addams, the settlement-house leader, and of Henry Demarest Lloyd, author of *Wealth Against Commonwealth*. These early associations with reformers continued, and it was typical that she was a director of the National Association for the Advancement of Colored People from 1909 to her death. Mrs. Kelley obtained practical experience in improving the conditions of labor after 1893, when she was appointed by Governor John P. Altgeld to be chief inspector of factories for Illinois. In 1899 she was called to New York to conduct the work of the National Consumers' League.

As we shall see, Mrs. Kelley understood the difficulties of improving the conditions of work throughout the country, and her strategy was as broad as the problems she faced. Her time was divided between lecturing, writing, and directing the organization of the Consumers' League at national headquarters on Henry Street in New York City. Felix Frankfurter recalled that "Florence Kelley was one of a galaxy of wonderful women with whom she worked—Jane Addams, Julia Lathrop, Lillian D. Wald, Grace and Edith Abbott, Alice Hamilton, among others. Florence Kelley seemed at the time, and remains in memory, the most salient, salty character of them all."[7]

On the professional staff of the National Consumers' League, Mrs. Kelley's main support came from Josephine Goldmark. As chairman of the league's important Committee on Legislation, Miss Goldmark directed some of the early campaigns for reform. Then from 1908 until 1915 she worked closely with Louis Brandeis, her brother-in-law, in the defense of legislation in the courts. She survived Mrs. Kelley by twenty years, during which time she provided a good deal of informal direction to league affairs. Her sister, Pauline Goldmark, working chiefly for the New York Consumers' League, contributed to the publications of the national league.

In the twenties, a new generation of women enlisted to carry on the work of the league. To the national office came Jeannette Rankin, who had, as congresswoman from Montana, cast a vote against America's entry into World War I in 1917 and was to do the same in 1941. Miss Rankin assisted Mrs. Kelley, traveling around the country as a lecturer. At the same time, Mary W. Dewson took over much of Josephine Goldmark's work in economic and social research.

The presidents of the National League during these years were a distinguished and active group of men. First was John Graham Brooks, Bostonian, Unitarian and independent social scientist who wrote many books, including *The Social Unrest* and *Labor's Challenge to the Social Order*. On vacating the office after sixteen years, Brooks was honorary president of the league until his death in 1938 at ninety-one. In 1915 Newton D. Baker succeeded to the presidency of the league. In 1923 John R. Commons became president and continued in office until 1935. The last in line for the period before 1938 under study was John G. Winant, liberal governor of New Hampshire, first chairman of the Social Security Board, and later American ambassador to Great Britain.

A number of college professors in the social sciences contributed intellectual assistance to the National Consumers' League during its most active years. Lawyers also played important functions in drafting model legislation, defending the position of the league in court cases, and advising on the constitutional problems of the day. Louis Brandeis was preeminent as counsel until 1916, when he was appointed to the Supreme Court. His successor was Felix Frankfurter, then a professor at Harvard Law School. Newton Baker, Benjamin Cohen and Dean Acheson were among the attorneys who assisted The National Consumers' League during the early New Deal.

Consumers' League Political Action

Early experience taught the National Consumers' League to take different actions to achieve its objective of raising standards of employment for women and children. Devoted supporters could make a personal contribution to the league's purpose through alert shopping. The principles of the organization declared it to be "the duty of consumers to find out under what conditions the articles they purchased are produced and distributed, and insist that these conditions shall be wholesome and consistent with a respectable existence on the part of the workers."[8]

The league made it practical for members to live up to these ideals. Led by Florence Kelley, volunteers acting as private factory inspectors persuaded manufacturers of ladies underwear to stitch on their goods the Consumers' League label signifying that production had taken place under satisfactory working conditions. In 1903, this meant that "the state factory law is obeyed; all the goods are made on the premises; overtime is not worked; children under sixteen years of age are not employed." Although the use of the label declined after 1917, when it was generally superseded by the union label, the Consumers' League continued through the years to emphasize direct action through boycotts by the shopping public.

Intelligent consumption based on investigation and education was an approach to the problem of working conditions which necessarily laid great stress on publicity. The location of the league with other organizations at the United Charities Building in New York afforded important advantages, as *The Survey*, *The Outlook* and related magazines edited there over a period of years served almost as house organs for the Consumers' League.

The legislative accomplishments of the Consumers' League came from careful research, clear goals and involved alliances. Commonly, after study and wide consultation, the league drafted a model bill on maximum hours, night work for women, child labor and other subjects. In 1910, for example, a model minimum wage bill was drawn up, and in 1912 it was first enacted in Massachusetts. Through the work of state and local consumers' leagues, especially the same model soon afterward became law in twelve other states and the District of Columbia. This pattern was repeated on other issues and at the national level, too, through alliances of the league with organizations like the American Association for Labor Legislation and the National Child Labor Committee.[9]

When statutes were on the books, Mrs. Kelley and Miss Goldmark, unlike some reformers, showed acute insight into the cycle of policy-making by focusing the attention of the National Consumers' League on public administration. Mrs. Kelley's experience in factory inspection for the state of Illinois had taught her useful lessons in dealing with the administrative branches of government, and she incorporated these in her teachings.

Following the work of getting legislation comes the less exciting task of enforcing it. Nowhere are there enough factory inspectors for the effective enforcement of the child labor laws. In some states, notably in Pennsylvania, an annual inspection is all that is regularly attempted. To meet this dearth women have made during the present year efforts to secure the appointment of women as inspectors in Minnesota and Connecticut.

It is desirable that in every state in which there is a Consumers' League the effort might be continued until crowned with success for the increase of the number of inspectors, and the addition of women to the staff.[10]

By 1906 fifteen states had women factory inspectors. Some of these women were also members of the Consumers' League, carrying organizational zeal directly into the job of enforcing the new laws. Where direct control of administration was absent, Mrs. Kelley requested "all state and local leagues to make investigations within their own territory into the hours of labor and the wages and cost of living of working women and girls." She would "gladly furnish suggestions as to methods of procedure." Mrs. Kelley's interest in conducting these inquiries meant that the league was armed with facts to use before legislative committees or to nudge officials charged with enforcing the law.

Defense of Maximum Hour Laws

The third branch of government was not neglected by Mrs. Kelley, for when the courts ruled against the constitutionality of statutes advocated by the league, she responded with the same methods of action used to win legislative and administrative victories. Her faith in organization, in fact finding, and in education, as well as her belief in eventual progress is shown in her reaction to an adverse judicial decision before the turn of the century. When the Illinois Supreme Court, in 1895, invalidated an eight-hour law for women,[11] Mrs. Kelley pointed out that maximum hours legislation had been upheld in many states and had long been in force in Europe. She continued, caustically,

It remained for the Supreme Court of Illinois to discover that the amendment to the Constitution of the United States passed for the purpose of guaranteeing the Negro from oppression, has become an insuperable obstacle to the protection of women and children. Nor is it reasonable to suppose that this unique interpretation of the fourteenth amendment will be permanently maintained, even in Illinois.[12]

Developments proved Mrs. Kelley right. The *Ritchie* decision with respect to maximum hours for women was reversed in 1910,[13] but the courts did not universally accept her view on minimum wages until twenty-five years later. Although Florence Kelley had a remarkable insight into the total governmental process, her own emphasis on the enforcement of laws left the direction of court cases to Josephine Goldmark. In dealing with problems, the leadership of the league was eminently practical.

By its 1905 decision in *Lochner v. New York*[14] holding unconstitutional a ten-hour law for bakers, the Supreme Court polarized itself and the nation between those who advocated or acquiesced in Progressive reform by legislation and those galvanized to stop most government regulation of employment practices. A five-to-four Court made clear through Mr. Justice Peckham it would decide whether a legislative act was within the constitutional police power of a state. Statistics about health might show the trade of a baker rife with health problems but, asked Peckham, "are we all, on that account, at the mercy of the legislative majorities?" It seemed capricious for the Supreme Court to uphold in 1898 a Utah act limiting mine workers to an eight-hour day[15] and seven years later to strike down a ten-hour law for bakers.

In *Lochner* separate dissents by Justices Harlan and Holmes showed somewhat different philosophies of the judicial function at work. Mr. Justice Harlan was satisfied the legislature had acted reasonably considering the abundance of medical testimony before them. But Mr. Justice Holmes was more deferential as he chastized the majority and contended that the Court should presume the validity of economic legislation. Only if a statute infringed "fundamental principles as they have been understood by the traditions of our people and our law" would Holmes move from a posture of judicial restraint to activism. This dissent won for Holmes something of a reputation as a supporter of reform though in the long run it has been well understood as a classic statement of his concept of the judicial function in a democratic society. The *Lochner* decision is a benchmark in many ways—too many to treat here—but by its retreat from 1898 by a close decision, the Court would move uncertainly for years on a case by case basis concerning varied kinds of protective labor legislation, maximum hour laws included.

Though it later approved many types of hour legislation, the Supreme Court has never had occasion to review *Lochner v. New York* and overrule that 1905 case explicitly.[16] It was this uncertainty that made the National Consumers' League determined to work fiercely for the constitutionality of the Oregon ten-hour law for women laundry workers, up for Supreme Court review in the 1907-08 term.

Some members of the NCL executive committee looked to Joseph H. Choate, the leader of the New York bar, as the natural man to defend the Oregon hour law. They felt that a first-class lawyer would make all the difference in the Supreme Court, and that Choate had knowledge of the subject. Florence Kelley did not agree as she recognized that the value preferences or opinions men have ordinarily affect how they utilize their skills. This applied to professional men, lawyers, too. Choate was not sympathetic to protective labor legislation. Even if he took the case it was doubtful he would or even could bring his ample imagination and legal scholarship fully to bear in its preparation. By chance Mrs. Kelley missed a meeting of the committee (a rarity for her) and she felt obliged to follow instructions and seek the services of Choate. To her relief, he declined. She and Josephine Goldmark were then free to follow their inclination to seek the aid of a lawyer whose passion would match his high ability.

Brandeis was fifty years old when Florency Kelley and Josephine Goldmark asked him in 1907 to guide the defense of the Oregon ten-hour law in the Supreme Court. Born in Louisville and educated in that city and in Dresden, Germany, and graduated from the Harvard Law School in 1877 as preeminent in student achievement of all classes, Brandeis practiced law briefly in St. Louis.

Soon he went back to Boston, where he built a lucrative law practice with Samuel D. Warren and the successor firm of Brandeis, Dunbar and Nutter. Brandeis attracted industrial, commercial and business clients by the score once his shrewdness as a counselor became well known. He was a millionaire by 1907 and many times that again by the time he reached the Supreme Court in 1916. His biographer has distilled the democratic outlook which won for Brandeis the sobriquet, "people's attorney," years before he became a justice:

Driving him on was the conviction that bigness and monopoly are inimical to efficiency, true *laissez faire*, and democracy. Brandeis saw the rise of the masses, organized in trade unions and other social groups, as the natural outcome of a changed and changing social order. Power was moving from the few to the many. It was not informed statesmanship to try to freeze privilege or to thwart change indiscriminately; neither was it desirable or safe to stand aloof from the struggle. The reformer's role was to guide the forces of social experimentation and thus to direct change along the lines of evolution rather than revolution.[17]

It was only in 1907 that Mrs. Kelley fully appreciated how unwilling employers would be to accept the program of the National Consumers' League, how quickly they would seek judicial relief and how successful they would be in thwarting unwanted legislation through litigation. Josephine Goldmark had been a member of the wedding when her eldest sister Alice Goldmark was married to Brandeis in 1891. Both spinsters who worked off and on with the National Consumers' League for a lifetime, Josephine and Pauline Goldmark were close to Louis and Alice Brandeis as family, as intellectuals, as reformers. Yet Josephine Goldmark was uncertain about the outcome as she and Mrs. Kelley went to Boston to ask for help.

As we know, Brandeis agreed to take command. His appearance as counsel for the State Industrial Commission in *Muller v. Oregon* was the first of a series of appellate court cases in which the National Consumers' League provided defenses of labor legislation.[18]

Josephine Goldmark has related further what Brandeis told her would be needed for a brief, "namely, *facts*, published by anyone with expert knowledge of industry in its relation to women's hours of labor, such as factory inspectors, physicians, trades unions, economists, social workers." If she could return in two weeks to Boston "with such printed matter, sufficiently authoritative to pass muster," she and Brandeis would then work up the material into a brief.[19] The *Outlook* magazine praised what then took place, as follows:

... Miss Josephine Goldmark, of the League, delved into the libraries—Columbia University Library, the Astor Library, and the Congressional Library were put at her service. Ten readers were employed. One, a young medical student, devoted himself solely to reading on the hygiene of occupation. It is significant that there is a lack of American statistics on this subject; there is plenty of opinion; the general conditions are a matter of common knowledge; but what we need are specific facts. Europe is ahead of America in this respect, and the foreign medical opinions are among the most impressive which were ultimately incorporated in the brief.

It is only a lawyer with a broad view and large mind who would do what Mr. Brandeis did—go before the Supreme Court of the United States with a brief of one hundred and thirteen pages, of which only two pages could be construed as a strictly legal argument. The result of this impressive presentation of facts was a unanimous decision by the Court that the present and future mothers of the race are worthy of defense against the greed of man.[20]

The Supreme Court in 1908, though little changed from its membership of three years before when it ruled against the New York bakery law for men, upheld the Oregon ten-hour law for women in laundries. The opinion of the Court by Mr. Justice David J. Brewer, moreover, not only cited but actually commended the brief submitted by Brandeis as providing convincing evidence that the Oregon legislature had acted reasonably. The facts that had impressed the legislators also impressed the justices, as Brandeis, Goldmark and Kelley had hoped. But because the *Muller* ruling was limited to one sex, in one industry, and for ten hours, it was not the end of uncertainty for hour legislation. Statutes for each sex, in other industries and for different hours, would also have to run the gauntlet of constitutional testing.

Much of the litigation ended in state courts, but Brandeis filed briefs in the three test cases carried by employers to the Supreme Court. Two of these from California concerned women and were unanimously approved by the Court in opinions by Mr. Justice Charles Evans Hughes prior to his resignation to become the Republican presidential candidate in 1916.[21] The subject of hour legislation was finally eased away from Supreme Court surveillance when the Oregon ten-hour law for men employed in manufacturing was sustained by a five to three division. This came in *Bunting v. Oregon,* a case also sponsored by the National Consumers' League. No mention of the *Lochner* case was made in either the *Muller* or *Bunting* opinions, but the constitutional power of states to regulate hours of employment for both men and women was thenceforth firmly established.

The alignment of justices sitting on six state maximum hour law cases from 1898 to 1917 shows unanimous approval in the three cases concerning women employees but dissents in all three cases concerning men (see table 7-1). The Brandeis-Goldmark briefs had stressed feminine frailty and Mr. Justice Brewer had made much of this in his opinion in *Muller v. Oregon.* This evidently appealed across the whole bench in *Muller, Miller* and *Bosley* as fourteen different justices approved of both ten-hour and eight-hour laws in varied occupations, none dangerous. Hour laws for men were a different matter. This seems never to have been analyzed carefully; Corwin is wrong in attributing the increase of two disapprovals of Utah mine hours to five of New York bakery hours to the predisposition of "a radically altered Court."[22] The changes in

Table 7-1

Justices' Alignment on Approval of State Maximum Hour Laws, 1898-1917

Appointment order of Justices from Harlan to Clarke	Dates of Service	Holden (1898) 7 to 2	Lochner (1905) 4 to 5	Muller (1908) 9 to 0	Miller (1915) 9 to 0	Bosley (1915) 9 to 0	Bunting (1917) 5 to 3
Harlan	1877-1911	+	+	+			
Woods	1880-1887						
Matthews	1881-1889						
Gray	1881-1902	+					
Blatchford	1882-1893						
Lamar, L.	1888-1893						
Fuller (C.J.)	1888-1910	+	−	+			
Brewer	1889-1910	−	−	+			
Brown	1890-1906	+	−				
Shiras	1892-1903	+					
Jackson	1893-1895						
White	1894-1921	+	+	+	+	+	−
White (C.J.)	1910-1921						
Peckham	1895-1910	−	−	+			
McKenna	1898-1925	+	−	+	+	+	+
Holmes	1902-1932		+	+	+	+	+
Day	1903-1922		+	+	+	+	+
Moody	1906-1910			+			
Lurton	1910-1914						
Hughes	1910-1916				+	+	
Van Devanter	1911-1937				+	+	−
Lamar, J.	1911-1916				+	+	
Pitney	1912-1922				+	+	+
McReynolds	1914-1941				+	+	−
Brandeis	1916-1939						n.p.
Clarke	1916-1922						+

Holden v. Hardy, 169 U.S. 366 (1898). An 1896 Utah statute limiting the period of employment of workmen in underground mines, or in the refining of ores or metals, to eight hours a day was ruled valid under the state police power by the Utah Supreme Court. U.S. Supreme Court affirmed, 7-2, in an opinion by Mr. Justice Brown. Brewer and Peckham dissented without opinion.

Lochner v. New York, 198 U.S. 46 (1905). The 1897 labor law of New York included a provision that "no employee shall be required or permitted to work in a biscuit, bread, or cake bakery or confectionary establishment more than sixty hours in any one week, or more than ten hours in any one day," with certain exceptions. Three state courts ruled this provision valid. The U.S. Supreme Court reversed, 5-4, in an opinion by Mr. Justice Peckham. Separate dissenting opinions were filed by Harlan and Holmes.

Muller v. Oregon, 208 U.S. 412 (1908). In 1903 the legislature of Oregon provided "that no female (shall) be employed in any mechanical establishment, or factory, or laundry in this state more than ten hours during any one day," a statute found valid by the state supreme court. The U.S. Supreme Court affirmed, unanimously, in an opinion by Mr. Justice Brewer.

Table 7-1 (cont.)

Miller v. Wilson, 236 U.S. 373 (1915). A California eight-hour statute, adopted in 1911, applied to forbid the employment of women in hotels was held valid by the Supreme Court of California. This was affirmed unanimously by the U.S. Supreme Court in an opinion by Mr. Justice Hughes.

Bosley v. McLaughlin, 236 U.S. 385 (1915). The same statute applied to limit the hours of work of a graduate woman pharmacist, student nurses and other hospital employees was approved by the courts in the same way they had acted upon *Miller v. Wilson,* above.

Bunting v. Oregon, 243 U.S. 426 (1917). A 1913 Oregon regulation of hours of service provided that "no person shall be employed in any mill, factory, or manufacturing establishment in this state more than ten hours in any one day" with some exception that there be time-and-a-half for overtime was approved by the Oregon courts. This was affirmed, 5-3, in an opinion by Mr. Justice McKenna. Chief Justice White and Justices Van Devanter and McReynolds dissented but without opinion. Mr. Justice Brandeis took no part in the consideration and decision of the case.

membership had nothing whatever to do with it as Gray was succeeded by Holmes and Shiras by Day, all justices who approved the hour laws in the respective cases they decided.

As table 7-1 shows, Brewer and Peckham held firm while Fuller, Brown and McKenna switched from endorsing the act under review in *Holden v. Hardy* to invalidating the statute in *Lochner v. New York.* They saw mining as a dangerous occupation justifying a state limitation on hours. This was absent in bakeries and the health argument did not persuade them. The votes by Chief Justice White and McKenna in *Bunting* seem inexplicable, but the dissents of Van Devanter and McReynolds are in keeping with their career-long rage against protective labor legislation. That they were recent appointees with twenty years of judicial service ahead meant stormy constitutional weather for future progressive legislation under Supreme Court review.

The National Consumers' League victory in *Muller v. Oregon* in 1908 increased the tempo of activity and also helped transform the organization. The NCL became systematically concerned with litigation, its likelihood, usefulness and the skilled preparation of cases. "While the brief provided once and for all a new method of defense and established its basis," Miss Goldmark knew that "it needed immediate reinforcement. For at any time, Mr. Brandeis warned us, new cases might arise needing new defense."[23] In 1909 the Russell Sage Foundation granted the sum of $2,500 to the National Consumers' League for an extended study of the literature on fatigue in relation to the number of working hours. During that winter, the new material was pressed into use in the defense of a new Illinois ten-hour law for women in a state supreme court case. That victory rewarded the diligence of Miss Goldmark and Mr. Brandeis as preparations for additional cases began.

The repeated needs of the league and the frequent demand from outsiders for basic health and social data led to the publication of a full-scale study of the problem by Josephine Goldmark. An extra grant by the Russell Sage Foundation assisted the appearance of *Fatigue and Efficiency*[24] in 1912. The first 302 pages of the book deal with the nature of fatigue, physical overstrain in industry, and the regulation of the problem by legislation. This section also contains a history of labor laws and their defense in the courts. The second part of *Fatigue and Efficiency*, 591 pages in length, titled "The World's Experience Upon Which Legislation Limiting the Hours of Labor for Women Is Based," consists of material contained in the first four briefs submitted to courts by Brandeis and Goldmark. Reliance on this compendium simplified the preparation of new legal briefs.

Legal Work and Publicity

As successive cases were dealt with in the courts, the league distributed its legal briefs to a wide audience. At the very beginning it was found that "the brief has attracted very wide attention; there is demand for it from lawyers, economists, college professors and publicists."[25] In the 1910 Illinois case, a special fund of $2,500 was raised to meet the expense of printing a large edition of the brief. "This brief then was available as ammunition whenever danger threatened the now rapidly increasing legislation regulating women's hours of labor."[26] In one year this brief was used to defend laws by state attorneys in Virginia, Michigan and Louisiana. The impact of the Brandeis-Consumers' League technique on the preparation of briefs would be difficult to estimate.

The concept of publicity held by the National Consumers' League was not a narrow one restricted to assisting lawyers defending labor legislation. Rather, the league's public relations approach was calculated to educate future opinion makers. Since a bulky sociological brief was a document of primary interest to the academic world, the league worked hard to bring its message in this long form to the attention of colleges and universities. In 1917, for example, Josephine Goldmark, then chairman of the committee on publications, reported:

By means of the generous gift of $5,000 from a friend interested in the defense of labor legislation, an edition of 4,000 copies of the Bunting brief was printed, a book of about 1,000 pages, in two volumes. This brief under the title of the 'Case for the Shorter Work Day' has been widely distributed. The aim has been particularly to reach students in law schools and colleges, and a gratifying response has followed the offer to send these volumes for educational purposes.[27]

The brief prepared in the Bunting case was distributed to 462 law schools, colleges and libraries in forty-five states and was sent to 717 individuals as well.

While the distribution of briefs was a major part of the league's publicity program, annual reports, flyers and leaflets such as "The National Consumers'

League, First Quarter Century" and "Thirty-five Years of Crusading, 1899-1935" were widely circulated. Scholarly articles were sometimes reprinted at league expense.[28] In 1925, the American Fund for Public Service paid for the publication of a collection of articles on the Adkins case compiled by the Consumers' League and published by the *New Republic*.[29] The book was then given wide distribution by the league.

Conclusion

The record of the National Consumers' League in working for improved labor standards offers an example of the range of activity and the degree of improvisation demanded of an organization agitating for change through the maze of government in the American federal system. In order to gain its ends the league was forced into the legislative, administrative, litigious and constituent processes at both state and national levels. The activities of the league, especially from 1908 to 1938, when many of its initial goals had been achieved, make up a veritable model of the strategies available to an interest group in modern America.

Organizations such as this, which do not serve their own members but rather work for the protection of others, constitute perhaps a distinct category in American politics. Some might argue that the key to their success was the rightness of a cause, but the political resources of the Consumers' League were also formidable. With its strong appeal to philanthropy, the league gained adequate financial support. This same appeal drew to its leadership a small but remarkable group of devoted people endowed with intellect, energy and resourcefulness. It is these strengths which appear to account for the development of the strategy, especially in manipulating the Brandeis brief, which was the hallmark of the Consumers' League.

This organization's interest in the outcome of court cases illuminates the political position of the state attorney general, for any number of things may influence the performance of his duty to enforce the statutes of his state and to defend their constitutionality when challenged. His own political philosophy, party, factional, or group affiliations may interfere. He may lack time, funds or an adequate staff to do the job properly. Under these circumstances, anyone concerned for the defense of legislation in the courts does well to see that the attorney general is ready, willing and able to do the job. It seems safe to assume that other organizations have had to deal with this necessity.

The National Consumers' League experience in Supreme Court cases suggests reasons why organized interest groups may quite often become involved in litigation. The league had a high stake in the legal defense of protective labor legislation. It was so much more concerned than were the state attorneys general that the league regularly volunteered to take over the main responsibility in preparing legal briefs. It was organized for sustained action in the defense of labor laws and also had the intellectual leadership, political skill, legal talent and financial resources necessary for success. Formidable equipment is apparently essential for an organization actively concerned with winning constitutional cases.

Early Minimum Wage Movement

Most professional economists today question the efficacy of minimum wage legislation. They believe such laws interfere with the proper functioning of a market economy and ultimately harm the genuine interests of the very persons intended to be helped. This is true not only of Milton Friedman, a celebrated conservative economist, but of Paul Samuelson, whose famous textbook has recently been fashioned to be "relevant" to the presumed radical student readers of the 1970s. Samuelson deplores "political pressures for wage and price freezes" except in emergency periods and says of minimum wage rates: "These often hurt those they are designed to help. What good does it do a black youth to know that an employer must pay him $1.60 per hour if the fact that he must be paid that amount is what keeps him from getting a job? Experience," according to Samuelson, "has taught most economists, whether they be liberals or conservatives, that such emergency measures work very well in short emergencies but do create more and more distortions the longer they are in effect."[1] Liberal and conservative economists today also evidently agree that minimum wage legislation is perhaps "the most drastic departure from traditional economic practice," with the Fair Labor Standards Act of 1938 taking the United States "a long way in the direction of the welfare state."[2] This is not a universal belief by any means and yet is an instance not dissimilar to the modern genetic scientist's criticism of mandatory eugenical sterilization laws. The beliefs of academic experts evidently do not always accord with the law of the land. Minimum wage laws today are on the lawbooks of every state and, on account of the Fair Labor Standards Act and its amendments, reside in the *United States Code* as well. The federal minimum started at forty cents an hour in a few occupations and has been raised by Congress several times. As the 1970s began, the minimum was $1.60 an hour. This congressional action has established the minimum wage provision as politically durable just as the Supreme Court settled its constitutionality in *United States v. Fred W. Darby* on February 3, 1941.[3] The last of the judicial archenemies of New Deal legislation, Mr. Justice McReynolds, retired two days before the decision was announced. Accordingly, the eight-member Court was unanimous as Mr. Justice Stone in his opinion in the *Darby* case gave positive answers to the two principal questions raised by the record in the case,

First, whether Congress has constitutional power to prohibit the shipment in interstate commerce of lumber manufactured by employees whose wages are less than a prescribed minimum or whose weekly hours of labor at that wage are greater than a prescribed maximum, and, second, whether it has power to prohibit the employment of workmen in the production of goods "for interstate commerce" at other than prescribed wages and hours.

This landmark decision settled many matters. Most important, the Court ruled that the Constitution virtually requires Congress to protect the broad facilities of "commerce among the states" from being used by anyone, in any way, to do harm. This doctrine meant, of course, that the Fair Labor Standards Act was a clearly valid undertaking. Although wage and hour provisions were under review in *Darby*, the Court there overruled the 1918 *Hammer v. Dagenhart* decision that Congress lacked constitutional power to exclude the products of child labor from interstate commerce.[4] This ended a long era of constitutional uncertainty; from then on Congress was able to enact statutes governing hours, wages, child labor and related matters without fear of judicial contradiction. *United States v. Darby* is perhaps most famous for a by-product. By taking a broad view of the commerce power the Court eliminated the need for the child labor amendment, whose ratification by the states had been incomplete since congressional proposal in 1924. Later this book will address itself to the highlights of the constitutional struggle, from 1906 to 1941, over federal power to regulate child labor. Now the interest is in considering the natural history of minimum wage laws in a long-dead age when their constitutionality was front and center in economic, political and judicial dispute.

Constitutional changes on minimum wage laws will be discussed in stages in this chapter. First will come a review of the origination of the idea of minimum wage laws in the United States along with a sketch of John A. Ryan, the Catholic priest who urged this as one of a cluster of Progressive reforms, beginning in 1903. This will be followed by the National Consumers' League adoption in 1910 of state minimum wage laws as a key part of its legislative program. The next topic will be the first state law, in Massachusetts, and the significant work of Mary W. Dewson; and another typical law, in California, under the leadership of Katherine Philips Edson. Then will come the litigation first treating the tie-vote Supreme Court decision upholding the Oregon minimum wage law and then moving on to the movement's traumatic constitutional setback by the Supreme Court in the 1923 case of *Adkins v. Children's Hospital*. These cases covered a full decade in the history of the National Consumers' League and witnessed a change from the lawyer-social worker team of Brandeis-Goldmark to that of Frankfurter-Dewson.

Finally, in examining the *Adkins* decision, an effort has been made to identify the influence such different elements as the judges, counsel, the bar, social movements and public opinion may have had on the outcome of constitutional litigation. Key elements are thus isolated and their interaction on the timing indicated as well as the nature of judicial decisions.

A companion chapter on minimum wage litigation will follow affording an account of the exact developments from *Adkins* in 1923 to its overruling in *West Coast Hotel Co. v. Parrish* in 1937. This will facilitate consideration of the ambiguous role of the lawyers for the militant National Woman's Party as well as a continuation of the work of the National Consumers' League on the constitutional and practical problems raised in managing delicate cases. Most important, this succeeding chapter will introduce a plan for understanding Supreme Court overrulings. This will be an important exercise because over-rulings have come to rival and perhaps outshine formal amendments as a means of constitutional change.

Father Ryan's "Living Wage"

John A. Ryan was a notable figure in the minimum wage movement in several ways. He was the earliest American scholar to advocate government-required minimums. An energetic publicist and a Progressive professor priest in the Roman Catholic Church, Ryan was a durable figure in the Progressive move-ment. Those who thought Catholicism a synonym of conservatism found Ryan an enigma but, of course, specific responses to him depended in the main on political, not religious beliefs. As a liberal Catholic and as a professional economist who argued the case for wage laws and related reforms, he deserves notice.

Ryan loved politics; he played both a practical and an intellectual game. He was born on a farm near Minneapolis-St. Paul, where his parents received the New York radical weekly newspaper, *Irish World and Industrial Liberator*, edited by Patrick Ford. Ryan's father belonged to the National Farmers' Alliance and John, at twenty-three, voted the Populist ticket in the 1892 presidential election. In 1896 he was for William Jennings Bryan. By then he was filled with idealism and could lose without sadness. Ryan's exemplars in Ireland and in the United States were opponents of the government in power.

While radical in politics, Ryan was relaxed in his Americanism and in his priestly positivism. Ryan's father left Ireland in 1834 before the famine of 1845-49 demarked the old and the new emigrants as masters of fate or victims of circumstance. John Ryan was the oldest of eleven children, ten of whom grew to adulthood, with a brother also ordained and two sisters taking vows. His mother doted on him and lived near him for a time after his father's death in 1917. He excelled in school and won the favor of John Ireland, the liberal archbishop of St. Paul, who opened the doors of education to Ryan and protected him against the intrusions of parish duties. This enabled Ryan to continue as a student until he was twenty-nine, first in St. Paul Seminary and, after his ordination in 1898, in the Catholic University of America. Ryan lived the life of a gentleman and a scholar with time to study, write, speak and travel. He visited Europe and crossed the United States, often driving his own car, many times. In addition to a good salary, he had royalties and lecture fees to ensure independence.

Early Minnesota Populism contributed a share of the morality and a share of the methods of thought which marked John A. Ryan. He developed a philosophy of social action and set exact standards that public policy should achieve. His concerns were as broad as any of the Progressives of his day; he really had no pet panacea but a total program. The idea of a minimum "living wage" was his first proposal, as well as proposed first by him, yet it was part of a broad-scale approach to reform. This approach was exhibited nicely in 1909 when he prepared for the *Catholic World* "A Programme of Social Reform by Legislation." In the field of labor legislation, Ryan advocated (1) a legal minimum wage, (2) an eight-hour law, (3) protective legislation for women and children, (4) legalization of peaceful picketing and boycotting, (5) unemployment insurance and employment bureaus, (6) state provision against accident, illness and old age, (7) municipal housing. Francis Broderick has noted that a second list of proposals going beyond these placed Ryan "among the more radical progressives like Henry Demarest Lloyd rather than Theodore Roosevelt."[5] These were (1) public ownership of public utilities, (2) and of mines and forests, (3) strict control of monopolies, (4) progressive income and inheritance taxes, (5) taxation of the future increase in land values, and (6) prohibition of speculation on the stock and commodity exchanges.

Within the minimum wage movement, among other Progressives, Father Ryan was never thought to be a Socialist or a pragmatist. His argument, developed in articles beginning in 1902 and in his doctoral dissertation published as *A Living Wage*, explains why. Every man has a God-given right to live on the earth's bounty, Ryan asserted. The unnatural development of industrialism does not alter this natural right but rather transmutes the worker's claim into a minimum wage requirement. Man's dignity as a creature of God is at stake and so a "decent livelihood" is a fundamental requirement for all humans. This theological basis gave Ryan's argument its uniqueness; it also was deeply felt by him. He often returned to these points in arguing the inadequacy of substitutes of work's worth derived from a cold analysis of value. Broderick explains Ryan's economic idealism this way: "On the authority of Sidney and Beatrice Webb, the English Fabians, he is convinced that a national minimum wage is no more open to economic objection than the factory legislation already on the books. He foresees political barriers, but he is not willing to surrender to them."

Consumers' League Program in the States

The movement for minimum wage legislation had a number of attributes familiar to American political reform. Minimum wage laws originated in Australia and were adopted in Great Britain just as interest spread to the United States. This reform appealed to three upper middle-class organizations: the National Consumers' League, the Woman's Trade Union League and the American Association for Labor Legislation. State branches of the National Consumers' League in Massachusetts, Oregon and Wisconsin were successful in carrying out the national pledge of making minimum wage laws its leading legislative goal in 1910.

Individuals associated with these organizations contributed through research, publicity, tactical skill in legislation and service in administrating newly enacted minimum wage laws. Father Ryan, with dedicated initiative, published an article in the *Catholic World* in 1909 entitled "A Legal Minimum Wage." Mrs. Florence Kelley on a trip abroad in 1908 learned about it directly from Beatrice Webb and then at home converted a host of followers to the primacy of this cause. In Massachusetts, Mary W. Dewson in 1910 served as executive secretary of a special commission of inquiry established by the legislature to study the wisdom of minimum wage legislation for women and children. Dewson's final commission report, based on her statistics on wages and expenditures, recommended enactment of legislation. In 1912 the Massachusetts minimum wage law became the first in the nation.

Minimum wage legislation did not, by any means, sweep the country. Success was marked in the first few years but only in the states where progressivism was already strong. Here is the full list in chronological order: 1912—Massachusetts; 1913—California, Colorado, Minnesota, Nebraska, Oregon, Utah, Washington and Wisconsin; 1915—Arkansas, Kansas; 1917—Arizona; 1918—District of Columbia; 1919—North Dakota, Texas and Puerto Rico; 1923—South Dakota.

At this point the movement was halted by the decision in *Adkins v. Children's Hospital*. Then, at the start of the New Deal in 1933, seven additional states enacted minimum wage laws: Connecticut, Illinois, New Hampshire, New Jersey, New York, Ohio and Utah. Utah, which had repealed in 1929 its law passed in 1913, again in 1933 adopted minimum wage legislation.

The altruism and logic of John A. Ryan, Florence Kelley and the National Consumers' League to favor state minimum wage laws for all workers early collided with the self-interest of the American Federation of Labor as seen by its President Samuel Gompers. His social outlook was colored with antagonism toward the state and suspicion of legislation which touched labor in any way. He quickly helped popularize the notion that "the minimum was the maximum" so that instead of a floor beneath wages the laws would in reality be malevolent and place a ceiling above them. Owing to this opposition the advocates of minimum wage legislation acquiesced and drafted bills which omitted male workers from their purview. The bills introduced in legislatures in 1911, 1912 and 1913 uniformly applied to women and children only and were also ordinarily limited to particular industries.

The question of broadening minimum wage legislation for women to cover all workers repeatedly arose over the years. The trade union opposition was profound and continuous until late in the New Deal so that until 1934 the question of including men in the coverage was scarcely broached. Meanwhile, leaders of the National Consumers' League like Mrs. Kelley, Josephine Goldmark and Mary Dewson did not seriously reconsider their position. When newcomers gave their attention to drafting and pushing for the round of women's wage laws after 1932 the question of including men was persistently asked. The older people of the movement, particularly Felix Frankfurter and Benjamin Cohen, insisted on following the line set by Gompers. But in the great experiment of the National Recovery Act from 1933 to 1935 men were covered by some industrial codes and in 1938 the National Fair Labor Standards Act set a minimum wage for all workers, men as well as women.

Mary Dewson, like many women of her time, was a purposeful feminist with a keen mind, college training and practical experience. Born in Quincy, she organized a Cleveland-for-President Club upon entering Wellesley College in 1893, then majored in history and economics and was elected president of her graduating class in 1897. She then came under the influence of Mrs. Elizabeth Evans, "a central figure in a close-knit group of pioneering social workers drawn from Boston's leading families."[6]

Here came Mary Dewson's experience in practical economics. From 1897 to 1900 she took a position under Mrs. Evans with the Woman's Educational and Industrial Union in Boston, where she analyzed the living costs of working women and turned out handy little record books for individual girls to keep track of their expenses. These simple budgets to be used for itemization of the costs of living were called *Twentieth Century Expense Books*. For the next decade Miss Dewson was superintendent of industrial probationers of Massachusetts and directed the woman's parole department of the state's industrial school system. By 1911, when Mrs. Evans asked her to lead the study of women's wages, Miss Dewson had a fully formed but naïve philosophy which Patterson has summed up in this way:

A minimum-wage for women was "socially just and economically advantageous." Not only would it provide adequate health and moral standards, it would benefit employers as well. Moreover, she claimed, it was also the most practical method of creating equal opportunities for women. Once women received a living wage, she believed they would be spared the immorality induced by poverty. Above all, Miss Dewson favored the minimum wage for women because it would enable them to take their place beside men in a society characterized by complete sexual equality, and not because it would *protect* them in an essentially male world. In this way, wedding social reform and feminism, Miss Dewson embraced a faith in legislation and in the democratic process which became an integral part of her social philosophy and which was of considerable importance in the reform methodology of the 1930s.[7]

In eight months Mary Dewson's committee prepared a statistical study of wages and expenditures and then recommended a minimum wage law for Massachusetts. The bill was adopted by the legislature in 1912 essentially as drafted by the Dewson committee.

This law set a pattern for other states but in many ways it was a markedly modest beginning. It was limited to women and children and was noncompulsory, depending on the good will of employers for meaning. This, in turn, would depend in large part on the diplomacy and skill of special boards created to set a minimum wage in particular industries. The wage to be established was labeled the "necessary cost of living" to be ascertained by statistical studies of living costs adequate for the "health and morals" of workers. A tripartite state commission was to establish and guide the special industrial boards, see that they followed fair procedures, consulted employers and employees and considered the financial condition of the industry and publicized recommendations. The publicity would come through public hearings and by newspaper publication of findings. Patterson has observed that the Massachusetts law expressed Progressive naïveté in believing that when the people had the facts they would, as consumers, oblige employers to comply with rational recommendations of the fact finders.

Yet it was a start and the noncompulsory feature was widely, though not universally copied in the states that adopted minimum wage laws during the next few years. It should be stressed that the essentially voluntary system in Massachusetts worked well and this feature ensured its survival as a state law until the New Deal, when both the courts and the public became willing to accept a higher degree of compulsion in protective labor legislation.

A careful account of the legislation in California shows how grudgingly modest these victories were even though, for the movement, they bestowed some benefit to recipients and important experience to their managers.[8] Under Governor Hiram Johnson, the state government of California drew a host of Progressives into public service between 1911 and 1917 and, like Wisconsin and Oregon, adopted much new social and economic legislation. Katherine Philips Edson was named a special agent for the Bureau of Labor Statistics for Southern California in 1912 and soon sponsored a legislative bill to provide a minimum wage for women in industry. Forty percent of the women workers of California were then earning less than $9 a week.

Her Labor Bureau studies were supplemented with information and arguments from Florence Kelley in New York. Katherine Edson worked out a proposal based on the Massachusetts law developed by Mary Dewson. She easily persuaded Governor Johnson to include the need for a minimum wage law as one of his "ten commandments" for legislative action in 1913. As finally introduced and enacted, the California bill established an Industrial Welfare Commission of five members with powers of investigation to be followed by setting minimum wages, maximum hours and conditions of work in selected industries. An employer refusing to obey a commission order and found guilty could be fined or imprisoned. The law, adopted by two-thirds of each house, was so strong that Edson advocated an amendment to the California constitution so that the legislature might, in the words of the amendment

provide for the establishment of a minimum wage for women and minors and may provide for the comfort, health, safety and general welfare of any and all employees. No provision of this constitution shall be construed as a limitation upon the legislature to confer upon any commission . . . such power and authority as the legislature may deem requisite to carry out the provisions of this section.[9]

Opposed officially by major trade unions and business organizations though it was, this amendment was adopted by a vote of 379,311 to 295,109.

It is notable that the California Industrial Welfare Commission declined to tempt fate through involving itself in litigation. As they organized in 1913, the commissioners were well aware that the National Consumers' League had used the talents of Brandeis and Goldmark in defending the similar Oregon law in the courts against a test case brought by employers. In light of this, Hundley tells us, the California commission worked gingerly, but he thinks adroitly and positively, to avoid commencement of similar legal action against them.

Frankfurter for Brandeis in Oregon

The constitutionality of the Oregon minimum wage law for women, along with that state's eight-hour law for men, had already been presented to the Supreme Court by Louis D. Brandeis. This caused a sensation in the Senate with Brandeis's reputation as a radical magnified in the national debate that ensued between his nomination on January 28, 1916, to confirmation, by a vote of 47 to 22, four months later on June 1.[10]

Although the case of *Bunting v. Oregon* and the wage case of *Stettler v. O'Hara* had been argued in December 1914, the Court had still not reached a decision a year later. Then a series of events upset the Court's routine and put off action indefinitely. These events were the death of Mr. Justice Lamar on January 2, 1916, Day's illness of several months, the delay in confirming Brandeis, and Hughes's resignation on June 10 to reenter politics. The nine-man Court was stabilized for the 1916-17 term after Day had recovered, Brandeis had been confirmed, and Clarke had succeeded to Hughes's seat. Not until 1917—four years from its beginning—did the Supreme Court announce a decision in the first minimum wage case to be adjudicated.

This first judicial challenge of a state minimum wage law was begun in 1913 in Portland, Oregon, by a manufacturer of boxes, F.C. Stettler. He sought to enjoin the Oregon Industrial Welfare Commission from enforcing its order, promulgated as required by law, to set a minimum weekly wage for women employed in factories in Portland. A leader in the campaign for the Oregon law had been Edwin V. O'Hara, a young Catholic priest who had studied under Ryan at St. Paul. Father O'Hara was then named chairman of the Oregon Industrial Welfare Commission; the equity action was brought by Stettler against him. The trial judge in 1913 ruled constitutional the Oregon minimum wage law as carried out by the commission and refused to issue the injunction Stettler sought. Backed by other manufacturers, Stettler appealed to the Oregon Supreme Court. O'Hara and the Consumers' League of Oregon countered by seeking the help of Father Ryan and Mrs. Kelley, who arranged for Josephine Goldmark and Louis Brandeis to defend the Oregon wage law there. Brandeis then submitted the first of the NCL briefs in a wage case to the state supreme court.

Josephine Goldmark has explained that in the O'Hara case she and Mr. Brandeis "submitted a brief of two hundred pages, which we prepared to show the world's experience with women's wages: the evil effects of low wages, and the benefits of an adequate wage from the physical, economic, and moral standpoints." The first Brandeis brief in defense of a minimum wage law worked—on March 17, 1914, the Oregon Supreme Court upheld the validity of the Industrial Welfare Commission's ruling.

Even so, the *Stettler* case was carried to the United States Supreme Court. The constitutional argument was that a labor agreement between an employer and an employee was a freely entered bargain which government could not disturb. This "freedom of contract" was said to be protected because the Fourteenth Amendment forbade a state from depriving any person of liberty without due process of law. We have seen that this view of "liberty of contract" was accepted by a Court majority in the ten-hour bakery case of *Lochner*. Many employers hoped the Court would be similarly persuaded to invalidate this state minimum wage law and stop the movement. Both sides watched the progress of *Stettler v. O'Hara* with high interest.

Working with the Oregon attorney general, Brandeis again filed the big brief he and Goldmark had organized to persuade the Supreme Court that the Oregon legislature had acted reasonably and the O'Hara commission fairly in requiring Stettler's company to pay a "living" wage to its women employees. On December 16 and 17, 1914, *Stettler v. O'Hara* was argued in Washington before the Court composed of Chief Justice White and associate justices, McKenna, Holmes, Day, Hughes, Lamar, Pitney and McReynolds. One lawyer who heard the case argued orally before the Court has left a warm account of the persuasive powers of Brandeis as an advocate. William Hitz, a lawyer and federal judge, wrote:

I have just heard Mr. Brandeis make one of the greatest arguments I have ever listened to. . . . When Brandeis began to speak, the Court showed all the inertia and elemental hostility which courts cherish for a new thought . . . but he visibly lifted all this burden, and without organizing or chewing the rag he reached them all and even held Pitney quiet.

He not only *reached* the Court but he *dwarfed the Court*, because it was clear that here stood a man who knew . . . and . . . cared infinitely more, for the vital daily rights of the people than the men who sat there sworn to protect them. It was so clear that something had happened in the Court today that even Chas. Henry Butler saw it and he stopped me afterwards on the coldest corner in town to say that no man this winter had received such close attention from the Court as B. got today, while one of the oldest members of the clerk's office remarked to me "that fellow Brandeis has got the impudence of the Devil to bring his socialism into the Supreme Court."[11]

Before a decision in *Stettler v. O'Hara* was made, Brandeis was named to the Court and Felix Frankfurter undertook to replace him as counsel for the National Consumers' League in representing Oregon. Frankfurter in 1915 was only thirty-three but, as a professor at Harvard Law School and converted to intense interest in public affairs by Brandeis himself ten years earlier, was an ardent believer in state protective labor legislation. A hallmark of his thought, even then, was that the states should initiate such legislation rather than have the federal government enter the field. Frankfurter thus felt with Brandeis that in the American constitutional system, states were social laboratories in which to try out novel legislation that might overcome some of the deficiencies of modern industrial life. Moreover, he agreed with Mr. Justice Holmes and with Roscoe Pound—the dean of Harvard Law School and the foremost philosopher of sociological jurisprudence—that courts should give legislatures the benefit of the doubt and permit them considerable discretion in experimentation. Maximum hour and minimum wage laws were among the kinds of new regulations Frankfurter particularly endorsed. These postures taken together meant that Frankfurter was committed fully to continuing the defense of the incomplete Oregon cases of *Bunting* on hours and *Stettler* on wages for well before the Brandeis nomination, Frankfurter was serving as "the 'watcher' for the Massachusetts field in regard to litigation on labor legislation."[12] This was enough to convince Newton D. Baker to become such a "watcher" in Ohio. Baker, soon to become secretary of war and later a perennial conservative prospect for the Democratic presidential nomination, expressed admiration of Frankfurter's work and ideas on labor legislation and for his idea "that some central authority in each state ought to be notified when the constitutionality of an act of the legislature is to be assailed."[13] This was an idea that became law in many states and for the federal government twenty years later. It is mentioned here to indicate the scope of Frankfurter's early activities, his connections with prominent men, his commitment to protective labor legislation and his alertness in understanding that procedures of the kind he suggested to Newton D. Baker would have a bearing on public policy.

As attorney general of Oregon, George M. Brown was prickly about having oral argument again in the *Stettler* case, apparently believing the Court should be permitted to make a clear call for it while the Consumers' League people wanted a chance for Frankfurter to appear and consequently pressed for reargument.

Brown thought the Court's rules left this to the justices and he declined to stipulate reargument orally, being willing to rest the case on the briefs. Josephine Goldmark was quite plain and direct in telling Brown she regretted he did not seem to agree with the league. She wrote:

The only reason for our inquiring whether you thought this change possible was because we have found the oral argument of so much value in the defense of a series of labor laws, and Mr. Frankfurter's practice before the Supreme Court has led him to the same belief.[14]

Brown was not the last attorney general to find himself grateful—but hardly acquiescent—in accepting help from an outside group. There appeared to be no question of his wish to defend the statute and win the case. For one thing, he thought that his opponents should be allowed to hang themselves if they were willing to go to the Court with a short brief against the opinion of the Oregon Supreme Court, a thousand-page brief prepared under the direction of Brandeis and filed by Frankfurter and Goldmark, "and also a brief prepared by this department which represents our best efforts."[15]

As matters turned out, the Court called for reargument in both *Bunting* and *Stettler* and heard Frankfurter as well as George M. Brown on January 18 and 19, 1917. As we have seen, the ten-hour law for men was sustained, in an opinion by McKenna, with White, Van Devanter and McReynolds dissenting, and Brandeis not sitting. Under custom dictated by elemental fairness, Brandeis could not have participated in these cases for he had first submitted them as counsel for Oregon. This was a misfortune for the National Consumers' League in the wage case, for while the remaining eight justices divided five to three in *Bunting* they divided evenly, four to four, in *Stettler v. O'Hara*. A tie vote has the effect of affirming the decision of the lower court meaning, in this instance, that the minimum wage law as sustained by the Oregon Supreme Court was upheld. This was fine for Father O'Hara's state commission but as the decision was issued *per curiam,* without an opinion, there was no precedent set and the constitutionality of such laws generally was left in doubt. How could one predict the outcome of future challenges to other statutes on the same subject with so uncertain an indication of judicial sentiment?

Clearly, litigation on minimum wage laws was just beginning, but already the National Consumers' League leadership was deeply informed and committed with valuable experience in litigation behind them. Even before the Court decisions in 1917, Florence Kelley sent Frankfurter a league resolution which she called a meager expression of the gratitude felt for his "unwearied, valuable help."[16]

After the Oregon law was sustained by the Court, Frankfurter wrote Father O'Hara a letter from the Harvard Law School, saying, "It is a distinct privilege to me to have been associated, as I feel I have been, with the pioneers in Oregon in their effort to establish those minimal standards of life on which alone a healthy society can be founded."[17]

Analysis of the Adkins Case

The train of events in the next constitutional test of a minimum wage law stretched from 1918, when Congress and President Wilson approved a statute "providing for the fixing of minimum wages for women and children in the District of Columbia," to 1923, when the Supreme Court ruled "that the act in question passes the limit prescribed by the Constitution."[18] Elizabeth Brandeis, an economist on the staff of the Minimum Wage Board of the District, wrote years later that for the fifteen years from 1917 to 1932 the *Adkins* case was "probably the most important decision on the constitutionality of a labor law."[19]

The *Adkins* case was, indeed, a major decision worth many pages in this book if either its significance in constitutional history or the quantity of available data on management of the litigation were the criterion. But since a legal defense pattern had been established by the National Consumers' League it is hoped that the economy of reducing this complex *Adkins* litigation into a simplified scheme will be useful.

Five elements will be examined: (1) the judges, (2) social movements, (3) counsel, (4) the bar, and (5) the public. The predispositions, alignments, vitality, values, intensity and many almost unascertainable qualities and unknown and unknowable facts concerning each of these elements would be needed to comprehend a constitutional decision like *Adkins*. Each seems to bear on time and timing, the ineluctable and perennial problem children of the historian's craft. The most specific yet, somehow simultaneously, the most general question here is this: How did it happen that on April 9, 1923, the Supreme Court of the United States, by a five-to-three division, ruled unconstitutional the District of Columbia minimum wage law? The elements that combined to produce this result interacted over many years and overlapped.

The simple outlines of *Adkins v. Children's Hospital* will suggest some of the crucial points. Friends of the 1918 act were named to the Minimum Wage Board of the District of Columbia with Jesse C. Adkins, then a lawyer in private practice, serving as chairman. One member of the Consumers' League, Ethel M. Smith, served on the board while two others, Clara Mortenson Beyer and Elizabeth Brandeis, were on the staff as secretary and assistant secretary. Under the law's requirement to organize industry-wide conferences, composed of an equal number of representatives of the employers and employees affected, the board convened a conference on the Hotel, Restaurant and Hospital Industries, and obtained a report recommending certain wage minimums.

After a public hearing, the Minimum Wage Board ordered that establishments serving food and hospitals must pay women employees no less than 34 1/2 cents per hour, $16.50 per week, or $71.50 per month. When meals were furnished as part payment to an employee, not more than 30 cents per meal could be deducted from the weekly wage. This minimum wage was found by the board necessary "to supply the necessary cost of living to ... women workers to maintain them in good health and to protect their morals," as the act required. The act declared any violation by an employer to be a misdemeanor, punishable by fine or imprisonment.

Two suits were commenced in the D.C. Supreme Court, a trial court, against the enforcement of this order, asking that the act be declared invalid and that permanent injunctions be issued against the Minimum Wage Board. Identical pleadings supported by the same brief, filed by the same counsel, supported each suit, one for the Children's Hospital of the District of Columbia and the other by Willie A. Lyons, a twenty-one-year-old woman elevator operator employed by the Congress Hall Hotel. They claimed the Fifth Amendment's due process clause, applicable to laws adopted by Congress for the District of Columbia, included freedom of contract and that the hospital in the one case and Miss Lyons in the other were thereby constitutionally protected in their employment arrangements.

Children's Hospital employed a large number of women in various capacities at rates agreed to by both sides even though they were admittedly less than the wage fixed by the board. Miss Lyons received a salary of $35 per month and two meals a day which she found most agreeable but, alas, under the board's order to raise her salary to $71.50 per month the Congress Hall Hotel "was obliged to dispense with her services." Precisely the fault of minimum wage legislation as argued by many economists today was here seen in practice. It is likely that both cases were initiated and sponsored by organized employers and that, in fact, Miss Lyons did not suffer a true pecuniary loss—but this is merely speculation.[20] The trial court dismissed the bills of the hospital and of Lyons to enjoin the enforcement of the Minimum Wage Law.

Upon appeal to the court of appeals of the district, a three-judge panel, by two to one, first on June 6, 1921, affirmed and, following a rehearing, on November 6, 1922, reversed the trial court. This snarl was occasioned by the illness of Judge Charles H. Robb, originally assigned to the panel, his substitution by a lower court judge, his subsequent recovery and insistence on a rehearing and, more than a year later, his vote to reverse. This was a coup for the opponents of the Minimum Wage Act; a setback for the board, the Consumers' League and other friends of the legislation. Speaking of timing, these events delayed review in the Supreme Court of the United States for eighteen months while significant changes in the membership took place. The final order of the court of appeals holding the act unconstitutional meant, too, that if only eight justices sat in the Supreme Court a tie would result in affirmance. The conditions in this respect were opposite those in *Stettler v. O'Hara*, where the Oregon Supreme Court had upheld a minimum wage law.

It was then the turn of the Minimum Wage Board to appeal the cases brought by the hospital and the elevator operator to the Supreme Court. The dates of the calendar to bear in mind are the following: March 4, 1921—Warren G. Harding inaugurated president; May 19, 1921–Chief Justice White died, and was succeeded by William Howard Taft; September 1, 1922–Justice Clark resigned, and was succeeded by George Sutherland; November 13, 1922–Justice Day retired, and was succeeded by Pierce Butler; December 31, 1922–Justice Pitney retired, and was succeeded by Edward T. Sanford.[21] Each Harding nomination was confirmed by the Senate within days, and those of former President Taft and Senator Sutherland on the same day their names were submitted. In less than two years, President Harding had named four men to the Court. March 14, 1923–*Adkins v. Children's Hospital* and *Adkins v. Lyons* were argued before the Supreme Court; April 9, 1923–the Court affirmed the decrees of the court below, by a five-to-three division, Mr. Justice Brandeis taking no part.

The timing and outcome of the *Adkins* case owed itself in at least some measure to the conduct of the litigation by opposing counsel, with the initiative very substantially in the hands of the lawyers who won. They were brothers, Wade H. Ellis and Challen B. Ellis, born in Covington, Kentucky, residents of Cincinnati as young lawyers, and partners in law practice in Washington beginning in 1912. Both men were well-trained college graduates with Wade holding the LL.B. from Washington and Lee, and Challen graduating from Harvard Law School. The elder brother had been editor of the *Cincinnati Tribune* in the 1890s, assistant corporation counsel of the city of Cincinnati for six years, attorney general of Ohio for four years, and, in the Taft administration, assistant to the attorney general of the United States in Washington. He drafted Taft's platform in 1912. He was at different times national president of Phi Beta Kappa and of the Sons of the American Revolution. The experience of Wade H. Ellis as a government attorney, success in private practice in the District of Columbia and acquaintance with the personalities and practices on the local judicial scene meant that he was remarkably well equipped to manage the litigation challenging the D.C. minimum wage law and to do so over the whole period from 1919 to 1923, from start to finish.

Their young partner in Washington then has recalled a comment, perhaps made by Owen J. Roberts, that "that juncture in the Court's history was the only time the *Adkins* case could have been won."[22] But the partner's belief is that "it was a very creditable piece of work done by Wade Ellis–a political man, beautifully spoken, a superb advocate." Challen Ellis, considered an excellent constitutional lawyer by his partner, did the spade work and prepared the ideas but the formulation was probably by Wade Ellis. The team on the final brief included Woodson Houghton, the young partner, and Joseph W. Folk, a former Missouri governor. These things stand out in their performance: initiating a test case that was jurisdictionally sound, persuading Court of Appeals Judge Robb to order a rehearing and to lead that court to invalidate the law as well, thus delaying the entire litigation to an opportune time, preparing an effective brief in both that court and in the Supreme Court and making an effective oral argument of the case in the Supreme Court. The oral argument was shared by Wade and Challen Ellis.

If there was a weakness on the other side of the counsel table it was the poor cooperation between Francis H. Stephens, corporation counsel for the Commissioners of the District of Columbia, whose equivalence to a city attorney or a state attorney general made the defense of the minimum wage law an official duty, and the team of Felix Frankfurter and Mary W. Dewson, who really did the work. The National Consumers' League people found Stephens inefficient, dull and uncommitted. A related handicap was the physical dispersion of the defenders of the law: Frankfurter was at the Harvard Law School in Cambridge, Mary W. Dewson was research secretary of the NCL in New York, Clara Beyer and Elizabeth Brandeis were at the Minimum Wage Board office in Washington, Jesse C. Adkins was at his law firm, and Francis H. Stephens was in the office of the corporation counsel with the Commissioners.

Stephens had to be prodded constantly by Adkins, Miss Brandeis and Mrs. Beyer to keep Frankfurter informed, file motions and briefs on time, cooperate in oral argument; and he failed in one way or another at many points. The failure may not have been fatal but it was surely counterproductive. While some polite, formal correspondence ensued with Stephens, Frankfurter easily saw him to be a "rather casual person" and turned to Adkins or the staff for simple information on the progress of the case. After the first argument of the *Adkins* case which they shared, Frankfurter wrote Stephens that he was "sorry I did not have a chance to say in person how generous it was of you to invite me into the case and how still more kind it was for you to let me have all the time."[23] Underneath this, Frankfurter was seething and he apologized to Mrs. Beyer "in blowing up for the failure to file the Stettler brief" which had been agreed to as a supplement to the material prepared by Mary Dewson. "I will not disguise my disappointment at the slip-up," Frankfurter wrote, adding: "However, I can well understand your difficulty in having an incompetent corporation counsel . . ."[24]

On a happier note, there was remarkable cooperation between Frankfurter—who in these years was regarded as general counsel of the National Consumers' League by leaders of the organization, though he held no title and received no pay—and Mary Dewson. During one six-month period Dewson wrote the factual part of 453 pages for the *Adkins* brief, preparing the copy, reading proof and distributing briefs far and wide.

Dewson and Frankfurter offered the judges impressive documentation on the cost of living and the desirability of good wages. But facts were used to make a moral claim of the government's duty and authority to require private employers to pay prescribed minimums. This may be the strength of this kind of assumption and argument, but the *Adkins* outcome shows that such a brief—and it is appropriate to use any of a number of labels for it: Brandeis brief, factual brief, sociological brief or economic brief—is far from convincing on all occasions. There are several answers to this argument. One is to counter the facts with detailed information arguing against them, a common approach in recent years.

What Wade and Challen Ellis did in *Adkins* was to concede the factual matters, acknowledge that higher pay would be nice, insist that the higher pay would have a consequence in unemployment (as the facts in the *Lyons* case proved) and then simply to argue that a law fixing wages in private employment was beyond legislative power. Here they made a distinction by not fighting again the old battle over maximum hour laws but agreeing that government could regulate hours and other matters directly promoting health and safety as these only indirectly affected the cost of labor. They distinguished wage legislation as an unconstitutional intrusion in the bargain between employer and employee.

These vistas on the respective qualities of counsel still make it impossible to weigh their effect on the outcome of the *Adkins* case. Nor can a relationship between the opposing interests be ascertained. The employer interest was not otherwise formally represented in the case than through the Ellis brothers as counsel for the parties. The National Consumers' League, on the other hand, had its position bolstered by two *amici curiae* briefs. They were filed on behalf of several of the states whose minimum wage laws would be affected by a constitutional ruling. One for the state of Oregon alone was filed by Attorney General Van Winkle and a Consumers' League leader in Portland, Joseph N. Teal. The other brief was for New York, California, Kansas, Wisconsin and Oregon signed by their attorneys general and several other lawyers, the most prominent being Hiram Johnson. While this formal support was intended to impress as well as inform the judges it is obvious that *only* five states filed and that forty-three did not. Although other states had minimum wage laws it was not yet an idea that had by any measure swept the country.

The judiciary inhabits a larger world than briefs and arguments, however, and there were many leading men at the bar in the 1920s, men fond of calling themselves "constitutional lawyers" who were opposed to protective labor legislation just as they were opposed to the prohibition amendment and the Volstead Act. They spoke out often in public: to bar association meetings, in the law reviews and in popular periodicals. With Harding's presidency a staunch conservative, James M. Beck, became solicitor general, whose duty it was to present the government's defense of all federal acts. But he was openly critical of child labor legislation, maternity legislation and minimum wage laws. Others with similar views included Louis Marshall, William D. Guthrie, Henry St. George Tucker, Elihu Root and William L. Marbury. Behind them were legions of lawyers who shared their values and outlook. These were men that many of the judges of the day admired and emulated as Twiss and others have shown.[25]

As for the Supreme Court, the most important single fact about the Harding appointments was that he named two ardent conservatives of the old school—Sutherland and Butler—to serve along with two justices similarly committed who were already sitting—Van Devanter and McReynolds. This meant that there were four votes against a minimum wage law before the case began; only one more vote was needed. As table 8-1 shows, Van Devanter, McReynolds, Sutherland

Table 8-1
Justices' Alignment on the Approval of Minimum Wage Laws, 1917-1941

Appointment order of Justices from White to Murphy	Dates of Service	O'Hara (1917) per curiam [4-4]	Adkins (1923) 3 to 5	Murphy (1925) per curiam 1 to 8	Donham (1927) per curiam 1 to 8	Tipaldo (1936) 4 to 5	Parrish (1937) 5 to 4	Darby (1941) 8 to 0
White	1894-1921	[−]						
White (C.J.)	1910-1921							
Peckham	1895-1910							
McKenna	1898-1925	[−]	−					
Holmes	1902-1932	[+]	+	−	−			
Day	1903-1922	[+]						
Moody	1906-1910							
Lurton	1910-1914							
Hughes	1910-1916							
Van Devanter	1911-1937	[−]	−	−	−	−	−	
Lamar	1911-1916							
Pitney	1912-1922	[+]						
McReynolds	1914-1941	[−]	−	−	−	−	−	
Brandeis	1916-1939	n.p.	n.p.	+	+	+	+	
Clarke	1916-1922	[+]						
Taft (C.J.)	1921-1930		+	−	−			
Sutherland	1922-1938		−	−	−	−	−	
Butler	1922-1939		−	−	−	−	−	
Sanford	1923-1930		+	−	−			
Stone	1925-1946			−	−	+	+	+
Stone (C.J.)	1941-1946							
Hughes (C.J.)	1930-1941					+	+	+
Roberts	1930-1945					−	+	+
Cardozo	1932-1938					+	+	
Black	1937-							+
Reed	1938-1957							+
Frankfurter	1939-1962							+
Douglas	1939-							+
Murphy	1940-1949							+

Stettler v. O'Hara, 243 U.S. 629 (1917). By even division [4-4], *per curiam*, without listing the alignment, the Court affirmed the Oregon Supreme Court's ruling that the Oregon minimum wage law for women was valid. Mr. Justice Brandeis did not participate. The votes indicated here are guesses based on the reasoning of T.R. Powell and Irving Dilliard.

Adkins v. Children's Hospital, 261 U.S. 525 (1923). A 1918 Act of Congress establishing a scheme for setting minimum wages for women in the District of Columbia was invalidated.

Table 8-1 (cont.)

Murphy v. Sardell, 269 U.S. 530 (1925). The Court, *per curiam*, held the 1917 Arizona minimum wage law for women invalid "upon the authority of *Adkins*." Also: "Mr. Justice Holmes requests that it be stated that his concurrence is solely upon the ground that he regards himself bound by the decision in *Adkins v. Children's Hospital*. Mr. Justice Brandeis dissents."

Donham v. West-Nelson Mfg. Co., 273 U.S. 657 (1927). Invalidation of the 1915 Arkansas minimum wage law for women affirmed, *per curiam*.

Morehead v. New York ex rel. Tipaldo, 298 U.S. 587 (1936). New York Court of Appeals invalidation of 1933 New York statute on minimum wages for women, affirmed.

West Coast Hotel Co. v. Parrish, 300 U.S. 379 (1937). Washington Supreme Court upheld validity of 1913 state minimum wage law for women. Affirmed. U.S. Supreme Court overruled *Adkins v. Children's Hospital*.

United States v. Fred W. Darby, 312 U.S. 100 (1941). In a case originating in Georgia, a three-judge Federal District Court ruled unconstitutional the minimum wage and maximum hour provisions of the Federal Fair Labor Standards Act of 1938 as beyond the scope of the commerce power. On direct appeal the Supreme Court reversed unanimously, 8-0. The case was decided on February 3, 1941. Mr. Justice McReynolds had retired from the Court on February 1, 1941.

and Butler voted consistently against all minimum wage laws tested in the Supreme Court. Their collective longevity kept them together on the bench until the end of the 1936-37 term. It was McKenna, then senile,[26] who supplied the needed fifth vote in the *Adkins* case.

We are left with the perplexing task of judging just why the *Adkins* case turned out as it did. It is evident that the judges were important, that the skill of counsel was not one-sided, that the result did not run counter to views of the bar nationally, that public opinion as registered in the election of Harding and in the paucity of state legislatures adopting minimum wage laws was unsettled at best and contrary-minded, possibly, and finally, that in the larger clash of social movements the advocates of protective labor legislation did not yet outweigh employers in their intense attachment to a point of view, in their connections to deeply felt values nor in their resourcefulness and organization. Yet *Adkins v. Children's Hospital* turned out in the longer run to be a landmark in a continuing struggle, not the end of an era. Two forks in that struggle will be examined in later chapters, one on the path of litigation and the other the path of seeking amendments to the Constitution to curb the Court or permit wage legislation. Constitutional change had been set in motion when John A. Ryan first urged minimum wage legislation in America, but that change would not be complete until such laws were legitimized through the judiciary or by the amendment process—or not completed, if the rule that "liberty of contract" which forbade wage controls should stand.

The Minimum Wage Overruling

When Florence Kelley died on February 17, 1932, the movement for protective labor legislation which she had championed for forty years seemed as uncertain of wide success as when her work began. The judiciary was one obstacle, for under constitutional interpretations then standing the states lacked power to enact and enforce minimum wage laws. The federal government lacked authority to regulate child labor. Yet the whole blame could not be placed on the judges. There were not enough votes in Congress to limit judicial review nor to propose an amendment empowering the states to adopt minimum wage laws. An insufficient number of state legislatures had ratified the child labor amendment as proposed by Congress in 1924. As will later be seen, the trade unions were weak and their right to collective bargaining not yet established under the Constitution. The Republican Party was dominant through the 1920s and the conservative wing of the Democratic Party was strong. Yet in 1932 there were glimmers of political change that might alter the Constitution profoundly.

There seemed by 1932 to be rising evidence that the Progressive faith in the states as social laboratories for innovative programs to protect working people would be justified. Experiments in social legislation had proceeded in New York State under Governors Alfred E. Smith and Franklin D. Roosevelt and in 1930, when Philip LaFollette was elected governor of Wisconsin, he soon began the kind of program in that state that came to be called a "Little New Deal." In a word, before Roosevelt was elected in November and took office in March 1933, there was a stirring in the states akin to the federal programs he came to sponsor in the years from 1933 to 1938.

The idea of minimum wage laws for women was merely one of these programs which were revived in the states in 1932 and then under Roosevelt had the endorsement of the federal government after 1933. One could have imagined a conservative vision of the Constitution welcoming such laws on grounds they came from the states and not from the national government. But this was not the actual practice as employers generally were unconcerned which government sought to regulate them in this way. Organized employers had opposed hour legislation, had fought workmen's compensation laws, had refused recognition of unions and criticized other measures advocated by organizations like the National Consumers' League, the National Child Labor Committee, the Woman's Trade Union League and the American Association for Labor Legislation.

But just as the campaign for maximum hour laws led to the development of the Brandeis brief and rulings that such legislation was constitutional so, too, did the movement of minimum wage laws happen to be a focal point in the struggle over constitutional change. We have seen that this campaign originated between 1903 and 1910, that the early legislation and litigation from 1912 to 1923 resulted in the *Adkins* case holding minimum wage laws unconstitutional. The abortive amendment campaigns were over. In 1932, especially after the November election, the National Consumers' League again took the initiative to develop new minimum wage laws and see them through constitutional tests in the courts.

It was not yet clear that the Supreme Court was prepared to change although the new members between the time of the *Adkins* decision in 1923 and the departure of Herbert Hoover from the White House on March 4, 1933, were not clearly hostile by any means. Harlan Stone was Coolidge's only appointment in a six-year presidency. Charles Evans Hughes succeeded Taft as Chief Justice, Owen J. Roberts succeeded Sanford and Benjamin Cardozo followed Holmes upon the nomination of President Hoover. If all four joined Brandeis, social and economic innovation by legislatures and by Congress would probably win judicial approval. Yet there would be no relenting by Van Devanter, McReynolds, Sutherland and Butler so that the prospect of favorable Supreme Court review of new legislation was hardly cheery.

As a voluntary organization, the National Consumers' League kept having its vitality renewed even beyond the time of Florence Kelley's death. Mary W. Dewson, Josephine Goldmark and Elizabeth Brandeis and other friends and sponsors continued their concern and interest for the national organization even though none held an official position. Upon the death of Mrs. Kelley, Mary Dewson arranged for Lucy Randolph Mason of Virginia, a suffragette who favored racial equality, union recognition and protective labor laws, to come to New York to be the second general secretary of the National Consumers' League.[1] She continued until July 1937, when she began work as an organizer for the Congress of Industrial Organizations under John L. Lewis. Mrs. Emily Sims Marconnier, a native of Wisconsin and admirer of the LaFollettes—her sister had married Robert Moses, the New York planner, in 1915—continued as an able associate secretary in the national office in New York.[2] There were also active chapters of the league in some states, notably in New Hampshire, Massachusetts, Rhode Island, Connecticut, New York, New Jersey, Ohio, Illinois, Wisconsin, California and Oregon. Felix Frankfurter continued to be fully available as informal general counsel of the National Consumers' League.

In 1932 many in the league who favored reform believed that much could be done and should be done in the states. That is where they first placed their energy, not exclusively but very heavily, toward a new campaign for enactment of a workable and valid minimum wage program. They would then cooperate in working for the constitutionality of state minimum wage legislation through litigation.

The ultimate goal was to draft new model legislation, see this adopted in several states, sponsor or support test cases in the courts, and then see that the wage laws spread to other states and were enforced effectively. At the constitutional level their goal was to obviate the *Adkins* rule. This chapter is designed to describe this complicated story and lay the basis for an examination of the elements in the new Supreme Court decisions on state minimum wage laws in the *Tipaldo* case from New York in 1936 and the *Parrish* case from the state of Washington in 1937. In reading these pages readers may wish to consult table 8-1 on the alignment of Supreme Court justices on the constitutionality of state minimum wage laws. The narration proceeds with the five elements presented in the chapter on the *Adkins* case in mind. These five aspects—the judges, the social movements and organizations, counsel in the cases, the bar and professional views, and public opinion—will be examined in relation to outcomes in the final section of this chapter.

Drafting the 1933 Standard Wage Bill

The swift construction of the National Consumers' League model minimum wage law in the winter of 1932-33 is a tribute to the virtue of a national organization coping with the American federal system. The NCL in the 1920s had become accustomed to losing; now the election results of 1932 gave them hope. They still saw a hostile judiciary and they deferred, perhaps too much, to the lawyers, especially their taskmaster, Felix Frankfurter. They could hardly anticipate—after years of disappointment in seeking to set minimum wages for women in a handful of states—the coming national laws on the subject. They would, of course, have a hand in drafting, advocating, explaining, and defending these laws: the ill-fated National Industrial Recovery Act of 1933 to be invalidated in the *Schechter* case in 1935, and the National Fair Labor Standards Act of 1938 to be declared constitutional by the Supreme Court in the *Darby* case in 1941. But the election of Roosevelt did not at the time point toward more economic regulation by the federal government. Nor could there be a proper expectation that eventually—five long years—the Supreme Court would accommodate the later New Deal to the Constitution. Before these events transformed the American constitutional system those reformers who wished to assure livable hours and wages for nonunion workers assumed that political action in the states was their only course.

There was nothing new about the idea of a "model bill" for the states, or a "model ordinance" for cities. Legislation abroad and at all levels in American government traditionally began by hammering out drafts which a sufficient number of sponsors had agreed to. W.W. Crosskey, perhaps the foremost, and certainly the most vociferous, critic of the American failure to achieve uniform legislation by a nationally imposed commercial code has stressed the numerous benefits in efficiency, surefootedness, economy and general sanity brought by identical laws within the nation.[3] Recognizing this need, each state legislature, at the turn of the century, appointed a commission on uniform state laws to meet annually, under the auspices of the Council of State Governments, to agree on texts of uniform laws on many subjects. This was a brave venture with at least three fundamental faults: (1) the commission itself became a target of conflicting interests with the resulting drafts models of contentious compromise, not of pristine artfulness; (2) the legislatures often changed key passages so the goal of uniformity failed; (3) courts in different states interpreted like legislative phrasing to suit themselves.

In a sense, and this is Crosskey's conclusion, the American experience with uniform state laws, contrary to proving federalism to be sound and workable, actually turned up a great deal of evidence that showed a modern federal system with a national economy was inherently chaotic, irrational, unworkable and ridiculous. While the Commission on Uniform State Laws and the American Law Institute functioned as quasi-official, neutral, "good government" organizations, there was a multitude of action groups working directly through state legislatures and they also developed "model bills." The American Association for Labor Legislation had drafted model measures on hours, wages, safety, health, social insurance and collective bargaining. Economists like John R. Commons and John B. Andrews spent their lives in drafting and promoting the adoption of such measures.[4] The first wave of minimum wage laws in the states had followed the proposed model legislation by the National Consumers' League in 1910.

The committee that drafted the "Standard Minimum Wage Bill" of 1933 backed by the NCL illustrates how many different hopes, fears, perceptions and blindnesses like-minded persons share. No doubt the NCL Labor Standards Committee, formed in December 1932, typifies conflict within most organizations—but conflict resolved *within* and a solid front result *without*. Mary W. Dewson was asked to appoint a committee to draft a model law. She set to work quickly, writing letters to five people to join her. Characteristically thinking ahead, and in confident good humor, she urged everyone to "pool the main ideas which we think should be covered before starting to draft the bill." Josephine Goldmark, experienced and esteemed, would be chairman. But Mary Dewson coordinated the work of the committee by correspondence, telegrams and occasional meetings of two or three committee members. In a month's time, on January 19, 1933, she was distributing the agreed-upon draft model for introduction into several state legislatures. During 1933, seven states actually adopted minimum wage laws for women identical with or very close to the NCL model bill.

If ever there was proof of the American predisposition to treat lawyers as soothsayers it lay in this committee's deference to the views of Felix Frankfurter in drafting the model bill. Charm, yes. Miss Dewson said toward the end of her letter of invitation, "Dear Felix, do not say the girls have gone bughouse, but think hard about these possibilities."[5] He replied: "Dear Molly: I think youse girls is swell. What the times need more than anything else is courageous demands intelligently expressed and massively documented." Frankfurter's wish to be heard but not seen registers in his order to Miss Dewson to put his friend Benjamin V. Cohen on the committee "at once and don't tell him that it had to be suggested to you."[6] This proved to be an absolutely superb idea. At times, Frankfurter was both help and hindrance.

On substance his preferences and his guesses were faulty, yet he seemed entirely self-assured. First, his judgment of the Court under Mr. Chief Justice Hughes was correct in the short run but woefully wrong in the long run of five October terms. It was "foolish beyond words to be cavalier about them and to be hopeful that a changed Court or changing times will make for a very liberal outlook on the part of the Court, and more particularly does it seem foolish to me beyond measure to build on expectations of a bouleversement [reversal] from the majority of nine. I can assure you that there is no right to any such hope, *under the leadership of Hughes*, let alone the others." [Italics mine.] [7]

More vital to the draft and ensuing litigation was Frankfurter's belief, at the outset of the new campaign, that there should be no quest for an overruling. Here, perhaps, he shows himself closer to the sense of judicial style expressed by Holmes, not Brandeis. Looking ahead to a test case, Frankfurter thought "the draftsman of a proposed law ought not to add more burdens than there will be at best for those who will have the responsibility to defend legislation before the Supreme Court nor more burdens than are indispensable *for those members of the Court who will seek to distinguish the Adkins case from the new proposal.*" [Italics mine.]

Some other Frankfurter forecasts were also wrong and may be quickly summarized. (1) "It is surely madness to tie up the case for women with that of men in drafting the model bill,"[8] he wrote in a letter to B.V. Cohen. (2) He insisted the test case should be from New York: "The make-up of the Court of Appeals of New York being what it now is, my own hunch is strongly for starting the litigation in the state courts and getting a favorable decision in the Court of Appeals. I should think we may safely count on Pound, Crane, Lehman, Crouch anyhow, and probably some of the others." We shall see that the *Tipaldo* test in the New York Court of Appeals lost four to three. (3) Frankfurter also was "all against [the] suggestion that the [Model] Act be based on the conception of an emergency and restricted to an emergency period. That seems to me to defeat the objective of the legislation, to be productive of very little good and to tender the wrong issue to the Court."[9] During the period 1933-37, this argument was used in many cases, often failing, sometimes winning. Hughes relied upon it in holding the Washington minimum wage law valid in 1937.

Frankfurter's good sense and mastery of administrative law contributed to his insistence that the NCL standard minimum wage bill of 1933 "have every protection of a procedural character indicating deliberation, ample opportunity for hearing to interested parties, disinterested and informed inquiry and elicitation of the specific facts in the different rates to be fixed." He wanted the wage boards to be kept with a fair amount of substantive power conferred upon them. This also must be quoted to round out the picture of Frankfurter's preoccupation with the job of the lawyers who would "come before the Court" to defend this act. "I think this is very important," he wrote to Josephine Goldmark; "perhaps more important than can possibly appear to those who have not the feel about what helps and what hurts before the Supreme Court, possessed by those whose business it is to watch the Supreme Court's doings as does a doctor that of the temperature of a pet patient."

Different tactics by Professor Joseph P. Chamberlain of Columbia were advocated to get the most fruitful test case before the Supreme Court. Chamberlain was both lawyer (Hastings LL.B., 1898) and political scientist (Columbia Ph.D., 1923). He practiced law in California for eight years before becoming a savant. At Columbia from 1909 to his death in 1951, Chamberlain was a member and then, after 1919, director of the Legislative Drafting Research Fund. Chamberlain's countertactics in nursing along the right test case enrich appreciation of the choices to be made. On this point, here are his views:

Miss Goldmark just 'phoned me about Felix Frankfurter's letter. I think he is right in believing that it would be easier to defend an act in which the Board was given quite complete power in view of the fact that both employer and employee are represented on the Board, but I think the problem is as to whether in New York State it would be administratively practicable to put so much work on a Board and expect to get any results. If you do not think so, I think the best way of handling the situation would be not to press legislation in New York but let Wisconsin or some other state, where the board system is practicable, go up to the Supreme Court as soon as possible on a compulsory act administered by a board, so as to get a decision, and then to follow along with an act like the one you proposed, giving more power to the Department.

I think that in any case it would be wiser to go up to the Supreme Court in a State like Wisconsin where you could get strong support from the labor movement and probably support from some manufacturers rather than in New York. This would be specially so since the situation is so much simpler there and the determination of what is a fair wage would not involve the immense complication that this determination would involve in a State like New York.[10]

Of the lawyers on the Labor Standards Committee, Benjamin V. Cohen did most of the work on the draft and his objective, like Frankfurter's, was to prepare a model law that would permit the Court to validate it by distinguishing, not by overruling. Prior to March 4, 1933, Cohen had been in private law practice in New York for ten years. Born in 1894 in Muncie, Indiana, he went to the University of Chicago as undergraduate and won two degrees later from the Harvard Law School. Cohen was first secretary to U.S. Circuit Court Judge Julian M. Mack in 1916-17, then he became an attorney to the United States Shipping Board in 1917 and counsel in the Paris Peace Conferences of 1919-21 to the American Zionists. Later during the New Deal he was prominently associated with Thomas Corcoran in assisting congressional committees on behalf of FDR in drafting the Securities Act of 1933, the Securities Exchanges Act of 1934, the Public Utility Holding Company Act of 1935 and, quite naturally, the Fair Labor Standards Act of 1938.

There were serious disagreements among the economists and lawyers on Mary Dewson's committee and these were reflected in the text of the bill. But the overarching quest to distinguish *Adkins*, to write a law that would be constitutional, was the approach taken by Benjamin Cohen. It should be a truism of political science, if it is not now one, that lawyers as draftsmen of statutes have their eye fully as sharply on the Constitution, as they understand the Court's view of it, as do those same lawyers performing as counsel in litigation. When the model state minimum wage law for women was completed in January 1933, Cohen helped prepare for the National Consumers' League a statement on why, when enacted and tested, the new model "may be declared constitutional." Cohen's explication of the aims of the draftsman is as follows:

The Law is the result of a conscientious and mature effort by counsel for the National Consumers' League to meet the objections which a majority of the Supreme Court found against the District of Columbia law in *Adkins v. Children's Hospital*, 261 U.S. 525. No one, of course, can venture certain prophecy in regard to a future action of the Supreme Court, particularly in a field so uncertain as that affecting minimum wage laws, for it is important to recall that only five members of the Supreme Court joined in the majority decision in the *Adkins* case over the very vigorous protest of Chief Justice Taft. But it is difficult to understand the references in the majority opinion by Mr. Justice Sutherland to the value of the service rendered save as a plain intimation that a properly drawn fair wage statute, such as is now proposed, would not run counter to the *Adkins* case. Mr. Justice Sutherland expressly states (261 U.S. 525, 559) that a statute requiring an employer to pay in money, to pay at prescribed intervals, to pay the value of services rendered, even to pay with fair relation to the extent of the benefit obtained from the service, would be understandable.[11]

Elizabeth Brandeis Raushenbusch's prowess on the committee is neatly documented by her already finished draft of a new law prepared for her husband's brother in Pennsylvania. One way to see this Pennsylvania draft is to draw in all the remaining commentators and set down their views, point by point on the model law in the making. Edwin A. Smith, Commissioner of Labor in Massachusetts was included particularly to interlock with a similar drafting group representing the national organization of state Labor Department officials. This was the full cast of the committee by the end of December 1932—Goldmark, Dewson, Brandeis, Smith, Chamberlain, Frankfurter and Cohen. Within five months, by May 1933, the New York legislature had voted this bill through almost unchanged and Governor Herbert Lehman signed it into law.

Court Test of New York's 1933 Wage Act

The new legislative policy embodied in the 1933 New York Minimum Wage Law was boldly administered by the state labor commissioner, Elmer F. Andrews, and vigorously enforced by the state attorney general, John J. Bennett, Jr. A key part of their strategy in applying the law was to invite a constitutional test—an almost certain reaction to a strongly enforced statute. A press release from Bennett's office on November 3, 1934, reported the first criminal prosecution under the act as applied to the laundry industry, following the indictment and arrest of Joseph Tipaldo and three other persons who were the managers, owners and bookkeeper of the Spotlight Laundry, 1061-61st Street, Brooklyn. "The indictments charge failure to pay at least the state minimum wage to the women and minors employed, forgery in the third degree in keeping false payrolls to conceal violation of the Minimum Wage Law, and conspiracy to violate the Minimum Wage Law and to forge the payrolls to conceal such violation."

The New York act declared it to be against public policy for any employer to employ any woman at an oppressive and unreasonable wage. This was defined as one which is "both less than the fair and reasonable value of the services rendered and less than sufficient to meet the minimum cost of living necessary for health." The act defined "a fair wage" as one "fairly and reasonably commensurate with the value of the service or class of service rendered."

Administrative procedures provided in the act called for a preliminary opinion by the labor commissioner of unreasonable wages in an occupation, followed by his appointment of an *ad hoc* wage board. That board, limited to not more than nine members, was to have equal representation of employers, employees and the public. The wage board possessed full authority to conduct a comprehensive investigation. The board might then recommend minimum fair wage rates to be approved at the discretion of the commissioner of labor. If the report of the board was approved, the commissioner would make a "directing order" defining the fair minimum and including appropriate administrative regulations. On the heels of this there would follow a ladder of sanctions starting with publicity and rising, after nine months of nonobservance, to a "mandatory order" and consequent punishment by fine and imprisonment for its violation.

The details of these procedures had been faithfully followed from June 1933 when Commissioner Andrews appointed the Laundry Wage Board, to November 1934 when Tipaldo and his associates were indicted by the Kings County Grand Jury. A "directory order" was in effect for nine months until August 6, 1934, when the "mandatory order" became effective. After investigations by the Labor Department's Bureau of Enforcement, the case was eventually referred to Attorney General Bennett for prosecution.

The grand jury heard testimony of employees who were found to have received from $7 to $10 for a work week as long as fifty-five hours. The legal minimum wage was $12.40 for a forty-hour week. Also testifying were

Commissioner Andrews, Raymond V. Ingersoll, chairman of the Laundry Wage Board, and Miss Frieda S. Miller, director of the Division of Women in Industry and Minimum Wage. Commenting on the indictments in the *Tipaldo* case, Commissioner Andrews said: "I believe Attorney General Bennett has developed an air-tight case against the Spotlight Laundry." Andrews's concluding remarks indicates a fine appreciation of the functions served by test cases in the administration of a program:

Attorney General Bennett has advised me that the case will be pushed through to an early decision. In the meantime, at his request, similar cases are being prepared for prosecution. . . . If 98 percent of the employers in an industry have been able to operate under a minimum fair wage law, I do not believe an inefficient or unscrupulous two per cent can successfully invoke the Constitution to protect them in the payment of antisocial wages.

The case which turned out to be the successful test of the New York State Minimum Wage Law of 1933 was an ordinary one until it reached the New York Court of Appeals, which held the Minimum Wage Act repugnant to the due process clauses of the state and federal constitutions on March 3, 1936. It directed that the order appealed from be reversed, the writ of habeas corpus sustained and the prisoner Tipaldo discharged. This was a four to three decision with Judge Lehman dissenting. An important victory had been won against the tide of social reform by legislation. The next move was up to the state of New York, specifically whether an appeal would be made and how conducted by Attorney General Bennett.

Consumers' League and Attorneys General on Appeal

Swiftly, within two weeks after announcement of the New York decision, Attorney General Bennett and Solicitor General Henry Epstein filed a petition for a writ of certiorari in the Supreme Court of the United States. Six reasons were advanced for allowing certiorari, as follows: (1) the meaning of the due process clause of the Fourteenth Amendment was drawn into question; (2) a new issue, distinguishable from that in the *Adkins* case was raised; (3) the *Adkins* rule should not be held controlling because conditions had changed since 1923; (4) provisions of the New York law differed from those of the District of Columbia law reviewed in *Adkins*; (5) "The construction and application of the Constitution of the United States and a prior decision of this, the Supreme Court of the United States, are necessarily involved in the case." (6) "The circumstances prevailing under which the New York law was enacted called for a reconsideration of the *Adkins* case in the light of the New York act and conditions aimed to be remedied thereby." These six contentions were contradictory but this is common practice in petitions seeking review. The quest is to give the Court some variety of reasons for review, not a single-minded, logical argument which might foreclose possible lines of thought which would gain the justices' approval.

The Supreme Court received an answering brief opposing certiorari from former Governor Miller and another from attorneys for the New York Hotel Association, as *amicus curiae*. In a matter of days briefs *amicus* in support of Bennett's petition were filed by Paul Windels, corporation counsel for the city of New York and Otto Kerner, attorney general for the state of Illinois. At the end of the remarkably short period of ten days, on March 30, 1936, the Supreme Court posted an order granting the writ of certiorari. The clear intention was to review the New York Court of Appeals ruling during the current term.

Briefs were due within the month. Oral argument before the Supreme Court in Washington was scheduled for April 29 and 30, 1936. All concerned faced a time of hectic exertion. Consumers' League workers were in for a grueling period of uncertainty and failure in putting established tactics to work. They first volunteered their services to Attorney General Bennett but, as Josephine Goldmark wrote in her *Impatient Crusader*, "For the first time the National Consumers' League was balked in its efforts to obtain an invitation for eminent counsel to join the state in this crucial defense, on which were set the hopes of the other states besides New York, which had in such rapid succession passed our Standard Minimum Wage Act."

Brandeis-type briefs were, in fact, prepared for the state of New York, under Attorney General Bennett's authority, by Henry Epstein and Frieda Miller. They were ample, up-to-date, masterful statements fully worthy of the Brandeis brief tradition. They were not massive as had been the brief by Frankfurter and Dewson in the *Adkins* case, but they were more than adequate and, most relevant, as intelligent and skillful as anyone in the league at that time could have produced under pressure. The appellant's brief on the law was seventy-seven pages, the companion factual brief on the economic background of the New York wage law was 201 pages.

The adverse ruling of the New York Court of Appeals mobilized the Consumers' League to action. Representatives of allied social, civic, labor and employer groups met immediately. On March 5, the Consumers' League issued this news release on the meeting:

Spokesmen for the group state that they feel strongly that the majority of the Court of Appeals has missed the entire point of the minimum wage legislation. This group announces its intention to wage a vigorous campaign to air the issues, radio time has already been arranged. Members of the laundry employers group present stated that they are mobilizing their forces to save the law and to educate their customers to the disastrous effect on the laundry industry of the Court's decision.

We heartily commend the Industrial Commissioner and the Attorney General on their announced intention to fight the minimum wage case to the highest court in the land. We will give them our support. Certainly the majority decision of the Court of Appeals gave them no alternative. That decision, we believe, was based on a total misapprehension of the provisions of the minimum wage law and a total failure to appreciate the significance of Justice Sutherland's decision in the Adkins case.

Clearly the two statutes—the old District of Columbia Law and the present New York law—are actually entirely different. The minority decision written by Judge Lehman makes this abundantly clear. As Justice Sutherland so aptly said in the Adkins case, a statute requiring an employer to pay the fair value of the services rendered would be "understandable." This is precisely what the New York Minimum Wage Law accomplished. The very language of the Adkins case is embodied in the New York law.

While everyone waited for the Supreme Court's action on New York's petition for certiorari, Clara Beyer and Frances Perkins in the Labor Department in Washington looked ahead to a way of presenting the Consumers' League point of view. A letter from Josephine Goldmark to the head of the Consumers' League of Rhode Island tells about one side of the activity:

At the invitation of the Secretary of Labor, a meeting was held in Washington on March 25th of the representatives of the attorneys general of states having minimum wage laws similar to the New York statute now in the courts. The idea of the meeting was that such states might desire to unite in intervening in the case. . . .

After considerable discussion the meeting decided that in view of the importance of the case it was desirable that other states having laws similar to that of New York should be represented before the United States Supreme Court both by joint brief and by oral argument, if possible.

In view of the difficulty of accomplishing this in the very short time available, the meeting decided that the National Consumers' League be requested to prepare a brief for submission to the states in question for their approval and signature. It was the sense of this meeting that the states which approve and sign the brief will desire that the National Consumers' League select some counsel of competence and standing to present the case to the Supreme Court as set forth in the brief. Ohio having litigation in the federal courts has filed its own brief.

After the Consumers' League's offer to help on the main brief for New York was rebuffed a new tack was taken. The league determined to represent its interest in seeing the New York law validated by making an argument to the Court in the name of the six other states which had adopted the NCL model law in 1933. Frankfurter would not serve as counsel; a new lawyer was needed. And each of the six attorney generals would need to be approached for permission on behalf of New Jersey, New Hampshire and Rhode Island.

The search for "some counsel of competence and standing" was entrusted to Josephine Goldmark and to Charles Burlingham, himself an eminent member of the bar of New York City. They decided to seek the services of Thomas Day

Thacher in preparing an *amicus curiae* brief on behalf of the six states. Thacher, after twenty years of practice in the city, had been named by President Coolidge in 1925 to be a judge of the United States District Court for the Southern District of New York. He served for five years, and then resigned to serve in Washington as solicitor general of the United States in the Hoover administration from 1930 to 1933. A Republican, Thacher was not known in the movement for minimum wages, but he was an experienced advocate, now returned to his practice in New York—and he agreed to serve.

Lucy Randolph Mason wrote at the time: "After a satisfactory conference with Mr. Henry Epstein, Solicitor General, who agreed to accept Mr. Thacher's cooperation, the National Consumers' League secured authorization from the attorneys general of the other states for Mr. Thacher to file his motion in the United States Supreme Court for leave to appear." Judge Thacher could be depended upon to be circumspect. He wrote to John J. Bennett, Jr., in Albany, requesting permission to deliver an oral argument in the case. In his reply Bennett wrote:

The matter has been very carefully and sympathetically considered by me, not only on receipt of your request, but prior thereto when suggestion was made to me that you be asked to join in the argument on behalf of the State of New York. I have reached the conclusion that the interests of the State and of our case will not be forwarded by argument of *amicus curiae* on behalf of the other states. It has always been the practice of this office in my administration to handle our own cases to which policy I have consistently adhered.

While, of course, I cannot and will not object to the filing of briefs by sister states as *amicus curiae* in aid of our position, I do not believe that added argument on their behalf will materially benefit the presentation of New York's case. I regret, therefore, that I cannot see my way clear to consent to such oral argument.

Without hesitation or questioning, Judge Thacher accepted Attorney General Bennett's word as final, telling him in reply: "In view of your conclusion that the interests of the State and of your case will not be forwarded by argument of *amicus curiae* on behalf of the other States, I am constrained to withdraw from the situation entirely and am advising the Attorneys General of the States . . . to this effect."

The next day Bennett confounded the leaders of the Consumers' League by consenting to the filing of a brief *amicus curiae* by the National Woman's Party. This organization was labeled by Lucy Mason as "a well-known opponent of all labor legislation." Earlier, Florence Kelley had seen its members as "a highly articulate minority of professional women, ignorant of the real needs of their wage earning sisters." True to form, the brief submitted by the Woman's Party argued the unconstitutionality of the New York law.

However much discomfort he caused the league, Bennett actually had a perfectly sound position on every count. He had granted permission to friend and foe to file *amicus curiae* briefs in the Supreme Court. This is in the best tradition. He had declined direct aid from a private organization in preparing New York's case but saw to it that the state's case under the detailed direction of Henry Epstein was competently planned. After all, Mrs. Kelley, thirty years earlier, first led the league to offer aid to state attorneys general when she saw their arguments were inadequately prepared. Bennett had not told Judge Thacher he could not approve a brief for the other states, only that he disapproved of an oral argument. This episode over, the league determined to involve itself in spite of Bennett's lack of cooperation and Thacher's withdrawal.

The Consumers' League, with its role limited by Bennett and with no time to lose, quickly got Dean Acheson to replace Judge Thacher. Acheson goes into no detail in his recollection of the arrangement, saying only that "Frankfurter thought a new face might bring a change of luck. Hence it fell to my lot to suffer martyrdom as counsel for *amici curiae* (six states) in the last of these cases to be lost, *Morehead v. New York* ex rel. Tipaldo."

Dean Acheson was then forty-two. He had been a student at Harvard Law School from 1915 to 1918, when Frankfurter was counsel in the Oregon wage and hour cases. Acheson went on to clerk for Mr. Justice Brandeis during the two terms of 1919-20 and 1920-21. Aside from several months during 1933 as an undersecretary of the Treasury, Acheson had been in practice in Washington with Covington and Burling since 1921. He then believed, and shows in his memoirs, a deep scorn for the "entrenched Old Guard on the Court" flying "the flag of Liberty of Contract." Acheson knew this Court and his commitment as a progressive and a Democrat was against the majority. Acheson's technical skills and his verbal mastery were already well established.

The content and functions of the Brandeis brief has nowhere been put better than in Dean Acheson's memoirs where he observes that it "sprang from a patient faith in the educative process and the power of reason." Acheson's statement, is in character with its witty and impeccable style:

These briefs proved with a wealth of authoritative detail what today is obvious—and, indeed, had been for some centuries to those whose minds, in Burke's phrase, the law had not sharpened by narrowing them. They proved that women were different than men and hence could be classified differently for protective measures; that their biological functions warranted protective measures; that necessitous women were not free women, and so on. The undeniable was added to the obvious, and the self-evident piled on top of that—"What Any Fool Should Know," as I described the Brandeis briefs to Frankfurter, quoting the Justice himself.

Compared to this, Acheson seems to have been ignorant of the traditions of the Consumers' League in using the Brandeis brief in litigation. He shows this misapprehension when he speaks of the Brandeis brief in Supreme Court cases as having been "filed for liberal organizations appearing as *amici curiae*, friends of the court." The statement is not merely false but, more pertinent, contrary to the essential philosophy of demonstrating on behalf of a state legislature the utter reasonableness of its laws. The approach to litigation stemming from this philosophy has been admirably put by one of its architects, Josephine Goldmark.

When we wanted Mr. Brandeis to enter a case—either by submitting a brief or taking part in the oral argument as he did in about a dozen cases—we had to secure an invitation for him to act on behalf of the state involved. He was unwilling to appear without such an invitation, merely as *amicus curiae*. The status of appearing as an official participant on behalf of the state seemed to him as an important element of strength for the defense. After the Brandeis brief had proved successful, Mrs. Kelley and I were sometimes hard put to secure the necessary official invitation; state officials were reluctant to lose any of the credit which they thought might accrue to themselves if they applied the same method alone—however inadequately equipped they were to do so. We had to walk warily indeed to avoid offending such officials. . . . Sometimes recourse to the governor was necessary. Somehow—with one exception—we always managed to secure the official invitation.

Even here in the *Tipaldo* case, Acheson was not officially to speak for "liberal organizations" as he put it, nor "on behalf of the state" whose law was challenged, but rather for six sister states. Still, it would be officially, with the Consumers' League role hidden from the Court's view, if consent could be gained from the attorneys general of the six states.

Because the states of Connecticut, Illinois, Massachusetts, New Hampshire, New Jersey and Rhode Island had enacted the model Minimum Wage Law in 1933, it seemed indispensable to a sound defense of the challenged New York law to have these states directly spoken for in the Supreme Court. Six state attorneys general had to be persuaded to allow Acheson to speak for them. Moreover, the task was doubly complex because the league had gained permission for Thacher's appearance when he withdrew. The attorneys general had to be approached again to approve Acheson. The league then learned that Attorney General Bennett of New York had written to his colleagues in the six states that their participation would not be appreciated.

The league pulled out all the stops. Frances Perkins and Clara Beyer wrote to the states. Trade union officers and state Consumers' League workers contacted state officials. Governor Wilbur Cross in Connecticut worked on Attorney General Daly. John G. Winant, then president of the National Consumers' League and serving on the Social Security Board in Washington, used his knowledge as former governor of New Hampshire to win the cooperation of Attorney General Francis U. Johnston of that state. Massachusetts was toughest. The Consumers' League there had to bring in an agreement from Paul Dever, the attorney general then campaigning for governor. After endless reports of failures the national office finally told the Massachusetts League:

Don't worry any more about your Attorney General. We have decided to give up because evidently Epstein and Bennett are determined not to let them cooperate. The brief will go to him in rough draft this week and if he wants to sign it, O.K., but at this point I do not care whether he does or not.

Finally, by April 24, all six agreed both to his brief and to Acheson's representation of their states in oral argument.

Years later Elinore Morehouse Herrick recalled how she had played the role of an innocent, anguished lady visiting Supreme Court Justices to obtain consent to the league's request that Acheson file a brief and make oral argument for the six states. That recollection is perfectly corroborated by notes and memorabilia in the Herrick Papers left by Mrs. Herrick to the Schlesinger Library at Radcliffe College. Handwritten in pencil on a yellow legal pad are these jottings under her caption: "Washington Min Wage Trip" which took place over the weekend of April 10-13, 1936:

Chronology of Weekend in Wash D.C.

Fri. April 10th 1:15 A.M. F.F. phoned & asked me to catch 2 A.M. train.

Sat. April 11th. Phoned Tom Corcoran & made apt. with H.F. Stone—Saw Stone & Cardozo with Corcoran. Stone looked into question of lack of consent from N.Y. Att'y Gen'l & necessity thereof—Also said he saw no reason why any question should be asked at time motion to intervene was made. Cardozo hesitant to discuss. Lunched with Acheson & Corcoran. Told Acheson we should be able to get authorization for oral argument from N.H. Ill. N.J. Mass. & Rhode Island but that Conn. was unfriendly. After lunch I started wheels in motion to get authorization.

Sun. April 12th. Worked at getting information Acheson wanted on facts.

Mon. April 13th. Acheson made motion which was granted. Spent balance of day trying to get authorizations. Learned on Mon April 13th that Bennett had written R.I. & Conn. Att Genls not to cooperate with us.

Discussing this weekend years later, Mrs. Herrick explained that the lawyers, especially Frankfurter, who had set the scheme in motion when he telephoned her from Cambridge, believed consent would more likely be granted if a woman in her position could directly complain to a justice of Bennett's foot-dragging. At the end of the day of Monday, April 13, 1936, she sent this telegram back to a colleague in New York:

COURT GRANTED ACHESON 30 MINUTES ORAL ARGUMENT HOORAY LEAVING ON SIX OCLOCK TRAIN PROBABLY ELINORE HERRICK

Woman's Party Against Wage Law Based on Sex

A group of feminists, organized as the National Woman's Party, went beyond advocacy of the equal rights amendment to work consistently against minimum wage legislation for women during the 1920s and 1930s. They did this in the conventional fashion of appearing at legislative hearings, writing letters to the editor of the *New York Times*, the *New York Herald Tribune* and other newspapers and magazines, instructing their own members through a house organ called *Equal Rights* and by litigation. Their private and official correspondence on this subject reveals an organization pursuing strategy and tactics essentially the same as its erstwhile opponent, the National Consumers' League. There were many differences in detail and in style and there was an antagonism of purpose which lay deep in the origins and outlooks of the women who worked for these rival organizations.

Disagreements within the National Woman's Party show that, while some members were conservative critics of labor legislation willing to work hand in glove with employers and their lawyers, those who worked in the *Tipaldo* case did so purely because they objected to a wage law applied to women only. The patron-saint was Alice Paul and the guiding spirit in the 1930s was Mrs. Jane Norman Smith in New York. The chief counsel was Mrs. Burnita Shelton Matthews, named by President Harry S. Truman in 1949 to be a judge of the United States District Court for the District of Columbia. Mrs. Matthews in 1936 was in practice with Laura M. Berrien and Rebekah Greathouse in the Southern Building in Washington.

Correspondence between one or another of the partners in the law firm of Matthews, Berrien and Greathouse and Mrs. Smith make up the bulk of available information on the role of the NWP in the minimum wage cases. This shows them appraising the *Tipaldo* case, deciding whether to file a brief, proceeding to prepare a brief *amicus*, soliciting funds to pay the printer, following the Ohio wage case of *Walker v. Chapmen* and frowning on an Ohio NWP lawyer allied too closely with employers. This is an episode in the history of a marginal organization with little experience in constitutional litigation before or since. Mrs. Smith and Mrs. Matthews consistently adhered in practice to the official doctrine of the party, as expressed in an editorial in *Equal Rights* praising the *Adkins* decision:

The Woman's Party stands for equality between men and women in all laws. This includes laws affecting the position of women in industry as well as all other laws. The Woman's Party does not take any position with regard to the merits of minimum wage legislation, but it does demand that such legislation, if passed shall be for both sexes. It is opposed to all legislation having a sex basis and applying to one sex alone.[12]

The Woman's Party probably would not have prepared a brief as *amicus curiae* in the *Tipaldo* case without suggestions by the employers' lawyers; yet they kept their distance and their independence. Before the New York Court of Appeals' decision Mrs. Smith wrote:

A few weeks ago, our New York office was approached by a lawyer for certain restaurants with regard to the case. An invitation was extended to the National Woman's Party to join in the argument before the Court of Appeals. The Minimum Wage order has not yet been extended to restaurants and hotels but they are naturally interested in the test case. . . .

Later, when the case was before the United States Supreme Court, Mrs. Matthews spurned the efforts of Challen B. Ellis to influence the shape of her brief. Mrs. Matthews wrote to Mrs. Smith:

Mr. Ellis telephoned me today. . . . [He asked] would the Woman's Party be agreeable to [my] appearing on the brief as OF counsel. He is an able person and a fine lawyer but I doubt if we could work satisfactorily with him as he is I think opposed to a minimum wage no matter who it covers. Our position is different. Besides, doing anything together might look like we were joining with the employers.

During the time *Tipaldo* and *Parrish* were becoming the crucial tests of minimum wage laws for women in the Supreme Court, the Ohio case of *Chapman v. Walker* was moving along in ways that made the test-case watchers feel that it might at any time blossom forth as the key litigation. It had a lot of potential. In one way it appealed greatly to Mrs. Smith as a case worthy of support from the Woman's Party; in another way it did not. Walker was a woman; Tipaldo was characterized by Mrs. Smith as a chiseler; she preferred support for the former. But the great drawback was that the feminist Agnes B. Dickinson of Columbus, who initiated the *Walker* case was cooperating with employers.

Moreover, in the *Tipaldo* case the Woman's Party would be coming in on its own with an *amicus curiae* brief where its ideological position could be set forth clearly. But in the *Walker* case, the whole burden of initiation and follow-through was being undertaken by Mrs. Dickinson. Working with the Ohio Laundryowners' Association and the Ohio State Association of Dyers and Cleaners, which were described as having given the feminists "much information in the past," Mrs. Dickinson began her action in January 1936. On the fourteenth she obtained an injunction against the state minimum wage division. "She agreed, on January 22, to permit the division to function provided there was no enforcement—which is another way of letting the women in the division draw their pay which had been stopped by the injunction. But there is no enforcement of the law."

Walker v. Chapman was not to be decided by the three-judge federal district court in Ohio until November 20, 1936, so that when the law was upheld the calendar of the United States Supreme Court had almost completely passed it by. The *Tipaldo* case had been decided on June 1 and the motion for reargument denied on October 14. Meanwhile, the *Parrish* case had been decided in Olympia in April, accepted by the Supreme Court on October 14 and already set for oral argument in December 1936.

There are four interesting aspects of *Walker v. Chapman.* First, the United States Supreme Court did not show any awareness that this case might eventually be available for its consideration along with the cases from New York and Washington, and the Court showed no inclination whatever to wait for as long as a term to allow this. Second, as the feminists and employers sponsoring Walker lost in the district court they had the choice of appeal, and chose not to. Third, here was a case where the antagonism of the Woman's Party and the Consumers' League was joined in court. The official report of the case shows Agnes B. Dickinson as counsel for Walker and the Ohio Consumers' League volunteer counsel, Marvin Harrison, acting as OF Counsel on the brief for the state of Ohio presented by Ohio Attorney General John W. Bricker. Fourth, this challenge to the Ohio minimum wage law led the Consumers' League of Ohio to work with Attorney General Bricker to prepare an *amicus* brief in the *Tipaldo* case for Ohio, separate from the brief of the six states offered by Dean Acheson. Finally, the New York and Washington women of the National Woman's Party were obliged to make a choice and to insist that their interests and the interests of the feminist movement should be sharply separated from the errant Mrs. Dickinson and her unholy alliance with the employers and their lawyers.

NWP frustration in gaining permission to file an *amicus curiae* brief in *Tipaldo* counters Consumers' League perception of instant cooperation from Bennett. When the New York attorney general finally yielded to the NWP, his press statement said permission had been granted on request. This was not true, although the view of the Consumers' League was never shaken. According to official Women's Party files, poor Bennett was a villian to the Woman's Party, too! Burnita Matthews was on top of the fast-breaking *Tipaldo* case in the spring of 1936. On March 30, the day the Court acted on the certiorari petition she telegraphed Mrs. Smith: WRIT GRANTED IN MINIMUM WAGE CASE ARGUMENT APRIL TWENTY-EIGHTH. Mrs. Matthews promptly asked permission to file as *amicus* from the two parties, as the Supreme Court rules required. Gates and Leavitt agreed; Bennett, so wrote Mrs. Matthews, "neither consented nor refused." She complained "the Court's rule is a bad one. The Court itself ought to decide whether other parties may join in as friends of the Court." To overcome Bennett's refusal Mrs. Matthews might seek permission directly from the Court and she acted quickly to arrange it. "I talked at length today to Mr. Cropley, the Clerk," she wrote, praising him as "a very fine and helpful person." She then drew up a motion seeking consent to file from the Court.

Simultaneously, Mrs. Matthews and especially Mrs. Smith went to work on Attorney General Bennett. "I think it would be well," wrote Mrs. Matthews, "to give some publicity out about the Attorney General if he is refusing us and letting the Hotel Association file a brief." Mrs. Smith did not hesitate. "I am going to the *Times* and *Herald Tribune* tomorrow," she announced. And she did, informally, and it worked, or at the least it coincided with consent from Bennett.

Money was needed to pay the printer for a NWP *amicus* brief. Mrs. Smith learned that about $200 would be needed and she readily agreed to help raise the sum and was sure she could, saying, "After all, there is some prestige to work of that kind." She sent letters out to several likely donors. Others sought funds, too, although Miss Berrien, the lawyer in Washington, cautioned against "asking Mrs. DuPont for a contribution for the brief." She felt that "in view of the kick-up the Black Committee is making about the organizations being supported by DuPont funds to attack the administration," that it would be better to get her to give to some other object. A feminist from California sent a small check with a note to Mrs. Smith that their cause was becoming an increasingly popular one.

Printed briefs must be filed with the clerk of the Supreme Court prior to the time of oral argument and this put great pressure on the office of Matthews, Berrien and Greathouse in Washington. They made it on April 27, with a day to spare.

The National Woman's Party *amicus* brief contended that wage laws were unpopular:

The laws of about sixteen states and various articles, reports and comments are cited by petitioner in support of minimum wage legislation for women. If the statute is constitutional it is not necessary to show any sentiment in favor of it. If it is unconstitutional, it cannot be sustained no matter how many people may desire it. But to whatever extent such considerations are material, we point out that the majority of the states have no minimum wage legislation and that there is considerable sentiment in this country against it. There is in addition organized opposition to minimum wage legislation which restricts women's freedom to contract while preserving that of men.

The brief of the National Woman's Party then proceeded to list about sixty organizations sharing this view. No doubt the power of an idea can be gauged, at least roughly, by knowing who supports it. Here the supporters included the Zonta Club of New York City and the Soroptomist Club, too. Also, the Business and Professional Women's Club of Vermont, the High School Teacher's Association of Los Angeles and the Women's Press Club of New York City.

The central argument of the National Woman's Party as *amicus* was the feminist view. The fund raising, the independence from Ellis and the employers, the work to gain consent to file—all the activity essential to getting a brief before the Court is important in this light. The activity meant that a strong statement, purely from the feminist outlook, would be available to the justices. The substance of the view had been shaped over the years, not simply by the NWP lawyers but by lay leaders as well. In an article in *Equal Rights* in 1936, Jane Norman Smith had explained the opposition of the NWP to minimum wage laws noting their protest when the bill was before the New York legislature in 1933. She stressed their agreement with Samuel Gompers' assertion that "the minimum tends to become the maximum." NWP members for years had recorded every example possible of women who had been thrown out of work owing to legal minima and replaced by a man to whom the law did not apply. They insisted that, "There is only one fair basis for minimum wage laws—and that is to place any wage minimum upon the *job*, rather than the sex of the worker." This was the argument of the party in their *amicus* brief in the *Tipaldo* case.

The Court Declines to Overrule Adkins

In the litigation after *Adkins* there is a tradition of judicial restraint on the readiness of courts to overrule. It is almost as though the decision invalidating the wage law for women achieved by the conservative activists then became almost sacrosanct to overruling by the true believers in restraint. Two years after *Adkins*, in the Arizona case, the reports noted: "Mr. Justice Holmes requests that it be stated that his concurrence is solely upon the ground that he regards himself bound by the decision in *Adkins v. Children's Hospital.*" The other dissenters in *Adkins*, Taft and Sanford, took Holmes's position but were silent on reasons. McKenna's replacement, Stone, had joined these three justices to side with Brandeis, the dissent of the Progressive activist Brandeis could have meant the overruling of *Adkins* then and there. But Holmes's view on restraint in overruling was not frivolous and his judicial attitude toward this cannot be dismissed as a cover for a change of heart on the issue of minimum wage laws. The position of the early Stone seems to be something else again.

Lower court judges have almost universally doubted their authority to overrule. When a Supreme Court doctrine stands in their way, they criticize and they distinguish, rarely do they overrule. When Judge Irving Lehman of the New York Court of Appeals dissented in *Tipaldo v. Morehead*, as that case was styled there, he expressed this traditional deference on the power to overrule by saying, "We start our consideration of the validity of the statute here challenged upon the assumption that the construction placed upon the Constitution by the decision of the Supreme Court in the *Adkins* case is open to attack only in that court. . . ." He insisted that when the Supreme Court construes the Constitution, others must accept it and illustrated the point by noting Holmes's acceptance in *Murphy v. Sardell.*

In writing that the New York law should be upheld, Judge Lehman made a beautiful statement on the wisdom of a readiness to reconsider and to overrule even though he felt constrained as a judge of a state court to distinguish *Adkins*. He declared that when convinced of error, courts must change their construction and admit it. Here is his formulation: "That courts have not been willing to perpetuate a construction after they have been convinced of its unsoundness, has been a source of strength to our system of constitutional government." Judge Lehman next speaks of the argument made in his court by Attorney General Bennett and Solicitor General Epstein and thereby sheds light on the subsequent disagreement in the United States Supreme Court over whether an overruling was sought by counsel. Clearly, Judge Lehman shows that a request was made in the state court at least, suggesting that the attorney general at that time was "overruling-minded." This is a continuation of what Judge Lehman said:

The Attorney General, upon this appeal, argues that the statute now under consideration is free from the objections to the earlier "Minimum Wage" legislation, which the Supreme Court, in the *Adkins* case, held to be in violation of the provisions of the Constitution; but that the Supreme Court would now decide differently if the same objections were now presented.

It was at this point that Judge Lehman excused himself by deferring to the Supreme Court as solely capable of overruling itself.

In delivering the opinion of the Court, Mr. Justice Butler displayed a restraint on procedure ironically in contrast to his activism on substance. Butler asserts that New York did "not ask to be heard upon the question whether the *Adkins* case should be overruled." As I have said elsewhere, Attorney General Bennett's brief says both things: *Adkins* can be distinguished *or* overruled. Mr. Justice Butler adopts the narrow ground that an overruling was not sought and hence an overruling cannot be considered. *Stare decisis*, like it or not, holds the Court in its grip: "The *Adkins* case, unless distinguishable, requires affirmance of the judgment below" (by the New York Court of Appeals in *Tipaldo*). This is Mr. Justice Butler's settled view of why the Court cannot countenance the overruling issue:

. . . . the petition for the writ sought review upon the ground that this case is distinguishable from *[Adkins]*. No application has been made for reconsideration of the constitutional question there decided. The validity of the principles upon which that decision rests are not challenged. This court confines itself to the ground upon which the writ was asked or granted.

There were three opinions by the nine U.S. Supreme Court Justices in affirming, five to four, the New York Court of Appeals invalidation of the 1933 New York State minimum wage law for women. Mr. Justice Butler spoke for himself, Van Devanter, McReynolds, Sutherland and Roberts, the five-man majority. Mr. Chief Justice Hughes wrote a dissenting opinion distinguishing the New York law from the federal statute applicable to the District of Columbia in the *Adkins* case. Mr. Justice Brandeis and Mr. Justice Cardozo joined in this opinion. The opinion by Hughes says *nothing* about overruling Adkins. By contrast, Mr. Justice Stone, dissenting separately in an opinion also joined by Mr. Justice Brandeis and Mr. Justice Cardozo, actively favored an overruling.

Thus, three of the four dissenters believe a reconsideration of *Adkins* was called for whether sought or not. Stone's words on this point are loud and clear, as follows:

I know of no rule or practice by which the arguments advanced in support of an application for certiorari restrict our choice between conflicting precedents in deciding a question of constitutional law which the petition, if granted, requires us to answer. Here the question which the petition specifically presents is whether the New York statute contravenes the Fourteenth Amendment. In addition, the petition [by the Attorney General for New York] assigns as a reason for granting it that "the construction and application of the Constitution of the United States and a prior decision" of this Court "are necessarily involved," and again, that "the circumstances prevailing under which the New York law was enacted call for a reconsideration of the Adkins Case in the light of the New York act and conditions aimed to be remedied thereby." Unless we are now to construe and apply the Fourteenth Amendment without regard to our decisions since the Adkins Case, we could not rightly avoid its reconsideration even if it were not asked.

Mr. Justice Roberts of Pennsylvania wrote no opinion in the *Tipaldo* case, but as four justices in the 1923 *Adkins* case were sitting in 1936 his position made all the difference. He made the Butler opinion the opinion of the Court. Ten months later, in April 1937, he took an opposition position and, again silently, joined in overruling *Adkins*. The *Literary Digest*, not yet plowed under, spoke of Roberts's "somersault," and featured his photograph. The National Woman's Party reported the case under a black headline "Surrender!" The editorial began, "As *Equal Rights* goes to press there comes the astounding news that the United States Supreme Court, through the switch of Justice Roberts, reverses itself on the constitutionality of minimum wage legislation discriminating against women." His actions in the *Tipaldo* case as well as in the *Parrish* case a year later quickly sealed Roberts's reputation, not as hero but as goat, as a man whose principles were so unsettled that he could switch expediently from a conservative to a liberal position.

Supreme Court justices do not write about their actions in cases. Has any justice written a memoir? No, nor do they later explain decisions. But Mr. Justice Roberts did prepare a statement explaining his actions and his thoughts in these minimum wage cases. At the urging of Mr. Justice Frankfurter, then his colleague but of course himself intimately involved in minimum wage cases, Roberts prepared a memorandum, dated November 9, 1945. He entrusted it to Frankfurter to be made public at his discretion. Roberts retired from the Supreme Court on July 31, 1945, and died on May 19, 1955. Mr. Justice Frankfurter then included the text of the Roberts testament in a memoir of Roberts in the *University of Pennsylvania Law Review* for December 1955. I will also reproduce the Roberts memorandum fully but in two sections, reserving his comments on the 1937 *Parrish* case. Roberts must have felt deeply misunderstood to prepare such a statement. Following is the first part of it, pertaining to his role in the 1936 decision:

A petition for certiorari was filed in *Morehead v. Tipaldo*, 298 U.S. 587, on March 16, 1936. When the petition came to be acted upon the Chief Justice spoke in favor of a grant, but several others spoke against it on the ground that the case was ruled by *Adkins v. Children's Hospital*, 261 U.S. 525. Justices Brandeis, Cardozo and Stone were in favor of a grant. They, with the Chief Justice, made up four votes for a grant.

When my turn came to speak I said I saw no reason to grant the writ unless the Court were prepared to re-examine and overrule the *Adkins* case. To this remark there was no response around the table, and the case was marked granted.

Both in the petition for certiorari, in the brief on the merits, and in oral argument, counsel for the State of New York took the position that it was unnecessary to overrule the *Adkins* case in order to sustain that position of the state of New York. It was urged that further data and experience and additional facts distinguished the case at bar from the *Adkins* case. The argument seemed to me to be disingenuous and born of timidity. I could find nothing in the record to substantiate the alleged distinction. At conference I so stated, and stated further that I was for taking the state of New York at its word. The state had not asked that the *Adkins* case be overruled but that it be distinguished. I said I was unwilling to put a decision on any such ground. The vote was five to four for affirmance, and the case was assigned to Justice Butler.

I stated to him that I could concur in any opinion which was based on the fact that the State had not asked us to re-examine or overrule *Adkins* and that, as we found no material difference in the facts of the two cases, we should therefore follow the *Adkins* case. The case was originally so written by Justice Butler, but after a dissent had been circulated he added matter to his opinion, seeking to sustain the *Adkins* case in principle. My proper course would have been to concur specially on the narrow ground I had taken. I did not do so. But at conference in the Court I said that I did not propose to review and re-examine the *Adkins* case until a case should come to the Court requiring that this should be done.

The student of Supreme Court overrulings will see three points of interest in this statement. The first is that he "saw no reason to grant the writ [of certiorari] unless the Court were prepared to re-examine and overrule the *Adkins* case." This view of the significance of a grant of certiorari differs sharply from the conventional explanation of Mr. Justice Frankfurter that a grant or denial tells nothing of the judicial attitude toward the merits in a case.

The second point is gleaned from Frankfurter's flat assertion that "when the *Tipaldo* case was before the Court in the spring of 1936, he [Roberts] was prepared to overrule the Adkins decision." This is of interest because it is a bald statement about this justice's policy predisposition. He had not as a justice of the Supreme Court yet reviewed a minimum wage case; yet in principle he had determined that such laws were, in general, constitutional. And in the greatest constitutional crisis in the Court's history he was ready to wait until a perfectly argued case came on for review.

This does clearly support, if taken at face value, the third point where Justice Roberts emphasizes that "in the petition for certiorari, in the brief on the merits, and in oral argument, counsel for the state of New York took the position that it was unnecessary to overrule the *Adkins* case in order to sustain the position of the state of New York." Everything Robert says about the argument by the state of New York leads one to think that their counsel was timid and incompetent. The records of the National Consumers' League suggest very strongly that there was another fault, namely the lack of interest of Attorney General Bennett in winning a great victory for the minimum wage. The record shows him to have been notably uncooperative with the league in preparing the case for the Supreme Court. Yet the view adopted by Mr. Justice Stone, joined by Brandeis and Cardozo shows that overruling *Adkins* had been sought and they were willing whether it had been or not.

The statement by Mr. Justice Roberts is simply incomprehensible when placed against the plain words of the briefs filed for New York State by Bennett and Epstein. Certainly their aim was to preserve the New York statute and so they invited the Court to distinguish *Adkins* if it could not overrule. But in seeking a writ of certiorari from the Court, two of the six points made in the petition by New York State centered on a purpose to see the *Adkins* case reappraised. These are the two points:

The construction and application of the Constitution of the United States and a prior decision of this, the Supreme Court of the United States are necessarily at issue.

The circumstances prevailing under which the New York law was enacted call for a reconsideration of the Adkins case in the light of the New York act and conditions aimed to be remedied thereby.

The main brief for New York State does not follow up strongly on these points but it does not abandon them.

"So far as American constitutional law is concerned," Professor Paul Freund has said, "the judge is a servant seated before his masters." The decision of the New York Court of Appeals in the *Tipaldo* case comes into view when Freund observes, "The company who share the lawmaking activity of Supreme Court judges include at least the lower tribunals as well as counsel. The deference paid to the views of other judicial and administrative officers will necessarily be affected by the regard in which they are held." Consigned as mossbacks unwilling to budge from reactionary paralysis, the four horsemen (of the Apocalypse one supposes and not of Notre Dame) were not isolated in thought or action. To speak only of the minimum wage cases before us, Sutherland,

Butler, Van Devanter and McReynolds were in league with and affirmed the court below in *Adkins, Murphy, Donham*, and *Tipaldo*. True, there were close divisions in the Supreme Court and in the lower courts as well. But they were not alone. *Tipaldo* in the New York Court of Appeals—over its history, perhaps the most august of the highest state courts—had been decided by a four-to-three split. The opinion there by Chief Justice Frederick E. Crews had its echo in the subsequent expressions in Mr. Justice Butler's *Tipaldo* opinion.

More than echo, Mr. Justice Butler said he was bound to follow the New York Court of Appeals on key points. "This court," said Butler, "is without power to put a different construction upon the state enactment from that adopted by the highest court of the state." Brushing petitioner's argument aside, Butler said further, "The meaning of the statute as fixed by its decision must be accepted here as if the meaning had been specifically expressed in the enactment." This was lovely reciprocity for the pledge of Chief Justice Crews in the case below where he vowed: "The interpretation of the federal Constitution by the United States Supreme Court is binding upon us; we are in duty bound to follow its decisions unless they are inapplicable."

In construing the 1933 New York law, Chief Justice Crews found it essentially like the 1918 federal law for the District of Columbia. The Act of Congress concerned "wages [that] were inadequate to maintain decent standards of living." The New York law provides a definite standard for wages paid—"at least the value of the services rendered." Crews declared this to be "a difference in phraseology and not in principle." He believed the distinctions between *Tipaldo* and *Adkins* to be "differences in details, methods and time; the exercise of legislative power to fix wages in any employment is the same." When all was said and done Crews concluded for the majority: "The order below should be reversed, the writ sustained, and the prisoner discharged, as chapter 584 of the laws of 1933, under which he is held, is unconstitutional according to *Adkins v. Children's Hospital.*"

In following the idea that "freedom of contract is the general rule and restraint the exception," Mr. Justice Butler was not simply repeating an argument at bar or a lower court opinion but a major theme in American constitutional law of that era. The Fourteenth Amendment's limitation against a state depriving any person of life, liberty or property had, since *Lochner v. New York* in 1905, been defined as protecting a "liberty of contract." This judicial slogan's history is complex. Suffice it to say that "liberty of contract" was invoked by Butler in *Tipaldo* just as Sutherland had done in *Adkins*. On this point Mr. Justice Butler really did not go as far in the direction argued by *Tipaldo's* counsel as they wished. Miller and Levitt had stressed freedom from price fixing, not only wage setting, but Butler's opinion took little notice of this theme.

But the National Woman's Party could correctly point to how its brief had been followed by the Court, and they did. On the night before the argument,

Bernita Matthews sent a copy of her brief to Governor Miller hoping "he would use some part of it pertaining to women." The questioning in oral argument convinced Mrs. Matthews that "Stone will be against us." Her perceptions were sharp as she added: "We feel that our four friends will remain firm—Sutherland, McReynolds, Van Devanter and Butler. The two on whom the case depends are Hughes and Roberts." In the oral argument, she reported, "they asked no questions and gave no sign." But their brief *amicus* was before the Court and they were sanguine. Mrs. Matthews was pleased to report that "Mr. Ellis says he has heard many compliments on our brief and commendations that the Woman's Organizations did this thing and did it independently of anyone else." The finest commendation of all resides in the opinion of Mr. Justice Butler in *Tipaldo* in a ruling supporting "the attitude consistently maintained by the National Woman's Party." Here the *Adkins* case was also closely followed, and at points quoted: "We cannot accept the doctrine that women of mature age, *sui juris*, require or may be subjected to restrictions upon their liberty of contract which could not lawfully be imposed in the case of men under similar circumstances."

In his dissent, Chief Justice Hughes would hold the New York law valid by distinguishing the law applied to the Children's Hospital in the District of Columbia case. He was impressed that New York had "been careful to adopt a different and improved standard, in order to meet the objection aimed at the earlier statutes, by requiring a fair equivalence of wage and service." Hughes followed the arguments of New York State, citing the statistics of the factual brief of New York and those "strikingly exhibited in the brief filed by the Corporation Counsel of the City as an *amicus curiae.*" As this brief had seen the handiwork of Frieda Miller, Dorothy Kenyon and Mrs. Herrick, the Consumers' League could take some pride in reaching Hughes. He followed the Consumers' League view that women must, sometimes, be specially protected by labor legislation of this character.

Mr. Justice Stone, as we have seen, would not distinguish, but would overrule *Adkins* and so he "would not make the differences between the present statute and that involved in the *Adkins Case* the sole basis of decision." Stone attached "little importance" to the fact that the law in the District was aimed at a "starvation wage" while the New York law required a "reasonable wage." In a searing paragraph he summed up the evidence for the reasonableness of minimum wage legislation. Low wages tend to bring ill health and immorality. Thirty-one foreign countries and seventeen states had enacted wage laws. This, for Justice Stone, proved minimum wage laws not to be "a remedy beyond the bounds of reason." His much quoted conclusion on this theme follows:

It is difficult to imagine any grounds, other than our own personal economic predilections, for saying that the contract of employment is any less an appropriate subject of legislation than are scores of others, in dealing with which this court has held that legislation may curtail individual freedom in the public interest.

Stone also made much of the Depression, the economic circumstances of the nation which had developed in the years since the 1923 *Adkins* case. Already the Court had acknowledged the bearing economic depression might have on constitutional interpretation in *Nebbia v. New York*. He insisted that *Nebbia* was a collateral case which "left the Court free of *[Adkins]* as a precedent, and free to declare that the choice of the particular form of regulation by which grave economic maladjustments are to be remedied is for legislatures and not the courts."

Glendon Schubert has explained that "on the heels of the announcement of an unfavorable decision" a loser "can ask the court to change its mind" in the case just decided. He makes an obvious point in observing that "a petition for rehearing has no chance unless at least one member of the former majority either leaves the Court or is willing to change his vote; but the rules of the Court do not necessarily stand in the way of obtaining such a rehearing, if a majority justice has been converted and the original decision was marginal." To permit this possibility, Attorney General Bennett had to prepare and file a petition for rehearing in *Morehead v. Tipaldo* within twenty days after the decision was announced on the last day of the October 1935 term of court—June 1, 1936.

Again the organizations became active, particularly the Consumers' League of New York, which took the decision as such a blow. Once more, the league had to deal with Bennett. And again, they did so indirectly by working through Governor Lehman. This time they achieved results. Just before the deadline, the good word came by Western Union from Governor Lehman's assistant, Charles Poletti, in Albany, to Mrs. Herrick in New York, June 18, 1936:

THE GOVERNOR HAS ASKED ME TO ADVISE YOU THAT AFTER AN EXCHANGE OF TELEGRAMS AND TELEPHONE CONVERSATIONS THE GOVERNOR THIS MORNING RECEIVED THIS TELEGRAM FROM THE ATTORNEY GENERAL QUOTE AFTER FULL CONSIDERATION OF THE WHOLE SITUATION I HAVE DECIDED TO PETITION THE SUPREME COURT FOR REHEARING IN MINIMUM WAGE CASE STOP I AM ISSUING A STATEMENT TO THIS EFFECT UNQUOTE PLEASE ADVISE BURLINGHAM CHEERIO—CHARLIE POLETTI.

By this time, Bennett and Epstein had fully digested the Court's opinions and the disagreement among them over whether an overruling of *Adkins* had been asked for by them. This they stressed in their petition for a rehearing. Unable to locate a copy of the petition itself we can see this charged theme clearly in an unusually full report of the request printed in the *New York Times*. Following are key parts of this newspaper report of the petition filed for New York:

Bennett and Epstein, in their brief, insisted that the court majority "misread the purport" of the petition which the State's lawyers originally submitted in the case, and the brief they presented in connection with the arguments.

The attorneys said that the court had ignored their request to reconsider the constitutional question involved in the Adkins case upon which the New York Court of Appeals had depended in holding the wage law invalid. . . .

"It is most respectfully submitted that the court misconstrued the basis of the petition and thereby needed properly to appraise the scope of review sought," the brief stated. . . .

To support their contentions Messrs. Bennett and Epstein quoted from their petition for a writ of certiorari asserting that the circumstances under which the New York law was enacted called for a reconsideration of the Adkins case.

This turned out to be nothing but ritual as the petition for rehearing in *Tipaldo* was denied without comment by the justices on October 12, 1936. But it could have had a subtle bearing on the eventual disposition of the Court on the constitutionality of minimum wage laws for women. On the same day, October 12, 1936, the Court agreed to review and hear on the merits the case of *West Coast Hotel Co. v. Parrish* to see whether the 1913 Washington state minimum wage law for women was constitutional.

Overruling Adkins in the Parrish Case

In Washington State between 1933 and 1937 the NCL guarded its interests without local organization and without a role in the climactic *Parrish* case. The league subscribed to Luce's Press Clipping Bureau in New York which blue-penciled and clipped from the *Seattle Times* for February 13, 1933, a listing of bills just introduced in the state legislature, this one: "H.B. 317, by Miller (D), King—Providing for a minimum wage of $15 a week based on a 48-hour week for women and all minors." Alert Mary Dewson wrote Miller, boasted of NCL experience and hoped "you will not press for the passage of your bill." The existing Washington statute, carried since 1913, was based on the cost of living and she feared "it might be considered unconstitutional. However if it is not brought before the courts it is the law of Washington and can be enforced." But whatever its fate, she was "absolutely certain that a flat and statutory rate will be declared unconstitutional." Representative Miller did not reply. No new legislation was enacted and the 1913 Washington law continued on the books.

Having discouraged new legislation, the league had next to discourage new litigation. An inquiry came from Henry M. Kaye, an attorney in Chewekah, Washington, dated May 1, 1935. He sought information and literature and had also written to Mr. Frankfurter. He told them his astonishing and disquieting plans: "I have filed suit recently under the provisions of the Washington Minimum Wage Law, and in view of the *Adkins* case, I have not the slightest doubt that the case will be taken to the state Supreme Court." The league sent Kaye their pamphlets and suggested a list of reading but the women also wrote each other, wondering what to do. They asked Mr. Kaye for details about his case.

Henry Kaye was representing a young woman working in a mercantile store, being paid less than the $13.20 per month provided by the state minimum law. When fired, she sued for back wages of $600, and in May 1935 Kaye wrote, "The trial court overruled the defendant's demurrer to the complaint and held that the case must go to trial." Kaye felt the state law could be distinguished as it "provides for remedies in laboring and working conditions aside from establishing minimum wages and in this respect avoids the criticism of the District of Columbia legislation which was simply and purely a price-fixing law." The women were sure Mr. Kaye should be dissuaded from continuing this court test, and as it happened, Kaye's case was not heard of again.

News of the test case that worked—brought by Mrs. Elsie Parrish against the West Coast Hotels—reached the Consumers' League through the good offices of Mary Anderson in the Woman's Bureau. Fret and worry marked her long letter to Josephine Goldmark since Superior Court Judge W.O. Parr had ruled the 1913 law invalid. Mr. Jay Olinger, supervisor of safety and industrial relations in Olympia, commented: "We regret the court decision very much as its effect will be far-reaching. The most we can say of it is that it is more good argument in favor of a constitutional amendment." Miss Anderson also told of trying to persuade minimum wage supporters in North Dakota to drop the *Neutmon v. Patterson* case scheduled to come to the district court there in December. In California, Mable Kinney wrote of her effective efforts to prevent test cases of their state minimum wage law for "to date we have been able to have them adjusted outside of court. . . ."

Sole dependence on the *Tipaldo* case was still the party line. Miss Anderson concluded her letter to Miss Goldmark: "We sincerely hope that the decision in the New York case will finally bring all of this disturbing uncertainty to a happy end."

While the Consumers' League placed all its eggs in one basket the New York office was apprised of developments in the *Parrish* case solely through Luce's Press Clipping Bureau. Emily Sims Marconnier wrote Louise Stitt at the Women's Bureau after the New York case was lost: "Do you know anything about the Washington State minimum wage case, which I understand is on its way to the U.S. Supreme Court? What little I have is from a newspaper clipping in a Seattle paper." All the while, the journalists of Seattle were alert and sanguine. The *Seattle Star* praised Chief Justice Millard's opinion in the *Parrish* case to the skies and predicted the case "will prove a hard nut for even that august body [the U.S. Supreme Court] to crack." These were the *Star's* conclusions:

. . . to an editor who is not so delicately attuned to the fine points of constitutional phraseology, it seems very plain that the Washington State supreme court has stated the case in terms of logic and simple justice.

It is greatly to be hoped that the Washington court has presented a case that will convince at least one justice of the highest court in the land—for that would make the Washington minimum-wage-for-women law virtually the law of the nation.

When the Supreme Court, made up of the same nine justices since Cardozo joined in 1932, convened for a new term the first Monday of October 1936 they were faced with a docket of cases raising the same old problems. The holdings against national New Deal legislation could not stop Congress and the president from reacting with essentially the same solutions to economic problems that had been tried before. Different phraseology, different agencies for enforcement, yes; but much the same philosophy of government was expressed. Now in the October 1936 term the constitutionality of the Social Security Act of 1935 and the National Labor Relations Act of 1935 was probably to be reviewed. The states, even more quickly than the national government, churned up similar issues to those supposedly laid to rest. On state minimum wage laws for women, the petition for rehearing in the *Tipaldo* case would be disposed of on October 10. That same day at least four justices, sufficient to grant the writ in response to a petition for certiorari, led the Court to agree to review the decision of the Supreme Court of the state of Washington that the 1913 wage law for women was constitutional.

The conservative justices of the Supreme Court were not feeling particularly unpopular as the October term began. Criticism of the Court there was. Condemnation by the president they expected. Attacks by Progressives had been their lot for years. Van Devanter could remember them since Teddy Roosevelt's attacks in the 1912 campaign. Sutherland, Butler, McReynolds were justices in 1924 when LaFollette's Progressive platform pledged court reform. There was nothing novel in the lambasting the Court took after its decision in the *Tipaldo* case, and in their invalidation of New Deal laws in the previous three terms.

Pictured, accurately enough, as reactionaries, the majority of the Court did not so much regard themselves as expressing an aristocratic viewpoint as they felt themselves stemming a temporary tide of "mobocracy" that would recede. The maxim that government never lets go of any power it gains had been shown to be foolish when the people repealed national prohibition of the liquor trade. In the *Tipaldo* case, the brief of the National Woman's Party had argued that since thirty states were without minimum wage laws for women, most people opposed such restrictions on employers. And now, early in the October 1936 term of Court a national presidential election would shed further light on what the people thought.

Many predictors of the time were with the majority of the Court. *The Literary Digest*, a weekly magazine with mass circulation, had been conducting public opinion polls for twenty years and had accurately anticipated the election of Harding in 1920, Coolidge in 1924, Hoover in 1928, and Roosevelt in 1932. The *Digest* boasted of seeking the opinions of the largest panel for a poll in history. As many as two million people were asked what they thought. But the questions were of a general character and it was later seen that those asked were people with automobiles and telephones so that there was an inadequate cross section of people questioned. But at the time the *Literary Digest* had great prestige as a soothsayer. On January 18, 1936, its poll reported that 62.66 percent of the American public opposed New Deal acts and policies while only 37.34 percent favored them. This from a sample of 1,907,800 persons. The attitude of the American public was pictured as overwhelmingly opposed to the New Deal even before the campaign began. In the final poll before the election, on October 31, 1936, the raw totals of voters questioned were reported as 1,293,669 favoring Landon with 972,897 for Roosevelt.

Under these general conditions of belief that the New Deal was unpopular, yet with the Court under severe criticism, the justices appreciated the fact, as Arthur Krock wrote in the *New York Times* on May 27, 1936, that the Court was on trial during the presidential campaign. The newspapers and magazines, the speeches and the letters to the editor were full of this major issue during the presidential campaign of 1936. After Roosevelt swept to a landslide victory, the Republican party, the *Literary Digest* poll and the Supreme Court all seemed crushed. Soon Krock was recalling Mr. Dooley's famous saying that the Supreme Court followed the election returns. As acute a contemporary observer as Dean Dinwoodey, then the Supreme Court correspondent of the *New York Times* (later he was president of the Bureau of National Affairs, publishers of *United States Law Week*) on December 13, 1936, discussed the possibility that the Court's attitude toward the New Deal had already changed or been influenced by the election returns.

A week after the election the Court agreed to review three cases concerning the constitutionality of the National Labor Relations Board. President Roosevelt's support of state minimum wage laws for women was so well known that the *Parrish* case, scheduled for argument just before Christmas would also, in effect, be a test of the New Deal spirit of the role of government.

The hopes of American conservatives in recent decades, and their belief in the wisdom of the people, have been highest just before presidential elections. This is shown in classic form in the summer and fall of 1936. Even the legal briefs in the minimum wage cases before the Supreme Court expressed this view. In the *Parrish* case, the reply brief for the appellants, filed in late October 1936, concluded with this statement: "We believe the considered judgment of the American people is that the majority opinion in [the *Adkins*] case was right." This reflected the buoyancy of businessmen (or at least hotel men in Washington State) and their lawyers in the coming election of Governor Landon and the defeat of President Roosevelt. These political and constitutional premises took a terrible tumble.

A by-product of the American federal system is that social and economic issues tend to have different histories in the different states. And the experience of litigation concerning those issues will be different within the different state courts. The next episode in the development of litigation on state minimum wage laws shows, too, that this history is not manipulated totally by a national organization.

At the time of the decision of the United States Supreme Court in the *Tipaldo* case on June 1, 1936, similar cases were in progress in three other states—Illinois, Ohio and Washington. The Ohio case, *Walker v. Chapman*, saw the Ohio wage law being defended by Attorney General John W. Bricker with a prominent Cleveland lawyer associated with the Ohio Consumers' League, Marvin C. Harrison, as special counsel. This would be decided favorably by the United States District Court for Southern Ohio with a woman, Judge Florence Allen, writing the opinion on November 20, 1936.

During this time the little noticed case was advancing in Washington State. It had begun with the filing of a complaint on July 12, 1935, that a Spokane hotel was not abiding by the still-in-force 1913 state minimum wage law. A labor lawyer named C.B. Conner brought the action on behalf of Elsie Parris, a chambermaid, and her husband. A trial was held before Judge W.D. Parr in the Superior Court of Chelan County, without a jury, on October 17, and his decision was announced on November 9. Judge Parr ruled that, in accord with the United States Supreme Court ruling in the *Adkins* case, the Washington minimum wage law of 1913 was ruled unconstitutional. The case was promptly appealed to the Supreme Court of the state of Washington, where a reversal was won. Chief Justice Millard, for a unanimous court voting *five to zero*, wrote an opinion which distinguished the case from Adkins and held the Washington law valid. The opinion was filed on April 2, 1936.

After a petition for rehearing was denied in May and the decision of the United States Supreme Court in the *Tipaldo* case announced on June 1, and lawyers for the West Coast Hotel Company proceeded on August 17 to file a jurisdictional statement seeking appeal in the United States Supreme Court. Of course, this statement sought a reversal in the *Parrish* case to be achieved by holding firm to the rule of the *Adkins* case as applied to *Tipaldo* that the setting of a minimum wage was beyond the constitutional authority of a state. It now becomes pertinent to consider in full the final half of the statement left to us by Mr. Justice Roberts concerning his part in the *Parrish* case.

August 17, 1936, an appeal was filed in *West Coast Hotel Company v. Parrish*, 300 U.S. 379. The Court as usual met to consider applications in the week of Monday, October 5, 1936, and concluded its work by Saturday, October 10. During the conferences the jurisdictional statement in the *Parrish* case was considered and the question arose whether the appeal should be dismissed [Here Mr. Justice Frankfurter notes of Roberts's statement: "Evidently he meant should be reversed summarily, since the Washington Supreme Court sustained the statute."] on the authority of *Adkins* and *Morehead*. Four of those who had voted in the *Morehead* case voted to dismiss the appeal in the *Parrish* case. I stated that I would vote for the notation of probable jurisdiction. I am not sure that I gave my reason, but it is that in the appeal in the *Parrish* case the authority of *Adkins* was definitely assailed and the Court was asked to reconsider and overrule it. Thus, for the first time, I was confronted with the necessity of facing the soundness of the *Adkins* case. Those who were in the majority in the *Morehead* case expressed some surprise at my vote, and I heard one of the brethren ask another, "What is the matter with Roberts?"

Justice Stone was taken ill about October 14. The case was argued December 16 and 17, 1936, in the absence of Justice Stone, who at that time was lying in a comatose condition at his home. It came on for consideration at the conference on December 19. I voted for an affirmance. There were three other such votes, those of the Chief Justice, Justice Brandeis, and Justice Cardozo. The other four voted for a reversal.

If a decision had then been announced, the case would have been affirmed by a divided Court. It was thought that this would be an unfortunate outcome, as everyone on the Court knew Justice Stone's views. The case was, therefore, laid over for further consideration when Justice Stone should be able to participate. Justice Stone was convalescent during January and returned to the sessions of the Court on February 1, 1937. I believe that the *Parrish* case was taken up at the conference on February 6, 1937, and Justice Stone then voted for affirmance. This made it possible to assign the case for an opinion, which was done. The decision affirming the lower court was announced March 29, 1937.

These facts make it evident that no action taken by the President in the interim had any causal relation to my action in the *Parrish* case.

Mr. Justice Roberts, by this statement, won the battle against the claim he switched because President Roosevelt sent his Court-packing message to Congress on February 1937, but he lost the war against the belief that his own role depended solely on the timid, disingenuous argument of Attorney General Bennett in the *Tipaldo* case and the definite request of C.B. Conner and Sam Driver in the *Parrish* case to reconsider and overrule the authority of Adkins. Justice Roberts's recollection of the briefs in the *Parrish* case turns out to be as faulty as it was in the *Tipaldo* case.

Key evidence shows Mr. Justice Roberts to be wrong in his recollection "that in the appeal in the *Parrish* case the authority of *Adkins* was definitely assailed and the Court was asked to reconsider it and overrule it." Chief Justice Hughes says as much in his majority opinion: "On the argument at bar, counsel for the appellees attempted to distinguish the *Adkins* case upon the ground that the appellee was employed in a hotel and that the business of an innkeeper was affected with a public interest." This distinction was rejected as "obviously futile, as it appears that in one of the cases ruled by the *Adkins* opinion the employee was a woman employed as an elevator operator in a hotel." Sure enough, the remarkable four-page brief on the law submitted by C.B. Conner and Sam M. Driver for the appellees does not at all ask for an overruling. Instead, the brief explains carefully and thoughtfully how the *Adkins* case can be distinguished.

The sustaining of the decision of the Supreme Court of the State of Washington in this matter is not in conflict with the decision of this Court in the case of *Adkins v. Children's Hospital*. This law was passed by virtue of the reserve police power of the State of Washington, and having received the approval of the highest Court of the State of Washington is entitled to approval by the Supreme Court of the United States. The Adkins Case construed an act of Congress which had received the disapproval of the highest Court of the District of Columbia, and we, of course, draw the conclusion that the act of Congress not having received the approval of that Court was not a reasonable and proper remedy for a condition existing in the District of Columbia.

The brief for the appellees goes on to argue that the decision in the *Parrish* case by the state supreme court "is not inconsistent with other decisions of the Supreme Court of the United States."

The brief of *amici curiae* state of Washington filed by G.W. Hamilton, attorney general, took a similar line. Noting the decision in the *Tipaldo* case, it supported the Supreme Court's refusal to consider overruling *Adkins* on grounds that the cases were distinguishable and that a review of the *Adkins* rule was not sought. Like the appellees in *Parrish* the state attorney general argued that the fact situation was different. The *Adkins* case was a review of a federal statute treated adversely by the lower appellate court; the *Parrish* case was a review of a state statute reviewed favorably by the highest appellate court of that state.

True, counsel for the appellant stressed the *Adkins* rule and insisted that the Supreme Court would have to follow it or make an overruling. Their answer to the argument of the appellee employee Parrish that the cases were distinguishable really had to be that they were not. In the last word, in the conclusion in a brief containing "Appellant's Answer to Brief for *Amici Curiae*," John W. Roberts and E.L. Skeel, attorneys for the appellant wrote:

In conclusion we contend that the issue before this Court is simply whether the Adkins case is to be reconsidered and reversed or whether its authority is to be sustained. We believe the considered judgment of the American people is that the majority opinion in that case was right. There may be authority that a minimum wage act based upon fair value of services might be upheld. That view, however, gives to the appellee no support in this case, because the Washington statute was passed prior to any decision on the minimum wage statutes, and is of the type held arbitrary, unreasonable and unconstitutional in the Adkins case and in the Tipaldo case. It follows that the judgment of the Supreme Court of the State of Washington must be reversed and the judgment of the Superior Court of Chelan County, Washington, set out in the record herein, affirmed.

The best proof that the Court was not asked to overrule *Adkins*, as Mr. Justice Roberts has asserted, comes from the contemporary report in *United States Law Week* for December 22, 1936. The report was prepared by Dinwoodey. It began:

As was held by the Court in the case involving the Minimum Wage Law for Women in the State of New York, so in the instant case counsel who defended the law did not ask the Supreme Court to reconsider and overrule its decision in the *Adkins* case rendered in 1923. . . .

The assistant attorney general of Washington, W.A. Toner, distinguished the *Parrish* case by stating that the hotel business was involved and that this was "a business affected with a public interest," different from the laundry business involved in the *Tipaldo* case. He also distinguished the Washington statute of 1913 from others considered by the Supreme Court by noting that the employee can bring a civil action against an employer who pays her less than the prescribed minimum. The important argument for our present theme is that Toner's argument on the point of overruling is emphasized further in Dinwoodey's report as having "*made it clear* [italics mine] that 'we don't take any such position' that the *Adkins* case must be overruled in order to sustain the Washington law."

If Chief Justice Hughes could overrule *Adkins* for a five-man majority which included Roberts, how could he do so in the face of the attempt of the lawyers for Parrish and for Washington State as well to distinguish only? Hughes faced the issue squarely, quoting and directly rejecting the position taken for the majority in *Tipaldo* by Mr. Justice Butler. Hughes did not touch upon the claims of Attorney General Bennett that an overruling had been sought in *Tipaldo*. Nor did he refer to Stone's dissenting position there that the Court should reconsider the *Adkins* rule whatever counsel said. All the same, Hughes did follow the earlier line of Stone.

He began: "We think that the question which was not deemed to be open in the *Morehead* case is open and *is necessarily presented here*" (Italics mine). Hughes then deferred to the supreme court of the state of Washington which "has refused to regard the decision in the *Adkins* case as determinative and has pointed to our decisions both before and since that case as justifying its position." Chief Justice Hughes did not dwell upon this conflict but hastily concluded "that this ruling of the state court demands on our part a re-examination of the Adkins Case." Then, in the terseness of a great lawgiver, the Chief Justice struck three distinct points speeding the Court toward its overruling quite apart from counsel's readiness to settle for distinguishing *Adkins*. These are Hughes's three points and his conclusion on this issue:

The importance of the question, in which many States having similar laws are concerned, the close division by which the decision in the Adkins Case was reached, and the economic conditions which have supervened, and in the light of which the reasonableness of the exercise of the protective power of the State must be considered, make it not only appropriate, but we think imperative, that in deciding the present case the subjects should receive fresh consideration.

This, then, is how Chief Justice Hughes led the majority into its great overruling, not through the reasoning of the Roberts memorandum based as it was on an incorrect recollection of the supplications of counsel, but on an appreciation of economic and, I think, political imperatives.

A remaining remark is due "counsel for the appellees [who] attempted to distinguish the Adkins case" and Assistant Attorney General Toner, as *amici curiae*, who "made it clear" in oral argument that *Adkins* need not be overruled. The 1913 Washington statute had been on the books twenty-three years. It had had a certain effectiveness. The supreme court of the state had ruled it was valid by distinguishing *Adkins* and with this success behind them the lawyers were taking a most intelligent tack in advising the Supreme Court of the United States that they, too, could distinguish. Their aim was to win this single case and continue the effectiveness of their own state minimum wage law. These lawyers were not representing in any direct way the minimum wage movement at large across the nation.

The tactics of the lawyers seeking to continue the validity and viability of the Washington state law and to win this single case is amply shown by the character of this answer to the jurisdictional statement filed by lawyers for the opponents of the law, by the main brief, by the state's *amici curiae* brief and by the fragmentary (but accurate and pertinent) report of their oral argument. They are also validated by the apparent disinterest of national organizations in the case. The election campaign certainly drew off the attention of active politicos like Mary W. Dewson. Liberal figures like Elinore Herrick and lawyers in the administration were dealing with the powers of the National Labor Relations Board and, on the other side, the Lawyers Committee of the American Liberty League were fast at work preparing the constitutional challenge of the board's powers. Lawyers in the National Woman's Party were watching the progress of Agnes Dickinson's Ohio case, *Walker v. Chapman*, until it was adversely decided on November 20. After that they puzzled over appealing, put off the choice and then went along with the decision of Mrs. Dickinson and Challen Ellis to drop it. There was awareness of the *Parrish* case; its progress was reported at key stages in brief reports in the *New York Times* and somewhat more fully in *United States Law Week*, but at that time it did not look like the landmark case it was to become.

I conclude that the testament of Mr. Justice Roberts is an inadequate guide to his part in the *Parrish* case in 1937. Frankfurter himself caught one error, where Roberts speaks of the question of whether the appeal "should be dismissed" when he meant "should be reversed summarily." An examination of the appeal papers in the *Parrish* case show Roberts to be wrong likewise in asserting that "in the *Parrish* case the authority of *Adkins* was definitely assailed and the Court was asked to reconsider and overrule it." No wonder that he heard one of the brethren ask another, "What is the matter with Roberts?"

Chronology and Supreme Court practice show that the crucial vote by

Roberts came at the conference on December 19, 1936, not in October when probable jurisdiction was noted. Stern and Gressman in their authoritative *Supreme Court Practice* make clear that the Court has treated appeal cases essentially like those coming up on certiorari. That is, the "rule of four" is followed in noting probable jurisdiction, which is the technical means for accepting the case for disposition on the merits. When the appeal in *Parrish* came up for consideration in conference on October 10, 1936, it was to be expected that the four dissenters in *Tipaldo* would favor review. Since no reasons are given for noting probable jurisdiction, and since none should be given according to Mr. Justice Frankfurter, and since the necessary four votes were sure to be cast by Mr. Chief Justice Hughes and Mr. Justices Brandeis, Stone and Cardozo, Roberts's vote was not needed at this stage. Roberts himself says, "I am not sure that I gave my reason."

The Roberts memorandum is a most unusual document. For one thing, there has never been anything like it in the history of the Court. While presidents who survive the presidency have often written extensive memoirs justices who retire or resign from the Court have never written about their judicial service (as witness in recent years Whittaker, Reed, Burton, Minton, and even Roberts other than in this case). The method of revelation was also unusual, although any method would be so for such a unique document. Above all, what is the reliability or unreliability of retrospective material? Roberts, under prodding by Frankfurter—whose mischievous style is famous—ten years after the events turns out a document which Frankfurter himself concedes is flawed and incomplete!

Among the general laws governing the psychology of memory, several that are relevant to judging the reliability of the Roberts memorandum are essential common sense. As Dibble has gleaned it from historians' manuals, (1) "testimony recorded shortly after an event took place is likely to be more accurate than testimony recorded long afterwards." Roberts prepared his statement nine years after the events occurred. Another, with a different premise is put this way by Dibble: (2) "disinterested testimony is likely to be more accurate than politically charged testimony." Roberts surely was seeking vindication even though Frankfurter says he was "indifferent to misrepresentation." A slightly different point: (3) "umprompted testimony is likely to be more accurate than prompted testimony." Mr. Justice Frankfurter spoke of this when he told us in publishing the Roberts memorandum that "it took not a little persuasion . . . to induce him to set [it] forth." Frankfurter's persuasion must be sharply set apart from the criteria of the "focused interview" so fully and artfully explained by Robert K. Merton and associates. It is also a rule of probability in inferring from documents to events that (4) "testimony recorded before many versions of the event in question have been heard is likely to be more accurate than testimony recorded after the witness has heard a variety of versions." In the eight years after 1937, the political explanations of the famous Roberts switch had entered our judicial folklore as a treasured piece of Americana. Another point (5) is that justices of the Supreme Court may have deep loyalties to the institution and the institutional powers call for explaining decisions in terms of constitutional doctrine and in terms of legal skills.

The trouble with the Roberts memorandum is not that it violates these probability laws but that measured against the plain record or petitions for certiorari, briefs and rehearing in the *Tipaldo* case and against the briefs and the report of the oral argument in the *Parrish* case, it is wrong. Skill of counsel cannot explain the switch. Whether the switch may be otherwise explained remains for examination.

Analysis of the Minimum Wage Overruling

As chance and the calendar would have it in the course of constitutional litigation in the minimum wage cases from 1914 to 1937, three elements or conditions which might have been crucial were minimized. They were surely present, they were even essential, but when it came down to the point of decision in the Supreme Court, announced in the *Parrish* case on March 29, 1937, overruling *Adkins*, they were not controlling. These were the skill of counsel, the nature of social movements and interest group leadership, and the views of the bar. Each of these influences must be measured against what can be seen of their impact on the Supreme Court of the time. This study is necessarily partial owing to the fragments of information available about how the thoughts of the justices ebbed and flowed through the years of consideration of these issues.

Consider the role of opposing counsel in these cases. In *Muller v. Oregon* in 1908 the brilliant sociological Brandeis brief was acknowledged to have been influential in winning the Court to accept the Oregon hour law. Brandeis and Goldmark perfected this argument in later cases. The brief in *Adkins* by Frankfurter and Dewson was overwhelming—two huge volumes of facts—and three Supreme Court justices followed their position. The factual argument as an idea well expressed in the briefs of New York in *Tipaldo* appears to have impressed Chief Justice Hughes and this was a fine achievement. Indeed, this may have been a crucial advance even though the case was lost because it settled Hughes in the pro-minimum wage camp. But in the end, in *Parrish*, the briefs of counsel appear to have had no bearing whatever on the result and, indeed, the overruling was made in the face of appellees' insistence none was requested or required.

On the other side, fending off the eventual validation of minimum wage laws surely owed something to the skill of counsel. Even in the favorable times and with the conservative justices on the bench in 1923 in the *Adkins* case, the skill of Challen B. Ellis and Wade H. Ellis must be acknowledged. In the *Tipaldo* case, counsel arguing against the law possessed fascinating charismatic qualities which dovetailed into the results. This included the prestige of Governor Nathan L. Miller, who had himself been a strong possibility for associate justice at the time Pierce Butler was nominated by President Harding. He shone high above Epstein and Bennett. And the *amicus curiae* brief of the National Woman's Party by Mrs. Matthews made a point with a difference probably more effectively than the opposing brief of Dean Acheson and the National Consumers' League for the six state attorneys general. If the effort was to reach Mr. Justice Roberts and hold the four conservatives, Governor Miller, Challen Ellis and Mrs. Matthews did it; Epstein and Acheson did not. But in the end, in the *Parrish* case, the briefs could not have accounted for the Roberts switch despite his self-testimony.

In these cases the role of social movements is seen in the capacity of organizations in reaching the Court by effectively suitable means. First, consider the leading part of the National Consumers' League and its state affiliates in sparking the movement to improve the lot of working women by conceiving of government-required wage minimums in private employment. The promotional, intellectual and tactical work of Kelley, Dewson, Brandeis, Goldmark, Commons, Paul Douglas, Frankfurter, Elizabeth Brandeis, Newton Baker, Herrick and others in the league won many over to their position. Their work, the work of others in and out of the league helped to bring state legislatures in sixteen states to enact minimum wage laws. Their work helped to bring enforcement of these laws in the states and their defense in the courts when challenged. The Consumers' League position of the reasonableness and constitutionality of minimum wage laws was adopted by four justices in *Stettler v. O'Hara* (1917), by three in *Adkins* (1923), by four in *Tipaldo* (1936). The fame of Louis Brandeis in developing the sociological brief with the league in 1908 and its application in other cases aided in giving him the prestige to win nomination to the Court by Wilson in 1916. His work also earned him enemies, but Brandeis was approved. Organizations like the Consumers' League whose own counsel become justices on the Supreme Court register success in this way.

But even with these skills, these attributes, the league in failing in 1923 lost momentum. Its new model law swept through seven legislatures in 1933 but the league's part in the ensuing litigation was not successful. In filing a short, nonfactual *amicus* brief in *Tipaldo*, Acheson broke tradition without bringing in a redeeming innovation. In the overruling case of *West Coast Hotel Co. v. Parrish* in 1937 the league did not participate at all. My conclusion is that the National Consumers' League helped generate the minimum wage movement, worked out its basic constitutional defense, shaped the legal thinking on the issue by countless lawyers, saw its own great advocate Brandeis on the Court, and influenced in some fashion the thinking of Holmes, Sanford, Taft, Stone, Cardozo and Hughes. But still, the absence of the NCL in the *Parrish* case does not even permit conjecture that their work led Mr. Justice Roberts to hold for the Washington Law in 1937 when he had held against the New York Law in 1936.

Organizations in the forefront of social movements tend to fulfill three functions in constitutional litigation: (1) They bring lawyers, related professionals like economists or geneticists, and laymen together to rally round a position and thereby become the recognized focus for doing battle; (2) They do this continuously over a period of years and thereby fill a time gap in contests over constitutional issues which, almost by definition, cannot be settled to *stay* settled in a day or a year but, rather, run a generation or more; (3) They provide vital resources like money, intelligence and information, mobilization at a crucial moment in time and supporting personnel as well. The opponents to minimum wage laws for women were a loose confederation of organizations, each highly specialized, and an array of lawyers whose own attributes were often a combination of skill and ideology. This often uncoordinated alliance complemented, and surely influenced a majority of the United States Supreme Court in *Adkins, Murphy, Donham*, and *Tipaldo* (see table 8-1, for details) as well as many of state and lower federal court judges in numerous cases during the period 1920-36. The judicial quartet of Van Devanter, McReynolds, Sutherland and Butler, together for the fifteen years from 1922 to 1937, played from the compositions of conservative lawyers sponsored by an array of business groups.

The organizations on this side were varied in size, makeup and effectiveness. There were particular corporations like the Children's Hospital, whose trustees opposed wage laws, the Spotlight Laundry and the West Coast Hotel Company, whose owners opposed them. There were state trade associations of hotels, laundrymen and restaurants—the largest employers of women. There were organizations of conservative intent specializing in fields adjacent to stopping wage laws whose activities to promote laissez faire aided the cause indirectly and sometimes directly. These included the Sentinels of the Republic and, especially here, the American Liberty League.

Perhaps most important of all was the National Woman's Party, whose collection of facts made a difference in *Adkins*, where Mr. Justice Sutherland expressed the feminist view along with his more profound liberty of contract position. The Woman's Party *amicus* brief in *Tipaldo* led to the same result in the majority opinion by Mr. Justice Butler. The party's work may have helped hold Roberts in *Tipaldo*. In the end, however, in *Parrish* the NWP dropped out and so played no direct part in the overruling case. Indeed, the premise of the party that they objected to wage laws for women only helped lay the foundation for the validity of minimum wage and price-fixing laws in principle without regard to sex.

Another element that was minimized was the bearing of the bar, of professional legal opinion, on the judiciary. Before 1900 law writers like Thomas Cooley, Christopher G. Tiedeman and John F. Dillon were thought to have extraordinary influence. The rise of professional law schools placed professors like C.C. Langdell and James Bradley Thayer in a strategic place to shape the views of lawyers-to-be. The professional associations with their national and state bar publications reached a wide audience of practitioners, often expressing and reinforcing less cosmopolitan ways of thought. More subtle, yet profound influences came from intellectuals who were not lawyers but whose powerfully expressed ideas about society, economics and political theory coursed into the underlying premises of legal thought. Mr. Justice Holmes detected the inarticulate notions of Herbert Spencer's laissez faire doctrines in the majority opinion holding New York's ten-hour law for bakers invalid in the *Lochner Case* in 1905. Liberal ideas on monopoly developed by Professor Richard T. Ely of Wisconsin silently entered Supreme Court opinion at about the same time. There are many ways in which a Supreme Court justice may be influenced by ideas—as many ways as any man, perhaps more ways than most—because a justice is not only a target but also in many instances a man who by his calling must be open and hospitable to the consideration of new paths of thoughts.

If the test of an idea is its ability to get itself accepted in the market place then there is, in the rough way of continents, a great divide between legal ideas on government regulation of property before and after March 29, 1937. Benjamin Twiss has shown us the influence of Evarts, Choate and Guthrie in bringing laissez faire into the Constitution. But the rise of the legal realists was expressed in the law reviews. The brilliance of Roscoe Pound, Thomas Reed Powell, Felix Frankfurter, Karl Llewellyn and Charles Groves Haines leveled the arguments of liberty of contract in the law school journals. Twelve articles attacking the decision of the Supreme Court in *Adkins v. Children's Hospital* were put together in book form by the National Consumers' League and sold by the *New Republic* in 1924. Justices then as now read law reviews as daily fare but no dent could be made on the four conservatives and there is no indication at all that Mr. Justice Roberts paid particular attention to the movement of scholarly thought and the currents of American intellectual life. The finality of the *Parrish* rule was sealed by the presence of this approval in the law schools as already registered in the law reviews. Yet this is a function different from persuading the swing man on a nine-man court to adopt a particular position in the first place.

Constitutional change in its pure meaning is the ultimate triumph of the preferences of one group of constituents over another. When the triumph is as permanent as the overruling of *Adkins* by *Parrish* then the specific swing of one justice to the new position becomes the means of ratifying significant constitutional change. Mr. Justice Roberts bore on his shoulders, in his mind and conscience the choice of switching. The element of *public opinion* seems to have eventually ripened and reached him. But this did not come about all at once. The focus in this 1936-37 era was on two *judges*, Roberts and Hughes.

Rarely has a nine-man court been composed of more men of settled views than the Supreme Court of the period from 1922 to 1937. A quartet of conservatives set themselves against the assertions of governmental authority to regulate business and the conditions of work. They were not moved by the liberal talent devoting itself to legal change. Opposite were Holmes, Brandeis, then Stone, and finally Cardozo who, for different reasons and not always jointly or consistently, believed the Constitution permitted the regulation of the private employment by both state and federal governments.

There has always been an appreciation by some justices of the United States Supreme Court when several state governments, Congress and the president imply that the Court cannot save the country. Although the Supreme Court interprets the Constitution it does not and cannot by itself set the ultimate course of constitutional development. Further, if the Court is to play a useful role, a constructive role, even any role at all, it must nurture its limited resources and see itself properly, in perspective, as the least and not the most powerful branch.

Chief Justice Charles Evans Hughes, after his second appointment to the Court in 1930, showed a high sense of the meaning of constitutional change. Years later Edwin McElwain demonstrated in a moving article the Hughes sense of justice toward indigent criminal defendants years before his concern and feeling became dominant in the country. Hughes decided that state minimum wage laws for women were valid in the *Tipaldo* case. He must already have felt this as a constitutional wave of the future and while he did not then lead Roberts to his side he was to do so during the next six months.

Three matters seem to have combined in bringing Roberts to support the wage law in the *Parrish* case during the summer and fall of 1936. One was the character and outlook of Roberts as a man and a judge. He was not wedded to laissez faire. This was in evidence in his opinion for the Court in the *Nebbia* case upholding state legislation fixing prices in the milk industry. His was not a complicated mind in the sense of embracing rich convolutions and complexities. His recollection of the arguments for an overruling in *Tipaldo* and *Parrish* was wrong but his readiness to base decisions on such points is an apt indicator of a simple legalistic style. If what counsel said (or what he thought counsel said) deserved to be taken at face value then similar thinking would be in harmony.

A relevant similarity lies in the record of the six minimum wage cases from *Stettler* in 1917 to *Parrish* in 1937: in each the lower court conclusion was affirmed by the Supreme Court of the United States (again, see table 8-1). This is a point that may have had real force for a man of Roberts's judicial temperament. Perhaps he would not strike out boldly and consciously in changing; his style was one where a result might seem different to others but where the elements of decision depended on simplistic and mechanical patterns of thought: what the lower court said or what counsel argued, for example. Justice Roberts had reduced judicial review to simple terms when, in *United States v. Butler* (1936) he declared that when an act is challenged as being unconstitutional, "the judicial branch of the Government has only one duty—to lay the article of the Constitution which is invoked beside the statute which is challenged and to decide whether the latter squares with the former."

Roberts made the famous switch in 1937 but it was Hughes's perception of the Court's participation in constitutional change which made a key difference. Among the justices in 1936, Hughes was the most experienced election-watcher and with "his great intellectual capacities," he surely anticipated Roosevelt's reelection and, moreover, knew its significance. Twice elected governor of New York (in 1906 and 1910), Hughes had resigned from his first service on the Supreme Court of the United States in June 1916 to accept the Republican party convention nomination for president. That was a sanguine moment. His dissent in *Tipaldo* was announced twenty years to the month of his resignation from the Court to enter politics. His view that President Wilson was beatable was nearly proved, but Hughes lost in one of the closest elections in American history, by an electoral vote of 277 to 254 and a popular vote of 9,129,606 to 8,538,221.

The election of 1936 bore a certain resemblance to 1916 with Roosevelt ending his first term in a position approximating 1916 when Wilson was completing his first term. The *Literary Digest* and Republican politicians this time could not have kept the sober, intelligent and experienced Hughes from believing that Alfred E. Landon represented the wave of the future. Hughes had all the earmarks of a Chief Justice who would, even on June 1, 1936, have been in part anticipating the verdict of the people for sweeping constitutional change. This could be, at least partially, the explanation of Hughes's dissent in *Morehead v. Tipaldo* on the last day of the term.

Hughes's biographer, Merlo J. Pusey, says that the Roberts switch was made in the *Parrish* case some time in the fall of 1936 but gives no date. Pusey, on the basis of an interview with Hughes ten years later, simply reports: "When Roberts, in a private chat, had divulged his intention of voting to sustain the Washington law, the Chief had almost hugged him." The decision in March 1937 was made possible by Roberts's change of mind. The landslide election of Roosevelt in November anticipated by Hughes and felt indirectly by Roberts permits a characterization of the overruling of *Adkins* as an occasion where Mr. Dooley's aphorism is the closest one can get to the tangled facts and swirling currents. The Supreme Court in the October 1936 term in holding state minimum wage laws constitutional, thereby overruling the *Adkins Case*, "followed the election returns."

Judicial Conservatism Overcome

10   The Amendment Stalemate

All at once, in the early 1920s, opposing groups perceived constitutional crises for which they prescribed amendments. Their efforts offset each other. Even as failures, they afford instruction into common behavioral patterns in the American system of government and also help to explain the paths taken by the groups in succeeding decades. The successful movement to repeal the Eighteenth Amendment has already been examined in detail. This chapter is devoted to amendment possibilities explored and expounded in reaction to two different constitutional events.

One exploration is the contrasting response of critics of national woman suffrage who wished to change the rules of the amendment procedure, set forth in Article Five, to cut the legislative role and get "back to the people." Having failed to stop the Nineteenth Amendment proposal by Congress, ratification by the legislatures or approval by the Supreme Court, these critics, in organizations like the Sentinels of the Republic and through publications like *The Woman Patriot*, worked for the "back-to-the-people" amendment. Quite a different reaction came from the National Woman's Party, which insisted that suffrage was merely a steppingstone to female economic liberation and advocated an equal rights amendment as a further, necessary measure.

These opposing aspirations became ensnarled in the moves attempted by LaFollette's Progressive Party, in the National Consumers' League, National Child Labor Committee and elsewhere, to utilize constitutional amendments to overcome adverse Supreme Court rulings in the child labor cases of *Hammer v. Dagenhart* in 1918 and *Bailey v. Drexel Furniture Company* in 1922, and in the minimum wage case of *Adkins v. Children's Hospital* in 1923. Again, two kinds of amendments were considered. One would change the rules and customs governing judicial review and in some fashion curb the powers of the Supreme Court. The other type of amendment, exemplified by the child labor amendment, actually proposed by Congress to the state legislatures in June 1924, would enlarge and clarify the constitutional authority of Congress to enact protective labor legislation.

These attempts to achieve constitutional change failed. The patriotic organizations never got the "back-to-the-people" amendment to a floor vote in either house of Congress. The woman's equal rights amendment was introduced in every Congress since the 1920s but it did not reach a floor vote until 1970 and then, in 1972 was finally proposed formally to the states. Consumers' League leaders could not agree among themselves on seeking a minimum wage amendment to overcome the *Adkins* rule, and the child labor amendment, though proposed by Congress, failed of ratification in the state legislatures. Revision of the power of the Supreme Court to pass on the constitutionality of federal legislation also foundered, first among critics of the Court who did not believe in going that far and then in failure to win sufficient support in Congress. Consideration was given in the 1920s to curbing the Court by ordinary legislation as an alternative to an amendment but this, too, failed then just as it did when submitted to Congress in a novel, politically loaded message by President Franklin D. Roosevelt in February 1937.

Several points may be made in this survey of amendment politics in the 1920s. One is the important symbolism which an amendment holds out to those who see their constitutional vision clouded, whether by a previously adopted amendment or by a Supreme Court decision. A clinician of constitutional change notices the readiness of losers in a political or legal encounter to blame the system as undemocratic. In the instances under study here we see that from the view of conservative patriots the amendment procedures failed to register the will of the people and that from the view of progressive reformers the Supreme Court subverted people's representatives in Congress and the state legislatures. The rhetoric was democratic. By their failures the creators and advocates of these amendments redeemed the truism that the most common method of constitutional change is through ordinary legislation, administrative innovation and litigation.

For those who witnessed the ratification of four amendments—establishing an income tax power, popular election of senators, national prohibition and woman suffrage—between 1913 and 1920, the idea of further constitutional change by this means was both attractive and believable. It also responded to what Edmond Cahn has brilliantly seen to have been a remarkable innovation in constitution-making by the framers of 1787. Article Five, providing for amendments, was a remarkable innovation, Cahn has observed, because most previous draftsmen had envisioned a document that would capture the ideal governmental arrangements and leave them static, for they believed this was the path to perpetuity.[1]

Although they foresaw the need to keep the Constitution abreast of newly felt needs, the formal amendment process proved inadequate. It is legitimate, but it does not have the political feasibility of ordinary legislation and follow-up litigation. Cahn believed Chief Justice John Marshall acknowledged this in *Marbury v. Madison* and, in fact, that first but effective claim for judicial review clearly opened an alternate path to constitutional change separate from amendments adopted under Article Five. This was the beginning of rivalry between different methods of constitutional change. In a relativist world, the spirit of the framers is discerned as recognizing a need for change and groping for a method; it is thought that the methods available today are equal in legitimacy but merely vary in their political utility from time to time.

In scrutinizing the campaigns for and against national prohibition, woman suffrage and the repeal of prohibition, we have seen wide sentiment harnessed by skillful leaders of organizations at work. The opposition was outflanked and outmanned. To estimate the effectiveness and mass appeal of one's own campaign or movement is, perhaps, among the most difficult of political arts. This is a different order of prediction from estimating the likely behavior of a nine-judge court. It happened that Wayne Bidwell Wheeler's American Anti-Saloon League was leading a social movement that could elect or persuade two-thirds of Congress and thirty-six or more state legislatures to approve the national prohibition amendment. It happened that Carrie Chapman Catt's National American Woman Suffrage Association did the same in seeing the Nineteenth Amendment adopted. Success in politics is often wrongly denigrated as not representing what the people want and it was not easy for Alexander Lincoln's Sentinels of the Republic, Harriet Frothingham's *Woman Patriot*, Alice Paul's National Woman's Party, Florence Kelley's National Consumers' League and Robert M. LaFollette's Progressive party to acknowledge that Wayne Wheeler and Carrie Catt were their political superiors and that winning approval of an amendment of broad scope in the American constitutional order was no mean achievement. This résumé of their difficulties will show that constitutional change is not an easy matter of manipulation but a rather profound political process.

The framers of the Constitution feared a majority faction enough to cause them to engineer the celebrated checks and balances as well as the continuation of a geographical division of powers we call federalism. They were to shore up their work with all manner of mathematical obstacles; enough to make the convention proceedings into a festival of fractions. This was one expression of their genius, for they were using fractions for purposes they well understood. Numerous fractions in addition to the bare majority required for ordinary business in Congress and the courts were inserted into the Constitution. Nine-thirteenths of the states were required to ratify the Constitution proposed by the framers. Apportionment of the House would be made by counting each free person as one but "three fifths of all other persons," namely slaves, a clause which Floyd McKissick, co-chairman of the Conference of Black Lawyers, has scornfully used as the title of a recent book.[2] Determination of taking roll calls on any question in Congress is "at the desire of one-fifth of those present." There are many uses of two-thirds votes in Congress: for a quorum of the House in electing a president should the electoral college fail, for expelling a member, for overriding a presidential veto, and for Senate ratification of a treaty and for conviction on an impeachment.

The amendment stalemate of the 1920s is a sample of the difficulties small organizations face in seeking adoption of amendments to the United States Constitution.[3]

Patriots' "Back-to-the-People" Amendment

The many conservative lawyers opposed to both prohibition and woman suffrage and who, additionally, were mainly unsympathetic to black suffrage and the income tax as well, could hardly have suspected that the amendment process would be utilized for a counterattack. At a given point in time, say January 1, 1921, opponents of the Eighteenth and Nineteenth Amendments could not hope to persuade two-thirds of each house of Congress to propose repeal amendments. Yet they ambitiously set forth to change the very method and procedure by which these amendments had been ratified. In the religion of fundamental constitutionalism "the people," as defined by practice in the states in 1789, were the holy of holies. To the high priests of this dogma, the evil and unrepresentative state legislatures could be shown in high relief by a measure to eliminate future unconstitutional change.

In form, the "back-to-the-people" amendment was a joint resolution to amend Article Five of the Constitution. It would require a two-thirds vote of Congress to be proposed to the states. But when proposed it emphatically specified referral not to legislatures but "to conventions of delegates in each state chosen by the people thereof." The key passage of this amendment would, in the words of *The Woman Patriot*, abolish "the power of minority lobbies to amend the supreme law of the land." This would be accomplished by retaining convention ratification (which was the preferred method of conservatives) and qualifying legislative ratification in these three ways: (1) that the members of at least one House in each of the legislatures which may ratify shall be elected after such amendments have been proposed; (2) that any state may require that ratification by its legislature be subject to confirmation by popular vote; and (3) that, until three-fourths of the states have ratified or more than one-fourth of the states have rejected or defeated a proposed amendment, any state may change its vote. The "back-to-the-people" amendment was introduced in the Senate on April 13, 1921, by Senator James W. Wadsworth, Jr., of New York and in the House a week later by Representative Finis J. Garrett of Tennessee.[4]

This was a quixotic gesture supported by the same sort of people who had broken their lances against black suffrage, woman suffrage and prohibition. They wished to change the rules of the game to make it more difficult for their enemies—the Progressives—to amend the Constitution. In an address before the Sentinels of the Republic and associated organizations in 1923, Thomas F. Cadwalader spoke of the origins of this corrective amendment in the blandest way:

A group of lawyers—one of the junior members of which I have the honor to be—have been giving this matter a great deal of study for several years, and when it was found that Senator Wadsworth and Representative Garrett were in hearty accord with the principles that we believed in, we were exceedingly glad and grateful that two such statesmen should lend it their active and enthusiastic support.[5]

Charles S. Fairchild, the American Constitution League and the lawyers Waldo G. Morse and Everett Wheeler appear by other accounts to have inspired the amendment. But there can be no question, from Cadwalader's account, that the Baltimore group, William L. Marbury, Arthur W. Machen, Jr., William P. Rawls and others were squarely in favor.

The Wadsworth amendment in 1924 was reported out favorably by a subcommittee of the Senate Judiciary Committee but never considered or voted upon by either House. The amendment showed how to think positively and served as a constant expression of disdain for the procedures followed in the adoption of the prohibition and woman suffrage amendments. Its importance was as a symbol for conservatives to rally to.

Stopping the Child Labor Amendment

Although the self-styled women patriots like Harriet Frothingham and their allies at the bar like Alexander Lincoln and William L. Marbury could not protect the Constitution in their view from being vitiated by national woman suffrage, nor reform Article Five by substituting the back-to-the-people amendment, they were able to acquire sufficient allies against a national child labor amendment to put a stop to it. There appear to be three related conditions that permitted what turned out to be merely rhetorical success for the patriotic alliance which put so much credence on the words of the Constitution.

The most important factor in the struggle for protective labor legislation, generally, and for the regulation of child labor in particular, was the unevenness of industrial development among the states. Thirteen state legislatures could prevent ratification of a constitutional amendment and there were more than that number even as late as the 1920s where agriculture predominated. The state legislatures in those states—and actually in many others—contained a bloc of rural and small-town representatives with a farmer's hostility toward regulating working conditions. This meant that a constitutional amendment empowering Congress to regulate child labor would have to win the support of the industrial states where the progressive tide was stronger.

Patriotic organizations opposed to the child labor amendment were preceded on the scene by organized manufacturers, most notably by David Clark, founding editor of the *Southern Textile Bulletin* in 1911, who engineered the invalidation of two federal statutes aimed at restricting the employment of children.[6]

Textile mills in England and in New England in the nineteenth century had children tending spindles for long hours on a regular basis. But as the South burgeoned with cotton mills after the Civil War thousands of hill folk entered the factories and brought their children, too. New Englanders felt the economic competition as well as twinges of conscience over the unspeakable conditions small children, many under the age of ten, worked under in the South. These conditions were studied, documented, photographed, and condemned endlessly in national magazines and in congressional reports.

The National Child Labor Committee was formed on April 15, 1904, to serve as "a great moral force for the protection of children." It was truly national in scope, although its leadership was similar in character to the National Consumers' League and, indeed, there was an overlapping membership. The NCLC chairman from 1904 to 1921 was Felix Adler, who was the founder of the Society for Ethical Culture in New York and the husband of Helen Goldmark. In Congress the movement for child labor reform was begun by the Indiana Progressive, Senator Albert Beveridge when he spoke for several consecutive days in 1906 describing conditions and prescribing suggested remedies by the National Child Labor Committee.

Two-thirds of each house proposed a child labor amendment in June 1924 in the language of the joint resolution as follows:

Resolved by the Senate and the House of Representatives of the United States of America in Congress assembled (two-thirds of each House concurring therein), That the following article is proposed as an amendment to the Constitution of the United States which, when ratified by the legislatures of three-fourths of the several States, shall be valid to all intents and purposes as a part of the Constitution:

ARTICLE

Section 1. The Congress shall have power to limit, regulate, and prohibit the labor of persons under 18 years of age.

Section 2. The power of the several States is unimpaired by this article except that the operation of State laws shall be suspended to the extent necessary to give effect to legislation enacted by the Congress.

The phrasing of the child labor amendment, and without doubt its principle and its feared potential, aroused vigorous and effective opposition from leaders of the American Catholic hierarchy. Patrick Joseph Cardinal Hayes in New York and James Cardinal O'Connell in Boston were outspoken critics of the proposed amendment. True, some members of the clergy, like John A. Ryan and Edwin V. O'Hara, and lay Catholics such as Frank P. Walsh, publicly advocated ratification. What Hayes and O'Connell, and such lawyers like William D. Guthrie believed was that the child labor amendment was an intrusion of the state into an area of parental control to be guided by the church. They felt this with a sincere conviction, in fact with a passion that sometimes seemed close to fanaticism, but this can be understood in the context of other threats they felt during the 1920s.

One was the national policy of prohibition with direct regulation of personal habits and the disturbing spectacle of power exercised by Protestant Fundamentalists which the Eighteenth Amendment displayed. The Oregon compulsory school law symbolized the movement to rely upon government-run schools only. The wording of the child labor amendment would not only permit limitations on work by children but might allow other regulations because they thought the word "labor" might be interpreted too broadly by Congress and the courts.

This suggests the range of the coalition that emerged to oppose ratification of the child labor amendment, a strange but understandable alliance of Southern mill operatives led by David Clark, scattered employers including the National Association of Manufacturers and its general counsel James A. Emery, the Sentinels of the Republic and associated patriotic organizations and, to cap it all, the leading Catholic bishops of the country. This was enough to stay ratification in several key, industrial states—notably New York and Massachusetts.

The Sentinels of the Republic and *The Woman Patriot* revived their argument that legislatures should not be permitted to amend the Constitution without consulting the people and they were successful in Massachusetts in causing an advisory referendum to show popular disapproval. They put out reams of propaganda, nicely complimenting the criticisms of Cardinal O'Connell, to stop the amendment at the polls. The Sentinels of the Republic could boast of the support of President A. Lawrence Lowell of Harvard University as well as the cardinal—a powerful combination in Massachusetts in the 1920s. Typical of the arguments made by the Sentinels was a one-page statement in *The Woman Patriot* headed "Submit Child Labor Amendment to Conventions" written by David Holmes Morton in March 1924. "Mere legislatures" take their lumps along with scorn for the so-called child labor amendment. Legislatures could too easily be stampeded to "adopt any kind of an amendment no matter how destructive of American principles." Still grumbling over the adoption of prohibition and woman suffrage, Morton complained particularly over ratification by legislatures, in these words:

Due to special sessions, stampeded legislatures, war hysteria and what not, there is grave doubt whether the 18th and 19th Amendments were sanctioned by the will of the American people. No candid citizen, who has examined the legislative ratifications, will reasonably dispute that statement or can in conscience do so.

In contrast, state conventions could not conceivably have blemishes.

Within two years of its proposal it was clear that the ratification of the child labor amendment would be impossible in the 1920s. Eventually some twenty-eight states ratified the amendment, but this was far too few and the steam was taken out of the movement once the decision in New York and Massachusetts was made.

The depth and sweep of change in 1933 took many conservatives by such surprise that they were quite unable to cope with it. Alexander Lincoln of the Sentinels of the Republic was never busier; but he also suffered deep frustration as the organization declined in size. SR had marked experience in beating social legislation in Congress, in helping to persuade the people of Massachusetts to vote "No" in the child labor amendment referendum of 1925, and in its leader's work in "test cases." Time showed SR to be too small, too static, too provincial—its recruits were older people—to fight anything but a losing guerrilla war against the new social welfare programs of the 1930s.

In choosing to concentrate on dampening the revival of the child labor amendment, Alexander Lincoln and the Sentinels were repeating themselves. They had thought their initiative in 1924-26 stopped the ratification process. As experts—and they had expertise—the Sentinels worked quickly to stop the child labor amendment as its ratification proponents brought it up after 1933 first in one state, then in another, in moves which seemed as calculated and sinister in purpose as they were swift and successful in execution. In repeating their campaign against child labor the Sentinels found themselves hopelessly out-flanked by events.

The inauguration of Franklin D. Roosevelt on March 4, 1933, coincided with a revival of interest in ratifying the child labor amendment; swiftly alerted, the Sentinels of America worked unceasingly for the next several years to stop it. In the end, they won the battle, but lost the war. Lincoln's correspondence records show us how the Sentinels worked in various states to stop ratification, how they immediately conceived of "test cases" to prevent state legislatures from changing their minds, and how they marshaled arguments in a new round to squash the revival of the amendment.

A Louisville lawyer, in February 1933, sent Lincoln what he called "an idiotic editorial" from the *Herald-Post* advocating adding the child labor amendment to the Constitution. The newspaper noted its submission nine years before and failure in twenty-six states. "But no time limit was put on it, and the courts have ruled that a state can change its position on the amendment." Oregon had just become the seventh state to ratify it. Asking for news, the lawyer recalled that "Florence Kelley declared that she would never quit the fight and would ultimately win, so there may be some backers left." Lincoln knew some would keep trying but doubted they would progress far. His Louisville correspondent wondered, in reply, "When the fight against ratification, if any, ought to be resumed." He was not sure how a flurry of state ratifications would stand in law. Concern over a revival did not take long to jell. Within a month, Cadwalader wrote Torbert: "I see in the papers that resolution to ratify the Child Labor Amendment has recently been passed in a few states including Ohio, and are pending in Alabama, Iowa, Pennsylvania, New Jersey, New York, Kansas, Wyoming and Michigan; and have passed the House in Minnesota." Cadwalader added, "I have still a few copies of the various pamphlets that we used in the big fight and I am enclosing you samples of them mellowed with the dust of years."

The American Bar Association, with its council organized on a federal basis, proved—on paper at least—to be a fine companion in arms to the Sentinels. Presidents of the ABA are elected annually and have considerable freedom in naming special committees to study and report on public issues. In 1934 the president was Earle W. Evans of Wichita, Kansas. Typical of his outlook is this offer in a letter to Alex Lincoln that year: "I will be indeed happy to have any other suggestions that you may care to make as to what we can do to defeat the amendment."[7]

This Bar Association interest led to the appointment of a "Special Committee to Oppose Ratification by States of Federal Child Labor Amendment and Promote Adoption of a Uniform Child Labor Act," with its letterhead, and far more important, a committee composed entirely of opponents. Its chairman was William D. Guthrie.

For years the ABA Committee on American Citizenship had worked to keep alien ideas from infecting society, economy and polity. This was a key committee, exemplifying the association's deepest feelings about the challenge to American life in the first third of the century. The committee's chairman in 1933-34, James M. Beck, far outshone his five colleagues in conservative fame and renown.

Facing the revival of ratification of the child labor amendment after 1933, the Sentinels of the Republic chose to specialize on the topic; a path leading it to sterility and eventual decline. Looking back it is easy to see that the organization could not even stay in the mainstream of reactionary opposition to the liberal tide exemplified by the New Deal, in the "Little New Deal" and eventually to the constitutional changes brought by the popular electoral support for liberalism.

The opponents of child labor were never persuasive in their claim that convention ratification was the only way and, as early as 1933, began planning litigation which eventually took the form of two test cases, decided adversely by the Supreme Court on June 1, 1939. *Coleman v. Miller* was prepared by lawyers in Kansas, particularly Robert Stone. *Chandler v. Wise* was directed by attorneys in Kentucky, particularly Lafon Allen. These lawyers were guided at every turn of their cases, chiefly through correspondents, by Alexander Lincoln and Sterling Edmunds of St. Louis, director of the League for the Protection of Home, Family, School and Child. From time to time, leading members of the American Bar Association offered suggestions.

All were opponents of federal limitations on child labor and as far as the "popular will" was concerned they evidenced no satisfaction that this reform would be acceptable. They could no more reconcile themselves to the possible good sense and validity of this reform whether it was voted by Congress, proclaimed by the president, or proposed as an amendment and ratified by referendum, legislatures or conventions.[8]

The National Child Labor Committee all these years continued to seek ratification of the amendment. This campaign was slowed as litigation in Kansas and Kentucky materialized. In 1937, for instance, the NCLC Board of Trustees agreed not to push further ratification but endorsed a request from William

Allen White "to give financial help to State Senator Payne Ratner, of Kansas," to prevent a United States Supreme Court reversal of the Kansas courts.[9] A committee of the trustees was appointed in 1938 to follow the litigation, but the main interest was already on enactment of the Fair Labor Standards Act, the best alternative to a constitutional amendment. The enactment of this statute made the test cases generated by the Sentinels and others something of a constitutional charade.

Feminine Factions on Equal Rights

The achievement of the vote for women through ratification of the Nineteenth Amendment in August 1920 had several fascinating political consequences. The most impressive result was in compliance. Except for the efforts of the Maryland League for State Defense and other small groups which tried to stop enforcement by litigation, and failed, there was official cooperation everywhere and no woman was kept from voting, in the words of the amendment, "on account of sex." Thus there was an entirely different experience with compliance than with the history of the Fifteenth Amendment with its similar phrasing that no person be denied the vote "on account of race, color or previous condition of servitude."

While there were no official barriers, large numbers of eligible women did not vote. In particular, black women were barred through the range of discouragements which continued to keep black men from voting. Nationally it is doubtful that more than 30 percent of eligible women voted in national elections in the 1920s while some 60 percent of men voted.[10] The voting in state and local elections would, ordinarily, be commensurately smaller. The official opportunity to vote is not to be confused with the social support and presence of the required individual knowledge and initiative to act. Of course, the Nineteenth Amendment did not *require* women to vote and the fact is that many did not. The wide acceptability of the Nineteenth Amendment as legitimate constitutional change helps to explain why public officials complied with its prescription and did not try to stop women from voting.

Another consequence was the breakup of the coalition of organizations which had joined together to back national woman suffrage. The consequences of the joint achievement varied. The generals in the campaign wished to remain at the head of their troups. Thus there were some transformations, but no sealing of the divisions that had been papered over during the final drive for ratification.

The National American Woman Suffrage Association led by Carrie Chapman Catt became the League of Women Voters led by her. The Congressional Union had already been renamed the National Woman's Party in 1916 and this organization continued through many years, by Alice Paul. We have seen that the opponents of woman suffrage also continued as small, cohesive organizations like the Woman Patriots. Other organizations led by women, but with varied political purposes related to the economic and moral welfare of women and children, continued untouched by their cooperation in endorsing the Nineteenth Amendment. Gertrude Folks Zimand continued her primary interest in the National Child Labor Committee while Florence Kelley did the same in the National Consumers' League.

In the readjustment among women's groups following adoption, perhaps the most striking controversy was over a new constitutional amendment advocated by the National Women's Party. For some years Alice Paul had had in mind a "Lucretia Mott Amendment" and had sought wider support from other organizations before having what has come to be called the equal rights amendment introduced in Congress on December 10, 1923 by Senator Charles Curtis and Representative Daniel R. Anthony, Jr., both of Kansas.[11] An equal rights amendment has been introduced in every Congress since 1923, usually taking this form: "Men and women shall have equal rights throughout the United States and every place subject to its jurisdiction. Congress shall have power to enforce this article by appropriate legislation."[12]

Even before the equal rights amendment was introduced in Congress in 1923 the idea had been considered and rejected by other women and their organizations, for different reasons. *The Woman Patriot* was vociferously opposed both because of the idea (after all, this included people who rejected woman suffrage) and because of the notoriety of the supporters. The Alice Paul group were the militant feminists of their day who picketed the White House and staged hunger strikes for suffrage. They had not lost their militancy and now they had a utopian vision that inequality between men and women could be eliminated once and for all through adoption of an equal rights amendment. For the right-wing women it was the objective as well as the tactics they found abhorrent. The pages of *The Woman Patriot* are replete with criticisms, close to libel, not only of Alice Paul's programs but those of Carrie Catt and Florence Kelley as well.[13]

The stalemate over Congressional approval of the equal rights amendment seems to have come from opposition by reformers like Florence Kelley rather than conservatives in the various patriotic organizations. Florence Kelley was committed to improving the lot of working women by seeking special legislation. She thought, with Josephine Goldmark and others in the Consumers' League, that the nature of women *as* women made special legislation essential. Moreover, they were not as readily organized into trade unions as men and consequently special legislation for women, as well as children, was needed. She came to feel that Alice Paul actually wanted to destroy protective legislation for women. Josephine Goldmark has reported that the National Woman's Party leaders declared "that a maximum hour law or a minimum wage law which applied to women but not to men was bound to hurt women more than it could possibly help them."[14] Following a meeting on December 4, 1921, between Miss Paul,

Mrs. Kelley and others, the board of directors of the National Consumers' League voted to oppose the equal rights amendment. Calling the idea "topsy-turvey feminism," Florence Kelley made opposition to this amendment a standard item in the league's program, believing it a substantial threat to the positive program for protective legislation for women. This is the most succinct summary of her objections:

Mrs. Kelley made in those early years the two major arguments against the "equal rights" amendment which remain the basic objections to this method of achieving women's rights. First, she declared that women cannot achieve true equality with men by securing identity of treatment under law. Because women are not identical with men they have certain different problems and need certain different legal remedies. Second, she saw that blanket action through a constitutional amendment would involve an interminable series of court decisions to determine what laws the amendment would permit or invalidate. Mrs. Kelley, who had spent a lifetime battling court interpretations of the "due process" clause of the Fourteenth Amendment, was especially fitted to recognize this danger in a new broad general amendment.[15]

There is something in the fifty-year campaign for an equal rights amendment that suggests, again, a kind of symbolic ritualistic quest to problem-solving. Constitutional change can have a tremendous bearing on the functioning of a society, but many critics of the amendment have looked upon it as a kind of moral and theatrical equivalent to the Kellogg-Briand Pact outlawing war. Just as the Woman's Party claimed to be, these critics were opposed to sex discrimination, but they did not think that a constitutional amendment would help. They believed the Nineteenth Amendment "made it possible in the two decades succeeding it to pass a host of state laws equalizing or at least improving the position of women with regard to guardianship of her children, jury duty, inheritance, property, citizenship, and many other legal rights."[16] Eleanor Flexner has quite correctly seen that the division over the equal rights amendment among women followed "the lines of income and social status." Members of the National Woman's Party were professional women who felt it an indignity to give special aid to women in more humble and less well-paid lines of work.

A recent study by a lawyer much concerned with perpetuation of discrimination against women has criticized the equal rights amendment as jeopardizing the advances made thus far and not promoting effectively those that, he believes, should be made in the future. The way to improve the lot of women is to work on particular subjects one by one on the merits. There should be equality where a functional analysis makes it sensible but he points out, for example, "that a law exempting women from strenuous military service is not one that denies or abridges any right (of men) on account of sex, but is one that is reasonably based upon the general physical (functional) differences between the sexes."[17]

Amendments as Legislative Politics

The voices of Ogg and Ray and other writers of standard American government texts echo in most academic accounts of the history of amendments to the United States Constitution of 1789. For instance, Pritchett has expressed his gratitude "that the Constitution is comparatively difficult to amend."[18] In his view it is essential "that the Constitution retain its brevity and be limited to fundamental structural arrangements and the protection of basic liberties. It would be disastrous if it became, through the amending power, a vehicle by which pressure groups and crackpots could impose their nostrums on the nation."

Philip L. Martin has praised convention ratification of amendments as a superior method over action by state legislatures, the alternative. The convention, he asserts, "is the only mechanism of ratification which assures the expression of the people."[19] If there is one cardinal principle of political science which all supplicants vow it is that unequivocal statements about the "general will" are suspect.[20] It is a difficult term, like "public interest," and is to be used cautiously. Consequently, Martin's flat preference for tapping "the expression of the people" is dubious both as political science and as political wisdom. He sees delegates to a convention as elected on a one-shot basis for a one-shot purpose; legislative elections as "confused by other issues." He repeats that "the most distinguishing characteristic of a state-ratifying convention is that it can more accurately reflect the popular will in the process of ratification than the state legislature."

If there is fault to find with this conclusion it must lie largely with the means followed in reaching it. My objections are of three sorts. First, Martin accepts words like "state sovereignty" and "popular will" at face value and does not look into the men, and the purposes of the men, who spoke them. Madison used these words in the late eighteenth century, which is one thing. But to quote Henry St. George Tucker without reference to his voting record or to his 1916 Storrs lectures attacking woman suffrage, is quite another. Political theory is impossible without an appreciation, a feeling, a recognition that knowing what a man says is not enough; what he is and what he represents in politics must be included.[21]

Second, the preference for convention over legislative ratification does not rest on a specific comparison informed by the political science of voting, elections and deliberative bodies. No one at all conversant with this vast literature could state flatly than any one of the several available electoral systems, taken alone, was absolutely most representative. The case for proportional, plurality or majority representation, and its variants, cannot be made without knowledge of other conditions.[22] By the same token, if legislatures in the states are inadequate mirrors of the popular will isn't there a faint prospect that conventions, specially arranged by those legislatures, could distort that will? The result of ignoring these qualifications is a flat conclusion that in all times under all circumstances state conventions are better than legislatures for ratifying federal constitutional amendments.

Third, there is little appreciation of the social and political history of the constitutional amendments of this century. The Supreme Court, that finely tuned instrument of the "popular will," was holding all manner of federal laws unconstitutional before 1937 so that, in the first part of the century, Progressives turned readily to constitutional amendments. Conservative opponents of Progressive legislative acts could occasionally overturn these laws in the courts. Progressives then moved the issue up a notch to the amendment level. Conservatives countered with claims that Progressive proposals were unconstitutional per se, whether in the form of amendments or as statutes. They went further and assaulted the method of amendment ratification by state legislatures as, of all things, undemocratic. Martin has insisted that these conservatives were sincere. One test might be to square their advocacy of state ratifying conventions on an *at-large basis* with their later embrace of electoral college reform on a *direct basis*.

Social Policies As Jurisdictional Issues

There are many reasons why those who initiate test cases for the resolution of substantive constitutional questions often fail to obtain a ruling on the merits. At a certain level of formality, the courts have adduced one set of reasons. At another level are commentaries on the reasons judges have offered. This chapter takes a perspective in keeping with the theme of constitutional change woven through this book. It is that ordinarily in constitutional cases the parties colliding on procedural grounds do so in pursuit of a larger purpose. Accordingly it is enlightening to consider the merits they had hoped to reach even though the Supreme Court may not go that far. The resulting jurisdictional and procedural rulings are important in themselves. They are simply better understood with this perspective.

In starting with the point that court decisions on questions of justiciability and standing and the like arise in cases someone hoped to see decided on the merits, we are looking again for that often elusive thread of the part played by social movements and organized interests in constitutional development. Lawyers concerned with policy cannot be unconcerned about procedure. The two are indissolubly mixed. It is safe to say that every social movement utilizing litigation to advance is forced to consider means of avoiding the shoals of jurisdictional and procedural grounds. In 1953, for instance, a law professor was urging "that the general rules governing litigable interest should not be applied so zealously as they have been recently where the issue in the case involves an alleged civil right."[1] His wish for a relaxation of older rules was certainly fulfilled—as it had to be if the civil rights movement was to advance.

Many new constitutional rules formulated since 1953 came only when the Supreme Court increased its zeal for civil rights and relaxed the "rules governing litigable interest." The Court relaxed its rule on standing against a plaintiff vindicating the constitutional rights of a third party in order to be sure a racial restrictive covenant would not be unenforced.[2] To overcome the old "separate but equal rule," and to decree the end of school segregation "with all deliberate speed," the Court took a generous view of a "class action" which made its decisions in the five cases before it broadly applicable.[3] It is well understood that the Court could reach the merits on legislative apportionment only after it softened its older measure of what the justices have termed "political questions."[4] The Court was also less zealous about its older rules when it agreed to entertain the possibility of determining the constitutionality of federal aid measures involving an alleged First Amendment right.[5] That organization's goal

257

is shown by the fact that lawyers for the NAACP Legal Defense Fund conducted the first litigations, lawyers associated with the National Institute of Municipal Law Officers and the National Municipal League overcame the "political question" obstacle, and lawyers for the American Jewish Congress and allied separatist groups sought the new rule for taxpayers.

This has ever been so. The present chapter is devoted to considering some of the procedural controversies generated by organized interests in the halcyon days before 1937. Some of the difficulties of organizing test cases in those years have already been touched upon. These kinds of procedural and jurisdictional obstacles are stressed here.

Likewise, the 1920s and 1930s produced controversies and, in some instances, changes in Supreme Court jurisdiction and practice. Litigation over new departures in social welfare laws clarified certain "rules governing litigable interest," emblematic of those decades. This string of cases affords an excursion into how a movement and a countermovement, for and against government-insured social security, churns up issues of justiciability. This is not to say that the courts decide each procedural or jurisdictional question raised by social movements in the same way they would determine the merits. Not at all. The variables in adjudication will not yield to such an analysis. What can be shown is that organized interests in pursuit of constitutional rulings on the merits sometimes end up with a judge-made rule on their litigable interest. In the early 1920s the first set of cases were *Massachusetts v. Mellon* and *Frothingham v. Mellon*, intended to put in question the grand scheme of federal grant-in-aid programs. The second set testing the constitutionality of the Social Security Act of 1935 also raised intriguing issues of the occasion and manner of invoking judicial review. This was in the cases of *Steward Machine Company v. Davis* and *Helvering v. Davis*, decided in 1937, which confirmed the changing views of the Court toward the New Deal.

Relatively slight attention has been paid social movements and organized interests as generators of constitutional cases having by-products in rules of jurisdiction and litigation. The leading writers on these subjects, Frankfurter and Landis, Hart and Wechsler, Stern and Gressman, and Charles Alan Wright, are quite aware of the social sources of litigation, but the scope of their task in setting forth the guiding principles of justiciability and practice has been too overwhelming by itself to permit much attention to these sources.[6] Moreover, they have a rather different perspective. They wish to instruct law students and practitioners in the rules and in the judicial rationale for them. Among legal historians, Willard Hurst has shown special sensitivity to procedure as the handmaiden of substantive policy. He believes "law has been more the creature than the creator of events" and that institutional structures and procedures have often been changed by the readiness of Americans to use law "as a means to bring about immediate practical results."[7] The judges who formulate the rules and the writers who explain them to the legal profession are engaged in a pressing and specialized subject which, ordinarily, does not permit commodious attention to the social origins and organized management of litigation.

By taking a close look at only a few cases developing out of controversies over social security during two decades, it will be possible in this chapter to consider the objectives of the litigants as well as the resulting rules on standing and justiciability.

Taxpayer Suits As a Progressive Idea

The judicial power of the United States extends, in the words of Article Three of the Constitution, to certain cases and controversies and leaves to the federal courts the determination of criteria of a proper case. An argument is not good enough. The argument must be endowed with specific attributes, ones the Supreme Court has identified in the natural history of litigation. This has not been static. An example of change is seen in the problem of what is known as the taxpayer suit. This is an action initiated by a private party against a frowned-upon legislative or executive policy. Many taxpayer suits are akin to man bites dog, for the action anticipates government action and tries to stop the Leviathan in its tracks. The advent of the taxpayer suit, its spread and use, has been an acknowledgment by lawyers and judges that the problem of bringing certain questions before the courts for adjudication requires novel methods. It is a method totally unknown to the Founding Fathers but recently included as part of the growing number of meanings the word "case" in Article Three describes.

The root of the matter is the idea of the adversary process, the notion that courts decide disputes between earnest parties with substantial stakes at issue. The adversary process insists that there be equal sides, that there be lawyers committed to its own side (with the subsidiary assumption not always true in fact) that the lawyers be in the same weight class with the same or similar resources of intellect, training, skill and zealousness.

Gradually, over a century, state courts have relaxed a strict adversary rule and permitted suits against local government policies by taxpaying citizens. Municipal action in virtually every state may be tested by altering the standing doctrine so that a plaintiff's status as a taxpayer "has been held sufficient to allow damage to him which is shared equally with all members of the public to form a judicially cognizable issue."[8] A taxpayer's suit has been defined as "a representative class action in equity, brought on behalf of all taxpayers against officials of the governmental unit challenged."[9] In practice, the word "taxpayer" has been treated so loosely that a group of persons wishing to question governmental action in the courts need only find the money and a nominal plaintiff to do so. This is why "taxpayers' suits" have functionally become "citizens' suits."[10]

A 1960 survey[11] showed that the objectives sought by plaintiff-taxpayers varied widely with the following in order of importance: (1) challenges to the use of the eminent domain power in connection with slum clearance, housing, highways, airport, and other public works projects; (2) attacks on the constitutionality of various methods of bond financing used by municipalities to circumvent limitations on indebtedness; (3) cases questioning the granting of franchises or licenses which represent public approval of privately owned but publicly used facilities; (4) efforts to withhold salary payments to civil servants who hold office in violation of statutory standards; (5) challenges to sales or donations of the public domain to private parties; (6) cases to achieve civil liberties objectives such as the prevention of expenditures for illegal methods of law enforcement or expenditures which would violate the separation of church and state; (7) suits to reapportion election or judicial districts.

Taxpayer suits were first allowed by American courts just prior to the Civil War but did not reach a great volume until the end of the nineteenth century. Then in the Progressive period a number of devices of democratic intent were fashioned to cope with entrenched officials and vested interests. In this connection the taxpayer's suit should be linked with the initiative, referendum and recall as a symbol of the Progressive era. In this century the taxpayer suit has been one of the chief weapons in the arsenal of the good government movement. William T. Evjue of the Madison, Wisconsin, *Capital Times*, with roots deep in the LaFollette movement, in 1960 established a special fund of $10,000 to be used, as he said, "in the protection of the public domain which is being raided periodically by private interests at the expense of the public interest."[12] He said that this fund would allow his newspaper "to start a taxpayer's suit where we believe that the state's lakes, rivers, streams, forests and parks are being taken over by private interests for private profit."[13] Similarly, the Citizens Union of the City of New York, described as "probably the most widely known and influential organization among the city's multitude of nongovernmental groups,"[14] and with origins before 1900 in the good government reform movement, has begun numerous taxpayers' actions throughout its history. Its activity in the courts has also taken other forms and has varied with the character of the local government. During the administrations of Mayors John F. Hylan and James J. Walker, between 1918 and 1932, the Citizens Union brought some nineteen lawsuits to restrain illegal expenditures of public funds and was successful in about twelve. Counsel of the Citizens Union more recently said he had "brought some half-dozen suits to restrain various governmental actions which we believed to be illegal. In addition, the Citizens Union occasionally intervenes, by leave of the court, as *amicus curiae* or friend of the court, in suits brought by others."[15] This use of taxpayers' suits by one newspaper and one civic organization is indicative of practices throughout the country in countering objectionable municipal expenditures.

The situation created by this easy access to the courts has been described by the *Yale Law Journal* in the following way:

Such litigation allows the courts, within the framework of traditional notions of "standing" to add to the controls over public officials inherent in the elective process the judicial scrutiny of the statutory and constitutional validity of their acts. Taxpayers' suits also extend the uniquely American concept of judicial review to legislative action by allowing minorities ineffective at the ballot box to invalidate statutes or ordinances on constitutional grounds. . . . Taxpayers' suits thus create an army of potential private attorneys general acting on whatever private incentives may induce them to spend the time and money to bring a taxpayer's suit: . . . And since group financing of such litigation is not infrequent, taxpayers' suits also mobilize various voluntary associations seeking private, economic, or social objectives to further law enforcement and prevention of corruption in government.[16]

The objections to the widespread use of taxpayers' suits are numerous. Even when unsuccessful the delay occasioned by such actions "may unduly obstruct the completion of public projects."[17] These suits may harass officials and immobilize local government, thereby inhibiting progressive community action. But most important of all, "taxpayers' suits may push the concept of judicial review of legislative and executive action too far."[18]

This should suggest that the concept of judicial review, which is usually thought of merely in terms of Supreme Court review of acts of Congress and of state legislatures deserves consideration from the viewpoint of the government of communities, as well. The vast array of state and federal courts which may review the actions of community governments means that this simple procedural device of loosening rules on standing has vast implications. Perhaps this fullness explains in large part why the Court up to that time had been so restrictive toward opportunities which arose from time to time to enlarge the routes and the means by which litigation could be brought. These appear to be the circumstantial reasons, which were in league with the rhetorical reasons, for a practically universal view among the justices that the case and controversy clause of Article Three should be construed narrowly.

Standing was severely drawn to rule out advisory opinions, taxpayer suits, friendly suits, declaratory judgments and the like. Moreover, the Court had itself developed the concept of casting certain constitutional litigation as raising "political questions" and its catalogue of such cases had been growing during recent decades. This was at least part of the Supreme Court's tradition with a salience for understanding some of the background circumstances on the occasion in the 1920s when the question of permitting taxpayer suits in federal court was urged more forcefully.

The Sheppard-Towner Maternity Act

The Sheppard-Towner Maternity Act of November 23, 1921, was one of a series of favorable congressional responses to the efforts of that notable band of women reformers including Florence Kelley, Julia Lathrop, Lillian D. Wald, Grace and Edith Abbott, Jane Addams, Alice Hamilton, Josephine Goldmark, Mary Anderson, Mary Dewson and others. They were college educated and instilled in themselves a sense of altruism which supported lifetime service in raising employment, education, health, nutrition and welfare standards. Hundreds enlisted with them in the settlement-house movement in numerous cities—Hull House in Chicago, the Henry Street Settlement House in New York being merely the most famous. They worked for protective labor legislation and government health and education programs. They were active in the National Consumers' League, and after 1906 in the Woman's Trade Union League and other organizations with their various state and local branches.

During the heyday of this push these women accumulated a huge store of expertise in substantive fields like industrial safety, medicine and demography, as well as in the most suitable methods of introducing improvements and gaining their adoption by government. An important milestone in this latter development was the congressional act creating the Children's Bureau.[19] Soon afterward, President Taft appointed Julia C. Lathrop chief of the new bureau, a position she held until 1921 when succeeded by a close associate, Grace Abbott. There is no single explanation to be made for the adoption of the Sheppard-Towner Act, but it was more than anything else a bill written in the Children's Bureau.

Under Julia Lathrop between 1912 and 1921 the Children's Bureau investigated infant mortality and crusaded for uniform birth registration under federal supervision. The bureau studied child labor and administered the first federal Child Labor Act in 1916 and 1917 until the Supreme Court held the measure beyond the power of Congress to regulate commerce among the states. The Children's Bureau worked with countless organizations outside the government in generating interest in and support for the protection of maternity and infancy with federal aid to the states.

By 1920, the federal grant-in-aid device was a common means of bringing national funds to bear on the solution of countrywide problems although defined as local matters. Dozens of programs had been initiated and all the states were then drawing federal funds, under Washington's guidelines, to employ county agents, conduct soil surveys, build roads and support the National Guard.

In 1919, Representative Jeannette Rankin (R., Montana) introduced a bill to provide federal grants to states willing to conduct health conferences, establish prenatal care centers and otherwise extend maternal aid. In 1920, this measure was endorsed in the party platforms of Democrats, Socialists, Prohibitionists and Farmer-Laborites. The Republican holdout was won over when Warren G. Harding, as the presidential candidate, pledged his support in a major campaign speech. In Congress in 1921, the maternity bill was reintroduced by Senator Morris Sheppard (D., Texas) and Representative Horace Towner (R., Iowa). It was adopted by substantial margins in Congress (63 to 7 in the Senate, 279 to 39 in the House), and signed into law by President Harding on November 23, 1921.

This act was an authorization providing for limited sums "to be paid to the several states for the purpose of cooperating with them in promoting the welfare and hygiene of maternity and infancy." The act created a Board of Maternity and Infant Hygiene to deal with certain appeals from decisions of the Children's Bureau which was charged with the duty of detailed administration. There was a privacy provision in sections 8 and 9 of the act, barring any federal or state official from entering "any home over the objection of the parents," and insisting, further, that nothing in the new law "shall be construed as limiting the power of a parent . . . to determine what treatment or correction shall be provided for a child or the agency or agencies to be employed for such purpose." There was also, in section 14, what might be called a "states-rights provision" one that has been typical of federal grant-in-aid legislation, stating that the act is intended "to secure to the states control of the administration of this act within their respective states, subject only to the provisions and purposes of this act."

The Sheppard-Towner Maternity Act authorized an appropriation of $1,480,000 for the fiscal year ending June 30, 1922, somewhat less for each of five subsequent years. To qualify, a state legislature must enact an enabling measure, including an implementation plan, and appropriate matching funds. Of the forty-eight states, thirty-eight joined the federal-state maternity program in 1922, seven others eventually joined, while three never participated. The three abstainers were Connecticut, Illinois and Massachusetts. In Congress, smaller appropriations were voted in 1926 for two more years, but intense opposition caused the Sheppard-Towner Maternity Act to expire on June 30, 1929.

It has been said that the scheme of maternity aid in the Sheppard-Towner program between 1921 and 1929 "was a link in a chain of ideas and actions from Roosevelt to Roosevelt, which began with the White House Conference on Child Welfare Standards in 1909 and ended with the Social Security Act of 1935."[20] Accordingly, the measure excited sanctimonious zealousness in its supporters (any opponent must wish women and children to die) and xenophobia in its critics (a vicious, un-American paternal step toward sovietism). This little-remembered, modest measure was, during the 1920s, a continuous source of passionate controversy.

The Attack on Federal Grants-in-Aid

Men and women actively opposed to federal maternity aid to the states were often associated together in a medley of patriotic societies. These were each small organizations, with few or no paid staff members, with life destinies of ten to twenty years. Behind them was a social impulse often felt by members of established families fearful of the rise in immigration, of broader social welfare programs, of financing and monitoring of new programs by the national government. Their anxieties over status, as much as anything, led them to celebrate their own family backgrounds in ways that gave them superior and self-serving claims as defenders of national values.

Specifically, many were experienced in the losing but hard-fought struggle against woman suffrage, both against adoption by individual state governments and against a national constitutional woman suffrage amendment. V.O. Key has wrongly treated this opposition as essentially silly and weak; on the contrary, it was in dead earnest, durable, intelligent and well organized. After all, the opposition to woman suffrage held off the likes of Susan B. Anthony, Lucy Stone, Elizabeth Cady Stanton, Carrie Chapman Catt and their national organizations for fifty years: from the introduction of the Anthony amendment in Congress in 1869 to ratification of this measure as the Nineteenth Amendment in August 1920. These opponents to woman suffrage, to the Sheppard-Towner Act and other governmental steps in social welfare and regulation deserve a closer look if we are to comprehend their objectives in the 1923 taxpayer cases.

Voluntary associations included the Woman Patriots, the American Constitutional League, the Maryland League for State Defense and, most aggressively, the Sentinels of the Republic. The first of these had begun in 1918 to publish a weekly newspaper called *The Woman Patriot* for the National Association Against Woman Suffrage, and after the Nineteenth Amendment was accepted as irreversible many in that association continued, up to 1940, to keep this organization going under its corporate name. Two officers with the most staying power, who got out the paper in Washington for years, were Mrs. Randolph Frothingham of Brookline, Massachusetts, and Mary G. Kilbreth of Southampton, Long Island. In 1920 and 1921, when only diehards stayed with the ship, Mrs. Frothingham was president of the Massachusetts Anti-Suffrage Association while Miss Kilbreth was president of the National. They also opposed much social legislation of the 1920s and were bitterly hostile to the New Deal.

The American Constitutional League had its roots in the New York Man Suffrage League, led from 1912 to 1920 by Everett Pepperell Wheeler, a lawyer who, it was said upon his death in 1925, had had more letters to the editor published in the *New York Times* than any contemporary. Most expressed his criticisms of the rising tide of woman suffrage. Wheeler was counsel to Charles S. Fairchild, president of the American Constitutional League, and in 1887 to 1889 secretary of the treasury under Cleveland, in the Supreme Court case of *Fairchild v. Hughes*, which aimed at voiding the Nineteenth Amendment. The Maryland League for State Defense likewise opposed the vote for women. It also sponsored a case, *Leser v. Garnett*, challenging the constitutionality of the Nineteenth Amendment in the Supreme Court with William Marbury and Thomas Cadwalader as counsel. Lawyers in this organization, centered in the Marbury law firm in Baltimore, also persistently worked for states rights, particularly against federal grants-in-aid for maternity and for education. Thus, in April 1924 Marbury and William Rawls appeared with Dr. Frank J. Goodnow, president of the Johns Hopkins University, to testify before the House Committee on Education against a bill to create a federal Department of Education.

The Sheppard-Towner Act led quite directly to the Sentinels of the Republic, organized in the spring of 1922 by a few persons meeting at the New York home of Charles S. Fairchild. "They viewed with alarm the constantly increasing list of measures designed to break down our dual system of government and to build up a strongly centralized bureaucracy in Washington." At that juncture, their concerns focused on these national legislative developments: "The 18th and 19th Amendments had recently been ratified, the Sheppard-Towner Maternity Act had been enacted, and the proposed Child Labor Amendment and bills to create a Department of Education and a Department of Public Welfare were then pending in Congress." The Sentinels of the Republic was incorporated in Massachusetts in August and sponsored its first public meeting, in Faneuil Hall on the two hundredth anniversary of the birth of Samuel Adams, on September 27, 1922. A history of the associations says: "Following their organization the Sentinels proceeded at once to attack the Sheppard-Towner Maternity Act. Largely through their influence Massachusetts refused to accept the Act and suits were brought by the State and an individual taxpayer, in the Supreme Court of the United States, to test its constitutionality."[21]

Looking back from the 1960s, Thomas Cadwalader, a surviving Sentinel from Baltimore, said that the association had no more than two hundred members and, in the main, its active membership held offices or were on the board of directors and hence could be identified on its letterhead. The Sentinels of the Republic's presidents were Louis A. Coolidge from 1922 to 1925, Bentley Wirt Warren from 1925 to 1927, and Alexander Lincoln from 1927 to 1940, when the Sentinels "simply expired." The last records of the Sentinels indicate they were survived, and partly transformed into the Woman Patriot Corporation, for in 1940 its president was Mrs. Randolph Frothingham and the treasurer Alexander Lincoln.

The affiliations and cross-membership of many Sentinels show that a voluntary organization probably can rarely be isolated out as an estate entirely separate from other associations or from institutions of government. This is especially important in gaining a realistic picture of the multiple loyalties of some lawyers when they also hold positions in government. Alexander Lincoln thus represented the Sentinels of the Republic's spirit while serving officially as assistant attorney general of Massachusetts. True, the state legislature declined to participate in the Sheppard-Towner program; yet, Lincoln helped push the state's negation much further by working up litigation challenging the entire program on a constitutional basis. Henry St. George Tucker, while a congressman, belonged to the Sentinels and also worked hard in the constitutional challenge to the maternity aid program in the courts. An even more prominent official opposed to the Sheppard-Towner Act was James M. Beck, solicitor general of the United States, whose official duty centered on representing the federal government before the Supreme Court. He served from 1921 to 1925.

Like so many losers in Congress, before and since, the opponents of the Maternity Act of 1921 cast the defeat in abstract constitutional terms and widened their complaint beyond this single statute to confront the very concept of the federal grant-in-aid. The goal was to have the Supreme Court of the United States declare such grant-in-aid programs violative of the Tenth Amendment (which reserves unstated power to the states) and the Fourteenth Amendment (which, among other things, forbids states from taking a person's property or liberty without due process of law) and the Fifth Amendment (which forbids property-taking without due process of law by the federal government). This sweeping goal would, the lawyers knew, be difficult to achieve because of the procedural difficulties inherent in developing suitable cases the Supreme Court would decide on the merits.

The Woman Patriot in 1922 featured attacks on the Sheppard-Towner Act by Governor Nathan L. Miller of New York, Attorney General J. Weston Allen of Massachusetts and Congressman Henry St. George Tucker of Virginia. Their criticisms were essentially like the arguments made in Congress against enactment in 1921 and would be reworked into briefs in the Supreme Court cases attacking the validity of the act in 1923. Miller insisted he had "no quarrel with the object sought by the sponsors of the Sheppard-Towner bill," and he applauded a state measure empowering localities to offer prenatal care. "That work can only be done effectively and economically by local agencies, public or private, and the will to do it, if it is to accomplish any good, must spring from the local spirit and enterprise, which cannot be created by a federal bureau." This objection was connected to constitutionality. Governor Miller said that the enumerated powers of Article One, Section 8 did not include the practice of medicine or midwifery. This was one step; others to control education and to gradually extend federal supervision over every state activity would surely follow.[22]

Attorney General Allen rendered an official opinion on the act to the Massachusetts Senate and House concerning the question of whether the Commonwealth has the right, "as a sovereign state" to question the constitutionality of the Maternity Act. His answers laid the basis for the original action he and Assistant Attorney General Alexander Lincoln brought in the Supreme Court.[23]

On August 17, 1922, Congressman Tucker delivered a speech on the floor of the House of Representatives on the duty of members of Congress to refrain from passing unconstitutional legislation. Tucker deplored remarks by a colleague like this: "I doubt whether this bill is unconstitutional, but we can pass it up to the courts and they can decide that question." He quoted Abraham Lincoln's 1860 Cooper Union speech, where Lincoln asserted that "No man who has sworn to support the Constitution can conscientiously vote for what he understands to be an unconstitutional measure, however expedient he may think it." Although Tucker wished congressmen had stopped the Sheppard-Towner Act because it was unconstitutional, he was gratified that at least the courts were open and that the Sentinels of the Republic could lay the question before them.[24]

It was decided to proceed in two ways to bring the claim of the Sheppard-Towner Act's unconstitutionality to the United States Supreme Court. One route would be in an original suit by the Commonwealth of Massachusetts, for herself and as representative of her citizens. This was conceived as possible from the sentence in Article Three of the Constitution which reads, "In all cases affecting ambassadors, other public ministers and consuls, and those in which a state shall be party, the Supreme Court shall have original jurisdiction." The term means in this context that the suit begins, or originates, in the Supreme Court and is not heard elsewhere beforehand. Such types of cases have never amounted to 5 percent of the Supreme Court's business in a term; original suits are rare and few are in fact decided on the merits. It was a gamble but one that Assistant Attorney General Alexander Lincoln eagerly, and Attorney General Jay R. Benton willingly took for the Commonwealth. Their brief emphasized the constitutional wrongs in federal grant-in-aid programs generally, in the Maternity Act specifically, and addressed the jurisdictional issue only after those assertions were fully aired.

The second case took the form of a taxpayer suit prepared by three Baltimore lawyers in federal court in the District of Columbia. The plaintiff taxpayer was Harriet Frothingham, an organization woman earlier sketched in brief.

It was a group of like-minded lawyers in William L. Marbury's Baltimore office who conducted the other constitutional challenge to the Sheppard-Towner Act. Then living in Washington, Mrs. Frothingham happened to be just right for the lawyers' idea of challenging the Maternity Act through a taxpayer suit to begin in the United States District Court in the District of Columbia. They had no suitable alternative as a form of action, for the maternity aid program was voluntary both on the part of each state and then also for the recipients of medical and other advice.

It was decided that an action could be brought not by someone in the program but on behalf of someone who was paying for it. A million dollar program made the per capita cost less than a penny each for the 1920 population of 105 million. Mrs. Frothingham doubtless paid more although the federal income tax at that time was modest by the rates today. But this was not the point, for she would have had standing in most state courts simply as a citizen. The question concerning her lawyers and which would concern the judges was whether the federal courts should permit a taxpayer suit and consider her challenge on the merits. The chief lawyer was William Lee Rawls, assisted on the brief by George Arnold Frick, and William H. Lamar. This suit was dismissed by the Supreme Court of the District of Columbia, the trial court, and the decree was affirmed by the Court of Appeals of the District. For this reason, Rawls's brief in the Supreme Court of the United States, where he appealed, concerned itself seriously with the question of standing.

The argument for Frothingham stressed the almost universal state practice "that a taxpayer has a sufficient interest to entitle him to maintain a suit against a public officer for the purpose of enjoining an unauthorized payment of public funds or disposition of public property." This state practice had even been recognized by the Supreme Court. Rawls, Frick and Lamar submitted there was no distinction between the right of a taxpayer to maintain a suit against a state officer and an officer of the federal government threatening to make an unauthorized expenditure of public money. This was tied to the assertion that the purposes of the Maternity Act were beyond the legislative power of Congress. Mrs. Frothingham could not resort to equity and so her lawyers claimed she had standing as a taxpayer, suffering a direct injury by being subjected to taxation to pay her proportionate part of the program's cost. "Her injury would be irreparable because it cannot be calculated."

These themes were supported in related briefs. One was filed by J. Weston Allen, a former attorney general of Massachusetts. Another was presented by the lawyers of the American Constitutional League, Everett P. Wheeler and Waldo G. Morse. An *amicus curiae* was also filed by Henry St. George Tucker, still a member of the House of Representatives from Virginia. These briefs were less concerned with the barrier of standing than with attacking the Maternity Act and the grants-in-aid principle.

Legal Defense of the Maternity Act

A coalition of twenty national women's organizations had helped move the Sheppard-Towner bill to passage in Congress. This was the first post-suffrage legislation directly affecting women, and historians have thought the then unclear power of women at the polls, said to present a threat of bloc voting in the midterm elections of 1922, accounted very largely for the statute. The coalition, called the Women's Joint Congressional Committee, placed Florence Kelley in charge of a subcommittee to work for enactment. Officially, the brunt of the defense was in the hands of the office of the solicitor general, but this was not sufficient for Mrs. Kelley, who worked to stimulate *amicus curiae* briefs.

The problem of ensuring strong defense for a statute in jeopardy is illustrated by Mrs. Kelley's efforts to persuade New York's attorney general to file an *amicus curiae* brief supporting the federal Maternity Act. After enactment of the Sheppard-Towner Act in November 1921, and with representatives of the League of Women Voters, the National Child Welfare Association, and other groups, Mrs. Kelley helped form an alliance to see that New York State took advantage of the generous federal aid provisions of the act. This was a struggle, as Governor Nathan Miller declared he would veto any such action by the state legislature. Miller's defeat at the hands of Al Smith in 1922 and vigorous lobbying by the women led to participation in the program by New York in 1923. Mrs. Kelley made an effort to have a number of states answer the attack of Massachusetts with one or more briefs *amicus curiae.*

Similar efforts were being made in other states with the result that ten attorneys general of the participating states joined together in a brief as *amicus curiae* in *Massachusetts v. Mellon.* The states so represented were Kentucky, Pennsylvania, Virginia, Minnesota, Colorado, Delaware, Indiana, Arkansas, Arizona and Ohio. This was a small number out of the more than forty participating states but large compared with the single state represented by Alexander Lincoln.

The Association of Land Grant Colleges also saw the issue in broad terms. The association employed a professor of constitutional law at Cornell University, Charles K. Burdick, to prepare and file a brief as *amicus curiae* on its behalf in the Massachusetts case. This is a most impressive document, showing the history of federal grants-in-aid, their efficacy and legality. The land-grant colleges had been established by the Morrill Act during the Civil War and their organization in Washington was an early entrant in the growth of lobbies for higher education. The brief by Burdick was one of the few, perhaps the only venture of the land-grant colleges in constitutional litigation. It recognized fully the calamity the state universities would suffer if the Frothingham-Massachusetts challenge to grants-in-aid was successful.

Professor Burdick used much of his *amicus* brief for the Association of Land Grant Colleges in a law review article on the political and constitutional history of grants-in-aid arguing that all of the questions raised about the use of the aid mechanism to induce states to venture new policy were issues for legislators, not judges.[25] He defined "federal aid" legislation as "legislation by Congress appropriating money from the national treasury or conveying public lands, to be used by the states or by state agencies." The donation of lands, in the Morrill Act of 1862 forming the basis of the land-grant colleges, for example, was rooted in the constitutional declaration that:

Congress shall have power to dispose of and make all needful rules and regulations respecting the territory or other property belonging to the United States; and nothing in this Constitution shall be so construed as to prejudice any claims of the United States, or of any particular state.[26]

After reviewing more than a century of experience under this clause, Burdick concluded in 1923 that it is

clear that public lands or their proceeds may be given or appropriated for use in the States for purposes which will be for "the common benefit," though they are purposes with regard to which Congress could not legislate directly, and that education, at least, is such a purpose.[27]

The other major theme in Burdick's review offered the orthodox, liberal view of the nature of the taxing power. He agreed that the power of Congress "to lay and collect taxes, duties, imposts and excises, to pay the debts and provide for the common defense and general welfare of the United States," provided in Article One, section 8, paragraph 1, was not a general, but a qualified, grant of legislative power. Madison had insisted that the power was limited to the purposes of the other enumerated powers in Article One, section 8, while Hamilton had taken a broader view that the phrase "general welfare" was comprehensive. In any event, Congress had often acted upon the liberal interpretation and appropriated money for welfare purposes not specifically within the scope of the enumerated powers. Burdick then detailed the history of federal aid legislation showing the breadth of congressionally supported activities. As the article was published during the time the Court was considering the cases of *Massachusetts v. Mellon* and *Frothingham v. Mellon*, Burdick was hoping for a decision on the merits that would directly uphold on the merits the constitutionality of federal grants-in-aid. The land-grant colleges had a heavy stake in this outcome.

Although a Republican Congress and a Republican president had supported the Sheppard-Towner Maternity Act, the chief defense of the law and of the principle of grants-in-aid in the test cases brought against the secretary of the Treasury and other administration officials was made by the Land Grant Colleges Association and the brief of the several state attorneys general. The Sentinels of the Republic actually had an ally in President Harding's Solicitor General James M. Beck, who was completely out of sympathy with Progressive social legislation and was to write, even in the age of the later Hoover presidency, a book attacking governmental growth titled *Our Wonderland of Bureaucracy*. By duty he was obliged to defend the government against the attack on the Sheppard-Towner Act and his brief did so ably, both on the jurisdictional issue and in defense of the federal aid principle. His biographer has reported Beck's unhappiness in defending a statute he disliked. Beck said that his brief was "largely prepared by the proponents at the Maternity Bureau" (confusing or joining together the new Women's Bureau with the Children's Bureau) and that the president had urged him "to let them say all they wanted to say in behalf of the constitutionality of the appropriation."[28] Keller summed up Beck's unhappiness this way:

Certainly, the brief's declaration—in italics—that *"the power of Congress to make appropriations from the general funds of the United States is almost unlimited"* was far from his own sentiment on the matter. He later recalled, "I was not in sympathy with the law," and tried to counter some of the damaging implications of the brief by declaring that the case was not "any authority for the United States government to spend money in non-federal projects in states." When the New Deal unveiled still more disturbing uses of the congressional power of appropriation for all that was "necessary and proper," he would bemoan "that unhappy expression in the taxing clause."[29]

Massachusetts and Frothingham Rules as Barriers

On June 4, 1923, the United States Supreme Court was unanimous in ordering *Massachusetts v. Mellon* dismissed and the dismissal by the District of Columbia courts of *Frothingham v. Mellon* affirmed.[30] The cases had been planned, argued, considered and disposed together with Mr. Justice Sutherland delivering a single opinion covering the two cases. After summarizing the nature of the challenge, Sutherland began his nine-page review with this announcement: "We have reached the conclusion that the cases must be disposed of without considering the merits of the constitutional questions."[31] In fact, his essay dealt with the constitutional question of standing to litigate in the federal courts but, of course, did not deal with the issue of the validity of the Maternity Act let alone the constitutionality of the principle of grants-in-aid. Thus, the Sentinels lost the case and the advocates of federal aid claimed to have won it. At least these advocates could later say that these were the results:

1. Federal grant-in-aid statutes, patterned after the Sheppard-Towner Act (which was typical of the modern grant form), will not be declared unconstitutional by the Supreme Court.
2. Neither a state nor a private citizen may ever had the merits of the constitutional questions involved in grants-in-aid considered by the Supreme Court, because of "want of jurisdiction."[32]

First, the Court ruled in *Massachusetts v. Mellon* that the state had presented "no justiciable controversy either in its own behalf or as a representative of its citizens." Mr. Justice Sutherland noted that the "statute imposes obligation but simply extends an option which the state is free to accept or reject." He went further by interpreting the constitutional provision that the Court has original jurisdiction "in all Cases . . . in which a State shall be Party."[33] "The effect of this is not to confer jurisdiction upon the Court merely because a state is a party," Sutherland wrote, "but only where it is a party to a proceeding of judicial cognizance. Proceedings not of a justiciable character are outside the contemplation of the constitutional grant." The state could not sue to stop a congressional statute; it could do that by simply refusing the moneys offered. Regarding the maintenance of a suit by the state as representative of its citizens the Court did not, in fact, give a sweeping answer covering all contingencies but it was definite that a state may not "institute judicial proceedings to protect citizens of the United States from the operation of the statutes thereof."[34]

Second, the Court disposed of the *Frothingham* case in the same style, noting that the right of a taxpayer to halt the execution of a federal appropriation act had never been passed upon there before. Mr. Justice Sutherland conceded that taxpayers could question municipal expenditures in state courts and he was willing to say that this was not only legal but proper. "The interest of a taxpayer of a municipality in the application of its moneys is direct and immediate and the remedy by injunction to prevent their misuse is not inappropriate."

Sutherland continued by conceding this to be true in many states and said it "is the rule of this Court."

The municipality was not merely fairly small but in legal theory local governments were corporations and this was also a persuasive point, as Sutherland noted. "The reasons which support the extension of the equitable remedy in such cases are based upon the peculiar relation of the corporate taxpayer to the corporation, which is not without some resemblance to that subsisting between stockholder and private corporation," he said, citing Dillon on municipal corporations.[35] For Sutherland, these concessions were the basis for a distinction, not an extension, of the doctrine that taxpayer suits are permissible in most state courts. The heart of his opinion is as follows:

[Compared to the municipal taxpayer] the relation of a taxpayer of the United States to the federal government is very different. His interest in the moneys of the Treasury—partly realized from taxation and partly from other sources—is shared with millions of others; is comparatively minute and indeterminable; and the effect upon future taxation, of any payment out of the funds, so remote, fluctuating and uncertain, that no basis is afforded for an appeal to the preventive powers of a court of equity.[36]

In denying standing to Harriet Frothingham, Mr. Justice Sutherland also feared that if one taxpayer were allowed "to champion and litigate" a cause, the fever would catch. Every appropriation and statute regarding expenditures would be open to question through taxpayer suits. It seemed to be this possibility that explained his decision as much as anything though he could show conclusively "that no precedence sustaining the right to maintain suits like this has been called to our attention."[37]

Remembering that Sutherland and several of his brethren on the Court in the 1920s were correctly regarded as judicial activists with conservative values, it is noteworthy that they pledged themselves to restraint in this instance. It cannot be overstressed that the differing postures of justices between activism and restraint have been within a framework of control over the judicial function. There has been some activism in champions of restraint like Holmes and Frankfurter; some restraint in a famous conservative activist like Sutherland and a famous liberal one like Douglas. The 1923 *Frothingham* rule, approved by justices who believed a federal child labor law and a District of Columbia minimum wage law invalid, shows they saw procedural limits to the power of judicial review. This is what Sutherland said about the barriers to judicial review:

We have no power *per se* to review and annul acts of Congress on the ground that they are unconstitutional. That question may be considered only when the justification for some direct injury suffered or threatened, presenting a justiciable issue, is made to rest upon such an act. Then the power exercised is that of ascertaining and declaring the law applicable to the controversy. . . . The party who invokes the power must be able to show not only that the statute is invalid but that he has sustained or is immediately in danger of sustaining some direct injury as the result of its enforcement, and not merely that he suffers in some indefinite way in common with people generally.[38]

In a discussion of the *Frothingham* rule years later, Hurst suggested that the decision was "born of a typical nineteenth-century American concern with tangibles."[39] It may also be looked upon as a concern with manners, formal manners, the legal equivalent of Emily Post's counsel on how Mr. Goodbody should enter a drawing room, a perspective taken by Rodell.[40] Charles P. Curtis has given a more rounded explication of the rule "that a taxpayer whose interest is 'undifferentiated from the mass of his fellow citizens' ought not to have standing."[41] He suggested three reasons why the Court limited its own power this way.

One is a matter of caution in the exercise of a great and a very hazardous power and the need of preserving the Court's power of timing its decisions.

The second is keeping at least the pretense of being nothing more than a court of law. And the third is to keep very far away, as far as possible, from undertaking the duty of what really amounts to giving advisory opinions where the request does not even come from the president (we know the Court refused an advisory opinion requested by President Washington) but from a private citizen.

I suggest that those three reasons may not amount to enough to justify the present practice, but they ought to be weighed before it is enlarged.

This was standard among most lawyers when Curtis spoke in 1953.[42]

It is safe to infer from the decision of the Court in the child labor cases and in cases concerning minimum wage laws for women that several members of the Court—Van Devanter, McReynolds, Butler and Sutherland—would not have considered the law valid. But they were not in favor of enlarging their jurisdiction at that time in that way. They preferred a different route and were in process of pursuing it through legislation. Chief Justice Taft had already named a committee of the Court to develop new legislation and this committee was doing so. This was to become the Judiciary Act of 1925.

The measure stemmed from a united view among the justices that greater control of their own business was essential. In a sense acceptance of taxpayers suits or suits by states in the manner of *Massachusetts v. Mellon*, would open the gates, not close and control them. For what was desired was a reduction of obligatory cases and an increase in cases the Court could accept or reject upon its own discretion. Thus there were not only broad policy reasons for refusing these cases in 1923 but also specific reasons of legislative strategy for the justices. In obtaining enactment of the Judiciary Act of 1925 the Court was acting as, and must be cast as, another agency of government seeking directly, and encouraging indirectly, favorable congressional action. This seems to be the appropriate context for understanding in part at least how the Supreme Court would deal with these cases at the procedural level even though some members of the Court, possibly even a majority of members, were not in sympathy with the Sheppard-Towner program.

Quite possibly, the unanimous decision of the Supreme Court holding that taxpayers lacked standing to question the constitutionality of congressional appropriations for a grant-in-aid program was, more than anything else, a strategic act. By not reaching the merits the Court held to a universal view among the justices that the institution was being swamped by cases it was obligated to decide. Taxpayer suits would add to that obligation. To permit them would be inconsistent with an important legislative reform measure the justices were then seeking and so an opposite, positive response to the claims of Massachusetts and Frothingham would be inconsistent. The reform proposal was eventually adopted by Congress and became law as the Judiciary Act of June 1, 1925. It was a law first officially proposed fifteen years earlier by President Taft and had been widely studied and discussed. It was being very strongly pressed upon Congress by members of the Court at the time of the decision in the taxpayer cases.

What the act did was to give the Supreme Court almost complete control of the cases it would decide on their merits. Its enactment, as Frankfurter and Landis said, came from congressional "deference to the prestige of the Supreme Court and its Chief Justice, whose energetic espousal helped to realize the Court's proposal. The opinion of the bar, within and without Congress, accepted the Court's prescription for the Court's needs."[43]

Social Security Act of 1935

The upsurge of domestic legislation under the New Deal is commonly divided into three phases—relief, recovery and reform, with war as a fourth—to acknowledge events and follow the Berryman cartoon of the transformation of President Roosevelt from "Dr. New Deal" to "Dr. Win-the-War." Each phase was marked by new definitions of crisis and an ever broadening role for the federal government. Conservatives like James M. Beck found the national government an uncontrollable bureaucracy in the 1920s under Coolidge and Hoover; they were apoplectic about the new departures of the 1930s. The ideas for the Roosevelt programs were ancient by some standards and it has been seen in these pages that the minimum wage movement was simply halted in its tracks by the Supreme Court in 1923. While the Court refused then to review the Sheppard-Towner Maternity Act, Congress itself was eventually persuaded to give up this grant-in-aid program and cut off appropriations after 1928. This type of program was one of many that was steamed up in the New Deal pressure-cooker.

The relief and recovery programs of the New Deal, adopted during the first hundred days after March 4, 1933, saw the bank holiday, job programs like the Works Progress Administration, the Civilian Conservation Corps, the National Youth Administration, the first Agricultural Adjustment Act and the National Industrial Recovery Act with its production codes. Some of these measures were so hastily prepared, badly administered, radically regarded and effectively opposed in litigation that they did not survive to the end of Roosevelt's first administration.

Now came permanent reform. Among the statutes which have become household words in American political life were those establishing the Securities Exchange Commission, the Agricultural Adjustment Administration, the National Labor Relations Board and, later, the Tennessee Valley Authority. The Fair Labor Standards Act of 1938 culminated the work of both the National Consumers' League and the National Child Labor Committee. Even in this impressive company of legislation it is easy to subscribe to this enthusiastic backward review of the significance of the Social Security Act of August 14, 1935.[44]

Perhaps no other single piece of social legislation concerned with domestic policy adopted in the past quarter-century has been more far-reaching than the Social Security Act in helping promote the well-being and happiness of the American people. Under this one Act, there exists programs of old-age, survivors, and disability insurance; federal grants to the states for the needy aged, the blind, dependent children, and the permanently and totally disabled; and maternal and child health, crippled children, and child welfare services. It can be said unequivocally that the social security system of nationwide social insurance and federal grants-in-aid programs for public welfare has become a permanent part of the basic fabric of the nation's social institutions, and that these programs have the support of both major political parties and the overwhelming majority of the American people.[45]

The Social Security Act had been nurtured by a specific organization, the American Association for Old Age Security, established in 1927. This complex movement has been described and analyzed at length in numerous studies not to be reviewed here.[46] The focus in the present chapter is on the way in which litigation was organized to challenge social policies in the courts and the jurisdictional problems this effort presented. Accordingly, we turn from the well-known story of social security legislation to the little-known background of the test cases which determined the fate of the 1935 act and the associated state laws in the Supreme Court.

Test Cases from Boston and Birmingham

The conventional saying that the Supreme Court decides great constitutional issues within a framework of a simple adversary case is disproved in many instances in the history of such adjudications. The Social Security Act of 1935 and the related state unemployment compensation laws, bitterly criticized in Congress and the legislatures and in the press, were naturally challenged in the courts, not in a single case, but in numerous cases brought in several states at about the same time and joined in, formally or informally, by hundreds of corporations. Nor were the cases truly adversary for they were mostly "typical cases" in which no penalty would be suffered and all sides agreed in advance to abide by the outcome. The National Lawyers' Committee of the American Liberty League was opposed to these statutes but the source of the litigation seems to have derived from a disinclination of businessmen to pay a new tax, a motive related less to doctrine than to dollars.

In its 1935-36 term the Supreme Court invalidated the tax features of the Agricultural Adjustment Act in *Butler v. United States*[47] and this aroused a belief among many employers that the federal and state social security acts were in constitutional jeopardy. They certainly were. Accordingly, the question of their validity was put to the test as swiftly as possible and all the courts responded on a remarkably prompt timetable. The really serious litigation did not get under way until late in 1936 and all the questions were resolved well before the end of the Supreme Court's 1936-37 term.

While threats of suits were made in many states, the chief cases reaching the appellate courts were from Boston, Massachusetts, and Birmingham, Alabama. The lawyers in Boston and Birmingham were not aware of each other's activities until their cases were accepted by the Supreme Court in Washington for review. The cases were cast similarly but the chief lawyers in the two cities had a quite different spirit in conducting them. In Birmingham, Borden Burr and William Logan Martin, each a committed conservative lawyer, managed the test cases. Burr's challenge to the Alabama Unemployment Compensation Act in the *Carmichael* case[48] became the leading Supreme Court ruling on that subject while Martin's case against the federal Social Security Act, *Steward Machine Company v. Davis*,[49] continues to be among the one hundred or so best-known Supreme Court decisions. Similar cases in Boston were carried forward by Edward F. McClennen, who was not particularly an advocate against the New Deal or modern social legislation as was William Logan Martin. His law office was not alone in having an interest, but his clients pressed him to question the new legislation and his challenge to state workmen's compensation was ventured in the *Howes Brothers* case in the Massachusetts Supreme Court and in what became the well-known United States Supreme Court case against the Social Security Act, *Helvering v. Davis*,[50] decided as a twin with the *Steward Machine Company* case.

The decisions of the Supreme Court of the United States on social security and unemployment compensation came in May of 1937, after the climactic rulings on state minimum wage laws and on the National Labor Relations Act. They were part of a piece in which the Nine Old Men themselves made the

Constitution conform to major social and economic reforms of a fundamental and permanent character. *Carmichael, Steward* and *Helvering* sped through the ordinarily slow judicial machinery in a matter of weeks, with the three decisions announced on Monday, May 24, 1937, three weeks after argument. Willis Van Devanter resigned nine days later, on June 2, 1937, and thereby vacated a seat soon to be filled by Hugo Black, a trusted Senate advocate of New Deal measures.

Here, interest focuses especially on the origin and management of the litigation from Boston, with attention on the lawyers and their clients, the problems of jurisdiction these cases raised and how they were dealt with differently by zealous judges than had been the Maternity Act in the *Massachusetts* and *Frothingham* cases of 1923.

Edward McClennen was driven more by the interest of dozens of business clients than by ideology to organize litigation challenging the constitutionality of the Social Security Act of 1935. A brilliant student, he was one of the last to skip college and go from high school to the Harvard Law School directly, yet he did so with high success, receiving his LL.B. *cum laude* at the age of twenty. In the summer of 1895, McClennen entered the office of Warren & Brandeis; he became a partner five years later. He spent his entire professional life in practice there and with succeeding firms: Brandeis, Dunbar & Nutter, 1897-1916; Dunbar, Nutter & McClennen, 1916-1929; Nutter, McClennen & Fish, after 1930. McClennen was prominent in public service and the most active member of the firm in litigation after 1900. He did not share Brandeis's reform interests but their values were compatible and their colleagueship agreeable.

In 1935 McClennen opposed the Society Security Act and the related Massachusetts unemployment compensation law; it is in this light that his association with Brandeis must be measured. These laws grew out of the progressive tradition of social and economic legislation for which Brandeis himself had been such an eloquent spokesman. To many opponents of the New Deal, as to opponents of the reforms advocated by President Wilson, Brandeis held social and economic views regarded as dangerous to the survival of the Republic. But while McClennen managed the test cases against these social innovations in the 1930s and had never, himself, advocated the kind of programs Brandeis worked for when they were law partners, they held each other in high esteem. The appointment of Brandeis to the Supreme Court was viciously attacked but his young partner McClennen was completely loyal. He knew from twenty years' daily association that Brandeis possessed uncommon character, high civic purpose and propriety as well as being a brilliant and compassionate person and he stuck by him unflinchingly. After confirmation McClennen and others in the firm continued on friendly terms with Mr. Justice Brandeis to the end of their days. Indeed, Brandeis visited his former associates at the office in Boston regularly each June on his way from Washington to Cape Cod for the summer and each September on his return for the Supreme Court's next term.[51]

By the mid-1930s some of the hundred or more corporate clients of Nutter, McClennen & Fish had been seeking legal advice from the firm from the time of its organization in 1879 and most had had a long-term association. The federal Social Security Act and the Massachusetts Unemployment Compensation Act affected most of them and they were consequently interested in learning what they should do. But their attitudes varied. Under McClennen's direction, several lawyers in the firm in the late summer and fall of 1935 canvassed their clients by letters, phone calls, and meetings and found a modest interest in a constitutional test mixed with a wish to conform to the letter of the new laws to avoid anything worse, such as a penalty. A lawyer who talked with five clients noted only one "with the litigation spirit" but even that company would consider $100 a large charge to contribute to challenging these statutes. Of the other four clients, the lawyer wrote this:

The rest were in favor of some social security legislation but did not want to pay under the particular acts and later find them invalid with no chance of recovering back their payments, but definitely did not wish to let themselves in for any considerable expense.[52]

This was typical. The clients and their lawyers wanted to cooperate with the law and yet, perhaps cooperatively, question it in the courts at the same time. Nutter, McClennen & Fish employed twenty lawyers and as many other secretaries and clerks. Its senior partners were also concerned about paying the new tax on employers. They took their own advice and conformed to the acts while proceeding guardedly down the path of litigation.

Business in New England in 1935 was not good. The textile mills, paper manufacturers, shoe companies, machine-tool plants, apparel specialties and banks among the firm's clients felt the pinch. There had been many business failures and any new government regulation, especially a tax, was regarded as a threat to the life of the company itself.

On November 12, 1935, Nutter, McClennen & Fish sent a form letter pointing out the provisions of the federal Social Security Act which deserved the immediate attention of their clients. The firm took pains to "express no opinion as to the constitutionality of the Act" and even warned, "Obviously the safest course is to proceed on the assumption that the Act is constitutional until it has been declared otherwise." The specific advice was a model of caution. First, for the tax on employers to provide funds for unemployment insurance, the tax computed on total wages would be at the rate of one percent for 1936, two percent for 1937, and three percent thereafter. Following a résumé of this requirement, the firm concluded with this advice:

We particularly call to your attention that it would be advisable to establish during 1936 a reserve to meet this tax, since it will be effective for the calendar year 1936, although not payable until 1937. Should the time come for payment of this tax, precautions should be taken at the time of payment to secure the right to have the amount paid refunded if the Act should be declared unconstitutional. [underlining in original letter][53]

Second, the old age assistance tax would become effective for the year 1937, computed on the total payroll for the first three years at one percent and not rising until 1949 to three percent. Third, the clients were told in detail about credits to be taken against the tax for unemployment insurance on account of contributions made to a State Unemployment Insurance Fund.

Edward F. McClennen had about ten lawyers in the firm working on the subject as he worked gingerly to develop test cases of both the Massachusetts and the federal legislation. Not a zealot in politics, he was sufficiently opposed personally to these measures to label the file "Social Security Act So-Called." Taking precautions against losing, he made sure that the government authorities understood that he was bringing test cases by an explicit agreement on paying or reserving the statutory tax in order to avoid penalties for noncompliance. He went further. There was a tacit agreement that if the test cases were lost his clients would conform without further question or litigation. This gentlemen's agreement gave the courts the last word but there would be strict compliance even before then.

A year passed. The quiet business of all sides burst into public and decisive activity starting in September 1936. The attack on the Massachusetts unemployment compensation program was first to blossom into appellate litigation. McClennen's case for Howes Brothers, Inc., against the state commission was reaching a climax. A batch of letters prepared by Nutter, McClennen & Fish went out over the signatures of executive officers for some fifty corporations to the commission. Each explained that having been "advised by counsel that in their opinion the Massachusetts Unemployment Compensation Law . . . is unconstitutional," a suit was before the courts and that the law did not provide for the return of reports or payments. While asking to be excused from making payments, each company agreed to give "adequate security for any payments you claim to be due." The letters then closed with this declaration:

Please understand that by making the foregoing requests the undersigned does not waive any claims which it may wish to make that said Massachusetts Unemployment Compensation Law is unconstitutional, or is inoperative by reason of the unconstitutionality of the Federal Social Security Act, . . . or otherwise.[54]

There were informal agreements among lawyers for companies wishing to challenge the state law and by the state attorney general's office. The Commission required submission of the taxes on employers,[55] but the attorney general's representatives sought to overcome this by suggesting that a special fund be established to hold the money intact to wait the conclusion of litigation.[56] An assistant attorney general for the Commonwealth urged upon a McClennen junior associate the desirability of agreeing "on one typical case to prosecute to a final judgment, and that we should make an agreement that the decision in that case will be binding in all pending cases."[57] McClennen's associate was wholly in accord with this.[58]

All sides, including the trial judge, then agreed that two cases would serve as tests of the state unemployment compensation provisions and these two, joined by numerous other companies formally or informally, were in the name of the Howes Bros. and Ellis companies. Thirteen corporations took the step of intervening to make the cases a class action and other companies stayed in the wings but contributed to the payment of counsel for handling the litigation. The entire bench of the Supreme Judicial Court of Massachusetts heard the cases argued in November and ruled against the corporate challenge on December 30, 1936. McClennen's clients agreed to continue the fight but in February 1937 his petition to the United States Supreme Court for review was denied. This left standing the Massachusetts Supreme Court's ruling that the Commonwealth's law was valid.[59]

The Supreme Court of the United States chose an Alabama case to rule directly on the merits that a state unemployment compensation law was valid.[60] It thus sidestepped the issue as raised by the two Massachusetts cases and by three New York cases. The Alabama test case had attributes making it different in several respects from the other litigations. For one, the *Howes* case in Boston and three cases in New York were pressed in the state courts and the highest state courts in each state upheld the respective state laws. As we have seen, the United States Supreme Court subsequently declined to review the affirmative ruling of the Supreme Judicial Court of Massachusetts in *Howes*. The same result was achieved in the New York cases but by a somewhat different procedural route and timing. The challenge in New York in *Chamberlin v. Andrews* was made earlier and decided earlier; the Supreme Court, indeed, considered a full review in the autumn of 1936 but simply announced, on November 23, that the judgments of the state court were severally affirmed, *per curiam*, that is, without decision.[61]

The other key reason for summary disposal of the *Howes* and *Chamberlin* cases seems surely to have been tied to the illness of Mr. Justice Stone during the middle of the 1936-37 term and the indication of Mr. Justice Roberts's readiness to join the wing of the Court prepared to uphold New Deal legislation. This is neatly supported by the action of November 23, 1936, when the Court announced publicly that the state court rulings in *Chamberlin* were "affirmed by an equally divided Court."[62] As the *United States Reports* made clear, Mr. Justice Stone took no part in numerous cases in the middle of the term so that Mr. Justice Roberts must, in a sense, have already changed his mind on fundamental social legislation under review in order to make a tie in *Chamberlin*. The consequence of an equally divided Court was to affirm the ruling below that the New York Unemployment Compensation Act was valid

The challenge from Alabama was different. Counsel for the companies had chosen the federal arena and won a ruling from the District Court of the United States for the Middle District of Alabama in their favor.[63] The United States Supreme Court was practically obliged to review this holding; moreover the case came onto the docket later in the term and with Mr. Justice Stone back, he not only filled the Court to its full complement and supplied the fifth vote needed for reversal but himself prepared the opinion for the Court. The case came on appeal, was argued April 7 and 8, 1937, and decided May 24, 1937. Even Sutherland joined the majority so that the vote was finally six to three in support of the Alabama Unemployment Compensation Act.

The *Carmichael* case on state unemployment compensation was argued and decided on the same schedule as the closely related cases centered on the federal Social Security Act. As the landmark cases on the federal matters were also from Boston and Birmingham we return to the counsel-client relations that successfully carried the constitutional issues to the Supreme Court. The final section of this chapter shows the procedural problems these cases presented to the justices and how they were resolved.

To Edward McClennen and his associates in Boston the loss of the *Howes* case was acceptable for they were making fine progress with their cases against the Social Security Act. Boston newspapers in November and December of 1936 afforded their readers prudently legalistic accounts of the developments. On November 10 the *Herald* reported:

The first test case in the nation on the constitutionality of the federal and state social security laws, and destined to reach the United States Supreme Court early next year, came before Federal Judge George C. Sweeney for a hearing yesterday.

The case, that of George P. Davis of Waltham, a Boston & Maine railroad stockholder, challenges the validity of the state as well as the social security act under which the Massachusetts unemployment law is operative.

Mr. Davis through counsel Edward F. McClennen, asked that a preliminary injunction be issued to restrain the Boston & Maine from paying taxes under the act. . . .

As the first test case, federal lawyers were alerted to intervene to defend the constitutionality of the Social Security Act of 1935. The decision to take action was made in Washington by Attorney General Robert H. Jackson and Social Security Board Chairman John G. Winant and carried out in Boston by subordinates. They included Francis J.W. Ford, United States attorney in Boston, later famed as the presiding judge in the Spock-Coffin conspiracy trial in the late 1960s, and Charles E. Wyzanski, then a special assistant to the attorney general in Washington, later a respected federal judge in Boston. Wyzanski petitioned to intervene, to become an actual party to the case on grounds that this was the first litigation in the country involving the legality of the federal act. Clearly, he feared the government's interest would not otherwise be adequately protected. This wish was granted and the commissioner of internal revenue and the collector of internal revenue for the district of Massachusetts were allowed by the district court to intervene as parties defendant. This meant that Davis, as plaintiff, and McClennen, as counsel, would be pitted directly against agents of the United States government and lawyers for the Department of Justice.

The courses of legal action open to the firm on behalf of its many corporate clients who objected to the social security tax were limited. The *Frothingham* rule meant they could not venture a taxpayer's suit. The penalty clauses of the Social Security Act were so severe that they dared not refuse to pay it and face prosecution. If prosecuted, they could raise constitutional issues, but the threat of losing such a case raised a risk of severe financial sacrifice. The firm came up with the alternative of having one of its own members, Davis, bring an action as a stockholder against companies that were hardly disposed to make a spirited defense of the law. This explains how Davis became the plaintiff[64] and makes clear how essential it was for the United States to intervene. This intervention rescued the litigation from the possibility of being defective as a friendly suit, though barely so.

Both of Davis's suits were dismissed by Judge Sweeney, that against the Boston & Maine Railroad on December 7, 1936; that against the Edison Electric Illuminating Company on January 27, 1937. The Circuit Court of Appeals for the First Circuit in Boston reviewed and affirmed these actions on April 14, 1937, and yet the Supreme Court found time to hear the further appeal on May 5 and to hand down a decision upholding Titles II and VIII on May 24. It did so, finally, only in the Edison case which was styled after the name of the then commissioner of internal revenue as the case of *Guy T. Helvering v. George P. Davis.* The ruling of the Court in *Helvering v. Davis* will be analyzed in the next section.[65]

Unknown to McClennen and Davis in Boston, lawyers in Birmingham, Alabama were moving at the same swift pace to challenge the constitutionality of government social security programs. The *Carmichael* case, conducted by Borden Burr, had resulted in the invalidation on December 15, 1936, of the Alabama Unemployment Compensation Act in a United States District Court and went directly to the Supreme Court for decision. That Court's reversal holding the Alabama act valid was announced May 24, 1937. A key companion case, *Steward Machine Company v. Davis* contending the Social Security Act of 1935, Titles III and IX, requiring a tax on certain employers, was unconstitutional on a number of counts went up at the same time. This case also originated in Alabama, prepared by William Logan Martin, with assistance from Borden Burr and others.

Borden Burr was a prominent southern opponent of the New Deal and a leader in the organized bar. He had been a delegate to Democratic National Conventions several times between 1904 and 1928 and was a friend and supporter of John W. Davis. After graduation from the University of Alabama in 1896, Burr earned a law degree at Washington and Lee, the alma mater of Henry St. George Tucker and Davis. Though not a member with Davis, Beck and others of the National Lawyers Committee of the American Liberty League (organized in 1934 to oppose Roosevelt's New Deal legislation), Burr had a continuous correspondence with Davis and Beck about test cases challenging these measures.[66]

William Logan Martin was born in Scottsboro, graduated from West Point in 1907, and won an LL.B. degree from the University of Alabama in 1908. A state prosecutor from 1909 to 1917, he was attorney general of Alabama for the two years before the entrance of the United States in World War I. Then he served in France as an army major. Service as judge of Montgomery Circuit Court for twenty months meant that he was thereafter known as Judge Martin. In 1921, Martin was appointed general attorney for Alabama Power Company, a position he held continuously until his death. This was, however, only part of his practice conducted from a thriving law firm in Birmingham. Nor does this depiction of his early career and professional base tell enough of his prominence in the organized bar and his position on public issues.

By the 1950s, Martin was supporting federal constitutional amendments to curb national power, especially as then exemplified by liberal presidential and Supreme Court decisions. His prominence in bar associations should be stressed. He chaired numerous committees of the American Bar Association over forty-five years, was a state delegate to the ABA from 1937 to 1959, and was president of the Alabama Bar Association in 1946 and 1947. Judge Martin was also very active in the Association of Graduates of the United States Military Academy, the Sons of the American Revolution and the Society of Colonial Wars. Upon his death a colleague wrote this estimate:

Judge Martin was a stalwart patriot with a penetrating insight into his country's founding and its subsequent history. His judgment and skill as a constitutional lawyer were known and respected. He was a crusader, seeking at every opportunity to preserve our inheritance and correct the evils which have crept into our political, economic and social life.[67]

Like McClennen's *Helvering* in Boston, Martin's *Steward Machine Co.* was a bona fide test case. Lawyers on all sides understood this. The courts cooperated in expedition. If it lost the case, the Steward Machine Company would suffer no penalty beyond an obligation to comply with the Social Security Act in the future. The case even took the modest form of a suit for refund of $46.14 already paid to the internal revenue collector under the act. The official Supreme Court reports, conforming to the practice of portraying constitutional battles as simply the pursuit of exclusively private claims, shows the Steward Company as the lone party against the statute. But true to the nature of many test cases, a news report in 1937 tells that "some 300 employers are attacking the constitutionality of the law."[68]

On April 8, 1937, Martin, McClennen and other lawyers opposing the Social Security Act of 1935 argued the case before the Supreme Court. If their standing was not accepted they could lose procedurally; if their arguments against national power under the welfare clause was not accepted they could lose on the merits. Thus there were two means of defeat and only one to the victory they sought. We turn to the response of the Supreme Court in the fateful spring of 1937.

Constitutionality of the Social Security Program

In the 1970s the durability and popularity of the federal social security program in the United States is completely settled. Political dispute nowadays concerns the size of the withholding bite, broadening the welfare features and the scheme of payments. Does anyone remember May 24, 1937, when the Supreme Court, barely by a five-to-four margin, ruled the key provisions of the basic 1935 act constitutional? Even parties to the legal challenge then have since accepted social security as wise national policy. "Social security checks give retired people options they didn't have earlier," George P. Davis recently remarked. Davis, the plaintiff in the *Helvering* case, became increasingly interested in problems of the aged in the 1940s and 1950s and gradually accepted social security as a helpful part of the solution. Congress has continually acted to broaden benefits and, even, to add on the Medicare program so that Davis's changing attitudes are emblematic of wide national sentiment. Yet the push to adopt the basic statute in 1935 and the test cases which followed in 1937 must be remembered as essential acts of creation and legitimization.

The division of the Court in 1937 on standing differed somewhat from the division on the merits. Four justices did not think a stockholder, like Davis, had standing to challenge the validity of the tax imposed on employers by section 804 of the Social Security Act. Mr. Justice Cardozo wrote for himself, Brandeis, Stone and Roberts their belief "that the remedy is ill conceived, that in a controversy such as this a court must refuse to give equitable relief when a cause of action in equity is neither pleaded nor proved, and that the suit for an injunction should be dismissed upon that ground."[69] He thought "this course should be followed in adherence to the general rule that constitutional questions are not to be determined in the absence of strict necessity." These four justices, especially Cardozo, Brandeis and Stone, had for a lifetime put stock in judicial restraint as appropriate to their democratic faith in majority rule. Had their view prevailed on another justice the case of *Helvering v. Davis* would have been dismissed under the spirit of abnegation in the *Mellon* cases and the federal social security programs would have stood without a direct Supreme Court ruling on the merits. But Mr. Justice Cardozo was obliged to say, however, that "a majority of the court have reached a different conclusion."

A surmise on why a majority to decide *Helvering v. Davis* on the merits surfaces readily. The four passionately conservative activists—Van Devanter, McReynolds, Sutherland and Butler—were eager to grasp the nettle in order to scorn the legality of so-called social security. Chief Justice Hughes exhibited a sagacious leadership in joining these four to permit standing and then deserting by moving with the four who espoused restraint—Cardozo, Brandeis, Stone and Roberts—to hold valid the Social Security Act of 1935. Hughes was the least doctrinaire of justices, the most visionary in preserving the institutional values. He must surely have known that government social security was here to stay and that the future of the program and the Court, too, would be better off with a flat decision on the merits. The four men of restraint gracefully accepted the wishes of Hughes and the four conservatives. Mr. Justice Cardozo spoke for them all in reporting that the other five found "in this case extraordinary features making it fitting in their judgment to determine whether the benefits and the taxes are valid or invalid." This ruling, he continued, "removes from the case the preliminary objection as to the nature of the remedy which we took of our own motion at the beginning of the argument. Under the compulsion of that ruling, the merits are now here."[70]

For the majority of Hughes, Brandeis, Stone, Roberts and himself, Mr. Justice Cardozo wrote separate opinions in the *Steward Machine Company* and *Helvering* cases. Of the eleven titles of the Social Security Act of 1935, Titles III and IX were upheld in *Steward* and Titles II and VIII were upheld in *Helvering*. All were constitutional because five justices accepted the idea that Congress could tax employers of eight or more and their employees, require the states to cooperate and establish a scheme of payment upon retirement or death of employees in the program. This was made possible by a generous view of the power to tax set forth in Article One, Section 8 of the Constitution and by rejecting the protests of Van Devanter, McReynolds, Sutherland and Butler that the Court should heed literally the limitations they read in the Fifth, Tenth and Fourteenth Amendments.

When the decision of the Court was announced, the Steward Machine Company and hundreds of other companies in the South along with the Edison Electric Illuminating Company of Boston and other New England firms complied fully with the requirements of the social security program. The Internal Revenue Service has found compliance with this program very close to total over nearly four decades. Only occasionally in that time have independent-minded employers, like Miss Vivian Kellems of Connecticut, refused as a matter of principle to abide by the requirements—and even they yielded under a modest but firm threat of legal action.

Among the factors working toward full compliance have been these: (1) The basic features of the social security program since 1935 have enjoyed the unequivocal approval of Congress, the president and the Supreme Court. (2) State governments, too, have been strongly supportive. (3) Public opinion has been increasingly favorable, allowing the program to be expanded and adjusted regularly to meet new expectations or objections. (4) Permanent administrative agencies, established to conduct the program, have had a quite clearly understood set of working principles and sanctions, especially the statutory tax and payment schedule, to make compliance possible to measure. Not all of these conditions have been present in policy-making on prohibition, the ban on school prayers, and racial integration requirements in housing, jobs and schools.

Thus, in 1937 the Supreme Court played its part in settling the constitutionality of a national social security program. In doing so a majority of justices indicated again that their own rules on standing could be relaxed. The rules in the *Mellon* cases were happily left untouched to stand for many more years against any wish or effort to upset the growing federal aid programs for social welfare. They would remain to do their protective work until a different group, in a later generation, with a different outlook and purpose, began in the late 1960s to chip away at the rules on standing. For the 1920s and 1930s, at any rate, the conservative opponents to federal spending like Alexander Lincoln of the Sentinels of the Republic, James Beck and John W. Davis of the American Liberty League, William Logan Martin of the American Bar Association and the unaffiliated like Burr, McClennen and George P. Davis were, one and all, held at bay, splendidly able lawyers and men of affairs though they were. Their vision of American constitutional law was not realized.

12 The White Primary Overruling 1921–1944

What were the "circumstances" V.O. Key found which "made the white primary an especially effective method for political neutralization of the Negro"?[1] The direct primary method of nomination arose generally in the United States and in the South only after 1900. At that time, most blacks were Republicans in keeping with the tradition of Abraham Lincoln and the position of the party before and after the Civil War. Most white southerners were Democrats, enough to make a one-party section. Intraparty contests settled in the Democratic primary could not be affected in the general election. These circumstances were "ideally suited for a solution of the Negro question in a manner satisfactory to the whites." If blacks were kept from an effective voice in government by this means, the southern states could continue indefinitely to segregate the races in services and accommodations, and to discriminate against blacks in any way the voters decided.

As black voting increased, and as many blacks became Democrats and appreciated the significance of primary elections, whites had to take increasingly stiff and obvious action. Over a period of two decades this action changed from being official state action to official action by the party until the exclusion of blacks from primaries became informal party practice. The constitutional issue therefore took slightly different form over the years, but always concerned the questions of "state action," the status of a primary as compared with a general election, the nature of a political party and deprivation of the suffrage rights of blacks.

Two groups of Texas blacks through many years brought court tests against their exclusion from Democratic primary elections.[2] Time frustrated both groups, but good fortune marked the NAACP cases in the United States Supreme Court in 1927, 1932 and 1944 in the two *Nixon* cases and *Smith v. Allwright*.[3] Of course, there were later cases, also. The same persistence, but with failure, disappointment, and understandable bitterness, attended sponsors of the other string of cases. In the 1920s these other cases were prepared by attorney R.D. Evans of Waco and the 1930s by a group led by J. Alston Atkins of Houston. Most of their cases stopped in Texas but two, *Love v. Griffith* in 1924 and *Grovey v. Townsend* in 1935, carried black claims to the United States Supreme Court where they were denied.[4] Mostly, the NAACP records show rivalry between the two sponsoring groups in a low key, only occasionally bursting out. But there was definite competition between the El Paso group and the group in Waco, Houston and other Texas cities for attention and support of

287

the NAACP in New York. This also appeared in the quest for victory in the courts, especially in the Supreme Court.

The story of the white primary cases will be told here through the Supreme Court cases. In the main, the story concerns the development of the NAACP cases. But to approximate the twenty-five year litigation agony of Texas blacks both sets of cases will be touched upon. Before considering the minute evolution of *Nixon v. Herndon*, the first NAACP case from El Paso, an earlier—indeed, the earliest—Texas white primary case to reach the United States Supreme Court will be examined.

Testing in Houston, 1921-1924

Love v. Griffith, decided by the United States Supreme Court in an opinion by Mr. Justice Holmes on October 20, 1924, had its beginning in Houston, On January 27, 1921, the city Democratic Executive Committee promulgated a rule that "Negroes will not be allowed to vote in the coming Democratic City Primary."[5] This rule was promptly published in the columns of the *Houston Post* and sent to election judges of the various voting boxes in the city. The primary would be held in a few days, on February 9. Attorney R.D. Evans of Waco, president of the Independent Colored Voters' League and a Democrat, acted quickly. Evans and several other Democrats, including C.N. Love and J.B. Grigsby "called on the chairman of the Democratic Executive Committee, James S. Griffith, in person and were told by him that only white people would be permitted to vote" in this primary election.

On February 2 these same men, Love, Grigsby, Newman Dudley, Jr., W.L. Davis, William Nickerson, Jr., and Perry Mack, with Evans as their lawyer, brought action in the Eleventh Judicial District Court of Harris County against the committee and the judges of the city Democratic primary election. The court was asked to issue "its most gracious writ of temporary injunction" restraining the committee and the judges from holding "a strictly white man's primary election" on February 9. Evans asked further that the temporary injunction later be made perpetual because the right to vote is a continuing one. He rightly saw if the rule was upheld "it can be applied by any political committee and will ultimately disfranchise" all blacks in Texas.

Evans's petition was promptly disposed of by Judge Charles E. Ashe of the Harris County District Court on February 5, in time to clear the election date, to support a white primary. The defendants demurred to the plaintiffs' petition, argument was heard, and the judge concluded that the law is for the defendant city Democratic Executive Committee and the election judges. The attorney for the defendants, Murray B. Jones, claimed the right for the committee, under provisions of state statutes and city ordinances, "to prescribe their own usages and establish their own rules." With this he also labeled the Democratic organization "a political and voluntary association for political purposes. Members of such parties may form them, reorganize them and dissolve them at their will." As this was a political and not a judicial question, Jones argued that the Fifteenth Amendment did not reach and could not be made to reach this matter. Judge Ashe wrote no opinion; he was at one with the defendants. The suit was dismissed. The judgment for Griffith carried an obligation on Love, Grigsby and the other plaintiffs to pay costs of $200. This they acknowledged and bound themselves to pay as an appeal was begun the week following the primary from which they were barred.

Love v. Griffith moved from Houston to the Court of Civil Appeals for the First Supreme Judicial District of Texas, at Galveston, where Evans again lost, in an opinion by Chief Justice R.A. Pleasants, on December 21, 1921.[6] He reasoned that since "the election has long since been held" it was impossible to grant the relief sought. Dwelling on the original request for admission to the February 9 primary, Justice Pleasants called the issue of the constitutionality of the statute and rule a moot question. The cause of action, he said, had "ceased to exist." The court declined to look ahead to the resurrection of the rule, on short notice, to disfranchise blacks in future primary elections, saying,

The constitutionality of a statute will not be inquired into by the courts unless the petition by which the question is presented shows that the statute affects some concrete right of the complainants. The rule of the executive committee applied only to the primary election of February 9, 1921, and we cannot assume either that the next Democratic primary election will be called under the same rule or instructions of the committee, or that appellants when such election may be called will be qualified voters in that city and desire to vote in such election.[7]

From this holding, Evans moved for a rehearing, lost and then sought review by the supreme court of Texas, which failed. He then sought higher review with Chief Justice Pleasants in Galveston who, "being desirous of giving the Petitioners an opportunity to present in the Supreme Court of the United States, the questions presented by the record," ordered and decreed that the Evans writ of error be allowed.[8] Although filed in the Supreme Court on June 23, 1922, *Love v. Griffith* had a long time to wait for disposition. The case was carried on the Supreme Court docket through the 1922-23 and 1923-24 terms.[9] Finally, the parties were told by the clerk to submit briefs in time for the beginning of the October term, 1924. R.D. Evans did so for Love and Grigsby, now denominated the plaintiffs in error, but there was no answering brief for Griffith and the city Democratic Executive Committee.

Evans's brief for plaintiffs in error shows him searching for a long-term solution. If the Texas courts were correct, he said, "there can never be a remedy for this wrong because there is not time enough allowed to completely adjudicate a question like this. But equity says there shall be no wrong without a remedy and so we think the law to be on this point."[10] The seventeen-page brief also urged, "The primary election is an election to all intents and purposes the same as the general election."[11] Evans reviewed Texas precedent to prove the point.

Read today, the argument is as convincing as any of the United States Supreme Court decisions to the same effect in recent years. The brief concluded with a broad attack on the significance of the all-white primary election, in these words:

> ... the attention of the court is called to the far-reaching influence of the questions presented in the foregoing pages of this brief, upon the rights of the Negro people, as protected by the Fifteenth Amendment to the federal Constitution. By this species of legislation the southern states have completely eliminated the Negro vote and influence in state, county and city government, notwithstanding their great property interest, education and general welfare. This very thing keeps the South solidly Democratic and it will remain so, as long as this kind of disfranchisement is allowed to go on. . . . This is the election that settles everything, the general election being now a mere ratification of what the primary election did.
>
> Further than this, it strikes at the vitals of the well-being of Negroes in all the nation, for if one state can pass, construe, and enforce such laws, and be within the purview of the Fifteenth Amendment any other state can do likewise, and in time the question can be nation-wide.
>
> It is therefore, most earnestly urged in the light of the statutes, constitutions, and decisions, thereunder, . . . that this court reverse the court of civil appeals, and construe the law in this case, with such directions as justice and the law may require.[12]

The fervor of Evans's brief for the plaintiffs in error was not matched by essential craftsmanship. Not only did the brief lack the stigmata of tables of cases and authorities it also did not rest on a statutory source for judicial remedy. The Supreme Court's accepted function is to hear cases, determine the law and make decrees sought by the parties. The Court requires precise guidance in construing the law and setting the "directions as justice and the law require." Evans really did not ask for a remedy that was within the authority and traditions of the Court to grant. His few sentences about equity were not informed by the vast literature on the subject and, less important, he did not refer to any of the treatises and law review articles which discussed the subject. To win this cause in the Supreme Court required canvassing alternative remedies rooted in laws and rules, specific remedies based on precedent and practice, and a persuasive argument of a high order. Unfortunately, Evans suffered from the weakness of many a "country lawyer" who has had the admirable temerity to carry a case to the Supreme Court of the United States. That Court is highly specialized (though it deals with a broad spectrum of cases), its members and their clerks are research-minded, professional and sophisticated. Emotion and outrage affect the Court in about the same way that grief and sadness touch a mortician. Their skills deal indirectly with misfortune. The justices who read Evans's brief must surely have regarded it as hopelessly amateurish.

The case was argued in Washington by Evans for plaintiffs in error but not answered by the Texas white Democrats. The argument on October 6, 1924, was followed precisely two weeks later by a denial of the black claim but with sweet dicta labeling that claim just. Mr. Justice Holmes, a model of judicial caution, wrote the opinion for a unanimous Supreme Court. This is the key passage ending the opinion:

If the case stood here as it stood before the court of first instance, it would present a grave question of constitutional law, and we should be astute to avoid hindrances in the way of taking it up. But that is not the situation. The rule promulgated by the Democratic executive committee was for a single election only, that had taken place long before the decision of the appellate court. No constitutional rights of the plaintiffs in error were infringed by holding that the cause of action had ceased to exist. The bill was for an injunction that could not be granted at that time. There was no constitutional obligation to extend the remedy beyond what was prayed.[13]

This disposition reflects its time in several ways. Evans had carried the case to the Supreme Court virtually alone. There was then in American jurisprudence no adequate remedy to a one-time deprivation; later the declaratory judgment would be available to dampen such a deprivation. Moreover, while Mr. Justice Holmes indulged in the conditional "if the case stood here as it stood in the court of first instance," he knew that the Supreme Court could not conceivably act fast enough. Later, the Court would develop means to act swiftly; as it then lacked them the case could never have stood there as it had in the trial court in February 1921. As it was, this simple case took three years for decision after docketing in the Supreme Court.

The 1910 map showing the percentage of blacks in the total population of Texas, by counties, makes understandable that this first effort as disfranchisement would occur by local action in the eastern part of the state (see figure 12-1). If a local white primary worked, then why not one for the whole state? This was soon done and then the source of opposition by blacks in the court shifted to the western part of Texas where the percentage of blacks was exceedingly small.

The Statutory White Primary

The Texas legislature in 1923, influenced by unhappy party rivalries in San Antonio, where blacks held a balance, flattered the Houston Democrats by passing their statute about disfranchisement into law, as follows:

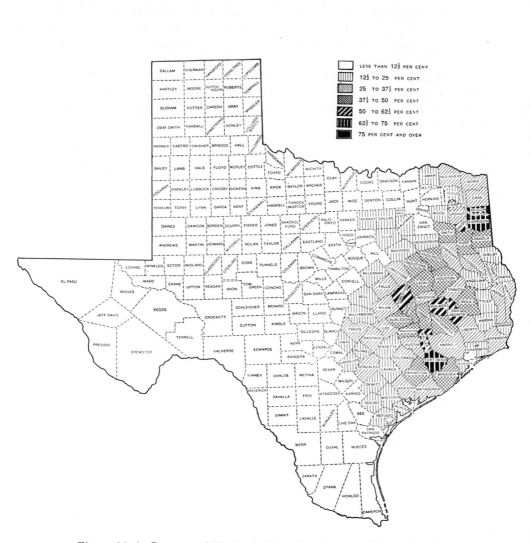

Figure 12-1. Percent of Blacks in Total Population of Texas, by Counties: 1910. Source: *Statistical Atlas of The United States*, prepared under the supervision of Charles S. Sloane, Geographer of the Census. Government Printing Office, Washington, D.C., 1914. Plate No. 199.

All qualified voters under the laws and Constitution of the state of Texas who are bona fide members of the Democratic party, shall be eligible to participate in any Democratic party primary election . . . however, in no event shall a Negro be eligible to participate in a Democratic party primary election held in the state of Texas. . . .[14]

An ill-fated suit was begun that year by two white lawyers in San Antonio, brought in behalf of Hurley C. Chandler, plaintiff, a black who had voted in past Democratic primary elections. The principal defendant was Pat M. Neff, governor of Texas. The suit was brought against the governor and attorney general of Texas, and the Bexar County Democratic chairman of the United States District Court in San Antonio. Counsel for Chandler, J.M. Woods and C.W. Johnson, wanted the defendants enjoined from enforcing the state white primary statute and, of course, they wanted Chandler accorded the right to vote in Democratic primaries.

Judge Duval West, on April 5, 1924, sustained the defendants' motion to dismiss the suit.[15] He mentioned the value of "elaborate and able briefs of authorities and arguments" but found no merit in Chandler's claim. There were two stumbling blocks. "The power of a court of equity by way of injunction has never in England, nor in America," he wrote, "been extended to political affairs."[16] He called this position in line with "elementary principles of jurisdiction"; among the authorities invoked was *Giles v. Harris.*[17] The second reason for dismissing the suit lay in Judge West's perception of political parties and primary elections. The legislature may regulate parties and primaries but they are nonetheless essentially voluntary and private. He felt that the Supreme Court of the United States had settled this in *Newberry v. United States*, where excessive campaign expenditures in a Republican Senate primary in Michigan were held not controlled by the federal Corrupt Practices Act of 1910.[18] He did not tarry to explain how this holding came from a four-four division in the Supreme Court but, cloudy or not, the *Newberry* precedent remained an obstacle to opponents of the white Democratic primary in the South for years and years.

One sentence from the *Newberry* case was sufficient for Judge West, who said, "It was held there that primary elections 'are in no sense elections for an office, but merely methods by which party adherents agree upon candidates whom they intend to offer and support for ultimate choices by all qualified electors.' "[19] Thus, as a constitutional law precedent *Chandler v. Neff* ruled that a state may regulate primaries as they pleased because the Fifteenth Amendment was not controlling.

Launching *Nixon v. Herndon*, 1924

The case of *Nixon v. Herndon*, in El Paso, was under way before the conclusion of *Love v. Griffith*. The El Paso branch of the NAACP was a going concern; its leaders offered the national office in New York a case, money, local lawyers, and responsibility for carrying the action to the higher courts. NAACP correspondence files are complete enough to give full strategy and tactics of *Nixon v. Herndon*, from its beginning in 1924 to the favorable Supreme Court outcome in 1927. The letters on the El Paso side reveal a devoted branch president, L.W. Washington, and a self-described country lawyer, Fred C. Knollenberg, each of whom acknowledged the superiority of the New York office in constant requests for support and guidance.

The NAACP in New York, then fifteen years old, was already developing a talented bureaucracy of civil rights professionals with a continuing wing of "eminent counsel" as volunteers. The New York end of the work was coordinated chiefly by Walter White, assistant secretary and, to a lesser extent, by James Weldon Johnson, secretary, and by Arthur B. Spingarn, chairman of the NAACP National Legal Committee. Decisions concerning the *Nixon v. Herndon* litigation were made only when Moorfield Storey in Boston and James Cobb in Washington had been consulted also.

Storey was now the senior survivor of his generation of post-Civil War abolitionists. A Fisk College and Harvard Law School graduate, in practice in Washington, D.C. since 1901, Cobb was in the vanguard of black civil rights lawyers working within the NAACP. By following *Nixon v. Herndon*—as the records permit a viewing—the feelings, motivations and style of the principals seeking enfranchisement will unfold.

The first news of *Nixon v. Herndon* reached New York in August 1924, in a letter from L.A. Washington to the director of NAACP branches, R.W. Bagnall.

The El Paso branch has labored for quite some time to work up a case regarding the Texas law, prohibiting Negroes from voting in the Democratic primary. It is not after all, the "DEMOCRATIC PRIMARY" that we clamor to enter, but to attempt our bit in fostering the great principles of the National Association for the Advancement of Colored People. It is a fact, however, that the Democratic primary election in Texas is the end of the election. That is to say, whoever is nominated in the primaries, under long existing circumstances, is the elected officer in the final analysis. In the meantime, during our fourteen years residence in El Paso, we have not been denied the right to vote in any election until July 26th, 1924. We were refused then as the result of the amendment, passed by the Texas Legislature, in its called session of last year. We are called on to pay taxes; we are tried by the courts; and yet we have not the right to vote for or against those who are up for election.

So, we had a "Democrat" to properly present himself at the polls on the day of the primary and he was refused. . . . It is to be noted that the branch is not mentioned in either of the articles, but the case is ours. This report is made to you so that you may be officially informed in the matter. We await any instructions from your office regarding the case.[20]

Four months passed before L.A. Washington wrote again, this time to send important news about the case and to seek a definite agreement of national support. The plaintiff was Lawrence A. Nixon, an El Paso dentist. "When Dr. Nixon was denied the right to vote," the letter explained, "our Branch immediately secured the services of Messrs. R.J. Channell and Fred C. Knollenberg to represent us in the Federal District Court. We raised and paid them a fee in the amount of $100.00."[21] But it was already thought that the case would go finally to the United States Supreme Court. "The attorneys will continue it by appeal," wrote Washington, "in the event $2500.00 is raised and placed in some bank subject to withdrawal in their favor." He was confident that "quite a sum of the above mentioned amount can be raised from among the Negroes of Texas." The El Paso branch looked to the NAACP for instructions and for some financial support, concluding with this deference and dependence: "In the event you decide to continue the case, we plan to collect and send all collections of funds direct to you." Documents in *Nixon v. Herndon* were enclosed.

The action was a suit for damages in the U.S. District Court in El Paso against two judges of elections who refused to let Dr. Nixon vote in the Democratic primary for Congress and state offices held on July 26, 1924. Nixon satisfied many criteria for a suitable plaintiff. As the official petition put it, he was "a negro, as defined by the statutes of the State of Texas, and belongs to the colored race."[22] He was a native-born Texan and American, forty-one years of age. He had resided and voted in El Paso since 1910, a duly registered and qualified voter. He was also a Democrat ready to pledge himself to support the party. His taxes, including the poll tax, were paid. He satisfied all the legal requirements of the suit by taking all necessary administrative steps in seeking to vote. Dr. Nixon was an educated, informed professional man and would induce any available sympathy for his cause. He was also personally committed to the cause and was prepared to last out the length of time litigation would need.

Nixon's "test case" avoided the equity trap, into which the *Giles, Love* and *Chandler* actions had fallen, and prayed judgment against the defendants in the sum of $5,000. The defendants, C.C. Herndon and Charles Porras, were then judge and associate judge of elections, respectively, in Precinct No. 9 in El Paso County. They refused a ballot to Nixon under an instruction by the chairman of the executive committee of the county Democratic organization based upon the state law of May 1923 excluding blacks. This, and more, was set forth in Knollenberg's amended petition, filed in the District Court October 15, 1924.

Attorneys for the defendant election judges moved for dismissal on several grounds in a one-page answer. They said the primary election "was not an election within the meaning of the Fourteenth and Fifteenth Amendments."[23] The white primary statute was valid and so the election judges, Herndon and Porras, were obliged to refuse the vote to Nixon. Thus they were not proper defendants, according to the motion to dismiss. The motion also called the subject matter of the suit "political in its nature" leaving the court without jurisdiction to determine the issues. Judge Duval West sustained the defendants' motion to dismiss Dr. Nixon's suit on December 3, 1924, in a judgment and order without opinion.[24] Losing the case in this court had been expected and accepted by Knollenberg, who said immediately that he would go to the Supreme Court. He had ninety days in which to perfect his appeal.

The NAACP–El Paso Agreement

The opportunity to sponsor the case begun in El Paso was studied quickly and thoroughly by NAACP leaders. Knollenberg's reputation was checked in *Martindale's Law Directory*; the hand-copied rating showed this: Born, 1877; Admitted to bar, 1901; (48 years old); b = good legal ability; v = very high moral character; 6 = estimated worth $5,000 to $10,000; g = good — promptness in paying bills.[25] Knollenberg's rating was very good. What of his work for Nixon?

The papers in the case were sent to Spingarn, then Storey, and then Cobb for judgment.[26] The three lawyers liked the documents they saw in *Nixon v. Herndon*. Spingarn thought the case seemed well prepared and would make a good test.[27] Storey found "good ground for pressing the suit," called the Texas statute absurd, and warned "if it is upheld there is no limit to the laws that can be passed against the rights of the colored people."[28] Cobb was enthusiastic. "It would be a dandy case to take up."[29] He went on:

I believe that the primary law in question is right in the teeth of the Fifteenth Amendment, and such a case would do the Association a great amount of good as well as the nation at large. Then too, I have gone very carefully over the papers filed in this case and I consider the same to be splendidly drawn.

Spingarn, Storey and Cobb named money as the only impediment to going forward with the case and this was up to headquarters. Cobb said: "I repeat that I think it a dandy case to take up and carry forward, provided the Association is in a position financially so to do." Storey felt the expense could be fairly calculated as it was purely a question of law with no evidence to be taken so that the record would not be voluminous. The printing bill would not be great. Storey concluded that "unless the Texas lawyers are very grasping I think the case could be tried within a reasonable sum, and I should be disposed to favor it, but I do not want to impose upon a financial burden which would embarrass you next year."[30] Spingarn warned Walter White that "this is a very important issue and cannot be taken up lightly." A long-term commitment was being made. "If we decide to get behind it," Spingarn warned, "it will mean the expenditure of a great deal of money, because no matter how competent these El Paso lawyers are, we would have to hire additional counsel when we got to the United States Supreme Court."[31]

On the basis of responses from the lawyers, White was in touch with Washington in El Paso to learn whether the estimated amount of $2,500 could be reduced and what amount Texas blacks would pledge toward the total.[32] The conference of executives of the NAACP in New York "made a favorable report upon the question of the National Office entering actively into this case." The Board of Directors on February 9 would act officially after these questions about finances were settled. Following the lines of Storey's questions, White concluded:

It seems to us therefore that such a fee is too high for the services which will be rendered. As I have said, if the fee is modified, there is a greater probability of favorable action by the Board.

Will you take up this matter with the attorneys and it might be well for them to write us directly, furnishing you with copy of that letter.

Letters came flooding back from El Paso to answer these questions.[33]

Lawyer Knollenberg reviewed all aspects of *Nixon v. Herndon* as it had developed in his mind before reaching the question of his fee in his long letter to Walter White. Knollenberg did not retreat an inch from his demand: $2,000 as his fee; $500 reserved for costs. He was adamant; anything less would provoke his withdrawal. L.W. Washington explained to White his realization that the fee was high but because of Knollenberg's "lucrative practice" in Texas and New Mexico, "because we could find none others to handle the case in the manner in which they have handled it; and because of its importance, we felt that we had better tentatively accept their proposition with the view of having the final decision from your office on all matters pertaining thereto."[34]

On February 9, 1925, the board of directors of the NAACP voted to sponsor the case of *Nixon v. Herndon*.[35] The motion to do so was made by W.E.B. Du Bois, seconded by The Reverend John Haynes Holmes. It was voted that $1,250 be appropriated by the national office for the case. The minutes show that "Mr. Spingarn, Chairman of the Legal Committee, explained that the contract with the lawyers in this case would be so drawn as to have it clearly understood that the Association shall have the right to have its counsel take part in the case when it reaches the United States Supreme Court." Telegrams were sent the next day to both lawyer Knollenberg and branch president Washington in El Paso.

White spelled out the financing and advised Knollenberg how important it would be to the national office to later associate their own counsel with him if the case reached the Supreme Court. In a formal declaration of agreement, Knollenberg was perfectly agreeable to having association counsel with him in the case.

Walter White's next task was to arrange for eminent counsel to serve. In *Nixon v. Herndon* they would be Moorfield Storey and James A. Cobb. Both men were not only remarkably adept lawyers but also were active members of the NAACP Board of Directors, fully committed to volunteering their time and services to black betterment. White explained to Cobb that the case would not require much work but it had to be carefully handled "to avoid any possible slip-up so that the decision we secure will have the widest possible effect."[36]

Knollenberg was proceeding. His petition to the District Court for United States Supreme Court review was granted by Judge West on February 27, 1925, who ordered the writ of error allowed.[37] Judge West was bound to do so when a losing party in his court petitioned for this writ and filed an assignment of error. This practice of review by right was so swamping the Supreme Court that in most cases two years or more was the wait for disposition of a case. Multiplied by other litigation in the country, the easy, sure, obligatory Supreme Court review in Nixon's case resulted in an unmanageable docket. This condition was then being repaired by adoption of new Supreme Court rules made possible under the Judiciary Act of 1925, signed into law by President Calvin Coolidge on February 13, 1925.[38] Review by right then sharply declined with the method by writ of error practically if not altogether dropped, replaced by control through certiorari. Centralization of review in the Court itself then became the predominant mode. Embedded in rules effective July 1, 1925, was the keystone theory.[39] "A review on writ of certiorari is not a matter of right, but of sound judicial discretion, and will be granted only where there are special and important reasons therefor." But in this changeover period all the cases docketed by the old writ of error would be dutifully processed by the Court. The transcript of record in *Nixon v. Herndon* was filed with the clerk of the Supreme Court of the United States on May 18, 1925.

Completion of a formal contract between the NAACP and the law firm of Knollenberg and Channell in El Paso gave the organization ownership of the case. The association did not wish to hold the prize in secret. Making its new case known to the world would gain prominence for the NAACP and prowess in the law.

Main Briefs in the Supreme Court

A year passed. Not until April 1926 was there again substantial correspondence concerning *Nixon v. Herndon* between El Paso and NAACP leaders in the East. By then the case had been lost in the district court and was ready for review in the Supreme Court of the United States. Knollenberg had drafted a brief and Dr. Nixon, the concerned plaintiff in error, promised to "send it to each of the other attorneys for their approval and suggestions."[40] Storey merely suggested that Knollenberg reduce the quotations from judicial opinions, saying "a short brief has a chance of being read, but a long brief you cannot be equally sure of."[41] Cobb corrected a number of points of form to coincide with prescriptions in the Supreme Court rules. He wrote Knollenberg, "The brief is an excellent one and I am quite sure that we will win the case."[42]

But then Cobb dwelt on what he called "the only question in the case of which there could be the slightest doubt" which was "whether or not a primary election is a public election reached by the Fifteenth Amendment of the Constitution." Now Cobb canvassed this question and reviewed the *Newberry* holding for Knollenberg's benefit. He, of course, believed that Dr. Nixon had been denied the vote in a public election definitely reached by the Fifteenth Amendment. Seeing how Cobb brought the precedents to bear affords appreciation of his abilities and an occasion to realize how cognizant a civil rights lawyer of that day was about the legal problems he faced.

That the Texas primary is such an election, as it is established by statute, there can not be the slightest doubt. It might be well in this connection to call the Court's attention to the case of *Love vs. Griffith*, 266 U.S. 32. It is true that that case went off on a question of jurisdiction as the case was then moot; however, Mr. Justice Holmes indicated very strongly what would have been the opinion of the Court had the case been seasonably before it. The case of *Newberry vs. U.S.* 256 U.S. 230, 65 Law Ed. 913, is easily distinguishable. It is to be noted that while the Court held the primary law in Michigan unconstitutional, it was so held for the reason that the law of Michigan was passed prior to the Seventeenth Amendment: and the majority opinion, five to four, simply held that the only authority for the regulation of elections in a state was under Article I, Section 4, which was not broad enough for the predication of the Michigan law. It clearly indicated in its opinion that if the law had been aided by the Seventeenth Amendment it would have been constitutional.

Mr. Justice McReynolds, speaking for the majority, observed referring to the adoption of the Constitution in its original, "primaries were then unknown. Moreover, they were in no sense elections for an office but merely methods by which party adherents agreed upon candidates whom they intended to offer and support for ultimate choice by all qualified electors. General provisions touching elections in constitutions or statutes are not necessarily applicable to primaries. The two things are radically different."

This rather loose and untenable expression, if attempted to be applied in this case, is reduced to an absurdity by the dissenting opinions both of Chief Justice White and Associate Justice Pitney; in which dissenting opinion Mr. Justice Brandeis and Mr. Justice Clarke concurred. And it is to be noted that Mr. Justice McKenna concurred in the majority result but not in the reasoning. The dissenting opinion is epitomized by Mr. Justice Pitney.

After stating that the result of primary elections in a number of places is decisive and final, the general election being only a ratification and mere form, he concluded by saying: "I conclude that it is free from doubt that Congress has power under the Constitution to regulate the conduct of primary elections and nominating conventions held for choosing candidates to be voted for in general elections for Representatives and Senators in Congress and that the provisions of the Act of August, 1911" (referring to the Michigan Act) "in that belief are valid." Having established that the primary election in Texas is a public election it necessarily follows, when the voting privilege is limited only to white citizens, that it falls athwart the Fifteenth Amendment. It has been held over and over again that the Fifteenth Amendment eliminated the word "white" from all the state statutes in which it appeared. It is true that the Fifteenth Amendment does not confer the right of suffrage, but it does invest citizens with a right from discrimination in the elective franchise on account of race, color, or previous condition of servitude. In other words, it says that while a state may have a qualified suffrage that any law passed must be applicable to all citizens irrespective of color or previous condition of servitude. *Myers vs. Anderson*, 238 U.S. 367; *Guinn vs. U.S.* 238 U.S. 347; *U.S. vs. Mosely, et al.*, 238 U.S. 382.

Knollenberg could not have been more cooperative. He cut down the questions, changed the form and followed other suggestions made by Storey and Cobb.

The clerk's stamp shows the brief for Nixon was filed in the office of the Supreme Court on May 22, 1928.[43] As is well known, the sponsoring organization of a test case is ordinarily omitted from all connecting official papers and documents. All that is shown are the parties and the lawyers; here L.A. Nixon, the plaintiff in error, and the attorneys, Storey, Cobb, Channell and Knollenberg. The thirty-two page brief elaborated, sometimes colorfully, on five points. (1) By asserting rights under the Constitution, the action was within the jurisdiction of the federal district court. (2) "A democratic primary election in Texas is a public election, recognized, and regulated by the Constitution and laws of said state." (3) Casting a ballot in such a primary "is an act of voting within the meaning of the Fifteenth Amendment." Discrimination on account of race or color therefore protects the plaintiff in his right to vote so guaranteed. (4) By denying a black "the same latitude in registering his preference as a member of any party of his choice that it allows to white members of such a party," the state legislature "abridges his right to vote under the Fifteenth Amendment and denies to him the equal protection of the law guaranteed by the Fourteenth Amendment." (5) The Texas white primary statute violates a state constitutional guarantee against disfranchisement. Finally, the Court was asked to "fix so definitely the rights of the Negro that the steps taken by the Texas legislature will not be followed by any other state."

It appeared that the Supreme Court would not reach *Nixon v. Herndon* until the fall term. This delay concerned Knollenberg, for this reason.

The last Saturday in July is the date fixed by statute for another primary election, and under the law of which we are complaining, the Negroes will again be denied the right to vote in the Democratic primaries. However, they can vote at the Republican primaries, this being the first time in history when the Republican party has held a primary here. I have sent Mr. Cobb a tentative motion to advance this case, hoping the Supreme Court of the United States will see fit to hear it and render decision before that time. Wish to ask you what you think of it?[44]

The lawyers and the national office were glad enough to support the advancement of the case but this was a blameless stance as there was practically no chance of a favorable response. Cobb explained: "While I shall make a motion to advance the cause as soon as the briefs are filed, it is not possible for it to be argued before the adjournment of Court. The Court adjourns in May and there are some eighty-three (83) cases of importance now for argument before the Court."[45] The motion was not filed until May 27 with the term fast running out.[46] *Nixon v. Herndon* would go over for consideration during the October term, 1926.

Oral argument in *Nixon v. Herndon* was heard by the Supreme Court on January 3, 1927, in its chambers in the basement of the United States Senate in the Capitol. No record of the argument remains but NAACP correspondence reveals that Knollenberg represented their side none too well. Also, Attorney General Dan Moody of Texas declared the state had not known about the suit and asked the Court to grant thirty days in which to submit a brief. The NAACP requested two weeks thereafter to file a brief in reply. Spingarn had joined in the oral argument but most of the time was allotted to Knollenberg. The NAACP contingent in the courtroom, including Cobb and William Pickens and Herbert Seligman of the NAACP publicity office were distressed and "Mr. Spingarn was not impressed with Mr. Knollenberg's argument."[47] Cobb had visited with Knollenberg in Washington before the argument and wrote of his performance: "He realizes thoroughly his mistake in the case and that he ought to have familiarized himself with the cases that I gave him on Sunday before the case was argued on Tuesday."[48] James Weldon Johnson was sanguine all the same:

Knollenberg was in the office the day after the argument and we had quite a conference with him. He himself confessed to me that he legally stubbed his toe once or twice, but he said he was aiming more after the psychological effect upon the court than upon the legal effect. I have a hunch that in spite of any slips that may have been made we will win this case. It will be a great victory if we do.[49]

The oral argument experience had been unsettling but the chance to prepare a reply brief was eagerly grabbed. Johnson, Cobb and Spingarn worked strenuously in planning the new brief. Cobb wrote Johnson that "it is of the greatest importance that we be alert" and urged that Louis Marshall be enlisted to review the reply brief."[50] As president of the American Jewish Committee, and through his experience in litigation on civil rights issues for many years, Marshall fitted the NAACP conception of "eminent counsel" perfectly. Knollenberg was only too happy to have the brief completed and filed by Cobb, Spingarn and Marshall. But when the brief was done, almost wholly by Marshall, Cobb asked that his name be omitted as he feared critics might charge a conflict with his new position of municipal judge of the District of Columbia.

The State of Texas Intervenes

The state of Texas had intervened by special leave of the Court; its role was in between a party to a case and an *amicus curiae*. A party is joined firmly, bearing direct responsibility in the litigation and consequences from its outcome. The *amicus curiae* in modern Supreme Court cases is ordinarily a concerned ally to one of the parties, definitely committed but without a concrete, legal stake in the immediate controversy. As an intervener, a less well understood position in court cases, Texas was joined practically as a party. Its statute was under fire and there was no appearance in the Supreme Court by lawyers for the nominal parties, Herndon and Porras, the election judges. The rub was that by filing a brief for the state, the attorney general of Texas implicitly acknowledged the primary election as an official enterprise.

The brief for Texas in *Nixon v. Herndon* argued five co-writer propositions against the points urged by the lawyers for the NAACP.[51] Its emphasis was on the political party as a purely voluntary association whose primary could not be reached from the limited jurisdiction of a federal court. Blacks, indeed, could form their own party and limit its membership as they wished.

The reply brief by Louis Marshall brought together constitutional theory with practical political facts. In a modest, not exhaustive way, it may be likened to the sociological briefs of Brandeis, Frankfurter and the women of the Consumers' League. The NAACP legal committee had been urged in 1916 to imitate this type of brief. Now in *Nixon v. Herndon*, Marshall did so in what was, as much as anything, a kind of political science brief, planned, written, and printed in less than a month's time and filed—with the names of Storey, Spingarn, Knollenberg and Channell added to Marshall's—on February 19, 1927.[52] This short reply brief of thirty-four pages cites only a few nonlegal sources but its brilliance lies in Marshall's mature skill in integrating those sources into his argument.

There are several points at which the brief demonstrates why Louis Marshall was ranked a great lawyer by contemporaries. Of course, the argument repeated, in improved style, points made in the earlier NAACP brief. But three examples of Marshall's craftsmanship will show the fundamental qualities of this reply brief. These are his analysis of the Fifteenth Amendment's phrasing and his utilization of black population and voting statistics.

"The right of citizens of the United States to vote," according to the Fifteenth Amendment, "shall not be denied or abridged by the United States or by any State on account of race, color, or previous condition of servitude." Marshall admired these broad, comprehensive terms of expression, unconfined to any particular time, occasion, manner, or mechanism. "It relates," he said, "to the exercise of the right of a citizen to give expression to his political ideas and predilections in such a way as to make them effective.[53] The brief expresses a fine sense of history, paralleling the kind of argument made for the expansion of governmental power under the commerce clause. Texas argued the literal line that the Fifteenth Amendment does not speak expressly of voting at primaries. True, said Marshall, "it does not descend to particulars." He went on:

It deals with the all-inclusive subject, "the right to vote," and, unless intellectual blindness were to be attributed to the earnest and high-minded statesmen who sponsored this Amendment, that right must be deemed to relate to any form of voting and for any purpose and to any part of the process whereby what is intended to be accomplished by voting is brought about. There is certainly nothing in the amendment which declares that voting at primaries is to be excepted from its scope.

It is said that in 1870, when the Fifteenth Amendment was adopted, there were no primary elections and that, therefore, the right to vote at a primary election could not have been contemplated. We reply that in 1870 the so-called Australian ballot was unknown. Voting machines had not been invented, and other possible methods of voting than the primitive then in vogue, e.g., voting *viva voce*, or by a show of hands, or by a ballot thrust into the hands of the voter by the poll workers, had not been conceived. Neither had the initiative, the referendum, the recall, been introduced into our political vocabulary. Can anybody have the hardihood to claim that for these reasons the newer methods and purposes of voting are not covered by the Constitution? Its language is adequate to include any act or conception or purpose which relates to or substantially affects the free exercise in its essence of the right to vote.[54]

Thus did Louis Marshall conceive of the "intention of the framers" of the Fifteenth Amendment to support his attack on the exclusion of blacks from the Texas Democratic primary.

To show the Court the significance of primaries, Marshall drew upon work of the Chicago political scientists, Charles E. Merriam and Louise Overacker.[55] As an academician who believed practical politics must inform social science which, in turn, must aid official action, Merriam would have taken great delight and pleasure to see his findings used in such a legal brief. Among the quotations Marshall used from the book was this one:

The theory of the party as a voluntary association has been completely overthrown by the contrary doctrine that the party is in reality a governmental agency subject to legal regulation and control. The element of public concern in the making of nominations has been strongly emphasized, and the right of the legislature to make reasonable regulations to protect and preserve the purity and honesty of elections has been vigorously asserted.

Statistical information in this reply brief supports the argument that the South is a one-party, biracial region. This is what makes exclusion of blacks from the key election of this single party significant. The census of 1920 is summarized in Marshall's brief (see table 12-1). The brief went on to show in detail how all United States senators from these states were Democrats, and how completely the Democratic Party was dominant by every available measure. There was also a demonstration of heavy candidate competition and voter turnout in the Democratic primary in Texas in contrast with the subsequent general election. This reply brief also used measured bitterness in condemning the white primary, altogether an impressive document, cogent and scholarly.

Marshall's NAACP colleagues were enthusiastic, as witness James Weldon Johnson's letter upon reading the brief:

In my opinion, it is absolutely unanswerable. I do not see for the life of me how the Supreme Court can sidestep or dodge the issue as you have raised it. Furthermore, the brief is a most valuable document for us and a splended piece of political propaganda. We shall send it to all of the colored newspapers and will also have it placed on file in the principal public libraries of the country.[56]

In its press release, the NAACP called the brief a group effort and "a stirring reply" to the state of Texas.[57] To think that the brief would never have been written but for a chance event—the late request of Texas to intervene—shows something of the unevenness of Supreme Court litigation at that time. There is no way to estimate the persuasiveness of this brief—in relation to other words, thoughts and influences—upon the justices of the Supreme Court. It surely helped, that much is certain.

Decision in *Nixon v. Herndon*, 1927

The Supreme Court decision in favor of Nixon came on Monday, March 7, 1927. Hearing the good word, James Weldon Johnson in New York wired Walter White in care of James Cobb in Washington to amplify.

ASSOCIATED PRESS JUST TELEPHONED SUPREME COURT HAS OVERTHROWN TEXAS PRIMARY LAW. STOP. FIND OUT FULL FACTS AND GIVE PRESS STORY GOING OUT OF WASHINGTON PROPER NAACP SLANT IF POSSIBLE. STOP.[58]

Table 12-1
White and Black Population in Ten Southern States, 1920*

State	White	Black
Alabama	1,447,032	900,652
Arkansas	1,279,757	472,220
Florida	638,153	329,487
Georgia	1,689,114	1,206,365
Louisiana	1,096,611	700,257
Mississippi	853,962	935,184
North Carolina	1,783,779	763,407
South Carolina	818,538	864,719
Texas	3,918,165	741,694
Virginia	1,617,909	690,017

*Source: Reply Brief for plaintiff in error, p. 34, *Nixon v. Herndon*, 273 U.S. 536 (1927). The information is in accord with the United States Census of Population for 1920.

White's telegram in reply was jubilant:

SUPREME COURT BY UNANIMOUS DECISION TODAY DECIDES TEXAS CASE IN OUR FAVOR. MR. JUSTICE HOLMES DELIVERING OPINION WHICH CLOSES QUOTE THE STATUTE OF TEXAS IN THE TEETH OF THE PROHIBITIONS REFERRED TO ASSUMES TO FORBID NEGROES TO TAKE PART IN A PRIMARY ELECTION, THE IMPORTANCE OF WHICH WE HAVE INDICATED, BY DISCRIMINATING AGAINST THEM BY THE DISTINCTION OF COLOR ALONE PERIOD. STATES MAY DO GOOD DEAL OF CLASSIFYING THAT IT IS DIFFICULT TO BELIEVE RATIONAL BUT THERE ARE LIMITS AND IT IS TOO CLEAR FOR EXTENDED ARGUMENT THAT COLOR CANNOT BE MADE THE BASIS OF A STATUTORY CLASSIFICATION EFFECTING THE RIGHT SET UP IN THIS CASE JUDGMENT REVERSED UNQUOTE. BUCHANAN VERSUS WARLEY DECISION PLAYED IMPORTANT PART IN WINNING THIS GREAT VICTORY WHICH MADE PROFOUND IMPRESSION BECAUSE OF ITS FAR-REACHING CONSEQUENCES YOU CAN WIRE COBB 613 F STREET. WALTER WHITE.[59]

White reported that the decision was creating a "sensation" in the Supreme Court clerk's office, which was "thronged with newspaper men and lawyers" copying the opinion. Senators David Walsh of Montana and David Reed were excited over the bearing *Nixon v. Herndon* might have on the Vare and Smith election cases before the Senate. These cases both concerned excessive and dubious expenditures in primary elections. White reported a general agreement that the decision nullified the ruling in the *Newberry* case and held that a primary is "an integral part of elections."[60]

NAACP lawyers reacted differently to the opinion of the Court, prepared by Mr. Justice Holmes, than they had to the holding. Everyone was delighted to win. But what Holmes had done was to bypass the Fifteenth Amendment and label the white primary statute a violation of the equal protection clause of the Fourteenth Amendment. As he said, "We find it unnecessary to consider the Fifteenth Amendment, because it seems to us hard to imagine a more direct and obvious infringement of the Fourteenth."[61] The Court had sidestepped the issue. In so doing it left a wide loophole available to opponents of black voting. For whatever reason, the Court had not accepted Louis Marshall's analysis of the right to vote and with characteristic caution Mr. Justice Holmes had written the simple and unilluminating opinion.

L.A. Nixon wrote a long letter to James Weldon Johnson five days after the *Herndon* decision was announced by the Supreme Court. Texas blacks were elated over the ruling, he said, judging from letters and telegrams he received. But he complained about the low financial support. Few had contributed money and while the El Paso blacks were proud of their work, they were only a few, and not well off. He hoped the national office might stimulate fund raising among them because he had had so little luck thus far. Dr. Nixon wisely appreciated the obstacles faced in the hearts of men and the psychological adjustments blacks who expected full victory would have to make. He wrote:

I hope our people realize the importance of this constitutional victory to our future efforts for complete emancipation. There is no doubt but that intimidation of Negroes at the polls in the South will continue in some degree at least. If we expect a complete change of Southern character as a result of this Court ruling there is danger that many of us are going to lose heart when we are disillusioned.[62]

But he was chiefly concerned about money. And he concluded with a pledge of continuing support: "El Paso is proud to have been instrumental in bringing this suit. There is nothing, I am sure, that she would not be willing to do—regardless of consequences—to further the Association's purposes."

He said nothing about white Texan Democratic reaction to the *Herndon* case, but Dr. Nixon included in his letter a clipping from the front page of the *El Paso Herald* for March 10, 1927. The news story read:

Negroes never will vote in Texas Democratic primaries, R.E. Cunningham and county judge E.B. McClintock agreed today.

"I know they will not vote in the city primaries two years from now," Mr. Cunningham, chairman of the city Democratic executive committee, said.

"Supreme Court or no supreme court, here is one executive chairman who will see that they do not vote. The supreme court has held the Texas Democratic primary law prohibiting negroes from voting unconstitutional, but that can't keep the various local executive committees from passing rules prohibiting the negro vote. . . ."

The final item in the NAACP file on *Nixon v. Herndon* is a press release on how much money the case took. They reported that the victory was won "at the unprecedentedly low cost of $2,909.31."[63] It was all because Storey, Marshall and Spingarn had donated their services. James Weldon Johnson was quoted in the release as saying:

To win a historic victory at the low cost of the Texas Primary Case, would be impossible for any individual. It is possible only through the generous and high-minded public service of the eminent counsel whose aid the N.A.A.C.P. has been enabled to enlist. If these gentlemen had been paid what their services command, the cost of the case would have been very high indeed.

Again, the men of prominence won more publicity by their gift. The unsung black lawyer, James A. Cobb of Washington, had prudently asked not to be included in such releases. Yet he had shrewdly seen Knollenberg's faults, tried to correct them, but calculated that Louis Marshall should be asked to write the important reply brief. Cobb was serving almost as a staff lawyer working with the impressive lay secretariat of the NAACP led by James Weldon Johnson and

Walter White. It is fair to think that three lawyers made the difference in *Nixon v. Herndon*, the first succession of the major white primary cases: a country lawyer Knollenberg who moved the case off the ground in El Paso, a black lawyer Cobb who worked intelligently in Washington on the case, and at the last minute, eminent counsel Louis Marshall, whose polished reply brief successfully answered the state of Texas. Arthur B. Spingarn and Moorfield Storey played less crucial roles.

NAACP Leadership Changes, 1927-1932

Supreme Court invalidation in *Nixon v. Condon* in 1927 of the four-year-old Texas white primary law set the stage for new lawmaking by opponents of black voting which, in turn, brought further litigation. Each side held to its own original purposes but the second time around there would be both similarities and differences. In particular, the NAACP leaders in New York who saw the case through now had practical knowledge about the tasks of running a test case on voting. This experience would condition their choices in further litigation.

The impressions formed by the NAACP leadership in the first *Nixon* case which would affect their judgment in a second round were these. The El Paso branch was faithful and cooperative, Dr. Nixon was a dependable plaintiff and attorney Knollenberg, though not sharp or learned, was dependable and pliable. Mercenary as Knollenberg seemed to be, the total outlay of under $3,000 for a Supreme Court victory was a superb bargain. A test case should be managed from the outset because choices of forms, type of action, pleadings, appeal papers and the like affect the outcome. When the case reaches the Supreme Court the briefs and oral argument must be planned carefully. The executive secretary needed guidance at many points by experienced counsel in order to deal adeptly with a developing case.

Continuation of the NAACP legal program required new faces, goals and techniques. Distinguished figures in the old leadership dropped out following *Nixon v. Herndon*. Death took Moorfield Storey, who had been NAACP president since its founding, and Louis Marshall, whose brilliant work in defense of Indians, Jews and Japanese Americans had lately been matched in his briefs in the first Texas white primary and the District of Columbia restrictive covenant cases for blacks. In 1930, James Weldon Johnson resigned as executive secretary to return to writing and teaching. Johnson was succeeded by the assistant secretary since 1918, Walter White, also a literary man as well as an activist who could conduct the administration of the NAACP with vigor.

Arthur B. Spingarn continued through these years to chair the National Legal Committee of the NAACP and during the 1920s legal work was becoming the hallmark of the NAACP. The well-advertised success in the first *Nixon* case helped them to raise money, draw prominent lawyers to join the legal committee and recruit young attorneys into the cause. This brought a subtle shift in emphasis and approach in legal work from dependence on "eminent counsel" toward the longer-range, in-house staff of vigorous younger men. Perhaps it was a function of its insecurity, or the noblesse oblige feelings of its founders, that the NAACP until 1930 counted on eminence when confronting the courts. But the generation of Storey, Marshall and Clarence Darrow was passing. Felix Frankfurter reluctantly agreed to become a member of the National Legal Committee as long as little would be expected of him. Little was and he and other members like Frank Murphy and Morris Ernst appear to have contributed little beyond their names on the letterhead. The vacuum left by the loss of Storey and Marshall would be filled in a different way.

A breakthrough into support by a philanthropic foundation enabled the NAACP to take a long look at appropriate strategies of constitutional change. In 1929 the American Fund for Public Service, established by the millionaire Charles Garland and run by a radical board of trustees, granted support for an NAACP assessment of its situation. This enabled the appointment of a lawyer as special counsel for the NAACP to draw up plans and begin implementation.

A thirty-year-old lawyer, Nathan Margold, conducted this work between 1930 and 1933 at a Depression salary and, as it turned out, with withered foundation support. As a youngster, Margold had been brought to America from Rumania and grew up in New York City. He graduated from CCNY and then, in 1923, from the Harvard Law School. In a short span he acquired experience in private practice, as an assistant United States attorney, as special counsel to the New York Transit Commission and as a legal administrator of Indian affairs. Margold was an instructor at the Harvard Law School in 1927-28.

His achievement for the NAACP was to draw up a remarkable litigation program aimed at reducing and eliminating segregation and discrimination in education, employment and housing. This is a substantial document which remains today a perceptive and ambitious blueprint of how an organization might cope with social disadvantage and legal invidiousness by planning and conducting test cases. This far-seeing assessment helped the association make tactical choices which made sense in contributing to the fulfillment of this larger plan. Margold's plan was not followed step by step at a time when depression crippled financial support and generated its own unique problems of despair. But the plan helped the leaders and members of the association understand how tactics should be chosen to contribute to strategic goals.

Continued attack on the Texas Democratic white primary was a part of this program, but Margold's contribution was not in drawing up plans for test cases but in working with the El Paso branch in carrying a new case in progress to the Supreme Court of the United States. Spingarn was an active elder statesman all through this litigation and he was well served by a young associate, William T. Andrews, who joined the NAACP staff in New York. After Louis Marshall's death in 1929, his son, James Marshall, came onto the NAACP board of trustees and worked particularly as counsel in the new *Nixon* case. James Marshall, born in 1896, graduated from Columbia Law School in 1920 and associated with his father's firm for ten years until 1930. He was in practice on his own between 1930 and 1934 when most active in NAACP legal affairs.

Between 1927 and 1932, Charles Houston emerged as the acknowledged leader of the black civil rights bar. Young as Houston was, his experience in his father's law firm in Washington and as a teacher after 1924 and vice dean after 1929 in the Howard University Law School gave him unmatched standing among black lawyers and their associates in NAACP branches around the country as well as with the New York leadership. A graduate of Amherst College and of the Harvard Law School in 1923, Houston saw the goals of the NAACP through a wide lens, which equipped him to work within the confines of a single litigation with larger purposes in mind. It was a canon with Houston that a test case must have a social purpose and that winning the case may not be as important as how it is won. He saw the courts much as Clarence Darrow did—as educational forums in which lessons could be taught to the public. But while Houston was in harmony with the large purposes being developed by Margold for purposes of master strategy, his affinity with other black lawyers occasioned some tactical differences. But Houston was always an NAACP man. Occasionally he worked out of the New York office and in 1935 moved there to become the first general counsel for the association.

These, then, were the men who kept the campaign of equality by lawsuit going and who contributed to a new stage of institutionalization in the NAACP. We may now turn to the events in the wake of *Nixon v. Herndon* to follow the association's further work against black disfranchisement in the South.

Nixon v. Condon, 1932

The behavior of white Democrats in Texas in response to the Supreme Court ruling against a statutory white primary forecast a good deal. They complied to the letter by wiping out the statute; they thumbed their noses at the spirit of the ruling by enacting a new law providing that state party committees had authority to prescribe voter qualifications in future primary elections. The Democratic state executive committee of Texas promptly acted as expected and adopted a resolution to open primaries in 1928 to "all white Democrats who are qualified" but to "none other." The committee acted on June 11, 1928, to cover the primary on July 28.

The El Paso NAACP had to contend with rivals in Houston and San Antonio in gaining national NAACP endorsement in preparing and appealing a test case against the 1928 rule. Lawyer Knollenberg drafted a letter for Dr. Nixon to send to the thirty-three members of the Democratic committee requesting a rule change. When Dr. Nixon went to the polls on July 28, he was accompanied by reliable witnesses who could testify later to the refusal to permit blacks to vote. The plan was to sue each of the members of the committee.

In Houston, attorney R.D. Evans of Waco (who had prepared the appeal in *Love v. Griffith*) took somewhat different action to stop the new rule. Evans himself was then president of an organization called the Independent Colored Voters' League. The plaintiffs he represented were J.B. Grigsby and O.P. DeWalt of Houston. Grigsby was president of the American Mutual Benefit Association while DeWalt owned the Lincoln Theatre in Houston, where he was also president of the local branch of the NAACP. Evans acted in advance of the primary and filed a petition in the United States District Court in Houston for an injunction restraining Guy Harris, chairman of the Harris County Democratic executive committee and the election judges from preventing blacks from participating in the July 28 primary. Four days before the primary, Judge C.C. Hutcheson ruled against Grigsby, DeWalt and Evans, ruling that political parties may prescribe their own membership qualifications and may bar black voters from their primaries.[64]

The third effort originated in San Antonio in an injunction action brought before federal Judge Duval West. This test case was begun by J.G. Wimberly. But Knollenberg in El Paso was asked about the prospects for this action and correctly predicted its failure on account of the views of Judge West, which had been made evident in the earlier case of *Chandler v. Neff*.[65] Judge West acted as predicted and blacks were not able to vote in El Paso, Houston or San Antonio in the July 28 Democratic primary in Texas.

Next came efforts of lawyers in each of the three cities to win the support of the NAACP Office in New York to their case. The El Paso group had the best chance to gain this endorsement even though the top NAACP lawyers in the East had doubts about Knollenberg's competence. The El Paso people had worked out the *Nixon v. Herndon* case successfully and their know-how was apparent early in the competition with other Texans opposed to the white primary. L.A. Washington was the chief informant for New York on the Texas scene. He quickly sent clippings and the text of the new Texas rule to New York and also spoke confidently of plans for legal action by the El Paso branch. On the morning of June 19, he reported that he had "conferred with Atty. F.C. Knollenberg and Dr. L.A. Nixon with the view of going into court again on the issue."[66] He stressed cooperation with New York, saying "We will attempt to set the stage as before and keep your department informed of each step taken."

Knollenberg asked New York for a fee of $4,000 to handle the new case in El Paso for the association.[67] The $2,500 paid in the *Herndon* case would not be sufficient for the new case which would be brought in Dr. Nixon's behalf against all thirty-three members of the State Democratic Committee. In New York, the opinion of Knollenberg's role in *Herndon* was low, the plans he had for suing all members of the executive committee dubious and his wish for a higher fee questionable. But the alternatives were worse. Moreover, Knollenberg kept insisting that while he needed a fee of $4,000 he would rather drop the whole matter than cause difficulty. He disliked having "any argument with respect to fees, and rather than to do this," he wrote, "we prefer the friendship to the business."[68] From New York, Knollenberg heard from the acting secretary of the NAACP, R.W. Bagnell, that the association wished him to handle the new El Paso case, that they would pay a fee of $2,500 and expenses up to $1,500 and that a retainer of $500 would be advanced immediately.[69] The New York office was obliged, too, to tell DeWalt and Evans of the decision to support the *Nixon* case in El Paso and not to aid them in following through on the litigation in Houston. "The Legal Committee is of the opinion," he wrote, "that the carrying of the Houston case up to the United States Supreme Court would be useless and result in needless expenditures of money."[70]

Only after Knollenberg was retained was the full NAACP Legal Committee brought into the matter and Louis Marshall hit the roof. He declared that Knollenberg's complaint was unsatisfactory and that he would prepare a short brief indicating the approach he advised. He doubted very much the advisability of making the thirty-three members of the Democratic executive committee of Texas individual parties defendant of this reasoning:

The action is one at law for damages against the election officers who refused to permit Dr. Nixon to participate in the primary election. There is no cause of action against the members of the committee and by making them parties one loses sight of the true significance of the action. The chances would be that the complaint would be dismissed as to each of the members of the committee, with costs, which might amount to a large sum if each of the members of the committee were to appear by a different lawyer.[71]

This view was relayed to Knollenberg, who protested it as wrong and complained that while "Mr. Marshall is a big lawyer, and has reached a place at the Bar of the United States which we can never reach, and we respect his judgment," there were predictions earlier that he, Knollenberg, could never win the *Herndon* case although he did it. After this bout of defensiveness, Knollenberg agreed to follow the wishes of the New York office.

Later, Knollenberg yielded to New York's advice, dropped action against the Texas Democratic leadership and made the case what it was later to become in the Supreme Court—a federal suit for $5,000 damages by Dr. L.A. Nixon against James Condon and C.H. Kolle, the election officials who refused to let him vote in the 1928 primary.

There was a judgment of dismissal in the U.S. District Court in 1929.[72] Knollenberg was so certain of also losing in the court of appeals in 1930 that he had his partner, Frank Cameron, travel to Fort Worth to make the argument before a three-judge panel of the Court of Appeals for the fifth circuit. The judges were Bryan, once a Democratic senator from Florida, appointed by President Wilson; Foster, identified only as a southern Democrat; and Dauthet, a

Republican formerly on the supreme court of Louisiana. Knollenberg and Cameron each wrote to Nathan R. Margold in New York about the extreme prejudice shown by these judges. Knollenberg and Cameron, of course, were both white lawyers from El Paso with considerable courtroom experience.

As expected, the court of appeals affirmed the lower court sustaining the statute and the authority of the Democratic State executive committee to exclude blacks from primary elections.[73]

Nixon v. Condon now came to the Supreme Court with Knollenberg prepared to cooperate completely with New York. He asked Arthur B. Spingarn if Margold and James Marshall, who were to work with him, would draw the petition for certiorari. Soon, Margold advised Knollenberg in El Paso that all of the work he had inquired about would be attended to in New York.

The writ was granted by the Supreme Court early in its 1931 October term, argued January 7, 1932, reargued March 15, 1932 and decided May 2, 1932.[74] The Supreme Court sided, five to four, with the NAACP contention that the authority exercised by the State Democratic executive committee to ordain a white primary was "state action" and hence violative of the Fourteenth Amendment. Mr. Justice Cardozo's opinion for the Court pinpointed the distinction of the committee in having carried out a power granted it by statute, not by vote of the party convention. "Whatever power of exclusion has been exercised by the members of the committee has come to them," wrote Cardozo, "not as the delegates of the party, but as the delegates of the state."[75]

The opinion for the majority declined to speculate on other constitutional schemes and, in a sense, seemed to invite Texas to try ones that might exclude blacks and still be valid. This is not to suggest anything about the racial attitudes of the justices but merely acknowledges the difficulty of drawing lines between the acceptable and the unacceptable at any time between state action and private action, between general elections and primaries, and between federal judiciary authority and state and local authority. It was probably not easy either to win five votes to this viewpoint as the *Newberry* rule was still standing and there were, in fact, four dissenting justices in *Nixon v. Condon* speaking through a long opinion by Mr. Justice McReynolds. His theme was that "political parties are fruits of voluntary action" and that the state statute of 1927 did not convert the Democratic party of Texas or its executive committee into a state agency.

There are four reactions to the Supreme Court's ruling in *Nixon v. Condon* to be noted. First, an interpretation of the five-to-four decision as essentially the function of the membership of the Court was made by Knollenberg in a letter to Walter White, saying

I want to tell you that you are entitled to the credit of making the five our way. Had it not been for your fight on Judge Parker, the five would have been against us, therefore, you are entitled to all the credit for this decision and I bow to your efforts. The results are now so apparent that there can be no question about the good the association has done for the Negroes.[76]

Second, Dr. Nixon did *not* gain the right to vote in the 1932 elections although he and the lawyers agreed to settle the *Condon* case with a minimum of fuss. The Democratic executive committee agreed to pay all the costs of the case if the NAACP agreed that Dr. Nixon would accept a judgment for one dollar only. (Although the official records of the case show that costs and the judgment were paid by the election judges, Condon and Kolle, they were paid by the committee, not by the parties or the state.) But at the time of settlement it was clear that the election judges in El Paso, acting upon the instructions of the county executive committee, would not let Dr. Nixon vote in either the general primary or the runoff primary in the fall of 1932. This prompted Knollenberg to play the same broken record a third time—"We have laid the basis for another suit . . . let me know whether or not we should file it . . . if you wish to continue the fight . . . it would be advantageous to have Dr. Nixon as plaintiff . . . for phychologically it has its effect upon the court."[77]

There was also the predictable behavior of the white Democrats of Texas who, acting without statutory authority in convention, assembled on May 24, 1932, resolved "that all white citizens of the State of Texas who are qualified to vote under the Constitution and laws of the state shall be eligible to membership in the Democratic party and as such entitled to participate in its deliberations." Fourthly, the leading NAACP lawyers were woefully concerned over how to attack this successfully in the courts. Nathan R. Margold, for example, was troubled and believed that there was possibly one way to win but that this would need to be studied and organized with the greatest possible care. This is what he wrote to his mentor, Professor Felix Frankfurter of the Harvard Law School:

My own opinion is that the strength of our case will depend largely upon how far we can convince the court that voting at a primary election—at least in states like Texas, where the primary election is practically determinative of the results at the final election—must be assimilated to voting at any final or public election, and not to voting at a private election of a private organization. Actually, the Supreme Court has already so decided both in *Nixon v. Herndon* and in *Nixon v. Condon*, for in each case the basis of liability was not a breach of the contractual right of a member of the Democratic Party to vote for its candidates but a tortuous deprivation of the right of a qualified voter to participate in a public election.

But we shall have to do more than rest on these decisions in order to bring home to the Supreme Court the thought that the situation is precisely the same as if the Democratic Party, or the Ku Klux Klan, had adopted a resolution prohibiting Negro citizens from voting at final elections in Texas, and as if the state courts had refused to entertain Nixon's action for damages against judges of election who denied him a vote on the basis of that resolution.

The opinion in the *Civil Rights Cases*, 109 U.S. 3, shows very clearly that the Supreme Court then would have reviewed and reversed such action by the state court as violative of the Fourteenth Amendments; and while it probably is futile to hope that all of the present justices could be gotten either to understand or to sympathize with the reasons for such action, it is not too much to hope that a majority of them can be won over by a really effective presentation of our side of the case.[78]

This problem, anticipated and understood so well by national leaders of the NAACP, would be unsolved for another twelve years. During this time, the association's legal program was transformed. The changes were accompanied by difficulties over local support, the participation of black lawyers in the program and a clear-cut defeat in the white primary case of *Grovey v. Townsend* in 1935. But this case did not have the endorsement or assistance of the National Legal Committee, a commentary in itself on the black movement. Would white allies drive off black allegiance to an organization like the NAACP?

The Unfortunate Case of Grovey v. Townsend

Treating a political party as a private association, the Supreme Court of the United States ruled on April 1, 1935, in *Grovey v. Townsend*,[79] that the denial of a ballot to a black for voting in a primary election, under a state-convention resolution restricting party membership to white persons, cannot be deemed state action inhibited by the Fourteenth or Fifteenth Amendment.

There are several remarkable things about this decision. For one, the opinion of the Court was prepared by Mr. Justice Roberts, whom many civil rights leaders had earlier been grateful to have on the bench instead of John J. Parker, the Hoover nominee rejected by the Senate partly in reponse to NAACP criticisms. For another, the decision was unanimous, nine to zero, and consequently the cause seemed hopeless in the wake of such a defeat. Of course, the ruling was made during a time when the Court was preoccupied with federal and state economic legislation aimed at alleviating the ills associated with the Great Depression. This probably goes far to explain the disaster for civil rights represented by the *Grovey* decision. But an inspection of the conduct of the case shows something more.

An off-the-cuff reaction by Roy Wilkins, then assistant secretary of the NAACP in New York, affords one view of this litigation. He regretted "that the fight was made" because, as he wrote a friend, "in many places in and out of Texas the very indecision on the point was resulting in more and more local communities granting the ballot to the Negro."[80] This expressed perfectly the incremental progress that the NAACP has been both praised and condemned for. Yet Wilkins also stressed that *Grovey v. Townsend* "was not handled by this association." This is important. It is important because it shows that one NAACP leader in 1935 was not anxious for more court tests but was judging progress in terms of whether blacks were, in fact, voting. True, many did not vote even after the victory of *Nixon v. Condon*, Dr. Nixon himself still being denied the right to vote in primaries. Wilkins was as realistic and cynical as he could be in noting the impact of *Grovey* as he said that

it appears that this decision is a great weapon for those sections of the Democratic party that wish to remain white. I do not think it will result in complete barring of the Negro from voting even in Texas because, as you well know, whenever the white man has some advantage he wishes to secure over other white men and thinks he can secure it through use of the Negro he will forget rules and regulations. Also, local political pressure and local machine politics, such as in San Antonio, will keep Negroes voting.[81]

Thus, Wilkins' view that the decision was unfortunate did not keep him from seeing that behavior—compliance or noncompliance—was affected by other factors than judicial pronouncements. This observation about the aftermath of *Grovey* is exceptional in recognizing that such a judicial setback might not be a total loss. This is true because of common concern that a civil rights victory that is not fully complied with is meaningless. Wilkins really suggests that expectations about judicial outcomes need to be tempered.

Black voting in Texas Democratic primaries was, in fact, stultified by the *Grovey* ruling. The day following its announcement in Washington, the El Paso County Democratic committee announced plans to adopt resolutions to bar blacks from future primary elections. An El Paso paper reported, however, that attorney Fred Knollenberg and Dr. L.A. Nixon would continue the court fight. This did not materialize. "Dr. Nixon voted in the last County primary, but said his ballot was not counted." He said that "Election officials marked 'Negro' across the face of the ballot."[82] Occasional correspondence between El Paso, particularly concerning full payment for Knollenberg's fee for legal services in the *Condon* case between 1928 and 1932, continued for another year. There is no record in the files of the NAACP concerning Knollenberg, Nixon and Washington in El Paso after that.

Grovey v. Townsend seemed like a total disaster; yet, the lawyers in Houston responsible for bringing the case were as militant afterward as they had been aggressive and independent in initiating this test case. They were black lawyers from Houston with a fervent interest in increasing black voting power. *Grovey* was brought by two lawyers, J. Alston Atkins, a graduate of the Yale Law School in the 1920s, and Carter Wesley, a graduate of Northwestern Law School in 1922. They had been joined by James M. Nabrit, Jr., in preparing an *amicus* brief in *Nixon v. Condon*, three years earlier. Nabrit was later, in the 1960s, president of Howard University in Washington. Atkins had tried but failed repeatedly to win in white primary cases. Thus he followed, or accompanied, R.D. Evans and other black lawyers in eastern Texas in consistently losing these cases while the white lawyers in El Paso in western Texas were winning *Nixon v. Herndon* and then *Nixon v. Condon*.[83]

But Atkins was not the least bit sheepish over the loss in *Grovey*. He had occasion to speak with feeling in letters to Charles H. Houston, a former associate in Houston, then vice dean of the Howard Law School just released for a year to be the first black lawyer to lead the NAACP legal program. Atkins looked upon this step as long overdue and blamed his own past failures on the presence of too many white lawyers in association cases. Excerpts from his letters to Charles Houston give this flavor. He first contratulated Houston on handling some of the key Supreme Court cases then pending and declared

I trust that this will be the beginning of a new policy, under which no case in the future will be presented in that tribunal without a Negro lawyer at the counsel table. Here's hoping you win; but the mere fact that you handled the case is a victory for Negro lawyers. I know that you did it as ably and effectively as any white member of the N.A.A.C.P. legal staff could have handled it. . . .

Had the N.A.A.C.P. had the wisdom to have built the fight in the Nixon cases around the Negro leadership which started the Texas Primary Law fight, and continued the fight around that leadership and those who in successive years have joined the fight, I feel certain that, instead of being practically a nonentity in Texas, the N.A.A.C.P. would have a strong and virile organization in Texas today. It was R.D. Evans of Waco, a Negro lawyer whom you know, that first indicated the possibilities of a fight upon the statutory Democratic primary elections of Texas. But, when the N.A.A.C.P. came to file its first Nixon Case, it ignored Evans, ignored the lay leadership in *Love v. Griffith*, paid its money to white lawyers, and went its merry way.

. . . if you are going to control the NAACP's legal policy and action, I would like to see this battle rounded into a great movement to win the franchise for Texas Negroes under your leadership. My own impression is that the one fundamental fight which all American Negroes must wage is the fight to place the ballot in the hands of the ten million Negroes of the South. The lack of this weapon is at bottom the foundation of most of the other wrongs from which all American Negroes suffer. This battle must be won if the net effect of other battles won is not to be an empty victory.

Charles Houston was most agreeable but he was not ready to share precisely Atkins's insistence on black lawyers and, indeed, defended past NAACP practice. This is what he wrote:

I believe that the N.A.A.C.P. must win the Negroes primarily to its program, and that it should be the great laboratory for developing Negro leadership wherever possible.

The other Texas cases came up before my active work in the Association began. I do not know the facts surrounding the choice of lawyers but I know that it is the general policy of the Association *to appoint Negro lawyers in all cases where considerations are otherwise equal.* [Italics supplied.]

I am sure that this general policy was followed in the Texas cases and that the Association must have had good reasons for the selection of counsel which actually happened.[84]

NAACP files bulge with correspondence from 1935 onward over possible new tests to again question the white primary in the Supreme Court. Not a month had passed since 1921 that black voters, NAACP branches and their lawyers in Texas had not been at work on litigation against the white primary; this continued long after the *Grovey* decision on April 1, 1935.

Toward the *Smith v. Allwright* Overruling, 1944

During the 1930s the NAACP legal program branched out in many directions and judicial victories mounted in several rather distinct fields. Black lawyers like Charles Houston, Thurgood Marshall and James Nabrit, Jr., became the dominant figures in the national program and they encountered the same problems in dealing with local lawyers confronted by Nathan Margold, James Marshall, Louis Marshall, Arthur Spingarn and Moorfield Storey, all white lawyers, when they conducted the national legal work earlier. The victories were infectious and strenghtened the vision of Houston, Marshall and Nabrit to improve the lot of blacks politically, educationally, economically and socially by proceeding to make a legal revolution. Thus they were deeply interested in voting cases, in opening access to higher education, in working for equal salaries for black teachers, in obtaining fairness in criminal procedures. Of all these, housing, voting, education and jobs continued through the whole history of the NAACP to be most emphasized in their legal program.

The installation of a full-time legal staff, the burdens of financing a legal program and the benefits of tax-free contributions offered by the Internal Revenue Code led, in 1939, to the establishment of a new organization apart from the National Association for the Advancement of Colored People. An organization qualifies for tax exemption so long as "no substantial part" of its activities is used to "carrying on propaganda, or otherwise attempting to influence legislation."[85] Out of these circumstances was formed the NAACP Legal Defense and Educational Fund, Inc. It shared an office with the NAACP in New York, until the early 1950s, when its endangered tax status forced a physical separation. The separation symbolized an increasing distinction in goals, style, economic base and personnel. This was an exceedingly slow, often cooperative but sometimes quarrelsome, separation of functions. It was not magnified until after the victory of the Legal Defense and Education Fund (also called the Legal Defense Fund, the Inc Fund, Ink Fund, or Fund) in the *School Segregation Cases* of 1954 and 1955.[86]

The growing experience of Thurgood Marshall in dealing with local NAACP branches, with lawyers across the country and with the nonlawyers in the NAACP in New York and Washington led him to formulate procedures to enable him to control litigation. During 1943, several memoranda expressed this interest and concern. One statement reveals Marshall's wish to get clear of Walter White and Roy Wilkins in controlling the legal work in the office. First, he stressed that NAACP branches should refer all legal cases directly to him, and not to White's office or to the bureau in Washington. He provided for clearance of questions of policy between himself and Walter White or their delegates. He specified that all correspondence about legal matters should be placed on his desk for review. He also covered outgoing communications by stating, "I am to approve all public statements concerning legal matters issued in any form. All press releases concerning legal work are to be approved by me before they are issued. . . . This approval is to be in addition to the approval of the Secretary [Walter White] or Assistant Secretary [Roy Wilkins]."[87]

In 1939 and 1941 the Supreme Court made decisions in election cases which buoyed the hopes of Thurgood Marshall and others in the Legal Defense Fund and the NAACP that the unfortunate outcome in *Grovey v. Townsend* might be changed. In *Lane v. Wilson*, the Court ruled, six to two, that Oklahoma's election registration scheme set up by statute in 1916 to reinstate the grandfather clause was unconstitutional. Why the 1916 law took twenty-three years to reach a constitutional test is difficult to explain. Clearly, no person or organization had the initiative to act against it. When a case was finally brought the Court had to reverse holdings in the U.S. Court of Appeals for the Tenth Circuit and the U.S. District Court for the Eastern District of Oklahoma. Those courts had upheld this plan: after the *Guinn* decision, Oklahoma opened the registration rolls for twelve days to enable persons not qualified to vote in 1914 to register. No later opportunity was provided. I.W. Lane was a black citizen of Wagoner County, Oklahoma, who was qualified for registration in 1916 but did not then get on the list. He sought to register on October 17, 1934, but this was denied and he sued Jess Wilson, former precinct registrar, and other county election officials for declining to register him. He sought damages for $5,000 under section 1979 of the Reconstruction statutes for this disfranchisement and this position was adopted by the Supreme Court in an opinion by Mr. Justice Frankfurter.

NAACP files reveal several intriguing sidelights about *Lane v. Wilson*. First, the case was initiated by a black attorney in Muskogee, Oklahoma, named Charles A. Chandler. Suit was filed in 1935 in the district court where Robert Lee Williams, former governor of Oklahoma, had worked for the grandfather clause twenty years earlier. After a long fight, Williams removed himself from hearing *Lane v. Wilson*. Later, he was elevated to the Court of Appeals for the Tenth Circuit in Denver and did sit on the case at that level.[88] Funds were provided by local sources in Oklahoma, particularly in Wagoner County, known as the "black county" of the state for having a black population of 6,753, representing about 30 percent of the total. The national office of the NAACP spent about $500 during 1937 and 1938 but funds were needed so badly that Charles Houston appealed to the American Civil Liberties Union for support.[89]

Meanwhile, Walter White received an extended complaint about finances from Roscoe Dunjee, editor of the *Black Dispatch* in Oklahoma City, said to be the

"Largest Circulated Negro Journal in the South." Dunjee agreed that Chandler was an outstanding attorney but asserted he was receiving funds from several sources, fund raising by NAACP branches and churches in Oklahoma had not been coordinated and now funds were coming in from New York. Dunjee also complained that Thurgood Marshall was making a visit to Oklahoma without touching the right bases, particularly snubbing him.[90] Marshall adroitly picked up the pieces by writing a detailed explanation of his travels (the visit to see Chandler in Muskogee had been impromptu, during a trip to Texas), and a thorough accounting of monies spent on the case. "I always hate to come into a state without seeing officers of our branches and especially state conferences," Marshall wrote Dunjee, "but I am sure you realize that under these circumstances time was more than limited and I had to be back in Dallas by early Monday morning." But this did not quiet Dunjee of the *Black Dispatch*, also a member of the NAACP Board of Directors, and soon the lawyer, Charles A. Chandler, was complaining that Dunjee's "damn pettiness and foolishness" was making the work intolerable."[91] While Chandler's criticisms of Dunjee were severe the lesson suggested was that a single state conference is not a dependable source of financial support for litigation—or it was not in Oklahoma in the late 1930s.

The Supreme Court granted certiorari to review the judgment of the Circuit Court of Appeals for the Tenth Circuit affirming the judgment against damages below.[92] Argument was set for March 3, 1939. The oral argument was to be made to the Supreme Court by Charles A. Chandler and James M. Nabrit, Jr., and Leon A. Ransom of the faculty at Howard Law School wrote urgently to Thurgood Marshall of the concern he and Charles Houston had over the quality of the presentation. He wrote this confidential letter:

Charlie and I are very much worried over the situation. Neither Nabrit nor Chandler having appeared before the Supreme Court before, we want to go over their arguments with them and then send them before the senior class at the law school, as we did Sidney [Redmond] in the *Gaines* [Missouri law school] case, to get the feel of their argument. In order to do this we must have Chandler here as soon as possible. . . .[93]

Arrangements were made. There was a dry run before the students at the Howard Law School and the briefs and arguments made to the Court by Chandler and Nabrit were successful. In invalidating the Oklahoma statute, Mr. Justice Frankfurter for the Court said that the Fifteenth Amendment "nullifies sophisticated as well as simple-minded modes of discrimination. It hits onerous procedural requirements which effectively handicap exercise of the franchise by the colored race though the abstract right to vote may remain unrestricted as to race."[94]

Even before this happy outcome in *Lane v. Wilson* was announced on May 22, contentiousness over funding the litigation worsened. Roscoe Dunjee persuaded the NAACP Board of Directors to pass a resolution requiring Charles A. Chandler to provide the national office with "an itemized account of receipts and disbursements" in the *Lane* case and a school bond case he had worked on. If he failed to comply within ten days, the resolution stated that "the Board will be compelled to remove him from the National Legal Committee."[95] Chandler had already filed a detailed breakdown of expenses on April 27 with Charles Houston showing that the total court costs for *Lane v. Wilson* amounted to $1,356.90, stressing that this "does not include any compensation for legal service, nor expense incurred in travel incident to promotional work, nor the effort to raise finances, nor compensation to stenographer in my office."[96] His receipts for this case were $23.28 less than expenditures. The Dunjee-Chandler money controversy, as it came to be known in the NAACP, was resolved when Charles Houston visited Dunjee in Oklahoma City and Chandler in Muskogee toward the end of May 1939. Houston's report was a model of solicitude for Dunjee, who believed in strict bookkeeping routines and Chandler, whose financial circumstances were so difficult he had been obliged to "spend any money coming into his hands rather than routing it thru Dunjee, advancing his own money and being reimbursed out of the state treasury of the N.A.A.C.P."[97]

Four minor points in the wake of the Oklahoma case concerned the NAACP and federal judges. The association had helped in 1930 to persuade the Senate to refuse confirmation of John J. Parker to the Supreme Court. In 1938 the association opposed the appointment of Robert Lee Williams to be on the Court of Appeals for the Ninth Circuit, but President Roosevelt named him under an agreement by which Williams would serve but two years until retirement. There were also federal judges with a predilection in favor of NAACP causes. Felix Frankfurter had been a member of the National Legal Committee during the 1920s and early 1930s although he seems not to have been especially active and he resigned once he was named to the Supreme Court. Charles Houston had been his student at the Harvard Law School but, again, Frankfurter had no contact after he came on the bench and even declined to contribute after Houston's early death in 1949 to a special educational fund for Houston's surviving child.[98] On the other hand, Judge Henry W. Edgerton of the Court of Appeals for the District of Columbia, whom Frankfurter once called the very model of the "disinterested" judge, mailed a check for $20 to the NAACP, apparently as a gesture of approval for its efforts in *Lane v. Wilson*.[99]

The case of *Lane v. Wilson* had shown that the emerging Roosevelt Court was, perhaps, different from the nine justices sitting less than five years earlier in *Grovey v. Townsend*. Thurgood Marshall was learning (and the association was learning) the complexities of handling cases from remote parts of the country. A black civil rights bar was being nationalized during these years. Now came a harbinger from out of the blue as the Department of Justice went to court in Louisiana to charge fraud in a primary election. On May 26, 1941, the Court took the opportunity to reconsider the rule in the *Newberry* case and all seven justices sitting agreed that Reconstruction civil rights laws were applicable to primary as well as to general elections. There were disagreements among the justices on other points but the case of *United States v. Classic* gave an enormous intellectual lift to NAACP lawyers because its basic premise seemed quite clearly to contradict that of *Grovey v. Townsend*. The NAACP lawyers were ready to move.

Lawyers in east Texas now had their innings as attorney W.J. Durham of Sherman began a case on behalf of Lonnie E. Smith against a Houston election judge named S.E. Allwright for being denied a ballot in the two 1940 Texas Democratic primaries. Smith sued for damages but this was dismissed on May 30, 1942, by the district court and this dismissal was affirmed by the court of appeals.[100] The case then came to the Supreme Court on certiorari[101] and argument was heard first November 10 and 12, 1943 and again on January 12, 1944. The case had been started in Houston by Carter Wesley but it became one of the first major cases to be handled almost completely by Thurgood Marshall and the NAACP Legal Defense Fund. Marshall and William H. Hastie made the oral argument before the Supreme Court. Others on the brief were Leon A. Ransom, Carter Wesley, W.J. Durham, W. Robert Ming, Jr., and George M. Johnson. There were also three briefs *amici curiae* supporting Marshall's position. One was by Whitney North Seymour for the American Civil Liberties Union, another by Osmond K. Fraenkel for the National Lawyers Guild and a third by John F. Finerty for the Workers Defense League.

Thurgood Marshall's expertise and confidence were growing. While working on litigation, he was also developing policies for his office. In addition to clarifying relations with the branches and with the Washington bureau and the national office in New York, Marshall saw that the scope of his domain as chief counsel needed to be registered and made known. Thus he ordered that "a detailed docket as to all court cases" be kept. This would be "an account book showing expenditures for each case broken down as to cases," to provide background for weekly and monthly reports of the legal department. In this same plan, Marshall also moved to make the National Legal Committee more than window dressing.

Starting with the Texas Primary case [Smith v. Allwright], we are to send members of the National Legal Committee from time to time specific requests for research, advice and work on pending legal cases. This is a two-fold object. One is to get the benefit of the advice of members of the National Legal Committee; the other is to weed out inactive members of the National Legal Committee.[102]

In November 1943 Marshall went further with a policy formula for the work of the Legal Defense Fund by preparing a guide for cases orginating in the branches. This lengthy document reveals the experience Marshall had gained in several years of work but only pertinent parts related to his view of the branches and the functions of his office will be indicated here. First, he stressed the diversity of the branches and the cases they might handle:

Legal work is one of the important phases of our program. Our branches and the national office will receive more and more requests for legal assistance. It is, therefore, necessary that our branches maintain an effective legal program. All legal work of the branches should be coordinated with the legal program of the national office.

With more than 400 branches of varying sizes in all sections of the country it is impossible to set up any type of model procedure that will fit all cases of all branches. This outline is merely an effort to set up certain basic principles to assist our branches in their legal cases. The outline will be revised from time to time.

After indicating the number of interlocking layers of bureaucracy in this huge federated organization with its separate Legal Defense Fund, Marshall stressed caution and cooperation:

The NAACP is not a legal-aid society. We can only take up cases where (a) there is injustice because of race or color, and (b) the case involves the establishing of a precedent which will benefit Negroes in general.[103]

These rules were evidently followed in *Smith v. Allwright*, an NAACP effort that was crowned with great success as it was decided April 3, 1944, by an eight to one margin that "*Grovey v. Townsend* is overruled."[104] This was the concluding line in Mr. Justice Reed's opinion for the Court.

As table 12-2 shows, the membership of the Supreme Court had changed almost entirely since the *Grovey* decision. Of the two justices remaining in 1943, Stone, who had been named Chief Justice by President Roosevelt (having served as an associate justice for fifteen years as a nominee of President Coolidge) sided with the majority, while Mr. Justice Roberts filed a bitter dissent. Stone had been the spokesman of the Court in the *Classic* case but did not speak of the *Grovey* case or of the white primary even though he then knew, according to his biographer, that he "had circumspectly brought traditional Southern election customs to the brink of destruction."[105]

Roberts, on the other hand, remained convinced that the *Grovey* rule was not only correct constitutional interpretation but also had sanctity because it had been decided unanimously only nine years before. There was no counsel serving Allwright and the other election judges, but Justice Roberts accepted the arguments made in separate *amici curiae* briefs by the attorney general of Texas and by Wright Morrow on behalf of George A. Butler, chairman of the State Democratic executive committee. Roberts stressed the distinction between *Nixon v. Condon* and *Grovey*. In *Condon*, he explained, the Court held that the

Table 12-2

Justices' Alignment on Holding Primary Elections to be "State Action" (Subject to Federal Law and Constitutional Standards, 1921-1953)[a]

Appointment order of Justices from White to Minton	Newberry (1921) 4-4	Love (1924) 0-9	Herndon (1927) 9-0	Condon (1932) 5-4	Grovey (1935) 0-9	Classic (1941) 7-0	Allwright (1944) 8-1	Terry (1953) 8-1
White, E.								
White (C.J.)	+							
Peckham								
McKenna	n.p.	—						
Holmes	—	—	+					
Day	—							
Moody								
Lurton								
Hughes								
Van Devanter	—	—	+	—	—			
Lamar, J.								
Pitney	+							
McReynolds	—	—	+	—	—			
Brandeis	+	—	+	+	—			
Clarke	+							
Taft (C.J.)		—	+					
Sutherland		—	+	—	—			
Butler		—	+	—	—			
Sanford		—	+					
Stone (C.J.)			+	+	—	+	+	
Hughes (C.J.)				+	—	n.p.		
Roberts				+	—	+	—	
Cardozo				+	—			
Black						+	+	+
Reed						+	+	+
Frankfurter						+	+	+
Douglas						+	+	+
Murphy						+	+	
Byrnes								
Jackson							+	+
Rutledge, W.							+	
Burton								+
Vinson (C.J.)								+
Clark								+
Minton								—

Table 12-2 (cont.)

aAlignments are on the central point only. In *Newberry* and *Classic* there were disagreements on other issues. In *Love*, the merits were not reached but no justice indicated a readiness to do so. See the remainder of this table for details of each case.

Newberry v. United States, *256 U.S. 232 (1921). Following heavy expenditures in Republican primary for the Senate from Michigan in 1918 between Henry Ford and Truman Newberry, Newberry was indicted for violating the Federal Corrupt Practices Act of 1910. The Act limited spending in campaigns for federal office but did not mention primary elections. The trial judge ruled the Act applied to primaries and Newberry was convicted of a violation. The U.S. Supreme Court, in a complicated ruling on May 2, 1921, set aside the conviction, 5 to 4. Mr. Justice McKenna took no position on the broad issue, leaving the Court tied 4 to 4 with the decided impression that such primary elections were beyond the reach of Congressional regulation.*b

Love v. Griffith, 266 U.S. 32 (1924). The city committee of the Democratic Party in Houston, Texas ruled on January 27, 1921 that "Negroes will not be allowed to vote" in the February primary for city offices. Blacks there promptly sought to have this enjoined but failed and were excluded from voting. Appeals after the election failed. On October 6, 1924 the U.S. Supreme Court by 9 to 0 ruled that the cause of action was moot as the Houston white primary was for a single, past election only. The merits were not reached.

Nixon v. Herndon, 273 U.S. 536 (1927). A 1923 Texas state statute barring blacks from voting in Democratic party primary elections held in the State for federal and state offices was ruled invalid violative of the Fourteenth Amendment's equal protection clause. The opinion for the Court by Mr. Justice Holmes, issued March 7, 1927, was for a unanimous, 9 to 0, Court.

Nixon v. Condon, 286 U.S. 73 (1932). A new 1927 Texas state statute repealed the 1923 law and provided that state party committees have authority to prescribe voter qualifications in future primary elections. The Democratic state committee of Texas then resolved that 1928 primaries would be open to "all white democrats who are qualified" but to "none other." Dr. L.A. Nixon of El Paso was denied the right to vote on account of race. On May 2, 1932, through an opinion by Mr. Justice Cardozo the Supreme Court, 5 to 4, ruled that because the committee's power came from the 1927 statute, not from the state party convention (that is from the power of the party as a voluntary association) this was state action within the meaning of the Fourteenth Amendment. The resulting discrimination was held to violate the Fourteenth Amendment. A dissenting opinion by McReynolds was supported by Van Devanter, Sutherland and Butler.

Grovey v. Townsend, 295 U.S. 45 (1935). The Democratic state convention of Texas adopted a resolution on May 24, 1932 restricting eligibility for membership in the Democratic Party to white persons. Blacks denied the right to vote in Houston in a primary held on July 28, 1934, contended the resolution was state action violative of the Fourteenth and Fifteenth Amendments. Mr. Justice Roberts, for a 9 to 0 Court, ruled otherwise, saying that even though nomination by the Democratic Party in Texas is equivalent to election, and exclusion virtually disfranchises the voter, this is worked by private action and is not a constitutionally forbidden discrimination. The case was decided April 1, 1935.

United States v. Classic, *313 U.S. 299 (1941). The Supreme Court on May 26, 1941, ruled that Reconstruction civil rights laws were properly applied to voting frauds in the 1940 Louisiana Democratic primary because citizens were deprived of their Constitutional guarantee to choose representatives to Congress. Chief Justice Hughes did not participate. McReynolds had retired but had not been replaced. The seven sitting Justices agreed that this* primary *election fraud did deny Constitutional rights. Douglas, Black, and Murphy went beyond the opinion of the Court, indicating they would have flatly overruled the import of the* Newberry *decision in that all primary elections involved Constitutional rights which Congress could protect by legislation. They dissented, however, from the application of broad civil rights legislation to criminal proceedings arising from primary election frauds on grounds that all criminal statutes should be strictly construed, applicable only to specific acts covered by such statutes. The opinion of the Court by Mr. Justice Stone did not men-*

Table 12-2 (cont.)

tion the white primary, but it was evident that the principles he laid down in the Classic *case conflicted with the* Grovey *rule.*

Smith v. Allwright, 321 U.S. 649 (1944). Smith, a black was refused a ballot to cast in the Democratic primary in Houston, Texas of July 27, 1940, for the nomination of candidates for the United States Senate, House of Representatives, Governor and other state officials. The refusal was solely on account of his race and color. By an 8 to 1 margin the Court held, in an opinion by Mr. Justice Reed, that the primary was "an integral part of the elective process," that state statutes were involved and that the rule of the Texas state convention taken with all of this "was State action in violation of the Fifteenth Amendment." *Grovey v. Townsend* was flatly overruled. Mr. Justice Roberts bitterly dissented against this overruling. The decision was announced on April 3, 1944.

Terry v. Adams, 345 U.S. 461 (1953). Apart from efforts by the State and the Party to exclude blacks from voting in Texas Democratic primaries, the Jaybird Democratic Association in Fort Bend County, Texas had, since 1889 conducted white preprimaries with the organization endorsed officials later winning the Democratic primary, after 1905, and the general election. Extending its *Allwright* ruling, the Court, per Justice Black held, 8 to 1, that the discriminatory practices of the Jaybird Democratic Association were prohibited as "state action" under the Fifteenth Amendment. Concurring opinion by Frankfurter and Clark developed somewhat different rationales and Minton filed a bitter dissent.

bThe *Newberry* and *Classic* cases in italics where Federal actions whose results had an impact on the Texas white primary cases described in this table.

state executive committee acted "solely by virtue of the statutory mandate and as delegate of state power." But in *Grovey* there was no state statute and, consequently, no "state action." The same condition prevailed in the denial of a ballot to Lonnie E. Smith. But Mr. Justice Roberts dwelled on the societal values of precedent and his complaints about overruling have gained some fame for this was but the beginning of a new flurry of overrulings which carried on through the period of the Warren Court.

But the majority had not overruled *Grovey v. Townsend* lightly. Their position seems explicable by noting that a combination of explanatory variables were present as the case came to decision. The nation was at war and, increasingly, World War II became a war celebrating the virtues in the breach so far as American blacks were concerned. The president had already shown a response to black claims to equality by establishing a Fair Employment Practices Committee by executive order. The Supreme Court had been turning away from the old domestic issues of governmental regulatory power over economic matters that marked its work so strongly into the late 1930s. Moreover, the *Smith v. Allwright* case was well briefed and argued as the skills of Thurgood Marshall and his team associated with the Legal Defense Fund sharpened. There were new members on the Supreme Court, too, seven of them appointed by President Roosevelt and, while they would have their disagreements on principle and innumerable personality conflicts, they tended strongly to join together in cases concerning race relations.

There remains one incident within the Supreme Court in disposing of *Smith v. Allwright* which indicates something of the confused attitudes of diplomacy that may occasionally mark judicial behavior. It was the assignment of the opinion by Mr. Chief Justice Stone. Immediately after hearing the case argued in January 1944, it was evident that eight members of the Court favored an overruling which would surely go far to extinguish the white primary in the South. Frankfurter was conversant with the subject; he had written the opinion in *Lane v. Wilson*, and Stone assigned the opinion in *Smith v. Allwright* to him. But in a gesture that surely expressed a latent, if not a patent, anti-Semitism, Robert H. Jackson, a recently named justice, urged Stone to change his mind because such an opinion by a man who was both a New Englander and a Jew would "grate on Southern sensibilities."[106] Stone changed his mind, asked Stanley Reed, a Democrat from Tennessee to prepare the opinion, which he did. Frankfurter then simply concurred but without opinion.

Jackson's judgment was wrong. Soon after the opinion was announced, the Texas State Bar Association condemned the Supreme Court in language that would not have been stronger had another written the opinion.

But now blacks were entitled to vote in primary elections in Texas and it was the belief of V.O. Key that *Smith v. Allwright* quite promptly had an effect on Texas campaigns and elections. Yet more litigation and, finally in the 1960s, national legislation would be needed to give to blacks substantial power at southern polls.

Part II: Findings and Recommendations

13 Litigation in the Web of Social Movements

Acknowledgment of litigation as a fundamental means of shaping public policy in the United States is a departure point for going beyond single case histories. The individual case must necessarily be the focus of counsel and judges whatever their vision of the larger social issues may be. Cases may be linked together when their relationship is evident and they appear at approximately the same time on the same docket. The law reporters and journalists likewise will report developments as cases are decided, and practitioners and law students absorb the new rulings as they are handed down. The particular case and the annual term of the Supreme Court are compelling frames for absorbing legal developments. A central point of this study has been that these necessary boundaries must be supplemented by students of constitutional law to embrace larger periods of time inhabited not only by judges and lawyers for particular voluntary associations but also by those rather amorphous institutions called social movements.

A social movement embraces varied, and to some extent discordant, collective efforts spread over a time span of one or more generations to achieve economic, social or political change. There may be social movements that never resort to litigation but this is uncommon in the United States. The term social movement is not used here for analysis, but simply to string together seemingly separate events to reveal relationships for purposes of a more adequate description of the nature of constitutional litigation. A conscious effort to see litigation in this light aids understanding of constitutional change and may, with application, provide a better means of analyzing judicial behavior than any other single methodology now available.

Taken alone in the casebook, *Buck v. Bell* broadens the policy power of a state under the Constitution. This case is understood in a different way in this book as a key episode in the eugenics movement. In this context the case is placed at the high point—in the middle 1920s—of a social movement that began at the end of the nineteenth century, gained many goals and then fell into disrepute through scientific criticism and political excess, especially in Nazi Germany, in the 1930s and 1940s. *Buck v. Bell* was not the brainchild of a single voluntary association. Although the Eugenics Records Office functioned very like a classic pressure group, it did not manage litigation as such. It has been shown that the gospel of eugenics and the teachings of the efficacy of compulsory procreative sterilization of mental misfits were widely disseminated. That these views were adopted in remote places and advanced in legislative and

329

judicial settings by humble social workers, physicians, nurses, doctors and others is exhibited in the story of the Virginia eugenics case of *Buck v. Bell.* It is simply one instance where a leading constitutional case can be linked to a social movement better than to the lawyers or to a voluntary association or interest group.

Because minority rights is a democratic value whose protection under the Constitution has traditionally been protected by the judiciary, there is a special appropriateness for small, organized interests to work through litigation. There is now sufficient evidence of participation in constitutional tests by organizations to advance with firmness the belief that organized interests turn to litigation as readily as they do to legislation. Twenty years ago there was almost no support for this idea in published scholarly work on the judicial process. Arthur F. Bentley in 1908 and then David B. Truman in 1951 asserted that interest groups dealt with public policy wherever formed, including the courts, but there were few findings to support the assertion, and Bentley and Truman provided almost no documentation. It is now clear that the phenomenon of interest group participation in constitutional cases was present long ago, when Bentley wrote as well as when Truman did. The simple fact is that studies of the way organizations sought their goals through the courts had not been undertaken partly because few held the needed explanatory concept of group politics and nobody undertook the research to provide documentary support.

Like journalists who accept official press releases as new, constitutional historians, legal scholars and social scientists have often taken the official styling of a case and the lawyers listed in the court reports as sufficient information about the participants in litigation. This feeling is exemplified in David Truman's *The Governmental Process*, wherein he names organizations listed in official reports as filing *amici curiae* briefs. No doubt this supports his point, but such evidence has been overused since it is easier to document than the much more significant fact that, if organizations are important in litigation, they will be found closely linked to the parties in the case.

Evidence in this book shows repeatedly how organizations that were exceedingly active in Supreme Court litigation never, or hardly ever, came in as *amicus curiae.* Eugenics organizations did not, either in the many state cases or in the Supreme Court test of *Buck v. Bell.* Their position was customarily represented by an attorney for the state government whom the Eugenics Records Office aided directly or indirectly. The Roman Catholic Church, the Scottish Rites Masons and the Ku Klux Klan were similarly quiet participants in the Oregon school monopoly case of *Pierce v. Society of the Sisters.* This book shows, for the first time, the numerous instances where the Anti-Saloon League of America argued in court in defense of prohibition laws. Similarly, the National Consumers' League worked closely with state governors and attorneys general in the constitutional defense of protective labor laws, introducing the Brandeis sociological brief in the process. The National Association for the

Advancement of Colored People has been very closely the most active of all organizations in Supreme Court litigation. In 1916 in its very first case, the NAACP appeared as *amicus curiae* to support the federal government's attack on the Oklahoma grandfather clause, and it is an organization that has filed other such briefs in recent years. For the most part, however, the NAACP has provided the direct legal defense of parties, usually defendants, in Supreme Court cases.

This study of constitutional change contributes an understanding of the development of American public law but falls far short of providing an adequate theory of it. A strong obstacle lies in the difficulty of speaking both concretely and abstractly about elements which promise to illuminate this subject. Individuals, voluntary associations and governmental organizations possess a certain concreteness. Concepts of interest groups and social movements have attractive appeal which is diminished by an elusive abstract quality when put to work. These are treacherous topics, calling for an effort to distinguish between clearly supportable findings and propositions that are more speculative.

Further study of the relationship between voluntary associations and constitutional change should also be stimulated by this study which certainly raises more questions than it answers. It is still not clear precisely how traits of associations such as membership size, wealth, intensity, alliances, skill, durability and persistence bear upon legal outcomes. Since we do not know, it would be foolish to claim that we do. It is appropriate, nevertheless, to summarize the findings about voluntary associations with appropriate qualifying points.

Names of organizations and claims of persons representing them are often poor guides to their size, wealth, cohesiveness, internal governance and representativeness. This is hardly a novel observation but yet deserves underlining. While it is true of associations in relation to newspaper advertisements directed at the public or statements aimed at legislators, it is uniquely relevant to a consideration of their participation in litigation.

Many legal action organizations have no members whatever, only a board and a legal staff, owing to the internal revenue code set by Congress in the 1930s. Under a key provision, tax exemption was permitted for organizations that litigated but barred for those that sought to influence legislation. NAACP leaders took advantage of this provision and incorporated an independent NAACP Legal Defense and Educational Fund. This Fund has gradually gained absolute independence from the NAACP and, consequently, in hundreds of cases its position is determined by an exceedingly small number of persons. In contrast, the NAACP itself has continued as a membership organization with thousands of chapters but with a litigation arm also. Also organized separately (as the NAACP Special Contribution Fund) but serving under NAACP trustees, its staff occasionally bridled over this dependence.

The range in types of voluntary associations having some role in constitutional litigation is remarkable. The *Pierce* case revealed that the Knights of Columbus and the Scottish Rites Masons provided funds and legal counsel. The

Prohibition cases, among others, saw Anti-Saloon League of America lawyers pitted against counsel for the American Brewers' Association. The Eugenics Records Office, with support from Mrs. Harriman and the Carnegie Institution of Washington, has also been typed as an organization engaged in litigation by fronting for the work of Harry H. Laughlin. Political parties have often been litigants, as seen by the activities of the Republican State Committee of Maryland in the grandfather clause case of 1907 to 1915 and the Texas Democrats in creating and defending the white primary between 1921 and 1944.

In cases contesting woman suffrage, maternity aid and child labor legislation in the 1920s and 1930s, a tiny organization called the Sentinels of the Republic sponsored Supreme Court cases. In 1970 one challenge to the validity of legislation permitting persons eighteen years old to vote was supported by the Conservative party of New York. In 1971 the new John Gardner group, Common Cause, began court action against the national party committees for ignoring statutory limits on campaign spending. Additionally there are numerous voluntary associations already well known as oriented toward legal action, including the National Consumers' League, the American Jewish Committee, the American Jewish Congress, the American Civil Liberties Union and the NAACP organizations.

Depicting relationships among organizations offers numerous difficulties which can be solved only when consistent measures of goals, size, leadership, finance, methods, success and so on are accurately determined. Investigation of groups opposing prohibition shows that they evolved into groups opposed to federal grants-in-aid for social welfare and to the New Deal. Members of these, in turn, were early comrades against woman suffrage and, for some, black suffrage as well. Looking at the organizations—most of which were shortlived—the idea of a genealogy was spawned. Figure 13-1 affords a ready view of the genealogy of some conservative organizations actively concerned with constitutional issues in the period from 1915 to 1945.

The proliferation of organizations today presents a tremendous problem for even the crudest analysis. In the environmental field, for example, one will go from office to office in New York and Washington only to learn that he has missed by chance the really critical, creative and significant lawyer or organization. The National Wildlife Federation prepares an annual directory of more than a thousand organizations concerned with the environment and a number of these are now considering or actually pressing litigation.[1]

In conclusion, these points are clear: (1) Most constitutional cases before the Supreme Court of the United States are sponsored or supported by an identifiable voluntary association. (2) This support is not new; it has been markedly true for decades. The fact that voluntary associations engage in constitutional litigation may simply be more visible today. This conclusion directly contradicts the impression that the Court does not deal with "planned litigation" and that attorneys and their clients mostly do not "raise funds, secure

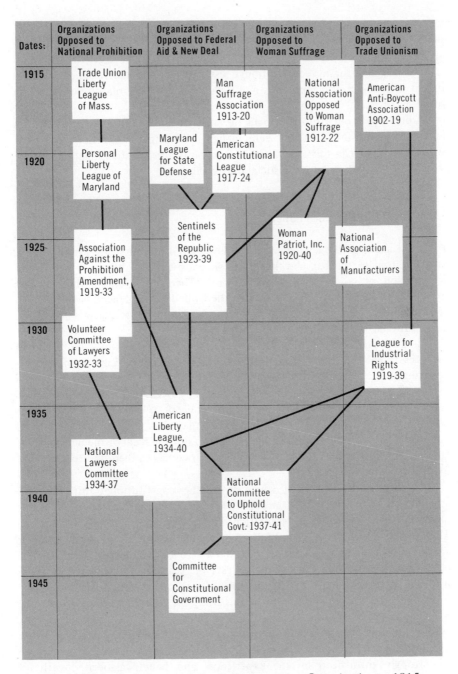

Figure 13-1. Genealogy of Some Conservative Organizations, 1915–1945.

additional representation, coordinate with other litigants, or employ research, publicity, or *amici curiae* activity to broaden the scope or political significance of their litigation efforts."[2] (3) It is believed that the role of voluntary associations in planning constitutional test cases is so pervasive and profound that it calls for careful reporting, and a close study by journalists, lawyers and social scientists.

As one moves out from the focus of single cases, however, new relationships in constitutional litigation are seen. In light of existing conceptions, the most significant finding in this study is that fluctuations in constitutional change are expressive of conflicts between social movements.

Lawyers on Constitutional Policy

Persons learned in the law, trained in a law school or apprenticed in an office, and admitted to the bar play key roles in constitutional litigation and in the formulation of constitutional amendments. The courts require that lawyers argue before them. Legislative bodies in the United States depend heavily, if not so exclusively, on the word of lawyers, especially in those matters felt to be constitutional.

The adversary system which pits lawyer against lawyer, assumes that each will bring essentially the same skills into service for his client. Like members of a debating society, each could as readily take the other side. This model, in fact, is achieved or comes close to achievement on many occasions. Its idealism led an earlier generation of lawyers to develop the concept of legal aid and provide for court-appointed attorneys for the indigent. Today that program is often looked back on with scorn as an inadequate palliative. But the ideal of the neutrality of lawyers and of their readiness to serve whoever comes to their door persists and is fulfilled on many occasions.

Yet this model does not square with the constitutional litigation and amendment skirmishes related in this study, where the representation of a client qua client is rare and the representation of a cause or point of view is common. The constitutional lawyer is committed to a goal and the clients in a particular adjudication are simply necessary instruments to be dealt with at the tactical level. To be sure, this generalization rests on scattered instances, but those instances have been made to yield up this truth through research far beyond the formal record. It can be inferred from this study that the same result will emerge from examination of other cases.

The findings presented here support the view that the types of cases a lawyer handles, the kinds of clients he represents, and his conception of counsel's role are strongly influenced by the experiences and beliefs associated with his nonlawyer characteristics.[3] The lawyers observed in this book offer several different kinds of proofs.

Some lawyers gain so strong a passion for a social objective that they never conduct a serious practice but move directly into whatever work they believe will advance their cause. Mrs. Florence Kelley and Madison Grant are examples. Their positions on public policy and on constitutional change were not merely different but antithetical, yet their behavior as lawyers was similar. Mrs. Kelley devoted her life to seeking protective labor legislation, to alleviating the difficulties immigrants and women and children faced in the industrial and urban jungle. She served on boards of directors of many Progressive action organizations and was noted for her leadership of the National Consumers' League. Madison Grant worked to conserve wildlife and to protect white, Anglo-Saxon Protestant society from immigration and other "defilements." Like Mrs. Kelley, Grant was a publicist and also a man who worked behind the scenes. Their legal training contributed to their skills, but did not affect their values. Nor did they ever do much in the way of practicing law.

Choice of a cause in advance of seeking the bar is most apposite to the principle that lawyers commonly make constitutional choices in accord with their personal, social and political attributes. The career of Wayne Bidwell Wheeler is an illustration. As an Oberlin College student in the 1890s Wheeler was persuaded that alcohol had to be eliminated because of its significant, immoral impact on society. He joined the Anti-Saloon League, and after some service in the field determined that legal training would help his effectiveness. He became a lawyer and a key draftsman as well as an enforcement agent and legal defender of numerous state, local and national temperance laws. His status as a lawyer meant that he was the chief prohibition lawyer in Supreme Court cases settling the constitutionality of the Webb-Kenyon Act, the Eighteenth Amendment and the Volstead Act.

Behind Wheeler's decision on the evils of drink lay the kind of family, social, religious and educational conditions which accounted for the kind of strong individual preferences which, in many cases, explain legal careers. This is not always easy to do and there are exceptions. Lawyers mature and change as does the world around them, but there is clearly some connection between early experience and outlook and the later constitutional stands of conservatives like William Marbury, Henry St. George Tucker, James M. Beck and William D. Guthrie, and lawyers like Louis D. Brandeis, Moorfield Storey and Louis Marshall.

Further efforts at explaining the attitudes of lawyers in relationship to background need to be undertaken. This study shows that black lawyers worked for the expansion of civil rights, but it does not explain why more did not nor why some white lawyers forwarded the NAACP cause. Women lawyers served the National Woman's party in minimum wage cases but other women opposed that organization. A single trait usually raises more questions than it answers. It seems true, nevertheless, that the single trait of being a lawyer contributes a small clue to a person's stance on a constitutional issue. Racial, religious, sex, regional and class traits contribute much more to understanding. Although there is danger in making this an exercise in circular reasoning by defining constitutional change in precisely these same terms of racial, religious and other social, economic and political traits, the characterization of lawyers as products of nonlegal influences holds much truth.

Nonlawyers sometimes assume the role of a lawyer in advancing particular social and constitutional objectives, which indicates how shaky professional distinctions can sometimes be. Josephine Goldmark served Brandeis and Mary W. Dewson served Frankfurter in preparing briefs in defense of protective labor legislation in major Supreme Court cases. Their names sometimes appeared on briefs and they did the substantial share of research and writing. We have seen that in 1912 a selection of the early Brandeis briefs was edited by Josephine Goldmark in the book *Fatigue and Efficiency*. On the subject of eugenics another nonlawyer, Harry Hamilton Laughlin, undertook the work of preparing a model law and a compendium of court rulings to guide advocates, whether lawyers or not, and legislators and judges. The result was that his *State Eugenical Sterilization* book of 1923 was the standard for the field. His role in advising lawyers in constitutional cases and in his appearance as an expert witness in *Buck v. Bell* indicates that he was active in promoting and defending the constitutionality of eugenical sterilization.

As the subject matter becomes specialized, it frequently happens that nonlawyers among the top experts function in ways that are essentially lawyerlike, a development concealed by rules and practices ordaining that only members of the bar conduct litigation. The examples of Goldmark, Dewson and Laughlin—again with dissimilar values though not in direct opposition—could easily be enlarged upon.

Attributes of Constitutional Litigation

By first placing the role of lawyers and the politics of litigation in the web of rival social movements it is now possible to define leading characteristics of the development of constitutional policy in the courts. In addition to support from the studies in this book, these characteristics rest on findings in other studies on the judicial process, especially in those listed in the bibliography, and on other developments observed but not yet described in print.

First, the Supreme Court ordinarily reaches a settled constitutional position only after decades of litigation on a subject. The right for blacks to vote was not assured by the Fifteenth Amendment in 1870 but rather by the destruction of the grandfather clause and of the white primary in litigation conducted almost constantly over a period of forty years. Nor was that all. There were many voting rights cases in the nineteenth century and there have been many others since the chief white primary cases from Texas were decided. Similar patterns mark the litigation over protective labor legislation, the right of trades unions to collective bargaining, the rights of persons accused of crime to counsel and other protections, judicial standards for the apportionment and districting of Congress and state legislatures and so on.

Second, persistent effort emanating from a social movement often marks the evolution of constitutional decision by the Supreme Court in a given field. These efforts will often be made by an organization that brings corporate traits to the task. Its resources include devotion to a cause with sensitivity to matters of timing, funds to pay mundane costs, members to serve as parties to an action, lawyers and others to manage long-term pursuit of remedies. These are the kinds of assets held by such organizations as the Anti-Saloon League, the NAACP, the National Consumers' League, the Jehovahs Witnesses, the American Jewish Congress, the American Civil Liberties Union, the Knights of Columbus and the Scottish Rites Masons.

In contrast, stray individuals do not normally possess the resources to conduct litigation over a long period. Those individuals who do figure in litigation independent of an organization may be mavericks who nonetheless serve the purposes of the larger social movement. This has been quite evidently true of Vashti McCullom and Madalyn Murray O'Hair in initiating challenges to sectarian practices in the public schools. It was certainly true of the lawyers who won validation of a state law requiring a minimum wage for women to the Supreme Court in *West Coast Hotel Company v. Parrish*, litigation about which the National Consumers' League was unaware until the case appeared on the 1936-37 docket.

When the Supreme Court ruled state legislative apportionment to be a subject for federal judiciary scrutiny, Carey McWilliams writing in the *Nation* depicted "the eleven individual plaintiffs" as irate city dwellers. He concluded that this was "in the American grain: on deadlocked issues, the individual citizen, rather than the organized interest groups, is most likely to set the democratic process in motion."[4] This is romantic stuff reflecting the populistic bias of the *Nation*. *Baker v. Carr* was litigation organized by a group of city attorneys in the big cities of Tennessee which enlisted the aid of the National Institute of Municipal Law Officers, the National Conference of Mayors, the National Municipal League and the League of Women Voters.

Third, to win judicial satisfaction, petitions to review numerous cases are made to the Supreme Court over a period of years. The initiative of counsel in starting litigation and carrying their cases to the Supreme Court is comparable to legislators who introduce the same bill in every term. A legislative majority cannot enact a statute unless a bill is introduced; this is the way the legislative process is set in motion. Legislators do not always expect to succeed the first time they try for passage. A judicial majority cannot make a decision unless a case is before them; this is the way the judicial process is set in motion. Those who seek major legal change through the courts also do not expect to succeed in the first case they bring. What gives hope to those who start these processes is a subject of some cultural, psychological and political depth—we know that many legislative and litigious campaigns have been failures—which will be given some attention in the events before us; it is clear, though, as a first proposition, that the mechanics are essential to make an overruling possible.

The persistence of the NAACP and its allies in voting cases, of the eugenics advocates, of the Consumers' League and others is a key feature of the moments of success these groups have enjoyed. Manwaring has shown that the Jehovahs Witnesses won review in 1940 of the compulsory flag salute only after six petitions had been rejected in the 1930s. Similarly, the Supreme Court failed on eleven occasions to grant review of legislative apportionment before doing so in *Baker v. Carr* in 1962. For twenty years the Supreme Court declined to consider on its merits the validity of a state miscegenation statute until it did so in *Loving v. Virginia* in 1971.

Fourth, when the United States appears in a case—whether as party, as intervenor or as *amicus curiae*—the know-how and resources of the solicitor general are of such a high order that this is very likely to determine the outcome. Professor Dixon has demonstrated this significance in the key reapportionment case of *Baker v. Carr* where Solicitor General Archibald Cox played a key role for the United States as *amicus curiae*. Mr. Justice Frankfurter has insisted in the first oral argument that Tennessee's apportionment could be a violation of the Tennessee constitution without also, necessarily, being a violation of the Fourteenth Amendment. He thus rejected a central assertion made by Charles S. Rhyne.[5] Professor Dixon believes it was not Rhyne who carried the chief burden in the case but Solicitor General Cox who presented "the ultimately victorious theory that Tennessee's current apportionment practice constituted a violation of a federal right—whatever the nature of the state constitution."[6]

This was Dixon's conclusion on this matter:

Although Mr. Rhyne was widely credited with bringing the courts into the political thicket in *Baker v. Carr*, one might wonder whether the outcome would have been the same without the *amicus* brief and argument of the solicitor general. This initial plaintiff theory, analyzed away by Justice Frankfurter, and deemed "manifestly untenable" by Justice Harlan, was ignored by the Court majority.[7]

The rules of the Supreme Court allow the solicitor general of the United States full freedom to enter a case as *amicus curiae*. Others must have permission of the parties, or of the Court as cases arise. This legal status combined with the expertise possessed by the office of the solicitor general, invariably aids the side of the case supported. As the solicitor general himself is ordinarily a distinguished and experienced advocate, his appearance as *amicus curiae* in oral argument before the Court taken together with the masterful written briefs of his office put strong weight behind his preferences. Since the outcome favored will quite certainly be a part of the program of the president and of the attorney general then the Court is assured that one co-equal branch of the government has weighted the policy issues raised in the litigation and has decided to support one solution. Where innovation in the law is called for, this assures the Court that its decision will be supported by the administration, particularly by the Department of Justice.

In the period since 1940 when the solicitor general acted as *amicus curiae* in litigation where the United States was not a party for the first time he has always been on the winning side. This was true in the *Mitchell* and *Henderson* cases, involving discrimination in railroad Pullman and dining cars, the *Restrictive Covenant Cases*, and the *School Segregation Cases*. In *Baker v. Carr* the lapse of time from May 1960 to March 1962 allowed solicitor generals in two administrations to declare themselves. Lee Rankin, solicitor general from 1956 to 1961, and Attorney General William Rogers under Republican President Eisenhower entered the case as *amicus curiae* in 1960 and this positive decision was reinforced under President Kennedy, Attorney General Robert Kennedy and Solicitor General Cox.

14 Amendment as Legislative Politics

The rarity of formal amendment under the American Constitution has been directly connected to the blossoming of judicial review in 1803. This happened early even though amendment was expressly provided for while judicial review was not. Edmond Cahn has argued that the triumph of judicial review was in keeping with the goal of the framers to make the Constitution open to change. Provision for any change was an eighteenth-century novelty, according to Cahn, but the experience of only a decade led Americans to accept judicial action as a better mode of change than amendment.

The small number of amendments adopted in this century—they are only eleven in number—attests to national satisfaction with governance by regular legislation, administration and judicial review. In contrast to these governing routines the amendment process is treacherous because it is so little used. Because amendments are needed only when other modes fail, they tend to deal with extreme situations and are thus either very concrete or quite abstract. So much can be accomplished in American government by regularly used means that special circumstances account for amendments.

Advocacy of constitutional change by amendment is often emblematic of frustrated causes. An amendment may be a last resort, a means of dramatizing a need and a claim on the future for the legitimacy of certain goals and values. Controversy over an amendment is ordinarily simply one part of wider political conflict but a part that is often highly symbolic. At its broadest level the amendments advocated by Progressives symbolized a distrust of the judiciary and of ordinary legislation in much the same way as the initiative, referendum, recall, taxpayer suits and other popular government programs of the day. In the same spirit in recent years conservatives have claimed the president and the Supreme Court were out of touch with the people and that constitutional amendments afforded a means of redress. If an amendment then fails even to be proposed, its supporters—like true believers in a small sect—undaunted, are likely to persist and become ever more zealous in carrying a conviction about the constitutional legitimacy of their position. They believe—and there are occasional historical proofs—that they will someday overcome. Meanwhile their amendment stands in their minds as a symbolic alternative to prevailing but illegitimate constitutional policy. Understanding of the amendment process has suffered through the years from a view that sees rules and procedures as less political than something called "substantive."

Discussions of the amendment process have been perennially couched in terms of whether it is too easy or difficult. When the Supreme Court treated ambiguities in the amendment procedure as political questions academic regrets were offered. Interest in amendments has often been in arid legality rather than in political realities. There has been insufficient recognition that controversy over the amendment process is a function of something else, a commitment for or against a government policy on social, economic or political matters. If a given amending procedure is deemed more or less likely to result in a certain amendment's proposal and ratification, then the attitudes about process have an anchor in policy preferences.

Amendment controversialists usually differ over social policy, government organization, power and procedure. Opponents to Amendments Fifteen, Eighteen, Nineteen, and child labor insisted that conventions in the states were an essential ingredient to the constitutionality of the process. They pointed to legislatures as easy marks for lobbyists, and argued state legislatures were often not representative of the people. They urged in unsuccessful litigation that the process of ratification was a justiciable question, properly resolved by the Supreme Court rather than by the political branches. But the great affection of these same interests and individuals for the "popular will," conventions, judicial review of amendments crumbled when American politics was transformed in the 1930s. Then they attacked the Court, sought amendments themselves and found the state legislatures more dependable allies than the people who elected Roosevelt, Truman, Eisenhower, Kennedy and Johnson.

In the 1910-40 period, the Progressive spirit expressed itself by supporting a string of constitutional amendments which were anathema to the social conservative, states rights mind. The circumstances of power distribution among major governmental institutions in the United States during this era, though complex and changing, made possible the formal proposal by Congress of several constitutional amendments. State legislatures, elected on a district basis, rightly were deemed sufficient carriers of the middle-class virtues to act as ratifying bodies for the prohibition and woman suffrage amendments. Surprisingly, because of their origins as Progressive reform mechanisms, taxpayer suits and state-wide referenda became favorite weapons of opponents of these amendments. When a federal child labor amendment was proposed to the legislatures in 1924, popular opposition was dramatized by a state-wide advisory referendum in Massachusetts. In 1933, when repeal could muster the requisite vote in Congress, wets regarded the legislatures as heavily weighted against them. Because legislatures were seen as obstacles to ratification of repeal Congress specified the State Convention method. This was in response to the urgings of the Association Against the Prohibition Amendment and the Voluntary Committee of Lawyers, who recommended at-large election of delegates to ratify the Twenty-first Amendment. This method worked.

That men had opposed national constitutional regulation of suffrage, alcoholic beverages or child labor made the wisest strategic and tactical moves possible for them occasions no surprise. But they were shortsighted in defining democracy essentially in terms of their temporary strategic posture. They attacked state legislative ratification in the federal judiciary. They praised state ratifying conventions and referenda until times changed and FDR's popularity at the polls dictated a strategy of legislative ratification of the Twenty-second Amendment limiting a president to two terms. In this instance the content of the amendment and the procedure for ratification showed the sponsors' distrust of popular, at-large elections.

Constitutional amendments are a form of legislation to be studied empirically by students of elections, of pressure groups, and of the lawmaking institutions. A knowledge of Congress, of propaganda and the climate of state legislation are all essential.

From the portrayal of amendment politics between 1910 and the 1940s six characteristics can be distilled.

First, a constitutional amendment is legislative in character, with specific alternative procedures so that proponents will choose strategies for proposal in Congress and ratification in the states which maximize support.

Second, advocates of states rights and state sovereignty during the period from 1865 to 1937 counted on the Supreme Court and judicial review as the best means to curb claims made for national power over social, economic and political subjects. Their basic position and theory was antagonistic to the growth of national authority whether by acts of Congress or by constitutional amendments.

And we know that Populists and Progressives, all who favored the extension of government power to regulate and correct social ills, tended in these years to have the greatest leverage in Congress and the state legislatures, relative to other governmental institutions. As these institutions represented one path of constitutional amendments this form of legislation became a viable means for seeking reform. Many ideas for progressive amendments failed in Congress. The child labor amendment succeeded there but failed ratification in the state legislatures. Prohibition, as well as the income tax, popular election of senators and woman suffrage must be counted as essentially Progressive amendments.

In defense of state sovereignty, a group of conservative lawyers—notably Arthur W. Machen, Jr., William L. Marbury and Henry St. George Tucker— spelled out a legal theory that placed intrinsic limits on constitutional amendments. By their theory, for example, enlargement of a state's constituency through suffrage amendments was not permissible. The total body of writing on the permissible scope of amendments shows this theory to be a transparent attack on the participation of blacks or women in elections and on government prohibition of liquor or child labor, a theory bolstered by the related attitudes on other public issues of these men and of Thomas F. Cadwalader, Alexander Lincoln, Elihu Root, William D. Guthrie, James M. Beck and of organizations such as the Sentinels of the Republic and the Woman Patriots.

Convention ratification was championed by critics of amendments proposed between 1918 and 1924 and by proponents of repeal in 1933 because of its strategic value. At-large election of convention delegates was preferred over district voting. In the 1940s conservatives shifted from this preference to favor legislative ratification. They also objected to at-large voting in presidential elections and favored an electoral college constituted by district elections. There is sufficient continuity among men and organizations with a states rights outlook to indicate that the preference for convention ratifications was strategic, not principled, as time and circumstance saw the preference evaporate.

Lastly, the comparative merits of legislatures and conventions as state ratifying bodies depend on the electoral system, the campaign and internal practices. Many considerations, such as the enormous experience Americans have had with legislatures as compared to special ratifying constitutions, should enter into the assessment. The single experience with convention ratification in 1933, where pledged delegations elected at-large were the rule, was much like a straight referendum. By so classifying the convention the basic issue becomes one of comparing referenda to legislatures as an instrument of the popular will. The literature on this subject is large and complex, but it strongly questions a conclusion that referendas or conventions represent the millennium for democracy.

The written United States Constitution needs constantly to be revised, and its revisions, whether by amendment, statute, ruling or order, also need clarification. There are an exceedingly high number of changes advocated compared with the number acceded to. This has been a general condition of American constitutional law through its history. While the ten amendments embodying the Bill of Rights were adopted early in the 1790s, only five amendments were added in the 1800s and eleven more in this century so far. In the last three decades the best-known measures, mostly nonamendments, have been provoked by the decisions of the Supreme Court and by presidential action. This is due to what Ralph Gabriel, in his *Course of American Democratic Thought*, called the cult of the Constitution and of the amendment procedure.

The cult of the American Constitution is akin to the reliance on Biblical text of religious fundamentalism, for it assumes that a written instrument has easily discernible meanings. It rests, also, on the inescapable fact that certain textual language is so specific that close to one hundred percent of the public are in agreement. For those parts especially concerning dates, very specific changes and rules of eligibility may be advocated. Otherwise, amendments are urged on occasions when the Court or the president has been thought to have misinterpreted the original, true meaning of the text. A clarifying amendment may be needed.

An attachment to formal amendments as having superior pedigree, virtue and legitimacy to the decisions of judges or presidents is normal. When a group gains satisfaction from the judges and presidents in power, it ordinarily sheds its preoccupation with formal amendment. The heirs of the Progressives were not much interested in amendments after about 1941, by which time the Supreme Court had upheld the constitutionality of federal power to regulate child labor and other New Deal measures.

After studying amendment politics for the period 1910 to the present, it comes as a surprise to conclude that an historical treatment of constitutional amendments—advocated, proposed or ratified—explains less about amendments themselves than about governmental structure and procedure. The subject matter, the motivations, the alliance of interests vary over the years, but the procedures, the arguments, the strategies and tactics have a certain consistency attached to the constitutional order itself. A long time-frame is critical to understanding because it shows how the same substantive sides reverse their procedural positions. Observations limited to one era will confuse this picture by making particular criticisms of institutions appear timeless when they are not. In adopting the structural approach for this chapter, past examples of the different types of amendments named above will be referred to in identifying some of the leading recent, current and prospective amendments.

Advocacy of an amemdment to the Constitution usually stems from one or a combination of these considerations: (1) As a higher law, the existing constitutional text cannot be changed by ordinary legislation and so both in a symbolic sense and in a technical sense an amendment appears to be required. (2) As a federal constitutional system in which some state practices cannot be reached by ordinary acts of the national government, an amendment may be required to apply practices of some states to recalcitrant states. (3) The reverse may come into play, when frustrated provincial interests seek amendments to regulate or limit national power. (4) Amendments are aimed at specific national institutions, occasionally Congress but more commonly the Supreme Court and the presidency. One purpose of such amendments is to alter the method of selection of, the authority of, or procedures followed by the president and the Supreme Court. (5) Amendments may be limited to overcoming particular acts or rulings of a governmental body, especially ones of the Supreme Court and the president.

Amendments against the Presidency

Franklin D. Roosevelt's bid in 1940 for a third term first evoked a rather comic effort to return to the "true principles of the Constitution" even though the text set no limit of presidential tenure. Opponents in Congress hastily called hearings to record their offense at Roosevelt's audacity. Those testifying had remarkable genealogical credentials but little else. Among them was a small collection of descendants of American presidents.[1] After FDR was elected to both a third term and a fourth, this opposition turned out to be something more than lampoon. The Republican Eightieth Congress in 1947 voted to propose an amendment limiting a president to two terms and the requisite number of states completed ratification in 1951. This Twenty-second Amendment did not apply to Harry Truman, who was then president, but it was otherwise strict by providing:

No person shall be elected to the office of the President more than twice, and no person who has held the office of President, or acted as President, for more than two years of a term to which some other person was elected President shall be elected to the office of President more than once.[2]

Although Dwight D. Eisenhower, the first president to be elected after the ratification of the Twenty-second Amendment, later repudiated this measure, there appears little chance and currently no interest for its repeal.[3]

Champions of presidential power as asserted by Roosevelt and Truman, and in the domestic field by Kennedy and Johnson, have been largely disenchanted with this resource. Where they once saw eternal verities they have come to see human failing and turned against the presidency as an institution in much the same way that conservative critics did in the 1930s and 1940s.[4]

The Bricker Amendment

As a constitutional barrier to the president and the national government no proposal generated as much political heat in the 1950s as the Bricker amendment. It became a rallying point for the modern states rights forces because it seemed calculated to give to the rural areas in the sparsely populated states some veto over the national government's treaty-making power, by declaring that no treaty shall affect the internal law of an individual state without the approval of the state. As governor of Ohio from 1939 to 1945 and as the Republican nominee for vice president of the United States in 1944, John W. Bricker was a practiced opponent of FDR's use of presidential power in foreign affairs. As a senator between 1946 and 1958 he made this his special focus. He particularly opposed the use by Roosevelt, Truman and Eisenhower of the executive agreement, a counterpart in foreign policy to the executive order in domestic policy. His formulation changed somewhat over the years but was consistently aimed at presidential reliance on the supremacy clause of the Constitution as a basis of discretion in international matters.[5]

The movement for the Bricker amendment was driven by a constitutional myth that formal limitations are more important than capabilities of power. One section of the proposal provides that any treaty contrary to constitutional restrictions would be void. Critics argued that this was already the case, but defenders pointed to the incontrovertible fact that no treaty had ever been declared unconstitutional. Despite the fact that no treaty can become the law of the land without presidential endorsement and a two-thirds vote of the United

States Senate, proponents of the Bricker scheme insisted that an amendment was needed to require review by the Supreme Court in case the Constitution were violated.

Although constitutional limitations would have been reinforced, the most significant goal was to cut into the power and independence of the president in foreign policy. The support given to this measure by John Foster Dulles when he was briefly a Republican senator from New York and then a preelection adviser to Eisenhower, suggested that the Bricker amendment was a partisan attack on Roosevelt and Truman, yet the switch made by Dulles in 1953 upon becoming secretary of state when he condemned the amendment indicates significantly that no active policy-maker could bear additional restrictions on his power to act in international politics. The same point was made in a different way when Senator Bricker later announced that the amendment was not aimed at President Eisenhower. He was correct. It was aimed at *any* president aggressive enough to favor agreements of consequence with other nations.

John W. Bricker's departure from the Senate in 1958 ended the active campaign for this amendment. Eisenhower's style and his luck in international diplomacy helped quell the movement. But a decade later the Vietnam War ended Lyndon B. Johnson's chance for a second elected term as president and was feeding Senate Democrats with a fear of power in the White House. This has not taken the form of advocacy of a constitutional amendment. Instead, the efforts have been to cut asunder the Tonkin Gulf resolution which was the basis of President Johnson's military buildup and engagement in Vietnam. After 1968 there were many Democratic senators—like Fulbright, McGovern, Church and Muskie—who, vis-à-vis presidential leadership in foreign policy, behaved like spiritual descendants of Senator John W. Bricker. Yet Bricker himself, in retirement in Ohio, opposed liberal attacks on the power of the President!

Equal Rights Amendment

There is such wide opportunity for those unhappy with the Supreme Court to express dissatisfaction that constitutional amendments must be understood to be but one opportunity to do so. Article Three of the Constitution merely says that there shall be one Supreme Court—leaving Congress with broad powers over the number of justices, their compensation and budget. Congress also has considerable control over the Court's jurisdiction and over the establishment of other federal courts. Since first exercising this authority by enacting the Judiciary Act of 1789 Congress has developed a complete statutory code, Title 16 in the *United States Code*, regulating numerous aspects of the business of the Supreme Court. Even in times of great constitutional crisis, as in 1937, the proposals of President Roosevelt to curb the Court took the form of a legislative bill rather than a constitutional amendment. Indeed, particular judicial decisions objected to by Congress may often be altered or countermanded by statutes.[6]

Statutes are only one means Congress has to correct, to modulate or harass the Court. Another means was shown by the Senate's refusal in 1968 to act favorably on President Johnson's elevation of Abe Fortas to be Chief Justice of the United States, followed by its outright rejection in 1969 and 1970 of President Nixon's nominations of Clement Haynesworth and G. Harrold Carswell to be associate justices of the Supreme Court. A possibly more explosive and damaging move lay in Representative Gerald Ford's efforts to have the House of Representatives vote to impeach Associate Justice William O. Douglas and to have the Senate proceed to try the justice on the charges, though it failed. There are also the routine matters of authorizing new federal judgeships, action on nominees to fill those and other vacant seats, annual consideration of appropriations for the judiciary and committee investigations of subjects bearing on the courts.

Constitutional amendments may nevertheless be needed to deal with limited situations. It is remarkable how many amendments have followed an unyielding Supreme Court ruling. Oftentimes the Court ruling has been only a minor obstacle faced by a cause. This seems true of the *Dred Scott* decision in 1856, which is sometimes pictured as a cause of the Civil War which, in turn, was corrected by the northern victory in the field and then the Thirteenth, Fourteenth and Fifteenth Amendments. A decision with an incidental effect was *Minor v. Happersett* in 1875, where the Court ruled that the Fourteenth and Fifteenth Amendments did not afford women the right to vote.[7] This made certain the need of a woman suffrage amendment, ratified as the Nineteenth in 1920.

The Equal Rights Amendment went to the states for ratification on March 22, 1972 when the required two-thirds was achieved in the Senate by vote of 84 to 8, having been passed by the House of Representatives, 354 to 28, in October 1971.[8] Representative Martha Griffiths, Republican of Michigan, was the chief sponsor in the House; Birch Bayh, Democrat of Indiana, in the Senate. As finally approved for action by the states the key section of ERA reads: "Equality of rights under the law shall not be denied or abridged by the United States or by any state on account of sex." Congress will have the power to legislate under the amendment but it will not take effect until two years after ratification.

Senator Sam Ervin insisted to the end of debate that women were adequately protected against sex discrimination by the due process clause of the Fifth Amendment and the Equal Protection Clause of the Fourteenth Amendment. But Congresswoman Griffiths had earlier despaired of this and insisted that a primary reason why the Equal Rights Amendment was needed was the Court's record. Even with the Fourteenth Amendment in the Constitution, the Court had "held for 98 years that women, as a class, are not entitled to equal protection of the laws."[9] She cast the issue directly as an amendment to overcome Supreme Court unwillingness to apply the Constitution to women's rights, saying "It is time, Mr. Speaker, that in this battle with the Supreme

Court, that this body and the legislatures of the states come to the aid of women by passing this amendment."[10]

Other Judicial Provocations

The Sixteenth Amendment of 1913 permitting the United States government to levy an income tax is the only clear instance in the twentieth century of ratification of an amendment which was virtually required by a Supreme Court ruling. In one of its most famous cases, the Court in 1895 held by a five-to-four margin that an income tax enacted in 1894 was beyond the power of Congress. As has been mentioned, the case was argued and won by Joseph H. Choate, Sr., and by William D. Guthrie, and these men were in the forefront of opponents to a constitutional amendment during the first decade of this century. In any event, the income tax was adopted and then, in litigation in which Guthrie participated, upheld as valid by the Supreme Court.[11]

Much is made of the unratified child labor amendment, as it should be, for its proposal in 1924 by Congress followed the Supreme Court's invalidation of two successive child labor statutes. But when Congress finally enacted a third law regulating child labor, the Court in 1941, changed its position and overruled the first of its decisions in the *Hammer v. Dagenhart* case of 1918. This quite correctly suggests that, given time, the Court might have cooperated with Congress in permitting an income tax, and even in watering down the prohibition amendment. These are all instances where congressional leadership and willpower may do things eventually accepted by the Court, even if reluctantly. The *National Prohibition Cases* of 1920 and *Sprague v. United States* in 1931 settled all hopes of judicial interference with the Eighteenth Amendment and, in a small way, required the repeal embodied in the Twenty-first Amendment if prohibition was to be ended.

This collection of cases rather distantly related to generating amendments could even include a legal action against the electoral college brought as an original case in 1967. The case of *Delaware v. New York* was sponsored by the Small Business Council "as a public service" and was prepared by Professor Robert G. Dixon, Jr., of the George Washington Law School.[12] The petition charged that small states were so underrepresented in the electoral college balloting that the Court should review the matter and invalidate the system. While the case was cast as an original action, presumably within the obligatory jurisdiction, the Supreme Court used its discretion and simply declined to consider the merits.

Some congressmen are certain to be tempted to advocate amendments in the face of Chief Justice Burger's *ex cathedra* opposition to federal legislation designed to grant to consumers and environmentalists standing to sue in federal court. Speaking before the annual meeting of the American Bar Association in St. Louis on August 10, 1970, the chief justice said that such measures would overburden the federal courts and, accordingly, action should be left to the states. But there is little reason to believe that state courts have a capacity superior to their federal counterparts to cope with these problems. Nor can it be thought that many of the pollution or consumer problems of significance are of a local or intrastate character. This evidently was in mind in 1968 when Congressman Richard L. Ottinger (D., New York) introduced a sweeping "Conservation Bill of Rights." The Ottinger conservation amendment would declare, as a matter of constitutional principle, that the "right of the people to clean air, pure water, freedom from excessive and unnecessary noise, and the natural, scenic, historic and esthetic qualities of their environment shall not be a-bridged."[13] The Ottinger idea was not one of Burger's targets but the legislators whose "class action" bills were singled out may now cast their bills as amendments to protect them against constitutional attack in the Supreme Court. Although the chief justice spoke against them only in terms of efficiency, economy and wisdom it will be difficult for advocates of these measures not to see this speech as a forecast of the judicial reaction to "class action" legislation.

The number of would-be amendments aimed at the Supreme Court is too large to attempt a review, but a few failures achieved sufficient prominence to require mention. Although each is a complicated story in itself they may be condensed to indicate their essence as protests against judicial rulings. Those to be reviewed here are the Becker amendment to overcome decisions forbidding prayers in public school, the Dirksen amendments in response to reapportionment and religious cases, and the amendment drafted by Judge Henry J. Friendly to revise the Fifth Amendment on account of judicial interpretations of the clause against self-incrimination. Each has so far failed but has gained considerable attention. It should be added that the failure of these amendments gives a certain negative endorsement by Congress and the states of the judicial decisions which provoked them. This is true, also, for the civil rights rulings of the Supreme Court so commonly attacked by southerners in Congress for, here again, the majority not only acquiesced but, in voting overwhelmingly for the Civil Rights Act of 1964 and the Voting Rights Act of 1965, really supported rulings of the Warren Court on race relations.

Becker School Prayer Amendment

The impression that American politicians prefer God as a running mate was mightily reinforced during the Eighty-eighth Congress, 1963-64 when some two hundred separate House joint resolutions were proposed to provide for the constitutionality of prayers and Bible reading in the public schools. This avalanche of amendments was triggered by three Supreme Court decisions. A denominationally neutral prayer adopted by the New York State Board of Regents for a program of daily classroom prayers in public schools was ruled invalid by the Supreme Court in the case of *Engle v. Vitale*, decided on June 25, 1962. The court ruled six to one that this was inconsistent with the First Amendment, which prohibits laws respecting an establishment of religion. The following year, on June 17, 1963, the Court upset Bible reading and the recitation of the Lord's Prayer by students in unison prescribed by a Pennsylvania statute and by a rule of the school board in Baltimore, Maryland.

These cases, *Abington School District v. Schempp* and *Murray v. Curlett*, were decided together in a flurry of opinions in which the Supreme Court held, eight to one, that the "establishment" clause of the First Amendment, as applied to the states through the Fourteenth Amendment, had been unconstitutionally breached.[14] There was an immediate outcry against the New York decision, intensified a year later by the Pennsylvania and Maryland cases. The criticism of the Court reached such an intensity that the phlegmatic chairman of the House Judiciary Committee, Emanuel R. Celler, finally called hearings to consider the hundreds of amendments put forward by members of Congress.

Representative Frank J. Becker, a Republican from Nassau County, New York, formulated the amendments that became the focus of the hearings. A Catholic and a veteran of World War I, Becker was prominent in the Knights of Columbus and the American Legion and it was thought that his motions were representative of the wishes and, perhaps, even directions of leading critics of the prayer decisions, such as Cardinal Spellman of New York. Becker was the first member of the House to submit an amendment in the Eighty-eighth Congress which opened in January 1963. This was just a sentence, reading "Prayers may be offered in the course of any program in any public school or other public place in the United States."[15]

This was sufficient in response to *Engle v. Vitale*, but when the Supreme Court reinforced that ruling in its decision in the *Schempp* and *Curlett* cases, Becker submitted a more elaborate resolution. This revised Becker amendment was drafted by an *ad hoc* committee of congressmen to satisfy all critics of the Court's rulings with a single resolution they could all support. The wording thus became more elaborate in a resolution submitted on September 10, 1963, with these provisions:

SEC. 1. Nothing in this Constitution shall be deemed to prohibit the offering, reading from, or listening to prayers or biblical scriptures, if participation therein is on a voluntary basis, in any governmental or public school, institution, or place.
SEC. 2. Nothing in this Constitution shall be deemed to prohibit making reference to belief in, reliance upon, or invoking the aid of God or a Supreme Being in any governmental or public document, proceeding, activity, ceremony, school institution, or place, or upon any coinage, currency, or obligation of the United States.
SEC. 3. Nothing in this article shall constitute an establishment of religion.[17]

The perfected Becker amendment of September 1963 had the stated support of fifty-eight other House members, but Chairman Celler opposed it and would not call hearings. In a familiar routine, efforts were made to bypass Celler by a petition to discharge the Judiciary Committee from considering it. But 218 signatures were needed. Had the measure come to the House floor it probably would have won many votes. Yet Celler gauged there was solid if not vocal support for his position and he held his ground. By April 1964 the discharge petition had gained 157 signatures and Celler felt it wise to hold hearings in the hope of stopping the amendment. The hearings in April, May and June 1964 are printed in three volumes, containing nearly 2,774 pages of testimony, exhibits and documents. But after the hearings ended on June 3, 1964, the House Judiciary Committee took no further action and Representative Becker's discharge petition drive also failed.

Ardor for the Becker school prayer amendment had peaked early and, gradually, it became evident through the 1964 hearings that it was insufficient. Mail to the Judiciary Committee changed from pro to anti, and Catholic interests, especially, retreated from support of Becker. The ideal of church-state separation was clearly strongly supported and while the Supreme Court's application of this ideal to exclude prayers from school was widely criticized, the decisions also were persuasive. Eventually opponents to these decisions were made to look like opponents of the First Amendment. Attacking the justices for their Godlessness was one thing but amending the Constitution's First Amendment came to seem like medicine too strong for the malady.

Dirksen Apportionment Convention Amendment

Senator Everett McKinley Dirksen's death on September 7, 1969, ended an intriguing crusade over several years to overturn the Supreme Court's "one man, one vote" ruling on apportionment of state legislatures. He had sought to accomplish this by an amendment to be proposed by a special constitutional convention, a never before used method of proposal provided by Article Five of the Constitution. Dirksen was reacting to the reapportionment rulings of *Baker v. Carr* and *Reynolds v. Sims.*[17] The Court had alarmed Dirksen by taking jurisdiction of cases where malapportionment was claimed and then, in *Reynolds v. Sims* on June 15, 1964, declaring that the equal protection clause requires that the seats in both houses of a bicameral state legislature be apportioned on a population basis. As the strongest objections to these rulings were from state legislators, especially those with rural constituencies, Dirksen and others determined that their initiative could register most effectively through voting to call a special constitutional convention to deal with this outrage. A majority of legislative bodies in thirty-four states (two-thirds of the fifty states in the Union after 1959) would be needed to support the petition.

In seeking to employ the untried procedure of having the state legislators apply to Congress to call a federal convention to consider an apportionment amendment, Senator Dirksen chose the most favorable procedural path to his goal. He had already failed to persuade congressional colleagues to order a delay in court-ordered reapportionment. Like the repeal leaders in 1932 and 1933, Dirksen quietly took an unused route, one that was most suited to capturing the political strength of hostility to the Supreme Court apportionment rulings. State chapters of the American Farm Bureau Federation worked closely with Dirksen through the entire campaign. In 1964 the general assembly of the Council of State Governments passed a resolution favoring an application to Congress for a constitutional amendment on apportionment. Almost before it was announced, sixteen state legislatures had voted for the Dirksen petition to Congress.[18] This swift start led to an awareness of danger which provoked supporters of reapportionment to worry about the procedures for a convention as well as the substance of any amendment that might be proposed.

The Constitution provides that, upon application of two-thirds of the states, Congress "shall call a convention." Dirksen's opponents began to talk darkly about the possible nightmare of a "runaway" convention which might propose any number of amendments or, even, an entirely new constitution. As the number of state legislatures to pass a "Dirksen resolution" increased to twenty and then twenty-five, the most constructive response to the threat of an unbridled constitutional convention was the introduction by Senator Sam Ervin of a bill to provide procedures for such an eventuality.

Ervin's "Federal Constitutional Convention Act"[19] would require particularly in the amendment or amendments to be proposed, uniformity in each application to Congress, place a six-year life on such applications and permit a state to rescind its application. When two-thirds of the states had made proper application, certified by the clerk of the House and the secretary of the Senate, each house would be duty-bound to agree to a concurrent resolution calling for the convening of a federal constitutional convention on the designated subject. Such a resolution would designate the place and time of meeting of the convention, set forth the nature of the amendment or amendments for consideration, specify the means of ratification and provide that the convention be convened within one year. Any such convention would "be composed of as many delegates from each State as it is entitled to Representatives in Congress." The states themselves would govern the method for selecting delegates and the vice president of the United States would convene the constitutional convention. The state delegations would each have but a single vote but in case "the delegates from any State present are evenly divided on any question before the convention, the vote of that State shall not be cast on the question." Ervin's bill also ruled out proposing an amendment "of a general nature different from that stated in the concurrent resolution calling the convention." This measure was not acted upon even though the number of "Dirksen resolutions" rose to thirty.

By June 1969, thirty-three states had passed resolutions to apply to Congress for a special constitutional convention to propose the Dirksen apportionment amendment. There was fear that the Senate might be obliged to drop other business to engage in "a chaotic fight over basic Constitutional law."[20] But a reporter for the *Wall Street Journal* made these speculations about the obscure motives behind this unique campaign against the apportionment rulings by justices on what Dirksen was fond of calling "the SOO-preme Court."

The prospect of chaos in the Senate is just what Sen. Dirksen is trying to promote, in a typically oblique assault on the court's ruling.

Most Dirksen-watchers agree he doesn't really want a Constitutional convention. The idea rather is to terrorize liberal Senators with the thoughts of a runaway convention that would start tinkering with the Bill of Rights.

To avoid such a calamity, the reasoning goes, Congress itself would propose to the states for ratification a Constitutional amendment specifying that one house of a state legislature could be apportioned on a basis other than strict population.[21]

Meanwhile an increasing number of states—over forty—were complying with *Reynolds v. Sims* and second thoughts about an amendment were spreading to the state legislatures. The North Carolina legislature rescinded its earlier resolution and the number of states was suddenly down to thirty-two. The campaign continued in the summer of 1969[22] but legislatures were going out of session without acting and, then, Senator Dirksen died in September. Finally, on November 4, 1969, the Wisconsin Assembly refused by a vote of 62 to 36 to support the "Dirksen resolution" and the idea of such an amendment was virtually abandoned.[23]

The Self-Incrimination Amendment

In another of its jeremiad rulings, the Warren Court on June 13, 1966, in *Miranda v. Arizona*, provided that the privilege against self-incrimination of the Fifth Amendment applies to "custodial interrogation."[24] Unless a suspect makes a clear, intelligent waiver of the constitutional right to remain silent, and is informed of his right to an attorney and knows what he says may be used as evidence against him, statements by a suspect may not be admitted at his trial. This extended a series of rulings on the constitutional limits on police interrogation and intensified the stormy opposition of this issue by law enforcement agencies, many congressmen and the press.

Congress is purported to have "repealed" the *Miranda* as applied to federal interrogation in *United States v. Wade* by Title II of the Crime Control Act of 1968.[25] But as these changes would not apply to the states, a constitutional amendment to stop the Supreme Court from treating the self-incrimination clause "with almost religious adulation" was written and publicized by Judge Henry J. Friendly of the Court of Appeals for the Second Circuit.[26]

Born in 1903 and trained in law at Harvard, Henry J. Friendly clerked for Mr. Justice Brandeis in the 1927-28 term and was then in private practice in New York for thirty years. President Eisenhower named him to the Second Circuit in 1959 and, though perhaps too old, Judge Friendly was spoken of after 1968 as a possible Nixon nominee to the Supreme Court. Judge Friendly admired the use of the protection against self-incrimination as a shield against governmental bullying over political and religious beliefs, but argued that the clause was being used increasingly to protect the guilty from fair and proper conviction for crime.

The Friendly amendment of 350 words would do several things. It would modify the *Miranda* rule and require an arrested person to identify himself and submit to reasonable scientific or medical tests. Compulsory production of records in response to reasonable subpoena would be provided. Warnings of the use of evidence against an accused need not be made unless a person had actually been charged with a crime. This last was the heart of Friendly's purpose.

Since the amendment was first advanced, nothing has happened to bring the measure into the Constitution. It thus stands as an idea, an obvious response to distasteful Supreme Court rulings and as further evidence of the difficulty in obtaining formal proposal and ratification of a constitutional amendment. Like many less heralded, the Friendly self-incrimination amendment must be added to the Dirksen apportionment convention amendment, the Becker school prayer amendment, the Bricker amendment and the child labor amendment as efforts at twentieth-century constitutional change that failed. There is a great deal of difference between attacking Supreme Court decisions and doing something about them. Correcting statutes are evidently more feasible and Court over-rulings often possible, but constitutional amendments have so far been almost impossible to achieve.

Amendments Against Tardy States

When several states do not follow strong trends in the rest of the nation a federal constitutional amendment may be advanced to bring them to heel. This was achieved in a number of instances beginning with the constitutional policy of racial equality set forth at the end of the Civil War in the Thirteenth, Fourteenth and Fifteenth Amendments. The provision that the states stop electing United States senators by vote of their legislatures and do so by popular ballot stemmed partially from a similar animus. As has been seen, prior to World War I most states had adopted prohibition laws and permitted women to vote but the Eighteenth and Nineteenth Amendments were essential to enforce this policy in a few remaining ones. The Twenty-fourth Amendment providing that the right to vote shall not be abridged by reason of failure to pay a poll tax has a kinship with the Civil War amendments as it was directed primarily at a few southern states.

This is not to say that amendments are often inspired by a single objective. They ordinarily have a complex purpose, usually a mixture of aims. Thus the amendment for equal rights for women, adopted by the House in August 1970, but defeated in the Senate, was aimed at broadening congressional power, overcoming some state practices and also augmenting the authority of the Supreme Court.

There are also amendments geared to changing constitutional provisions, whether vague or specific, which cannot be altered by an ordinary statute. The Twentieth Amendment in 1933 exemplified this by resetting exact dates for assembling Congress (from March 4 to January 3) and for inaugurating the president and vice president (from March 4 to January 20). The two-term limit for president could not have been set by statute; hence, the Twenty-second Amendment. While the admission of new states into the Union is a subject of ordinary legislation, provisions for District of Columbia representation in Congress and participation in presidential elections are subjects requiring constitutional amendments. The District was granted electors for president by the Twenty-third Amendment ratified in 1961. An amendment for congressional representation for the District of Columbia has been before Congress for many years and there has been an increased interest in this possibility in 1970. Another illustration of a technical amendment, one needed because no other form of legislation could legitimately achieve the objective in mind, is the Twenty-fifth Amendment put forward by Senator Birch Bayh of Indiana to clean up ambiguity over presidential disability, removal and succession. This was ratified in 1967.

The question of whether a problem can be dealt with by a statute instead of a constitutional amendment recurs often. The child labor issue early in the century shows how changing times and outlooks gave this question different answers. In 1916 Congress and President Wilson believed the commerce clause justified a child labor law but the Supreme Court said no in 1918 in *Hammer v. Dagenhart*. After another law, this one based on the tax power, and another judicial invalidation, the country was treated to fifteen years of controversy over the wisdom of a child labor amendment proposed by Congress in 1924. Then Congress again passed a child labor statute based on the commerce clause and this time in 1941 the Supreme Court upheld it and overruled *Hammer v. Dagenhart*. In years when the Supreme Court is indulgent toward congressional power—when the justices have a spirit of restraint regarding the national legislature, in other words—much can be done by statute that might in another era call for an amendment. If the Supreme Court had not taken a generous view of the authority of Congress, there are many basic statutes that would have had to await adoption of new amendments. Since the 1930s these include the National Labor Relations Act and the Social Security Act of 1935, the Fair Labor Standards Act of 1938, and the Civil Rights Act of 1964.

The Eighteen-Year-Old Vote

It is clear that these and many other statutes are directed in part at bringing a few recalcitrant states into line, at setting national standards in a particular field and ensuring that the sanctions are sufficient to bring the desired result. The legal mind is stretched and the lay mind bewildered by a statute-or-amendment cacophony. There seems little doubt that a national abortion act to legalize abortions throughout the United States or Supreme Court rulings holding antiabortion statutes invalid would make the slow, state-by-state process of reform unnecessary.[27] But very serious doubt about the constitutionality of reducing the voting age to eighteen in federal, state, and local elections by means of a simple statute led to the passage of the Twenty-Sixth Amendment.

The eighteen-year old vote was granted by Title III of the Voting Rights Act Amendments of 1970, approved by President Nixon June 22, 1970.[28] The key part of the text is as follows:

Sec. 302. Except as required by the Constitution, no citizen of the United States who is otherwise qualified to vote in any State or political subdivision in any primary or in any election shall be denied the right to vote in any such primary or election on account of age if such citizen is eighteen years of age or older.

Senator Edward Kennedy of Massachusetts had championed this statutory solution by contending that the approval of the Voting Rights Act of 1965 in the case of *Katzenbach v. Morgan*[29] explicitly recognized that Congress had broad power to legislate to enforce the equal protection clause. The Court by a seven to two margin upheld the provision that no person who has completed the sixth grade in Puerto Rico shall be denied the right to vote in any election because of his inability to read or write English. These are among the most pointed paragraphs in Senator Kennedy's argument:

Seen in perspective, the *Morgan* case was not a new departure in American constitutional law. Rather, it was a decision characterized by clear judicial restraint and exhibiting generous deference by the Supreme Court toward the actions of Congress. . . .

In essence, the *Morgan* case stands for the proposition that Congress has broad power to weigh the facts and make its own determination under the Equal Protection Clause. If the Supreme Court determines that there is a reasonable basis for legislation by Congress in this area, then the legislation will be sustained . . .

Yet there was sufficient doubt within Congress that the measure had to be tacked on to the extension of the Voting Rights Act and also had to include a proviso for enforcement which anticipated a Supreme Court test.

Congress could not, directly and explicitly, seek from the Supreme Court an advisory opinion on the eighteen-year-old vote statute. It could and did authorize and direct the attorney general "to institute in the name of the United States such actions against states or political subdivisions, including actions for injunctive relief, as he may determine to be necessary to implement" the law. Initial proceedings fall under the jurisdiction of three-judge United States district courts and "any appeal shall lie to the Supreme Court." The statute further provides that judges sitting on eighteen-year-old vote cases have "the duty" to cause them "to be in every way expedited." This act took effect on January 1, 1971.

While Senator Kennedy's position that a statute was adequate and constitutional was supported by Paul A. Freund and Archibald Cox of the Harvard Law School,[30] the Department of Justice and President Richard Nixon insisted that an amendment was required, a view taken by Professors Bickel, Black, Bork, Ely, Pollak and Rostow of the Yale Law School.[31] They contended that *Katzenbach v. Morgan* "makes sense as part of the mainstream of Fourteenth Amendment litigation, policing state restrictions on ethnic minorities. But it has little apparent application to a restriction affecting all Americans in forty-six states." The Yale Law School faculty members' letter continued:

A statute lowering the voting age would raise the expectations of ten million young Americans—expectations likely to be dashed by a judicial determination that the statute is unconstitutional. This lends point to the fact that when heretofore the nation decided upon a fundamental change in the composition of the electorate, the consensus was embodied, in permanent and unchallengeable form, in a constitutional amendment. One hundred years ago the 15th Amendment, enfranchising blacks, was added to the Constitution.

Fifty years ago the 19th Amendment, enfranchising women, was added to the Constitution. If, in 1970, the nation is ready to welcome into the political process Americans who have reached the age of eighteen, Congress should, in fidelity to our constitutional traditions, submit to the states for ratification a new constitutional amendment embodying that new consensus.

President Nixon canvassed "many of the nation's leading constitutional scholars" and found that the "great majority" regarded a statute providing the eighteen-year-old vote by statute "as unconstitutional."[32]

The tactic of placing the eighteeen-year-old vote provision in the Voting Rights Act Amendments of 1970 helped ensure its adoption by both Houses of Congress. It is interesting to observe how this tactic affected the president, the attorney general, state compliance, the development of litigation and the response of the courts. President Nixon favored voting at age eighteen but believed this should be done state by state or by federal constitutional amendment and yet he signed the measure because he lacked an item veto and could not have killed Title III without vetoing the first two titles of the Voting Rights Act Amendments. Attorney General John Mitchell promptly sought letters of compliance from all governors and had received positive assurances from twenty by the end of July, 1970.

The Supreme Court held, in December 1970, that Congress could validly lower the voting age to eighteen for federal but not state and local elections.[33] This decision presented state and local election officials with the expensive prospect of providing separate balloting arrangements for voters of different ages whenever national and state elections coincided. This would next occur across the nation in 1972. Many persons who had been reluctant to afford the vote to eighteen year olds now agreed to move swiftly toward a constitutional amendment to make voting eligibility by age equivalent in all elections. In March 1971 Congress approved and thus officially proposed this amendment to the states:

The right of citizens of the United States, who are 18 years of age or older, to vote shall not be denied or abridged by the United States or by any state on account of age.

The two-thirds majority was easily achieved as the Senate vote on March 10 was unanimous at 94 to 0 and the House vote on March 23 was 401 to 19.[34] Ratification began immediately and was completed in the record time of three months on June 30, 1971 when Ohio became the thirty-eighth and final state to approve the amendment.[35]

15 Recommendations

Confidence in Supreme Court litigation and amendments as proper means for guiding Constitutional change will be enhanced by a handful of reforms. Actual practice should be appropriately regulated, simplified and be as open and public as suits each mode. Four recommendations deal with litigation. One is concerned with disclosing information about sponsors of litigation, another with providing specialized knowledge to the Supreme Court. The practice of Congressmen arguing cases in the federal courts is criticized and the association of judges with organized groups questioned. The infrequency of successful constitutional amendment calls for statutory regulations to govern procedure and one recommendation on this subject is now presented.

Litigant Registration

The idea of disclosure of the activities of voluntary associations is a continuing and vexing one in the American democracy. This is so because of the conflict between the idea of free association and the activities of associations conducted as a private enterprise. Against this value of privacy is the public interest in knowing who pays for what and represents whom in the complex interrelationships between the body politic and its rulers. The battle over disclosure has been fought on many grounds.

For example, the efforts to limit financial contributions to political parties was one battle early in the century. Another came with the efforts to have lobbying groups file basic information with the United States Congress. And the problem of influence is not easily discerned by even the most careful and thorough kinds of disclosure. However, it appears that the courts have operated on a myth that cases are between private parties and that the questions before the court are to be decided entirely on rational grounds according to the skill of argument.

This book has shown that a substantial number of major constitutional cases before the Supreme Court are sponsored by particular organizations operating as parts of amorphous social movements. This fact should be apprehended not only by the Court but also by the public, or at any rate by those members of the public whose knowledge is most germane to the functioning of the courts. Thus, the recommendation here follows the viewpoint which was behind the Regulation of Lobbying Act of 1945. This act provided that organizations seeking legislation from Congress file quarterly statements of their purposes and their financial expenditures with the clerk of the House of Representatives and, while loopholes exist, this information be made available to the press and to the public. Similar legislation should now be adopted—or similar provisions provided for in the rules of the Court—pertaining to the organizations and their lawyers who appear before them.

For scholars, detailed information will aid understanding of the relationships between individual lawyers and associations, and those more abstract concepts of interest groups and social movements. Depicting relationships among organizations offers numerous difficulties which can be solved only when consistent measures of such items as goals, size, leadership, finance, methods and success are accurately settled.

There appears to have been a proliferation of legal action organizations, each with quite limited concerns, marching under the banner of the public interest. In late 1970 the Internal Revenue Service accorded tax exemption to numerous "public interest law firms" but at the same time required each organization to file more detailed reports about finances and activities than had ever been the case before. If large numbers of constitutional cases are prepared by organizations in the public interest it will be important to judge that interest not merely by the contentions of the organizations in court but also by the source and extent of their financing, the nature of their staff and the scope of their numbers.

Filing information with the Internal Revenue Service serves one purpose, but associational participation in constitutional cases is so widespread that disclosure of finances and membership totals should be made by parties and organizations appearing in the Supreme Court. This disclosure should be simple, should be filed with the clerk or the Administrative Office of United States Courts, be subject to corroboration, and be made public in regular reports.

Disinterestedness of Judges

It is a corollary that lawyers who become United States judges, whether sitting or in retirement, should not compromise their disinterestedness by associating with legal action groups. They should also be careful of accepting honors from them. This is an exceedingly slippery subject deserving careful evaluation for we would not want judges who were so divorced from reality they could not act wisely in their official capacities. Even while urging judges to be aloof one cannot disagree with Chief Justice Warren's insistence that "Our judges are not monks or scientists, but participants in the living stream of our national life."[1]

While judges can never be angels, they should take care not to engage in activities which give the suggestion of a conflict of interest, an impropriety, or an indication that they have chosen sides before a case has been decided. The most sensational exposures of such compromises with evil have come in recent years in the Senate investigations of the roles of Mr. Justice Fortas of the United States Supreme Court and of Judge Clement Haynsworth of the Court of Appeals for the Fourth Circuit. Those investigations showed that the judges in question had either (Fortas) accepted money from a private foundation to give private counsel and advice to that foundation or (Haynsworth) participated in cases concerning corporations in which he had a financial interest. These instances were exaggerated by the press and by opponents in the Senate. But they suggested a problem of widespread concern. There is an additional problem not touched on by those instances in the attitudinal relationships which develop when a man becomes a judge and must shed his numerous associational relationships. This recommendation that judges not counsel legal action groups or accept honors from them would help to solve this problem.

Several instances of the kind of judicial connections to action organizations alluded to here have been described in this study. A number deserve to be recited in brief to show the unusual complexity of the problem that this recommendation is aimed at curing. It may be that the problem is so complex that no simple nostrum will work. Yet one can proceed to consider a cure only when the instances which seem to be aberrations of a proper norm are made explicit:

Item. Judge Julius J. Hoffman, United States district judge in the Northern District of Illinois, was given a testimonial dinner in May 1970 by the Veterans of Foreign Wars. It was clear from the speeches made on that occasion and from the whole intent of the program that Judge Hoffman was being honored and toasted for his stiff sentences and stiffer handling of the defendants in the trial of the Chicago Seven during the winter and spring of 1970. His attitudes, shared as they were by members of this large veterans' organization, were being rewarded.

Item. In May 1970 the retired Chief Justice of the United States, Earl Warren, was acclaimed at a conference of the NAACP Legal Defense and Education Fund, Inc., in New York City. Mr. Warren on that occasion gave a speech criticizing trends in the United States, particularly, by inference, the practice of the president of the United States and of the attorney general. Although the chief justice is in retirement he continues to receive a full salary under the provisions of the *United States Code*, and his association with an organization that has sponsored hundreds of cases in the federal courts and dozens in the United States Supreme Court placed Mr. Warren's position as a disinterested judge in jeopardy.

Item. In the early 1950s Judge Waites Waring, a United States district judge in Charleston, South Carolina, made a number of decisions forwarding the claims of equality by American blacks who were parties in cases before his court. His position in these cases was ordinarily a dissenting one and those dissents were able and wise statements of what the law should be. Many were later adopted, in effect, by the Supreme Court of the United States. Judge Waring thereby earned an enduring reputation as a courageous judge in a hostile environment, for he and his wife were subjected to a considerable amount of abuse and to a weakening of their numerous social ties in Charleston. Stories about their situation appeared often in the liberal press of the time and have been repeated since. The papers of Judge Waring and the book by his friend Walter White indicate[2] an association close to counseling. So far so good. The problem comes from the fact that Judge Waring seemed to be engaged in actually counseling Mr. White, then the secretary of the NAACP, about the appropriate kinds of action that he and the association should take. Such a relationship between a judge and the head of a major action organization was out of place.

Item. Charles F. Amidon, a United States judge in the Dakotas in the first two decades of the century, was a constant adviser to President Theodore Roosevelt and to Mrs. Florence Kelley, executive director of the National Consumers' League. It was Amidon who advised Theodore Roosevelt on his famous proposal for the recall of federal judges. In the early 1920s Judge Amidon was a very active adviser to Mrs. Kelley on how to amend the Constitution in order to cut the Supreme Court's power of judicial review. The idea that a sitting federal judge would help draft such proposals seems wrong.

The recommendation made here is a difficult one to implement. It probably can only be cautionary and this caution may properly fall within the code of behavior prescribed for judges by the United States Judicial Conference. But the conference, or some other agency or scholar should amplify the study of compromising practices and recommend some further remedy.

As Chief Justice Warren put it upon the occasion of his retirement in June of 1969, the task of judging

is made more difficult in this Court because we have no constituency. We serve no majority. We serve no minority. We serve only the public interest as we see it, guided only by the Constitution and our own consciences.[3]

If the federal judge has no constituency but the public interest, he should demonstrate this to the satisfaction of the public.

Congressmen Not to Serve As Counsel

The special position members of the bar hold in conducting litigation should be limited when lawyers obtain legislative office. In particular, sitting members of the United States Congress should not represent parties, sign briefs or present oral arguments in United States courts.

A handful of instances of congressmen in court cases dealing with constitutional issues may be cited. Henry St. George Tucker in the early 1920s helped the attack in *Frothingham v. Mellon* against the constitutionality of the Sheppard-Towner Act while he was a representative from Virginia. Congressman Patrick Kelley of Michigan did the same in cases challenging the validity of the Volstead Act and the Eighteenth Amendment. Senator Matthew Neeley of West Virginia participated in cases in the early 1950s and other congressmen defended racial segregation in the courts at that time. In the 1960s Senator Sam Ervin of North Carolina filed briefs and made arguments before the Supreme Court in the *Darlington Mills* labor case and, for a group of churches, in the case of *Flast v. Cohen* to broaden taxpayer participation in the federal courts. In 1970 Senator Edward Kennedy made an oral argument in defense of the eighteen-year-old-vote statute in a case before the court of appeals for the District of Columbia. A thorough documentation of the participation of congressmen in court cases is needed. But these examples suggest that the occurrence is not a sport and that it deserves study and a suitable remedy.

That the remedy should be the exclusion of congressmen from participating in court cases stems from several sources. For one, the principle of the separation of powers suggests that the duty of defending acts of Congress lies with the Justice Department, particularly in the office of the solicitor general. This is right and proper, but it is not appropriate for United States congressmen who have been in a minority in voting on an action—as was Congressman Tucker and Congressman Kelley in the 1920s and as was Senator Ervin in the 1960s—to then appear in the courts to challenge legislation which they opposed. Other means to perform this function exist. Private associations can employ their own lawyers and private parties should bear the brunt of the cost of challenging acts of Congress in the courts. When an organization—brewers, conservatives or churchmen—oppose a particular policy, it should not employ the services of lawyers who are sitting members of the United States Congress. Nor should the Department of Justice enlist or feel obliged to accept a senator as an ally in defending a statute.

A member of Congress who participates in a Supreme Court case has many silent, hidden threats at his disposal to use against the institution and its members before whom he appears. He has an opportunity to consider and vote upon the appropriations for the judiciary, the addition of judges to the judiciary and on many statutes governing the power of the courts. He has the power, possibly, to investigate members of the Court and may be called upon to sit on matters of impeachment. If he is a United States senator, he will consider judicial nominations and vote upon these. Moreover, in the instances cited in the study, we have seen that congressmen are taking positions in court which are identical with those that they have taken on substantive policy questions as members of Congress. For them to leave the legislative halls and enter the courtroom to argue that position is improper, not so much out of a conflict in interest as through lack of propriety.

The propriety versus conflict of interest distinction was first made in the study by the Senate of the qualifications of Mr. Justice Fortas to be Chief Justice of the United States in 1968. The questions of his activity as an adviser to President Johnson, for example, and for his position in defending the Vietnam policies of the administration to private citizens at that time were thoroughly castigated. There was no specific breach of law, no specific violation of a rule, but the notion that a sitting member of the Supreme Court should advise a president about a policy which might come under assault in the courts seemed plainly wrong to many observers. It was wrong as a matter of judicial good sense. By the same token, the notion that sitting members of Congress may argue cases before the courts is a violation of the canons of good sense and of ethics, which should guide the behavior of all congressmen.

A particularly difficult and thorny problem arises when a member of Congress is employed by a private organization to represent it in a challenge to a federal statute. The congressman who has taken a position on the statute is placed in a situation where he is employed by an organization to represent it in assaulting the statute which he has opposed. Whether he is paid by an organization is in a sense beside the point. His attitudes are also in play and to represent a private association whose attitudes he shares is wrong.

This recommendation could be implemented by statute, or alternatively by the rules of the Court. It should be studied also by the organized bar based on a full survey of members of Congress, and it should be extended to the study of conflicts of interest and improprieties by lawyers who sit in state legislatures.[4]

Independent Research for the Supreme Court

The Supreme Court should have substantial funds available to employ expert assistance in analyzing questions raised in cases under consideration. The Court needs help—to paraphrase the Brownlow Commission—with various aspects of its work and this recommendation is meant to overcome some of the perennial difficulties which the judiciary faces in dealing with a multiplicity of urgent social, economic and other problems raised in ordinary litigation. The adversary process is often insufficient in formulating modern public law.

Suggestions from many sources have been made on how a nine-man Court can cope with the tremendous burdens of decisions placed upon it by a country as industrialized, as urbanized, as complex and as large as the United States of America is in the 1970s. They have also included recommendations that the Supreme Court be enlarged and be split up or reorganized in fundamental ways. These recommendations all seem unwise. We have had a nine-man Supreme Court for a hundred years and a somewhat different sized Supreme Court from the beginning of the republic. It is the authoritative judicial body, the court of last resort, and its traditions and its power and authority should continue in order to provide a reliable, legitimate basis for the formulation of our constitutional law from the side of the judiciary. But the adversary process has numerous limitations and the Court needs help.

The chief problem with the adversary process as practiced in the Supreme Court over many decades is the imbalance in money, in other resources of skill and legal talent, and of persistence and of information with the parties likely to be unable to give the Court the kind of equal aid and competitive argument upon which the adversary idea is based in theory. At the turn of the century it was the great corporations which had the upper hand in conflicts with impecunious trade unions. At other times it has been a particular church, a particular trade association, or a particular organization, even one championing civil rights or civil liberties, which has had by far the superior talent and resources over, say, a particular municipality or a particular state. In any event, imbalances have developed and these imbalances are not correctable by the ordinary adversary proceeding.

Recent studies of the business of the Supreme Court have shown that perhaps the greatest difficulty is the diverse academic subjects such as psychology, sociology, economics, history, political science and technological, scientific issues. The Court is presented with mathematical studies, with survey research, with Rorschach tests and with historical interpretations in which it possesses no special expertise. It is often true that one side in a litigation is able to conduct a study which has all of the earmarks of a dispassionate social science survey but which, on inspection, has flaws. It is often beyond the intellectual training and intellectual capacity of the judges and their young law clerks to analyze these studies and correct them. It is also impossible for the other side to do so.

Background studies performed on behalf of a litigant by his counsel or by an organization devoted to forwarding his cause need the scrutiny of experts and the Court needs their help in being guided to a full understanding of the possible misconceptions, sloppy thinking, poor theory or other weaknesses that such reports and studies may contain. Examples abound. For example, in *Brown v. Board of Education* the NAACP Legal Defense and Educational Fund, Inc., brought into Court nationally recognized sociologists and psychologists to testify at the trial level to show the patterns of discrimination that were inherent in a separate school system. It was simply beyond the intellectual capacity of the opposition to meet the factual and conceptual arguments set forth by these nationally renowned sociologists and psychologists, but it would have been of value to the Court to have had some rebuttal provided to them by experts who served the Court alone.

In the recent capital punishment cases a survey of persons under sentence to be executed was made by students from the University of Pennsylvania Law School under the guidance of a sociology and law professor. This study was not answered by the briefs on the other side and here again the weakness of a state attorney general trying to debate scholars of national reputation who are specialists in a field beyond the knowledge and appreciation of such a man or such an office.

Studies by Martin Shapiro, a political scientist, and Charles A. Miller, a historian,[5] have shown that the justices are frequently out of their depth in dealing with a multitude of specialized subjects. The justices themselves are simply too hard pressed for time, lack the original training necessary to check on subjects even if they had the time, and employ clerks in turnover positions one or two years at a time. While the clerks are usually brilliant students not long out of the leading law schools, they are not adequately equipped to aid the justices on all of the complex matters which come before the Court in a given term. After all, many of the most important issues which the Court must resolve are relatively new issues and have been presented to the Court in an adversary proceeding in which there is an imbalance in the scholarly work done by the advocates.

With the justices and their clerks unable to cope with the new material adequately, the Court needs some kind of resource beyond its own skills. An example of the way the Court has conceded the principal point at issue in this discussion has been shown in the drafting of the rules of the Supreme Court itself. These rules were revised thoroughly in 1954 and again, just as thoroughly, in 1967. On both occasions the Supreme Court created a committee on the revision of the rules and named a group of lawyers with experience before the Court to serve on the committee and to develop the rules.[6] If the Supreme Court needs guidance from an outside committee in preparing its own rules with which the Court and its staff are thoroughly conversant and as fully expert as they could be on any topic under the sun, it seems reasonable to suppose that it needs such committees or advisory groups in connection with ordinary litigation and ordinary questions which come before it.

The suggestion being made here is that the Court have funds available to it at its own discretion to employ an individual or a group of experts to advise the Court on substantive matters under consideration. Expert advice will not technocratically decide things for the court, however, since experts disagree among themselves. But more frequent use of experts will open judicial eyes to the pitfalls of such use. In a discussion of the problem a court faces in coping with an imbalance of information and of conceptualization by counsel, Paul A. Freund has apparently dismissed the idea of providing for the courts an equivalent to the Legislative Reference Service for Congress. But he does not do so without indicating the strong basic need for such a service and its probable value to the disinterested decision-making process which is exalted as the proper role for judges. It is worth quoting his comment at some length:

One final objection to the so-called Brandeis brief is that it places an inappropriate task on counsel. Is the adversary method the most suitable one for dealing with economic data? Someone has said that there are three sides to every lawsuit—my side, your side, and the truth. Should the responsibility for developing the background facts be placed on counsel, or should it be borne by some disinterested source? Should there be established for the courts something equivalent to the legislative reference service organized in a number of states for the benefit of the legislature? This would perhaps be a more radical innovation than the Brandeis brief itself, and yet it is not altogether fanciful.

We owe much of our commercial law to the boldness of Lord Mansfield in seeking advice from experienced merchants regarding mercantile practices. The English admiralty courts have utilized the services of retired mariners drawn from the Royal Navy and the Merchant Marine—the celebrated "elder brethren of Trinity House." Some of our courts are beginning to employ disinterested medical and psychiatric advisers. The great difficulty with this idea in constitutional litigation is that the experts would be tempted to intrude their views on the merits of the legislation instead of helping the court to understand other people's views. Perhaps the right place for nonlegal experts in constitutional law is in the legislative process. If records of hearings and committee reports, particularly in state legislatures, were more illuminating and accessible, the task of the advocate in court would be simpler, and the court itself would be more disposed to display that basic judicial virtue, humility.[7]

We see that Freund is attracted to the idea of providing counsel to the Court beyond the advocates for the parties and the briefs of *amici curiae*, but then he quickly draws back from it. It is probable that the Legislative Reference Service of the Library of Congress and the many similar services which abound in the states and municipalities of the country are not suitable models for what the Court needs. It needs something more like the professional staff that some committees of Congress have developed or the professional staffs available to the Executive Office of the President, such as the Council of Economic Advisers. The Court, after all, has a magnificent library and it, too, can draw on the resources of the Library of Congress. There should be no development of a permanent bureaucracy which advises the Court although there could be a small staff to aid the Court in seeking out and assembling the material which it requests. There should not be a permanent clerking system as occurs in the courts in some other countries, Australia, for example. Rather the Court needs funds to employ qualified persons to make special studies.

There are at least two clear models available for implementing this recommendation. One is the traditional *amicus curiae* brief which, unfortunately, has moved from being in the service of the Court to the service of one or another of the advocates.[8] The Court could invite an *amicus curiae* brief to answer specific questions, which would mean that the brief would be prepared under the guidance of a member of the bar of the Court and would have the resources and the suggestions of the Court to work with. Thus the whole idea of the traditional *amicus curiae* would be redeemed and utilized, and this possibly is the most appropriate approach toward carrying out the recommendation. Indeed, this approach was employed in the case of *Brown v. Board of Education* (1954, 1955) when the Court in trying to determine what type of decree to issue, invited *amici curiae* briefs from the attorney general of the United States and from several states which were not parties. In the Court's order the questions, five in number, were put to all of these officers and the briefs answered or tried to answer all of them; while they did so in a manner which recommended policy, this broadened the case and gave the Court much more information and insight than it would otherwise have had available to it.

My suggestion then is that the Court name particular lawyers known to be conversant with certain subjects such as psychiatry, antitrust economics, or survey research so that they could then employ experts who would aid them and the Court in presenting a position for the Court rather than for the advocates. If this were done it would be important that the document produced for the Court be made public and be available for refutation by the advocates in the case.

The special committee idea offers another means to help the Court when there is an imbalance between the advocates, and the judges and their clerks are unable by themselves, either through lack of time or training, to deal with a particularly troublesome issue. Perhaps the Court, say, is faced with deciding whether a public opinion poll or two public opinion polls, in a change of venue case, would pass muster in the scholarly community. If so, the Court might request the Survey Research Center at the University of Michigan to make an independent study for the Court. Its report also should be made public, made part of the record and open to refutation by the advocates. Other examples could be cited.

There is a constantly increasing use of expert economists and other social scientists by the advocates themselves and the Court should have some means to correct the imbalance, and the direct expert advice of a particular institution may be in order. The Court also needs some means for an independent investigation of the background of cases. It may be that a permanent office—possibly by the expansion of the office of the clerk of the Supreme Court—should be attempted in order to scrutinize the background history of litigation. We have seen in the important case of *Buck v. Bell* that a friendly suit was presented to the Court, adjudicated and decided. The lower court determined that the child of Carrie Buck was an imbecile when she was not. Moreover, the case was a friendly suit from beginning to end. The Supreme Court has the power and authority under the Constitution to decide cases in controversies, and it has determined that it will not decide friendly suits or give advisory opinions. It could change its practice on these matters. The Court should have the resources to investigate the parties and to be certain that the cases it hears are fully and adequately briefed, and if they are not they should either not be heard or they should seek outside help. Such an investigatory mechanism would have been most salutary in the case of *Buck v. Bell*. This is not to imply that more and better information would eliminate the effect of differences in ideology among the justices. But more and better information would produce clearer, more logically consistent results at a minimum.

An Amendment Procedure Statute

Congress should adopt a constitutional amendment procedure measure, under Article Five, to regularize and improve ratification practices in the states.

Amendment ratification practices have been uneven, uncertain and fickle when they should be ordered, scheduled and more rational. There is either too much publicity, as in the case of the abortive child labor amendment, or too little, as in the adoption of the Twenty-second Amendment limiting the tenure of American presidents to two terms. The specter of the Dirksen amendment and the problems of state ratification of amendments which may run on for a considerable period of time are each in their own way undesirable.

The convention ratification of the Twenty-first Amendment repealing prohibition was an example of a powerful reaction mounted by several different organizations to repeal prohibition through a unique method which gave to those interests the advantage of a state convention arrangement amounting almost to a national referendum. But today, under the reapportionment rulings of the Supreme Court, the state legislatures much more adequately reflect their constituencies (to mirror public opinion in as honest and adequate manner as representative institutions are ever likely to be able to achieve). Consequently, it is appropriate that Congress refer constitutional amendments which it proposes to the state legislatures. In anticipation, a basic procedural statute should be adopted by Congress to govern all of the various amendments which may be propsed. Such a measure might be called the "Constitutional Amendment Procedure Act."

This act would attempt to cope with a number of problems traditionally associated with the ratification process which, in the age of television and abundant federal resources, should include the following: The Congress should provide that within a period of, say, ninety days, there would be a conference—financed by the federal government—in Washington to inform members of the state legislatures about the new measure proposed for their consideration. The conference should be conducted by the presiding officers of the House and Senate in cooperation with the leadership of both parties. It should take pains to ensure that the leading congressional advocates and opponents of the proposed amendment have ample opportunity to present the basic arguments, which would obviously draw national attention and publicity and the presence of lobbyists on both sides of whatever measure was under consideration.

A second feature of the Constitutional Amendment Procedure Act concerns the composition of the conference which would be made up of delegates from each of the fifty states. Each state would consider the question of ratification of a proposed amendment and the delegates at the conference should come from the state institutions involved. The governor or his representative would be one delegate while the leadership of the state House of Representatives and of the state Senate should send between four and six delegates chosen in a uniform manner. The likely total of the assembly under this plan would be between 250 and 300, a body not inappropriate for a three-day conference. Expenses should be set and paid for by the government.

A third provision should be a timetable for consideration of the proposed amendment. If the special conference is held within ninety days following the proposal of each amendment, then a similar schedule should be provided for ratification. There are always dangers in providing that a particular event must take place on a particular day, but this practice has been a common practice in the United States government where presidential elections are held on a particular day known years in advance and when Congress meets on a particular day also known well in advance. The advantages outweigh the possible losses in seeking to set a particular time for a vote on a constitutional amendment by the state legislatures.

Indeed, there might be an annual date set so that state legislatures would be obliged to vote on a constitutional amendment, say, during the first week of February as long as the amendment proposed was adopted by the Congress at least six months beforehand. Again, this would focus national publicity on the actions of the legislatures; they would all vote on the same day and they would all have considered the issue through both their own local channels and from national television, national news magazines and the publicity generated by the special conference. It would also clear the decks so that an amendment which failed of ratification would not be permitted to be presented to the legislatures again until repassed by a subsequent Congress. An amendment could not drag on for decades as did the child labor amendment proposed in 1924. It is a much better thing from the point of view of the conduct of such important business that the amendment process be brought to the fore and that the procedures be spelled out in advance.

If constitutional change expresses shifting social conflict, the rules under which both litigation and amendment politics are conducted need to be well-settled in advance. Already the 1970s have seen ratification of an amendment assuring the vote to eighteen-year-olds and proposal of the equal rights amendment. There is the perennial discussion about amendments prescribing the nomination of the president, perhaps through adoption of nationwide primaries, and his election by some means other than the Electoral College. Agitation for modification of court orders utilizing busing as one means of school integration has raised the spectre of a constitutional amendment on this subject. The emotional peaks reached in the national debate about busing are similar to those seen during the controversy over national prohibition. A "Constitutional Amendment Procedure Act" is needed to lay down rules that will give all sides confidence that future amendments are carefully weighed, openly pursued, widely supported and legitimately adopted as part of the Constitution.

Bibliography

Bibliography

Manuscript Sources

If we know more about the past than those who lived in it, this condition owes itself to the availability of diaries, letters and documents which those living then did not widely share with contemporaries. Time thus reveals some of the prevailing inhibitions that helped the past keep its secrets. The duration of time before these secrets are yielded up depends on specific directions of the deceased, on chance, on the zealousness of the search, and on modern efforts to organize and study manuscripts, all this is, in a sense, simply a literate brand of archaeology. To a student of American constitutional change in this century there are many wonderful "finds" alongside an endless parade of tantalizing mysteries. In other words, there is nothing regular or regularizing about manuscript sources.

Two great centralizing government agencies, the National Archives and the Library of Congress, have in the last decade given more coherence to the manuscript collections scattered around the country than has ever been done in the United States or elsewhere. There were many earlier efforts at cataloguing, but the most complete and recent in a single volume is Philip Hamer, *A Guide to Archives and Manuscripts in the United States*, prepared for the National Archives, and published by Yale University Press in 1961. The descriptions of even huge collections are uniformly a sentence or less, but the organization by states, cities and libraries makes the volume a convenient starting point in any search. Unfortunately it is rapidly becoming outdated and its usefulness diminishes as the growth of manuscript collections accelerates.

There is also the vastly more complete *National Union Catalog of Manuscript Collections*, prepared by the Card Division of the Library of Congress. By the end of 1971 this ran to ten large volumes and brought the total collection described to 27,312 representing holdings in 805 repositories. The advantages of the *NUCMC* series include up-to-dateness, a master index of repositories and descriptive statements about each of the collections. There is also a subject index. Like most multivolume reference sets, the *National Union Catalog of Manuscript Collections* is difficult to use and master. An inherent weakness is its dependence for information and descriptions of collections on the far-flung repositories in the country. It remains enormously useful in checking upon what papers do not exist as well as getting a preliminary hint of what a collection may obtain.

Although many manuscript collections already present and open in libraries are not listed in *A Guide to Archives and Manuscripts in the United States* or in the *National Union Catalog of Manuscript Collections*, others are announced in annual reports, periodicals or specialized publications about particular libraries.

Thus the *Quarterly Journal of the Library of Congress* and that library's *Information Bulletin* are helpful preliminary sources of news. Separate catalogues are published, some collections among these being the *Guide to Manuscript Collections of The American Philosophical Library*. G.K. Hall & Co. has published a volume of all catalogue cards to the manuscript collection in the New York Public Library. The biennial reports of the Schlesinger Library at Radcliffe College contain good descriptions of new materials.

The register to a manuscript collection can be an enormously useful tool to the researcher. Sometimes called an inventory, the register as a technique was developed at the Manuscript Collection of the Library of Congress. It is prepared as the collection is organized and boxed so that there is a master list or index to all the major features of the collection and, when done well, includes a descriptive analysis of its significance. Today a library will ordinarily send an interested researcher a photocopy of a register and in some instances registers have been published. Perhaps the most outstanding registers are those prepared during the 1960s for some of the collections at Syracuse University as, for example, the *Register to the Papers of Dorothy Thompson*. The Library of Congress has published about 75 registers including the *Register to the Papers of Felix Frankfurter* and a *Register to the Papers of Charles J. Bonaparte*. Unpublished registers are easily photocopied.

The search for sources on constitutional change has led also to law offices and to the files of voluntary associations, materials which are not yet and may never be in library manuscript collections. None of these are listed in the Hamer *Guide* or in *NUCMC*. Except for the fact that these materials are not listed in the library catalogues to manuscript collections, they fulfill all the requirements of true archival resources. They are primary materials, they bear on important events, they are available to researchers and they are authentic. As indicated above, this is where manuscript collections begin in any event so that when a researcher examines them in the office of a lawyer or a voluntary association he is simply getting a jump on those who wait for the materials to appear in a library. Indeed, the researcher may actually facilitate having the material moved along toward a permanent library destination. In the course of my work I have aided in placing some of the papers of the National Consumers League in the Library of Congress, and the papers of the Voluntary Committee of Lawyers, Inc., in the Wesleyan University Library, where a special Collection on Legal Change has begun. Numerous other papers studied in private surroundings have not yet gone to public repositories.

Manuscript Collections[a]

American Jewish Congress. Files of the Commission on Law and Social Action.

---

[a]Entry numbers to NUCMC in this bibliography lead to concise descriptions in the *National Union Catalog of Manuscript Collections*, published annually by the Card Division of the Library of Congress, 1959-.

Office of the American Jewish Congress, 15 East 84th Street, New York, N.Y.

Amidon, Charles Fremont, 1856-1937. Papers in the Orin G. Libby Manuscript Collection, Chester Fritz Library, University of North Dakota, Grand Forks, N.D.

Anti-Saloon League of America. Records, 1893-1945, including its successor organization, the American Council on Alcohol Problems. Michigan Historical Collections, Ann Arbor, Michigan.

Association Against the Prohibition Amendment. Records, 1920-1933, in U.S. Library of Congress, Manuscript Division. NUCMC No. *MS 59-249.*

_____. Maryland Division. Papers in the Enoch Pratt Free Library, Maryland Collection, Baltimore, Maryland.

Bonaparte, Charles Joseph, 1851-1921. Papers in the U.S. Library of Congress, Manuscript Division (220C). NUCMC No. *MS 60-2031.*

Catt, Carrie (Lane) Chapman, 1859-1947. Papers in U.S. Library of Congress, Manuscript Division. NUCMC No. *MS 59-54* and *MS 68-2014.*

Consumers' League of Massachusetts. Records, 1891-1955, in Schlesinger Library on the History of Women in America, Radcliffe College (B-24). NUCMC No. *MS 64-715.*

Davenport, Charles Benedict, 1866-1944. Papers in American Philosophical Society Library, Philadelphia. NUCMC No. *MS 68-1468.*

Davis, John W., 1873-1955. Oral history memoir in Special Collections, Butler Library, Columbia University, New York, N.Y.

_____. Papers in Yale University Library. NUCMC No. *MS 64-1291.*

Fairchild, Charles Stebbins, 1842-1924. Papers in New York Historical Society.

Frankfurter, Felix, 1882-1965. Papers in U.S. Library of Congress, Manuscript Division. NUCMC No. *MS 68-2033.*

Frost, William Goodell, 1854-1938. Papers in the Hutchins Library, Berea College, Berea, Kentucky.

Hayes, Patrick Joseph Cardinal, 1867-1938. Papers in the Archives of the Archdiocese of New York, Corrigan Library, St. Joseph's Seminary, Yonkers, N.Y.

Herrick, Elinore (Morehouse), 1895-1964. Papers in Schlesinger Library on the History of Women in America, Radcliffe College (A-156). NUCMC No. *MS 66-493.*

Hobson, Richmond Pearson, 1870-1937. Papers in U.S. Library of Congress, Manuscript Division.

Jackson, Gardner, 1896-1965. Oral history memoir in Special Collections, Butler Library, Columbia University, New York, N.Y.

Joy, Henry Bourne, 1864-1936. Papers in Michigan Historical Collections, Ann Arbor, Michigan. NUCMC No. *MS 65-343.*

Laughlin, Harry Hamilton, 1880-1943. Papers in Northeast Missouri State College Library, Kirksville, Missouri. NUCMC No. *MS 68-1368.*

Lincoln, Alexander, 1873-1954. Papers in Schlesinger Library on the History of Women in America, Radcliffe College (A-109). NUCMC No. *MS 62-1127.*

Lutz, Alma. Papers on National Woman's Party. Schlesinger Library on the History of Women in America, Radcliffe College.

Lynchburg Training School and Hospital, Records of Carrie Buck case file [Buck v. Bell, 1924-1930]. Lynchburg Training School and Hospital, Department of Mental Hygiene and Hospitals, Lynchburg, Virginia.

Marbury, William L., 1858-1935. Items in possession of his son, William L. Marbury, 900 First National Bank Building, Baltimore, Maryland.

Massachusetts Anti-Suffrage Association. Papers in Massachusetts Historical Society, Boston, Mass.

Merritt, Walter Gordon, 1880-1968. Pamphlet collection in Windels, Merritt & Ingraham, 40 Wall Street, New York, N.Y.

———. Items in possession of Mrs. Walter Gordon Merritt, Route 4, New Fairfield, Conn.

National American Woman Suffrage Association. Records, 1900-1920, in U.S. Library of Congress, Manuscript Division.

National Association for the Advancement of Colored People. Records, 1909-1949, in U.S. Library of Congress, Manuscript Division (352A). NUCMC No. *MS 68-2057*.

National Consumers' League. Papers, 1898-1952, in U.S. Library of Congress, Manuscript Division.

———. Microfilm copy of Minutes of the Executive Committee, Board of Directors, and Annual Meetings drawn from the Papers in U.S. Library of Congress, Manuscript Division. Available in many subscribing libraries.

New York Society for the Suppression of Vice. Records, 1872-1950, in U.S. Library of Congress, Manuscript Division. NUCMC No. *MS 59-253*.

Nutter, McClennen & Fish. Official files on Social Security Act Cases conducted by this law firm, 1935-1937. Nutter, McClennen & Fish, 75 Federal Street, Boston, Mass.

Ohio Council on Alcohol Problems, Inc. Records, chiefly of Ohio Anti-Saloon League, 1915-1938. Michigan Historical Collections, Ann Arbor (4754).

Oregon Attorney General's case files Nos. 470A and 470B [Pierce v. Society, 1922-1925]. Oregon State Archives Division, Oregon State Library, Salem, Oregon.

Prohibition Party. National Committee Minutes, 1908-1919. Michigan Historical Collections, Ann Arbor.

Sanger, Margaret Higgins (Mrs. J. Noah H. Slee), 1879-1966. Papers in the Sophia Smith Collection, Smith College Library, Northampton, Massachusetts.

———. Papers in U.S. Library of Congress, Manuscript Division (622A). NUCMC No. *MS 60-153*.

Shouse, Jouett, b. 1879. Papers in the Margaret I. King Library, University of Kentucky, Lexington, Kentucky (59M61). NUCMC No. *MS 60-1214*.

Smith, Jane (Norman), 1874-1953. Papers in Schlesinger Library on the History of Women in America, Radcliffe College (A-116). NUCMC No. *MS 62-3414.*

Spingarn, Arthur Barnett, 1878-1971. Papers, 1911-1964, in U.S. Library of Congress, Manuscript Division (323G). NUCMC No. *MS 66-1458.*

Storey, Moorfield, 1845-1929. Papers in U.S. Library of Congress, Manuscript Division (327L).

Tucker, Henry St. George, 1853-1932. Papers in University of North Carolina Library, Southern Regional Collection. NUCMC No. *MS 60-779.*

Voluntary Committee of Lawyers, Inc. Papers, 1927-1934, of Joseph H. Choate, Jr. (1877-1968), in Collection on Legal Change, Wesleyan University, Middletown, Conn.

_____. Financial Records of V.C.L., 1927-1934, of Harrison Tweed (1884-1969), in Collection on Legal Change, Wesleyan University.

Walsh, Frank P., 1864-1939. Papers in New York Public Library, Manuscript Room.

West, Helen (Hunt), 1892-1963. Papers in Schlesinger Library on the History of Women in America, Radcliffe College (A-140). NUCMC No. *MS 65-842.*

Wheeler, Everett Pepperell, 1840-1925. Papers in New York Public Library, Manuscript Room.

White, Sue Shelton, 1887-1943. Papers, 1913-1943, in Schlesinger Library on the History of Women in America, Radcliffe College (A-74). NUCMC No. *MS-2655.*

White, Walter Francis, 1893-1955. Papers in James Weldon Johnson Collection, Beinecke Library of Yale University Library, New Haven, Conn.

Wister, Owen, 1860-1938. Papers in U.S. Library of Congress, Manuscript Division (315G). NUCMC No. *MS 59-232.*

Selected Published Works

This is a working bibliography compiled to aid study of relationships between social movements, voluntary associations, lawyers and constitutional change in the United States in this century. If relentlessly pursued these topics would lead to a book-length bibliography; here the list is selective and limited. Its emphasis is on empirical studies, the concrete not the abstract, the factual not the speculative. Recent studies are emphasized because from the standpoint of empirical investigation of litigation most of the work has occurred in the last two decades. Most of these studies have been of recent events, too, although there are notable exceptions—Magrath's account of *Fletcher v. Peck* (1810) and Olson's discoveries about the background to *Plessy v. Ferguson* (1896).

The most obvious omissions from this bibliography are the standard, contemporary accounts of developments of Supreme Court doctrine. This literature is familiar to all students of the Court and of constitutional law and is relatively easy to locate. There is no single perfect bibliography but the standard casebooks and histories, the *Index to Legal Periodicals* are built around established topics like capital punishment, equal protection and freedom of speech.

The present bibliography attempts something different. It has grown out of a search for social science studies of the courts and of litigation. It has drawn from *Dissertation Abstracts*, journals like *Labor History* and the *Western Political Quarterly* and anthologies or books of readings put together by political scientists and sociologists.

Another feature of this bibliography is its inclusion of specific Supreme Court cases which stress process and impact. In doing this it has been thought wise to include the pertinent citations. In the section on these cases, accordingly, there is a cross-reference feature running from author and study to the case citation itself.

Interest Groups in Litigation

Barker, Lucius J. "Third Parties in Litigation: A Systematic View of the Judicial Function." *Journal of Politics* 29 (February 1967): 41-69.

Bentley, Arthur. *The Process of Government: A Study of Social Pressures.* Chicago: University of Chicago Press, 1908. Chapter 16, "The Pressure of Interests in the Judiciary," pp. 382-99, is the pioneer statement of the theme.

Berns, Walter F. *Freedom, Virtue and the First Amendment.* Baton Rouge: Louisiana State University Press, 1957. Includes a short critique of David Truman's approach to the judicial process. At pp. 130-33, 160-62.

Birkby, Robert H. and Murphy, Walter F. "Interest Group Conflict in the Judicial Arena: The First Amendment and Group Access to the Courts." *Texas Law Review* 42 (1964): 1018-48.

Blaisdell, Donald C. *American Democracy Under Pressure.* New York: Ronald, 1957. See especially pp. 261-68.

Carter, Robert L. "Civil Liberties and the Civil Rights Movement." In *Legal Aspects of the Civil Rights Movement*, edited by Donald B. King and Charles W. Quick, pp. 181-93. Detroit: Wayne State University Press, 1965. Deals with rights of association.

"Class Actions." *Race Relations Law Reporter* 1 (1956): 991-1010.

Danelski, David J. "Public Law: I. The Field." *International Encyclopedia of the Social Sciences* 13 (1968): 175-81.

Fellman, David. "Adjudication: I. Domestic Adjudication." *International Encyclopedia of the Social Sciences* 1 (1968): 43-49.

_____. Review of *Dred Scott's Case*, by Vincent C. Hopkins. *Annals of the American Academy of Political and Social Science* 280 (1952): 182.

_____. "Constitutional Rights of Association." *Supreme Court Review* (1961): 74-134.

"Freedom of Association." *Race Relations Law Reporter* 4 (1959): 207-236.

Ginger, Ann Fagan. "Litigation as a Form of Political Action." In *Legal Aspects of the Civil Rights Movement*, edited by Donald B. King and Charles W. Quick, pp. 195-217. Detroit: Wayne State University Press, 1965.

Grossman, Joel B. and Tanenhaus, Joseph. *Frontiers of Judicial Research.* New York: Wiley, 1969.

Hakman, Nathan. "Lobbying the Supreme Court: An Appraisal of 'Political Science Folklore.' " *Fordham Law Review* 35 (October 1966): 15-50.

_____. "Old and New Left Activity in the Legal Order: An Interpretation." *Journal of Social Issues* 27 (1971): 105-121.

Horn, Robert A. Groups and the Constitution. Stanford, Calif: Stanford University Press, 1956. Deals with the modern law of association concerning churches, trade unions, political parties and other organizations.

Howe, Mark DeWolfe. "Political Theory and the Nature of Liberty." *Harvard Law Review* 67 (1953): 91-95.

"Inciting Litigation." *Race Relations Law Reporter* 3 (1958): 1257-77.

Jaffe, Louis. "Standing to Secure Judicial Review: Public Actions." *Harvard Law Review* 74 (1961): 1265-1314.

Krislov, Samuel. "The Amicus Curiae Brief: From Friendship to Advocacy." *Yale Law Journal* 72 (1963): 694-721.

_____. "Constituency Versus Constitutionalism: The Desegregation Issue and Tensions and Aspirations of Southern Attorneys General." *Midwest Journal of Political Science* 3 (February 1959): 75-92.

Marshall, Thurgood. "Group Action in the Pursuit of Justice." *New York University Law Review* 44 (October 1969): 661-672.

Murphy, Walter F. "The South Counter-Attacks: The Anti-NAACP Laws." *Western Political Quarterly* 12 (1959): 371-390.

_____, and Pritchett, C. Herman. *Courts, Judges, and Politics: An Introduction to the Judicial Process.* New York: Random House, 1961. Chapter 8. "Interest Groups and Litigations," an essay at pp. 274-282, followed by reprinted readings.

Peltason, Jack. *Federal Courts in the Political Process.* New York: Random House, 1955.

_____. "Judicial Process: I. Introduction." *International Encyclopedia of the Social Sciences* 8 (1968); 283-91.

"Private Attorneys-General: Group Action in the Fight for Civil Liberties." *Yale Law Journal* 58 (1949) 574-98.

Rheingold, Paul D. "The MER/29 Story—An Instance of Successful Mass Disaster Litigation." *California Law Review* 56 (1968): 116-48.

_____. "Mass Litigation Affecting Many Persons." *Trial*, December 1965, p. 29.

Robison, Joseph B. "Organizations Promoting Civil Rights and Liberties."

Annals of the American Academy of Political and Social Science 275 (1951): 18-26.

Schubert, Glendon. "Judiciary: I. Judicial Behavior." *International Encyclopedia of the Social Sciences* 8 (1968): 307-315. Deals with history, analysis and prospects, followed by a large bibliography.

Sills, David L. "Voluntary Associations: I. Sociological Aspects." *International Encyclopedia of the Social Sciences* 16 (1968): 262-279.

"The South's Amended Barratry Laws: An Attempt to End Group Pressure Through the Courts." *Yale Law Journal* 72 (1963): 1613-45.

"Taxpayers' Suits: A Survey and a Summary." *Yale Law Journal* 69 (1960): 895-924.

Truman, David B. "Political Group Analysis." *International Encyclopedia of the Social Sciences* 12 (1968): 241-45.

Vose, Clement E. "Interest Groups, Judicial Review, and Local Government." *Western Political Quarterly* 19 (March 1966): 85-100.

_____. "Litigation as a Form of Pressure Group Activity." *Annals of the American Academy of Political and Social Science* 319 (1958): 20-31.

Studies of Organizations that Litigate

Bonnett, Clarence E. *Employers' Associations in the United States: A Study of Typical Associations.* New York: Macmillan, 1922.

Ehrmann, Henry W. "Interest Groups." *International Encyclopedia of the Social Sciences* 7 (1968): 486-92.

Goldmark, Josephine. *Impatient Crusader: Florence Kelley's Life Story.* Urbana: University of Illinois Press, 1953. An admiring history of the National Consumers' League and its most outstanding leader.

Kellogg, Charles Flint. *NAACP: A History of the National Association for the Advancement of Colored People.* Vol. 1, 1909-1920. Baltimore: Johns Hopkins Press, 1967.

Markmann, Charles Lam. *The Noblest Cry: A History of the American Civil Liberties Union.* New York: St. Martin's Press, 1965.

Miller, Loren. *The Petitioners: The Story of the Supreme Court of the United States and the Negro.* Cleveland: World Publishing Co., 1966, Meridian Books No. M222.

Morgan, Richard E. "Backs to the Wall: A Study in the Contemporary Politics of Church and State." Ph.D. dissertation in political science, Columbia University, 1967. Protestants and Other Americans United for the Separation of Church and State—POAU.

Roche, John P. *The Quest for the Dream: The Development of Civil Rights and Human Relations in Modern America.* New York: Macmillan Company, 1964. Describes the roles of the Anti-Defamation League, the American Civil Liberties Union and the NAACP among others.

Sills, David. "Voluntary Associations: Sociological Aspects." *International Encyclopedia of the Social Sciences* 15 (1968): 362-79.

Wolfskill, George. *The Revolt of the Conservatives: A History of the American Liberty League, 1934-1940.* Boston: Houghton Mifflin Co., 1962.

Constitutional Litigation

Studies of Supreme Court Cases: The Judicial Process.

Barker, Lucius J., and Barker, Twiley W., Jr. *Freedoms, Courts, Politics: Studies in Civil Liberties.* Englewood Cliffs, N.J.: Prentice Hall, 1965.

Berman, Daniel M. *It Is So Ordered: The Supreme Court Rules on Schools Desegregation.* New York: W.W. Norton & Company, 1966.

    Brown v. Board of Education, 347 U.S. 483 (1954), 349 U.S. 294 (1955).

Berns, Walter. "Buck v. Bell: Due Process of Law?," *Western Political Quarterly* 6 (1953): 762-773.

    Buck v. Bell, 274 U.S. 200 (1927).

Bickel, Alexander. *The Unpublished Opinions of Mr. Justice Brandeis: The Supreme Court at Work.* Cambridge: Harvard University Press, Belknap Press, 1957.

    Atherton Mills v. Johnston, 259 U.S. 13 (1922), in Bickel at pp. 1-20;

    St. Louis, Iron Mountain & Southern Ry. v. Starbird, 243 U.S. 592 (1917), in Bickel at pp. 21-33;

    Strathearn S.S. Co. v. Dillon, 252 U.S. 348 (1920), in Bickel at pp. 34-60;

    Arizona Employers' Liability Cases, 250 U.S. 400 (1919), in Bickel at pp. 61-76;

    United Mine Workers v. Coronado, 259 U.S. 344 (1922), in Bickel at pp. 77-99;

    Sonneborn Bros. v. Cureton, 262 U.S. 506 (1923), in Bickel at pp. 100-118;

    Stratton v. St. Louis Southwestern Ry., 282 U.S. 10 (1930), 284 U.S. 530 (1932), in Bickel at pp. 119-163;

    Shafer v. Farmers Grain Co., 268 U.S. 189 (1925), in Bickel at pp. 164-201;

    Railroad Commission v. Southern Pacific Ry., 264 U.S. 331 (1924) and American Railway Express Co. v. Kentucky, 273 U.S. 269 (1927), in Bickel at pp. 202-219;

    Bullock v. Florida, 254 U.S. 513 (1921), in Bickel at pp. 220-238.

———. "The Voting Rights Cases." *Supreme Court Review* (1966): 79-166.

    South Carolina v. Katzenbach, 383 U.S. 301 (1966).

Blaustein, Albert P., and Ferguson, Clarence Clyde, Jr. *Desegregation and the Law: The Meaning and Effect of the School Desegregation Cases.* New York:

Vintage Books, 1957.

  Brown v. Board of Education, 347 U.S. 483 (1954), 349 U.S. 294 (1955).

Boles, Donald E. *The Bible, Religion, and the Public Schools.* 3d ed. Ames: Iowa State University Press, 1965.

Chambers, John W. "The Big Switch: Justice Roberts and the Minimum-Wage Cases." *Labor History* 10 (Winter 1969): 44-73.

  Morehead v. New York ex rel. Tipaldo, 298 U.S. 587 (1936),

  West Coast Hotel Co. v. Parrish, 300 U.S. 379 (1937).

Cortner, Richard C. *The Apportionment Cases.* Knoxville, Tenn.: University of Tennessee Press, 1970.

  Baker v. Carr, 369 U.S. 186 (1962).

  Reynolds v. Sims, 377 U.S. 533 (1964).

_____ . *The Arizona Train Limit Case: Southern Pacific Co. v. Arizona.* The Institute of Government Research, Arizona Government Studies, no. 8. Tucson: University of Arizona Press, 1970.

  Southern Pacific Co. v. Arizona, 325 U.S. 761 (1945).

_____ . *The Jones & Laughlin Case.* Borzoi Series in United States Constitutional History. New York: Alfred A. Knopf, 1970.

  National Labor Relations Board v. Jones & Laughlin Steel Corp., 301 U.S. 1 (1937).

_____ . *The Wagner Act Cases.* Knoxville, Tenn.: University of Tennessee Press, 1964.

  National Labor Relations Board v. Jones & Laughlin, 301 U.S. 1 (1937).

Eggert, Gerald G. "Richard Olney and the Income Tax Cases." *Mississippi Valley Historical Review* 48 (June 1961): 24-41.

  Pollack v. Farmers' Loan & Trust Co., 157 U.S. 429 (1895), 158 U.S. 601 (1895).

Fine, Sidney. "Frank Murphy, the Thornhill Decision, and Picketing as Free Speech." *Labor History* 6 (Spring 1965): 99-120.

  Thornhill v. Alabama, 310 U.S. 88 (1940).

_____ . "Mr. Justice Murphy and the Hirabayashi Case." *Pacific Historical Review* 33 (May 1964): 195-209.

  Hirabayashi v. United States, 320 U.S. 81 (1943).

Garraty, John A., ed. *Quarrels That Have Shaped the Constitution.* New York: Harper & Row, Harper Colophon Books, 1964.

  Marbury v. Madison, 1 Cr. 137 (1803), by John A. Garraty in Garraty at pp. 1-14;

  Dartmouth College v. Woodward, 4 Wheat. 518 (1819), by Richard N. Current in Garraty at pp. 15-29;

  McCulloch v. Maryland, 4 Wheat. 316 (1819), by Bray Hammond in Garraty at pp. 30-49;

  Gibbons v. Ogden, 9 Wheat. 269 (1824), By George Dangerfield in Garraty at pp. 49-62;

Charles River Bridge v. Warren Bridge, 11 Pet. 420 (1837), by Henry F. Graff in Garraty at pp. 62-76;

Scott v. Sandford, 19 How. 393 (1857), by Bruce Catton in Garraty at pp. 77-90;

Ex parte Milligan, 4 Wall. 2 (1866), by Allan Nevins in Garraty at pp. 90-109;

Munn v. Illinois, 94 U.S. 113 (1877) by C. Peter Magrath in Garraty at pp. 109-128;

Civil Rights Cases, 109 U.S. 3 (1883), by Alan Westin in Garraty at pp. 128-145;

Plessy v. Ferguson, 163 U.S. 537 (1896), by C. Vann Woodward in Garraty at pp. 145-159;

Northern Securities Co. v. United States, 193 U.S. 197 (1904), by R.W. Apple, Jr. in Garraty at pp. 159-176;

Muller v. Oregon, 208 U.S. 412 (1908), by Alpheus Thomas Mason in Garraty at pp. 176-191;

Schechter Poultry Corporation v. United States, 295 U.S. 495 (1935), by Frank Freidel in Garraty at pp. 191-210;

United States v. Curtiss-Wright Corporation, 299 U.S. 304 (1936), by Robert A. Divine in Garraty at pp. 210-222;

West Virginia State Board of Education v. Barnette, 319 U.S. 624 (1943), by Irving Dilliard in Garraty at pp. 222-243;

Brown v. Board of Education, 347 U.S. 483 (1954), 349 U.S. 294 (1955), by Alfred H. Kelley in Garraty at pp. 243-269.

Goodman, Walter. "A Victory for 400,000 Children—The Case of Mrs. Sylvester Smith." *New York Times Magazine,* August 25, 1968, p. 28.

King v. Smith, 392 U.S. 309 (1968).

Grodzins, Morton. *Americans Betrayed: Politics and the Japanese Evacuation.* Chicago: University of Chicago Press, 1949.

Korematsu v. United States, 323 U.S. 214 (1944).

Heckman, Richard Allen, and Hall, Betty Jean. "Berea College and the Day Law." *Register of the Kentucky Historical Society* 66 (January 1968): 35-52.

Berea College v. Kentucky, 211 U.S. 45 (1908).

Hill, Herbert, and Greenberg, Jack. *Citizen's Guide to De-Segregation: A Story of Social and Legal Change in America.* Boston: Beacon Press, 1955.

Brown v. Board of Education, 347 U.S. 483 (1954), 349 U.S. 294 (1955).

Hopkins, Vincent C. *Dred Scott's Case.* New York: Fordham University Press, 1951. Atheneum, 1967.

Scott v. Sandford, 19 How. 393 (1857).

Howard, J. Woodford, and Bushoven, Cornelieus. "The Screws Case Revisited." *Journal of Politics* 29 (August 1967): 617-36.

Screws v. United States, 325 U.S. 9 (1945).

Katz, Ellis. "The Supreme Court in the Web of Government: The ACLU, the

Supreme Court and the Bible." Ph.D. dissertation, Columbia University. *University Microfilms Dissertation Abstracts Number 67-9346*, 1967.

　　Abington School District v. Schempp, 374 U.S. 203 (1965).

Kutler, Stanley I., ed. *The Dred Scott Decision: Law or Politics?* Boston: Houghton Mifflin Co., 1967.

　　Scott v. Sandford, 19 How. 393 (1857).

Kutler, Stanley I. *Privilege and Creative Destruction: The Charles River Bridge Case.* New York: J.B. Lippincott Co., 1971.

　　Charles River Bridge v. Warren Bridge, 11 Pet. 420 (1837).

Lee, Calvin B.T. *One Man, One Vote: WMCA and the Struggle for Equal Representation.* New York: Charles Scribner's Sons, 1967.

　　WMCA, Inc. v. Lomenzo, 377 U.S. 633 (1964).

Leuchtenburg, William E. "The Case of the Contentions Commissioner: Humphrey's Executor v. U.S." In *Freedom and Reform: Essays in Honor of Henry Steele Commage*, edited by Harold M. Hyman and Leonard W. Levy, pp. 276-312. New York: Harper & Row, 1967.

　　Humphrey's Executor v. United States, 295 U.S. 602 (1935).

Levy, Leonard W. and Phillips, Harlan B. "The Roberts Case: Source of the 'Separate But Equal' Doctrine." *American Historical Review* 56 (1951): 510-18.

　　Roberts v. City of Boston, 59 Mass. 198 (1849).

Lewis, Anthony. *Gideon's Trumpet.* New York: Random House, Vintage, 1964.

　　Gideon v. Wainwright, 372 U.S. 355 (1963).

Lieberman, Elias. *Unions Before the Bar: Historic Trials Showing the Evolution of Labor Rights in the United States.* New York: Harper, 1950; revised edition, New York: Oxford Book Co., 1960.

　　In re Debs, 158 U.S. 564 (1895), in Lieberman at pp. 29-43;

　　Adair v. United States, 208 U.S. 161 (1908), in Lieberman at pp. 44-55;

　　Loewe v. Lawlor, 208 U.S. 274 (1908), in Lieberman at pp. 56-71;

　　Bucks Stove and Range Co. v. Gompers, 219 U.S. 581 (1913), in Lieberman, at pp. 71-83;

　　Hitchman Coal Co. v. Mitchell, 245 U.S. 229 (1917), in Lieberman at pp. 96-107;

　　American Steel Foundries v. Tri-City Central Trades Council, 257 U.S. 184 (1921), in Lieberman at pp. 108-117;

　　Truax v. Corrigan, 257 U.S. 312 (1921), in Lieberman at pp. 118-26;

　　Wolff Packing Co. v. Court of Industrial Relations of Kansas, 262 U.S. 522 (1923), 267 U.S. 522 (1925), in Lieberman at pp. 127-40;

　　United Mine Workers v. Coronado Coal Co., 259 U.S. 344 (1922); Coronado Coal Co. v. United Mine Workers, 268 U.S. 295 (1925), in Lieberman at pp. 141-63;

　　Bedford Cut Stone Co. v. Journeymen Stone Cutter's Association, 274 U.S. 37 (1927), in Lieberman at pp. 164-72;

Senn v. Tile Layers Protective Union, 301 U.S. 468 (1937), in Lieberman
   at pp. 173-80;

National Labor Relations Board v. Jones & Laughlin Steel Corporation,
   301 U.S. 1 (1937), in Lieberman at pp. 181-203;

National Labor Relations Board v. Fansteel Metallurgical Co., 98 F.2d 375
   (1938), in Lieberman at pp. 204-16;

Thornhill v. Alabama, 310 U.S. 88 (1940), in Lieberman at pp. 217-24;

United States v. Hutcheson, 312 U.S. 219 (1941), in Lieberman at pp.
   241-52;

Steele v. Louisville & Nashville Railroad, 323 U.S. 192 (1944), in
   Lieberman at pp. 252-62;

Wallace Corporation v. National Labor Relations Board, 323 U.S. 248
   (1944), in Lieberman at pp. 263-71;

Allen Bradley Co. v. Local Union No. 3, I.B.E.W., 325 U.S. 797 (1945), in
   Lieberman at pp. 272-86;

United States v. United Mine Workers of America and John L. Lewis, 330
   U.S. 258 (1947), in Lieberman at pp. 287-302;

Lincoln Federal Labor Union No. 19129 v. Northwestern Iron and Metal
   Co., 69 S.Ct. 251 (1949); Whitaker v. North Carolina, 69 S.Ct. 251
   (1949); A.F. of L. v. American Sash & Door Co., 69 U.S. 258 (1949),
   in Lieberman at pp. 330-43.

Magrath, C. Peter. *Yazoo: The Case of Fletcher v. Peck*. Providence: Brown
University Press, 1966. New York: W.W. Norton, 1967.

Fletcher v. Peck, 6 Cr. 87 (1810).

Malick, Clay P. "Terry v. Adams: Governmental Responsibility for the Protection of Civil Rights." *Western Political Quarterly* 7 (March, 1954): 51-64.

Terry v. Adams, 345 U.S. 461 (1953).

Manwaring, David R. *Render Unto Caesar: The Flag Salute Controversy*.
Chicago: University of Chicago Press, 1962.

West Virginia State Board of Education v. Barnette, 319 U.S. 624 (1943).

Minersville School District v. Gobitis, 310 U.S. 586 (1940).

Marke, Julius J. *Vignettes of Legal History*. Introduction by Bernard Schwartz.
South Hackensack, New Jersey: F.B. Rothman, 1965.

Marbury v. Madison, 1 Cr. 137 (1803), in Marke at pp. 1-18;

United States v. Peters, 5 Cr. 115 (1809), in Marke at pp. 19-32;

McCulloch v. Maryland, 4 Wheat. 316 (1819), in Marke at pp. 33-50;

Wheaton v. Peters, 8 Pet. 591 (1834), in Marke at pp. 51-64;

Luther v. Borden, 7 How. 1 (1849), in Marke at pp. 65-80;

Scott v. Sandford, 19 How. 393 (1857), in Marke at pp. 81-104;

Ex parte Merryman, 17 Fed. Cas. 144 (No. 9487) (1861); Ex parte
   Vallandigham, 1 Wall, 243 (1864); Ex parte Milligan, 4 Wall. 2 (1866),
   in Marke at pp. 105-140;

Ex parte McCardle, 7 Wall. 506 (1868), in Marke at pp. 141-68;

Slaughter-House Cases, 16 Wall. 36 (1873), in Marke at pp. 169-90.

Mathis, Doyle. "Chisholm v. Georgia: Background and Settlement." *Journal of American History* 54 (June 1967): 19-29.

Chisholm v. Georgia, 2 Dall. 419 (1793).

McCollum, Vashti Cromwell. *One Woman's Fight.* Boston: Beacon Press, 1951, rev. ed. 1961.

McCollum v. Board of Education, 333 U.S. 203 (1948).

Metcalfe, William K. "The Tidelands Controversy: A Study in the Development of a Political-Legal Problem." *Syracuse Law Review* 4 (Fall 1952): 39-89.

United States v. California, 332 U.S. 19 (1947).

Olson, Otto H., ed. *The Thin Disguise: Turning Point in Negro History. Plessy v. Ferguson: A Documentary Presentation, 1864-1896.* New York: Humanities Press, 1967.

Plessy v. Ferguson, 163 U.S. 537 (1896).

Peirce, Neal R. "The Electoral College Goes to Court," *The Reporter*, October 6, 1966, pp. 34-37.

Delaware v. New York, motion to file a bill of complaint denied, 385 U.S. 895 (1966), rehearing denied, 385 U.S. 964 (1966).

Prettyman, Barrett, Jr. *Death and the Supreme Court.* New York: Harcourt, Brace & World, Inc., Harvest Book, 1961.

Fikes v. Alabama, 252 U.S. 191 (1957), in Prettyman at pp. 5-46;

Green v. United States, 365 U.S. 301 (1961), in Prettyman at pp. 47-89;

Francis v. Resweber, 329 U.S. 459 (1947), in Prettyman at pp. 90-128;

Griffin v. United States, 336 U.S. 704 (1949), in Prettyman at pp. 129-66;

Crooker v. California, 357 U.S. 433 (1958), in Prettyman at pp. 167-257;

Williams v. Georgia, 349 U.S. 375 (1955), in Prettyman at pp. 258-94.

Pritchett, C. Herman and Westin, Alan F., eds. *The Third Branch of Government: Eight Cases in Constitutional Politics.* New York: Harcourt, Brace & World, Inc., 1963.

West Virginia State Board of Education v. Barnette, 319 U.S. 624 (1943), by David R. Manwaring in Pritchett and Westin at pp. 19-49;

Anderson v. Mt. Clemens Pottery Co. (Portal-to-Portal Pay Case), 328 U.S. 680 (1945), by Richard E. Morgan in Pritchett and Westin at pp. 50-82;

Francis v. Resweber, 329 U.S. 459 (1947), by Barrett Prettyman, Jr. in Pritchett and Westin at pp. 83-117;

Zorach v. Clauson, 343 U.S. 306 (1952), by Frank J. Sorauf in Pritchett and Westin at pp. 118-148;

N.A.A.C.P. v. Alabama, 357 U.S. 449 (1958), by George R. Osborne in Pritchett and Westin at pp. 149-203;

Vitarelli v. Seaton, 359 U.S. 535 (1959), by Leonard G. Miller in Pritchett and Westin at pp. 204-233;

United States v. California, 332 U.S. 19 (1947), United States v. Louisiana, 339 U.S. 699 (1950), United States v. Texas, 339 U.S. 707 (1950),

Alabama v. Texas, 347 U.S. 272 (1954), United States v. Louisiana, 363 U.S. 1 (1960), by Lucius J. Barker in Pritchett and Westin at pp. 234-74;

Gallagher v. Crown Kosher Super Market, Inc., 366 U.S. 617 (1961), Two Guys from Harrison-Allentown, Inc. v. McGinley, 366 U.S. 582 (1961), by Sister Candida Lund in Pritchett and Westin at pp. 275-308.

Rembar, Charles. *The End of Obscenity: The Trials of Lady Chatterley, Tropic of Cancer and Fanny Hill.* New York: Random House, Bantam Books, 1969.

Robinson, Donald B. *Spotlight on a Union: The Story of the United Hatters, Cap and Millinery Workers International Union.* New York: Dial Press, 1948. See Chapter 5, "Battle of the Century," at pp. 77-101.

Loewe v. Lawlor, 208 U.S. 274 (1908).

Schubert, Glendon, ed. *Reapportionment.* New York: Charles Scribner's Sons, 1965. Baker v. Carr, 369 U.S. 186 (1962);

Reynolds, v. Sims, 377 U.S. 533 (1964).

Taper, Bernard. *Gomillion v. Lightfoot.* New York: McGraw-Hill Book Co., 1962.

Gomillion v. Lightfoot, 364 U.S. 339 (1960).

Taylor, Telford. *Two Studies in Constitutional Interpretation: Search, Seizure, and Surveillance and Fair Trial and Free Press.* Columbus: Ohio State University Press, 1969.

tenBroek, Jacobus; Barnhart, Edward N.; and Matson, Floyd W. *Prejudice, War and the Constitution: Causes and Consequences of the Evacuation of the Japanese Americans in World War II.* Japanese American Evacuation and Resettlement Study. Berkeley and Los Angeles: University of California Press, 1958. Reissued 1968.

Korematsu v. United States, 323 U.S. 214 (1944).

Tyack, David B. "The Perils of Pluralism: The Background of the Pierce Case." *American Historical Review* 74 (1968): 74-98.

Society of the Sisters v. Pierce, 268 U.S. 510 (1925).

Vose, Clement E. Review of *Anatomy of a Constitutional Law Case*, by Alan F. Westin. *Yale Law Journal* 69 (1969): 716-24.

——. *Caucasians Only: The Supreme Court, the NAACP and the Restrictive Covenant Cases.* Berkeley and Los Angeles: University of California Press, 1959. Campus Editions No. 1, 1968.

Shelley v. Kraemer, 334 U.S. 1 (1968);

Hurd v. Hodge, 344 U.S. 24 (1948);

Barrows v. Jackson, 346 U.S. 249 (1953).

——. "NAACP Strategy in the Covenant Cases." *Western Reserve Law Review* 6 (1955): 101-145.

Shelley v. Kraemer, 334 U.S. 1 (1948).

——. "National Consumers' League and the Brandeis Brief." *Midwest Journal of Political Science* 1 (1957): 178-190.

Muller v. Oregon, 208 U.S. 412 (1908).

Westin, Alan F. *The Anatomy of a Constitutional Law Case.* New York: Macmillan Company, 1958.

Youngstown Sheet & Tube Co. v. Sawyer, 343 U.S. 579 (1952).

Westin, Alan F. "Bookies and 'Bugs' in California: Judicial Control of Police Practices." In *The Centers of Power: 3 Cases in American National Government*, edited by Alan F. Westin, pp. 107-160. New York: Harcourt, Brace & World, Inc., 1964.

Irvine v. California, 347 U.S. 128 (1954).

Wood, Stephen B. *Constitutional Politics in the Progressive Era: Child Labor and the Law.* Chicago: University of Chicago Press, 1967.

Hammer v. Dagenhart, 247 U.S. 251 (1918);

Bailey v. Drexel Furniture Co., 259 U.S. 20 (1922).

Studies of Supreme Court Cases: Impact of Decision.

Beaney, William M. and Beiser, Edward N. "Prayer and Politics: The Impact of Engel and Schempp on the Political Process." *Journal of Public Law* 13 (1964): 475-503. Reprinted in Becker, *The Impact of Supreme Court Decisions*, at pp. 20-34.

Engle v. Vitale, 370 U.S. 421 (1962);

School District v. Schempp, 374 U.S. 203 (1963).

Becker, Theodore L., ed. *The Impact of Supreme Court Decisions: Empirical Studies.* New York: Oxford University Press, 1969.

Birkby, Robert H. "The Supreme Court and the Bible Belt: Tennessee Reaction to the 'Schempp' Decision." *Midwest Journal of Political Science* 10 (1966): 304-315. Reprinted in Becker, at pp. 106-114.

School District v. Schempp, 374 U.S. 203 (1963).

Dolbeare, Kenneth M. "The Supreme Court and the States: From Abstract Doctrine to Local Behavioral Conformity." Original essay in Becker, at pp. 206-213.

Engel v. Vitale, 370 U.S. 421 (1962);

School District v. Schempp, 374 U.S. 203 (1963).

———, and Hammond, Phillip E. *The School Prayer Decisions: From Court Policy to Local Practice.* Chicago: University of Chicago Press, 1971.

Johnson, Richard M. "Compliance and Supreme Court Decision-Making." *Wisconsin Law Review* (Winter 1967): 170-85. Reprinted in Becker, at pp. 115-28.

School District v. Schempp, 374 U.S. 203 (1963);

Engel v. Vitale, 370 U.S. 421 (1962);

Zorach v. Clauson, 343 U.S. 306 (1952);

McCollum v. Board of Education, 333 U.S. 203 (1948);

Everson v. Board of Education, 330 U.S. 1 (1947).

_____. *The Dynamics of Compliance: Supreme Court Decision-Making in a New Perspective.* Evanston, Ill.: Northwestern University Press, 1967.

Levine, James P. "Constitutional Law and Obscene Literature: An Investigation of Bookseller Censorship Practices." Original essay in Becker, *Impact*, at pp. 129-48.

Roth v. United States, 354 U.S. 476 (1957).

Manwaring, David R. "The Impact of Mapp v. Ohio." In *The Supreme Court as Policy-Maker: Three Studies on the Impact of Judicial Decisions*, edited by David H. Everson, pp. 1-43. Carbondale, Ill.: Public Affairs Research Bureau, Southern Illinois University, 1968.

Mapp v. Ohio, 367 U.S. 643 (1961).

Medalie, Richard J.; Zeitz, Leonard; and Alexander, Paul. "Custodial Police Interrogation in Our Nation's Capital: The Attempt to Implement Miranda." *Michigan Law Review* 66 (1968): 1347-422. Reprinted in Becker, *Impact*, at pp. 165-75.

Miranda v. Arizona, 384 U.S. 436 (1966).

Muir, William K., Jr. *Prayer in the Public Schools: Law and Attitude Change.* Chicago: University of Chicago Press, 1967.

Engle v. Vitale, 370 U.S. 421 (1962);

School District v. Schempp, 374 U.S. 203 (1963).

Orfield, Gary. *The Reconstruction of Southern Education: The Schools and the 1964 Civil Rights Act.* New York: Wiley, 1969. A study of the impact of the 1964 Act on school desegregation.

Patric, Gordon. "The Impact of a Court Decision: Aftermath of the McCollum Case." *Journal of Public Law* 6 (1957): 455-64.

McCollum v. Board of Education, 333 U.S. 203 (1948).

Peltason, Jack W. "After the Lawsuit Is Over." In *Federal Courts in the Political Process*, edited by Jack W. Peltason, pp. 55-64. New York: Random House, 1955.

_____. *Fifty-Eight Lonely Men.* New York: Harcourt, Brace and World, 1961.

Brown v. Board of Education, 347 U.S. 483 (1954); 349 U.S. 294 (1955).

Reich, Donald R. "The Impact of Judicial Decision Making: The School Prayer Cases." In Everson, *The Supreme Court as Policy-Maker*, at pp. 44-81.

School District v. Schempp, 374 U.S. 203 (1963);

Engel v. Vitale, 370 U.S. 421 (1962).

Sorauf, Frank J. "Zorach v. Clauson: The Impact of A Supreme Court Decision." *American Political Science Review* 53 (1959): 777-91.

Zorach v. Clauson, 343 U.S. 306 (1952).

Souris, Theodore. "Stop and Frisk or Arrest and Search—The Use and Misuse of Euphemisms." *Journal of Criminal Law, Criminology and Political Science* 57 (1966): 251-64. Reprinted in Becker, *Impact*, at pp. 176-80.

Escobedo v. Illinois, 378 U.S. 478 (1964).

Steamer, Robert. "The Role of the Federal District Courts in the Segregation Controversy." *Journal of Politics* 22 (1960): 417-38.

    Brown v. Board of Education, 347 U.S. 483 (1954); 349 U.S. 294 (1955).

Vines, Kenneth N. "Federal District Judges and Race Relations Cases in the South." *Journal of Politics* 26 (1964): 337-57. Reprinted in Becker, *Impact*, at pp. 76-87.

    Brown v. Board of Education, 347 U.S. 483 (1954); 349 U.S. 294 (1955).

Wald, Michael S.; Ayers, Richard; Hess, David W.; Schantz, Mark; and Whitebread, Charles H. III. "Interrogations in New Haven: The Impact of *Miranda.*" *Yale Law Journal* 76 (1967): 1519-648. Reprinted in Becker, *Impact*, at pp. 149-64.

    Miranda v. Arizona, 384 U.S. 436 (1966).

Wasby, Stephen L. *The Impact of the United States Supreme Court: Some Perspectives.* Homewood, Ill.: Dorsey Press, 1970.

    _____. "The Pure and the Prurient: The Supreme Court, Obscenity, and Oregon Policy." In Everson, *The Supreme Court as Policy-Maker*, at pp. 82-116.

    Roth v. United States, 354 U.S. 476 (1957), and related cases.

Notes

Notes

Preface

1. Clement E. Vose, University of California Press, Berkeley and Los Angeles, 1959; Campus Editions no. 1, 1968.
2. Buck v. Bell, 274 U.S. 200 (1927).
3. Pierce v. Society of the Sisters, 268 U.S. 510 (1925).
4. Steward Machine v. Davis, 301 U.S. 548 (1937); Helvering v. Davis, 301 U.S. 619 (1937).
5. Bobbs-Merrill, Indianapolis and New York 1969 and 1970.
6. Harper & Row, New York, 1971; Harper & Row, New York, 1972.
7. 2 vols. to date, vols. 1 and 6: Macmillan Co., New York, 1971.
8. National Prohibition Cases, 253 U.S. 350 (1920).
9. *Notable American Women, 1607-1950*, 3 vols. Belknap Press of Harvard University Press, Cambridge, 1971.

Introduction: Approaches to Constitutional Change

1. Remarks by Hugo Black in "Tribute to Alexander Meiklejohn," *AAUP Bulletin* 54 (September 1965), pp. 367-68.
2. Information about the habits of the justices comes from published sources and from conversations with Justices Frankfurter, Black and Burton as well as with numerous former clerks in conversations over the years.
3. Morehead v. New York *ex rel.* Tipaldo, 298 U.S. 587, 633 (1936) (dissenting opinion). When the Court ruled that state courts may not constitutionally award damages when a racial restrictive covenant is broken, Chief Justice Fred M. Vinson felt his colleagues had followed their personal "predilections on social policy" and "a simple self-serving process of argument" in reaching the result. Barrows v. Jackson, 346 U.S. 249, 266, 269 (1953) (dissenting opinion).
4. Fred Rodell, *Nine Men: A Political History of the Supreme Court from 1790 to 1955*, Random House, New York, 1955.
5. John Schmidhauser, "The Justices of the Supreme Court: A Collective Portrait," *Midwest Journal of Political Science* 3 (1959), pp. 1, 2.
6. Ibid., p. 49.
7. See C. Herman Pritchett, *The Roosevelt Court*, Macmillan Company, New York, 1948; idem, *Civil Liberties and the Vinson Court*, University of Chicago Press, Chicago, 1954.
8. See Glendon A. Schubert, "The Study of Judicial Decision-Making as an Aspect of Political Behavior," *American Political Science Review* 52 (1958), p.

1007; Fred Kort, "Predicting Supreme Court Decisions Mathematically: A Quantitative Analysis of the 'Right to Counsel' Cases," *American Political Science Review* 51 (1957), p. 1; Franklin M. Fisher, "The Mathematical Analysis of Supreme Court Decisions: The Use and Abuse of Quantitative Methods," *American Political Science Review* 52 (1958), p. 321; John P. Roche, "Political Science and Science Fiction," *American Political Science Review* 52 (1958), p. 1026.

9. It was said of Mr. Justice Brandeis that "almost the paramount quality of a good judge was the capacity to be reached by reason, the freedom from self-pride that without embarrassment permits a change of mind." Paul A. Freund, "Introduction" to Alexander M. Bickel, *The Unpublished Opinions of Mr. Justice Brandeis*, Belknap Press of Harvard University Press, Cambridge, 1957, p. xx. See also Paul A. Freund, *On Understanding the Supreme Court*, Little Brown, Boston, 1949, pp. 45-75. And Mr. Justice Frankfurter, speaking of "the qualities which should be sought for in members of the Supreme Court," has said, "The first requisite is disinterestedness; the second requisite is disinterestedness; the third is disinterestedness." Felix Frankfurter, "Judge Henry W. Edgerton," *Cornell Law Quarterly* 43 (1957), pp. 161, 162.

10. See, e.g., Drew Pearson and Robert S. Allen, *The Nine Old Men*, Doubleday, Doran, Garden City, New York, 1937; Arthur M. Schlesinger, Jr., "Supreme Court, 1947," *Fortune*, January 1947, p. 73.

11. Alan F. Westin, "Stephen J. Field and the Headnote to O'Neil v. Vermont: A Snapshot of the Fuller Court at Work," *Yale Law Journal* 67 (1958), p. 363.

12. Bickel, *Unpublished Opinions of Mr. Justice Brandeis*.

13. Discussions of this problem are to be found in ibid, pp. vii-ix; Westin, book review, *Yale Law Journal* 66 (1957), pp. 462, 468-69. Studies that treat the Court as an ever-changing "small group" contribute a helpful thought. See Eloise C. Snyder, "The Supreme Court as a Small Group," *Social Forces* 36 (1958), 232. That hard bargaining goes on among judges is amply shown in a recent study of the United States Court of Appeals for the Second Circuit. Marvin Schick, *Learned Hand's Court*, Johns Hopkins Press, Baltimore, 1970. Harsh language and troubled relations in the Supreme Court during the 1940s is convincingly documented in J. Woodford Howard, *Mr. Justice Murphy: A Political Biography*, Princeton University Press, Princeton, 1968.

14. Quoted in Benjamin R. Twiss, *Lawyers and the Constitution*, Russell and Russell, New York, 1962, p. 2. Reprint of the 1942 edition.

15. Ibid. That a similar role has been played by lawyers on other questions in other eras is suggested by the careers of Daniel Webster and Thurgood Marshall, but the precise place of counsel in relation to other factors in Supreme Court cases remains to be spelled out. For a classic discussion, see the chapter on constitutional law and Daniel Webster in Charles Warren, *The Supreme Court in United States History*, rev. ed., vol. 1, Houghton Mifflin, Cambridge, 1928, pp.

686-728. On Thurgood Marshall, see Saunders Redding, *The Lonesome Road*, Doubleday and Company, Garden City, New York, 1958, pp. 315-29. See also John Frank, *Marble Palace*, Alfred A. Knopf, New York, 1958, pp. 97-101.

16. Clyde Jacobs, *Law Writers and the Courts*, University of California Press, Berkeley, 1954, p. v.

17. Abe Fortas, "Thurman Arnold and the Theatre of the Law," *Yale Law Journal* 79 (1970), pp. 1003-004.

18. Lochner v. New York, 198 U.S. 75 (1904).

19. C.E.M. Joad, "Herbert Spencer (1820-1903)," *Encyclopedia of the Social Sciences* 14 (1934), 295. Less attention is paid *Social Statics* in R.L. Carneiro, "Herbert Spencer," *International Encyclopedia of the Social Sciences* 15 (1968), pp. 121-28.

20. Ely to Holmes, October 24, 1906, reprinted in Benjamin G. Rader and Barbara K. Rader, "The Ely-Holmes Friendship, 1901-1914," *American Journal of Legal History* 10 (1966), p. 138.

21. Edward S. Corwin, "The Supreme Court as a National School Board," *Law and Contemporary Problems* 14 (Winter 1949), p. 22; Martin Shapiro, *Law and Politics in the Supreme Court*, Free Press, Glencoe, Ill., 1964; Charles A. Miller, *The Supreme Court and the Uses of History*, Belknap Press of Harvard University Press, Cambridge, 1969.

22. Arthur F. Bentley, *The Process of Government*, Principia Press, Bloomington, Ind., 1935, p. 388.

23. Ibid., p. 393.

24. Walter Berns, *Freedom, Virtue and the First Amendment*, Louisiana State University Press, Baton Rouge, 1957, p. 133. His criticism was leveled at David Truman, *The Governmental Process*, Alfred A. Knopf, New York, 1951, especially chapter 15.

25. Darryl Baskin, "American Pluralism: Theory, Practice, and Ideology," *Journal of Politics* 32 (February 1970), p. 71. Baskin's article contains an ample bibliography of the subject.

26. V.O. Key, Jr., *Politics, Parties and Pressure Groups*, Thomas Y. Crowell, New York. This was true of all the editions until 1958. Later editions, reflected the findings of studies in constitutional litigation.

27. The discussion here expresses the outlook prevailing during the first years such studies were undertaken and is drawn from C.E. Vose, "Litigation as a Form of Pressure Group Activity," *Annals of the American Academy of Political and Social Science* 319 (September 1958), pp. 20-31. By 1972 there were numerous studies of particular cases and these are listed in the bibliography.

28. Robert A. Horn, *Groups and the Constitution*, Stanford University Press, Stanford, Calif., 1956. See also Elias Lieberman, *Unions Before the Bar*, Harper & Brothers, New York 1950.

29. Richard Harris, "I'd Like to Talk With You for a Minute." *New Yorker*, June 16, 1956, pp. 72,88.

30. David J. Danelski, "Public Law: The Field," *International Encyclopedia of the Social Sciences* 13 (1968), p. 179.

31. Nathan Hakman, "The Supreme Court's Political Environment: The Process of Noncommercial Litigation," *Frontiers of Judicial Research*, eds. Joel B. Grossman and Joseph Tanenhaus, John Wiley and Sons, New York, 1969, p. 199. See Hakman, "Lobbying the Supreme Court—An Appraisal of 'Political Science Folklore,' " *Fordham Law Review* 35 (1966), p. 15.

32. Robert H. Jackson, *The Struggle for Judicial Supremacy*, Alfred A. Knopf, New York, 1941, p. 311.

33. Ibid., pp. 311-12.

34. Felix Frankfurter and Henry Hart, "The Business of the Supreme Court at October Term, 1933," *Harvard Law Review* 48 (1934), p. 238. Corwin has observed "that for considerable intervals it [the Supreme Court] will be found to be under the sway of a particular 'social philosophy,' the operation of which in important cases becomes a matter of fairly easy prediction on the part of those who follow the Court's work with some care." Corwin, *The Constitution and What It Means Today*, 12th ed., Princeton University Press, Princeton, 1958, p. 253. Corwin had in mind the outlook of the judges, but apparently, when the *New York Times* declared, the day after the Court announced its decision in the *School Segregation Cases*, that the result had been "inevitable," it was speaking of the "spirit of the times." *New York Times*, May 18, 1954, p. 28.

35. Rudolph Heberle, "Types and Functions of Social Movements," *International Encyclopedia of the Social Sciences* 14 (1968), p. 438; Joseph R. Gusfield, "The Study of Social Movements," ibid., p. 445. These articles each supply ample bibliographies of the subject.

36. Truman, *The Governmental Process*, p. 33.

37. Ibid., p. 34.

Chapter 1
The Eugenics Movement

1. Buck v. Bell, 274 U.S. 200 (1927).

2. Ibid., p. 207.

3. Act of Virginia, March 20, 1924, ch. 394.

4. Ibid., p. 207.

5. Jacobson v. Massachusetts, 197 U.S. 11 (1905).

6. David W. Meyers, *The Human Body and the Law: A Medico-legal Study*, Aldine Publishing Co., Chicago, 1970, p. 40.

7. Gordon Allen, "Eugenics," *International Encyclopedia of the Social Sciences* 5 (1968), pp. 193-97, at 193.

8. Donald K. Pickens, *Eugenics and the Progressives*, Vanderbilt University

Press, Nashville, 1968, p. 5. The fullest assessment of the movement is Mark H. Haller, *Eugenics: Hereditarian Attitudes in American Thought*, Rutgers University Press, New Brunswick, N.J., 1963.

9. Brief for Plaintiff in Error at 18, Buck v. Bell, 274 U.S. 200 (1927).

10. F.N. David, "Francis Galton," *International Encyclopedia of the Social Sciences* 6 (1968), pp. 48-53.

11. Pickens, *Eugenics and the Progressives*, p. 55.

12. Persia Campbell, with a foreword by Grayson Kirk, *Mary Williamson Harriman*, Columbia University Press, New York, 1960. *National Cyclopedia of Biography*, vol. 23, p. 376.

13. Quoted in Walter F. Berns, "Buck v. Bell: Due Process of Law?," *Western Political Quarterly* 6 (1953), pp. 762-75, at p. 767, from B.O. Owen-Adair, *Human Sterilization: Its Social and Legislative Aspects*, published by the author, Portland, Oregon, 1922, p. 157.

14. Charles B. Davenport and Harry H. Laughlin, ". . . How to Make a Eugenical Family Study," *Bulletin no. 13*, Eugenics Record Office, Cold Spring Harbor, New York, 1915.

15. *Eugenics, Genetics and the Family*, vol. 1 (Scientific Papers of the Second International Congress of Eugenics), Williams & Wilkins Co., Baltimore, 1923, p. 2.

16. Ibid., p. 4.

17. Ibid., pp. 329-39.

18. Texts of statutes, administrative and judiciary rulings from Indiana together with excerpts of correspondence between state officials and the Eugenics Records Office are printed in Harry H. Laughlin, *Eugenical Sterilization in the United States*, published by the Psychopathic Laboratory of the Municipal Court of Chicago, Chicago, Ill., 1922, pp. 6, 15, 63, 145, and especially pp. 256-70.

19. Ibid., p. 255.

20. Letter of April 29, 1921, to H.H. Laughlin, quoted in ibid., p. 255.

21. Ibid.

22. Ibid.

23. The seven states were New Jersey, 1913; Iowa, 1914; Michigan, 1918; New York, 1918; Nevada, 1918; Indiana, 1921; and Oregon, 1921. There is a detailed review of litigation growing out of the several eugenical sterilization statutes enacted prior to 1922 in Laughlin, *Eugenical Sterilization*, 1922, pp. 142-290. This includes all case citations and judicial opinions. There are also case and family histories of the individual subjects of litigation in the eight states. Four were "moral perverts," two "feeble-minded," one "epileptic and feeble-minded," and one a "felon." Laughlin, pp. 291-321.

24. Laughlin, *Eugenical Sterilization*, p. vii.

25. Ibid., p. 446.

26. Berns, "Buck v. Bell," p. 762.

27. My thanks to Frances Hassencahl of Euclid, Ohio, for providing me with a record of this correspondence, which she discovered in her research on eugenics for her doctorate in speech. This material is in the manuscript collection of Harry H. Laughlin in the library of Northeast Missouri State College.

28. Documents on the Virginia sterilization statute of 1924 were supplied to the author by Dr. Benedict Nagler, Superintendent, Lynchburg Training School and Hospital, Virginia.

29. C. Herman Pritchett, *The American Constitution*, McGraw-Hill Book Company, New York, 1959, p. 144.

30. Thurman W. Arnold, *Symbols of Government*, Yale University Press, New Haven, 1935.

31. Walter Berns correctly judged this was a "friendly suit" but did not pursue the point in his article, "Buck v. Bell."

32. See David J. Danelski, *A Supreme Court Justice Is Appointed*, Random House, New York, 1964, p. 226, n. 28.

33. Boston spoke on December 14, 1911. His paper was later published as an article, "A Protest Against Laws Authorizing the Sterilization of Criminals and Imbeciles," *Journal of the American Institute of Criminal Law and Criminology* 4, no. 3 (1913-14), pp. 326-58. Boston was an early advocate of NAACP legal action for black rights, an authority on medical and legal ethics and, in 1931, president of the American Bar Association. Lynn Boston, "Memorial of Charles Anderson Boston," The Association of the Bar of the City of New York *Year Book*, 1935, pp. 287-92.

34. G.K. Chesterton, *Eugenics and Other Evils*, Dodd, Mead & Company, New York, 1927, p. vi.

35. Pius XI, *Casti Connaubi* (Encyclical on *Christian Marriage in Our Day*), December 31, 1930, secs. 68-71.

36. T.J. O'Donnell, "Sterilization," *New Catholic Encyclopedia*, McGraw-Hill Book Company, New York, 1967, vol. 13, p. 704.

37. Ibid.

38. Ibid.

39. Pickens, *Eugenics and the Progressives*, p. 204, referring to the work of the British sociologist, Morris Ginsberg.

40. Ibid., pp. 204-05, citing Herbert J. Muller, "The Dominance of Eugenics," *Birth Control Review* 16 (October 1932), pp. 236-38.

41. 316 U.S. 535 (1942).

42. Letter, John R. Rague, executive director, Association for Voluntary Sterilization, Inc., to C.E. Vose, November 10, 1969.

43. Dr. Paul R. Ehrlich, author of *The Population Bomb*, had a sterilization operation after one child. *New York Times*, October 2, 1969.

44. "Resolution on the Desirability of the Two-Child Family," September 17, 1969. The full resolution is available from AVS, 14 West 40th Street, New York City 10018.

45. Letter, Rague to Vose, November 10, 1969.

46. Developments in many states are regularly reported in *AVS News.*

47. Probable jurisdiction noted, 37 LW 3308 (1969), to review *Nebraska v. Cavitt*, 182 Neb. 712 (1968).

48. Vincent L. Dowding to C.E. Vose, December 10, 1969.

49. Letters of Vincent L. Dowding to C.E. Vose, November 24, December 10, 1969.

50. Jurisdictional Statement filed by R.A. Huebner and V.L. Dowding, *Cavitt v. Nebraska*, October term, 1969, no. 54.

51. Kindregan, "Sixty Years of Compulsory Eugenic Sterilization: 'Three Generations of Imbeciles' and the Constitution of the United States,"*Chicago-Kent Law Review* 43 (1966), p. 123, cited in Jurisdictional Statement, ibid., p. 10.

Chapter 2
The Grandfather Clause

1. Four sources of information have been indispensable in preparing this account of the twin "test cases" on the constitutionality of grandfather clauses in state voter registration laws, Guinn v. United States, 238 U.S. 347 (1915) and Myers v. Anderson, 238 U.S. 368 (1915), aff'g 182 F. 223 (C.C.Md. 1911). Briefs and records filed in the Supreme Court of the United States were consulted in the depository at the Connecticut State Library in Hartford. Other depositories are listed in Robert Stern and Paul Gressman, *Supreme Court Practice*, 3d ed., BNA Books, Washington, D.C., 1962, pp. 7-15. Two other sources were local information from the states of Oklahoma and Maryland, where the cases originated. The Oklahoma Historical Library in Oklahoma City yielded much on the grandfather clause from the Fred S. Barde collection in the research library and from the Newspaper Collection. I am indebted to Mrs. Manon B. Atkins of the Research Library and Mr. Jack Wettengal of the Newspaper Department for their assistance. For Maryland, a visit to Baltimore enabled me to examine news clippings in the Sunpapers Library and files in the Maryland Room of the Enoch Pratt Free Library. In Baltimore I interviewed Thomas F. Cadwalader, at eighty-eight an unabashed advocate of white supremacy, who vividly remembered these cases. Most profitable were interviews with William L. Marbury, about his father, William L. Marbury, who led the legal defense of the grandfather clause in the Myers case. He also gave me a copy of his privately published book, William L. Marbury, *The Story of a Maryland Family*, Baltimore, 1966, a most helpful document. Finally, the papers of Charles J. Bonaparte, Moorfield Storey, Arthur Spingarn and the NAACP in the Manuscript Division of the Library of Congress were studied.

2. Accounts of the grandfather clause as one device among many to ban Negro political participation include Gilbert T. Stephenson, *Race Distinctions in*

American Law (1910); C. Vann Woodward, *Origins of the New South, 1877-1913*, Baton Rouge, Louisiana State University Press, 1951; and Woodward, *The Strange Career of Jim Crow*, 3d rev. ed., Oxford University Press, New York, 1967.

3. V.O. Key's, Jr., *Politics, Parties and Pressure Groups*, obviously regards parties and groups as distinct types of organizations. Such a distinction is found questionable in David Sills, "Voluntary Associations: Sociological Aspects," *International Encyclopedia of the Social Sciences* 16 (1968), pp. 362-79.

4. Hamilton Owens, *Baltimore on the Chesapeake*, Doubleday, Doran, Garden City, 1941, p. 289.

5. Ibid., pp. 292-93.

6. Scott v. Sanford, 19 How. 393 (1857).

7. Frank R. Kent, *The Story of Maryland Politics: An Outline History of the Big Political Battles of the State from 1864-1910*, Thomas and Evans Printing Co., Baltimore, 1911, p. 22.

8. Ibid., p. 108.

9. Eric F. Goldman, *Charles J. Bonaparte: Patrician Reformer*, Johns Hopkins, Baltimore, 1943. This study ends at the year 1900.

10. Charles J. Bonaparte, "Experiences of a Cabinet Officer Under Roosevelt," *The Century Magazine* 19 (March 1910), pp. 572-78, at p. 753.

11. Vern Countryman, book review, *New York Review of Books*, 13, July 31, 1969, p. 35.

12. This campaign is well-exhibited in the papers of Charles J. Bonaparte, notably in a pamphlet by Cyrus Field Adams, "The Republican Party and the Afro-American," 1908, 32 pages. The text of the Straus amendment is printed at p. 25. The Republican National Committee printed 104,000 copies of the pamphlet for the 1908 campaign. Adams to Bonaparte, Oct. 21, 1908, Bonaparte Papers, Library of Congress, box 127.

13. Kent, *The Story of Maryland Politics*, pp. 386-87.

14. Bureau of the Census, *Thirteenth Census of the United States Taken in the Year 1910: Statistics for Maryland*, Government Printing Office, Washington, D.C., 1913.

15. Maryland Laws of 1908, c. 525, p. 347.

16. William L. Marbury, Jr., to C.E. Vose, June 11, 1968.

17. Record, p. 24, Myers v. Anderson, 238 U.S. 368 (1915).

18. Ibid., pp. 24-25.

19. Act of April 20, 1871, Sec. 1979, Rev. Stat.

20. Bonaparte to J. Wirt Randall, June 25, 1909, Bonaparte Papers, box 164.

21. Record, p. 3, Myers v. Anderson.

22. Harry Kalven, *The Negro and the First Amendment*, Ohio State University Press, Columbus, 1965.

23. Record, p. 5, Myers v. Anderson.

24. Bonaparte to Daniel R. Randall, October 27, 1913, Bonaparte Papers, box 238.

25. 182 Fed. 223 (C.C. Md., 1910).

26. An authorized biography contains many unexpurgated details from the Williams papers. Edward Everett Dale and James D. Morrison, *Pioneer Judge: The Life of Robert Lee Williams*, Torch Press, Cedar Rapids, Iowa, 1958.

27. Irvin Hurst, *The 46th Star: A History of Oklahoma's Constitutional Convention and Early Statehood*, Semco Color Press, Inc., Oklahoma City, 1957, p. 10.

28. W.A. Robinson, "George Franklin Edmunds," *Dictionary of American Biography.* Edmunds's address is reported in *Congressional Globe*, 39th Cong., 1st Sess., p. 2176.

29. Leo E. Burnett to Bonaparte, October 28, 1907, Bonaparte Papers, box 127.

30. Coyle v. Smith, 113 Pac. 944, *affirmed*, 221 U.S. 559 (1911).

31. W.B. Munro, "Initiative and Referendum," *Encyclopedia for the Social Sciences*, 8 (1932), pp. 50-52.

32. Atwater v. Hassett, 111 Pac. 802 (1910).

33. News dispatch from Chickasha, October 14, 1910, unidentified newspaper in Barde Collection, Research Library, Oklahoma Historical Collection.

34. Williams v. Mississippi, 170 U.S. 220 (1898).

35. Atwater v. Hassett, 111 Pac. 802, 812 (1910).

36. Ibid.

37. Bureau of the Census, *Thirteenth Census of the United States Taken in the Year 1910: Statistics for Oklahoma*, Government Printing Office, Washington, D.C., 1913.

38. Republican party platform, 1908, in Kirk H. Porter and Donald Bruce Johnson, *National Party Platforms*, University of Illinois Press, Urbana, 1965.

39. *Kingfisher Midget*, October 29, 1910. Copy in Oklahoma Historical Collection.

40. Dale and Morrison, *Pioneer Judge*, p. 195.

41. Record, p. 1. Guinn v. United States, 238 U.S. 347 (1915).

42. Certificate, p. 1, Guinn v. United States, 238 U.S. 347 (1915).

43. Record, p. 34, Myers v. Anderson, 238 U.S. 368 (1915).

44. Brief for Plaintiff in Error, Myers v. Anderson.

45. Arthur W. Machen, Jr., "Is the Fifteenth Amendment Void?," *Harvard Law Review* 23 (January 1910), pp. 169-93.

46. Brief for Plaintiff in Error, p. 107.

47. Texas v. White, 7 Wall. 700 (1869).

48. Brief for Plaintiff in Error, pp. 119-20.

49. Brief for Plaintiffs in Error, Guinn v. United States.

50. Brief for Appellant, Guinn v. United States.

51. Sam Acheson, *Joseph W. Bailey* (1921); Acheson, "Joseph Weldon Bailey," *Dictionary of American Biography*, Supp. I.

52. Brief of J.H. Adriaans as *amicus curiae*, p. 1, Guinn v. United States.

53. Ibid., p. 33.

54. Ibid., p. 38.

55. Brief for Defendants in Error, Myers v. Anderson.

56. Brief for the United States, Guinn v. United States. Nothing of the Guinn case is revealed in the papers of John W. Davis in Sterling Library, Yale University, New Haven, Conn. This was among the first of scores of cases Davis argued before the Supreme Court. As this was in alliance with the NAACP, his last, Brown v. Board of Education, 347 U.S. 483 (1954), was in opposition.

57. Brief *amicus curiae*, by permission of the attorney general in support of the government's position, by Burford and Embry, Guinn v. United States.

58. Brief for NAACP, *amicus curiae*, Guinn v. United States.

59. Elliott M. Rudwick, "The Niagara Movement," *Journal of Negro History* 42 (1957), pp. 177-200.

60. C.F. Kellogg, *NAACP, 1909-1920*, vol. 1, Johns Hopkins Press, Baltimore, 1967, pp. 42, 57-62.

61. State v. Curry, 121 Md. 534 (1913).

62. Four years later the Supreme Court ruled racial residential segregation invalid in test cases from Louisville, Buchanan v. Warley, 245 U.S. 60 (1917). Baltimore's Caucasian interest was represented in a brief by S.S. Field. Moorfield Storey prepared the Supreme Court case for the NAACP. W. Ashbie Hawkins filed a brief *amicus curiae* for the Baltimore Branch of the NAACP.

63. Bonaparte to Storey, November 8, 1909, Bonaparte Papers, box 164.

64. Bonaparte to Daniel R. Randall, October 27, 1913, Bonaparte Papers, box 238.

65. Kellogg, *NAACP*, p. 260.

66. *Amicus curiae* brief of NAACP, pp. 16-17, Guinn v. United States.

67. Marbury, *The Story of a Maryland Family*, p. 102.

68. *Daily Oklahoman*, June 23, 1915.

69. Ibid.

70. Ibid.

71. Ibid.

72. Ibid.

73. U.S. Const., Art. II, Sec. 2. For the essentials of the subject of the president's legal power to pardon, see *U.S. Constitution, Analysis and Interpretation* (1964), pp. 456-61.

74. 1916 Atty. Gen. Ann. Rep. 356.

75. Dale and Morrison, *Pioneer Judge*, p. 251.

76. Lane v. Wilson, 307 U.S. 268 (1939).

Chapter 3
Woman Suffrage

1. See Key, *Politics, Parties and Pressure Groups*, p. 613. Key has chosen the least sophisticated, most rustic, silliest quotations available dated in the nineteenth century to ridicule woman suffrage.

2. Mrs. Charles Eliot Guild, "The Early Days of the Remonstrants Against Woman Suffrage; A Memory Sketch by Their First Secretary," 12 pp., at p. 1, Massachusetts Anti-Suffrage Association Papers, box 1, Massachusetts Historical Society.

3. Ibid., p. 2. See Francis Parkman, "The Woman Question," *North American Review* 129 (October 1879), pp. 303-21.

4. Parkman, p. 320.

5. Guild, "The Early Days," p. 8.

6. Melvin I. Urofsky to C.E. Vose, October 2, 1969.

7. Guild, "The Early Days," p. 2.

8. T. Burges Johnson, "Memorial of Everett P. Wheeler," The Association of the Bar of the City of New York *Year Book, 1925*, p. 521.

9. *New York Times*, September 3, 1912 (letter to the Editor), Everett P. Wheeler Papers, New York Public Library, box 1.

10. Carrie Chapman Catt to Everett P. Wheeler, October 20, 26, 1915, Catt Papers in the Library of Congress, box 9.

11. Baltimore *American*, August 16, 1919, quoted in *The Woman Patriot*, 3, no. 20, August 30, 1919, p. 7.

12. Eleanor Flexner, *Century of Struggle: The Woman's Rights Movement in the United States*, Belknap Press of Harvard University Press, Cambridge, 1959, p. 296.

13. *The Woman Patriot*, 3, no. 25, October 4, 1919, p. 3.

14. *The Woman Patriot*, 3, no. 23, September 20, 1919, p. 5.

15. Hawke v. Smith (no. 1, Eighteenth Amendment), 100 Ohio St. 385, 126 N.E. 400 (1919).

16. Hawke v. Smith (no. 1, Eighteenth Amendment), 253 U.S. 221 (1920).

17. Hawke v. Smith (no. 2, Nineteenth Amendment), 100 Ohio St. 540, 127 N.E. 924 (1919).

18. Hawke v. Smith (no. 2, Nineteenth Amendment), 253 U.S. 231 (1920).

19. Hawke v. Smith (no. 1, Eighteenth Amendment), 253 U.S. 221 (1920).

20. Hawke v. Smith (no. 2, Nineteenth Amendment), 253 U.S. 231 (1920).

21. These cases were reported zealously in *The Woman Patriot*: "Ohio's Supreme Court Case," 4, no. 10, March 6, 1920, p. 2; "The Case for Referenda," 4, no. 17, April 24, 1920, p. 3; report of the oral argument under "The Rights of the People Before the Supreme Court," 4, no. 18, May 1, 1920, p. 2; and "The Ohio Campaign," by Hulbert Taft, Editor, *Cincinnati Times-Star*, 4, no. 19, May 8, 1920, p. 8.

22. George S. Hawke to Carrie Chapman Catt, July 6, 1920. Catt Papers, box 22.

23. Ibid.

24. "Faith in the Supreme Court," *The Woman Patriot*, 4, no. 42, October 16, 1920, p. 4.

25. Eichelberger to Kilbreth, April 6, 1920, Papers of Everett P. Wheeler, box 10.

26. Marbury to Kilbreth (copies to Wheeler, Eichelberger and Mrs. Gibbs), April 7, 1920, Wheeler Papers, box 10.

27. Henry St. George Tucker to Wheeler, April 27, 1920, Wheeler Papers, box 10.

28. Fairchild v. Hughes, 258 U.S. 126 (1922); Leser v. Garnett, 258 U.S. 130 (1922).

29. Fairchild v. Hughes, 258 U.S. 126 (1922).

30. *Baltimore Evening Sun*, October 30, 1920, reprinted in *The Woman Patriot*, 4, no. 44, November 13, 1920, p. 2.

31. *The Woman Patriot*, 4, nos. 51 and 52, December 25, 1920, pp. 1-4, at p. 1.

32. *Baltimore Sun*, November 25, 1941.

33. Leser v. Garnett, 139 Md. 46, 114 Atl. 840, (1921).

34. Machen, "Is the Fifteenth Amendment Void?," p. 169; Henry St. George Tucker, *Woman Suffrage by Constitutional Amendment*, Yale University Press, 1916; William L. Marbury, "The Limitations Upon the Amending Power," *Harvard Law Review* 33 (December 1919), pp. 223-35; idem., "The Nineteenth and After," *Virginia Law Review* 7 (October 1920), pp. 1-29.

35. *The Woman Patriot*, 6, no. 3, February 1, 1922, p. 4.

36. Fairchild v. Hughes, 258 U.S. 126 (1922); Leser v. Garnett, 258 U.S. 130 (1922).

37. Melvin I. Urofsky to C.E. Vose, October 2, 1969.

38. Author's interview with Cadwalader, Baltimore, August, 1967.

39. Fairchild v. Hughes, 258 U.S. 126 (1922) at 129, quoting Muskrat v. United States, 219 U.S. 346 (1911), at 357.

40. Ibid., pp. 129-130.

41. Leser v. Garnett, 258 U.S. 130, at 137.

42. There are fewer than 500 cases for all American jurisdictions, from the beginning to the present, listed in a recent, careful survey of the subject. See Leo Kanowitz, *Women and the Law: The Unfinished Revolution*, University of New Mexico Press, Albuquerque, 1969, pp. 306-10. But very few cases have raised constitutional issues in the Supreme Court. Ibid., pp. 149-96.

43. Flexner, *Century of Struggle*, p. 170.

Chapter 4
Prohibition

1. The seven cases were briefed, argued and decided as one with the reporter of the Supreme Court collecting them under the title, *National Prohibition Cases*, but the seven are frequently cited by the name of the first of the cases, *Rhode Island v. Palmer*, 253 U.S. 393 (1920).

2. Bernard Hershkopf interview with C.E. Vose, February 12, 1970.

3. 277 U.S. 438 (1928).

4. 273 U.S. 510 (1927).

5. Prohibition party platform of 1872, in Kirk H. Porter and Donald Bruce Johnson, *National Party Platforms, 1840-1956*, University of Illinois Press, Urbana, 1956, p. 45.

6. Katherine Anthony, "Frances Elizabeth Caroline Willard," *Dictionary of American Biography* 20 (1936), p. 234.

7. Mrs. Herman Stanley, Promotion Secretary, National Woman's Christian Temperance Union, Evanston, Illinois, to C.E. Vose, January 7, 1970. In 1970 the WCTU claimed 250,000 members, each paying annual dues of $3.65—"a prayer and a penny a day"—but while the president, Mrs. Fred J. Tooze, says the union is "committed to prohibition," she adds that they are "not working on it now." *Wall Street Journal*, January 16, 1970, p. 1.

8. The absence of WCTU litigation is evidenced by the fact that there is no information on the subject in the Frances E. Willard Memorial Library for Alcohol Research, said to be the largest temperance library in the world. The NWCTU president writes, "I do not know of any litigation in the courts ever carried on by any national, state or local facet of our organization." Mrs. Fred J. Tooze to C.E. Vose, November 21, 1969.

9. Kenneth M. Gould, "Carry Amelia Moore Nation," *Dictionary of American Biography* 13 (1934), p. 394.

10. Ibid., p. 395.

11. Justin Steuart, *Wayne Wheeler: Dry Boss*, Fleming H. Revell Company, New York, 1928, pp. 38-39.

12. Ibid., p. 47.

13. These pamphlets are contained in the Ohio Anti-Saloon League Collection of the Michigan Historical Collections, University of Michigan. I am indebted to Kenneth P. Sheffel for bringing this material to my attention.

14. Ernest H. Cherrington, *The Evolution of Prohibition in the United States of America*, American Issue Press, Westerville, Ohio, 1920, p. 151.

15. Mugler v. Kansas, 123 U.S. 623 (1888), at p. 665.

16. Bowman v. Chicago & Railway Co., 125 U.S. 465 (1888).

17. Leisy v. Hardin, 135 U.S. 100 (1890); Brown v. Maryland, 12 Wheat. 419 (1827).

18. 26 Stat. 313.

19. In re Rahrer, 140 U.S. 545 (1891).

20. *Proceedings of the 16th National Convention of the Anti-Saloon League of America*, July 6-9, 1915, pp. 533-37.

21. 248 U.S. 276 (1919).

22. U.S. Const., Art. I, Sec. 7, Cl. 2.

23. Quoted in Steuart, *Wayne Wheeler: Dry Boss*, pp. 95-96.

24. My discussion is based primarily on the careful study of the League in James H. Timberlake, *Prohibition and the Progressive Movement, 1900-1920*,

Harvard University Press, Cambridge, 1963, pp. 125-84. This is more concise, yet in many ways more complete, than the original and still classic study undertaken during prohibition, Peter H. Odegard's *Pressure Politics: The Story of the Anti-Saloon League*, Columbia University Press, New York, 1928. I was also able to study scattered records of the Anti-Saloon League of America at the offices of the American Council on Alcoholism in Washington in 1969 prior to their permanent deposit in the Michigan Historical Collection in Ann Arbor.

25. Timberlake, *Prohibition and the Progressive Movement*, pp. 128-29.

26. Ibid., p. 135.

27. Joseph R. Gusfield, *Symbolic Crusade: Status Politics and the American Temperance Movement*, University of Illinois Press, Urbana, 1966.

28. Const., Art. I, Sec. 1, Cl. 3.

29. Virginius Dabney, *Dry Messiah: The Life of Bishop Cannon*, A.A. Knopf, New York, 1949, pp. 296-97.

30. The Fugitive Slave Acts, were based on the Constitution, Art. 4, Sec. 2, which read, "No person held to service or labor in one state under the laws thereof, escaping into another, shall, in consequence of any law or regulation therein, be discharged from such service or labor, but shall be delivered up on claim of the party to whom such service or labor may be due." For a discussion of the Fugitive Slave Acts and the personal liberty laws, see Dwight Lowell Dumond, *Anti-Slavery: The Crusade for Freedom in America*, University of Michigan Press, Ann Arbor, 1961, pp. 305-14.

31. These papers were opened by the author in the Enoch Pratt Free Library, Baltimore, Maryland.

32. Carl Brent Swisher, *American Constitutional Development*, 2d ed., Houghton Mifflin Co., Boston, 1954, p. 705, citing Edward S. Corwin, "Constitutional Law in 1919-1920," *American Political Science Review* 14 (November 1920), pp. 635, 651.

33. *Documentary History of the United States Brewers' Association*, published by the Association, New York, 1898, p. 111.

34. Ibid., pp. 470-71.

35. United States Brewers' Association *Yearbook* (with Proceedings of the Fifty-Third Annual Convention held in Atlantic City, N.J., Oct., 1913), published by the Association, New York, 1914.

36. The information here is drawn from Stanley Baron, *Brewed in America: A History of Beer and Ale in the United States*, Little, Brown, Boston, 1962; from the United States Brewers' Association *Yearbooks*, particularly those issued from 1901 to 1920; and from interviews in New York with officials of the United States Brewers' Association. I have also utilized the library of Joseph E. Seagram's Sons and relied upon occasional publications of the Distilled Spirits Institute, Washington, D.C. and the Licensed Beverage Industries of New York.

37. Baron, *Brewed in America*, p. 284.

38. Ibid., p. 283.

39. Ibid., pp. 220-22.

40. Ibid., p. 225.

41. Ibid., p. 301.

42. Ibid.

43. Ibid., quoting Odegard, *Pressure Politics*, p. 163.

44. The statute at issue was the Wartime Prohibition Act of November 21, 1918, ch. 212, 40 Stat. 1045. The Kentucky case was Hamilton v. Kentucky Distilleries & Warehouse Company; the New York case was Dryfoos v. Edwards, Collector. The cases were decided together on December 15, 1919, and are reported as 251 U.S. 146 (1919).

45. United States v. Standard Brewery, United States v. American Brewing Co., 251 U.S. 210 (1920).

46. Benjamin R. Twiss, *Lawyers and the Constitution: How Laissez Faire Came to the Supreme Court*, Princeton University Press, Princeton, 1942, pp. 215-17.

47. Barnard Hershkopf interview with C.E. Vose, February 19, 1970. Also, see Baron, *Brewed in America*, p. 314.

48. Dillon v. Gloss, 256 U.S. 376 (1921).

49. United States v. Sprague, 282 U.S. 716 (1931).

50. United States v. Sprague, 44 Fed. 2d 967 (1930).

51. Jeremiah M. Evarts, who filed an *amicus curiae* brief with the Supreme Court in *Sprague*, and agreed with the conclusions of the district court has recently said that Clark was "showing off." Evarts interview with C.E. Vose, April 17, 1969. Harrison Tweed had earlier told me that everyone considered Judge Clark to be something more than merely eccentric.

52. Bernard Hershkopf to C.E. Vose, February 19, 1970.

Chapter 5
Lawyers for Repeal

1. U.S. Const. Amend. XVIII; Amend. XXI.

2. James H. Timberlake, *Prohibition and the Progressive Movement*.

3. Joseph R. Gusfield, *Symbolic Crusade*.

4. Ibid., p. 126.

5. VCL Financial Records, Harrison Tweed Papers.

6. VCL, "Certificate of Incorporation of the Voluntary Committee of Lawyers, Inc." (1929), J.H. Choate, Jr., Papers.

7. VCL, "By-laws of the Voluntary Committee of Lawyers, Inc." n.d. [1929], Choate Papers.

8. "The Voluntary Committee of Lawyers, Inc." n.d. [1929], 8 pp.

9. VCL, "Bar Association on Record for Repeal: State and City Bar Associations (Either by Resolutions or Referenda)" (April 1932), 1 p.

10. VCL, "[2nd] Report of Executive Committee, May, 1930" (May 30, 1930), 4 pp.

11. VCL, "[3rd] Report of Executive Committee, November 1930" (Nov. 26, 1930), p. 4.

12. Prohibition of alcoholic beverages, expansion of the suffrage and regulation of child labor were often considered unsuited for action by national constitutional amendment. See, for example, Arthur W. Machen, Jr., "Is the Fifteenth Amendment Void?," *Harvard Law Review* 23 (January 1910), p. 169; Henry St. George Tucker, *Woman Suffrage by Constitutional Amendment*, Yale University Press, New Haven, 1916; William L. Marbury, "The Limitations Upon the Amending Power," *Harvard Law Review* 33 (December 1919), p. 223; Calvin Coolidge, "Enemies of the Republic," *The Delineator* 98 (June 1921), pp. 4, 5, 66; (July 1921), pp. 10, 11, 38-39; 99 (August 1921), pp. 10, 11, 42.

13. *Inaugural Addresses of the Presidents of the United States*, House Doc. No. 218, 87th Cong., 1st Sess. (1961), p. 288.

14. *New York Times*, May 21, 1929, p. 1.

15. For the complete, official results, see U.S. National Commission on Law Observance and Enforcement, Publications Number 1-14, U.S. Government Printing Office, Washington, D.C., 1929-31.

16. Zechariah Chafee, Jr., and others, *The Mooney-Billings Report: Suppressed by the Wickersham Commission*, Gotham House, New York, 1932.

17. House Doc. No. 722, 71st Cong., 3rd Sess. (1931).

18. Ibid., p. 83.

19. Ibid., p. iv.

20. *Statement of the Board of Managers of the Voluntary Committee, Inc. Based on and Citing from Report of the Wickersham Commission*, March 22, 1931, 14 pp., at p. 3.

21. Ibid., p. 14.

22. AAPA, *Handy Digest of the Wickersham Report*, Washington, D.C., January 1932, 17 pp.

23. *Statement of the Board of Managers*, p. 4.

24. *Philadelphia Record*, February 9, 1932, p. 15. Other information on the hoax is drawn from the Choate Collection.

25. Pitcairn to Choate, February 10, 1932.

26. The letter was printed, legal size, on one page, undated. Copies were mailed May 31, 1932.

27. Porter and Johnson, *National Party Platforms*, p. 349.

28. VCL, "[6th] Report," February 25, 1933, p. 4.

29. Porter and Johnson, p. 332.

30. U.S. Const. Amend. XX.

31. For a superb biography, see Morton Keller, *In Defense of Yesterday*, J.B. Lippincott, Philadelphia, 1959.

32. Choate to Palmer, December 9, 1932.

33. Palmer to Choate, December 8, 1932.

34. Corwin to Choate, December 8, 1932.

35. Palmer to Choate, December 16, 1932.

36. Choate to Palmer, December 15, 1932.

37. Palmer to Choate, December 16, 1932.

38. Ibid.

39. Johnston to Palmer, December 16, 1932.

40. Choate to Palmer, December 15, 1932.

41. Choate to Davis, Choate to Beck, November 30, 1932.

42. Choate to Palmer, December 2, 1932.

43. Ibid.

44. Johnston to Jouett Shouse, December 2, 1932.

45. Johnston to Shouse, November 3, 1932.

46. Choate to Shouse, December 7, 1932.

47. Choate to Palmer, December 23, 1932.

48. Johnston to Palmer, January 9, 1933.

49. Machen to Choate, January 30, 1933.

50. Choate to Machen, February 3, 1933.

51. Machen to Choate, February 4, 1933.

52. Johnston to Palmer, January 9, 1933.

53. Const. Amend. XXI.

54. Stebbins to Mrs. Frances C. Smith, January 25, 1933.

55. Choate to Stebbins, January 28, 1933.

56. Choate to Stebbins, January 30, 1933.

57. Telegram, executive committee to VCL state representatives, January 30, 1933.

58. Choate to VCL state representatives, January 30, 1933.

59. Choate to Palmer, January 30, 1933.

60, Dowling to Choate, January 31, 1933.

61. Choate to Dowling, February 2, 1933.

62. Choate to C.E. Moore, February 3, 1933.

63. Choate to A.S. Gilbert, February 3, 1933.

64. W.L. Walls to VCL, February 6, 1933.

65. Rogers MacVeagh to Choate, February 3, 1933.

66. Ibid.

67. Robert H. Anderson to Choate, February 9, 1933.

68. Shouse to Choate, February 9, 1933.

69. Choate to Shouse; Choate to Mrs. Charles H. Sabin, February 11, 1933.

70. Everett S. Brown (compiler), *Ratification of the Twenty-first Amendment to the Constitution of the United States: State Convention Records and Laws*, University of Michigan Press, Ann Arbor, 1932, p. 5.

71. VCL executive committee to state governors, February 24, 1933.

72. Sidney G. Stricker to Atlee Pomerene, February 27, 1933.

73. During national prohibition drys frequently aided government prosecutions, as witness the appearances in the Supreme Court of Wayne Wheeler, counsel to the Anti-Saloon League of America. Wet forces, marshaled at first by the distillers, challenged the validity of the Eighteenth Amendment and the laws and procedures adopted for enforcement, in a number of cases from the National Prohibition Cases, 253 U.S. 350 (1920) to United States v. Sprague, 282 U.S. 716 (1931).

74. Lucien H. Boggs to Choate, December 20, 1932.

75. Choate to Boggs, January 4, 1933.

76. Edgar Allan Poe, Jr., to Choate, April 6, 1933.

77. Shouse to Poe, April 11, 1933.

78. Choate to Shouse, April 10, 1933.

79. Choate to Poe, April 10, 1933.

80. Hartman and Disney v. Beamish, October 1933, not reported.

81. W.S. Chase, brief *amicus curiae*, for International Reform Society, et al., in Hartman Disney v. Beamish, Ct. of Common Pleas of Dauphin County, Penna., October, 1933, not reported.

82. Ibid.

83. Noel Dowling, "A New Experiment in Ratification," *American Bar Association Journal* (July, 1933), pp. 383-87.

84. Chase, brief *amicus curiae*, p. 3.

85. Ibid. The case was dropped just as ratification by thirty-six states seemed assured. Wilbur Morse to Shouse, November 2, 1933.

86. Robinson Verrill to Choate, March 8, 1933.

87. Ibid., pp. 1-2.

88. Choate to Verrill, March 9, 1933, 4 pp.

89. Verrill to Choate, March 10, 1933.

90. Robert Hale to VCL, March 11, 1933.

91. Choate to Hale, March 16, 1933.

92. See Felix Frankfurter, "Advisory Opinions, National," *Encyclopedia of the Social Sciences* 1 (1930), pp. 475-78. For the report of the decision, see 167 Atl. 178 (1933).

93. Hale to Choate, March 31, 1933.

94. Hale to Choate, April 3, 1933.

95. Robert Hale, "But I, Too, Hate Roosevelt," *Harper's Magazine*, August 1936, pp. 268-73.

96. C.B. Ryan, Jr. to Choate, April 7, 1933.

97. Louis J. Brann to Arthur L. Race, April 4, 1933.

98. March 7, 1933.

99. Choate to Thomas F. Cadwalader, March 10, 1933.

100. Cadwalader to Choate, March 11, 1933.

101. Choate to Cadwalader, March 13, 1933.

102. Choate to George W. Martin, June 28, 1933.

103. Ibid.

104. Choate to John S. Wise, Jr., July 6, 1933.

105. Williamson to Choate, June 30, 1933.

106. Johnston to Choate, July 6, 1933.

107. Martin to Choate, June 30, 1933.

108. "The Repeal Victory," *Literary Digest*, December 10, 1933.

109. *New York Times*, January 20, 1968, p. 29.

110. Pollock v. Farmers' Loan & Trust Co., 175 U.S. 429 (1895).

111. See brief in opposition to the proposed income tax amendment submitted to the New York State Legislature by Victor Morawetz, William D. Guthrie, Austen G. Fox and Choate, Sr. The endorsement was by Joseph H. Choate, William D. Guthrie, Victor Morawetz, Austen G. Fox, and John G. Milburn. A separate statement was included by Francis Lynde Stetson.

112. Mugler v. Kansas, 123 U.S. 623 (1887).

113. Josephine Goldmark, *Impatient Crusader: Florence Kelley's Life Story*, University of Illinois Press, Urbana, 1953, pp. 151-55.

114. *The Chemical Foundation, Inc.*: a booklet containing A. Mitchell Palmer, "Aims and Purposes of the Chemical Foundation, Inc. and the Reasons for its Organization," and an address to the National Cotton Manufacturers Association (New York, 1919), 70 pp.

115. 72 U.S. 1 (1926).

116. "Joseph Hodges Choate," in *Dictionary of American Biography*, Scribners, New York, 1930.

117. Leonard Harrison and Elizabeth Laine, *After Repeal*, Harper & Brothers, New York, 1936.

118. Irenee du Pont to Choate, April 10, 1933.

119. Pierre S. du Pont to Choate, April 20, 1933.

120. Telegram, Shouse to Choate, November 8, 1933.

121. Otis Seabury Cook to Choate, November 28, 1933.

122. Clyde A. Dewitt to Choate, December 6, 1933.

123. H.P. Rhudy, "Memorandum on Finances," April 7, 1931, in VCL Financial Records, Tweed Collection.

124. Choate to Tweed, July 5, 1932, Choate Collection.

125. I am indebted to Brian Rogers of Wesleyan University for assembling this material from standard biographical sources, especially *Who's Who in America* and *Who Was Who in America*. This was supplemented by information found in the *Memorial Book* published annually by the Association of the Bar of the City of New York.

126. James H. Timberlake, *Prohibition and the Progressive Movement*; Joseph R. Gusfield, *Symbolic Crusade*.

127. V.O. Key, Jr., "A Theory of Critical Elections," *Journal of Politics* 17 (February 1955), pp. 3-18.

Chapter 6
The Catholic School Issue

1. Pierce v. Society of the Sisters of the Holy Names of Jesus and Mary, Pierce v. Hill Military Academy, 268 U.S. 510 (1925), affirming, Society v. Pierce, Hill v. Pierce, 296 Fed. 928 (1924).

2. *New York Times*, June 2, 1925, p. 22.

3. For the ineffectiveness of parochial schools in instilling religious belief, see Peter Rossi and Andrew M. Greeley, *The Education of American Catholics*, Doubleday and Company, Anchor Books, New York, 1966.

4. David B. Tyack, "The Perils of Pluralism: The Background of the Pierce Case," *American Historical Review* 74 (1968), pp. 74-98; Lloyd P. Jorgenson, "The Oregon School Law of 1922: Passage and Sequel," *Catholic Historical Review* 54 (1968), pp. 455-66.

5. *New York Times*, June 5, 1925, p. 16. Letter to the editor from Felix Frankfurter.

6. 268 U.S. 530, at 536.

7. 268 U.S. 530, at 534-535.

8. 268 U.S. 530, at 535.

9. Compulsory Education Act, Oregon Laws, Sec. 5259 (1923). The text is also printed in Pierce v. Society, 268 U.S. 510, 530.

10. Oregon Laws, Sec. 4103. Details of early experience with the law are neatly and charmingly explained in Gilbert L. Hedges, *Where the People Rule* or *The Initiative and Referendum, Direct Primary Law and the Recall in Use in the State of Oregon*, Bender-Moss Co., San Francisco, 1914, pp. 29-44.

11. *Official Pamphlet Distributed among Voters Prior to Election of Nov. 7, 1922*, State of Oregon. Printed in Brief for Appellee, Appendix I, pp. 19-43, Pierce v. Society, 268 U.S. 510 (1925).

12. Argument (Affirmative) submitted by H. Baldwin and others, in behalf of the Compulsory Education Bill, *Official Pamphlet . . . Election of Nov. 7, 1922*, p. 25.

13. Ibid., p. 24.

14. The major statements, issued between 1738 and 1902, are cited in the carefully detailed article by W.J. Whalen, "Freemasonry," *New Catholic Encyclopedia* 6 (1967), pp. 132-39, at 134.

15. Ibid., p. 137.

16. Tyack, "The Perils of Pluralism," p. 77.

17. Argument (Negative) submitted by the Catholic Civil Rights Association of Oregon, by J.P. Kavanaugh and others, opposing the Compulsory Education Bill, *Official Pamphlet . . . Election of Nov. 7, 1922.* Brief for Appellee, Appendix I, pp. 41-43, Pierce v. Society.

18. J.G. Shaw, *Edwin Vincent O'Hara: American Prelate*, Farrar, Straus and Cudahy, New York, 1957. A chapter on "The Oregon School Question" is at 98-105.

19. I am indebted to Mr. Jack F. Thompson, assistant secretary of state, letter of February 25, 1970, for the "Official Abstract of Votes" for 1922 showing: Yes, 115,506; and No, 103,685. The unreliability of newspaper reports is shown by the differences in the figure of 115,506 to 103,685 given by Tyack, "Perils of Pluralism," p. 91, from the Portland *Oregonian*, November 9, 1922, compared with 107,498 to 97,204 given by Kenneth T. Jackson, *The Ku Klux Klan in the City, 1919-1930*, Oxford University Press, New York, 1967, p. 207, from the *Oregon Daily Journal*, November 9, 1922.

20. U.S. Congress, House, *Congressional Record*, 83rd Cong., 2d sess., 1954, 100, pt. 4: 4605-4607. These remarks honoring Pierce include obituaries from the *Portland Oregonian* and the *Portland Journal.*

21. Papers of Margaret Sanger in the Library of Congress include correspondence with Pierce and drafts of bills he introduced on behalf of the birth control movement.

22. "Wallace McCamant," *Cyclopedia of American Biography*, vol. 34, p. 34.

23. Tyack, "The Perils of Pluralism," p. 93, quoting from *The Oregon School Fight: A True History*, Portland, Oregon, 1924, p. 118.

24. John C. Veatch to C.E. Vose, January 7, 1970.

25. Daniel A. Tobin, state deputy, New York State Council, Knights of Columbus to M.J. Madigan, editor, *Catholic News*, July 20, 1925, in Papers of Joseph Cardinal Hayes, box 15, Archives of the Archdiocese of New York, Corrigan Library, St. Joseph's Seminary, Yonkers, N.Y.

26. Ibid., p. 2.

27. Ibid., quoting Minutes of Meeting of Supreme Council, Knights of Columbus for January 6, 1923.

28. Quoted from the resolution of September 24, 1919, in F.T. Hurley, "National Catholic Welfare Conference (NCWC)," *New Catholic Encyclopedia* 10 (1967), p. 225.

29. G.E. Reed, "Oregon School Case," *New Catholic Encyclopedia* 10 (1967), p. 738, quoting *St. Louis Progress*, January 25, 1923.

30. Edward J. Hanna, Archbishop of San Francisco to Hayes, November 4, 1926, Hayes Papers, box Q-26.

31. Hayes to Hanna, November 27, 1926, Hayes Papers, box Q-26. The tenor of the correspondence suggests that all the details of the litigation had been forgotten as Archbishop Hanna spoke of a committee in the state of Washington and an appeal from the bishop of Seattle. Hanna may have confused Washington with Oregon or this may have been still another source of outside funds for Archbishop Christie. In his reply, Cardinal Hayes said, matter-of-factly, his check was for "the Oregon Fund."

32. *Official Catholic Directory*, P.J. Kennedy & Sons, New York, 1967, pp. 251, 988.

33. Record, at p. 8, Pierce v. Society, 368 U.S. 510 (1925).

34. *Handbook of Private Schools for American Boys and Girls, An Annual Survey*, 11th ed., 1927, Porter Sargent, Boston, p. 546. The elder Hill died in

1930; two sons then carried on the school until the early 1960s. *Handbook of Private Schools: An Annual Descriptive Survey of Independent Education*, 42nd ed., 1961, Porter Sargent, Boston, pp. 657-58.

35. Ibid.

36. Veatch to Vose, January 7, 1970.

37. Society of the Sisters v. Pierce, Governor of Oregon; Hill Military Academy v. Pierce, 296 Fed. 928 (1924).

38. McCamant to Willis S. Moore, April 1, 1924, Records of Attorney General, case file 470A, Oregon State Archives.

39. Ibid.

40. Moore to McCamant, April 8, 1924. Ibid.

41. McCamant to Moore, April 9, 1924. Ibid.

42. McCamant to Van Winkle, June 4, 1924; McCamant to Moore, August 8, 1924; Van Winkle to McCamant, August 9, 1924; Van Winkle to Koser, August 13, 1924, ibid.

43. McCamant to Van Winkle, June 4, 1925, ibid.

44. Ibid.

45. Ibid.

46. Ibid.

47. *New York Times*, July 10, 1928, p. 23.

48. Chamberlain to Van Winkle, January 10, February 2, 1925; Van Winkle to Chamberlain, January 27, 1925; Van Winkle to McCamant, January 24, February 20, 1925. Records of Attorney General case file 470A, Oregon State Archives.

49. *New York Times*, May 12, 1925, p. 24.

50. Leave to File Brief by Public School Defense League, Pierce v. Society, pp. 13-14.

51. Ibid.

52. Brief for Appellant Governor of Oregon, Pierce v. Society, Pierce v. Academy, at 36-37, citing Truax v. Raich, 239 U.S. 33 (1915).

53. Ibid., at 41, citing Meyer v. Nebraska, 262 U.S. 390 (1923).

54. Ibid., at 38-39, citing Jacobson v. Massachusetts, 197 U.S. 11 (1905).

55. City of New York v. Miln, 11 Peters 102 (1837).

56. Brief for Appellant Governor of Oregon, Pierce v. Society, Pierce v. Academy, at 39-40.

57. Ibid., at 46.

58. See Twiss, *Lawyers and the Constitution*.

59. For a sketch of his career, listing major litigation and providing the chief printed sources, see John J. Dolan, "William Dameron Guthrie," *Dictionary of American Biography*, Supp. 1 (1946), pp. 367-68. His writings were voluminous. There seems to be no body of legal papers or manuscripts of Guthrie's remaining but, for the present study, Guthrie correspondence has been located in the Patrick Cardinal Hayes Papers, in the Louis Marshall Papers and in the Alexander Lincoln Papers.

60. Guthrie to the Reverend John J. Wynne, September 14, 1915, Patrick Cardinal Hayes Papers, Archives of the Archdiocese of New York, Corrigan Library, St. Joseph's Seminary, Yonkers, N.Y.

61. Address by William D. Guthrie, "Dedication of the Roman Catholic Parochial School at Glen Cove, Long Island, N.Y.," Sept. 6, 1915, privately printed, 12 pages. Copy in Hayes Papers.

62. Guthrie to Wynne, September 14, 1915, Hayes Papers.

63. Guthrie to Hayes, September 15, 1915, Hayes Papers.

64. The Reverend Joseph P. Dineen to the Reverend Francis W. Howard, April 12, 1920, Hayes Papers, Box P-13.

65. This is familiar, popular humor used in reference to the American Legion in Charles G. Bolte, *The New Veteran*, Reynal & Hitchcock, New York, 1945.

66. Griffith R. Dye, Jr., "Louis Marshall: Defender of the Constitution" (M.A. thesis, University of Cincinnati, 1967), p. 126.

67. Ibid., pp. 130-31.

68. William H. Harbaugh, "The Papers of John W. Davis (1873-1955)," *Yale University Library Gazette* 37 (1963), p. 13.

69. Dye, "Louis Marshall," at p. 152 citing correspondence from Guthrie in the Marshall Papers, American Jewish Archives, Cincinnati. Also, see William D. Guthrie, in "Tributes to Louis Marshall," *The Jewish Tribune and Hebrew Standard* 89 (December 10, 1926), p. 9.

Chapter 7
The Brandeis Brief

1. Lottery Case (Champion v. Ames), 188 U.S. 321 (1903).

2. 36 Stat. 825 (1910), Mann Act: 18 U.S.C. 2421-2423. Hoke v. United States, 227 U.S. 308 (1913); Caminetti v. United States, 242 U.S. 470 (1917).

3. Donald E. Richberg, *Labor Standards Conference*, Second Annual Report, 1933, back cover.

4. There is no full history of the NCL. For accounts, see Josephine Goldmark, *Impatient Crusader: Florence Kelley's Life Story*; foreword by Felix Frankfurter; preface by Elizabeth Brandeis, University of Illinois Press, Urbana, 1953; and Maud Nathan, *The Story of an Epoch-Making Movement*; foreword by Newton D. Baker, Mary Anderson and Edward A. Filene, Doubleday, Page, Garden City, 1926. For brief accounts stressing the league's importance in general historical developments, see Robert H. Bremmer, *From the Depths: The Discovery of Poverty in the United States*, New York University Press, New York, 1956, pp. 232-43; Arthur M. Schlesinger, Jr., *The Age of Roosevelt: The Crisis of the Old Order, 1919-1933*, Houghton Mifflin, Boston, 1957, pp. 23-26; and George Soule, "Consumers' League," *Encyclopedia of the Social Sciences* 4 (1948), pp. 291-93.

5. Louis Filler, "Edward Albert Filene," *Dictionary of American Biography*, Supp. 2, pp. 183-85.

6. For her Socialist commitment as a young woman, see Dorothy Rose Blumberg, *Florence Kelley: The Making of a Social Pioneer*, Augustus M. Kelley Publishers, New York, 1966. In 1926 the child labor amendment was denounced in the United States Senate as "part of the Engels-Kelley program . . . derived straight from the fundamental Communist manifesto of 1848." *Congressional Record*, July 3, 1926, p. 12919. Sure enough, this was repeated endlessly. The best all-round account of her full life and contribution to social change is Louise C. Wade, "Florence Molthrop Kelley," *Notable American Women*, 1971. (All *NAW* biographies read in draft form by permission of individual authors and of Edward T. James, Editor.)

7. Goldmark, *Impatient Crusader*, p. ix.

8. NCL *Fourth Annual Report* (1903). See John Graham Brooks, "The Label of the Consumers' League," *Publication of the American Economic Association*, 3rd series, Macmillan Company, New York, 1900, I, pp. 250-58. Also, see "The Consumers' League Label and Its Offspring," *Survey* 32, August 8, 1914, p. 478.

9. See Elizabeth Brandeis, *Labor Legislation*, in *History of Labor in the United States, 1896-1932*, vol. 3, introduction by John R. Commons, Macmillan Company, New York, 1935.

10. NCL *Eighth Annual Report* (1970).

11. Ritchie v. People, 155 Ill. 98, 40 N.E. 454 (1895).

12. Florence Kelley, *Some Ethical Gains Through Legislation*, Macmillan Company, New York, 1905, p. 141.

13. Ritchie v. Wayman, 244 Ill. 509, 91 N.E. 695 (1910).

14. 198 U.S. 45 (1905).

15. Holden v. Hardy, 169 U.S. 366 (1898).

16. One authority speaks on Bunting v. Oregon, 243 U.S. 426 (1917), and Muller v. Oregon, 208 U.S. 412 (1908), as "decisions overruling the Lochner case" but omits this from an elaborate appendix titled "Supreme Court decisions overruled by subsequent decision." *Constitution of the United States of America: Analysis and Interpretation*, prepared by the Legislative Reference Service, Library of Congress, 1964. For the quotation see p. 1096. The list of overrulings is at pp. 1539-51.

17. A.T. Mason, "Louis Dembitz Brandeis," *International Encyclopedia of the Social Sciences* 2 (1968), pp. 143-45, at p. 144.

18. A National Consumer's League pamphlet states that the organization prepared briefs in the support of fifteen cases. *Thirty-Five Years of Crusading, 1899-1935*, National Consumers' League, New York, 1935, p. 10. While no official listing is available, a compilation of known cases in which the league was involved is given below. Where two courts are cited for a single case, the league

participated in both proceedings; one citation for a case signifies more limited involvement by the league. Muller v. Oregon, 208 U.W. 412 (1908); Ritchie v. Wayman, 244 Ill. 509, 91 N.E. 695 (1910); People v. Elerding, 254 Ill. 579, 98 N.E. 982 (1912); Ex parte Hawley, 85 Ohio 495, 98 N.E. 1126 (1911), affirmed, Hawley v. Walker, 232 U.S. 718 (1914); Ex parte Miller, 162 Cal. 687, 124 Pac. 427 (1912), affirmed, Miller v. Wilson, 236 U.S. 373 (1915); Bosley v. McLaughlin, 236 U.S. 385 (1915); Bunting v. Oregon, 243 U.S. 426 (1917); Stettler v. O'Hara, 69 Ore. 519, 139 Pac. 743 (1914), affirmed 243 U.S. 629 (1917); People v. Charles Schweinler Press, 214 N.Y. 395, 108 N.E. 639 (1915), affirmed, 163 App. Div. 620, 148 N.Y.S. 725 (1914); Children's Hospital v. Adkins, 284 Fed. 613 (D.C.C.A., 1922), affirmed, Adkins v. Children's Hospital, 261 U.S. 525 (1923); Radice v. New York, 264 U.S. 292 (1924); Gainer v. Dohrman, S.F. No. 10, 990, Sup. Ct. Calif (1924); Morehead v. New York ex rel. Tipaldo, 298   U.S. 587 (1936).

19. Goldmark, *Impatient Crusader*, p. 155.

20. *The Outlook*, March 21, 1908, quoted in NCL *Tenth Annual Report* (1909).

21. Miller v. Wilson, 236 U.S. 373 (1915); Bosley v. McLaughlin, 236 U.S. 382 (1915).

22. Edward S. Corwin, *Constitution: Analysis and Interpretation*, 1964, p. 1094.

23. Goldmark, *Impatient Crusader*, p. 160.

24. Josephine Goldmark, *Fatigue and Efficiency*, Russell Sage Foundation, New York, 1912.

25. NCL *Tenth Annual Report* (1909).

26. NCL *Twelfth Annual Report* (1911).

27. NCL *Seventeenth Annual Report* (1917).

28. For example, Thomas Reed Powell, "The Oregon Minimum-Wage Cases," reprinted from *Political Science Quarterly* 32 (June 1917), pp. 296-311.

29. National Consumers' League, *The Supreme Court and Minimum Wage Legislation*; Introduction by Roscoe Pound, New Republic, Inc., New York, 1925.

Chapter 8
Early Minimum Wage Movement

1. Paul A. Samuelson, *Economics*, 8th ed., McGraw-Hill Book Company, New York, 1970, p. 372.

2. Harry K. Girvetz, "Welfare State," *International Encyclopedia of the Social Sciences* 16 (1968), p. 516. A recent survey of the subject with a superb bibliography is N. Arnold Tolles, "Wage and Hour Legislation," *IESS* 16 (1968), pp. 418-24.

3. 312 U.S. 100 (1941). The F.L.S.A. was approved June 25, 1938, ch. 676, 52 Stat. 1060, 29 U.S.C., secs. 201-219.

4. 247 U.S. 251 (1918).

5. This section draws heavily from Francis L. Broderick, *Right Reverend New Dealer: John A. Ryan*, Macmillan Company, New York, 1963. Ryan's own works have also been consulted. See especially, John A. Ryan, *A Living Wage*, Macmillan Company, New York, 1906, rev. ed. 1920.

6. Paul Taylor, "Elizabeth Glendower Evans," *Notable American Women*.

7. James T. Patterson, "Mary Dewson and The American Minimum Wage Movement," *Labor History* 5 (1964), pp. 141-142.

8. Norris C. Hundley, Jr., "Katherine Philips Edson and the Fight for the California Minimum Wage, 1912-1923," *Pacific Historical Review* 29 (1960), pp. 271-85. Also, see Norris C. Hundley, Jr., "Edson," *Notable American Women*.

9. Amendments to Constitution . . . to be Submitted to the Electors of the State of California at the General Election on Tuesday, November 3, 1914, p. 29, as cited in Hundley, "Katherine Phillips Edson," p. 277.

10. The political story of the Brandeis appointment is lucidly told in A.L. Todd, *Justice on Trial: The Case of Louis D. Brandeis*, McGraw-Hill Book Company, New York, 1964. Todd dedicates his book "To the President who next appoints a Louis D. Brandeis."

11. William Hitz to Felix Frankfurter, December [?], 1914, handwritten copy, NCL Papers, Library of Congress, folder C, item 1.

12. Josephine Goldmark to Felix Frankfurter, November 19, 1915, Frankfurter Papers, Library of Congress, box 60.

13. Baker to Frankfurter, February 2, 1916, ibid.

14. Josephine Goldmark to George M. Brown, October 23, 1916, ibid.

15. Brown to Joseph N. Teal, October 19, 1916, ibid.

16. Kelley to Frankfurter, November 23, 1916. The resolution was passed at the Seventeenth Annual Meeting of the National Consumers' League, Springfield, Mass., November 16, 1917.

17. Quoted in J.G. Shaw, *Edwin Vincent O'Hara: American Prelate*, Farar, Straus and Cudahy, New York, 1957, p. 44.

18. The act of September 19, 1918, 40 Stat. 960, ch. 174 was ruled valid by a three-judge panel of the Court of Appeals of the District of Columbia, June 6, 1921, but on rehearing this was overruled and the statute invalidated, November 6, 1922. Children's Hospital v. Adkins, 284 Fed. 613 (1922). On appeal by the Minimum Wage Board, Adkins being chairman, argument was heard March 14, 1923, in the Supreme Court and the decision was announced April 9, 1923. Adkins v. Children's Hospital, 261 U.S. 525 (1923).

19. Brandeis, *Labor Legislation*, p. 688.

20. A federal district judge in North Dakota, Charles F. Amidon, a close student of such litigation, said this of the hospital and the elevator girl: "It

should be shown that the plaintiffs do not represent the great body of working women intended to be protected by the law. It should be plainly proven that the whole suit is based on falsehood and hypocracy *[sic.]*. It is A.B.C. that the laboring women are substantially in favor of the minimum wage law. The real plaintiffs in the suit are the employers. It is their 'liberty' to exploit that is skulking behind the 'liberty' and 'property' of the nominal plaintiffs." Amidon to Florence Kelley, March 12, 1923, National Consumers' League Papers, Library of Congress, folder F, item 5.

21. A comprehensive list of appointments to the Supreme Court with dates of nomination, confirmation, retirements, resignations, deaths and other notations is in *Congress and the Nation, 1945-1964*, edited and published by Congressional Quarterly Service, Washington, D.C., 1965, pp. 1452-53.

22. Interview with Woodson P. Houghton by C.E. Vose, Washington, D.C., June 13, 1967.

23. Frankfurter to Stephens, February 16, 1921, Frankfurter Papers, box 57.

24. Frankfurter to Clara Beyer, February 23, 1921, ibid.

25. Benjamin Twiss, *Lawyers and the Constitution: How Laissez-Faire Came to the Supreme Court*.

26. For an engrossing account of the finessing to persuade McKenna to quit the Court, see David J. Danelski, "A Supreme Court Justice Steps Down," *Yale Review* 54 (March 1965), pp. 411-25.

Chapter 9
The Minimum Wage Overruling

1. Lucy Randolph Mason, *To Win These Rights: A Personal Story of the CIO in the South*, foreword by Eleanor Roosevelt, introduction by George Sinclair Mitchell, Harper & Brothers, New York, 1952, pp. 11-18.

2. Emily Sims Marconnier interview with C.E. Vose, August 1967.

3. W.W. Crosskey, *Politics and the Constitution*, 2 vols., University of Chicago Press, Chicago, 1953.

4. See John R. Commons and John B. Andrews, *Principles of Labor Legislation*, Harper & Brothers, New York, 1916.

5. Dewson to Frankfurter, December 14, 1932, Frankfurter Papers, box 58, folder 3.

6. Frankfurter to Dewson, December 30, 1932, ibid.

7. Frankfurter to Goldmark, January 10, 1933.

8. Frankfurter to B.V. Cohen, February 1933.

9. Frankfurter to Goldmark, January 10, 1933.

10. J.P. Chamberlain to Mary Dewson, January 13, 1933, NCL Papers, box 44 (R-9), folder 1.

11. "Why We Believe the Standard Minimum Wage Bill May be Declared Constitutional," NCL Statement, mimeographed, January 1933, NCL Papers, box 44.

12. *Equal Rights* 1 (March 31, 1923), p. 56.

Chapter 10
The Amendment Stalemate

1. Edmond Cahn, "An American Contribution," in *Supreme Court and Supreme Law*, ed. Edmond Cahn, Indiana University Press, Bloomington, 1954.

2. Floyd McKissick, *Three-fifths of a Man*, Macmillan Company, New York, 1969.

3. In *The Federalist*, no. 85, Alexander Hamilton, in discussing the difficulty of uniting two-thirds, three-fourths or nine-thirteenths of the state legislatures for their possible action in the amendment process, speaks in language that will delight many modern behavioral scientists when he calls this "one of those rare instances in which a political truth can be brought to the test of mathematical demonstration." *The Federalist*, edited, with introduction and notes, by Jacob E. Cooke, Wesleyan University Press, Middletown, Conn., 1961, p. 594.

4. S.J. Res. 40 – H.J. Res. 69, 66th Congress (1921).

5. *Woman Patriot* 8 (March 1, 1924), p. 5.

6. This section draws heavily from Stephen B. Wood, *Constitutional Politics in the Progressive Era: Child Labor and the Law*, University of Chicago Press, Chicago, 1968. The book is a thorough account of the start of the movement and the work of the National Child Labor Committee, the complex legislative work in Congress and, most revealing, the part played by men like Clark who represented the interests felt by owners and managers of cotton mills in the South in managing the test cases. Wood's account ends in 1924 and is relied upon here for a summary of the events to that point; thereafter, the story in this section draws on heretofore unpublished materials from the papers of Alexander Lincoln on the Sentinels of the Republic, located in the Schlesinger Library, Radcliffe College, Cambridge, Massachusetts.

7. Evans to Lincoln, December 6, 1934, Alexander Lincoln Papers, folder 28.

8. After Guthrie's death in 1935, Lincoln corresponded at length with the attorneys who challenged ratification of the child labor amendment in Kentucky and in Kansas. The Child Labor Amendment Cases were: Coleman v. Miller, 307 U.S. 433 (1939) and Chandler v. Wise, 307 U.S. 474 (1939). The cases were argued together on October 10 and 11, 1938, reargued on April 18, 1939 and decided on June 5, 1939. Counsel, arguing against the validity of ratification, in the Kansas case (Coleman v. Miller) were Robert Stone and Rolla W. Coleman; in

the Kentucky case (Chandler v. Wise) were Lafon Allen and Oldham Clarke. Alexander Lincoln corresponded particularly with Robert Stone of Topeka, Kansas and Lafon Allen of Louisville.

9. NCLC Board of Trustees, 132nd meeting, December 7, 1937, in NCLC Papers, container 9.

10. The most reliable information, from the Survey Research Center of the University of Michigan, is that "the vote participation rate among women in our samples is consistently 10 percent below that of men, as an over-all estimate." To reach this level there was a slow increase in vote participation since 1920. Angus Campbell, Philip E. Converse, Warren E. Miller, Donald E. Stokes, *The American Voter*, John Wiley & Sons, New York, 1960, p. 484.

11. S. J. Res. 21 and H.-J. Res. 75, 68 Cong., 1st Sess., providing for equal rights for men and women throughout the United States.

12. This language is quoted from the discussion in Carl B. Swisher, *American Constitutional Development*, 2nd ed., Houghton Mifflin, Boston, 1954, pp. 702-03.

13. A content analysis would show the treatment accorded the three groups to contain degrees of difference. Mrs. Catt's League of Women Voters was merely "the feminist lobby" seeking radical programs to serve "political jobhunters." *Woman Patriot*, March 19, 1921, p. 4. An article condemning Miss Paul's work was entitled, "The Woman's Party and Communism" and asserted that the National Woman's Party was organizing twenty-four *soviets. Woman Patriot*, October 1 & 15, 1922, p. 12. The attack on Mrs. Kelley stated the child labor amendment "was drafted principally by Mrs. Florence Kelley, the Socialist friend of Frederich Engels and translator of Karl Marx, etc." *Woman Patriot*, August 1, 1924, p. 6.

14. Goldmark, *Impatient Crusader*, p. 182.

15. Ibid., p. 183.

16. Eleanor Flexner, *Century of Struggle: The Woman's Rights Movement in the United States*, Belknap Press of Harvard University Press, Cambridge, 1959, p. 328.

17. Leo Kanowitz, *Women and the Law: The Unfinished Revolution*, University of New Mexico Press, Albuquerque, 1969, p. 195. Kanowitz repented in 1971 and publicly supported the equal rights amendment before Congress.

18. C. Herman Pritchett, *The American Constitution*, McGraw-Hill Book Company, New York, 1959, p. 41.

19. Philip L. Martin, "Convention Ratification of Federal Constitutional Amendments," *Political Science Quarterly* 82 (1967), pp. 61-71.

20. For a recent sophisticated analysis of this kind of problem, see Patrick Riley, "A Possible Explanation of Rousseau's General Will," *American Political Science Review* 64 (1970), pp. 86-97.

21. See my earlier discussion of Tucker's opposition to woman suffrage in Chapter 3.

22. There has been remarkably slight empirical study of direct democracy, but a recent analysis of open housing referenda demonstrates that "outcomes are affected by differences in the scope of the laws, in timing and the nature of communities." The author concludes that direct democracy, of which voting on slates of delegates to special ratifying conventions is surely an example, is very regularly "governance by a minority." Howard D. Hamilton, "Direct Legislation: Some Implications of Open Housing Referenda," *American Political Science Review* 64 (March 1970), pp. 124-37, at pp. 136-37.

Chapter 11
Social Policies as Jurisdictional Issues

1. Ralph F. Bischoff, "Status to Challenge Constitutionality," in *Supreme Court and Supreme Law*, ed. Edmond Cahn, Indiana University Press, Bloomington, 1954, p. 26.
2. Barrows v. Jackson, 346 U.S. 249 (1953).
3. Brown v. Board of Education, 347 U.S. 483 (1954).
4. Baker v. Carr, 369 U.S. 186 (1962).
5. Flast v. Cohen, 392 U.S. 83 (1968).
6. See Felix Frankfurter and James K. Landis, *The Business of the Supreme Court*, Macmillan Company, New York, 1927; Henry Hart and Herbert Wechsler, *The Federal Court and the Federal System*, Foundation Press, Brooklyn, 1953; Robert M. Stern and Eugene Gressman, *Supreme Court Practice*, 4th ed., BNA Books, Washington, D.C., 1969; Charles Alan Wright, *Handbook on the Law of Federal Courts*, West Publishing Company, St. Paul, Minn., 1963.
7. James Willard Hurst, *The Growth of American Law: The Law Makers*, Little, Brown and Company, Boston, 1950, pp. 4, 6.
8. This section is drawn largely from Comment, "Taxpayers' Suits: A Survey and a Summary," *Yale Law Journal* 69 (April 1960), pp. 895-925, at p. 898.
9. Ibid., p. 906.
10. Ibid.
11. Ibid., pp. 907-08.
12. Madison, Wisconsin, *Capital Times*, February 22, 1960, p. 1.
13. Ibid.
14. Wallace S. Sayre and Herbert Kaufman, *Governing New York City: Politics in the Metropolis*, Russell Sage Foundation, New York, 1960, p. 497.
15. See letters of Samuel D. Smoleff to C.E. Vose, July 7, 1960, August 29, 1969, December 11, 1969, April 22, 1970 and July 13, 1970. The Citizens Union of New York cases include the following: Childs v. Moses, 290 N.Y. 828, 50 N.E. 2d 235 (1943); Bergerman v. Murphy, 303 N.Y. 762, 103 N.E. 2d 545 (1952); Bergerman v. Byrnes, 305 N.Y. 811, 113 N.E. 2d 557 (1953); Berger-

man v. Gerosa, 3 N.Y. 2d 855, 166 N.Y. Supp. 2d 306 (1957); Bergerman v. Wagner, 2 N.Y. 2d 908, 161 N.Y. Supp. 2d 434 (1957); Bergerman v. Lindsay, 25 N.Y. 2d 405, 306 N.Y.S. 2d 898 (1969), 2d 405, 306 N.Y. Supp. 2d 898 (1969), *cert. denied*, 38 L.W. 3496 (1970).

16. Comment, "Taxpayers' Suits," p. 904.

17. Ibid.

18. Ibid., p. 910.

19. Children's Bureau Act of April 9, 1912, c. 73, 37 Stat. 79.

20. J. Stanley Lemons, "The Sheppard-Towner Act: Progressivism in the 1920s," *Journal of American History* 55 (March 1969), p. 776.

21. "Brief History of the Sentinels of the Republic," n.d., p. 2, Alexander Lincoln Papers, folder 5, Radcliffe College, Cambridge, Mass.

22. *Woman Patriot*, February 1, 1922, p. 1.

23. Ibid., May 15, 1922, p. 1.

24. Ibid., October 1-15, 1922, p. 15.

25. Charles K. Burdick, "Federal Aid Legislation," *Cornell Law Quarterly* 8 (1923), pp. 324-37.

26. Constitution, Art. IV, Sec. 3, Par. 2. Also, see the discussion in *The Constitution, Analysis and Interpretation*, Library of Congress, Washington, 1964, pp. 791-95.

27. Burdick, "Federal Aid Legislation," p. 327.

28. Morton Keller, *In Defense of Yesterday*, J.B. Lippincott, Philadelphia, 1959, p. 177.

29. Ibid.

30. 262 U.S. 447 (1923).

31. 262 U.S. 447, 480.

32. *Federal Grants in Aid*, Report of the Committee on Federal Grants-in-Aid, Council of State Governments, 1949, p. 24.

33. U.S. Const., Art. III, Sec. 2.

34. In 1970, a Massachusetts "Anti-Vietnam" statute declared that no inhabitant of the Commonwealth shall be required to serve in the military services of the United States outside territorial limits in an undeclared war. The statute specifically commands the state attorney general to bring "an original action" in the United States Supreme Court to enforce the law. If this does not work, the attorney general is to proceed through an inferior federal court. There is no other means provided for the enforcement of this state policy. The similarity of the peace movement in Massachusetts in the 1970s to the patriotic movement to stop federal maternity aid in the 1920s is striking. The following commentary suggests that the course of litigation may be as frustrating:

"The Supreme Court has heretofore refused to entertain appeals involving the constitutional power to draft and dispatch troops abroad in aid of the undeclared war in Vietnam. It will have no difficulty in rejecting the proposed action by the state of Massachusetts. In the famous case of *Massachusetts v.*

Mellon the Court held that a state has 'no standing' to sue on a claim that federal action unconstitutionally affected its citizenry. The Court can, of course, find differences between that case and future cases, and reach a different result, if it chooses." *New Republic*, April 18, 1970, p. 11.

35. 262 U.S. 447, 487, citing John F. Dillon, *Municipal Corporations*, 5th ed., vol. 4, sec. 1580.

36. Ibid.

37. Ibid.

38. Ibid., p. 488.

39. Remarks of James Willard Hurst on the condition and scope of constitutional review in *Supreme Court and Supreme Law*, ed. Cahn, p. 33.

40. Fred Rodell, *Nine Men: A Political History of the Supreme Court from 1790 to 1955*, Random House, New York, 1955.

41. Remarks of Charles P. Curtis in *Supreme Court and Supreme Law*, ed. Cahn, p. 35.

42. Ibid., pp. 31-32.

43. *The Business of the Supreme Court*, p. 280.

44. Social Security Act of Aug. 14, 1935, c. 531, 49 Stat. 620.

45. Wilbur J. Cohen, "The First Twenty-Five Years of the Social Security Act, 1935-1960," *Social Work Yearbook 1960*, 14th issue, ed. Russell H. Kurtz, National Association of Social Workers, New York, 1960, pp. 49-62, at p. 49.

46. For a contemporaneous account by an economist who later served in the United States Senate, see Paul H. Douglas, *Social Security in the United States; Analysis and Appraisal of the Federal Social Security Act*, McGraw-Hill Book Company, New York, 1936.

47. 297 U.S. 1 (1936).

48. Carmichael v. Southern Coal & Coke Co., 301 U.S. 495 (1937), *reversing*, 17 F. Supp. 225 (1936).

49. 301 U.S. 548 (1937), *affirming* 89 Fed. 2d 207 (1937).

50. Howes Brothers Co. v. Massachusetts Unemployment Compensation Commission, 296 U.S. 275 (1936), *cert. den.*, 300 U.S. 657 (1937). Helvering v. Davis, 301 U.S. 619 (1937), *reversing*, 89 Fed. 2d 393 (1937), *but affirming*, 18 Fed. Supp. 1 (1937).

51. A member of the firm from 1918 into the 1970s has recalled the relationship. George P. Davis interview with C.E. Vose, September 1969.

52. A.L. Newton, undated notes, in Nutter, McClennen & Fish office records, File 42572.

53. "To our Clients," November 12, 1935. Nutter, McClennen & Fish, File 42572.

54. The particular form letter quoted here is for S.D. Warren Company to Massachusetts Unemployment Compensation Commission, September 15, 1936. Nutter, McClennen & Fish, File 42572.

55. Joseph McCartin to Nutter, McClennen & Fish, September 16, 1936.

56. James J. Ronan, assistant attorney general, to E. Curtiss Mower, Jr., September 23, 1936.

57. Ibid.

58. Mower to Ronan, September 26, 1936.

59. Howes Brothers Co. v. Massachusetts Unemployment Compensation Commission, 296 U.S. 275 (1936), *cert. den.*, 300 U.S. 657 (1937).

60. Carmichael v. Southern Coal & Coke Co., Carmichael v. Gulf States Paper Co., 301 U.S. 495 (1937), *reversing*, 17 F. Supp. 225 (1937).

61. Chamberlin v. Andrews, Stearns & Co. v. Andrews, Associated Industries v. Dept. of Labor of New York, 299 U.S. 515 (1936), *affirming* 159 Misc. 124, 286 N.Y.S. 242; 271 N.Y. 1, 2 N.E. 2d 22, 106 A.L.R. 1519 (1936).

62. Ibid.

63. Southern Coal & Coke Co. v. Carmichael, 17 F. Supp. 225 (1937).

64. The Davis-McClennen relationship was learned by locating the names listed in the *United States Reports* as counsel in the case and checking them in the *Martindale-Hubbell Law Directory*. It was found that all of McClennen's associates in the case, along with the plaintiff, were listed in the firm. This was not a secret among Boston lawyers, or judges for that matter, and the details of the relationship were cheerfully and fully explained by George P. Davis in correspondence and conversations in September 1969 with C.E. Vose.

65. Helvering v. Davis, 301 U.S. 619 (1937), *reversing* Davis v. Edison Electric Illuminating Co. of Boston, 89 F. 2d 393 (1st Cir. 1937), *reversing* 18 F. Supp. 1 (1937). Davis v. Boston & Maine Railroad, *cert. denied*, 299 U.S. 614 (1937). For this case below, see 89 F. 2d 368 (1st Cir. 1937), *reversing* 17 F. Supp. 97 (1936). Evidently the parties agreed informally that the railroad case was to be governed by the Supreme Court's ruling in Helvering v. Davis. The official reports leave this issue in limbo.

66. Papers of John W. Davis, Beinecke Library, Yale University Library. Especially see 1934-1935 correspondence between Burr and Davis on United States v. Belcher, *appeal dismissed*, 294 U.S. 736 (1935), concerning the constitutionality of the National Industrial Recovery Act.

67. Alvin W. Vogtle, "William Logan Martin," *Memorial Book 1960*, Association of the Bar of the City of New York, p. 54. This is supported by a letter with other details, S. Eason Balch to C.E. Vose, September 25, 1969.

68. *Mobile Press Register*, January 3, 1937. A copy of this story came from Judge Martin's office files in Birmingham.

69. Helvering v. Davis, 301 U.S. 619, 639 (1937).

70. Ibid., 639-640.

Chapter 12
The White Primary Overruling, 1921-1944

1. V.O. Key, Jr., *Politics, Parties and Pressure Groups*, Thomas Y. Crowell Co., 5th ed., New York, 1964, pp. 601-612. A fuller explanation is Key,

Southern Politics in State and Nation, A.A. Knopf, New York, 1950, pp. 531-674.

2. Records and briefs in Supreme Court cases were consulted in the Connecticut State Library, Hartford, Conn. Correspondence on the white primary litigation was found in the Arthur B. Spingarn Papers and the Legal Files in the NAACP Records, all in the Manuscript Division, Library of Congress. The papers of Moorfield Storey and Felix Frankfurter there were also consulted.

3. Nixon v. Herndon, 273 U.S. 536 (1927); Nixon v. Condon, 286 U.S. 73 (1932); Smith v. Allwright, 321 U.S. 649 (1944).

4. Love v. Griffith, 266 U.S. 32 (1924); Grovey v. Townsend, 295 U.S. 45 (1935).

5. Transcript of Record, p. 3, Love v. Griffith. All quotations in these two paragraphs are from this Record.

6. 236 S.W. 239 (Tex. Civ. App. 1921).

7. 236 S.W. 239, 240 (1921).

8. Record, p. 20, Love v. Griffith.

9. Love v. Griffith (No. 444, 1922 Term; renumbered No. 60, 1923 term; renumbered No. 12, 1924 term).

10. Brief for Plaintiffs in Error, p. 5, Love v. Griffith.

11. Ibid., p. 9.

12. Ibid., pp. 16-17.

13. Love v. Griffith, 266 U.S. 32, p. 34 (1924).

14. Tex. Civ. Stats., Art. 3093-A (1923).

15. Chandler v. Neff, 298 Fed. 515 (W.D. Tex. 1924).

16. Ibid.

17. Giles v. Harris, 189 U.S. 475 (1903).

18. Newberry v. United States, 256 U.S. 232 (1921).

19. Chandler v. Neff, 298 Fed. 515, 519.

20. L.W. Washington to R.W. Bagnell, August 2, 1924. NAACP box D-63.

21. Washington to Bagnell, December 18, 1924, ibid.

22. Transcript of Record, p. 5, Nixon v. Herndon (No. 480, 1925 term; renumbered No. 117, 1926 term).

23. Record, p. 8.

24. Record, p. 9.

25. This directory has flourished and continues today, in five huge volumes, as a standard reference. *Martindale-Hubbell America Law Directory*, Summit, N.J., 102nd annual edition, 5 vols., 1970. The nice treatment of Knollenberg contrasts with the simple identification for counsel in Love v. Griffith, R.D. Evans, whose name is misspelled "Evan" with the notation, "(colored)." *Martindale's American Law Directory*, New York, 57th year, 1 vol., 1925.

26. W.F. White to A.B. Spingarn, January 12, 1925. NAACP D-63.

27. Spingarn to White, January 6, 1925, ibid.

28. Storey to White, January 10, 1925, ibid.

29. J.A. Cobb to White, January 29, 1925, ibid.

30. Storey to White, January 10, 1925, ibid.

31. Spingarn to White, January 6, 1925, ibid.

32. White to Washington, January 16, 22, 30 and February 16, 1925, ibid.

33. L.W. Washington to White, January 26, February 5, 1925; Knollenberg to White, January 30, February 28, 1925, ibid.

34. Washington to White, February 5, 1925, ibid.

35. Extract from the minutes of the February 9, 1925, meeting of the Board of Directors, ibid.

36. White to Cobb, March 13, 1925, ibid.

37. Record, p. 10, Nixon v. Herndon (No. 117, 1926 Term).

38. Act of February 13, 1925, 43 Stat. 936. Supreme Court Revised Rules, 266 U.S. 645 (1925).

39. Rule 35, 266 U.S. 645 (1925). The classic study of the revolution attempted by the 1925 act is Felix Frankfurter and James M. Landis, *The Business of the Supreme Court*, Macmillan & Company, New York, 1927.

40. L.A. Nixon to William Pickens, January 9, 1926, ibid.

41. Storey to Spingarn, April 8, 1926, ibid.

42. Cobb to Knollenberg, April 7, 1926, ibid.

43. Brief for Plaintiff in Error, Nixon v. Herndon.

44. Knollenberg to White, April 3, 1926. NAACP D-63.

45. Cobb to J.W. Johnson, April 12, 1926, ibid.

46. Motion to Advance, 3 pp., Nixon v. Herndon, No. 480, 1925 term.

47. Louis Marshall to J.W. Johnson, January 13, 1927. NAACP D-64.

48. Cobb to J.W. Johnson, January 11, 1927, ibid.

49. J.W. Johnson to Cobb, January 10, 1927, ibid.

50. Cobb to J.W. Johnson, Jan. 8, 1927, ibid.

51. Brief for the State of Texas 13 pp., Nixon v. Herndon. Special leave to file the brief was granted on January 4, 1927, to Dan Moody, former attorney general of Texas. The brief was submitted on February 4, by Claude Pollard, attorney general, and D.A. Simmons, first assistant attorney general, for the state of Texas.

52. Reply brief for plaintiff in error, 34 pp. Nixon v. Herndon.

53. Ibid., p. 3.

54. Ibid., p. 12.

55. Ibid., pp. 8, 9, 11. The book was Charles E. Merriam and Louise Overacker, *Primary Elections*, University of Chicago Press, Chicago, 1908. For an assessment of this political scientist, see Barry G. Karl, "Charles E. Merriam," *International Encyclopedia of the Social Sciences* 10 (1968), pp. 245-59.

56. Johnson to Marshall, February 21, 1927. NAACP D-64.

57. NAACP, "Release to Colored Press," February 25, 1927, ibid.

58. Telegram, J.W. Johnson to White, March 7, 1927, ibid.

59. Telegram, White to Johnson, March 7, 1927, ibid.

60. The Senate, in 1928, excluded both Vare of Pennsylvania and Smith of Illinois for overspending, thereby indicating again the growing belief that primaries were integral to the election system, regulated by the government. Arthur W. Macmahon, "First Session of the Seventieth Congress," *American Political Science Review* 22 (August 1928), pp. 650, 651-652.

61. Nixon v. Herndon, 273 U.S. 536, 551-52 (1927).

62. L.A. Nixon to J.W. Johnson, March 12, 1927, NAACP box D-64.

63. NAACP Press Release, March 25, 1927, ibid.

64. NAACP Press Release, July 27, 1928, NAACP Papers, box D-64. *Houston Sentinel*, July 13, 1928. *New York World* (editorial), July 26, 1928.

65. Knollenberg to R.A. Campbell of San Antonio, June 28, 1928, NAACP Papers, box D-64.

66. Washington to William T. Andrews, special legal assistant, NAACP, New York City, June 20, 1928, ibid.

67. Knollenberg to James Weldon Johnson, July 10, 1928, ibid.

68. Knollenberg to NAACP, New York, August 6, 1928, NAACP Legal Files, box D-64.

69. Bagnell to Knollenberg, August 29, 1928, ibid.

70. R.W. Bagnell to O.P. DeWalt, September 13, 1928, ibid.

71. Louis Marshall to William T. Andrews, November 9, 1928, ibid.

72. Nixon v. Condon, 34 F.2d. 464 (1929).

73. Nixon v. Condon, 49 F.2d 1012 (1931).

74. Nixon v. Condon, *cert. granted*, 284 U.S. 601 (1931); 286 U.S. 73 (1932).

75. Nixon v. Condon, 286 U.S. 73, 85 (1932).

76. Knollenberg to White, May 5, 1932, Spingarn Papers, box 65.

77. Knollenberg to White, October 20, 1932, ibid.

78. Margold to Felix Frankfurter, May 5, 1932, ibid.

79. 295 U.S. 45 (1935).

80. Wilkins to P.L. Prattis, April 4, 1935, NAACP Legal Files, box D-92.

81. Ibid.

82. Clipping dated April 2, 1935, accompanying letter from Knollenberg to Walter White, April 4, 1935, ibid.

83. Evans failed in these efforts: Love v. Griffith, 236 S.W. 239 (Tex. Civ. App. 1921), *affirmed*, 266 U.S. 32 (1924); Grigsby v. Harris, 27 F.2d (S.D. Tex., 1928), *application to appeal denied*, 27 F.2d 945 (1928). W. Owen Dailey of Houston was the losing attorney in White v. Lubbock, 30 S.W.2d 722 (Tex. Civ. App. 1930). Atkins and Wesley had failed in Love v. Democratic Executive Committee of Houston, Equity No. 438, S.D. Tex., Jan. 23, 1931 (moot); White v. Democratic Executive Committee of Harris County, 60 F.2d 973 (S.D. Tex., 1932); Drake v. Executive Committee of the Democratic Party for the City of Houston, 2 F.Supp. 486 (S.D. Tex., 1933); and the case here of Grovey v. Townsend, 295 U.S. 45 (1935).

84. Houston to Atkins, May 15, 1935, NAACP Legal Files, box D-92.

85. 26 U.S. Code sec. 170 (c) (2).

86. The relationships during the 1940s are discussed in detail in C.E. Vose, *Caucasians Only*.

87. Memorandum from Marshall to White, Wilkins and Perry, July 20, 1943, NAACP Papers, box 266.

88. 98 F.2d 980 (1938).

89. Houston for NAACP to ACLU, November 1, 1937, NAACP Legal Files, box D-92.

90. Dunjee to Walter White, October 17, 1938; White to Dunjee, October 17, 1938; NAACP Legal Files, box D-92.

91. Chandler to Thurgood Marshall, January 23, 1939, ibid.

92. 305 U.S. 559 (1938).

93. Leon A. Ransom to Thurgood Marshall, February 2, 1939, NAACP Legal Files, box D-92.

94. Lane v. Wilson, 307 U.S. 268, 275 (1939).

95. The resolution was passed on May 8, 1939. White to Houston, May 15, 1939, NAACP Legal Files, box D-92.

96. Charles A. Chandler, "State of Court Costs, Lane v. Wilson," April 27 1939, 2 pages, ibid.

97. Charles Houston, "Confidential Memorandum to the Office," June 8, 1939, received by Walter White, June 9, 1939, ibid.

98. This is spelled out in correspondence in the Frankfurter Papers, Manuscript Division, Library of Congress.

99. Edgerton to NAACP, June 1, 1939, NAACP Legal Files, box D-92.

100. Smith v. Allwright, 131 F.2d 593 (1943).

101. Smith v. Allwright, *cert. granted*, 319 U.S. 738 (1943).

102. Memorandum from Marshall to White, Wilkins and Perry, July 20, 1943, NAACP Legal Files box 266.

103. "Outline of Procedure for Legal Cases, NAACP Branches," September 1943, ibid.

104. Smith v. Allwright, 321 U.S. 649 (1944).

105. A.T. Mason, *Harlan Fiske Stone: Pillar of the Law*, Viking Press, New York, 1956, p. 614.

106. Jackson to Stone, January 17, 1944. Quoted in full in Mason, *Harlan Fiske Stone*, p. 615.

Chapter 13
Litigation in the Web of Social Movements

1. *The Conservation Directory*, National Wildlife Federation, Washington, D.C., 1970. For a select, breezy organizational who's who, see Ann Cottrell Free,

"The Conservation Establishment," *The Washington*, April 1970, pp. 42-45, 93, 94.

2. Nathan Hakman, "Lobbying the Supreme Court," *Fordham Law Review* 35 (1966), p. 47; Hakman, "The Supreme Court's Political Environment," *Frontiers of Judicial Research*, ed. Joel B. Grossman and Joseph Tanenhaus, John Wiley and Sons, New York, 1969, p. 246. It appears that Hakman reached his conclusions by asking large numbers of lawyers engaged in both commercial and noncommercial litigation about their cases. Most declared that they served individual clients. The method of the current study has been directly opposite as decided cases were looked into and the lawyers reached by looking at a litigation as a tangled web of conflicting interests.

3. See Hubert J. O'Gorman, *Lawyers and Matrimonial Cases: A Study of Informal Pressures in Private Professional Practice*, The Free Press, Glencoe, Ill., 1963, pp. 36-64 and 119-145.

4. Carey McWilliams, *The Nation* 194 (April 7, 1962), p. 293.

5. This is the passage spotted by Professor Dixon in the Rhyne brief: "The complaining voters are not charging inequality of representation under the Fourteenth Amendment.... On the contrary, they claim equality of voting rights as provided by the constitution of Tennessee, and charge that the legislative attempt (successful so far) to deny that equality results in a violation of equal protection of the laws. This is an important distinction, which reflects the manner in which the Fourteenth Amendment operates. It *does not in itself decree equality in voting rights.* It says that *if* the state policy is to afford equal voting rights (expressed here by the people of Tennessee in their organic law), the attempt by state officers, under color of law, to deny such equality to *some* of the citizens is a denial of equal protection." (Emphasis added by Dixon. *Democratic Representation*, pp. 128-29, n. 25.) Reply to Appellees' Statement in Opposition and Motion to Dismiss, p. 2, Baker v. Carr, 369 U.S. 196 (1962).

6. Dixon, *Democratic Representation*, pp. 128-29.

7. Ibid.

Chapter 14
Amendment as Legislative Politics

1. See *Third Term for Presidents of the United States*, Hearings before a Subcommittee of the Senate Committee on the Judiciary, 76th Cong., 3d Sess., September 4-October 30 (1940). Conservative opposition to Roosevelt was, of course, well established long before the third term effort. For information about one link between the earlier American Liberty League and support for an anti-third term amendment, see Richard Polenberg, "The National Committee to Uphold Constitutional Government, 1937-1941," *Journal of American History* 52 (December 1965), pp. 582, 597.

2. See Paul G. Willis and George L. Willis, "The Politics of the Twenty-Second Amendment," *Western Political Quarterly* 5 (September 1952), pp. 469-82.

3. Dwight D. Eisenhower, *Public Papers of the Presidents of the United States*, 1956, p. 862. A leading conservative columnist even believed the Twenty-second Amendment should be repealed to enable Eisenhower to run again in 1960. David Lawrence, "Today in National Affairs," *New York Herald Tribune*, July 10, 1956, p. 19.

4. For a criticism that the office isolates the president from reality and that the erosion of power is profound, and should be, see George E. Reedy, *The Twilight of the Presidency*, World Publishing Company, New York and Cleveland, 1970, p. 137. Reedy is particularly critical of a suggestion that the president be restricted to one six-year term.

5. Senator Bricker's sixth version was introduced as S.J. Res. 1, 84th Cong., 1st sess. (1955). For a summary of the history of the Bricker amendment, see *Congressional Quarterly Weekly*, July 1, 1955, p. 768. His latest version was as follows:

SECTION 1—A provision of a treaty or other international agreement which conflicts with this Constitution, or which is made in pursuance thereof, shall not be the supreme law of the land nor be of any force or effect.

SECTION 2—A treaty or other international agreement shall become effective as internal law in the United States only through legislation valid in the absence of international agreement.

SECTION 3—On the question of advising and consenting to the ratification of a treaty, the vote shall be determined by yeas and nays, and the names of the persons voting for and against shall be entered on the Journal of the Senate.

SECTION 4—This article shall be inoperative unless it shall have been ratified as an amendment to the Constitution by the legislatures of three-fourths of the several states or in seven years from the date of its submission.

6. An excellent, though hardly exhaustive summary, of some twenty-five instances of this is to be seen in Comment, "Congressional Reversal of Supreme Court Decisions, 1945-1957," *Harvard Law Review* 81 (1958), pp. 1324-37.

7. 21 Wall. 162 (1875).

8. The Equal Rights Amendment officially proposed to the states for ratification took the form in Congress of H.J. Res. 208, 92nd Cong. For excerpts from the majority report of the Senate Committee on the Judiciary on the ERA, see *Congressional Record*, Daily ed., March 22, 1972, vol. 118, pp. S4582-4587. This issue of the *Record* contains a veritable anthology of law review articles on sex discrimination and women's rights as well as the Senate debate. The vote is recorded at p. S4612.

9. *Congressional Record*, August 10, 1970, vol. 116, p. H7953.

10. Ibid., p. H7948.

11. The income tax provisions of the Tariff Act of 1894, Act of August 27,

1894, 28 Stat. 553-560, secs. 27-37, were invalidated in Pollock v. Farmers' Loan & Trust Co., 157 U.S. 429 (April 8, 1895) and rehearing, 158 U.S. 601 (May 20, 1895). The Sixteenth Amendment was proposed by Congress on July 2, 1909, and ratification was completed on February 3, 1913. The constitutionality of the Sixteenth Amendment was upheld by the Supreme Court in Dodge v. Brady, Collector, 240 U.S. 122, on February 21, 1916. William D. Guthrie, argued against constitutionality while John W. Davis, as solicitor general, prepared and won for the United States government.

12. Attorneys general of twelve states filed motions in the case, which was brought by David P. Buckson, attorney general of Delaware, with Dixon as counsel. The motion for leave to file a bill of complaint was denied. Delaware v. New York, 385 U.S. 895 (1966), *rehearing denied*, 385 U.S. 964 (1966). The litigation is described in Neal R. Peirce, "The Electoral College Goes to Court," *Reporter*, October 6, 1966, pp. 34-37.

13. H.J. Res. 1321, 90th Cong. 2d sess., 1968.

14. Engle v. Vitale, 370 U.S. 421 (1962); Abington School District v. Schempp and Murray v. Curlett, 374 U.S. 203 (1963).

15. H.J. Res. 9, 88th Cong., 1st sess.

16. H.J. Res. 693, 88th Cong., 1st sess.

17. Baker v. Carr, 369 U.S. 186 (1962); Reynolds v. Sims, 377 U.S. 533 (1964).

18. *New York Times*, December 13, 1964.

19. S. 2307, 90th Cong., 1st sess.

20. Arlen J. Large, "Dirksen's Crusade," *Wall Street Journal*, June 2, 1969, p. 1.

21. Ibid.

22. Comments of Esther H. Esmond, office of Senator Dirksen, to C.E. Vose, July 31, 1969.

23. *New York Times*, November 5, 1969.

24. Miranda v. Arizona, 384 U.S. 436 (1966).

25. United States v. Wade, 388 U.S. 218 (1967), Act of June 19, 1968, secs. 3501, 3502.

26. Henry J. Friendly, "Fifth Amendment Tomorrow: The Case for Constitutional Change," *University of Cincinnati Law Review* 37 (Fall 1968), p. 671; idem, "Fifth Amendment: The Case for a Constitutional Change," *Pennsylvania Bar Association Quarterly* 40 (June 1969), p. 524. Also, see *New York Times*, November 10, 1968.

27. The National Abortion Act was introduced by Senator Robert W. Packwood of Oregon. S. 3746, 91st Cong., 2d Sess., 1970.

28. Public Law 91-285, 91st Cong., H.R. 4249, 1970.

29. 384 U.S. 641 (1966). For Senator Kennedy's speech, see *Congressional Record*, March 5, 1970.

30. Letter to the Editor, *New York Times*, April 12, 1970.

31. Letter to the Editor, *New York Times*, April 5, 1970. President Nixon's views were elaborated in a letter to the speaker of the House and others on April 27, 1970. *Weekly Compilation of Presidential Documents*, May 4, 1970, pp. 588-90.

32. *Weekly Compilation of Presidential Documents*, May 4, 1970, p. 590.

33. United States v. Arizona, 400 U.S. 112 (1970) and Oregon v. Mitchell, 400 U.S. 112 (1970).

34. *Congressional Quarterly Weekly*, March 26, 1971, p. 691.

35. *Congressional Quarterly Weekly*, July 2, 1971, pp. 1436-39.

Chapter 15
Recommendations

1. Earl Warren, "The Law and the Future," *Fortune,* November 1955, p. 107.

2. Walter White, *A Man Called White*, Viking Press, New York, 1955.

3. 23 L Ed 2d, p. xlii.

4. For discussions of the somewhat harder "conflicts" as against the softer "improprieties," see Clement E. Vose, "Conflict of Interest," *International Encyclopedia of the Social Sciences* 3, (1968), pp. 242-46; and Jerry Landauer, "Judicial Propriety: The Fortas Case," *Wall Street Journal*, September 18, 1968.

5. Martin Shapiro, *Law and Politics in the Supreme Court: New Approaches to Political Jurisprudence*, The Free Press of Glencoe, Ill., 1964; and Charles A. Miller, *The Supreme Court and the Uses of History*, Belknap Press of Harvard University Press, Cambridge, 1969.

6. Frederick Bernays Wiener, "The Supreme Court's New Rules," *Harvard Law Review* 68 (November 1954), pp. 20-94.

7. Paul A. Freund, *The Supreme Court of the United States: Its Business, Purposes, and Performance*, Meridian Books, World Publishing Company, Cleveland and New York, 1965, pp. 153-54.

8. Samuel Krislov, "The Amicus Curiae Brief: From Friendship to Advocacy," *Yale Law Journal* 72 (March 1963), pp. 694-721.

Index

Abbott, Edith, 106, 167; Sheppard-Towner Maternity Act, 262
Abbott, Grace, 48, 167; Childrens' Bureau, 248; Sheppard-Towner Maternity Act, 262
Abington School District v. Schempp, 351
Acheson, Dean, National Consumers League, 168; as *amicus curiae* in 1933 minimum wage law, 209
Act of Congress of April 20, 1871, 30
Addams, Jane, 48, 164; and Florence Kelley, 167; and Sheppard-Towner Maternity Act, 262
Adkins, Jesse C., 190
Adkins v. Childrens Hospital: origin, 180; lawyers, 191–192; *amici curiae* briefs, 194; decision, 216, 243
Adler, Felix, 248
Adriaans, J. H., 40, 41, 58
Allen, Judge Florence, 228
Allen, Lafon, 251, 423
Allwright, S. E., 321
Altgeld, Governor John P., 164, 167
American Anti-Boycott Association, 164
American Association for Labor Legislation, 165, 183, 200
American Bar Association, 104; and Twenty-first Amendment, 111; and child labor amendment, 250, 251
American Constitutional League, leaders and policy, 50; *Fairchild v. Colby,* 51; woman suffrage, 58; back-to-the-people amendment, 247; *Fairchild v. Hughes,* 264
American Federation of Labor, 165
American Fund for Public Service, 308
American Genetics Association, 8
American Hotel Association, 108
American Jewish Committee, 157; as *amicus curiae* in *Pierce v. Society of the Sisters,* 147
American Law Institute, 200
American Legion, 111
American Liberty League, 86, 165
American Woman Suffrage Association, 64
Amicus curiae, 369; filed by Charles Evans Hughes, 93; by Anti-Saloon League, 94; by William Sheafe Chase, 122; by Seventh Day Adventists, 157; by American Jewish Committee, 159; by National Women's Party, 208; by Dean Acheson, 209; by Henry St. George Tucker, 268; in *Guinn and Beal v. United States,* 40,

41; in *Hawke v. Smith,* 57; in *Racial Restriction Covenant Cases,* 61; in *United States v. Standard Brewery,* 92, 93; in *United States v. Sprague,* 98; in *Pierce v. Society of the Sisters,* 157–159; in *Adkins v. Childrens' Hospital,* 194; in 1933 minimum wage law, 208; in *Morehead v. New York,* 209; in *Walker v. Chapman,* 214; in *West Coast Hotel Co. v. Parrish,* 230–232; in *Massachusetts v. Mellon,* 269–272; in *Baker v. Carr,* 338; in *Buchanan v. Morley,* 404; and relationship with office of Solicitor General, 339
Amidon, Charles F., 420
Anderson, Henry W., 106
Anderson, John B., 28
Anderson, Mary, 262
Anderson v. Myers: origin, 30; counsel, 35–37; brief to Supreme Court, 39; opinion, 41
Andrews, Elmer F., 204
Andrews, John B., 200
Andrews, William T., 308
Ansel, Martin F., 42
Anthony, Daniel R., Jr., 253
Anthony, Susan B., 64
Anti-Catholicism, 143
Anti-Saloon League, 57; leadership, 69, 72, 76, 77; origin, 81; and immigrants, 84, 85; and apportionment of Congress, 84; briefs in Supreme Court cases, 95–97
Anti-Vietnam statute, 425
Arnold, Thurman, 16
Article Five, 246; opinion of Mr. Justice Day in *Hawke v. Smith,* 55, 56
Ashe, Judge Charles E., 288
Association Against the Prohibition Amendment, 107
Association for Voluntary Sterilization, 18
Association of Amalgamated Negro Organizations, 34, 35
Association of Land Grant Colleges, 269
Atkins, J. Alston, 287, 315
Atwater v. Hassett: origin, 33; *amicus curiae* brief by John Burford, 34; opinion, 35

"Back-to-the-people" amendment, 246, 247
Bacon, Selden, 98
Baez, Joan, 66
Bagnalt, R. W., 294
Bailey v. Drexel Furniture Co., 243
Bailey, Joseph Weldon, 40
Baker, Newton D., 106, 109, 168, 188

437

Baker, Reverend Purley A., 82
Baker v. Carr, 352, 432; *amicus curiae* brief
    in, 338
Baldwin, Roger, 144
Baltimore Sun, 24
Bayh, Birch, 348
Bean, Robert S., 150
Beatrice State Home, 19
James M. Beck, 61, 112, 127, 194; and Shep-
    pard-Towner Maternity Act, 266, 270,
    271
Becker School Prayer Amendment, 350
Bell, John Hendren, 14
Bennett, John J., Jr., 204, 205, 208
Bentley, Arthur F., 330
Berne, Walter, 12
Berrien, Laura M., 212
Beveridge, Senator Albert, 248
Beyer, Clara, 190, 207
Bingham, James, 56
Blue, Fred O., 79
Board of Examiners of the Mentally Defi-
    cient, 19
Board of Maternity and Infant Hygiene, 263
Bonaparte, Charles J., 25; grandfather clause
    strategy, 29; concept of defamation, 30;
    and Consumers League of Maryland, 167
Boston, Charles A., 17
Brandeis, Elizabeth, 190
Brandeis, Louis D., and woman suffrage, 49;
    on *Fairchild v. Colby,* 62; on *Leser v.*
    Garnett, 62; and progressive spirit, 164–
    166; judicial philosophy, 169–172; on *Mul-*
ler v. Oregon, 275
Brann, Louis J., 125
Branson, Fred P., 32
Brewer, David J., 173
Bricker, John W., 214, 228
Bricker Amendment, 346
Brooks, A. Ames, 43
Brooks, John Graham, 168
Brown, George M., 188
Brown, Robert, 29
Brown v. Board of Education, 367–369
Brown v. Maryland, 78
Brownlow Commission, 366
Buchanan, C. A., 34
Buck, Carrie, 13–15
Buck v. Bell: origin, 5, 10; Holmes opinion,
    15, 16
Bullitt, William Marshall, 92
Bunting v. Oregon, 173, 186
Burdick, Charles K. 269
Burford, John, 41; *amicus curiae* in *Atwater*
    v. Hassett, 34
Burlingham, Charles, 207
Burr, Borden, 276
Butler, Pierce, 235

Butler v. United States, 276

Cadwalader, Thomas F., 59; and the Twenty-
    first amendment, 112; and Voluntary
    Committee of Lawyers, 126, 127; back-
    to-the-people amendment, 246; *Leser v.*
    Garnett, 60
Cahn, Edmond, 244, 341
California Industrial Welfare Commission,
    185
Cannon, James J., 84
Cardozo, Benjamin, 198
Carnegie Institution of Washington, 7
Catholic Civil Rights Association, 144
Catholic Education Association, 156, 157
Catholic World, 183
Catt, Carrie Chapman, 47, 51, 57, 65, 245
Cavitt, Gloria, 19
Cavitt v. Nebraska, 19
Celler, Emanuel R., 351
Chaffee, Zechariah, Jr., 106
Chamberlain, George Earle, 151, 152
Chamberlain, Joseph P., 202
Chamberlin v. Andrews, 280
Chandler, Charles A., 318
Chandler v. Neff, 293
Chandler v. Wise, 251
Channell, R. J., 295
Chase, William Sheafe, 122
Cherrington, Ernest H., 82
Childrens' Bureau, 262–267
Child Labor Act, 262
Child labor amendment, 248; proposed text,
    249–250
Chisholm, Shirley, 66
Choate, Joseph Hodge, Jr., 77, 92, 112; and
    Twenty-first Amendment, 103, 109,
    118; and chemical industry, 128, 129
Christie, Archbishop Alexander, 147
Citizens Union of the City of New York,
    260
Class actions, 350
Clark, David, 247
Clark, William, 98
Cleveland, Grover, 50
Cobb, James, 294
Cohen, Benjamin, 168; and draft of model
    wage law, 201; personal background,
    202; explication of wage law, 203
Cohen, Juilius Henry, 98
Colby, Bainbridge, 59
Coleman, Rolla W., 422
Coleman v. Miller, 251
Commission on Uniform State Laws, 200
Common Cause, 332
Commons, John R., 168, 200
Compulsory Education Act of 1922, 143
Comstock, Ada L., 106

Confederate veterans, 72
Conference of Black Lawyers, 245
Congressional Union, 66, 252
Congressmen: conflict of interest, 364, 365
Congress of Industrial Organizations, 198
Conner, C. B., 228, 229
Constitutional amendments: politics of, 243; state ratifying conventions, 116, 117, 342; state legislative ratification, 343; advocacy of, 345; against the presidency, 345; against the Supreme Court, 347; against tardy states, 355, 356; procedure statute, 371; suitability of, 410
Constitutional League, 33, 42
Constitutional litigations: attributes of, 336
Coolidge, Louis A., 265
Cooley, Thomas, 236
Corcoran, Thomas, 203
Corwin, Edward S., 112
Council of State Governments, 200
Cox, Archibald, 338, 339
Coyle v. Smith, 32, 33
Crain, Robert, 69, 91
Crichton-Clarke, William H., 98
Crosskey, W. W., 199
Crowthers, Governor Austin, 26
Cruce, A. C., 40
Cumming, Robert C., 118
Curran, Henry H., 111
Curtis, Charles P., 253, 273

Dabney, Virginius, 85
Daily Oklahoman, 44
Daugherty, Harry, 59
Davenport, Charles Benedict, 7
Davis, John W., 41, 79, 109, 158
Debs, Eugene V., 164
DeForest, Henry W., 103
Delaware v. New York, 349
Democratic State Central Committee, 32
Dawson, Mary W., 180, 262; and National Committee of Lawyers, 168; philosophy of, 184; and minimum wage law, 198–200
Dibble, Vernon, 233
Dickinson, Agnes, 214, 232
Dillon, John F., 236
Dinwoodey, Dean, 227
Dirksen Apportionment Convention Amendment, 352
Disenfranchisement, 25, 290; in Oklahoma, 31; in Maryland, 33; and *Lane v. Wilson,* 318
Dixon, Robert G., Jr., 349
Dooling, John T., 118
Dow, Neal, 71
Dowding, Vincent L., 19
Dowling, Noel T., 118, 122

Dred Scott case, 24
Driver, Sam, 229
Dry states: in 1916, 74; in 1920, 73
DuBois, W. E. B., 297
Dugdale, Richard Louis, 7
Dulles, John Foster, 347
Dunjee, Roscoe: *Lane v. Wilson,* 318
Durnham, W. J., 321

Edmunds, George F., 32
Edson, Katherine Phillips, 180, 185
Eichelberger, J. S., 58
Eighteenth Amendment, 55, 69; and apportionment of Congress, 83, 84
Ellis, Challen B., 192; skill of, 234
Ellis, Wade H., 134, 192
Ely, Richard T., 237
Embry, John: *amicus curiae* brief in *Guinn and Beal v. United States,* 41
Emery, James A., 249
Enforcement Acts, 45
Engle v. Vitale, 351
Epstein, Henry, 204
Equal Rights Amendment, 348
Ervin, Senator Sam, 348; uniformity in amendments, 353
Estabrook, Arthur H., 7, 8, 10
Eugenical Sterilization in the United States, 11
Eugenical Sterilization Law, 12
Eugenics and Other Evils, 17
Eugenics Record Office, 8, 14, 15
Eugenics Record office Bulletin, 8
Evangelical Lutheran Synod, 145
Evans, Earle W., 251
Evans, Elizabeth, 184
Evans, R. D.: in *Grigsby and DeWalt,* 287, 288, 310
Evarts, Jeremiah M., 98
Evjue, William T., 260

Fairchild, Charles S., 59, 247, 264
Fairchild v. Colby, 51, 59; opinion of Brandeis, 62
Fairchild v. Hughes, 264
Fair Employment Practices Commission, 325
Fair Labor Standards Act of 1938, 179
Farley, John Cardinal, 156
Fatigue and Efficiency, 176
Federal Bureau of Investigation, 106
Federalist, 422
Federal Constitutional Convention Act, 353
Feigenspan, Christian, 92
Christian Feigenspan, Inc. v. Bodine, 93
Fifth Amendment: and opponents to Sheppard-Towner Maternity Act, 266
Fifteenth Amendment: grandfather clause,

21, 29; interpretation of William L. Marbury, 39, 40; in *Guinn and Beal v. United States*, 40–44; and Cadwalader, 62; and primary elections, 288
Filene, Edward A., 167
Finerty, John H., 321
Fitzgerald, John J., 90
Flast v. Cohen, 365
Flexner, Eleanor, 254
Fourth and Fifth Congressional League, 33
Fourteenth Amendment, 22; in *Guinn and Beal v. United States*, 40; and residential segregation, 43; in *Pierce v. the Society of the Sisters*, 156; and the Oregon Compulsory Education Act, 150; in *Stettler v. O'Hara*, 187; and opponents to Sheppard-Towner Maternity Act, 266; and primary elections, 288
Fox, Austen G., 98, 105
Fox, Wilmer T., 10, 11
Foxcroft, Frank, 49
Fraenkel, Osmond K., 321
Frankfurter, Felix, 165; and draft of model wage bill, 200–202
Franklin, Pink, 42
Freedman, John J., 88
Freemasonry, 140
Freund, Paul, 220; reference service for judiciary, 368
Frick, George Arnold, 60, 267
Friedman, Milton, 189
Friendly, Judge Henry J., 355
Friendly suit: *Bell v. Buck*, 16
Frierson, William L., 92, 94
Frothingham, 50, 264, 267; and child labor amendment, 247
Frothingham v. Mellon, 270–272
Fugitive Slave Acts, 85, 408

Gabriel, Ralph, 344
Galton, Sir Francis, 6
Gardner, John, 109, 332
Garland, Charles, 308
Garrett, Earle W., 106
Garrett, Finis J., 246
Garrisson, William Lloyd: woman's rights, 49
Gearheart, B. W., 57
Giddings, E. J., 45
Gilbert, Abraham S., 118
Gilbert, William B., 150
Goddard, Henry H., 8
Goldmark, Josephine, 198; draft of model wage bill, 168, 200; further support of 1933 New York minimum wage law, 207; feminine chauvinist, 253;
Goldmark, Pauline, 168
Gompers, Samuel, 165

Goodnow, Dr. Frank J., 264
Goodrich, James P., 10
Gorman, Arthur Pue, 24, 25
Gorham-Rasin: machine against black suffrage, 25
Grand Army of the Republic, 72
Grandfather clause, 21
Grant, Madison, 335
Greathouse, Rebekah, 212
Green, Edith, 66
Griffiths, Martha, 348
Grovey v. Townsend, 287
Grubb, William I., 106
Guinn, Frank, 37
Guinn and Beal v. United States: origin, 38; *amicus curiae* brief by J. H. Adriaans, 40; *amicus curiae* brief by NAACP, 41; opinion, 41
Guthrie, W. D., 69, 92, 112, 194; child labor 248; *Pierce v. the Society of the Sisters*, 148, 154–156
Gusfield, Joseph, 101
Gaines, Charles Groves, 237

Hamilton, Alexander, 422
Hamilton, G. W., 230
Hamilton, Alice, 167; Sheppard-Towner Maternity bill, 262
Hale, Robert, 123–125
Hammer v. Degenhart, 180, 243, 349
Hanley, J. Frank, 56
Hanley, Brother P. J., 147
Harmon, Judson, 57
Harriman, Mary Williamson, 8
Harrison, Marvin C., 214, 228
Hart, Luke E., 147
Haskall, Norman: brief for Guinn and Beal, 40
Hastie, 321
Hawke, George S., 55
Hawke v. Smith, 94; counsel, 55, 56; *amici curiae* briefs, 57
Hawkens, W. Ashbie, 43, 404
Hayes, Patrick Joseph Cardinal, 156; child labor amendment, 248
Hellen, Arthur, 56
Helvering v. Davis, 276–285, 427; opinions, 285
Henry Street Settlement House, 262
Hereditary Genius, 7
Heredity of Feeblemindedness, 8
Herndon, C. C., 295
Herrick, Elinore Morehouse, 211, 222
Hershkopf, Bernard, 69, 92, 98–99
Hill Military Academy, 139
Hitz, William, 187
Holmes, Reverend John Haynes, 297
Holmes, Mr. Justice Oliver Wendell, Jr., 38;

on *Buck v. Bell*, 5; on the Oregon school laws, **140**; on *Nixon v. Herndon,* 305
Hornor, C. G., 40
Houghton, Woodson, 192
Houston, Charles H., 309; defense of white counsel in NAACP, 316
Howard, William H., grandfather clause, 29
Hughes, Chief Justice Charles Evans, 38, 59, 238; and Social Security Act of 1935
Hull House, 262
Hylan, John F., 260

Ingersoll, Raymond V., 205
Interest group participation, 330–333
International Lady Garment Workers Union, 164
International Reform Federation, 122
Ireland, John, 81

Jessup, Henry W., 98
Johnson, George M., 321
Johnson, Hiram, 185
Johnson, J. A., 34
Johnson, James Weldon, 294, 304
Johnson, Reverdy, 23, 24
Johnston, Henry Alan, 113
Jones, Clarence M., 29
Jones, Murray B., 288
Jones, Wiley, 34
Jordan, David Stan, 7
Judiciary: alignment, 195–196; conflicts of interest, 362–364; review, 341; quality, 396
Judiciary Act of 1789, 347
Judiciary Act of 1925, 298

Kalmey, Claude, 29
Kalven, Harry, 30
Katzenbach v. Morgan, 357
Kavanough, John P., 144, 147
Kelley, Florence, 128, 197; and the National Committee of Lawyers, 167; policy of, 169; eight-hour work day and *Ritchie v. People,* 170; opposition to Alice Paul, 254; and Sheppard-Towner bill, 262; and Womens Joint Congressional Committee, 268
Kelley, Patrick Henry, 93
Kellog, Charles F., 43
Kent, Frank, grandfather clause, 24, 26
Kentucky Distilleries and Warehouse Co. v. Gregory, 93
Kenyon, Dorothy, 106, 222
Kenyon, William S., 106
Key, V. O., Jr.
Kilbreth, Mary G., 58, 264
Kimball, Sarah Louise, 9
King, Alex C., 92, 94

Knights of Columbus, 147, 148
Knollenberg, 294, 295; and finances, 297; *Nixon v. Congdon,* 311
Kozer, Sam A., 142, 151
Krock, Arthur, 227
Ku Klux Klan, 139; *Pierce v.,* 157, 158
Kynett, Reverend Alpha J., 81

Labor Standards Committee, 202
LaFollette, Robert M., 53, 158
Lamar, Joseph R., 38
Lamar, William H., 267
Lane v. Wilson: origin, 318; *certiorari,* 319; oral argument, 319–320
Langdell, C. C., 236
Lathrop, Julia C., 48; Childrens Bureau, 167; Sheppard-Towner Act, 262
Laughlin, Harry, 11, 13, 14
League for State Defense, 58
Ledbetter, W. A., 34, 40
Legal, Legislative and Administrative Aspects of Sterilization, 9
Legislative Drafting Research Fund, 202
Lehman, Irving, 217
Lemann, Monte M., 106
Leser, Oscar, 60
Leser v. Garnett, 60–63, 264
Lewis, John L., 198
Lincoln, Alex, 93, 112; child labor amendment, 247–251; *Sentinels of the Republic,* 265, 266
Literary Digest: opinion polls, 226
Llewellyn, Karl, 237
Lloyd, Henry Demarest, 167
Lochner v. New York, 170
Loesch, Frank J., 106
Lottery Act of 1895, 163
Love v. Griffith: origin, 287; disenfranchisement, 290; Mr. Justice Holmes' opinion, 291
Loving v. Virginia, 338
Lowell, A. Lawrence, 249
Lowell, John, 49
Lowenthal, Max, 106
Lurton, Justice Horace H., 38, 44
Luce, Clare Boothe, 66
Lucy Stone League, 66
Lyons, Willie A., 191

McCamant, Wallace, 145, 150
McClennen, Edward F., 276
McCormick, Paul J., 106
McElwain, Edwin, 238
Mach, Julian M., 202
Machen, Arthur W., Jr., 39, 61; back-to-the-people amendment, 247; Twenty-first Amendment, 115
McKenna, Joseph, 38

Mackintosh, Kenneth, 106

McReynolds, Mr. Justice James Clark: opinion in Pierce, 160

McWilliams, Carey, 337

Mann "White Slave Traffic" Act of 1910, 163

Man Suffrage Association Opposed to Political Suffrage for Women, 50, 51

Marbury, William L.: disenfranchisement, 22–28; brief for plaintiff Myers, 39; in *State v. Gurry,* 43; resistance to womans suffrage, 51, 52; argument against Nineteenth Amendment, 61; and the Twenty-first Amendment, 115; and Adkins, 194; child labor amendment, 247; back-to-the-people amendment; in *Leser v. Garnett,* 264

Marbury v. Madison, 244

Marconnier, Emily Sims, 198

Margold, Nathan, 308

Marshall, Charles, 24

Marshall, Louis: in *Nixon v. Herndon,* 301–303; as a conservative, 157, 194

Marshall, James, 308

Marshall, Chief Justice John, 244

Marshall, Thomas R., 10

Marshall, Thurgood: rise of, 317

Martin, George W., 103

Maryland, black population of, 27

Maryland Division of the Association Against the Prohibition Amendment, 86

Maryland League for State Defense, 51, 252, 264

Mason, Lucy Randolph, 198; and the New Work minimum wage law, 208

Massachusetts Anti-Suffrage Association, 50

Massachusetts v. Mellon: amicus curiae brief, 269

Martin, William Logan, 276

Masten, Arthur H., 103

Maternity Act of 1921, 266

Matthews, Burnita, 214

Maxwell, Lawrence, 57

Mayer, Levy, 92

Mayor, etc. of *New York v. Miln,* 154

Melvin, Ridgely P., 30, 39

Mental Deficiency Act, 15

Merriam, Charles E., 303

Marton, Robert K., 233

Milholland, John E., 42

Miller, Charles A., 368

Miller, Frieda S., 205, 222

Miller, Nathan L., 235

Minimum wage bill of 1933: *amicus curiae* brief filed by National Womans Party, 208; Supreme Court disposition, 179, 198

Minor v. Happersett, 65, 348

Miranda v. Arizona, 354

Missouri Pacific Railway Co. v. Kansas, 80

Monroe, David H., 106

Montgomery, W.W., Jr., 109

Moody, Dan, 429

Moore, Willis S., 152

Morehead v. New York: amicus curiae brief, 209

Morehead v. Tipaldo, 223

Morris, Judge Thomas J., 30

Morrow, Dwight, 111

Morse, Waldo G., 59, 61, 241

Morton, David Holmes, 249

Moses, Robert, 198

Mitley, Constance Baker, 66

Mugler v. Kansas, 128

Muller, Herbert J., 18

Muller v. Oregon, 172

Murphy v. Sardell, 216

Murray v. Curlett, 351

Myers, Charles E., 29

Myers, Stanley, 150

Myers v. Anderson, 38

Nabrit, James M., Jr., 315

Nagle, Patrick S., 35, 37

Nation, Carry, 72

National American Woman Suffrage Association, 57

NAACP: beginnings of, 42; in Guinn and Beal, 41; Legal Redress and Legislative Committee, 43; Moorfield Storey, 44; residential segregation, 42, 43; and Florence Kelley, 167; the El Paso agreement, 296; assessment, 308; test cases against primaries, 309, 310; and federal judges, 320; formation of Legal Defense and Educational Fund, 317, 321, 322; Dunjee-Chandler controversy, 320

National Association of Manufacturers, 249

National Association Opposed to Women Suffrage, 48, 58

National Catholic Welfare Conference, 148

National Civic League, 122

National Commission on Law Observance and Enforcement, 105

National Child Labor: leaders, 248, 251

National Child Labor Conference, 165

National Consumer's League: supporters and staff, 166–168; political action, 168; *Bunting v. Oregon,* 173 –175; *Muller v. Wilson,* 173; *Muller v. Oregon,* 173; *Bosely v. McLaughlin,* 173–175; Russell Sage Foundation, 175; publications of, 176; and minimum wages, 180; *Adkins v. Childrens Hospital,* 180; and Samuel Gompers, 183; *Stettler v. O'Hara,* 186;

and Felix Frankfurter, 193; and Labor Standards Committee, 200; and model minimum wage law, 200; and the Standard Minimum wage bill of 1933, 200, 207; and Dean Acheson, 209
National Fair Labor Standards Act of 1938, 184, 199
National Industrial Recovery Act of 1933, 199
National Labor Relations Act of 1935, 226
National Lawyers' Committee, 165
National League of Women Voters, 65; beginnings, 47
National Popular Government League, 53
National Prohibition Cases, 94, 349
National Prohibition Convention, 71
National Recovery Act, 184
National Woman Suffrage Association, 64
National Temperance Society, 122
National United Committee for Law Enforcement, 122
National WCTU, 122
National Woman's Party, 47, 66, 243, 165; against wage legislation for women, 211; leaders, 212; attitude toward separatism, 253
Nebbia v. New York, 223
Negro and the First Amendment, 30
New Age, 143
New Deal Programs, 275
New York Man Suffrage League, 264
New York Minimum Wage Law, 1933: strategy and origins, 204; writ for certiorari, 205
Niagara Movement, 42
Nineteenth Amendment, 47; court cases, 53; arguments of William Marbury, 61; Leser v. Garnett, 264; Fairchild v. Hughes, 264
Nixon, Lawrence A., 295
Nixon v. Condon: origin, 307–309; preparations, 310; counsel, 311; Louis Marshall, 311; Frank Cameron, 311; petition for certiorari, 312; opinion of Mr. Justice Cardozo and Mr. Justice McReynold, 312; reactions, 312, 313
Nixon v. Herndon: origin, 288, 293; preparation, 296, 298; collaboration, 301; Louis Marshall, 303; opinion, 305
North American Review, 38
Noyes, Walter C., 92
Nyce, Peter Q., 152

O'Connell, James Cardinal: child labor amendment, 248
Odegard, Peter, 101
Office of State Eugenicist, 12
Official Pamphlet, 143, 145

O'Hara, Edwin V., 144; child labor amendment, 248
Ohio Anti-Saloon League, 75, 87
Oklahoma: 1907 Census, 31; 1910 Census, 35; Socialists, 35, 37; Supreme Court, 34
Olcott, Ben, 142
Olmstead v. United States, 70
Open housing, 424
Ordway, Samuel H., 103
Oregon Compulsory Education Act: origins, 139, 140; supporters, 141, 142; detractors, 143; adoption, 145; and the Ku Klux Klan, 145
Oregon Industrial Welfare Commission, 186
Osborn, Henry Fairfield, 9
Ottinger, Richard L., 350
Outlook, 169, 172
Overacher, Louise, 303
Owens, Hamilton, 23

Palmer, A. Mitchell, 59, 94, 112, 113–115
Parker, John J., 164
Parr, Judge W. D., 228
Parkman, Francis: woman's rights, 48, 49
Parrish, Elsie, 228
Parrish v. West Coast Hotel Co., 181, 228; amicus curiae brief, 230–232; Chief Justice Hughes' views, 231
Paul, Alice: National Woman's Party, 47; Lucretia Mott Amendment, 212, 245, 253
Perkins, Frances: 1933 New York Minimum Wage Law, 66, 207
Personal liberty leagues: origins, 85; roots, 86; leaders, 87
Pickens, Donald, 6
Pickens, William, 301
Pierce, Walter M., 139, 146, 145
Pierce v. the Society of the Sisters: origins and development, 141–159; legal expenses, 148; opinions, 160
Pitcairn, Raymond, 108
Pleasants, Chief Justice R. A., 289
Poe amendment: understanding clause, 25
Poe, Edgar Allen: and the Twenty-first Amendment, 43, 121
Poe, John P., 25
Pollard, Claude, 429
Pollak, Walter H., 106
Population: white and black in south in 1920, 304
Porras, Charles, 295
Pound, Roscoe, 106
Powell, Thomas Reed, 237
Progressives, 342
Protective League, 33
Price, John G., 57

Priddy, A. S., 14
Primaries, 430
Public Interests League, 50
Public School Defense League, 153
Putney, Albert H., 152

Race, Arthur L., 125
Randall, Daniel R., 41
Randolph, Mary D., 60
Rankin, Lee, 339
Rankin, Jeannette, 48, 165, 262; and health care centers, 168
Ransom, Leon A., 321
Rasin, I. Freeman, 24
Raushenbusch, Elizabeth Brandeis, 203
Rawls, William Lee, 39, 92, 264, 267; back-to-the-people amendment, 247
Reed, David, 305
Regulation of Lobbying Act of 1945, 361
Remonstrance, 49
Report on the Enforcement of the Prohibition Laws of the United States, 106
Republican party: and the grandfather clause, 26; platform of 1908, 35; state central committee of Maryland, 30
Restrictive Covenant Cases, 339
Revenue Act of 1862, 88, 90
Reynolds v. Sims, 352, 354
Rhyne, Charles S., 338
Rice, Herbert A., 93
Ritchie, Albert C., 109
Ritchie v. Wayman, 170
Robb, Charles H., 191
Roberts, George, 102
Roberts, John W., 230
Roberts, Owen J., 192
Roberts memorandum, 233, 234
Roosevelt, Eleanor, 66
Roosevelt, Franklin, 109
Roosevelt, Theodore, 53
Root, Elihu, 69, 79, 93, 194
Rhudy, Helena P., 103
Russell, Reverend Howard Hyde, 75, 87
Russell Sage Foundation: National Consumers League, 175
Ryan, Father John A., 144; background, 181; philosophy, 182; minimum wage laws, 180; child labor amendment, 248

Sabin, Mrs. Charles H., 135
Safeguard, 34
Salpingectomy, 18
Samuelson, Paul, 179
Saunders, Charles R., 49
Saxe, John Godfrey, 21, 118
School Segregation Cases, 339
Schubert, Glendon, 223
Schwimmer, Rosika, 66, 165

Second International Congress of Eugenics, 9
Self-Incrimination Amendment, 354
Seligman, Herbert, 301
Sentinels of the Republic, 93, 249, 250, 264; attacks on the Sheppard-Towner Maternity Act, 265
Seventh Day Adventists, 145; amicus curiae brief, 157
Sexual sterilization, 5
Seymour, Whitney North, 321
Shapiro, Martin, 368
Sharp, Dr. H. C., 10
Shaw, Ralph M., 109, 112
Sheppard, Morris, 262
Sheppard-Towner Maternity Act, 48, 261, 262; test of constitutionality, 267
Shelton, Burnita, 212
Shelton, Robert G., 13, 14
Sherman Anti-Trust Act of 1890, 89
Shouse, Jouett, 116, 119, 135
Skeel, E. L., 230
Socialists: Florence Kelley, 48
Social reform: opponents, 263–264
Social Security Act of 1935, 226, 263, 274; legal challenges, 276–282
Society of the Sisters, 139
Sons of Temperance, 71
Sons of the American Revolution, 140
Soper, Morris A., 41
Spence, Kenneth M., 103
Sprague v. United States, 349
Stalker, Gale H., 84
Stanton, Elizabeth Cody, 64
State maximum hour laws, 174
State v. Gurry, 43
States rights: in Oklahoma, 33
State sterilization legislation, 9
Statutes, 348
Stayton, William H., 135
Steffens, Lincoln, 163; Boston 1915 movement, 167
Stephens, Frances H., 193
Sterilization: in Germany, 6
Stettler v. O'Hara: George M. Brown, 186, 188; Brandeis, 186, 187
Stewart, Gilchrist, 42
Steward Machine Co.. v. Davis: opinion, 285
Simmons, D. A., 429
Sinclair, Upton, 163
Sixteenth Amendment, 349
Skinner v. Oklahoma, 18
Smith, Alfred E., 109
Smith, Charles B., 56
Smith, Edwin A., 203
Smith, Ethel M., 190
Smith, Harvey C., 55
Smith, Jane Norman, 212, 215

Smith, Lonnie E., 321
Smith, Margaret Chase, 66
Smith v. Allwright, 287, 317;
Smith, Warren Wallace, 10
Spingarn, Arthur B., 295; *Nixon v. Herndon,*
    296
Stimson, Henry L., 120
Stone, Harlan, 198
Stone, Lucy, 64
Stone, Robert, 251, 422
Storey, Moorfield, 23, 42; *amicus curiae*
    brief in *Guinn and Beals; Nixon v.*
    Herndon, 294, 296
Straus, Isaac: grandfather clause, 28
Strode, Aubrey E., 14
Stuart, Charles B., 34, 40
Studin, Charles H., 42
Supreme Court: decisions, 37; membership,
    323–325
Survey, 167
Sutherland, George, 79

Taft, William Howard, 38, 78; and *Pierce v.*
    the Society of the Sisters, 153
Taxpayer suits, 259; provocations, 260; and
    the courts, 261
Teal, Joseph N., 194
Tenth Amendment: and the Maternity Act
    of 1921, 266
Texas v. White, 39, 40
Thatcher, Thomas Day: *amicus curiae* in
    1933 minimum wage bill, 208
Thayer, James Bradley, 236
Third International Eugenics Congress, 18
Tiedeman, Christopher, 236
Tilden, Samuel J., 50
Timberlake, James, 101
Tipaldo, Joseph, 204
Tipaldo v. Morehead, 119, 120
Towner, Horace, 262
Toner, W. A., 231; *amicus curiae* in *Parrish,*
    232
Truman, David, 330
Tucker, Henry St. George, 194; Sentinels of
    the Republic, 266
Tuckerman, Eliot, 98
Tumey v. Ohio, 70
Twentieth Century Fund, 167
Twenty-first Amendment, 118, 346; bill
    proposals, 70, 102; champions of the
    wets, 112; political realignment, 136,
    137
Twentieth century expense books, 184
Tweed, Harrison: and the Voluntary
    Committee of Lawyers, 130
Twiss, Benjamin, 237

Understanding clause, 44, 45

Uniform Crime Reports, 106
United States Brewers Association, 87;
    objectives, 88; labor, 89; ethnicity and
    religion, 90
United States Code, 179, 347
United States Law Week, 230, 231
United States v. Butler, 238
United States v. Chemical Foundation, Inc.,
    129
United States v. Classic, 321
United States v. Fred W. Darby, 179
United States v. Sprague, 98
United States v. Standard Brewery, 92
United States v. Wade, 354

Van Devantes, Willis, 38
Van Waters, Miriam, 106
Van Winkle, General Isaac: in *Adkins,* 144
Veatch, John C., 147
Verrill, Robinson, 123
Vinson, Chief Justice Fred M., 395
Volstead Act, 76; supporting opinion, 94
Voluntary Committee of Lawyers: members,
    103; objectives, 103, 104; and Wicker-
    sham Committee, 107; repeal amend-
    ments, 109; constitutional conventions
    and ratifying conventions, 117;
    drafting bills, 119; in Maine, 124, 125,
    126; finances, 130, 131
Vote participation of women, 423
Voting Rights Act Amendments of 1970,
    357

Wadsworth, James W., Jr., 246
Wald, Lillian D., 167; Sheppard-Towner
    Maternity Act, 262
Walker, James J., 260
Walker v. Chapman, 214–232; *amicus curiae*
    brief, 214; *certiorari,* 214
Walsh, David, 305
Walsh, Frank P: child labor amendment, 248
Walters, Alexander, 42
Warren, Bentley Wirt: Sentinels of the
    Republic, 265
Washington, L. W., 294
Waters, Cecilia S., 60
Webb, Beatrice, 183
Webb-Kenyon Act of 1914, 76, 90; Supreme
    Court cases, 79; Taft veto, 83
Wesley, Carter, 315, 321
West, Judge Duval, 295; G. G. Wimberly,
    310
Westervelt, George, 103
West Virginia League, 79
Wheeler, Everett Pepperell, 50, 52, 59, 247
Wheeler, Wayne B., 57, 58; in Washington,
    80; and Webb Kenyon Act, 75, 79; in
    Ohio, 76; preparation of legislation,

Anti-Saloon League, 76
White House Conference on Child Welfare
    Standards, 263
White, James A., 57
Whitehead, I. P., 14; brief for Carrie Buck, 6
White, Walter, 294–296
White, William Allen, 252
Whyte, William Pinkney, 23, 24
Wickersham Commission: origin, 102;
    members, 106; staff, 106; reports, 107
Williams, George Washington, 61
Williams, Robert Lee, 31; opinion in *Atwater
    v. Hassett,* 34
Williams v. Mississippi, 34
Wilkins, Roy: in *Grovey v. Townsend,* 314
Willard, Frances E., 71
Wilson Act of 1890, 77–78

Wilson, Reverend Luther B., 81
Winant, John G., 168
Wise, John S., Jr., 127
Wolverton, Charles E., 150
Woman Patriot, 48, 52, 253, 264
Woman's Anti-Suffrage Association of
    Massachusetts, 50
Woman's Christian Temperance Union, 71
Woman's Educational and Industrial Union,
    184
Woman's Joint Congressional Committee,
    268
Woman's Organization for National Prohibi-
    tion Reform, 135
Woman's Trade Union League, 183, 262

Zimand, Gertrude Folks, 253